The Ormond Lordship in County Kilkenny, 1515–1642

Cork Studies in History & Culture

The Ormond Lordship in County Kilkenny, 1515–1642

The rise and fall of Butler feudal power

DAVID EDWARDS

FOUR COURTS PRESS

Set in 10.5 pt on 12 pt Bembo for
FOUR COURTS PRESS LTD
7 Malpas Street, Dublin 8, Ireland
e-mail: info@four-courts-press.ie
http://www.four-courts-press.ie
and in North America by
FOUR COURTS PRESS
c/o ISBS, 920 N.E. 58th Street, Suite 300, Portland, OR 97213.

A catalogue record for this title
is available from the British Library.

ISBN 1–85182–578–9

Printed by Creative Print and Design (Wales), Ebbw Vale.

To Harry and Helen Edwards, my parents

Contents

Part I
The Passage of Power: A Structural Account

Part II
The Rise and Fall of the Ormond Lordship: A Political Narrative

Illustrations

Acknowledgements

This book began its life fifteen years ago. Originally it was intended to be a study of the Kilkenny county gentry *c.*1540–1640, and to be broadly similar in approach to the various county community studies that have characterised the historiography of late medieval and early modern England. After a while, however, I realised that to properly reconstruct the political and social texture of an Irish local community during the sixteenth and early seventeenth centuries it is not enough to simply borrow from English historical models. Just one word separates Tudor and early Stewart England from Ireland, yet it leaves the two countries worlds apart: lordship. The more documents I consulted, the more I realised Co. Kilkenny, ostensibly a very English part of Ireland, was dominated by its local overlords, the Butler earls of Ormond, in a way that was utterly unknown on the other side of George's Channel and the Irish Sea. And so it was that a study of the gentry metamorphosed into a study of a great feudal lordship.

There are many people I must thank for helping me with this project. During my time as an undergraduate at Trinity College, Dublin, two great teachers, Helga Robinson-Hammerstein and Ciaran Brady, first aroused my interest in the sixteenth century. Dr Brady oversaw my subsequent postgraduate studies, on which this book is partly based, and though we have come to differ in certain areas of interpretation, my work has benefited considerably from his input. Since coming to Cork I have been lucky to work with Kenneth Nicholls, who unselfishly has made his unrivalled knowledge of the archives available to me and enabled me to locate many obscure documents and references that might otherwise have escaped my attention. Only one other person has helped me as much as Kenneth – my friend and former flatmate Brian Donovan, with whom I have enjoyed a hugely rewarding scholarly partnership over the years.

I must acknowledge the assistance of the staff of all the various libraries and record offices in Ireland and the United Kingdom that I have visited in the course of my research. In the National Library of Ireland, special thanks are due to Rachel Scahill of the archives task force, who allowed me consult her catalogue of the Prior-Wandesford Papers before it was finished, and also to Tom Desmond. In Kilkenny Peter Farrelly kindly volunteered to act as my guide when I requested access to the Corporation Archives. At UCC, the prolonged writing-up of this book was greatly assisted by Helen Davis and the staff of

Special Collections in the Boole Library, especially the late Patricia Connolly; by the secretarial staff in the History Department, particularly Charlotte Holland and Margaret McAllister; and by Gabriel Doherty and Trixi Faber, to whom I will be eternally grateful for rescuing Chapter 1 from the jaws of a Microsoft 'application error'. The maps and graphs were completed with the assistance of Colin Rynne and Brian Donovan. Additional research undertaken since October 1999 was aided by a HEA grant to the Department of History, UCC; the cost of illustrations was met by the Arts Faculty Publications Fund, UCC.

For furnishing me with references to evidence, or otherwise offering valuable advice, I wish to thank the following: Margaret Curtis, Jim Delaney, Adrian Empey, Jane Fenlon, Raymond Gillespie, Con Manning, Hiram Morgan, James Murray, Timothy O'Connor, Hilary Ryan, David Starkey, Clodagh Tait, and Julian Walton. I must also thank Nicholas Canny and Aidan Clarke for their helpful comments when assessing an earlier version of the study when it was submitted as a doctoral dissertation for their examination. Finally, special thanks are due to Ronnie Wallace, once my History teacher in secondary school, who has never ceased to take an interest in my work, and took me on a memorable 'field trip' of his own devising so that I could view some of the castles and topography of the Ormond country.

Family and friends have also been supportive: hence my thanks to my wife Clodagh Caulfield, and my mother- and father-in-law, Aileen and Maurice Caulfield. I thank Patrick Roycroft, a geologist and my oldest friend, for listening to me drone on and on about the Ormonds over the years, and for asking sometimes startling questions. My debt to Harry and Helen Edwards, my parents, is evident from the dedication.

D. Ed
University College Cork,
March 2003

Conventions

The following should be noted:

1 Precise dates are given in old style, in accordance with the Julian Calendar that was in use in Ireland throughout the sixteenth and early seventeenth century, but the year is taken as beginning on 1 January.

2 In most places I have endeavoured to give recognisable modern forms of personal names: hence Butler not Butiller, Botyller or Boteler, Comerford not Quemeforde, and Grace not Gras. Likewise with placenames: Burnchurch not Bronchurch or Brantchurch, Derrynahinch not Durrenehenche, Higginstown not Ballyhyggyne, etc. However, I have not always been consistent in this. I have retained some old placenames, such as Cantwell's Court (presently Sandford's Court) and Drumroe (now Mount Loftus), as their modern names, deriving from post-Cromwellian settlers, seem anachronistic in a work dealing with the pre-1650 period. Elsewhere, in order to avoid confusion I have chosen what are now unusual, even archaic, spellings of certain names. Thus I have followed Edmund Curtis in rendering the Archdeacon family as Archdekin in order to differentiate them from church officials of the same name.

3 When giving quotations I have modernised the spelling and punctuation.

4 All currency denominations are given in pounds sterling unless otherwise indicated.

Map of the baronies of County Kilkenny

Abbreviations

Anal. Hib.	*Analecta Hibernica*
AO	Archive Office
BL	British Library
Bod. Lib.	Bodleian Library, Oxford University
Butler Soc. Jn.	*Butler Society Journal*
Cal. Carew MSS	*Calendar of the Carew manuscripts preserved in the archiepiscopal library at Lambeth, 1515–1624*, ed. J.S. Brewer & W. Bullen, 6 vols. (London 1867–73)
CPRI	*Calendar of patent & close rolls of chancery in Ireland for the reigns of Henry VIII to Elizabeth I, and Charles I*, ed. James Morrin (Dublin 1861–3)
Cal. SP, Dom.	*Calendar of state papers relating to English affairs, Domestic*, ed. R. Lemon & M.A.E. Green, 12 vols., London, 1856–72
Cal. SP, Spanish	*Calendar of state papers relating to English affairs, Spanish, preserved in the Archives of Simancas*, ed. R. Tyler & M.A.S. Hume, 8 vols. (London 1892–9)
Carrigan, *Ossory*	William Carrigan, *History & antiquities of the diocese of Ossory* (4 vols., Dublin 1905)
Carte, *Ormond*	T. Carte, *Life of James Butler, duke of Ormond* (6 vols., Oxford 1851)
COD	*Calendar of Ormond deeds*, ed. Edmund Curtis, 6 vols. (Irish Manuscripts Commission, Dublin, 1932–43)
CP	Chancery Pleadings
CSPI	*Calendar of state papers relating to Ireland*, ed. H.C. Hamilton, E.G. Atkinson & R.P Mahaffy, 24 vols., London 1860– 1912
D	Deed
GEC, *Complete peerage*	George Edward Cockayne, *The complete peerage of Britain & Ireland,* new edition ed. V.H. Gibbs and others (13 vols., London 1910–59)
Hore & Graves (ed.), *Social state*	H.F. Hore & J. Graves (ed.), *The social state of south-eastern Ireland in the sixteenth century* (RHAAI, Dublin 1870)
HMC	Historical Manuscripts Commission
IHS	*Irish Historical Studies*

Inq. Lagenia	*Inquisitionum in Officio Rotulorum Cancellarie Hiberniae asservatum, Reportorium, i* (Dublin 1827)
IESH	*Irish Economic and Social History*
Ir. Fiants	*Irish fiants of the Tudor sovereigns* (Dublin 1994)
Ir. mon & ep deeds	*Irish monastic & episcopal deeds, 1200–1600*, ed. Newport B. White (Dublin 1931)
Jn.	Journal
JRSAI	*Journal of the Royal Society of Antiquaries of Ireland*
KCA	Kilkenny Corporation Archives
KSEIAS	*Kilkenny & South-East of Ireland Archaeological Society*
Lamacraft (ed.), *Ir. funeral entries*	C.T. Lamacraft (ed.), *Irish funeral entries in the British Museum*, special volume of *Irish memorials of the dead* (Dublin 1907)
LP Henry VIII	*Letters and papers, foreign and domestic, of the reign of Henry VIII*, ed. J.S. Brewer and others (21 vols. in 32 parts, London 1862–1932)
Ms/MSS	Manuscript/Manuscripts
NA	National Archives of Ireland
NHI	*New history of Ireland*
NLI	National Library of *Ireland*
Ossory Arch Soc.Jn.	*Ossory Archaeological Society Journal*
PRO	Public Record Office, London
PRONI	Public Record Office of Northern Ireland
RC	Record Commissioners (Ireland)
RHAAI	*Royal Historical & Archaeological Association of Ireland*
PRIA	*Proceedings of the Royal Irish Academy*
RO	Record Office
Soc.	Society
SP	State Papers
SP, Henry VIII	*State papers, Henry VIII* (11 vols., London 1830–52)
TCD	Trinity College, Dublin
WSEIAS	*Waterford & South-East of Ireland Archaeological Society*

Introduction

It is well known that during the late medieval and early modern period most regions of Ireland were closely identified with the aristocratic lineages that ruled them. Much of Wicklow, for example, was known to contemporaries as the Byrnes' country (*Crioch Branach*) in deference to the O'Byrnes, who controlled the area from Greystones to Glenmalure,[1] most of Tyrone and part of Derry and Armagh was the O'Neills' country (*Duiche Neill/Tir Eoghain*),[2] and Co. Cork was divided between the countries of the Barretts, Barrys, Courcys, Roches, Condons and, of increasing influence, the countries of MacCarthy Reagh, MacCarthy Muskerry and the Desmond Fitzgeralds.[3] In all, according to one source, by the beginning of the sixteenth century there may have been as many as 90 such 'countries' in Ireland existing as autonomous and semi-autonomous territories under the sway of native lords and chiefs.[4] In the absence of a strong central government these countries, also known as lordships, were the key components of political life. Power was measured by the size and prosperity, and the military capacity, of each aristocratic territory. Great lordships expanded, or at least preserved the integrity of their frontiers, while weaker ones contracted, unable to defend their boundaries.[5] Until the late 1500s Ireland was primarily a land of lordships, a place of constantly shifting frontiers where, above all, politics was usually conducted locally.

Despite acknowledging the importance of the native lordships in the framework of everyday life before 1641, Irish historians know relatively little about them. In part this has been due to a shortfall in the availability of surviving archival material: the letters and papers of many of the old ruling lineages of Ireland are no longer extant, having been lost through destruction, dispersal and neglect.[6] But it is also true that, until recently, historians have been so preoc-

---

1 L. Price, 'The Byrnes Country in the 16th century and the manor of Arklow', *JRSAI* 66 (1936), 41–66; K. Nicholls, 'Crioch Branach: the O'Byrnes and their country', in C. O'Brien (ed.), *Feagh McHugh O'Byrne: the Wicklow firebrand* (Rathdrum Historical Soc., 1998), 7–39. 2 E. Ó Doibhlin, 'O'Neill's "own country" and its families', *Seanchas Ard Mhaca* 6 (1971), 3–23. 3 K. Nicholls, 'The development of lordship in County Cork, 1300–1600', in P. O'Flanagan & C.G. Buttimer (ed.), *Cork: history & society* (Dublin 1993), 157–97. 4 *S.P., Henry VIII*, ii, 1–31. 5 K. Nicholls, *Gaelic and gaelicised Ireland in the Middle Ages* (Dublin 1972), 21–5; K. Simms, *From kings to warlords: the changing political structure of Gaelic Ireland in the later Middle Ages* (London 1987), 10–20. See also M. O'Dowd, 'Gaelic economy and society', in C. Brady & R. Gillespie (ed.), *Natives & newcomers: the making of Irish colonial society, 1534–1641* (Dublin 1986), 120–47. 6 Many more documents con-

cupied with the 'grand narrative' of sixteenth- and early seventeenth-century
Ireland – essentially a story of English reconquest and native aristocratic revolt
– that, often, it has not been possible to include discussion of the intricate, highly
local, worlds of the lordships in the general histories of the period.[7] Although
there have been fine case studies of individual ruling families, in general such
studies have been confined to the great lordships as and when they impacted
on the main narrative, that is, when they engaged in rebellion and were overthrown. Hence the growing body of work dealing with the Kildare rising of
1534, the many rebellions of the Offaly O'Connors and Wicklow O'Byrnes,
the risings of Shane O'Neill in the 1560s, the Kavanagh-Butler rising of 1569,
the Desmond and Fitzmaurice risings of 1569–73 and 1579, those of Rory Oge
O'More in the 1570s, and, even more so, the Tyrone rising of the 1590s.[8]

cerning the lordships have survived than was previously thought: see esp. B.C. Donovan & D.
Edwards, *British sources for Irish history, 1485–1641* (Dublin 1997); idem, 'British sources for Irish
history before 1485: a preliminary handlist of documents', *Anal. Hib.* 37 (1998). **7** There are signs
that this has started to change, with two of the most important recent general studies of the sixteenth century attempting to follow the trail blazed by Nicholls in 1972 (Nicholls, *Gaelic & gaelicised Ire.*, 126–77) in making the provincial lordships more central to the analysis: C. Lennon,
Sixteenth-century Ireland: the incomplete conquest (Dublin 1994); C. Brady, *The chief governors: the rise
and fall of reform government in Tudor Ireland, 1536–1588* (Cambridge 1994). As yet, however, general studies of the seventeenth century have failed to pay more than passing attention to life in the
lordships. **8** E.g., for the Kildare rising see B. Bradshaw, 'Cromwellian reform and the origins of
the Kildare rebellion, 1533–4', *Transactions of the Royal Historical Soc.*, 5th series, 27 (1977); S.G.
Ellis, 'Tudor policy and the Kildare ascendancy, 1496–1534', *IHS* 20 (1977); idem, 'The Kildare
rebellion and the early Henrician Reformation', *Historical Jn.* 19 (1976); L. McCorristine, *The revolt
of Silken Thomas: a challenge to Henry VIII* (Dublin 1987); M. Ó Siochrú, 'Foreign intervention in
the revolt of Silken Thomas, 1534–5', *PRIA*, C 96 (1996). For the O'Connors: F. Fitzsimons,
'The lordship of O'Connor Faly, 1520–70', in W. Nolan & T.P. O'Neill (ed.), *Offaly: history &
society* (Dublin 1998). For the O'Byrnes: B. Donovan, 'Tudor rule in Gaelic Leinster and the rise
of Feagh McHugh O'Byrne', E. O'Byrne, 'The battle of Glenmalure, 25 August 1580: cause and
course', and D. Edwards, 'In Tyrone's shadow: Feagh McHugh O'Byrne, forgotten leader of the
Nine Years War', all in O'Brien (ed.), *Feagh McHugh O'Byrne*; L. Price, 'Notes on Feagh McHugh
O'Byrne', *Kildare Arch. Soc. Jnl.* 11 (1931–3); C. O'Brien, 'Feagh McHugh O'Byrne: firebrand of
the Wicklow Mountains', *History Ireland* 8/1 (Spring 2000). For Shane O'Neill: J. Hogan, 'Shane
O'Neill comes to the court of Elizabeth', in S. Pender (ed.), *Feilscríbhinn Torna* (Cork 1947); C.
Brady, *Shane O'Neill* (Dublin 1996); Idem, 'The killing of Shane O'Neill: some new evidence',
Irish Sword 15 (1982); H. Morgan, 'The end of Gaelic Ulster: a thematic interpretation of events
between 1534 and 1610', *IHS* 26/101 (May 1988); C. Breathnach, 'The murder of Shane O'Neill:
Oidheadh Chuinn Cheadchathaigh', *Ériú* 43 (1992). For the Kavanagh-Butler revolt: D. Moore,
English action, Irish reaction: the MacMurrough Kavanaghs, 1530–1630 (Maynooth 1987); J. Hughes,
'Sir Edmund Butler of the Dullough', *RHAAI* 1 (1870); H. Butler, 'An anti-English Butler', *Butler
Soc. Jn.* 1 (1968). For the Desmond-Fitzmaurice revolt: C.R. Sasso, *The Desmond rebellions, 1569–73
and 1579–83* (University Microfilms International, Michigan 1984); C. Brady, 'Faction and the origins of the Desmond rebellion of 1579', *IHS* 22 (1979). For Rory O'More: V. Carey, 'The end
of the Gaelic political order: the O'More lordship of Laois, 1536–1603', in P.G. Lane & W. Nolan
(ed.), *Laois: history & society* (Dublin 1999). And for Tyrone's rebellion: C. Brady, 'Sixteenth century Ulster and the failure of Tudor reform', in C. Brady, M. O'Dowd & B. Walker (ed.), *Ulster:
an illustrated history* (London 1989); P. Walsh, *The will and family of Hugh O'Neill* (Dublin 1930);
C. Falls, 'Hugh O'Neill the Great', *Irish Sword* 6 (1963); F.M. Jones, 'Pope Clement VIII

Although not all lords and chiefs rebelled, it could be argued that explaining native revolt has occupied Irish historians inordinately, with comparatively few attempts made to explain the decidedly thorny issue of native collaboration with the crown, which was widespread though often ambivalent.[9] Furthermore, and again largely because of the preoccupation with revolt, but also because of the slow development of Irish social and economic history, studies of the lordships have been primarily focused on external relations and on the dealings of their rulers with the English royal government or with international forces such as France, Spain and the papacy. The internal workings of the lordships have usually been treated as of only secondary importance.[10] Helping to rectify this imbalance is one of the principal objectives of this book, which draws upon the extensive archive of arguably the greatest 'collaborators' of all, the Butlers, earls of Ormond, to examine in detail the ebb and flow of aristocratic control in a major Irish lordship during the sixteenth and seventeenth centuries, a period of massive upheaval when the composition of the native noble elite was wholly transformed by English reintervention.

Ironically, the present work took shape in research for an essay dealing with a rebellion – the 1569 Butler revolt – during which the author discovered that the insurrection was as much due to internal as external pressures.[11] Previous studies of the revolt had concentrated almost entirely on external elements, laying great stress on the instability caused by factional intrigues against the Butlers at the English royal court,[12] but an examination of the actual movements

(1592–1603) and Hugh O'Neill', *Bulletin of the Irish Committee for Historical Sciences*, new series, 2/73 (1953); N. Canny, 'Hugh O'Neill and the changing face of Gaelic Ulster', *Studia Hibernica* 10 (1970); H. Morgan, *Tyrone's rebellion: the outbreak of the Nine Years War in Tudor Ireland* (Dublin 1993); idem, 'Hugh O'Neill and the Nine Years War in Tudor Ireland', *Historical Jn.* 36 (1993); idem, 'Faith and fatherland in sixteenth century Ireland', *History Ireland* 3/2 (Summer 1995); J.J. Silke, 'Hugh O'Neill, the Catholic question and the papacy', *Irish Ecclesiastical Record*, 5th series, 94 (1965). **9** Although the term 'collaboration' has acquired a pejorative meaning, I use it only as defined by the *Oxford English Dictionary* – that is, as 'working in combination with another'. Native collaborators have appeared only fitfully in the secondary literature, despite their numerous and various nature. For the O'Connors Sligo, see M. O'Dowd, *Power, politics and land: early modern Sligo, 1568–1688* (Belfast 1991). Otherwise, see A. Chambers, *Chieftain to knight: Tibbot Burke, 1567–1629, 1st Viscount Mayo* (Dublin 1983); C. Brady, 'The O'Reillys of East Breifne and the problem of Surrender and Regrant', *Breifne* 6 (1985); D. Edwards, 'The MacGiollapadraigs (Fitzpatricks) of Upper Ossory, 1532–1641', in Lane & Nolan (ed.), *Laois*; idem, 'Collaboration without Anglicisation: the MacGiollapadraig lordship and Tudor reform', in P.J. Duffy, D. Edwards & E. FitzPatrick (ed.), *Gaelic Ireland: land, lordship and settlement, c.1250–c.1650* (Dublin 2001). **10** This said, there are nonetheless some valuable insights into local power arrangements in O'Neill country in Canny, 'Hugh O'Neill', passim, Morgan, *Tyrone's rebellion*, 85–135, and Brady, *Shane O'Neill*, 8–21. Knowledge of the mechanics of Kildare power have been advanced by S.G. Ellis, *Tudor frontiers and noble power: the making of the British state* (Oxford 1995), ch. 4. For the MacDomnaills of Antrim, see S. Kingston, 'Trans-Insular lordship in the fifteenth century', in T.M. Devine & J.F. McMillan (ed.), *Celebrating Columba: Irish-Scottish connections, 597–1997* (Edinburgh 1999). **11** D. Edwards, 'The Butler revolt of 1569', *IHS* 28/111 (May 1993), 228–55. **12** J. Curtis, 'The Butler revolt of 1569' (unpublished M.A. dissertation, St Patrick's College, Maynooth, 1983); N. Canny, *The Elizabethan conquest of Ireland: a pattern established, 1565–76*

of the Butler rebels before and during their rebellion did not find this persua-
sive. On the contrary, it emerged that those of the Butlers who rebelled did so
because of changes made, against their wishes, to the military and political structures of their territories by the head of the dynasty, 'Black' Thomas Butler, tenth
earl of Ormond. Far from being simply an anti-English revolt, it seemed the
rising was also a family dispute, an anti-Ormond revolt, and the result of a profound crisis within the ranks of the Butler lineage. The added fact, previously
overlooked, that the Butler rebels faced considerable local opposition within
Kilkenny and Tipperary, mainly from the local gentry and merchants, only
pointed to one conclusion: the exercise of authority within 'the Ormond country' was more complex, more multi-dimensional, than historians of the sixteenth century had previously suggested. To understand the politics of the
Butlers of Ormond, one needed to investigate not only the Butlers, but other
local families too. The merchants and gentry were important players in the affairs
of the area, crucial to the power of the earl of Ormond, yet little was known
of them. Who were they? Why did they support Ormond against his rebel kinsmen in 1569? What could the earl offer them that the rest of the Butlers could
not? Was their support actually more important to the earl than that of his
family? Any major study of the Ormond lordship must also contain an account
of the gentry of the earldom.

What follows attempts to explore the ways in which aristocratic power relationships operated within the Ormond lordship in Co. Kilkenny, not only at a
high political level between lord and state, but from top to bottom, between
the lord, his immediate family, his more distant kin, his clients, tenants and
neighbours, his supporters and enemies. Implicitly it rejects the idea, pedalled
by hostile English officials such as Edmund Spenser and Sir John Davies, that
the nature of noble power in all the Irish lordships was uniformly, and excessively, tyrannical.[13] On the contrary, as far as we can tell, each lordship, or country, had its own customs, its own level of tyranny.[14] If the Ormond lordship in
Kilkenny was typical of the great Anglo-Irish lordships – a question that must
seek its answer elsewhere, being outside the confines of this study – then it
would seem that demands could vary considerably over time, depending on circumstances. Crucially, it was only in periods of major crisis that the overlords,
the earls of Ormond, were openly tyrannical, seeking without consent to impose
heavier exactions than was customary. At most other times, consent was vital
to the exercise of lordship, and it was achieved as it had been throughout the

(Hassocks 1976), 52–3, 149–50; S.G. Ellis, *Tudor Ireland: crown, community and the conflict of cultures,
1470–1603* (London 1985), 260–1; idem, *Ireland in the age of the Tudors, 1447–1603: English expansion
and the end of Gaelic rule* (London 1998), 297. **13** Edmund Spenser, *A view of the present state of
Ireland*, ed. W.L. Renwick (Oxford 1970); Sir John Davies, 'A discovery of the true causes why
Ireland was never entirely subdued [1612]', in H. Morley (ed.), *Ireland under Elizabeth and James I*
(London 1890), 295–6. **14** Nicholls, *Gaelic & gaelicised Ire.*, 31–40. As Canny has noted, it is difficult to be sure of the extent of the differences between Gaelic Irish and Anglo-Irish lordships,
because unlike Anglo-Irish sources, Gaelic sources are predominantly the product of a warlord
culture, and rarely contain complaints of abuses (Canny, *Elizabethan conquest*, 21)

late Middle Ages – partly through bullying, partly through compromise, after
an 'assembly' of the leaders of the local gentry and merchants, a gathering which
served a similar function to the *oireachtas* of Gaelic territories.[15] It is interesting
to note in this regard that, in order to sustain the notion of unrestrained tyranny
to his English readership, Spenser derided public assemblies in Irish lordships as
being commonly attended by 'all the scum of loose people' of the country.[16]
Whatever of conditions elsewhere, this definitely was not the case in the
Ormond country, where assemblies continued to be held as late as 1608,
attended by the gentlemen and freeholders (or petty nobility) of the area.[17]
Though the earls jealously guarded their power, they usually attempted to reach
a consensus with the local gentry regarding the management and regulation of
various aspects of local life. In contrast, the royal government that Spenser and
Davies served was inclined less and less to seek support for its policies through
parliament, the national assembly, ever more eager to impose its will by decree,
by *diktat*.

　　In order to chart how the authority of the earls of Ormond developed at a
time of fundamental change in Ireland, what follows will endeavour to measure the impact of English governmental expansion on the county. Increasingly
Irish historians are becoming aware of just how disruptive the English re-inter-
vention was to provincial life. The crown government's underlying antipathy
to the principle of devolution meant that initial efforts to control Ireland through
reform and assimilation gave way inexorably to more aggressive methods
designed to destroy the independence of all its various lordships.[18] It is often
overlooked that the Ormond lordship was adversely affected by the royal assault
on aristocratic power. While historians have noted the benefits of collaboration
that accrued to successive earls during the sixteenth century – particularly to
Thomas, the tenth earl, in the reign of Elizabeth I[19] – close attention has not
been paid to the often uneasy relations that existed between the earls and government officialdom. In fact, periodically, from as early as the 1530s, the earls
faced serious denunciations of their power by members of the colonial administration in Dublin, and this even though their cooperation was sometimes critical to the success of the government's plans. Time and again before 1603 the
earls were forced to expend their energies in trying to neuter such criticisms,

15 C.A. Empey & K. Simms, 'The ordinances of the White Earl and the problem of coign in the
Middle Ages', *PRIA*, C 75 (1975), 161–87.　**16** Spenser, *View*, 77–9. For scholarly discussion of
the Irish assembly (*oireachtas*), see Simms, *From kings to warlords*, 60–78, esp. 69–75, and E. FitzPatrick,
'An Tulach Tinóil: Gathering-sites and Meeting-culture in Gaelic Lordships', *History Ireland* 9/1
(Spring 2001), 22–6, the best statements on the matter to date.　**17** NLI, Ms 11,044, and n. 15
above.　**18** For the ongoing debate surrounding the chronology of the crown's replacement of a
programme of reform with one of re-conquest, see Brady, *The chief governors*, passim; Canny,
Elizabethan conquest, ch. 3 and 8; Idem, 'Revising the revisionist', *IHS* 30/118 (Nov. 1996), 242–54;
D. Edwards, 'Beyond Reform: Martial Law and the Tudor reconquest of Ireland', *History Ireland*
5/2 (Summer 1997), 16–21.　**19** C. Brady, 'Thomas Butler, earl of Ormond (1531–1614) and
reform in Tudor Ireland', in idem (ed.), *Worsted in the game: losers in Irish history* (Dublin 1989); C.
Falls, 'Black Tom of Ormonde', *Irish Sword* v (1961–2).

generally through court intrigue, but also through temporary withdrawal of cooperation with Dublin, so that they rarely felt totally secure.

Paradoxically, it was under Queen Elizabeth I (1558–1603), the monarch who was most protective of Ormond interests, that these defensive strategies became most urgent, as crown officials in Dublin became less tolerant of the privileged position of the Ormond territories and began working tirelessly to undermine the earldom. Following the queen's death the assault gathered pace. In a political, religious and legal confrontation with the eleventh earl, the Catholic Walter Butler, that has rarely been noted in the histories of seventeenth-century Ireland,[20] the Ormond lordship was finally overthrown under a less sympathetic monarch, James I (1603–25). Despite long years of collaboration with the state, by the early seventeenth century the earldom's autonomous status and its public association with Counter-Reformation Catholicism left it exposed to new royal demands, and it was ruthlessly cut down by Protestant government officials.

Historians have ignored the dramatic reduction of the earldom primarily because the Ormond dynasty survived its Jacobean downfall to stage something of a comeback under Charles I (1625–49), before going on to greater glory under Charles II (1660–85). Indeed, having succeeded to the title in 1633 its most famous representative, the Protestant twelfth earl of Ormond, James Butler (1610–88) – the future first duke of Ormonde – subsequently ascended the ladder of state power with such speed before 1641 that historians have generally celebrated him as the apparent saviour of his lineage. As will be shown below, it is difficult to sustain such an interpretation. Quite apart from his shortcomings as a politician, which were considerable, the twelfth earl found it impossible to repair the damage that had been done to his dynasty while he was a child, during the 1610s and '20s, when the government's anti-Catholic programme was at its peak.

As I have suggested elsewhere, it is only possible to appreciate the quite miserable state of his inheritance, and the devastating impact of the crown's hostility to his grandfather, Earl Walter, by examining in detail extant local evidence, looking beyond the lives of the earls to (once again) assess the condition of their friends and followers among the Kilkenny gentry.[21] By pursuing this broader perspective a totally different impression emerges of political trends in the Ormond country during the early-to-mid seventeenth century. Essentially, while James, the Protestant twelfth earl, soared to prominence in Dublin after 1633, befriending his masters in the colonial administration and making a string of concessions to facilitate the centralisation of state power, his authority at home in Kilkenny deteriorated rapidly. The anti-Catholic policies that had humbled

---

20 It is completely ignored in the most recent textbook of the period, B. Fitzpatrick, *Seventeenth century Ireland: the war of religions* (Dublin 1988). A useful outline has recently appeared in V. Treadwell, *Buckingham & Ireland, 1616–28: a study in Anglo-Irish politics* (Dublin 1998).   **21** D. Edwards, 'The poisoned chalice: the Ormond inheritance, sectarian division, and the emergence of James Butler, 1614–42', in T. Barnard & J. Fenlon (ed.), *The dukes of Ormonde, 1610–1745* (Woodbridge 2000), 55–82.

his grandfather Earl Walter remained in place to worry the traditional clients of his house, the local gentry and merchants. Hence, regarding those accusations of tyranny which have so hampered our understanding of the world of the Irish lordships, it will be argued here that in Kilkenny the development of greater control over the county by the central government, and the complete acquies-cence to crown policy of Earl James, the ruling lord, before 1640, led to cries of misrule by the local community. The great Kilkenny revolt of 1641–2 was aimed not just at the recovery of recently lost local privileges, but also at the overthrow of what the county community perceived as English governmental tyranny. Harsh as Ormond rule had sometimes been in the time of the twelfth earl's predecessors, by the beginning of the 1640s the Kilkenny gentry preferred the return of the old feudal order to the continued growth of state power. To attain this goal they rose up against Earl James, their nominal overlord, whom they perceived as an 'Unkinde Deserter', a traitor to his blood and to the polit-ical customs of the Ormond country.

What follows, then, is not a standard biographical account of the Butlers, earls of Ormond, during the sixteenth and early seventeenth centuries, but rather a history of their earldom. Although endeavouring, as it must do, to paint detailed individual portraits of each of the five earls that ruled Kilkenny between 1515 and 1642, it also attempts to explain how each of the earls interacted with the county community. It is as much a work of social and economic history, and even historical geography, as it is of political history, for in order to recon-struct the skeleton of the Ormond power structure, and to measure how it changed and evolved over time, it was necessary to rediscover such aspects of local life as rents charged per acre, land quality and land use, the strength of commerce, trade routes, urban and rural population distribution and clientage and kinship networks. By thus broadening the scope of my analysis to examine the earldom as much as the earls I am afraid I have written a very big history, much bigger than I anticipated when commencing my work. I only hope it provides sufficient new insights to justify its bulk.

PART I

The Passage of Power: A Structural Account

CHAPTER I

County Kilkenny, Ormond country

In many ways later medieval and early modern Co. Kilkenny was different from what it is today, a quietly prosperous corner of the province of Leinster. In those times it stood out among its neighbours, and was by far one of the most impor-tant areas of Ireland. As scholars have noted, it was only 'in theory an ordinary county subject to the Dublin administration'; in reality it was a centre of power, a regional capital in the mid-south of the country.[1] This was not unusual. For much of the sixteenth and early seventeenth centuries Ireland was more a patch-work of regions, great and small, than a unified country or state, and in many places the authority of individual families counted for much more than that of the royal government in far-away Dublin.[2] Co. Kilkenny owed its high status almost entirely to the presence of one family, the Butlers of Ormond, Anglo-Irish magnates who had chosen it as the centre of their lordship in the course of the Middle Ages. Thanks mainly to the Butlers' prominence, Kilkenny had its golden age between 1515 and the 1640s, possessing a strategic signifi-cance in national affairs that it has rarely enjoyed since.

Physical geography was the foundation upon which the Butlers of Ormond built. Kilkenny's situation was highly advantageous, ideal as a power-base. According to one observer who wrote of it in the 1580s, Co. Kilkenny lay almost at the centre of the southern Leinster borderlands, holding a strong phys-ical frontier with the territories of the MacGiollapadraigs (or Fitzpatricks) and the O'Mores in Laois, and with various branches of the Kavanaghs in Cos. Carlow and Wexford.[3] Indeed, centrality was arguably its greatest asset. Standing more or less equidistant between Dublin and Cork, it was also a useful mid-point between Leinster and Munster. In 1536 a crown official had recommended that the royal courts be transferred from Dublin to Kilkenny in order to make them more accessible to suitors from the two provinces.[4] The shire capital, Kilkenny city, was a hive of inter-provincial business, a popular overnight stop for travellers.[5] By the standards of the time the county was a crossroads, a place where the south-east of the country encountered the south-west, and vice versa.

---

1 D.B. Quinn & K.W. Nicholls. 'Ireland in 1534', *NHI*, iii, 8.   2 Ibid., 1–38; P. Wilson, *The beginnings of modern Ireland* (Dublin 1914), ch. 1; M. O'Dowd, 'Gaelic economy and society', in C. Brady & R. Gillespie (ed.), *Natives & newcomers*, 120–47.   3 Colm Lennon, *Richard Stanihurst: the Dubliner, 1547–1618* (Dublin 1981), 141.   4 *LP Henry VIII*, xi, no. 521.   5 E.g., NLI, Ms 13,236 (7); Lamacraft (ed.), *Ir. funeral entries*, 141; Grosart (ed.), *Lismore papers,* 1st series, i, 29, 70.

Its physical centrality gave the county a hybrid identity, for it belonged almost as much to Munster as it did to Leinster. This was widely recognised at a high political level. Commissions issued to Kilkenny county officials often required them to take control of Munster shires like Waterford, Limerick and Cork along with Kilkenny itself.[6] As late as the early seventeenth century, Kilkenny remained something of a geographical and administrative oddity, most of the time included on the Leinster assize circuit, but occasionally, when circumstances dictated, lumped in with Munster as well.[7]

This inter-provincial centrality was ideally suited to the Butlers' needs. Holding Kilkenny, they controlled a critical avenue between the two most densely populated provinces of Ireland. It followed logically that, should the need to do so ever arise, by threatening to cut this avenue off, the dynasty could hold the Dublin executive to ransom and exact guarantees for the maintenance of its powerful position. For this reason alone, Kilkenny had become the capital of the Ormond lordship during the medieval period.[8]

The fact that the Butlers of Ormond were able to continue to dominate Kilkenny after 1515 – and even to increase their standing there – is ample testament to their power and ability, for the sixteenth and early seventeenth century is generally regarded by historians as a time when the central government expanded at the expense of regional lords such as they.[9] This is not to say that the Ormond Butlers were left unmolested by the state after 1515 – nothing of the sort – but it does indicate that the government was more respectful of the family than it would otherwise have been had they been based somewhere else.

In general, mainly because of its anxiety over access to the south, the Dublin administration allowed the Butlers, strong and relatively loyal, a freer hand than most in the conduct of their affairs. The policy had dramatic results. By 1603 the house of Ormond had developed an extraordinary territorial hegemony in Kilkenny and the mid-south, so much so that the government had to change its policy and was compelled to spend much of the early seventeenth century trying to chop the dynasty down to a more manageable size. In particular, the eleventh earl of Ormond, Walter Butler (1614–33), suffered reverse after reverse because of the extent of his inheritance and personal authority. Eventually the crown's attempt to weaken the Ormond lordship in Kilkenny, and to remould it in its own image, would end in failure, serving only to alienate many among the shire community, who for reasons of their own greatly resented the state's interference. This chapter will seek to (i) examine just how powerful the Ormond presence was across later medieval and early modern Co. Kilkenny, in order to discover if the post-1614 assault by the state stood any chance of

6 *Ir. Fiants*, Eliz. I, nos. 469, 542, 666, 725, 828, 2430, 3860, 4776; NA, M 7008, 2a. 7 J. McCavitt, '"Good planets in their several spheares": the establishment of the assize circuit in early seventeenth century Ireland', *Irish Jurist* 24 (1989), 266, 273. 8 C.A. Empey, 'The Butler lordship', *Butler Soc. Jn.* 3 (1970–1), 174–87. 9 Brady, *Chief governors*; Canny, *Elizabethan conquest*; A. Clarke & R. Dudley Edwards, 'Pacification, plantation and the Catholic question, 1603–23', *NHI*, iii, 187–232.

success, and (ii) determine how much and what sort of support existed in the shire for what was, after all, an over-mighty earldom. To begin this analysis, and draw attention to the highly localised nature of political power in the sixteenth and seventeenth centuries, it will be necessary to describe the earls' lands, which formed the very foundation of their authority.

THE ORMOND PRESENCE

It was only a matter of time before the sheer scale of the Ormonds' power-base in the shire concerned the government. Even in 1515 the ancestral estate of the head of the dynasty, the seventh earl of Ormond, Thomas Butler (1478–1515), was very large: sprawling across the county, it accounted for approximately 40–45,000 acres[10](nearly one-sixth of all available land).[11]At the time of the earl's death, in August 1515, the Ormond estate already had a firm hold over the Kilkenny countryside. The estate was then cross-shaped, and as such it affected most parts of the county, stretching from the manor of Kilmocar in the north to Grannagh near Waterford in the south, while simultaneously fanning out to embrace Gowran in the east and Callan in the west. Great as this was, however, it was merely a platform for a much greater estate in the years ahead.

The seventh earl's death provided the turning point. Thomas was the last of what could be called the medieval earls of Ormond – the Carrick line of earls, descended directly from Edmund Butler, earl of Carrick (1318) – and when he died without sons, he cleared the way for the rise of the gaelicised Pottlerath branch of the family, headed by Piers Butler, a distant relative. Piers, or Piers Ruadh (Red Piers), to give him his contemporary alias,[12] was just what the crown government was looking for in the early sixteenth century. Unlike Thomas, who lived in London and had long been an absentee landlord, Piers had a strong presence in the county, and was a major military figure. The government hoped that by recruiting him it would be able to improve its grip over the south and south-east of the country. In time Piers benefited hugely from the crown's favour. The strongest candidate in Ireland, he was recognised as the heir to the earldom of Ormond and eventually became eighth earl in 1538, once all the other claimants had been silenced.[13] His succession had major implications for the size of the Ormond estate. Immediately he was able to add his own holdings to it, some 19,000 acres by the mid-1530s,[14] an increase of more than 40 per cent on the estate as it stood in 1515. This was just the beginning, for under the new Pottlerath line of earls, the Ormond patrimony in Kilkenny

---

10 Plantation acres. 1654 measurement. For the pre-1515 Ormond estate see *COD*, iii, nos. 70, 95, 110, 119, 160, 172, 218–20, 234: D.B. Quinn (ed.), 'Ormond papers, 1480–1535', ibid., iv, 312, 328–9, 344–5. 11 Co. Kilkenny had about 263,000 acres according to 1654 measurements (Appendix I below). 12 Quinn (ed.), 'Ormond papers', 345; J. Carney (ed.), *Poems on the Butlers* (Dublin 1945), 8–11. 13 Chapter 2 below. 14 *COD*, iv, nos. 127, 134, 172, 176, 179, 182.

was set to more than double in size before the death of Piers' grandson, the tenth earl, 'Black' Thomas, in November 1614.

The government greatly facilitated the expansion of the estate between 1536 and 1542, the era of the suppression of the monasteries. Eager to persuade the Butlers to go along with Henry VIII's breach with Rome, the royal administration resorted to bribery, offering Piers and his family a major share of the spoils of the suppression in return for their support of the king's religious changes.[15] The offer was accepted, and by August 1542 Piers' successor as ninth earl, his eldest son James (1539–46), had been granted four ex-monastic sites in the shire, the Cistercian abbeys of Duiske and Jerpoint, the priory of Kells, and the Augustinian friary of Callan, grants which added a further 14,000 acres to his holdings.[16]

In quantitative terms these grants had a profound impact on landholding patterns in Co. Kilkenny. Prior to 1542 the religious orders, taken together, had ranked as the second largest landowners in the shire, behind the Butlers of Ormond. Now they were gone, swept away overnight, and largely because of the government's policy towards their former estates the distance separating the Ormond Butlers from the rest of the local proprietors was greatly enhanced. The Ormonds had been given almost 75 per cent of all the land that the religious orders had possessed in the county, and if the grant of Inistioge priory to Earl James' younger brother, Richard Butler (the future first Viscount Mountgarret), is taken into account, then the dynasty's share of the spoils was closer to 80 per cent of the total acreage seized by the crown.[17] For them, the dissolution of the monasteries was a bonanza.

The dissolved estates were destined to remain in Butler hands for more than a hundred years, a notable fact, in stark contrast with trends in England. There many of the noble families who profited from the suppression quickly transferred their ex-religious possessions to the land-hungry gentry in return for ready money. English historians have consequently often viewed the latter part of the reign of Henry VIII as vital in the development of the gentry as a powerful group in society.[18] Thanks to the Butlers' good fortune, however, Co. Kilkenny followed an entirely different path. Here the dynasty's long-term monopolisation of all grants acted as a stumbling-block for the shire gentry, preventing the emergence of a local market in ex-monastic land such as appeared all over England and Wales after the 1530s.[19] In short, in Kilkenny the dissolution stifled the progress of the gentry by increasing the Ormonds' dominance over them.

15 Ellis, *Tudor Ireland,* 200–4; B. Bradshaw, *The dissolution of the religious orders in Ireland under Henry VIII* (Cambridge 1974). 16 *Ir. Fiants,* Henry VIII, nos. 161, 241–3: N.B. White (ed.). *Extents of Irish monastic possessions. 1540–1* (Dublin 1943), 197; NLI, D.2337, 2350. 17 *Ir. Fiants,* Henry VIII, no. 239. 18 J. Youings, *Sixteenth Century England* (London 1984), 161–4; R.H. Tawney, 'The rise of the gentry', *Economic History Review* 11 (1941); H.J. Habbakuk, 'The market for monastic property. 1539–1603', ibid. 28 (1958). 19 D.M. Palliser, *The age of Elizabeth* (London 1983), 87, 89–90.

The Ormond Butlers would not have been able to curtail the Kilkenny land market without the continuance of royal favour. All the ex-monastic land that James the ninth earl had received by 1542 had come in the form of 21-year leases, implying that the interest of his successor, his eldest son and heir, Earl Thomas, in the temporal possessions of such jewels as Jerpoint Abbey and Callan Friary was set to expire in the early 1560s. But 'Black' Thomas (as the tenth earl was known) never needed to renew the leasehold. Reared at the royal court since the mid–1540s, he stood well with successive English monarchs, who because of his court background felt sure of his loyalty, and they allowed the monastic lands to become the *permanent* property of his family. This was done by changing the form of tenure under which the lands were held: Jerpoint and Callan were re-granted to him by Queen Mary in 1558 to hold in *capite* for-ever, and in 1578 Elizabeth I gave him Kells Priory, also for ever, but this time in free socage. The Kells grant was particularly advantageous. Under socage tenure, the crown gave up its claim to various feudal dues, including the ward-ship of the land during a minority.[20]

Thanks to grants like these, the tenth earl's long career (1546–1614) was a high point for the Kilkenny estate of the Butlers, earls of Ormond. In addition to consolidating the gains made by his father James and his grandfather Piers, Earl Thomas also bought a great deal of land in his own right. In plain statisti-cal terms he acquired approximately 13,050 acres in the shire. He continued to drink deep of the well of royal favour as long as Elizabeth I remained on the throne, gaining a string of grants and privileges that greatly enhanced his wealth. An occasional debt to the crown notwithstanding, Black Thomas of Ormond was far and away one of the richest men in Elizabethan Ireland. All the land that he bought in Co. Kilkenny he gained absolutely, paying hard cash for it, and by the time of his death in 1614 his purchases had taken his ancestral estate to unparalleled heights. No less than 90,000 plantation acres – about one acre in three – belonged to him.[21]

The massive growth of the estate under the eighth, ninth and tenth earls had major implications for the scope of Ormond power in the shire. Quite simply, the authority of the earldom was no longer a major factor in local life; it was instead *the* major factor. The Ormond estate was everywhere, covering upland and lowland alike, densely distributed across 78 of the shire's 139 parishes.[22] For the ordinary people it must have had a claustrophobic presence. By the begin-ning of the seventeenth century there were at least 25 castles in the county that belonged to the earl and were manned by his men; these overlooked most of the main highways and thoroughfares, and enabled a close watch to be kept on all travellers coming into and going out of the shire. In a real and physical sense,

---

20 NA, Lodge MSS, Rolls, i, 127–31, 401. The Jerpoint-Callan grant was confirmed to him in 1563, when the crown rent (£IR49 3s. 9d.) was also abolished *(Ir. Fiants*, Eliz. I, no. 504); A.K.R. Kiralfy (ed.), *Potter's historical introduction to the English law* (4th edn., London 1962), 494–5. **21** For a list of his purchases, see NLI, Ms 2506, fol. 22r. **22** Ibid., MSS 975. 2543, 2560; Appendix I below.

Co. Kilkenny was just what outsiders often called it – 'the earl of Ormond's country'. With the earl's servants spread so widely across the shire very little happened without his knowledge or without his consent.

Like a giant modern industrial concern such as General Motors in Detroit, the earldom affected the fortunes of the great majority of the county's inhabitants, rural as well as urban, rich as well as poor. Each year the yield of its vast acreage swamped the local markets and fairs, so that more than any other estate, it probably played a major part in determining food prices in the area. Because of the size of its estate, the earldom would have had an inordinate influence on the relationship between supply and demand.

The earldom's influence could also be felt in other ways. Apart from some of the town-based industries, the Ormond household was one of the biggest employers in the shire. All year round it required a host of domestic servants to tend to its daily needs: ushers and porters to guard access to its many castles and tend to its guests; victuallers and cooks to provide and prepare food; maids and laundresses to do the cleaning; blacksmiths, saddlers and stable-boys to care for its horses; woodsmen to chop fuel, and so on. At any one time these domestic servants numbered in the low hundreds, and through their family connections the influence of their aristocratic employers reached down to touch the lives of thousands more in the county. The management and exploitation of the estate likewise necessitated the hiring of a multitude of agricultural workers, either specialist drovers and shepherds, retained throughout the year, or general farm labourers, engaged during the summer and at harvest time.[23]

Noble power on such a grand scale was increasingly rare in Ireland in the early seventeenth century, a time when the expanding centralised government rapidly reduced the native nobility.[24] But the decision taken by the crown after 1614 to divide up the estate and dismantle the lordship was destined to have far-reaching and counter-productive results partly because the government did not fully appreciate how important the earldom had become to local life.

Each region of the shire had its own special relationship with the earls. In some areas there were very strong ties indeed, for during the course of the sixteenth century, while their estate was growing, the earls had taken the opportunity to develop certain regions in a manner that furthered their interests. It should be pointed out that this did not necessarily improve each area very much. However, it did often improve the earls' influence, for they recruited local supporters everywhere in the shire, and as we shall see, in some places they managed to create a community of friends and clients that was sometimes wholly dependent upon them. All over the county the earldom of Ormond had friends and allies. Even where it came into conflict with local vested interests it often had the means to make useful friendships (through financial inducements and

23 The Ormond household account book for 1630/1 (NLI, Ms 2549) provides a detailed picture of the importance of the estate in local affairs.   24 N. Canny, *From Reformation to Restoration: Ireland, 1534–1660* (Dublin 1987), ch. 6; W.F.T. Butler, *Confiscations in Irish history* (Dublin 1917), ch. 1–4.

other strategies) that could overcome or sidestep the difficulties. As the royal government would eventually discover to its cost, too many of the most important people in Co. Kilkenny – landlords, merchants, lawyers, soldiers, clergy – were Ormond people, just as acre by acre and field by field the shire was Ormond country. Of course, the irony for the crown after 1614 was that many of these friendships and alliances had been forged during the preceding century, the very time when it had actively facilitated the expansion of the earls' influence.

THE NORTHERN UPLANDS

Nowhere in the county was the growth of Ormond power felt so profoundly as it was in the north, in the baronies of Galmoy and Fassadmin and the northernmost parts of Crannagh and Gowran. Upland country, with hills to the east and west guarding entry into the Nore Valley, it was of immense strategic importance to the shire economy. Possession of it was a prerequisite of meaningful overlordship. Commencing in the 1510s and continuing well into the early seventeenth century, successive earls of Ormond made control of the 20-mile area stretching from Urlingford to Castlecomer one of their principal territorial objectives. In doing so, they transformed the character of the region. Not necessarily for the better: at their instigation, between *c.*1515 and 1640 northern Co. Kilkenny experienced a protracted three-stage development which, as it worked itself out, entailed as much suffering as progress for the local people.

Initially, before the Ormond expansion got under way, the north had been a quietly prosperous, occasionally dangerous, inter-ethnic zone, a place where (usually) little happened and the Gaelic Irish and Anglo-Irish lived side by side. Relations were made easier by the fact that in the course of the fifteenth century the Anglo-Irish had become increasingly gaelicised. Families such as the Graces had commenced acting as patrons to Gaelic scribes, and their leaders had adopted laudatory Gaelic pseudonyms, such as *féasóg*, the bearded (Oliver Grace, *c.*1470), and *crios iaraan*, the iron-belted (John Grace, *c.*1520).[25] However, the peace was soon shattered by the rebirth of Ormond power after 1515. Immediately the north of the county became a battleground, providing the setting for a bitter struggle between the Butlers of Ormond and their most threatening neighbours, principally the Gaelic MacGiollapadraigs (alias Fitzpatricks) of Upper Ossory and the O'Brennans of Idough in Fassadinin, but also including the Anglo-Irish earls of Kildare, who owned an important fort at Glashare in Galmoy.[26]

With the eruption of these conflicts the north of the shire took on its present appearance, becoming shorter but broader in shape, as the borders with Cos. Laois and Carlow changed forever. Previously, ever since the early thirteenth century, northern Co. Kilkenny had been a long strip of land more or

25 NLI, Ms 8315 (9); O. O'Kelly, *Placenames of County Kilkenny* (Kilkenny Arch. Soc., 1985), 29.
26 See Chapters 3–4 below for the border wars.

less coterminous with the diocese of Ossory. Running north as far as
Slievebloom in Upper Ossory, it had included the medieval fees of Offerlane,
Coolbally, Gortnycross, Aghmacart, Ballygennan and Gortreny in the
modern-day baronies of Upperwoods, Clarmallagh and Clandonagh, Co. Laois.²⁷

After 1515, however, the county and the diocese diverged, with the northernmost lands overrun by the MacGiollapadraigs, who expelled their Anglo-Irish
occupants (chiefly the Graces), and proceeded to withdraw the entire territory
of Upper Ossory from Co. Kilkenny. They did this mainly to evade the jurisdiction of the Kilkenny sheriffs, who were usually Butler creatures, and as such
unlikely to grant the MacGiollapadraigs a fair trial for alleged offences.²⁸ The
fact that the office of sheriff stayed in the hands of the Butlers of Ormond and
their supporters until the 1580s (see Appendix 3) insured that Upper Ossory
never returned to Co. Kilkenny. Instead it remained unshired and aloof, existing as an autonomous Gaelic lordship under the MacGiollapadraigs until 1600,
when it was finally re-shired by the government as part of Queen's County
(Co. Laois), to which it has been attached ever since.²⁹ After 1515 the bound-
ary that separated it from north Co. Kilkenny soon became a hard frontier made
up of a series of woodlands and man-made ditches stretching from Coolnacrutta
through Coolcashin to Kilmenan and Loughill.³⁰

It is important to realise that the Kilkenny/Upper Ossory border was a political frontier only. It was *not* characterised by a hard ethnic divide. Although the
MacGiollapadraigs retained hardly any Anglo-Irish followers in Ossory, in north
Kilkenny the Butlers, Graces, Shortals and Purcells commanded Gaelic Irish as
well as Anglo-Irish support, and all the major local landowners had Irish tenants, spoke at least some Irish, and practiced Irish customs.³¹ Members of the
MacGiollapadraigs' famous medical school at Aghmacart were able to cross the
frontier seemingly at will, writing parts of their surviving texts in Upper Ossory,
other parts at Ballyragget and Courtstown, under the patronage of the
Mountgarret Butlers and the Graces.³² Likewise, members of the O'Doran law
school, also based in Upper Ossory, acted as brehons to Viscount Mountgarret
as well as to the MacGiollapadraig chieftains. Occasionally, as in 1559, in an
effort to restore the peace, the brehons could play an important part in negotiating a 'slanety' or *sláinte* (a Gaelic bond of guarantee) between the Butlers and
the MacGiollapadraigs;³³ so too could the primarily Anglo-Irish merchants of

27 St John Brooks (ed.), *Knight's fees*, 227, 265, 270–2. **28** C. McNeill (ed.), 'Lord Chancellor
Gerrard's Notes of his Report of Ireland', *Anal. Hib.* 2 (1931), 162–3, 167–8, 219; Alnwick Castle,
Ms 476, ff 32v–33r. **29** Edwards, 'MacGiollapadraigs', 354. **30** Details of this frontier can be gleaned
from an Elizabethan description of the Ormond lands: *COD*, vi, Appendix 1. **31** E.g., soldiers of
Gaelic Irish origin were maintained by the Ormond Butlers at Kilmocar and Glashare (*Ir. Fiants*,
Eliz. I, nos. 950, 1065, 2031, 2058) and by the Mountgarret Butlers at Ballyragget (ibid., no.1057).
The use of the Irish language is confirmed by the gaelicised names of some of the Purcell troops
housed at Kilderry – William fitz Redmund Reagh and Richard Mór Purcell (ibid., no. 950). For
Gaelic tenants, in addition to evidence contained in the pardons in government fiants (ibid., passim)
see esp. NLI, Ms 9081; NA, CP E/48; ibid., CP G/66; ibid., CP I/180; ibid., CP Aa/5. **32** RIA
Ms 439 (3 C 19), ff 13r–234v, a treatise of 1590 by Risteard Ó Conchubhair. **33** Ibid., Ms D 5 3,

Kilkenny city. Like many frontier parts of sixteenth-century Ireland, the North Kilkenny/Upper Ossory border was an area of cultural and ethnic intermixing, not separation.

The other Gaelic territory in the north, *Hy-Duach* or Idough in Fassadinin – a place of bleak, wet, cold hills – had a comparable experience, though its native inhabitants, the O'Brennans, did not fare nearly as well as the MacGiollapadraigs. Like the MacGiollapadraigs, the O'Brennans saw their territory change counties following the Butler resurgence, but whereas Upper Ossory escaped from Co. Kilkenny, Idough was drawn into it as the sixteenth century progressed. During the Middle Ages it had been included in Co. Carlow as part of the Irish inheritance of the Bigods, dukes of Norfolk.[34] However, by the 1540s (if not a lot earlier)[35] Idough was being claimed by the Ormond Butlers, and they had their claims recorded formally in an official document in March 1547, when an inquisition post mortem was made for the estate of the ninth earl, James Butler, who had died six months earlier. Though it was admitted in court that the earl had received no rent for it from the O'Brennans, and although the lineage were unable to object, Idough was registered as part of his Kilkenny estate to be passed on to his son and heir 'Black' Thomas, the tenth earl.[36] Under Earl Thomas the territory was inescapably joined to Co. Kilkenny.

By the early 1560s, as Earl Thomas' power was growing in Dublin and London, members of his family increased their grip on Idough to such an extent that the Clan Wickelow sept of the O'Brennans were powerless to prevent a major military incursion onto their lands by the tenth earl's brother, Sir Edmund Butler of Cloghgrenan, and some of the O'Brennans began enlisting as soldiers in the Butler forces.[37] The process of aggrandisement continued throughout the reign of Elizabeth 1, and in the 1580s many of the O'Brennans entered into a last desperate (and unfortunately poorly documented) battle for survival, refusing to acknowledge the authority of the sheriff of Co. Kilkenny,[38] and in *c.*1590–1 they ambushed Edmund Butler, second Viscount Mountgarret, when he and his forces dared to parade through Idough.[39] In the next few years, however, O'Brennan resistance petered out. In 1594 the tenth earl received a grant of several pieces of land in the area forfeited to the crown by attainder, and he also began buying out other parcels of O'Brennan land. All told, through his agent, Patrick Grant, he acquired more than 5,000 acres across Idough in little over a year.[40]

By 1604 the O'Brennans realised that they had no choice but to accept the earl's overlordship, and Gilpatrick O'Brennan, the chief of the strongest sept, the Clan Moriertagh, duly became friendly with the earl.[41] Soon afterwards, with

item 4. **34** McNeill (ed.), 'Lord Chancellor Gerrard's Notes', 219; BL, Harleian Ms 430, ff 204v–206r. **35** The O'Brennans may have been drawn into Kilkenny temporarily *c.*1400: J. Graves, 'The Ancient Tribes and Territories of Ossory, No. 1', *KSEIAS*, 1 (1849–51), 238. **36** *COD*, iv, no. 361. **37** PRO, SP 63/11/4; N. Murphy, 'The O'Brennans and the ancient territory of Hy-Duach', *Ossory Arch. Soc. Jn.* 1 (1874–9), 399; *Ir. Fiants*, Eliz. I, no. 911. **38** PRO, SP 63/108/34; *COD*, vi, no. 89 (2). **39** HMC, *Egmont MSS*, i, 23. **40** *COD*, vi, nos. 89 (2), 99. **41** NLI, D 3340.

the O'Brennans' agreement, the entire territory was included within the boundaries of Co. Kilkenny, becoming part of the barony of 'Fassadinin and Idough',
as the earl of Ormond wanted. One of the constables of the barony was William
O'Brennan of Ballyhomyn (one of the Clan Moriertagh), and the chieftains of
all four O'Brennan septs were named among its 'principal gentlemen'.[42]

Thus the rebirth of Ormond power after 1515 changed the boundaries of
north Kilkenny forever, sundering the county's age-old ties with a strong Gaelic
dynastic region while annexing a weaker one that had once been part of Carlow.
But not just the Gaelic dynastic lands along the northern borders were affected
by the Ormond resurgence. For the Anglo-Irish too, the entire late medieval
settlement pattern was overturned following the outbreak of hostilities in 1515.
Several of the oldest Anglo-Irish landowning families in the area were forced
to sell up and leave, among them the Launts of Coulshill, the Pembrokes of
Ballyragget and the Freneys of Clone and Rathbeagh, each of whom had lived
in the north since the fourteenth century or earlier.[43] Without exception they
sold or mortgaged their lands to the Butlers of Ormond,[44] and by the 1540s the
dynasty had moved into the area in earnest, pushing its estate further north
towards the present border with Laois.

The net result of Ormond expansion was that large parts of the baronies of
Fassadinin, Galmoy and northern Crannagh and Gowran were cordoned off as
military zones under Butler control. Existing castles were renovated and new
ones constructed as the Ormonds established a string of garrisons in the area,
situated at Glashare (which the earls got in 1537 after the collapse of the
Kildares), Foulkscourt, Tubbrid, Coulshill, Ballyragget, and Kilmocar. Backing
them up in this enterprise were several 'gaelicised' Anglo-Irish client families:
the Butlers, Viscounts Mountgarret, the Graces – a major lineage based at
Courtstown Castle who controlled 'Grace's country' in the Slieveardagh hills
– and the Shortals, Purcells and Archdekins (alias MacCodys or McOdos).
Although freeholders, most of these families were creatures of the earldom,
feudal subjects who held their lands directly in fee of the earls, the lords of the
fee, usually in return for fealty, military service, suit of court, and a nominal
rent charge. This was the case with the Mountgarret Butlers, the Courtstown
Graces, the Shortals of Ballylorcaine, and the Archdekins of Bawnballinlogh,
who held their lands in fee by knight's service of the earls' manor of Kilkenny,
and the Purcells of Ballyfoyle and Foulkesrath, who held of Gowran manor.[45]
As late as the 1620s, long after the border wars had ended, the earls continued
to keep account of the local landlords who owed them fealty and suit of court.[46]
Feudalism (in a bastard form) was the backbone of the Ormond lordship
throughout the county, but it was especially important in the north, where the
earls' demands for military service were most often required.

42 *Cal. Carew MSS, 1603–24*, 29.   **43** *COD*, ii, nos. 258, 377, 397; ibid., iii, nos. 50, 127, 144,
209.   **44** Ibid., iv, nos. 69, 134, 176, 182; ibid., v, nos. 7, 14 (1), 46, 127, 145, 267; ibid., vi, nos.
89 (2), 99 (1), NLI, Ms 2506, fol. 22r.   **45** *Cal. Carew MSS, 1515–74*, no. 273.   **46** NLI, Ms 11,053
(3); ibid., Ms 2509, passim.

The feudal client families of the region gave frequent military support to their overlords. Sometimes they established new garrisons of their own, or else they supplied many of the officers and troops who served in the Ormond forts.[47] The Graces were perhaps the most useful in this regard, with various members of the family taking charge of the Ormond castles at Rathvilly, Co. Carlow, Glashare and Foulkscourt, Co. Kilkenny, and Kilcooley, Boulick and Roscrea, Co. Tipperary.[48] Within barely a generation, northern Co. Kilkenny (and the territory to either side) had become a no-go area patrolled by marauding gangs of pro-Ormond soldiers who cared little for the rule of law. It remained like this for most of the sixteenth century.

The effect on the northern economy was catastrophic. As the level of violence intensified, important local commercial and population centres shrivelled up. The manorial village at Durrow on the Laois-Kilkenny frontier was badly hit. Church property, held by the bishops of Ossory, it had prospered late in the fifteenth century, apparently thriving as a neutral trading post between Kilkenny and Upper Ossory. After 1515 the Butler resurgence sent it into decline. The Purcells of Foulkesrath, longstanding Butler supporters, began illegally exploiting the bishops' lands in the area.[49] By the 1540s, rather than attracting merchants and skilled craftsmen, Durrow was receiving the undivided attention of the Butler and MacGiollapadraig armies, for fear that the bridge it guarded connecting Kilkenny to Laois would fall into the hands of the other.[50] The boundaries of Durrow manor, and the range of its manorial rights and privileges, were disputed by the rival dynasties for a long time afterwards. As late as 1635, the sheriff of Co. Kilkenny was compelled to intervene there in order to prevent the chief of the MacGiollapadraigs, the fifth baron of Upper Ossory, from encroaching any further on its lands, which were normally controlled by the servants of the earl of Ormond. Consequently, Durrow village failed to develop as it should have, into an important market town, and instead it had to eke out a humble existence as a small border settlement, becoming the sort of place that attracted members of the underworld, thieves, smugglers, and cattle rustlers looking to sell their stolen commodities far from more advanced market centres where government officials might be found.[51] (It remained a detached part of Co. Kilkenny until 1837).

The village of Freshford – like Durrow, an episcopal manor – had a similar experience; here too the re-emergence of the Butlers apparently put paid to its growth and development.[52] By the 1560s the manor house of the bishop of Ossory

---

47 *Ir. Fiants*, Eliz. I, nos. 90, 787, 950, 1057, 1065, 1184, 1899, 1903, 1933, 2013, 2025, 2058, 2064. **48** Lambeth, Ms 601, 40 (Rathvilly); PRO, SP 63/68/16 (Roscrea); HMC, *Haliday MSS*, 100 (Glashare & Foulkscourt); NLI, Ms 2507, fol. 17v (Boulick); St Kieran's College, Kilkenny, Carrigan MSS, Vol. 18, 23 (Kilcoooley). **49** *COD*, iv, no. 39. **50** Much of the history of Tudor-era Durrow can be gleaned from a series of depositions made in 1577: N.B. White (ed.), *Ir. mon & ep deeds, 1200–1600* (Dublin 1936), 213–21. **51** NA, Co. 1759; ibid., RC 6/2, 141–2; McNeill (ed.), 'Lord Chancellor Gerrard's Notes', 165–6. **52** Freshord's growth in the fifteenth century was aided by some major building works commissioned by the bishops: Carrigan, *Ossory*, ii, 251; Moran, 'Bishops', 247.

and the bishop's sturdy little castle at Upper Court were both dilapidated, and the surrounding area was described as 'depopulated, deserted and not yielding any rent'.[53] Conditions thereabouts did not improve for a long time, and it was well into the seventeenth century before Freshford became a sizeable population centre again, finally counted as one of the lesser towns in the county in the 1650s.[54] Had it not been for the series of local wars sparked off by the rise of the Ormond Butlers after 1515, Freshford might have become a town much earlier.

Across the north, the expansion of the Ormond lordship brought considerable dislocation, and with population levels shrinking, land values also fell. Early in the sixteenth century the local land market had apparently been quite buoyant, if a series of deeds from north western Fassadinin are anything to go by. Commencing in the mid-1490s and continuing until the late 1530s, the townlands of Rosconnell, Loughill and Ballyoskill, situated next to the border with Laois, had been the subject of five leases made by the St Leger family, the owners. Despite the fact that the land involved was frontier land, the St Legers had had no trouble getting a good return from it, for as yet there was no shortage of willing tenants. Accordingly, each of their five leases had been made for short periods of time – 7 years, 5 years, 3 years, 9 years and 3 years respectively – and the rent demanded by the St Legers had continued to rise, from 10 shillings (Ir.), a summer sheep (that is, one sheep out of every flock) and 10 gallons of butter *c*.1495, to £4 (Ir.), a pig and a sheep in 1537, that is, an eightfold increase or thereabouts in forty years.[55]

But even by 1537 conditions had begun to change. The re-emergence of the Butlers of Ormond led to a rise in violence and the new tenant, the Gaelic rector of Rosconnell, Rory O' Bergin, felt compelled to ask the St Legers for a guarantee that they would only come to visit Rosconnell 'in good faith and not otherwise'; in other words, he feared that the St Legers would station their troops on his leasehold as they joined with the Butlers in waging war against the MacGiollapadraigs.[56] His fears were soon realised. By 1549/50 there was all-out war between the St Legers and the MacGiollapadraigs, and Rosconnell was overrun by both their armies.[57] The MacGiollapadraigs proved the stronger, constantly preying upon the local inhabitants, raiding and burning their farms, and eventually the St Legers were forced to leave the area. Sometime before the 1570s they handed over their Rosconnell estate to 'Black' Thomas Butler, tenth earl of Ormond, in exchange for lands elsewhere in the county.[58]

Earl Thomas did not take possession of the land in order to exploit it economically; rather, he intended to transform it into a buffer zone for the protection of his lands at Kilmocar and Dunmore further to the south. Hence his decision to sub-let Rosconnell and Ballyoskill to one of his most experienced captains, the Gaelic constable of Kilmocar fort, Donill Mac Shane, a pro-Butler member of the MacGiollapadraig lineage and head of the MacGiollapadraigs of

53 NA, M 2816, 3–4. **54** Ibid., Prim Mss, no. 32 – *Mercurius Politicus*, 436 (1658). **55** *COD*, iv, nos. 4 (1)–(5). **56** Ibid., no. 4 (5). **57** Ibid., v, nos. 31 (1)–(3); *Ir. Fiants*, Edward VI, no. 399. **58** *COD*, vi, Appendix 1, 144–5.

Formoyle, who remained in forcible possession there until the closing years of the sixteenth century. By this time the value of the area had noticeably stagnated, bringing the earl a rent of a mere £5 (stg) per annum.[59] Had it not been for the disturbances of the previous sixty years it would doubtless have been worth a great deal more. Once peace returned early in the seventeenth century Rosconnell, Ballyoskill and Loughill quadrupled in value in the space of less than ten years, producing a rent return of £20 (stg) per annum by Easter 1610.[60]

Rosconnell's experience was not untypical of other estates in the north of the shire. As Chart 1.1 demonstrates, by the 1560s, after more than fifty years of political violence, the value of property in Galmoy, Fassadinin and northern Crannagh and Gowran was lagging far behind the value of property in Co. Kilkenny's midland basin. Although a certain disparity between the two regions was inevitable – after all, the midland basin was the economic heartland of the county – the fact that land anywhere in the midlands was worth on average three times as much as land in the north was significant. In strict economic terms, the north had much going for it – mineral deposits, some of the best arable land in the county, and high quality grasslands for grazing horses, cattle and sheep in the Slieveardagh and Johnswell hills. As Professor Smyth has observed, there were 'pockets of superb [farming] land ... at Lisdowney and Ballyragget', and some of the county's best champion ground ran through Freshford, Dunmore and Mayne. By and large, only the wet, damp hill country around Idough and Castlecomer provided a tough environment for agriculture.[61] Yet, despite all this, land across the region struggled to reach a valuation of even 3.7*d.* per acre, a trivial amount by the second half of the sixteenth century.

Conditions were worst at Kilmocar – it was Ormond land, and therefore a target for MacGiollapadraig attacks – but even the most valuable holding in the north, that belonging to the Ormond client family, the Purcells of Ballyfoyle, was worth relatively little. The Ballyfoyle estate in Fassadinin and northern Gowran, which included lands at Muccully and Kilmadum, was quite highly developed in the reign of Elizabeth I. A schedule of goods drawn up after 1578 recorded that the deceased head of the family, Geoffrey Purcell, had made the most of the rolling hill country, breeding horses on an extensive stud farm, and keeping large numbers of cows, sheep and pigs as well.[62] Nonetheless, the Ballyfoyle land was worth little more than 5*d.* per acre, its economic potential clearly unrealised in a time of local turmoil. Until the close of the Elizabethan period the Purcell family had constantly to be on their guard against armed incursions onto their lands by night-time interlopers looking to steal their livestock or plunder and intimidate their tenants.[63]

The same was true of the Graces of Courtstown and the Shortals of Ballylorcaine, the principal landowners on the other side of the Nore Valley, in north-

---

59 NLI, Ms 2506, fol. 10v, which gives the half-yearly rent charge of £2 10s. 0d. **60** Ibid., fol. 36v. **61** W.J. Smyth, 'Territorial, social and settlement hierarchies in seventeenth century Kilkenny', in W. Nolan & K. Whelan (ed.), *Kilkenny: history & society* (Dublin, 1991), 127–8. **62** NA, CP F/33. **63** *Ir. Fiants*, Eliz. I, no. 3816.

Chart 1.1   *The wealth of the Kilkenny gentry, c.1560*

Landowner's name	Main estate	Acreage	Total value (£stg)	Value per acre (pence)
Northern uplands				
J. Grace	Courtstown	c.10,000	£120	2.9
O. Shortal	Ballylorcaine	5,380	£80	3.6
G. Purcell	Ballyfoyle	c.4,500	£67	3.7
P. St Leger	Tullaghanbroge	1,400	£27	4.6
D MacShane Fitzpatrick	Kilmocar	1,300	£10	1.9
R. Purcell	Foulkesrath	550	£10	4.4
Midland basin				
W. Sweetman	Castle Eve	1,210	£74	14.7
G. Blanchville	Blanchvillstown	2,950	£67	5.7
J. Cantwell	Cantwell's Court	3,550	£60	4.1
P. Forstall	Kilferagh	1,530	£51	8.0
T. Den	Grenan	2,600	£51	4.7
E. Butler	Paulstown	3,240	£40	3.0
N. White	Knocktopher	850	£40	11.3
T. Dobbin	Lisnetane	c.850	£40	11.3
T. Comerford	Ballymack	580	£40	16.5
F. Comerford	Callan	c.400	£40	24.0
R. Comerford	Ballybur	390	£30	18.5
R. Fitzgerald	Bunchurch	1,420	£30	5.0
W. Forstall	Kilmanehine	350	£20	13.7
J. Rochford	Killary	590	£20	8.1
R. Shee	Kilkenny	c.400	£20	12.0
J. Tobyn	Cahirlesky	1,070	£20	4.5
E. Walton	Waltonsgrove	1050	£20	4.6
P. Dobbin	Thomastown	c.200	£12	14.4
N. Devreux & W. Lincoll	Mallardstown	550	£10	4.4
R. Twye	Tuitestown	200	£10	12.0
D. Rothe	Kilkenny	150	£10	16.0
P. Fitzgerald	Danginmore	190	£6	7.6
D. Howling	Kilree	220	£5	5.5
Southern uplands				
E. Walsh	Castlehowell	c.13,000	£151	2.8
P. Walsh	Listerlin	2,390	£27	2.7
J. Butler	Duiske	8,600	£20	0.5

J. Tobyn	Killosnory	720	£10	3.3
J. Howling	Derrinahinch	1,060	£7	1.6
	Southern lowlands			
W. Dalton	Kilmodally	2,850	£67	5.6
P. Strange	Dunkitt	5,650	£51	2.2
W. Gall	Gaulskill	1,910	£30	3.8
J. Freney	Ballyreddy	2,080	£60	6.9
E. Fitzgerald	Brownsford	1,950	£50	6.2
T. O'Dea Fitzgerald	Gurtines	2,000	£20	2.4
W. Power	Powerswood	400	£5	3.6
J. Aylward	Aylwardstown	870	£13	3.6

Source: Lambeth MS 611, fol. 87

---

ern Crannagh. Like the Purcells they were steadfast supporters of the Butlers of Ormond, but because their lands were closer to the MacGiollapadraigs' territory in Laois, they paid more heavily for their allegiance than the Ballyfoyle Purcells. By the early 1560s the Graces and the Shortals could expect as little as 2.9*d.*–3.6*d.* per acre from their respective estates, having suffered more than most as a result of the increase in violence following the rise in Ormond power.[64]

Ironically families like these could not have survived the strain of the mid-to-late sixteenth century without economic aid from the earls of Ormond. Although loyalty to the Ormond banner was directly responsible for their predicament, only the Ormonds had the capacity to nurse them through their difficulties. As we have seen, the earls possessed a huge ancestral estate – and one which was growing rapidly, especially in the north – and from 1550 onwards they placed this at the service of the northern landowning community, offering cheap tenancies as a reward to the Graces and their ilk for their continued loyalty. According to the Ormond rental for Michaelmas 1593, the tenth earl's tenants in Fassadinin and Galmoy were charged barely 2*d.* per acre for some very large lease-holds there. Details of some of the tenancies are set out in Chart 1.2 below. The lesser Purcells were particularly fortunate, three of them occupying almost 3,600 acres in Fassadinin in return for a rent charge of just 1.6*d.* per acre. Of these Robert Purcell of Foulkesrath got easily the best deal. Possessing a modest 550-acre estate of his own at Foulkesrath, he was able to more than double the amount of land available to him by leasing a further 700 acres at Shanganagh and Coolcrahin close by, for which the tenth earl asked just 1.2*d.* per acre.

Leases such as these strengthened greatly the bonds that tied the northern squires and gentry to the earls of Ormond, and helped the much older feudal ties to continue in operation. By offering such big leaseholds for very little

64 Ibid., Edward VI, no. 946.

Chart 1.2 *Northern tenancies on the Ormond estate, c.1593*

Tenant	Leasehold	Acreage	£ value	Rent per acre
Robert Purcell of Foulkesrath	Shanganagh & Coolcrahin	c.700	£3.10s.	1.2d.
Richard Mor Purcell of Kilmocar	Kilmocar, Connohy, etc.	2,410	£15	1.5d.
Redmund Reagh Purcell of Esker	Graigerawe	450	£4	2.1d.
Donill Fitzpatrick of Kilmocar	Rosconnell & Marketcastle	1,300	£5	0.9d.
John Butler of Castlecomer	Aghtubbrid & Clogh	c.1,050	£10	2.4d.
Garret O'Dowill of Baleen	Ballyspellane & Borresmore	1,000	£20	4.8d.
Barnaby fitz Donill Fitzpatrick of Kilmocar	Durrow	1,340	£10	1.8d.

Source: NLI, Ms 2506, ff 10v–11v; *Ir. Fiants*, Eliz. I, nos. 3948, 4329; *COD*, vi, no. 99 (3)

money, the earls made the majority of the local landlords economically dependent upon them to some extent, buying their loyalty through an unusual system
of estate management that defined profit in political, not financial, terms. Thanks
to these giveaway Ormond leases, the landowning community that still existed
in north Co. Kilkenny *c.*1540 remained in place until 1600 and beyond, possessing a considerable amount of cheap leasehold land to exploit as best they
could and thereby cushion the blow of the overall decline in local property
values that accompanied the Ormond–MacGiollapadraig border wars.

The economic protection offered by the Ormonds should not be underestimated. It had at least one major effect on the north that outlasted the Ormonds'
own predominance, as it helped to accelerate the decline of the Gaelic lineages
there. Early in the seventeenth century, the local Anglo-Irish landowners
(Ormond associates all) began to expand into Idough, previously the most
unreachable part of the north. They continued doing so even after the earldom
fell into decline following the accession of the eleventh earl, Walter, in 1614.

The principal Anglo-Irish families involved were the Mountgarret Butlers
and various branches of the Purcells, Shortals and Comerfords,[65] and between
them they brought to its logical conclusion a policy begun by the earls of
Ormond in the sixteenth century. Capitalising on the O'Brennans' economic
weakness,[66] by the beginning of the 1630s they had managed to acquire perhaps

65 NLI, Ms 11,044 (92); ibid., Prior-Wandesford Papers, Irish material.   66 The poverty of the

as much as a quarter of the entire territory of Idough, thereby insuring its transformation from a wholly Gaelic region to one of mixed ownership where the Anglo-Irish were rapidly gaining the upper hand. The cultural ramifications of their expansion were soon widened with the arrival by their sides of local New English adventurers such as Sir Cyprian Horsfall, Oliver Wheeler, Henry Mainwaring and the Ridgeways, earls of Londonderry.[67] Within barely a generation, between 1600 and 1630, Idough had succumbed to the power of outside money, with larger and larger parts of it yielded up by the O'Brennans, first to Anglo-Irish, then New English, investors. And so it was that the Anglo-Irish families of the north – so often the oppressors of commerce before 1600 – acted as harbingers of the market economy after that date. Without the Ormonds' previous protection, they would probably not have been able to do so.

Eventually, however, the great strides that the Anglo-Irish landowners had managed to make in Idough were undone because of the earldom's collapse. In 1635/6, cursed with soaring financial problems, Earl Walter's successor, James, the twelfth earl and future duke (succ. 1633–d. 1688), agreed terms with leading members of the royal administration in Dublin to pass Idough in its entirety over to Christopher Wandesford, the master of the rolls. It will be shown in Chapter 5 below that he had no right to do so. For the present purposes it will be enough to examine the impact of Wandesford's arrival, insofar as it affected the locals and helped to alter their hitherto quite positive view of the earldom of Ormond. The twelfth earl's deal with Wandesford threatened to bring wholesale change in its wake. At once the proprietorial rights of all the other landowners in the area, Gaelic Irish, Anglo-Irish and New English, were overthrown by the state. Idough seemed set for a massive upheaval. Wandesford envisaged establishing a private plantation there centred around Castlecomer, bringing in colonists from England as tenants, skilled farmers and artisans who he hoped would transform the landscape and revolutionise the local economy. His tenants duly began arriving in Idough from 1638 onwards, and by 1641 they had managed to build a small English-style village of 500 people at Castlecomer, to create a 4,000-acre parkland in the adjoining hill country, and to open new mining works there.[68] Had the twelfth earl of Ormond not been close to bankruptcy, Wandesford might never have gained entry to the region.

Traditionally the general improvement in the economy of north Co. Kilkenny after 1600 has been associated with the arrival of Wandesford's little colony at Castlecomer. To an extent this is plausible: with the development of Castlecomer the north began to take on its modern form. However, there is reason to believe

O'Brennans is illustrated by a 1621 deed of mortgage, wherein Donogh McFirr O'Brennan (the mortgager) spoke of his 'urgent and necessary uses' of £18 (stg), a relatively modest sum at that date: H.B. McCall, *The family of Wandesford of Kirklington & Castlecomer* (London 1904), 262. **67** *Inq. Lagenia*, Co. Kilkenny, Charles I (64). **68** McCall, *Family of Wandesford*, 77–8; W. Nolan, *Fassidinin: Land, settlement & society in south-east Ireland, 1600–1850* (Dublin 1979), 54–6. The village population is given in 'The case concerning the territory of Idough', n.d., 1641 (NLI, Prior-Wandesford Papers, Irish material).

that, for the period up to 1642, the economic importance of the Wandesfords' arrival has been exaggerated. For one thing, the changes at Castlecomer and its surrounding area were actually quite modest. The village of Castlecomer, the centre of the little colony, struggled to come to life. Mines were already in operation in the area long before the Wandesfords came – there are references to a mine (probably a coalmine) operating in the 1490s, and to a furnace being worked at Kildergan (alias Kildroyn or Killerghan) in 1622 – and by the 1630s an ironworks belonging to the earl of Londonderry was also up and running.[69] Likewise, the Wandesfords' plans to establish an iron pot manufactory at Castlecomer were frustrated by a long battle over the sale of a pot-making patent.[70]

Admittedly the arrival of the Wandesfords and their tenants did bring some profound changes, especially outside Castlecomer village, in the surrounding countryside. Hitherto, because of its mountainous terrain and inhospitable climate, Idough had been predominantly an area of pastoral farming. During the late sixteenth century, for example, it was stated that the tenants of the earl of Ormond 'did manure and sow' only a small part of the earl's land there, preferring instead to have his lands divided up into 'booleys or dairy places' where they could graze their cattle.[71] Immediately after the annexation of the territory by Christopher Wandesford in 1635 it seems a lot more land was given over to arable farming. One of Wandesford's tenants is known to have had a malthouse attached to his home at Castlecomer,[72] while another operated a scythe mill. The scythe mill was especially important. According to one of Wandesford's earliest biographers, 'it wrought scythes in such abundance that the Irish, who had hitherto suffered their grass … to rot on the ground, now imitated the English manner of mowing and preserving hay'.[73] As Nolan has noted, there is no reason to cast doubt on the local tradition that the Wandesfords introduced the art of haymaking to Idough.[74]

Yet this was not so remarkable as it might seem. The changes the Wandesfords made to Idough's economy were in step with the trends emerging elsewhere in the north of the county in the seventeenth century. With the coming of peace after 1603, more people were able to live in the region, and as already noted, old rural population centres such as Freshford experienced re-expansion. New centres also emerged. In the north-west, for example, Foulkescourt grew significantly, becoming an important rural settlement with 32 cottages springing up near the castle bawn.[75] The rise in numbers brought a corresponding increase in the

69 *CSPI, 1601–3 & Addenda, 1565–1654*, 671; Indenture between Walter Archer, Tirlagh fitz Thomas, and Lawrence, Lord Esmond, 8 Dec. 1622 (NLI, Prior-Wandesford Papers, Irish material); McCall, *Family of Wandesford*, Appendix, no. 178.   **70** Bod. Lib., Ms Add. C 286, ff 1, 16–18, 22; Articles of agreement, 27 July and 10 Aug. 1637 (NLI, Prior-Wandesford Papers, Irish material).   **71** NA, CP F/42.   **72** TCD, Ms 812, ff 190r–192r.   **73** T. Comber, *The life of Christopher Wandesford* (London 1778), 70.   **74** Nolan, *Fassidinin*, 55. But only to the Gaelic part of the territory. Anglo-Irish parts, such as Castledough/Odagh (parcel of the medieval cantred of Idough, but now in Crannagh) already had some expertise in haymaking in the 1540s: *COD*, iv, no. 317 (3).   **75** NLI, Ms 2560, 40.

Chart 1.3 Regional corn varieties, c.1621

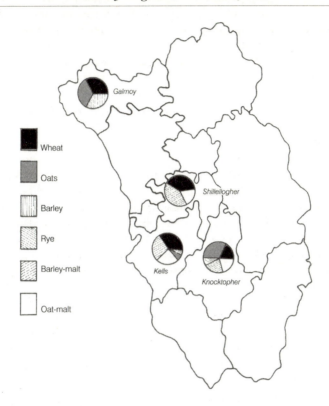

Wheat

Oats

Barley

Rye

Barley-malt

Oat-malt

Source: Michaelmas & Easter rents, 1621 (NLI, MS 11,063)

amount of land under tillage. There was probably a good financial return from arable farming. At Ballyragget one of the Mountgarret tenant families (who also kept cattle and sheep) set aside two fields for wheat, from which they claimed to anticipate an income of £80 per annum in the early 1600s.[76] By 1641 approximately 60 per cent of the entire barony of Fassadinin – not just Idough – was given over to arable farming.[77] Moreover, according to a document among the Ormond papers, by 1621 barley was being sown quite widely in the barony of Galmoy, along with wheat and oats (see Chart 1.3). There is also evidence to show that, by the reign of Charles I, potatoes had been introduced to the north, evidently grown as a luxury high-value crop, as one Gaelic farmer had his potato crop stolen in 1636.[78] All told, the demand for land across the area probably increased radically at this time, with the duration of leases on some estates drop-

76 NA, CP I/180.   **77** 9,789 plantation acres out of a total of 16,309: Nolan, *Fassidinin*, 60.   **78** NLI, D. 4052.

ping to five years, as at Urlingford in 1623, and rents rocketing upwards, as at Rathely in 1640, where a leasehold of arable and pasture fetched 2s. per acre.[79] In other words, the economic changes that the Wandesfords achieved in Idough via the forceful dispossession of the local proprietors were matched elsewhere across the northern uplands – but without recourse to such extreme measures. Ultimately, the most important thing about the Wandesfords' arrival was their displacement of the pre-existing, ethnically mixed, landowning community, not least because in 1640/1 this came to have a direct bearing on the future of the earldom of Ormond in the county. Understandably, those who had been displaced by Wandesford could not forgive the twelfth earl, James Butler, for having brought Wandesford in by selling them out.

However, by producing such a tense political climate, the events in Idough were quite exceptional. Elsewhere in the north the decline of the earldom of Ormond did not lead to any similar drastic challenges to settlement patterns. Instead, in Galmoy, northern Crannagh and Gowran, and the rest of Fassadinin, things carried on much as they had been doing before their downfall. As such, the local proprietorial structures that the earldom had helped to create before 1614 remained in place afterwards. The same families as had dominated the landscape in the late sixteenth century continued to do so in the seventeenth, not least the Ormonds' near relatives the Mountgarret Butlers, but also the Purcells, Archdekins, Shortals, and Graces. Only the Purcells of Ballyfoyle experienced serious economic problems, forced by a succession of wardships to mortgage or sell land with regularity between 1618 and 1640.[80] The other local families seem to have purchased at least some land after 1603, especially in Idough, and some, such as the Archdekins, added to their possessions through improvement and investment, acquiring the right to hold a market and two fairs at Bawnballinlogh in 1611.[81] And this at a time when all across Ireland comparable local elites were falling away, displaced by a growing class of New English colonists. Not so in north Kilkenny. Across the area, apart from the fall of the O'Brennans, the Elizabethan status quo survived almost untouched down to 1641.

This lengthy continuity gave northern Kilkenny a strong regional character. The tightly knit nature of the local Anglo-Irish families, something which had helped them survive the border wars of the sixteenth century, remained in force as late as the 1640s, when English officials in Dublin saw little difference between their methods of family organisation and those of their Gaelic neighbours. The 1641 depositions sought information concerning the 'sept' of the Butlers in Idough and 'the sept of the Codies [Archdekins]' in Galmoy.[82]

Underpinning the continued prevalence of tight, almost clannish, family units in the north was the fact that, even in the reign of Charles I, it was still a

---

79 NA, Thrift Abstracts, no. 2968; J. Ainsworth & E. MacLysaght (ed.), 'The Power-O'Shee papers', *Anal. Hib.* 20 (1959), 257. **80** Carrigan, *Ossory*, iii, 466–71. **81** Land purchases in Idough are discussed in Chapter 5 below. See also NA, Lodge MSS, Vol. 14: Fairs & Markets, 86; M. O'Dowd (ed.), 'Irish concealed lands papers', *Anal. Hib.* 31 (1984), 88, 91. **82** TCD, Ms 812, ff 166r, 169r.

place dominated by big estates. Along with the earls of Ormond, the other major Anglo-Irish landowners in the area – the Mountgarret Butlers, the Graces of Courtstown, the Shortals of Ballylorcaine, the Purcells of Ballyfoyle – held about 50 per cent of all the land in Fassadinin in 1641[83] and 65 per cent of Galmoy.[84] This meant that the younger sons of these families had no need to leave the familial estate, for there was enough land to go round between them *and* the heads of their line when circumstances demanded. And so it was that a local variation of the Gaelic custom of partible inheritance was found among some of the Anglo-Irish squires and gentry of Co. Kilkenny. For instance, during the period 1450–1600 both the Purcells of Ballyfoyle and the Shortals of Ballylorcaine set aside some of their patrimonial lands to establish lesser scion branches nearby: this was how the Purcells of Lismaine and Ballysallagh, and the Shortals of Tubbrid and Kildrinagh originated. No wonder crown officials described these families as septs. On the whole, however, partible inheritance was only practised occasionally in the north – for the most part, the big estates remained big down to 1641.

Considering that the north of the county was frontier land for most of the period 1500–1640, there is reason to believe that the large sprawling familial estates produced a much lower level of outwards migration than might otherwise have materialised. Instead of leaving for the towns, many of the 'poor relations' of the northern landowners stayed put, rooted to a particular area that was often named after them, that is, to Purcell country in northern Gowran and southern Fassadinin, or to Grace country in upland Crannagh. Surviving records from the sixteenth century show that many of the tenants on the Shortal and Purcell lands were themselves Shortals and Purcells, and that, moreover, many more again of their more distant relatives eked out a living as tenants on the lands of neighbouring families.[85] Because of all this, the northern squires and gentry were like the Butlers of Ormond in miniature: themselves the heads of large family groups, they were often responsible for huge numbers of dependants. Figures from the era of the Cromwellian transplantation show that the Purcells of Ballyfoyle had an extended family of 121 persons made up of immediate family, kindred and servants, in 1654. All of these would have lived within a few miles of Ballyfoyle castle, on Purcell land, or else on the land of well-inclined neighbours and kin.[86]

The clannishness of the northern Anglo-Irish families was further compounded by the fact that they were all very closely related to each other. Generation after generation, Purcells married Shortals, Shortals married

83 See Appendix 1 below. As with all mountain areas, the acreage for Fassidinin as given in the 1654 Book of Survey and Distribution is wildly inaccurate, omitting at least 10,000 acres of Wandesford land from the barony: NLI, Ms 975, 187–94. **84** Ibid., 196–201. **85** Government pardons are a rich source for settlement patterns in the sixteenth century. For Shortals at Rathely and Baleen, see *Ir. Fiants*, Eliz. I, nos. 927, 1057, 1076; for Purcells at Rathbeagh, Graigerawe, Ballyragget, Ballyspellane, Kirrehill, Donaghmore, and elsewhere, ibid.., nos. 950, 1057, 1065, 1068, 1184. **86** Persons transplanted to Connaught, *c*.March 1654 (St Kieran's College, Carrigan MSS, Vol. 21).

Archdekins, Butlers married Graces, and so on, thereby creating a thick web of kinship in the area that outsiders found hard to penetrate.[87] In 1588 a Co. Meath gentleman felt he had been denied a fair trial in Kilkenny because his adversary, Edmund Purcell of Ballysallagh, who held a small estate near Ossory Hill in northern Gowran, was 'greatly allied and friended in all wheres [that is, places]'.[88] This was even the case for some of the inhabitants of the Co. Kilkenny midlands. Late in the reign of Elizabeth I, the Kilkenny lawyer Walter Archer stated in a Dublin Court that he was unable to get compensation against one of the Ballyfoyle Purcells who had seized some of his pasture land, because Purcell lived in a 'remote part' of the county, and was too well connected with the local gentry for justice to be done.[89] Indeed, well into the seventeenth century it remained difficult for outsiders to prosecute the northern landlords in the local courts as, 'well allied' and clannish, they were not easily persuaded to find against one of their own when serving as jurors.[90]

The earls of Ormond had of course played a major part in creating this densely insular community. The large estates of the area would not have survived without their help before 1603. Moreover, their influence could still be felt after their post-1614 downfall. The survival of the landlords under their protection guaranteed the continuance of something increasingly out of step with trends elsewhere in Ireland – the old feudalistic principles of lordship and patronage. For it was during the early seventeenth century that the next most senior Butler lord, Richard Butler, third Viscount Mountgarret, began operating as the earls had done, using his own land in the area to develop a clientage relationship with the local gentry, recruiting middlemen tenants such as Richard Browne, a merchant from Kilkenny, at Urlingford, John O'Loughlin, a minor Gaelic gentleman, at Ballyragget, and Richard Butler, a kinsman, at Rathelty. The rents he charged could be very low: another Kilkennyman, Robert Shee, paid him just 2*d.* per acre for a smallholding. And just as on the pre-1614 Ormond estate, some of these sub-let the viscount's land at a profit to the ordinary tenant farmers of the region.[91] An impression of the value of these leases to Mountgarret's clients can be seen at Ballyragget, where by 1618 John O'Loughlin, his wife and five children, survived very comfortably on a farm estimated to be worth more than £600 (stg) in land, livestock and crops.[92]

Plainly, like an old habit, the feudalistic order of Galmoy, Fassadinin and northern Crannagh and Gowran was hard to break. Unlike many other places in Ireland, north Co. Kilkenny was a place where the traditional elite had successfully adapted to survive. Admittedly the general economic improvements in the area after 1603 helped them to do this, but so too did a strong opportunistic streak that was the product of life in the borderlands. Although they had been nurtured by the earls of Ormond, they proved themselves a tough and resilient lot once the mantle of Ormond protection was lost, capable of carry-

---

87 Carrigan, *Ossory*, ii, 284; ibid., iii, 156–7, 158–9; Empey (ed.), *A worthy foundation*, 90–1. 88 NA, CP A/183. 89 Ibid., CP K/223. 90 Ibid., CP B/25, 127, 302; CP E/20, 289; CP G/124. 91 NA, Thrift Abstracts, no. 2968; ibid., CP Aa/5; CP T/112. 92 Ibid., CP I/180.

ing on the traditions of lordship, kinship and resistance to outside interference in which their ancestors had been raised by the local overlords. Eventually, in 1640/1, their leaders would play a leading part in challenging the royal administration in Dublin. In doing so, they would instigate the collapse of the Ormond lordship in the county, as one of the principal royal councillors to earn their wrath was the twelfth earl of Ormond, James Butler, a man whom they perceived as betraying the noble traditions of his predecessors, in Idough trading 'good lordship' for personal gain at their expense. Like so many other rebels of this period that posed as loyal subjects while attacking their rulers, in 1641 the Kilkenny northern community would see themselves as better Ormondists than Ormond himself. It was a curious effect of more than a century of Ormond patronage.

THE MIDLAND BASIN I: THE AGRICULTURAL HEARTLAND

The ramifications of the re-shaping of north Kilkenny between 1515 and 1640 by the earls of Ormond and their clients seem greater still when the focus of attention is switched south to the centre of the county. Before 1603, by turning the north into a military borderland, the eighth, ninth and tenth earls insured the security and prosperity of the county's low-lying midland basin, which was then the agricultural heartland of the shire even more than it is at present. Nowadays the Co. Kilkenny midland plain is mainly a region of dairy farming, with about 20–25 per cent of the available land given over to tillage.[93] In the later medieval and early modern period, however, tillage was much more important, and the low-lying central plains acted as a breadbasket for much of the rest of the county. Stretching out on both sides of the Nore valley, and ranging across the baronial districts of Shillellogher, Kells, mid-Gowran, southern Crannagh, northern Knocktopher, and the liberties of Kilkenny and Callan, the fertile plains of the midlands were ideally suited to arable production. So much so, in fact, that by the middle years of the seventeenth century it had made Co. Kilkenny the fourth biggest grain producer in Ireland (behind Wexford, Meath and Louth).[94]

The soil quality is generally very good all across the central plain, and it enabled farmers to produce a rich variety of crops. Smyth has noted that the dominant feature over most of lowland Kilkenny was an open-field tillage economy geared to grain production, chiefly wheat, barley and oats; the information in Chart 1.3 above bears him out. Wheat, barley-malt and oat-malt were the principal crops in the baronies of Shillellogher and Kells, with oats more to

---

93 This is a 1965 estimate; tillage has probably declined even further since then: D.A. Gillmor, 'The agricultural regions of the Republic of Ireland', *Irish Geography* 5/4 (1967), 255. 94 Smyth, 'Territorial, social and settlement hierarchies', 133. This remained the case late in the eighteenth century, when it was described as 'one of the great corn counties': D. Beaufort, *Memoir of a map of Ireland* (Dublin 1792), 52.

Chart 1.4   Blanchvillestown crops, 1601 (bushels)

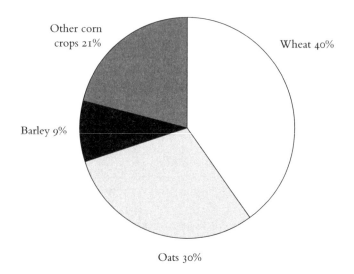

Other corn crops 21%

Wheat 40%

Barley 9%

Oats 30%

Source data:

Wheat	109 bushels
Oats	81 bushels
Barley	24 bushels
Other corn crops	56 bushels

Note: Co. Kilkenny bushels probably followed the 'great Irish measure' of 32 gallons per bushel

Source: NA, CP/M 102

the fore in Knocktopher. Productivity was especially high in Kells barony, where the widest range of grain crops was sown. The average yield approached a bushel per acre, with almost two bushels per acre on the best farms. Further to the east the Blanchville estate at Blanchvillestown was probably fairly typical of the farms in southern Gowran. Chart 1.4 demonstrates how in 1601 their farm was heavily geared towards grain production, with wheat and oats once more leading the way, and with some other grain types also sown.

    Mid-Kilkenny's river system underpinned its arable economy.[95] Fed by the Nore and its tributaries – the King's River, the Gloragh and the Lingaun – the region had an abundant water supply, crucial for arable farming, not least because

95 A.A. Miller, 'River development in southern Ireland', *PRIA*, 45 B (1938–40), 321–54; Beaufort, *Memoir*, 53.

it allowed mills for grinding and pounding corn to be built along the riverbanks. The midlands were dotted with watermills of all types and sizes. For instance, there was a pounding mill at Tullaghanbroge belonging to the St Legers, a grinding mill at 'Piers Rothe's Croft' near Washeshayes on the Nore belonging to the Shees, and a Comerford mill at Kilbrican on the King's River.[96] A rare fragment of the 1654 Civil Survey for Co. Kilkenny mentions mills at Haggardstown (where there were two), Dunmore, Woollengrange, Dunbill and Kilmanagh.[97] But these were only a few of the mills that existed. Recently a local scholar has accounted for another 15 mills, all within a four-mile radius of Kilkenny city.[98] To them should be added a further 27 at least, mainly from a little further afield,[99] giving the shire midlands a rough total of some 50 mills that were in operation between 1500 and 1640.

Yet pastoral farming was not neglected. Sheep farming was carried on in many places, such as Kilferagh, where there was a fulling mill belonging to the Forstalls, who in the 1540s secured a license to export wool beyond the seas.[100] Jerpoint was likewise part of the county's sheep country, and there is a reference to a flock of 300 sheep being put out to graze on a nearby hill in the 1630s.[101] Nor was dairy farming neglected. During the Elizabethan period, the Gaelic and Anglo-Irish tenants of the Fitzgeralds of Burnchurch were allowed to pasture or booley their cattle on a large piece of ground called 'Skeagh Farren Connowe', now part of the modern townland of Bewly. There were several other pasturelands or booleys nearby.[102] A seventeenth-century farm account that covers the Ormond lands at Dunmore, Kells and Jerpoint (as well as other lands in the north of the shire) records how tenants at Pottlerath and Keappaheddin leased 30 Irish cows from one of the dynasty's estate agents in 1620.[103] There were different breeds of cattle on the Ormond lands. In the previous year 17 'English cows' had been leased to the tenants, in return for 51 gallons of butter.[104] There were likewise different breeds of sheep.[105] Nevertheless, though pastoral farming remained an important part of the midlands economy, there is no doubt that arable production maintained its primacy, and may even have increased in importance after 1603, when the shire population began recovering after a century of war. According to a Jerpoint document of Charles I's time, Richard Sherlock, an Ormond client, was trying to turn 200 acres of pastureland over to tillage, albeit against the wishes of the local herdsmen.[106]

---

96 NA, CP Q/70; ibid., CP O/27; T.G. Fewer & K.W. Nicholls, 'The will of Robert Forstall of Kilferagh, 1645', *Decies* 48 (1993), 15–16. 97 NLI, Ms 2560, 37–9, 45. 98 J. Doyle, 'The water mills of Kilkenny', *Old Kilkenny Review*, 3/2 (1985), 147–59. 99 At Kells manor, Kilinny, Kellsgrange, Carrengair in Thomastown, Archersgrove, Cloghalea, Dysert in Pleberdstown, Cantwell's Court (2), Dunamaggan, Rahine, Callan (2), Kilferagh, Ballyfrunk, Gowran (2), Kilkrine, Joelstown (alias St Martin's), Rosbercon, Maddockstown, Jerpoint, Newtown Jerpoint, Dunbill, Inistioge (2), and Bennettsbridge: *Inq. Lagenia*, Co. Kilkenny, passim. 100 *Ir. Fiants*, Henry VIII, no. 59. The Forstalls kept part of their flock at Castlegarden: Fewer & Nicholls, 'Will of Robert Forstall', 14. 101 NLI, Ms 11,053 (12). 102 *COD*, vi, Appendix 1, 127–30. 103 NLI, Ms 2506, fol. 112r. 104 Ibid., fol. 111r. 105 Ibid., Ms 2552, fol. 7r. 106 Ibid., Ms 11,053 (12).

Good farming conditions, whether arable or pastoral, insured a high population. It is well known that by the early seventeenth century the region was home to five towns and a city, making it one of the most urbanised areas of Ireland. The towns played a crucial role in the shire economy and they are discussed separately below, but even outside their walls population levels were high. Across the Nore valley and up into the surrounding foothills there were dozens of small manorial villages and hamlets, made up of clusters of thatched cabins. The aforementioned fragment of the Civil Survey perfectly illustrates the varying density of settlement in this prosperous rural world. In Crannagh barony a rural hamlet of 30 cabins was to be found beside the stone slate house at Dammagh, while there were 24 cabins beside Ballycallan Castle, and 15 cabins beside the two 'chimney houses' at Corrohy.[107]

For most of the period under review the teeming populace of the midland plain faced intense competition for land, something that greatly benefited the local landlords. As shown earlier in Chart 1.1, at the start of Elizabeth I's reign landlord estates in the Kilkenny midlands were worth on average three times more than those situated in the northern and southern uplands and the southern lowlands of the shire, with values of 1s. an acre typical of many farms. Indeed, on some estates values were already approaching 1s. 4d.–1s. 8d. per acre even at this early date, as on the Comerford lands at Ballybur and Ballymack. Land was especially valuable (and scarce) in the environs of Kilkenny city and Callan town. There is some evidence to show that short-term leases were used by landlords in Callan, with land being let to the Gaelic Merry (alias O'Houlighane) family 'for the time being' in 1595, and by the reign of Charles I lands at Bootstown in the foothills overlooking the town were worth approximately 3s. 6d. per acre.[108] The population pressure was far greater at Kilkenny where arable lands in the city liberties had risen to £1 per acre by 1641.[109]

Thriving economic conditions such as these persuaded successive earls of Ormond to concentrate on protecting the midland basin. Some of their own most valuable manorial lands lay here, in Kilkenny city itself, in Callan, and at Dunmore, Dunfert, Dammagh, Pottlerath, Ballycallan, Gowran and Knocktopher. Remarkably, the high value of these midlands manors is borne out by government sources as well as by the Ormond family papers. As early as the reign of Henry VIII the crown had enough knowledge at its disposal to appreciate that the heart of the Ormond lordship lay in mid-Kilkenny, something not always made clear by the actions of some of its leading officials who, obsessed by the heavy concentrations of the Ormond forces elsewhere in the north and east, often mistook the military zones as the earls' main bases. According to a royal estimate of 1547 the most valuable Ormond manor was Kilkenny, followed at a distance by Callan and Gowran, but rural manors such as Dammagh and Dunfert also added considerably to the earls' wealth.[110]

---

107 As Note 97 above. **108** White (ed.), *Ir. mon & ep deeds*, 223–5; Ainsworth & MacLysaght (ed.), 'Power-O'Shee papers', 258. **109** Ibid., 257–8. **110** NLI, Ms 2507, ff 1r–2r.

Subsequent Ormond rentals confirm this picture. Until well into the seventeenth century, the earls' most valuable lands, rural as well as urban, were confined to the central plains of the county.[111]

What made their midlands estates so valuable was not high cash rents so much as high agricultural levies. This was most obvious at Kells Abbey. Early in the reign of Elizabeth I, though it brought in a money rent of £20 per annum paid by the tenant-in-chief, Kells was worth a great deal more. The sub-tenants were liable to an additional charge in kind, expected to hand over a proportion of their grain to the earldom in the form of a levy known as port grain.[112] This was where the big money lay. An estate account of August 1559 shows that the 'port of grain belonging to the Abbey of Kells' amounted to 220 bushels of wheat and 250 bushels of oats that lay on the ground, worth perhaps £210 (stg), and a further £280 in ready cash, apparently the result of various sales of grain that already had been completed.[113] Port grain was a major component of the Ormond income in Co. Kilkenny, and it helped the earls to survive the economic uncertainties of the later sixteenth century. Indeed, from the 1540s onwards, following a series of royal currency devaluations, port grain and other dues in kind became increasingly useful to them. With the coinage losing some of its value, the earls and their estate agents hoped to change from cash rents to rents in kind wherever possible, but especially in the midlands. By the mid-1570s port grain was also being charged at Kilkenny manor and Burgessmore, while Kilmore mill was set for an unspecified rent in corn, and some of the Dunfert and Pottlerath demesne lands were set for 60 and 80 bushels respectively.[114] The policy paid dividends. By 1597 the earldom's corn yield had risen so much that Earl Thomas was able to supply the English army in Brittany with victuals, selling a major consignment of wheat and oats for £1,100 (stg) to its commanders.[115]

To ordinary countryfolk, the earls of Ormond may have seemed most exploitative in the shire midlands. With a strong vested interest in the local agricultural yields, the Ormonds kept a close watch on their sub-tenants. In 1577 the tenth earl employed Thomas Archer (a Kilkenny merchant) to make a survey of all the tithes that were due from his lands. The earl specified that above all there was to be no leniency shown to the tenants of the midlands breadbasket, who had been trying to evade payment in recent times. He stated, 'I do much wonder how all my corn is consumed this last year, [for] I looked it should have made me a good sum of money, but I perceive I am not honestly dealt with, which I cannot like of.' Sub-tenants owing pastoral dues did not escape either. Earl Thomas wanted the inhabitants of Callan and other places, probably Jerpoint, forced to meet his demands for such things as summer sheep (a sheep

111 Ibid., Ms 2506, passim. 112 Ibid., fol. 4v; ibid., Ms 2507, fol. 18r. 113 Ibid., ff 20r–21r. Although the price of wheat and oats varied considerably across the period, a value of 13s. 4d. (Ir) per bushel was not unusual: 'Report on the Fitzwilliam manuscripts at Wilton', *Anal. Hib.* 4 (1932), 290–2. 114 NLI, Ms 2506, ff 4v, 10r; ibid., Ms 2507, fol. 5r–v. 115 HMC, *Salisbury MSS*, vii, 113.

of every flock), poundage hogs (a hog of every herd) and watch hens,[116] and from the 1570s onwards meticulous accounts were kept of all these levies. The accounts show that the sub-tenants of the Kilkenny midlands were more carefully managed than those of other regions.[117]

Crucially, the earls' pronounced economic interest in the area did not affect the midlands elite. Only the poorer elements suffered from the earls' demands. As in the north of the county, the local squires and gentry provided the earls' main tenants-in-chief and they were the chief beneficiaries of Ormond patronage. The leaseholds of Ormond land that were given to them were every bit as lucrative as anything on offer elsewhere. The Anglo-Irish Graces of Ballylinch paid a fixed rent of just £8 for a manor and castle and more than 1,000 acres near Jerpoint reckoned to be worth £300 per annum by Jacobean times; likewise the Gaelic Shees (originally O'Shees) of Kilkenny and Upper Court paid the earls about £11 rent for various properties in the county, including Jenkin's Mill in Kilkenny city, that were valued at £100. Other major midlands beneficiaries of Ormond largesse were the Rothes and Bryans (alias O'Byrnes) of Kilkenny and the Cantwells of Cantwell's Court, who each received land worth £100 from the earls before the accession of James I.[118]

In truth the earls of Ormond were more concerned to purchase the support of the midlands landowners and merchants than they were even to bind the northern border families to their side. It is not hard to discover the reason for this. Most of the main midlands gentry families – the Blanchvilles, Comerfords, Sweetmans, Cantwells, Dens and Burnchurch Fitzgeralds – were wealthy enough to be independent. Surviving evidence indicates that the landlords and merchants of the Kilkenny breadbasket were among the richest in the whole country. They lived a life of luxury, able to afford expensive imports from England, France, Spain, Portugal, the Canaries and the Americas, and their appetite for material comfort acted as a spur to the trading activities of the Kilkenny merchants.[119] The gentry were accordingly a proud and haughty lot, used to putting their wealth on display and acting like little nobles, entertaining important visitors to the shire in order to have their opinions heard in the wider world. To take just the Comerford lineage: Fulk Comerford had the lord deputy, Sir Henry Sidney, dine with him at his house in Callan in 1569; Garret Comerford of Inchyhologhan entertained the earl of Cork, the wealthiest lord in Ireland, in his castle in May 1625; and John Comerford of Ballybur was one of those with whom the papal nuncio, Cardinal Rinuccini, stayed following his arrival in Ireland in 1645.[120] Some of the marriages contracted by the mid-Kilkenny families also bore witness to their economic and political clout in southern Ireland

---

116 Bod. Lib., Carte Ms 1, fol. 22.   **117** NLI, Ms 2508, ff 11, 32.   **118** *Inq. Lagenia*, Co. Kilkenny, James I (22); NLI, D. 3295; ibid., Ms 2506, fol. 36r–v.   **119** Knowledge about imports from Europe and further afield has been dramatically improved by J.C. Appleby (ed.), *Calendar of material relating to Ireland in the high court of admiralty examinations, 1536–1641* (Dublin 1992). See also J.G. Hurst & J.M. Lewis, 'The Spanish olive jar in Ireland', *PRIA* 75 C (1975), 115–17.   **120** TCD, Ms 660, 78; Grosart (ed.), *Lismore papers*, 1st series, ii, 103–4; Moran, 'Bishops', 323.

and further afield. Early in the seventeenth century the Butlers of Callan found wives among the English Catholic gentry, forming unions with the Audleys of Norfolk and the Knatchbulls (alias Nashpoles) of Kent.[121] More typically, at about the same time the Ballybur Comerfords married into the Kavanaghs of Borris in Carlow, the O'Kennedys of Ballingarry in north Tipperary, and the MacGiollapadraigs of Upper Ossory.[122]

The political and economic importance of the mid-Kilkenny landlords was further enhanced by the fact that several of them had urban as well as rural interests, and held influential positions in the towns. Ever since the early thirteenth century the Archdekins and the Dens had dominated Thomastown, first through their co-ownership of the manor of Grenan, and subsequently (having formally partitioned it), via the two manors of Grenan and Dangin.[123] Similarly, the Fitzgeralds of Burnchurch were important figures in Callan.[124]

The midlands gentry were politically empowered in their own right, and the earls of Ormond made special concessions to them in order to retain their loyalty. Thus many of the offices in local government were largely the preserve of the midlands gentry – especially during the sixteenth century, when the nomination of officials was *de facto* in the Ormonds' gift. In Appendix 3 below it can be seen how, for long periods before 1603, the post of county sheriff was monopolised by the Fitzgeralds of Burnchurch, the Comerfords of Ballymack and the Dens of Grenan. Possession of the shrievalty added to the wealth of these families and bound them closer to the earldom. According to a 1580s reference, for much of the preceding century the earls of Ormond and the sheriffs of the county had carved up – illegally – the profits of royal justice between them, splitting the proceeds of the sale of traitors' and felons' goods, with the earls taking one half, the sheriffs the other; the crown had reportedly received nothing by this arrangement.[125]

The earls viewed the Kilkenny midlands elite as their junior partners in government, and often called on their services. Some they employed in Tipperary, as legal and administrative officials in their palatine liberty, centred at Clonmel. The Rothes, Archers and Shees, all from Kilkenny city, were especially prominent among the earls' officers in Tipperary, regularly summoned to serve as seneschals, treasurers, attorneys, and clerks of the liberty before 1621 (the year in which the earls forfeited the liberty to the crown). The same was true of the Fitzgeralds of Burnchurch and the Howths of Dammagh, who occupied the Tipperary seneschalship in 1533–45 and 1556–7 respectively, and also of the Cantwells of Cantwell's Court, the Comerfords of Ballybur and the Butlers of Knocktopher, who provided sheriffs for the liberty in 1602, 1603, 1613 and 1614.[126] Beyond the liberty lands, in the cross of Tipperary – that part of

---

121 St Kieran's College, Carrigan MSS, Vol. 3, unpaginated. **122** Ibid., Vol. 21, unpaginated. **123** Carrigan, *Ossory*, iv, 267. **124** NA, M 2835. **125** PRO, SP 63/115/10. **126** For Tipperary liberty officials see in general T. Blake Butler, 'Seneschals of the Liberty of Tipperary', *Ir. Gen.* 3/2 (1957), 46–59; 'Sheriffs of the Liberty of Tipperary', ibid., 3/5 (1960), 158. The latter article, however, is erroneous in places – Richard Comerford of Ballybur (sheriff 1603) is misidentified

Tipperary that was the preserve of the archbishops of Cashel – the gentry of mid-Kilkenny also occasionally did service on the earls' behalf. In 1560, for example, Oliver Grace of Ballylinch, one of the tenth earl's most trusted agents, served in Cashel as the sheriff of the cross.[127] This latter appointment probably needed royal support as, at least in theory, the Ormonds and their representatives had no business meddling in archiepiscopal territory. But for much of the Elizabethan period, of course, crown backing for Ormond servants willing to officiate outside Co. Kilkenny was often readily forthcoming. It is very likely that the tenth earl, Black Thomas, secured royal approval for the promotion of Patrick St Leger of Kilkenny to the post of clerk of the peace for Munster in 1584, for the queen received 'good commendation of [his] sufficiency and loyalty' at a time when the earl attended upon her at court.[128] Earl Thomas also used his influence in government to help Jasper Shee of Kilkenny become an officer of the royal ordnance at Waterford in the early 1580s.[129]

The esteem in which the earls held the Kilkenny midlands elite is also illustrated by their involvement in high politics. Time and again the earls looked to the local gentry, especially those from the towns, to represent them in Dublin during periods of tension. Many of the midlands families were well versed in English law, sending their sons to be educated at the inns of court in London,[130] and some of them, such as the Archers and Cowleys of Kilkenny and the Comerfords of Callan, became very well known as lawyers in the crown courts in Dublin. Their legal renown made them ideal spokesmen for the Ormond interest whenever the earls feared trouble with the royal administration. Successive earls saw to it that the midlands gentry also dominated the county's parliamentary elections. In the early 1530s, when Earl Piers was busy undermining the national ascendancy of the earls of Kildare, he had his henchman Roland Fitzgerald of Burnchurch represent him as a 'knight of the shire' in the Irish house of commons.[131] The tenth earl had Gerald Blanchville of Blanchvillestown and Robert Rothe of Kilkenny elected for the shire in 1585/6, a time when he was in danger of losing out to a hostile lord deputy in the apportionment of land in the projected plantation of Munster.[132]

Most striking of all, however, when the national power of the earls of Ormond was reborn after 1515, the midlands families gained entry to the central government itself. Ormond patronage saw to it that, beginning in 1522 (when Earl Piers briefly became lord deputy) and continuing until the early 1600s (when Earl Thomas began to decline), a steady stream of Kilkennymen

as 'of Rathelty, Co. Tipperary' – and it should be checked against documents in NLI, Ms 11,044. **127** Butler, 'Sheriffs', *Ir. Gen.* 3/4 (1959), 122. Similarly, in 1597 Thomas Cantwell of Cantwell's Court was made collector of the composition money and subsidy in Co. Tipperary and the cross of Tipperary: *Ir. Fiants*, Eliz. I, no. 6172. **128** *CSPI, 1574–85*, 545; *APC, 1581–2*, 441. **129** PRO, SP 63/134/41. **130** The Kilkenny families went mainly to Gray's Inn and the Inner Temple: D. Cregan, 'Irish Catholic admissions to the English Inns of Court, 1558–1625', *Irish Jurist* 5 (1970), 107–13; J. Foster (ed.), *Register of admissions to Gray's Inn* (London 1889), 2, 10, 23, 27. **131** G.D. Burtchaell, 'The Geraldines of County Kilkenny, Pt. 1', *JRSAI* 22 (1892), 366. **132** *CSPI, 1586–8*, 52–3.

made it up the slippery pole to high government office.[133] The father and son team of Robert and Walter Cowley of Kilkenny and Brownestown were among the earliest beneficiaries of mounting Ormond influence. Robert first emerged as a prominent figure in 1520, when made clerk of the Irish privy council by the earl of Surrey.[134] His fortunes continued to rise after the collapse of the Kildare Fitzgeralds in 1534, and in 1538 he was appointed master of the rolls, the second most senior office in chancery. He held this post for four years, before losing it in 1542 as a result of a row with Lord Deputy St Leger. His son Walter quickly filled his shoes, rising from a clerkship in chancery to become successively solicitor general and surveyor general of Ireland.[135] The Cowleys aside, in 1521 Earl Piers had persuaded Surrey to make James Cantwell, bachelor-at-law, a commissioner for maritime affairs in Munster.[136] Walter Archer of Kilkenny was another Ormond client; in 1536 he received royal letters patent installing him as clerk of the common pleas of the exchequer.[137]

More Ormond nominees found their way to high office in the reign of Elizabeth I, thanks to the extraordinary level of influence enjoyed by the tenth earl, Black Thomas. Edmund Butler of Callan was the first of a new batch of magistrates to emerge through the earl's patronage. Having first served as an agent of Ormond expansion in north Tipperary and Ely O'Carroll in 1567, by 1572 Earl Thomas had introduced Edmund to the inner circle of Irish government, where he quickly won a reputation as a 'just dealer'.[138] Official commissions followed, including one for the division of Munster into counties in 1576 (something of obvious interest to Ormond). Eventually, in 1582, he attained high office, becoming attorney general of Ireland, and a year later he was made second justice of queen's bench.[139] Two more Ormond clients from the shire midlands broke into the state service in the 1580s, James Ryan of Kilkenny and Gerald Comerford of Callan and Inchyhologhan. Ryan, an obscure figure, moved to Dublin sometime before 1577 to work as a government clerk under Nicholas White in chancery,[140] and in 1591 he was made one of the masters of chancery, with power to run the court during the absence of the lord chancellor and master of the rolls.[141] Historians, in contrast, know more of Comerford. During the final years of the sixteenth century he became one of Earl Thomas' most important mouthpieces west of Kilkenny, first serving Ormond interests in Connaught, where from 1585–1600 he acted as royal attorney-at-law, before moving on to Munster, where he was successively second justice and then chief justice of the province.[142]

133 For many years before 1515 the Ormond dynasty had lacked representatives in Dublin, except for the period 1492–4: S.G. Ellis, *Reform & revival: English government in Ireland, 1470–1534* (London 1986), 220–5. 134 Ibid., 37, 170, 225. 135 *Ir. Fiants*, Henry VIII, nos. 50, 68; ibid., Edward VI, no. 219; *CPRI, Henry VIII–Eliz. I*, 37, 165–6; *APC, 1542–7*, 42; ibid., *1550–2*, 365. 136 *Cal. Carew MSS, 1515–74*, 20. 137 NA, Ferguson MSS, Exchequer Memoranda Rolls, Henry VIII, 191. 138 *CPRI, Henry VIII–Eliz. I*, 509; PRO, SP 63/36/4. 139 *Ir. Fiants*, Eliz. I, nos. 2323, 2543, 2758, 2860, 3558, 4010, 4211. 140 PRO, SP 63/64/8. 141 *Ir. Fiants*, Eliz. I, nos. 4430, 5527. For his Kilkenny background, see NA, CP A/286. 142 For brief accounts of his life, see

Most of these office-holders were little more than creatures of the earldom. Despite their work for the state none of them – except Walter Cowley[143] – ever broke free of their noble patrons or supported a government policy that might harm the Ormond interest. By and large, their careers were marked by their capacity to serve the Butlers as much as the crown.

The downfall of the house of Ormond in the reign of James I impacted severely upon the Kilkenny midlands elite. Once the earldom began to decline they too slipped from power, because of their Catholicism no longer adjudged members of the country's ruling elite. The fact that they never regained a governmental role was profound, for it transformed them overnight into a potential source of danger to the crown. Long accustomed to power, they were cut adrift by a change in government policy. They even struggled to keep a hold of the county shrievalty (see Appendix 3). Their resentment became a major political problem, and increasingly after 1614 they turned away from the royal administration and sought affirmation instead in the networks of relatives and allies that they possessed among the Catholics of the south, from Dublin to Galway to Cork. In this lay a source of the crown's collapse in 1641. The Catholic Confederation of Kilkenny of 1642 was, at least in its early stages, in part an assembly of friends and kindred of the Kilkenny squires and gentry, all intent on reclaiming the ground they had lost since Jacobean times.[144] The influence they had enjoyed while the earls of Ormond had been central to crown policy was ultimately to cost the crown dear.

THE MIDLAND BASIN II: THE URBAN WORLD

The midlands community was accustomed to power not just because of the gentry's importance to the earldom. The central basin of Co. Kilkenny was remarkable in later medieval and early modern times in that it contained six walled towns situated within a 20-mile radius. Each one of the towns was a power centre, vital to both the Ormond lordship and the English monarchy because of the wealth of their markets and their strategic value as defensible sites. Moreover, merchant families of considerable antiquity and influence governed these towns. Ever since the high Middle Ages, when the towns were first founded, the merchants had built up their corporate rights and privileges, and in exchange for their loyalty they had grown used to the exercise of authority with crown consent. Like the gentry who controlled the countryside, the merchants were a force to be reckoned with, and their activities as financiers,

Carrigan, *Ossory*, iv, 230–1; *Irish memorials of the dead*, ii (1892–4), 146. See also N. Fallon, *The Armada in Ireland* (London, 1978), 71–3; Bagwell, *Tudors*, iii, 206, 215. **143** Cowley only helped the government against the earldom after falling into disgrace in 1546: D. Edwards, 'Malice Aforethought? The death of the ninth earl of Ormond, 1546', *Butler Soc. Jn.* 3/1 (1987), 37. **144** The members of the Confederate general assembly are conveniently gathered in M. Ó Siochrú, *Confederate Ireland, 1642–1649: a constitutional and political analysis* (Dublin 1999), 256–9.

investors and employers gave them a grip over the economy of southern Leinster, and parts of Munster.

Principal among the towns was Kilkenny city, variously described by visitors as 'a beautiful town', 'the best dry town in Ireland', and most significantly, as the chief inland town in Ireland.[145] This latter description was a fitting one, for Kilkenny played a crucial role in the economy of the mid-south of the country. Standing at the heart of the Nore river valley, it provided the commercial engine not just for Co. Kilkenny, but for parts of Tipperary, Laois, Carlow and Kildare as well.

Kilkenny was the major entrepôt for the mid-south. Its merchants strived constantly to overcome the physical limitations of its inland position. Utilising the nearest seaports, New Ross and especially Waterford, they carried on a regular overseas trade with England and continental Europe. The city enjoyed a special relationship with Bristol. Ever since 1510 its burgesses had been treated as freemen there,[146] a privilege that insured that the great Bristol fair, held in August every year, was an important date in the Kilkenny calendar: each August a dozen or more Kilkenny merchants made the voyage across George's Channel to open stalls there, selling woven cloth, wool and animal hides, and buying minor manufactured goods, housewares and some English cloth in return.[147] So great was the tie with Bristol that several Kilkenny families sent their sons there to be trained as apprentices,[148] while others (such as the Shees) established a permanent base in the port by initiating a Bristol branch of their family.[149] But important as it was, Bristol was not the only destination of the local trading houses. Kilkenny merchants also turned up at London, Chester, Bridgwater and Plymouth in England,[150] Milford and Pembroke in Wales,[151] and further afield at Antwerp, Middleburg and Lisbon in Europe.[152] Suffice it to say that the merchants of Kilkenny did *not* depend completely on the hinterland of their city, as one expert has suggested.[153] In an age of European colonial expansion, when more and more goods were reaching Europe from Africa, Asia and the Americas, enormous riches could be had through seafaring. The merchants of landlocked Kilkenny were determined to participate.

145 Lennon, *Richard Stanihurst*, 141; E. Campion, 'A historie of Ireland, 1571', in *Ancient Irish histories* (2 vols., Dublin 1809), i, 2; Fynes Moryson, *An itinerary of his travels*, ed. C. Hughes (4 vols., Glasgow 1907–8), iii, 157. **146** C. McNeill (ed.), *Liber Primus Kilkenniensis* (Dublin 1931), 118. **147** E.g., in 1535, 1565 and 1637: PRO, E/122/21/7, ff 25r–29r; ibid., E190/1128/2, ff 10v–11v; ibid., E190/1128/3, ff 5r–6v; ibid., E190/1128/5, fol.5; ibid., E190/1136/8, ff 17r, 18, 20v–21v. **148** Bristol City RO, Ms 04352 (2), sub 18 Aug. 1572; D. Holles (ed.), *Calendar of the Bristol apprentice book, 1532–42* (Bristol 1949), 70, 89, 123, 181; E. Ralph & N. Hardwick (ed.), ibid., *1542–52* (Bristol 1980), 16, 31–2. **149** Ibid., 7, 30, 89; H. Cotton, *Fasti Ecclesiae Hibernicae: Leinster* (Dublin 1848), 412; J. Vanes (ed.), *The ledger of John Smyth, 1538–50* (Bristol 1974), 10, 113, 203. **150** NA, CP B/127; Guildhall Library, London, Ms 9051/5, ff 135r, 403r, 462r; Chester City RO, Ms SB 10, fol. 53r; PRO, E190/1082/4, fol. 3v; ibid., HCA 1/44, fol. 217r. **151** E.A. Lewis (ed.), *The Welsh port books, 1550–1603* (London 1927), 189, 193; HMC, *Fifth Report* (London 1876), 5. **152** *COD*, v, nos. 162, 176; *Ir. Fiants*, Eliz. I, no. 3948 (John Cleere); NLI, D. 3335 (Richard Forstall); W. Carrigan, 'Old Waterford Wills, iii: Alderman Nicholas Ley, 1585', *WSEIAS* 9 (1906), 209–16. **153** A. Sheehan, 'Irish towns in a period of change, 1558–1625', in Brady & Gillespie (ed.), *Natives & newcomers*, 96.

The overseas trade, so doggedly pursued, gave Kilkenny an edge over the other inland towns in the mid-south. Although the merchants of Gowran, Thomastown and Callan sometimes got in on the act, their participation in overseas ventures was irregular at best, nothing like the persistence exhibited by their Kilkenny counterparts.[154] As a result, for an inland town Kilkenny city soon developed an unusual commercial empire during the sixteenth century, distributing foreign goods to neighbouring areas to the north, east and west. Extant sources record several instances of persons from Tipperary and Laois who purchased imported items from Kilkenny merchants,[155] but other markets also fell within the town's grasp. About 1560, for example, the Kilkennyman James Cantwell set himself up in Baltinglass as a fruit and spice merchant, selling 'a confection of quinces, pears and plums called marmalade', as well as Asian and New World commodities such as sugar, ginger and nutmeg.[156] At about the same time, Kilkenny's vintners were to be found selling high quality white wine to the residents of Kilkee Castle, Co. Kildare.[157] By the close of the sixteenth century this inland trade with Kildare – something that would have been unthinkable in the 1520s and '30s because of Butler/Fitzgerald enmity – was firmly established. In 1584, the empire advanced to Naas, where special arrangements were made to ensure that all such 'wares or merchandises' that the Kilkenny merchants brought there would go on sale in the market place without the usual tolls being charged.[158] The high reputation of Kilkenny's craftsmen broadened its horizons still further. In 1610 the vice-president of Munster, based in Cork, sent the great mace of Munster to Kilkenny to be repaired by a famous goldsmith of the city.[159]

Viewed against this background it is not surprising that on a local level Kilkenny city increased its hold over the county economy in the period before 1640. The import trade was clearly very profitable, and the merchants of Kilkenny looked to develop the other towns in the shire as suitable markets for their goods. The extent of their success was remarkable. In Callan, Thomastown and Knocktopher the Kilkenny merchant elite began to dominate affairs. They established a series of cadet branches, attempting to infiltrate each of the oligarchies that existed in these lesser towns. The strategy had succeeded by the early years of the seventeenth century. In 1613 William Rothe, the grandson of a prominent Kilkenny merchant, was elected MP for Callan, the third member of his branch of the family to have attained high office there since the 1580s.[160] The Rothes also elbowed their way into Thomastown, building up a

---

154 One merchant from Gowran appeared in Bristol in 1566, one from Thomastown in 1570, and one from Callan in 1577 (PRO, E190/1128/8, fol. 2v; ibid., E190/1128/16, fol. 6v; ibid., E190 1130/1, ff 5v–6r). 155 NA, CP I/5; ibid., CP K/294; ibid., CP L/54; ibid., RC 6/1, 230; Carrigan, *Ossory*, i, 84–6, 94–5; BL, Add. Ms 19,843, 53–4, 62, 106–7, 198. 156 *Ir. Fiants*, Eliz. I, no. 327. 157 Kent AO, Ms U1475 025/1, fol. 203r. 158 NA, RC 6/1, 159; ibid., CP B/302; ibid., CP O/1, 66. 159 BL, Harleian Ms 697, fol. 73r. 160 G.D. Burtchaell, 'The family of Rothe of Kilkenny', *RHAAI*, 4th series, 7/2 (1886), 508, 521; *COD*, v, no. 243 (1c); ibid., vi, no. 2 (13). For the Callan Archers see ibid., vi, no. 5 (3); *Ir. Fiants*, Eliz. I, no. 4979.

small estate from the Elizabethan period and becoming sovereigns of the town a generation later.[161] It was in Knocktopher, however, where the Kilkenny elite scored their biggest victory. According to a surviving manorial court roll they had annexed control of the town as early as 1586, for in that year its three leading burgesses hailed from Kilkenny, Richard Shee, Edward Langton and Walter Archer.[162] The Kilkenny merchants do not seem to have penetrated the governing cliques of Gowran and Inistioge to anything like the same extent, but this impression may simply be due to the paucity of extant evidence concerning both those places.[163] Certainly, Kilkenny's great civic families were involved in the impressive growth of Freshford after 1603, wherein it had outstripped both Knocktopher and Inistioge by the 1650s: for many years beforehand a representative of the ubiquitous Rothe dynasty, Jasper Rothe, had been settled there, seizing his chance to become one of the very first merchants of this newly emerging town.[164]

Underpinning the influence of its leading families was Kilkenny's status as the administrative centre of the shire. The inhabitants of the other regions of the county were accustomed to journeying there for all manner of business. Although the pleas of the crown were sometimes held in Gowran, Callan or Thomastown, the main county court was held in Kilkenny sessions house, an ex-monastic building known as Blackfriars; the county treasury, where the sheriff deposited his receipts, was located somewhere in the city.[165] Likewise, from 1566 the county gaol was stationed at Grace's Castle in Parliament Street, and thereafter its dank cells provided an uncomfortable prison for criminals from inside and outside the shire.[166] Over the years Kilkenny acquired all the trappings of a government centre. It had several legal firms of note, chief amongst them those run by the Archer and Cowley families,[167] and consequently the county landlords often tried to have their disputes settled in the city, where traditionally witnesses were publicly examined 'at the great [market] cross in the middle of the royal square'.[168] The market cross was also the place where royal proclamations were posted, and copies of various government orders were first sent to the city before being dispatched elsewhere around the shire.[169] As the

---

161 *COD*, vi, no. 6; Burtchaell, 'Family of Rothe', 509; NA, CP K/24. Likewise the Raggets, who had acquired property in Thomastown by 1612: Richard Ragget's will, 1612 (St Kieran's College, Carrigan MSS, Vol. 83, unpaginated). **162** NLI, Ms 2551 (6). **163** In 1607 one of the Rothes occupied a small castle in Inistioge (Burtchaell, 'Family of Rothe', 506; C. Manning, 'A 16th century Rothe in stone', *Archaeology Ireland* 7/2 (1993), 12–13). The same year one of the Archers was constable of the Ormond manor of Gowran, but it is not known if he owned any property in the town: NLI, Ms 11,053 (9). **164** TCD, Ms 812, fol. 182r. Richard Cromwell was proclaimed lord protector at six places in the shire in 1658, including Freshford, but neither Knocktopher nor Inistioge were deemed important enough to be included (NA, Prim MSS, no. 32: *Mercurius Politicus*, 436). **165** *Inq. Lagenia*, Co. Kilkenny, passim. The treasury is alluded to in NLI, D 3928. **166** *CPRI., Henry VIII–Eliz. I*, 522; Grosart (ed.), *Lismore papers*, 1st series, i, 16; NLI, Ms 11,053 (9); KCA, Ms CR/K 59; Bod. Lib., Carte Ms 62, no. 51. **167** NA, CP G/34, for Walter Archer, 'learned in the laws', at work *c.*1638; Nottingham University Library, Ms Mi.Da. 57/1q, for Michael Cowley *c.*1640. **168** *COD*, iv, no. 183. **169** KCA, Ms CR/K 27, 33, 37,

capital of the Ormond lordship its role as a centre of secular government was guaranteed, but it was a focal point for religious affairs too. Like the earl of Ormond at Kilkenny Castle, the bishop of Ossory had his principal seat in the city, residing in the episcopal palace beside St Canice's Cathedral. The Reformation and Counter-Reformation enhanced Kilkenny's religious importance, for by the beginning of the seventeenth century both Protestant and Catholic bishops were housed in the city, and clergy of both churches were arriving there in increasing numbers.[170]

Kilkenny's industrial strength put the cap on its regional supremacy in the mid-south of Ireland. It was home to four major industries, each of which capitalised in one way or another on the natural resources of its hinterland. By far the best known of these was the cloth-making industry, which thrived on the wool produced on the county's sheep pastures. Probably the city's main employer, it was organised into five guilds (at least): the guilds for merchant-tailors and cordwainers in the Hightown, or 'Englishtown', directly supervised by the corporation, and those for the weavers, cotners and tailors in the Irishtown, the northern part of the city that lay under the jurisdiction of the bishop of Ossory.[171] The other corporate towns in the shire seem not to have offered much competition. Presumably the industry was too far advanced in Kilkenny to enable a rival centre to appear somewhere else.[172]

The leather-working industry was found in several towns in the county as well as Kilkenny. Indeed, after 1576 tanning, a vital part of the leather trade (in which animal hides were coated or 'tanned' to give them a soft surface), should have been confined to Gowran. In accordance with a statute passed in the Irish parliament a few years earlier, the government had settled upon Gowran as a suitable place where the tanning of hides would be carried on as a state-sponsored local monopoly, under license from Dublin.[173] The scheme failed, however, probably because it was unworkable, and Gowran did not become the centre of the tanning trade in the shire. Instead it had to bow to Kilkenny in this as in everything else, and right down to 1640 the tan-houses of the Rothes and others continued to turn out finished and semi-finished leather in Kilkenny, either for export overseas, or else for sale to other local craftsmen involved in the industry, such as saddlemakers, shoemakers and glovers, of whom Kilkenny had many.[174]

The building and fruit-growing industries were much the same, existing on a moderate scale in other towns but based principally in Kilkenny city. According to observers, both of these industries were pursued so actively in Kilkenny that they lent it an unusually pleasant appearance when compared with other Irish towns. As Luke Gernon said around 1620, Kilkenny was a city

for proclamations of 1622, 1632 and 1637. **170** Chapter 5 below. **171** Neely, 'Kilkenny city', 158–60; J. Ainsworth (ed.), 'The Irishtown Corporation Book, 1537–1628', *Anal. Hib.* 28 (1978), 53. **172** One tailor is recorded in Gowran in 1608: NLI, Ms 11,053 (9). **173** *CPRI, Eliz. I*, 208. **174** Burtchaell, 'Family of Rothe', 529; PRO, E190/1136/10, ff 9v, 22v. During Elizabeth I's reign there were 18 master glovers and 13 master shoemakers in Kilkenny city, each employing several apprentices: *Ir. Fiants*, Eliz. I, no. 2424.

of stone and marble archways, a place where 'the houses are of grey marble fairly built, the fronts … supported with pillars or arches, under which there is an open pavement to walk on'. He found the city's appearance further enhanced by its 'wholesome and delightful orchards and gardens, which are somewhat rare in Ireland'.[175] Kilkenny's lowland climate, dry with extreme heat and cold, was ideal for growing fruit, and its inhabitants exploited its commercial potential. The quality of its apples and pears seems to have enjoyed a high reputation, sold as far away as Co. Kildare,[176] while lower quality fruits did not go to waste, used in marmalades and other preserves by local confectioners. Beekeeping was also carried on as an associated craft, and honey was added to fruit to produce a local form of mead that was highly prized.[177] By 1640 there were no fewer than 30 orchards situated around the city, most of them along the banks of the Nore.[178]

The building industry was also considerable. Blessed with a steady source of good quality building stone from nearby quarries,[179] the local builders plied their trade over a wide area. As well as periodically being called upon to work at Kilkenny Castle and other Ormond properties around the shire,[180] the local builders could be found delivering stone to Lismore Castle, Co. Waterford in 1615, and the Catholic prelate, David Rothe, stated that they even exported building stone overseas.[181] One overseas destination is recorded. In 1637 the master of the king's works, Inigo Jones, requested delivery of 'black Irish marble' from Kilkenny for the new steps he had designed for the rebuilding of St Paul's Cathedral in London.[182]

The vitality of its industries and the scale of its trade made Kilkenny an attractive place to settle, and its population grew steadily. Described in 1536 by one of Henry VIII's agents as 'well replenished of people and wealthy',[183] in 1577 the government recognised its growth and planned in future parliamentary legislation to allow the corporation to extend its liberties.[184] Historians have acknowledged its importance, and it has been suggested that by the seventeenth century its population numbered between 2,000 and 3,000 people, making it

175 BL, Stowe Ms 180, fol. 39. **176** Kent AO, Ms U1475 025/1, fol. 65r; HMC, *Ormonde MSS, 1572–1660*, 36. **177** S. Lang & M. McGregor (ed.), *Tudor wills proved in Bristol, 1546–1603* (Bristol 1993), no. 192; *Ir. Fiants*, Eliz. I, no. 327. **178** R.C. Simington (ed.), *Civil Survey for County Waterford, Muskerry & Kilkenny City* (Dublin 1942), 504–6, 508, 514–5, 517, 519–20, 522, 525–6, 528, an incomplete source that list 16 orchards owned by Catholics in 1650. A further 9 orchards of the Protestant marquis of Ormond are given in H. Butler (ed.), 'Occupants of Ormond houses in Kilkenny, 1641–61', *Butler Soc. Jn.* vii (1977), 545–50. Otherwise, see White (ed.) *Extents*, 201; *Ir. Fiants*, Eliz. I, no. 4420; NA, Lodge MSS, Wardships, I, 257 (Protestant property); Ainsworth & MacLysaght (ed.), 'Power-O'Shee papers', 238 (Fowlingsrath outside the walls); NLI, Ms 975, pp 218, 220 (St John's, outside the walls). **179** KCA, Ms CR/J 18, 27, 29; J. Graves, 'The history, architecture and antiquities of the city of Kilkenny, *KSEIAS* Jn., 2nd series, ii (1858), 324; Doyle, 'Water mills', 148, 153–4. **180** Clonalis House, O'Conor Don Ms 6.4HN002; NLI, Ms 2549, passim. **181** Grosart (ed.), *Lismore papers*, i, 67; Graves, 'History', 324. **182** Sheffield City Library, Ms WWM Str. P. 24–25/133. **183** *Cal. Carew MSS, 1515–74*, 105. **184** PRO, SP 63/59/78.

by far the largest inland town in the country.[185] Yet there is reason to suspect that it may have been larger still. Irish scholars have tended in the main to adopt English demographic norms when making their population estimates, and they have done so without trying to adapt them to local circumstances. In particular, the figure of 4.5–5.0 persons per family that was established for pre-modern England by the Cambridge Group for Population History[186] has been too readily applied to Ireland, where people of all classes tended to marry younger and so breed longer.[187] Certainly, it makes little sense where Kilkenny is concerned. According to a sample study of 32 local gentry families given in Appendix 2, the average elite family in Kilkenny was dramatically different from its English counterpart, containing 7.4 persons (English elite families averaged just 3.0 to 5.0 children per marriage between 1550 and 1650).[188] Other scattered fragments of evidence indicate that in Co. Kilkenny the families of well-to-do tenants and peasants could also be large, with six children per marriage not unusual.[189] Taking this latter figure (6.0) as a more plausible locally specific multiplier it emerges that by 1640 Kilkenny's urban population must have exceeded that suggested by previous estimates. The city then had 500 houses in the Hightown,[190] and perhaps as many as 125 houses in the Irishtown,[191] signifying a minimum city population of perhaps 4,000 people. Indeed, it may have been still higher, as many houses would have contained more than one family.

Of the county's other urban centres, population estimates can now be hazarded for Callan and Inistioge, but not for anywhere else. Recent research has succeeded in retrieving long-lost mid-seventeenth century descriptions of the two towns. Callan was much the bigger, having 166 houses in five streets within its liberties (plus another 5 houses owned by the Ormonds), while Inistioge was tiny, little more than a village, with just 27 houses in two streets (and an unknown number, perhaps 30 or so, that were Ormond property).[192] Using the

---

185 Ellis, *Tudor Ireland*, 38, suggests 3,000 for the 1530s; Sheehan, 'Irish towns', 97, gives 2,000 *c*.1600; Neely, 'Kilkenny city', has 2,000–2,500 for 1640. **186** See Palliser, *Age of Elizabeth*, 40–6. **187** Sir William Petty, writing in the late seventeenth century, assumed a *minimum* of 5 persons per one-chimney and 6 persons per two-chimney household in Ireland: G. Mac Niocaill, *Irish population before Petty* (Dublin 1981), 1–2. See also R.A. Houston, *The population history of Britain and Ireland, 1500–1750* (Cambridge 1995), 26–7; L.M. Cullen, *The emergence of modern Ireland, 1600–1850* (Dublin 1981), 83–4. **188** L. Stone & J. Fawtier-Stone, *An open elite? England, 1540–1880* (abridged edn., Oxford 1986), 60–1. **189** E.g., the five sons of James O'Loughlin, tenants at Ballyragget, *c*.1600 (NA, CP I/180); the six children of Leonard Blanchville, husbandman, *c*.1654 (St Kieran's College, Carrigan MSS, Vol. 21, unpaginated). Government pardons sometimes record soldiers and farmers with three or even four sons (*Ir. Fiants*, passim). **190** Not 308, as stated in Neely, 'Kilkenny city', 163–4, which does not take account of an additional 184 houses that belonged to the Ormonds in 1641: Butler (ed.), 'Occupants', passim. **191** According to surviving Elizabethan annals of Kilkenny, in August 1575 six score, or 120, houses were 'burned at Kilkenny in the Irishtown and Hightown' (Clonalis House, O'Conor Don Ms 6.4 HN002), but it does not say that Irishtown was completely destroyed by the fire. The fire is not noted in the Irishtown Corporation Book. **192** C. Manning, 'The finding of the Civil Survey of Inistioge and Callan', *Archaeology Ireland* 14/3 (Autumn 2000), 18–23; 'The Civil Survey of Inistioge and Callan, Co. Kilkenny', *JRSAI* 128 (1998), 48–73. My thanks to Conleth Manning for helping me

same multiplication figure that I have used for Kilkenny, it can be suggested that Callan had in the region of 1,100 inhabitants by 1641, and Inistioge barely 400. Thomastown, the third biggest town in the county, was much closer to Callan than Inistioge in size. It was deemed large enough to be included on the government muster commissions in the sixteenth century, and (unlike Inistioge) it was mentioned as important by David Wolfe the Jesuit, writing in 1574, and by Richard Stanihurst, writing ten years later.[193]

Gowran did not qualify as a major population centre. A frontier town for much of the Tudor period, it was situated near one of the most concentrated military zones in the shire, in the Barrow borderlands, and even with the joint assistance of the earls of Ormond and the Dublin executive it experienced difficulty controlling its hinterland. In 1552 and again in 1567 it was given an exemption from the cess, the government army tax,[194] but its development was constantly frustrated by circumstances beyond its control. Early in the 1580s Gowran was badly affected by wartime famine[195] and in 1604 it was hit by a serious outbreak of plague. Happily the early seventeenth century saw an improvement in Gowran's fortunes, and in 1650 Oliver Cromwell described it as a populous town when he brought his forces there.[196]

Gowran's recovery, significant as it was, should not be exaggerated. In general, the first half of the seventeenth century was a time of growth for all of the shire's towns. Migrants were attracted to Co. Kilkenny from across the country, and from England and Scotland too. Thus while Gowran gained new settlers such as the Everards from Tipperary, the Kellys from Laois-Offaly, and the O'Loughlins from Leitrim,[197] Thomastown was regularly colonised by Waterford families such as the Whites, Dobbins and Sherlocks,[198] as was Inistioge, which also got the Evelyns and Sherwoods from England,[199] and Callan received the native Irish Kavanaghs from Carlow and the New English families of Adams and Aungier.[200]

THE MIDLAND BASIN III: THE BUTLERS AND THE TOWNS

Outsiders like the anonymous 'H.C.', author of a late Elizabethan tract on Ireland, had no doubt that the county's towns owed their well being to the Butlers of Ormond. The dynasty, said 'H.C.', had always defended the local

---

with these estimates. The 5 Ormond houses in Callan are noted in 'Chief rents of Callan due to the lady marchioness of Ormond', n.d., *c*.1650 (NLI, Ms 11,063 (1)). **193** *Ir. Fiants*, Eliz. I, nos. 2117, 2444; NA, Lodge MSS, Articles with Irish chiefs, etc., 94; *CSP Rome, 1572–8*, 157; Lennon, *Richard Stanihurst*, 141. **194** *Ir. Fiants*, Edward VI, no. 1101; *COD*, v, no. 146. **195** HMC, *Salisbury MSS*, ii, 507. **196** M. Sparks, 'Gowran', *Old Kilkenny Review* 3 (1950), 45–6. **197** TCD Ms 2512: 23, 108; Notes from the Kelly Manuscript (St Kieran's College, Carrigan MSS, un-numbered volume, unpaginated); NLI, Ms 11,053 (9). **198** NA, Chancery MSS, Catalogue of Deeds, Pt. 1, nos. 18, 34, 52, 60, 63, 65, 68, 71; *CSPI, 1586–8*, 52–3, *COD*, v, nos. 155, 182, 287; ibid., vi, no. 145. **199** Ibid.; NLI, D. 4009; NA, Ferguson MSS, Revenue Exchequer Orders, 1592–1657, 323. **200** *COD*, v, no. 109; ibid., vi, no. 58; NA, CP B/33; ibid., CP C/184.

merchants and artisans and helped them 'to apply their trades and crafts without any impediment'. To his eyes this made the Ormond country unusual
among the southern Irish lordships. Because of the Butlers' encouragement, Co.
Kilkenny (and to a lesser extent Tipperary) was an area where young men
'scorned not to get their living' through commerce and hard work; above all,
it was a place where money was respected.[201]

Insiders such as Robert Rothe, the seneschal of the Ormond estate, agreed
wholeheartedly with these comments. In his pedigree of the family, compiled
in 1616, he recorded how a hundred years earlier the eighth earl, Piers Ruadh,
and his imposing countess, Margaret Fitzgerald, had brought a number of
Flemish weavers to Kilkenny to set its citizens a good example, manufacturing
'tapestries, Turkey carpets, cushions and other like works'.[202] They improved
the urban infrastructure in other ways too. According to Stanihurst it was Piers
and Margaret who first established the Ormond school at Kilkenny, from which,
he said, educated men sprang 'as if from a Trojan horse' (though Rothe indicated the schoolhouse was built entirely at Countess Margaret's cost). By the
1550s the fame of the school had spread and students came to Kilkenny from
as far away as Dublin to be educated, Stanihurst himself among them.[203] In 1565
the Black Earl, Thomas, allowed the citizens a right of way beside his 'great
orchard'.[204] The same earl paid for the 'Hospital of the Blessed Saviour of the
City of Kilkenny' – built by November 1611 – when he received a royal license
to purchase lands for its maintenance by statute of mortmain; it was re-estab-
lished with a charter of incorporation by his successor, Earl Walter, in 1630.[205]

The earls often involved themselves directly in urban affairs. Notwithstanding
their classification as territorial magnates, they lived mainly in towns like
Kilkenny, Carrick, Clonmel and Gowran, where their principal seats lay.
Occasionally they participated in commercial ventures. In 1517–18, for instance,
Piers Ruadh sold a large number of wool fleeces and animal hides to one of his
Butler kinsmen in Waterford,[206] while in the 1590s his grandson Earl Thomas
is recorded as doing the same, selling £60 (stg) worth of wool to a merchant of
London.[207] The Black Earl also profited from Kilkenny's export trade, in 1597
employing a Waterford factor, Nicholas Ley, to sell a cargo of locally manu-
factured cloth on his behalf in the south-west of England valued at £260 (stg).[208]
As Chart 1.5 shows, it contained various products of Kilkenny-Tipperary.

The quantity of cloth items in the cargo is noteworthy. The earls maintained
a keen watch on the progress of the cloth-making industry in the shire capital.
As late as 1639 the twelfth earl, James Butler, attempted to boost the industry
(and line his own pockets into the bargain) by soliciting a government contract
for the manufacture of frieze for the army. In the event his initiative was unsuc-

201 PRO, SP 63/203/119, pp 127–8. **202** HMC, *Second report*, 224–5; TCD, Ms 842, fol. 156r.
203 Lennon, *Richard Stanihurst*, 246, 142; TCD, Ms 842, fol. 156v. **204** NLI, Ms 2510, fol. 32v.
205 Bod. Lib., Carte Ms 62, no. 18; Ledwich, *Antiquities*, 484. **206** *COD*, iv, no. 41. **207** R.B.
Wernham (ed.), *List & analysis of state papers, foreign, Eliz. I, July 1593–Dec. 1594*, 238. **208** *APC*,
1597, 116; G.B. Harrison (ed.), *A second Elizabethan journal, 1595–8* (London 1974), 187.

Chart 1.5 The earl of Ormond's exports to Plymouth, 1597

Cloth products	*Other products*
12 double gowns	120 quarter boards
20 white mantles	260 pack hides
30 double coverlets	
40 set coverlets	
40 grey mantles	
40 single caddows	
60 grey caddows	
260 yards of frieze	

Source: PRO, HCA, 1/44, fol. 217r

---

cessful – the local cloth that he offered as a sample to the army commissioners was deemed sub-standard, too coarse for soldiers' uniforms[209] –but even so his effort showed that like many of his predecessors, he recognised the value of the industry to the city community.

It was as patrons that the Ormonds played a key role in the development of urban life in the county. Powerful in national politics, they were often able to gain important concessions for the towns. Sometimes this merely meant intervening whenever local burgesses ran into trouble with the government. In 1576, for instance, 47 townsmen from Inistioge received a royal pardon 'at the suit of Thomas, earl of Ormond'.[210] In 1603 Earl Thomas likewise insured that Kilkenny city was not heavily penalised for its part in religious disturbances in the south following the accession of James I.[211]

Butler patronage could be constructive as well as protective, as the people of Inistioge discovered early in the seventeenth century. In 1604, like Gowran, Inistioge had been ravaged by plague, leaving it 'much dispeopled and impoverished'.[212] Three years later the tenth earl's heir-apparent, Theobald Butler, Viscount Tulleophelim (alias Tully), greatly aided the town's recovery when he persuaded the government to grant Inistioge the right to hold a Tuesday market and two annual fairs, and in 1609 he improved things still further by securing a third yearly fair for it.[213] These grants secured Inistioge's future as the Irish economy experienced change after the Elizabethan wars. Under the new monarch, King James, the Dublin government attempted simultaneously to improve and to regulate the business infrastructure of the country, and accordingly whenever it made a grant of a fair or a market it was not just attempting

---

209 *CSPI, 1633–47*, 228. **210** *Ir. Fiants*, Eliz. I, nos. 2799–2802. For a 1566 example involving Kilkenny city, see KCA, Ms CR/K 4. **211** Chapter 5 below. **212** Erck, *Reportory*, ii, 425. **213** NA, Lodge MSS, Rolls, Vol. 2, 287–8; HMC, *Hastings MSS*, iv, 30–1; CPRI, *James I*, 155.

to extend the urban network, it was also choosing which town or village was suitable for inclusion within it.[214] For a town as small as Inistioge it was imperative that it did not miss out. The grants of 1607 and 1609 allowed it to steal a march on Knocktopher, another tiny town, which had to wait until 1635 before getting its own government-sanctioned fairs and a Thursday market.[215]

The reason for the crown's delay in validating Knocktopher's commercial status is difficult to pinpoint precisely, but religion may have had something to do with it. When Inistioge had benefited earlier, its overlord, Viscount Tully, had been publicly attached to the Protestant faith, and a committed supporter of the government. After his death in 1613, however, the Butler dynasty had become openly associated with the Catholic opposition, a development that instigated a political confrontation with the Dublin administration that lasted on and off for twenty years, until James Butler – another Protestant – succeeded to the earldom of Ormond in 1633. Viewed against this background, Knocktopher's belated acquisition of two fairs and a market in December 1635 makes sense in a politico-religious context, for the grant was made as a direct government favour to Earl James. The suspicion that religion was the bottom line when grants of fairs and markets were being prepared is strengthened considerably by reference to some of the other towns and villages in the shire. When Kilmanagh and Tullaghmaine, Ormond estate villages, received their grants in 1608, the incumbent earl, Earl Thomas, was reckoned to be a Protestant. Likewise, although both Richard Butler, third Viscount Mountgarret, and Walter Butler, eleventh earl of Ormond, were prominent Catholic leaders, when they secured grants of fairs and markets for Ballyragget and Callan (in 1622 and 1631 respectively) they did so at a time when their religious differences with the crown were temporarily on hold and their standing in Dublin was higher than normal.[216] Had the Butlers all been Protestants, how much more extensive might Co. Kilkenny's economic infrastructure have been by 1640?

By securing officially sanctioned markets and fairs for the local towns, the Butlers, like other landlords, were not acting selflessly. Markets were potentially very valuable not just for the towns involved. As the patentees, the Ormond and Mountgarret Butlers were lords of the market at six places: Inistioge, Ballyragget, Kilmanagh, Tullaghmaine, Graiguenamanagh and Knocktopher. As such, they were entitled to collect (or lease) the profits of the market court in each one of these. They would also have expected the new markets and fairs to have attracted more settlers to their territories and increase the value of their urban rents.[217]

The extent to which self-interest motivated the Butlers in their dealings with Co. Kilkenny's towns has tended to be overlooked by local historians, many of

214 R. Gillespie, *The transformation of the Irish economy, 1550–1700* (Dublin 1991), 28. **215** NLI, D 4011. **216** NA, Lodge MSS, Fairs & Markets, 86; Chapter 5 below. **217** *Circa* 1623 the Butlers leased the profits of Inistioge to New English arrivals: NA, Ferguson MSS, Revenue Exchequer Orders, 1592–1657, 323. For landlords and markets in Ulster, see R. Gillespie, 'The origins of the Ulster urban network, 1600–41', *IHS* 24/93 (May 1984), 18–19.

whom have presented a somewhat romanticised version of events. Based largely on the seventeenth-century writings of Robert and David Rothe, both of whom depended to a large extent on Butler support, a view has been handed down of Co. Kilkenny as an area where, in the towns at least, 'good lordship' and aristocratic benevolence were the order of the day. Although it contains a large measure of truth – the Ormond Butlers *did* identify more strongly with urban interests than many other Irish lords – nevertheless the emphasis on their patronage has been exaggerated.

There are many instances of the dynasty acting contrary to the interests of the towns, especially in the early-to-mid sixteenth century, when the Butlers were primarily military overlords and some of their servants best described as armed thugs. In 1526 Earl Piers' retinue threatened to destroy Kilkenny/Bristol relations. His men conducted themselves so badly in the English port that they incited a riot there, wherein 600 Bristolmen surrounded Piers' lodgings and swore to burn it to the ground.[218] A generation later, in 1559, Piers' grandson, Sir Edmund Butler of Cloghgrenan, ordered his troops to prevent the inhabitants of Upper Ossory travelling south to trade in Kilkenny city, a decision clearly not designed to enhance his popularity in the shire capital. In 1569 Sir Edmund and his two younger brothers, Edward and Piers Butler, actually laid siege to the city and ravaged its immediate hinterland in the course of an ill-fated rebellion.[219] Actions like these guaranteed that the towns were often the most strident critics of the Butler family, urging it to reform its ways or suffer the withdrawal of support as a result.[220]

As overlords the Ormond Butlers were almost bound to come into conflict with the local towns. The sixteenth century is known to have been a period when Irish towns in general sought greater autonomy,[221] and those in Co. Kilkenny were no exception. The world they inhabited was still a feudalistic one, and although each of the shire's six main towns already possessed a considerable degree of self-government, still they had to render obedience to the manorial rights and privileges of landlords such as the Butlers. These could be very extensive. According to the Knocktopher manor court roll, in 1586 the burgesses had to join with the rest of its inhabitants in delivering timber, slates and other building materials to the constable of the Ormond manor whenever repairs were needed to be made to the earl's manor house. In addition, the roll states that 'the burgesses, commonalty and other inhabitants of the said town were accustomed to convey, at their own expense, as often as they were requested … all salt, iron and wine which the lord [Ormond] or his constable … [purchased] in the city of Waterford, or in the towns of Thomastown, [New] Ross, Jerpoint and Inistioge'. In recompense for their services Earl Thomas gave the Knocktophermen just one meal for each day such duties required their absence from home.[222]

218 PRO, SP 60/1/48. **219** HMC, *Haliday MSS*, 72; Edwards, 'Butler revolt', 249–50. **220** Ibid., 235–40. **221** Sheehan, 'Irish towns', 105–12. **222** Empey, 'Medieval Knocktopher', 445–7.

The rights of the earls were equally imposing in Gowran. There the heir of a burgess was formally enfeoffed of his inheritance by the portreeve *and* the earl's constable 'according to the laudable customs of that town'.[223] As the sixteenth century wore on the burgesses sought to shake themselves free of some of the earls' demands. By the 1590s they were engaged in a bitter row with Earl Thomas over the duties expected of them regarding his manorial mill. In particular, they objected to his demand that they, not his servants, should repair and renovate the mill. The earl would not let the matter drop. Determined to hang onto his feudal privileges he brought forward witnesses to swear that, in his father's time (1539–46), the townsmen of Gowran had without protest joined with his tenants from nearby lands to carry timber 'and other necessaries' needed for the repair of the mill.[224] Relations worsened in 1608 when Gowran received a new charter from the government enhancing its autonomy as a parliamentary borough. Immediately the burgesses tried to undermine the tenth earl's authority. They stopped paying him his annual chief rent of £5, and some refused to render suit at his manor court. Finally, in November 1608 when the earl despatched two servants to the town to seize cattle by distraint as punishment, the locals reacted angrily, and ten of them chased after Ormond's men, captured one of them and beat him up, before leaving him to chill in the town stocks all through the cold winter night. An ugly affair, it reflected the sort of despair that the power of the earls could induce among sections of the urban community. It was only settled three years later, early in 1611, after the chief governor of Ireland, Sir Arthur Chichester, was compelled to intervene.[225]

The Gowran dispute is an important episode in the history of the Ormond lordship in Co. Kilkenny, not just because it signals the emergence of stubborn urban opposition to aspects of feudalism, but also because it helps to debunk one of the principal myths about the role played by the Butler dynasty in the economic development of the shire. Contrary to general opinion, it seems most unlikely that the earls of Ormond helped the local towns to get their charters renewed or extended. It was not in their interest to do so. When Kilkenny received city status by virtue of a new royal charter on 11 April 1609, it had nothing whatsoever to do with Butler influence. Rather, Kilkenny's leading merchants, always an ambitious lot, went to London and secured the charter themselves. In fact the 1609 charter, known as 'the Great Charter', was the second one that the Kilkenny merchants extracted from James I. An earlier one, dated 16 October 1608, had not been to their liking, and they had given Nicholas Langton the task of persuading the king to grant their wish for full-blown civic status. Kilkenny's subsequent elevation to the dignity of a city, governed by a mayor, aldermen and common council, was ultimately Langton's doing, and a testament to the wealth of the merchants (charters cost money).[226]

---

223 *COD*, iv, no. 188.   224 Ibid., vi, Appendix 1, 126–7.   225 NLI, Ms 11,053 (9); ibid., D. 3486; KCA, Ms CR/K 15.   226 J.G.A. Prim, 'Memorials of the family of Langton', *KSEIAS* Jn, 2nd series, 5/1 (1864), 72–3; and Murphy, 'Ten civic families', 8–12, provide the best accounts of the getting of the charter.

The Ormonds for their part did not react well to the change. In June 1610 the tenth earl complained to the English privy council about the matter, stating that 'the officers of the town (*sic*) of Kilkenny, by colour of a new charter lately granted ... do now go about to encroach upon his privileges'. Despite his advanced years Earl Thomas – almost eighty – was still able to pull strings in high places, and the lord deputy of Ireland was ordered to see to it that, in the course of the subsequent government inquiry, there should be shown 'as much favour to the nobleman as may be agreeable to equity'.[227] Unfortunately as it turned out for the city, these instructions suited Lord Deputy Chichester, who mistrusted Kilkenny as a Catholic stronghold. Even in 1609, no sooner had Kilkenny gained its civic charter than he had set his exchequer officials the task of querying the extent of its jurisdiction.[228] He was happy to consider Ormond's complaints, and the city subsequently underwent a lengthy period of uncertainty over its future, in 1611/12 being forced to compromise with Earl Thomas over his privileges, while simultaneously being put to great expense in Dublin where a series of technical objections were made in the exchequer over the sort of fines that could be collected by the city sheriffs.[229] Far from encouraging Kilkenny's emergence as a city, the Butlers of Ormond played instead a small but significant part in its post-1609 difficulties, troubles which only ended in 1616 when Chichester's successor, Lord Deputy St John, decided not to strip Kilkenny of its charter and liberties, despite a strong desire to do so in government circles.[230] For all that it was the capital of their lordship, the earls of Ormond were not prepared to sponsor a development that would mean relinquishing some of their power.

Perhaps one of the most telling facts about the Ormond overlordship is that the dynasty seems never to have taken sides with the towns against any of the local gentry. At its most basic level Ormond power was landlord power. For example, when in 1543 the townsmen of Callan complained about the extortionate practices of the sheriff, James Sweetman, a leading gentleman, the Ormonds did not become involved, but left it to the Dublin Council to settle the matter.[231] Likewise, they consistently ignored the actions south of Inistioge of two major landowners, the bishops of Ossory and the Fitzgeralds of Brownesford, who between them almost monopolised the salmon fisheries on the River Nore there – thus threatening the livelihoods of Inistioge's fishermen – by constructing large fishing weirs on both sides of the river, contrary to a statute of Henry VIII. In this instance, the Butlers' non-involvement was entirely self-interested; especially after 1568 when, as the new owners of Inistioge Priory, they too came to possess a number of fishing weirs on the river.[232] Clearly, to

---

227 Bod. Lib., Carte Ms 30, fol. 219.   228 NA, Ferguson MSS, Revenue Exchequer Orders, 1592–1657, 70–1, 79.   229 Ibid., 105, 116, 118–9, 159; KCA, MSS CR/J 36–7, CR/K 16, 18, 22. Chichester's actions are discussed in Chapter 5 below.   230 *APC, 1615–16*, 689–90; ibid., *1616–17*, 91–2.   231 *COD*, iv, no. 295.   232 NA, CP E/99; A.E.J. Went, 'A short history of the fisheries of the River Nore', *JRSAI* 85 (1955), 22–5.

have spoken out against the exploitative practices of either the Fitzgeralds or
the bishops would have meant jeopardising their own river profits, something
they were not prepared to do.[233]

In the final analysis the relationship between the Ormonds and the towns is
probably best described as one of mutual dependence and a little ambivalence.
The earls needed to retain the support of the towns – especially Kilkenny city
– in order to consolidate their grip on local society. Hence their tendency to
offer employment to so many of the shire's leading townsmen. During the sixteenth century the most important posts in Ormond service – seneschal of the
earls' estate, steward of the earls' household, earls' secretary and earls' attorney
– were invariably filled by members of the Archer, Rothe, Shee and Cowley
families of Kilkenny.[234] In this way the earls succeeded in building an effective
body of support on Kilkenny's city council. Many of the principal councillors,
and several of the city's sovereigns and mayors, were Ormond creatures, agents
of feudalism in the civic chamber who often put their loyalty to the earldom
ahead of their loyalty to the city.[235] Chart 1.6 below shows the extent to which
Thomas, the tenth earl, managed to recruit the most important members of the
civic elite before his death in 1614. Six of the city's first eighteen aldermen were
the earl's servants, each day working on his behalf, taking care of his interests.
Presumably it was largely through the representations of these men – some of
who were referred to by contemporaries as 'the earl's men' – that Ormond was
so often able to patch up his differences with Kilkenny corporation (even when
daring to challenge the terms of the charter of 1609).

Earl Thomas was more mindful of the need for a civic lobby than many of
his predecessors. Though he preferred when he was in Ireland to live in his
English-style manor house at Carrick-on-Suir (built to his specifications in
1565),[236] he usually spent a large part of each year in residence at Kilkenny Castle.
In effect, rather like a minor royal prince, he made Carrick his private abode
and Kilkenny his public one, and as a result Kilkenny became much more the
capital of the Ormond lordship than had previously been the case. His father
and grandfather had spread themselves more thinly around the Ormond territories, residing variously at Gowran, Callan, Clonmel, Pottlerath and
Keappahedin as well as at Kilkenny,[237] but it was the tenth earl who based the
earldom mainly in the city. Towards this end, in 1580 he modernised Kilkenny
Castle, hiring the local builder, Robert Freney, to construct a 'great gallery'
there,[238] a place where major political receptions and other important gather-

233 Hore & Graves (ed.), *Social state*, 131. When the twelfth earl mortgaged his Inistioge estate to
Marcus Knaresborough in 1635/6, he made sure to retain its fisheries: NLI, D 4004, D 4009, D 4027.
234 *COD*, iv, no. 352 (5); ibid., v, nos. 40, 45, 72a (5), 95, 181 (7), 199, 210, 239.   235 E.g., in April
1631 the mayor of Kilkenny, John Shee, decided to quit his mayoral office several months before
his term expired, in order the better to serve Earl Walter: NLI, Ms 2505, 3.   236 For Carrick, its
architecture and contruction, see esp. Jane Fenlon's superb OPW guide, *Ormond Castle* (Stationery
Office, Dublin 1996).   237 *SP Henry VIII*, iii, nos. 240, 242, 254; *COD*, iv, nos. 37, 222; *CSPI,
1509–73*, 6, 37, 45, 50, 53.   238 Clonalis House, O'Conor Don MSS, Ms 6.4 HN002.

Chart 1.6 *Ormond's servants: the civic connection*

The first 18 aldermen of Kilkenny city, 1609	*Ormond estate officials 1610*	*Officers of Tipperary liberty, c.1613*
Robert Rothe, mayor	Seneschal: Robert Rothe	Seneschal: Sir Walter Butler of Kilcash
Patrick Archer	Steward I: Thomas Archer	Treasurer: Robert Rothe
Thomas Archer	Steward II: Henry Shee	Chancellor: Dr John Haly of Cashel
Walter Archer	Secretary: Henry Shee	Attorney: Patrick Archer
Michael Cowley	Attorney: Patrick Archer	Clerk: Helias Shee
Nicholas Langton	Trustee: Walter Lawless	Justice I: Sir John Everard of Fethard
Walter Lawless		Justice II: John Meade of Cork
Thomas Ley		Custos Rotulorum: Sir James Craig
Richard Ragget		
Edward Rothe		
John Rothe fitz Piers		
Arthur Shee		
Edward Shee		
Helias Shee		
Henry Shee		
Luke Shee		
Thomas Shee		

Sources: NLI, Ms 2531, p.109; ibid., Ms 11,044, passim; ibid., D. 3326, 3340, 3366

---

ings could be held (and, presumably, where his large collection of Renaissance paintings could be exhibited). The castle was transformed during his years in power. Previously an urban fortress, manned by a large garrison of private retainers, Earl Thomas removed the troops from the castle as part of his reform of the Butler army, an important gesture that symbolised his intention to preside over a less militarised lordship than his forebears.[239]

By and large the Kilkenny civic elite responded favourably to these changes. The disappearance of a permanent garrison from the earl's castle removed one of the thorniest problems affecting Ormond/Kilkenny relations during the middle years of the sixteenth century, namely the behaviour of the Butler soldiers, who were not always as disciplined or law-abiding as they might have been. This is not to say that the city corporation had always been opposed to the dynasty's military strength; nothing of the sort. In the past, when circumstances had demanded, the city had been quite willing to encourage the Butlers in their use of force. The damage inflicted on the shire economy by the MacGiollapadraigs and their supporters early in the sixteenth century – a time

---

239 Edwards, 'Butler revolt', 234.

when the Ormond dynasty had been relatively weak and divided – had meant that temporarily at least, the citizens of Kilkenny had a vested interest in fostering the re-emergence of a large Butler army in the county. The fact that the army subsequently became a blight on the local economy, with the Butler soldiers robbing Kilkenny merchants on the highways, should not disguise the fact that the army could not have grown significantly without some level of support from the merchants. Indeed, for all its ills, from c1515 to 1550 the Butler army had given the civic leaders what they had then most wanted, that is, greater protection against the external threat posed to their interests by the MacGiollapadraigs, the Kildare Fitzgeralds, the O'Brennans, and hostile branches of the Kavanaghs, who hindered them when bringing their merchandise north or east of the shire heartland.[240]

THE EAST MARCH: THE BARROW BORDERLANDS

Although from the Ormonds' point of view the greatest threat to the Kilkenny midlands after 1515 came from the north of the county, there was also a considerable security problem in the east, in the southern part of Gowran barony and the north of Ida, another area with distinct geographical and political characteristics. Here weak physical boundaries caused by the Barrow's floodplain left the shire heartland exposed. Forests made it more dangerous still. Some of the densest woodland in the county was to be found hereabouts, part of a great forest and bog that stretched into the shire from St Mullins in Co. Carlow.[241] As such it was vulnerable to attack from hostile neighbours based in the present-day counties of Carlow and Wexford, principally the forces of the Fitzgeralds, earls of Kildare, and their allies among sections of the MacMurrough Kavanaghs. The weak topography of the region insured that armed gangs were able to sweep through the forests into central Kilkenny from southern Carlow or northern Wexford to waylay local merchants travelling along the roads from market to market. Even in the reign of Charles I, long after the Elizabethan border wars had ended, the eastern frontier of Kilkenny continued to attract criminals and outlaws. In 1626, for instance, a crown official reported that three 'notorious malefactors' – Lionel Blanchville, Murrough Backagh Kavanagh and Brian Kavanagh – were finding it easy in the thickly wooded landscape to evade the local authorities, sometimes hiding out 'in a cave over the Barrow' near St Mullins, while at other times slipping across the river into Co. Kilkenny.[242]

   At the start of the sixteenth century, concern about the unruliness of the east was compounded by the fact that it was still very much part of Gaelic Leinster. Indeed, in 1515 large parts of it were quite separate from Kilkenny. This was particularly true of the Rower, a boggy, thickly wooded territory con-

---

taining over 6,000 acres facing the Blackstairs mountain, now part of the barony of Ida. The Rower was a place apart. On the back of a hill, it was cut off from the Butler country by the confluence of the Nore and the Barrow; it was even described as 'half an island' in a document of Elizabethan date.[243] Much earlier, during the 1400s, the Rower had belonged to the MacMurrough Kavanaghs, the Gaelic kings of Leinster, who seem to have held it as part of their kingdom, and sometime before 1476 the head of the dynasty, Donal Reagh Kavanagh, had granted possession of it to one of his sons, Cahir.[244] A new Kavanagh branch was thereby established, the Rower sept, which made the townland of Coolhill the centre of a new lordship. By 1500 or thereabouts Cahir's son, Gerald Kavanagh, had consolidated the Kavanaghs' hold in the region, building a strong stone fort there, *Cloch Gherailt,* the ruins of which can still be seen today.

The Rower was not the only Gaelic lordship in what became east Co. Kilkenny. To the north of it was the territory of Farren O'Ryan, occupied by the O'Ryan lineage that, like the Kavanaghs, also had lands on the other side of the Barrow in Co. Carlow. Unfortunately, it is difficult to discover much about the history of this family. Weaker than the O'Brennans, but stronger than lesser families such as the O'Dorans and the little-known O'Hennessys,[245] at the start of the sixteenth century the O'Ryans clung on to a small territorial lordship that was roughly equivalent to the modern parish of Ullard and part of neighbouring Powerstown. In all, their lands in the county amounted to perhaps 3,500–4,000 plantation acres in 1515.

They had probably held a lot more land during the Middle Ages, but the expansion of the Kildare Fitzgeralds and the MacMurrough Kavanaghs pushed them into retreat long before the Ormond revival got under way. As will be seen in Chapter 3 below, by the early 1500s their nearest and most dangerous neighbours were not the Butlers, but the Fitzgeralds and the Kavanaghs at Drumroe and Powerstown. Of course, the proximity of these greatly encouraged the Butlers of Ormond to seek to control the O'Ryans' land after 1515. As a result, for fifty or sixty years afterwards the O'Ryans found themselves ripped asunder by powerful outside forces, divided up between pro-Butler, pro-Fitzgerald and pro-Kavanagh factions,[246] a development which hastened their decline.

What made Farren O'Ryan so tempting was not the O'Ryans' strength. They had no major castles or strongholds worth fighting over. Nor could they raise much of an army. According to a late fifteenth century estimate, they could muster only 36 men for battle, a pitiable levy that made theirs one of the small-

---

243 Lambeth Ms 635: 55.   **244** Ibid., Ms 614: 141. Although the document (also of Elizabethan date) claims the Rower was given to another of Donal's sons, Art Buidhe, Cahir was clearly the recipient. See White (ed.) *Ir. mon & ep deeds*, 176–8.   **245** For the O'Dorans, see D. Moore, 'English action, Irish reaction: The MacMurrough Kavanaghs, *c.*1530–*c.*1630' (MA thesis, NUI Maynooth, 1985), ch. 1. For the O'Hennessys, NA, Lodge MSS, Wardships, I, 255; *Ir. Fiants*, Edward VI, no. 384.   **246** In the 1560s the sons of Cahir MacArt Kavanagh seem to have supported the O'Ryans of Ballyshanboy (ibid., Eliz. I, no. 751).

est forces in Ireland.[247] Rather, what made the Butlers, Fitzgeralds and Kavanaghs compete for the O'Ryans' land was the fear that it would fall into the hands of the others. Hence, like the inhabitants of other borderlands, the O'Ryans were mere pawns in a struggle for the dominance of mid-Leinster.

The key to controlling both Farren O'Ryan and the Rower was possession of the upland territory in between, at Graiguenamanagh. Since the late Middle Ages its strategic importance had been widely acknowledged on a provincial level; even in far-off Dublin, royal officials regularly toyed with the idea of taking it into crown hands.[248] In the early sixteenth century Graiguenamanagh belonged to the monks of the Cistercian order, headed by their abbot Cahir Kavanagh, who held a large and prosperous monastery at Duiske (as well as the parish of Grangesylva further north), possessing in all about 12,000 acres. By itself Duiske Abbey was a prize worth having, dominating the local economy. Better still, its outlying lands included the Coppanagh Gap, a crucial avenue of access into Kilkenny's midland plain from the mountains and woods of north Wexford. Unsurprisingly, while one of their number was abbot, the Kavanaghs remained a force to be reckoned with in west Carlow/east Kilkenny.[249]

Although the eighth earl of Ormond, Piers Ruadh, attempted to secure the borders with Wexford and Carlow shortly after 1515, he and his family did not get very far until Duiske Abbey became available following the dissolution of the monasteries, for he found the Kavanaghs and the Fitzgeralds hard to shift. True, as regards the Kavanaghs, Piers had some allies among them (partly through the connections of his mother, Saiv Kavanagh), and in 1530 some of the Rower sept had agreed to sell him a share of their lands.[250] Yet none of this negated the fact that the clan retained a strong presence in east Kilkenny,[251] one that might turn against Piers' family in the future. Everything changed, however, in the mid-to-late 1530s: the Kildare Fitzgeralds were destroyed, the Kavanaghs exposed, and the religious orders abolished. Suddenly the abbey became available, and in the early 1540s it was granted to his son James, the ninth earl. Henceforth the Ormond Butlers surged ahead of the Kavanaghs as the dominant force in Kilkenny's eastern Barrow borderlands. Kavanagh attacks on Graiguenamanagh, which had reached a peak in the late 1530s,[252] subsequently fell away, and the earls of Ormond were at last able to develop the area into a highly effective buffer-zone against their outside enemies.

Further Ormond expansion soon followed in the surrounding area. In 1542 James the ninth earl consolidated his hold over the Kavanaghs of the Rower by compelling the Roches of Drumdowney – Anglo-Irish gentry in decline – to grant him possession of their manor in the Rower.[253] In the meantime he posed as the protector of the local Kavanagh sept and its leader, the pro-Butler Cahir

247 L. Price, 'Armed forces of the Irish chiefs in the sixteenth century', *JRSAI* 62 (1932), 203–4. **248** E.g., *Cal. Carew MSS, 1515–74*, 6, 134.   **249** Moore, 'English action, Irish reaction', 22–3. **250** Ibid., 21–2; White (ed.), *Ir. mon & ep deeds*, 176–8.   **251** The Rower sept was active nearby at New Ross: Hore & Graves (ed.), *Social state*, 68.   **252** White (ed.), *Extents*, 202–3.   **253** *COD*, iv, no. 270.

Mac Gerald, when the latter was prey to the suspicions of the Dublin govern-ment in 1545.[254] Progress was also made in Farren O'Ryan. Most of the O'Ryans effectively capitulated to the Butlers around 1549, as the ninth earl's widow, the dowager countess of Ormond, Joan Fitzgerald, and the earl's younger brother, the future Viscount Mountgarret, Richard Butler, persuaded the clan to surrender their lands to the earldom in return for Butler protection. A treaty followed, the details of which remain unclear, but by the 1560s it was widely recognised that all the septs of the O'Ryans held their lands in fee by knight's service of the Ormond manor of Gowran.[255] Once more, feudalism provided the basis for Ormond expansion.

The Butlers assimilated the O'Ryans with extraordinary ease. Presumably the clan feared harsher treatment from the Kavanaghs or the Kinsellaghs across the river.[256] Whatever the case, from the 1540s onwards many of the O'Ryans embraced the Ormond lordship, and in return some of them began receiving tenancies and sub-tenancies on Ormond and pro-Ormond lands elsewhere in Kilkenny (and in Carlow too). A junior line of the lineage was established on the Ormond estate at Dunbill, a grange of Jerpoint near Kilkenny. Others became Ormond tenants at Dunfert in the midlands and at Clontubbrid in the north.[257] Nor was this all. The O'Ryans who remained in the east – the major-ity of the family – were encouraged to participate in Co. Kilkenny's legal system, and some of their leaders served as jurors for the barony of Gowran alongside the Butlers, Blanchvilles and Archdekins.[258]

At first, having secured possession of Duiske Abbey and the hill country around Graiguenamanagh, the earls of Ormond looked to dominate Farren O'Ryan and the Rower through military might. By Elizabeth I's time they had established permanent garrisons in the region at the forts of Graigue, Grange MacWilliam Carrogh and Cloghasty.[259] Within the Ormond dynastic structure, the main responsibility for the east devolved upon the tenth earl's younger brother James Butler, who had been assigned Duiske by the terms of their father's will. However, despite receiving a fee farm regrant of the abbey estate from the queen in 1566, James and his son failed to make a lasting impression in the area, as both died prematurely.[260] It therefore fell to another Butler branch, the Butlers, viscounts Mountgarret, to move in and consolidate part of the area as the representatives of the dynasty. Already possessing lands across the Barrow in Fassagh Bantry, Co. Wexford, the Mountgarrets made short work of pene-trating the Rower. Sometime after 1571 the second viscount, Edmund Butler,

254 Ibid., no. 341. **255** *Cal. Carew MSS, 1515–74*, no. 273. **256** The O'Ryans occasionally ran up against the Kinsellaghs: NLI, Ainsworth Reports, Vol. 1, 136. **257** *Ir. Fiants*, Eliz. I, no. 1873; *COD*, v, no. 133; ibid., vi, 126; *CPRI, James I*, 25. Likewise one Muurough O'Ryan, who was settled at Cottrellsboley *c*.1552 and subsequently moved to Burnchurch, where he was still living in the 1590s: *COD*, vi, 127. **258** Ibid., v, no. 95; BL, Add Ms 47,172, fol. 35r. Thomas McMurrough, the sergeant of Gowran barony in 1593, was almost certainly an O'Ryan: NLI, Ms 2506, fol. 11r. **259** *Ir. Fiants*, Eliz. I, no. 921. Cloghasty was acquired by the Ormonds quite late, around 1570/1: *COD*, v, no. 181 (4). **260** J. Hughes, 'The Butlers of Duiske Abbey', *RHAAI*, 3rd series, 1/1, 64–8.

took possession of most of the area from the Kavanaghs – possibly by mortgage, but more likely by force.[261] He was equally assertive in Farren O'Ryan. When he rose in revolt at the end of the sixteenth century, he was supported by 'a rabble of O'Ryan rebels', 'all the Ryans, his followers'.[262]

Mountgarret's success on the eastern frontier acted as a harbinger of further Anglo-Irish expansion. In the mid-1580s the last remnants of meaningful Gaelic autonomy in the region shrivelled up and collapsed. The Duiske Butlers were reactivated as Earl Thomas' favourite bastard son, Piers Dubh (or Black Piers), received possession of the abbey estate from his father. This time a lasting lineage was established. Over the next forty years Piers and his heir, Sir Edward Butler of Duiske, pushed forward on the O'Ryan lands. By the early 1630s the Duiske Butlers had received twelve separate conveyances of O'Ryan land in western Carlow and eastern Kilkenny from sixteen members of the O'Ryan lineage and one of the O'Hennessys, with the result that in the space of just two generations, they gained an interest in approximately 2,500 acres in Farren O'Ryan, the greater part of the territory.[263]

Lesser Anglo-Irish families gradually followed the Butlers into the area. The O'Ryans were economically marginalised and, already Ormond subjects, they seem to have been fair game for Anglo-Irish money. By 1607 the Blanchvilles of Milltown and the McCody Archdekins of Cloghlea had bought their way into Farren O'Ryan, and later still they were joined by the Sweetmans of Hodsgrove and the native Irish Kellys of Gowran. Again, as with similar developments in the north of the shire, it is important to avoid portraying this simplistically as the colonisation of the 'Irishry' by the 'Englishry' of Kilkenny. In cultural terms, it was the the intermixing, or hybridisation, of Gaelic and Anglo-Irish modes of transfer that transformed the ownership of land in the area. The Blanchvilles and McCody Archdekins as often accepted traditional Gaelic pledges as they did English-style mortgages from the O'Ryans.[264]

Meanwhile in the Rower, to complement the Mountgarrets' earlier gains there, a second large part of the Kavanaghs' territory fell into the hands of Sir Nicholas Walsh of Clonmore, a distinguished legal official and follower of the tenth earl of Ormond. Sometime before 1587 he secured a lease of the lands of Tincorran, Tinscolly, Coulreny and Tentwine from Derby McCahir Kavanagh, the head of the Rower sept, and 'divers of his kinsmen'.[265] In time this lease seems to have led to a more lasting transfer of title, for in February 1608 he (not the Kavanaghs) was recognised as the lawful owner of the lands, which he held in fee of the king by socage tenure.[266] His successor Thomas Walsh was still in

---

261 Donal Spaniagh Kavanagh claimed that Mountgarret pretended a title by mortgage (Lambeth Ms 614: 141). Evidence that the viscount used force in the Rower comes from a statement of Sir Nicholas Walsh that his tenants there had been attacked and terrorised by Mountgarret's men c.1587: NA, CP E/246. **262** PRO, SP 63/205/74. **263** *Inq. Lagenia*, Co. Carlow, Charles I (40); NA, Lodge MSS, Wardships, Vol. 1, 181, 255; NLI, Ms 975: 224–7. **264** Ibid., 225–7, 233; *Inq. Lagenia*, Co. Kilkenny, James I (4). **265** NA, CP E/246. **266** *Inq. Lagenia*, Co. Kilkenny, James I (5).

occupation in 1641, by which date it seems there were no longer any Kavanaghs who owned land in the area. Instead the Rower was uniformly the property of the Ormond and Mountgarret Butlers, the Clonmore Walshes and two other Kilkenny-based Anglo-Irish families, the Graces of Killrindowney and the Stranges of Drumdowney. The Gaelic Bolgers (or O'Bolgers), a medical family closely linked to the Blanchvilles of Milltown, also entered the area.[267] More so than in any other ethnically Gaelic zone of Kilkenny, in the Rower the Anglo-Irish expansion initiated by the earls of Ormond in the sixteenth century had led to the complete dispossession of the traditional Gaelic lineages within less than a hundred years. At least in Farren O'Ryan, and even in Idough, patches of land remained the property of some of the O'Ryans and O'Brennans in Charles I's reign. Not so in the Rower, where the Kavanaghs are noticeable only by their absence after 1600.

There was a larger context to events in the Barrow borderlands than first meets the eye. Just as in the north, where the territories of Upper Ossory and Idough were each the subject of important changes in the county boundaries, so significant cartographic and administrative alterations were required in the east. It is sometimes overlooked that by colonising what is now east Co. Kilkenny, the Butlers of Ormond and their supporters effectively annexed the region from neighbouring Co. Carlow, to which it had belonged in medieval times. As no history of Irish county boundaries yet exists, some comments about how this transfer was viewed by the government may be useful: all the more so as the assignment of the Barrow area reveals much about the change in royal attitudes towards the Ormond Butlers that took place after 1603.

Before that date the earls of Ormond were able to enlarge Kilkenny at Carlow's expense principally because they enjoyed a measure of crown support. Throughout much of the sixteenth century any expansion of the Butlers was acceptable in government circles if it occurred at the expense of Gaelic lineages such as the Kavanaghs, who were normally viewed with unyielding suspicion in Dublin and London.[268] Moreover, the Butler carve-up of (new) east Kilkenny/ (old) west Carlow may also have been deemed permissible on the grounds of expediency insofar as the area was not easily governable from Carlow Castle, where the local English administration was based. One thing is clear: in tolerating Ormond aggrandisement in the Barrow flood plain, the crown probably gave no consideration to the fact that, geographically, the area belongs more naturally to the lowlands of Kilkenny than it does to Carlow. By failing to do so, the crown laid the foundations for fresh problems after 1603, when its leniency towards the earldom ended. Suddenly suspicious of the Butlers as a leading Catholic dynasty, and increasingly aware that Co. Kilkenny was a hive of popery, the royal authorities were no longer prepared to concede that it had grown in size. The area of immediate Ormond dominance was about to be curtailed.

---

267 NLI, Ms 975: 139; Blanchville feoffment, 1618 (St Kieran's College, Carrigan MSS, Vol. 3, unpaginated). **268** Moore, 'English action, Irish reaction', ch. 2–4.

Following the accession of James I the six eastern parishes of Shankill, Kilmacahill, Wells, Grangesylva, Powerstown and Ullard, once part of medieval Carlow,[269] began to oscillate between Kilkenny and that county, sometimes still counted part of Kilkenny, more often included with Carlow.[270] This sudden state of flux had some curious results. Overnight the tiny market town of Wells, just a few miles east of Gowran, rose to become an administrative centre, a regular part of the Carlow assize circuit and a place where courts of inquisition were held. This would not have occurred had it remained shired with Kilkenny.[271] Odder still, despite not owning any land in the aforementioned six parishes, some major Kilkenny landlords found themselves occasionally drawn into the Carlow county administration. In 1631, for instance, two of the principal landowners of the east Kilkenny midlands, Sir Oliver Shortal and Sir Edmund Blanchville, were named as commissioners for the Carlow corn supply, a strange choice, as the main bulk of their estates lay towards the centre of Co. Kilkenny, and neither of them owned any land east of the Barrow.[272] More logical choices for the task would have been Walter Butler, eleventh earl of Ormond, Richard Butler, third viscount Mountgarret, Sir Edward Butler of Duiske, or Edmund Butler of Paulstown, each of whom owned extensive estates in the six parishes' district and all of whom had property east of the Barrow in either Carlow or Wexford. Presumably the main reason for overlooking them was to prevent them, as Butlers, from controlling affairs in Co. Carlow as much as they controlled them in Co. Kilkenny.

Ultimately, the most significant thing about the crown's meddling with Kilkenny's Barrow borderlands is that the return of the six parishes to Carlow failed to reduce the level of Butler influence in the area. Each of the main Butler branches enjoyed extensive connections with some of the major Carlow families, especially the Kavanaghs and the Bagenals. Furthermore, there was nothing the crown could do to stop the lesser landowners of the borderlands – the junior lines of the Graces, Sweetmans, Blanchvilles, Archdekins, etc. – from viewing either the earl of Ormond or Viscount Mountgarret as their overlord. The fact remained that first the Ormonds and then the Mountgarrets had spearheaded the colonisation of the region by the Kilkenny gentry. As elsewhere in Co. Kilkenny the feudal ties of patronage and clientage were hard to dissolve. As if to reject the crown's policy, it was commonplace in the early seventeenth century for the eastern border squires and gentry to describe themselves as 'of Kilkenny', and their land as Kilkenny land, when appearing in a Dublin court.[273]

---

269 C.A. Empey, 'County Kilkenny in the Anglo-Norman period', in Nolan & Whelan (ed.), *Kilkenny*, 75–6. **270** *Eighth report of the Irish Record Commission* (Dublin 1819), 432–3; NA, Lodge MSS, Wardships, Vol. 1, 180–2. For the sheriff of Carlow at work in the area in 1640, see NA, Carte Transcripts, Vol. 1, 118. **271** HMC, *Third Report*, 52, where the date should read 1605, not 1695. **272** R. Caulfield (ed.), *The council book of Youghal* (London 1878), 164. **273** E.g., Shankill in the common pleas in 1609 (TCD, Ms 2512: 20); Grangesylva and Graiguenamanagh in the exchequer in 1605, 1611 and 1614 (NA, Ferguson MSS, Revenue Exchequer Orders, 1592–1657, 34, 143, 160).

Irrespective of its official designation as part of Carlow, the six parishes' district was a Kilkenny colony, and as such, even in the reign of Charles I, its little community saw itself as belonging to the Ormond country in Co. Kilkenny.

THE SOUTHERN UPLANDS: WALSH COUNTRY

In the next distinct zone of the county, the southern uplands below Inistioge, Knocktopher and Kells, the Butlers' influence was also quite extensive. Less immediate than in the north and east, it was similar to the situation in the midlands, in that the Ormonds did not seek to, literally, possess the other landowners, but were content to cooperate with them and delegate power to them. The mountainous terrain was probably responsible for this. The Walsh Mountains, as they are known, rise to a height of just below 1,000 feet in some places, and spanning more than fifteen miles in width, they provide a poor environment for farming, with sticky soils and inadequate natural drainage. The earls of Ormond, together with the rest of the Butlers, had little interest in the land here. Instead of seeking to establish a territorial monopoly they were content simply to control the uplands' flanks, to the east holding Duiske and the surrounding lands, as already noted, while to the west, near the Tipperary border, the Ormonds possessed Clonmacshanboy Castle and a few hundred acres in Kilmaganny parish, and two old branches of minor Butlers, dating back to the late Middle Ages, were based at Kirrihill and Rossenarrow. By these means the Butlers hemmed the mountains in and avoided the worst land, leaving the vast bulk of the area to the care of the principal local family, the Walshes (alias Brenaghs) of the Mountains.

The Walshes were one of the main client families of the house of Ormond. An ancient lineage of Cambro–Norman descent, they had been in Co. Kilkenny and its environs at least as long as the ancestors of the earls, having come to Ireland in the late twelfth century, *c.*1180 in Wexford, and they had settled in south Kilkenny by 1285.[274] Their main seat at Castlehowell was one of the most important castles in the county, overlooking the western midlands of the shire. Their close relationship with the Butlers was well known, and they are referred to in a sixteenth-century state paper as 'the Walshes, at the earl of Ormond's command'.[275] They held their land by knight's service of the earls' manor of Knocktopher, and down to Elizabethan times they provided one of the main segments of the Ormond army.[276]

In return the degree of control that the earls exercised over the Walsh family was generally very lax. Even if owed money by some of the junior Walshes,

274 St John Brooks (ed.), *Knights' fees*, 100–1, has the best account of the Walshes' origins. Some highly fanciful accounts, as passed on by local seanchai in the mid-eighteenth century, can be found in W. Carrigan, 'Scraps of Walsh Mountain History, No. 4', *WSEIAS* 12 (1909), 173–8. **275** Alnwick Castle, Ms 476 GC 26, ff 32v–33r.   **276** *Cal. Carew MSS, 1515–74*, no. 273; NLI, Ms 2507, fol. 22v.

the earls respected the rights of the head of the lineage, Walsh of Castlehowell, to intervene in the matter to arrange the best terms for his kinsmen.[277] As a direct consequence the Walsh country became semi-autonomous. Though it belonged indisputably to the county of Kilkenny, it was often only loosely attached, and for much of the sixteenth century its occupants avoided contact with the formal shire administration. In fact, left to their own devices, the Walshes achieved considerable notoriety as bandits, raiding anyone within reach who was not tied to the earldom, but committing their worst acts far from home, across the eastern and southern frontiers of the shire in Wexford and Waterford.[278] The mountains that they inhabited became one of the great criminal districts of the south of Ireland, offering a safe haven to thieves and cattle rustlers such as Shane Brenagh fitz Robert (alias John Walsh), one of the fiercest outlaws of the Elizabethan era. For a number of years before he was caught and hanged in the 1580s Shane played cat and mouse with government officials in Kilkenny, Tipperary, Wexford and Waterford, leading a gang of about a dozen men – nearly all Walshes, but including some Butlers too – in various feats of banditry.[279]

Free of outside interference, the Walshes became one of the most gaelicised Anglo-Irish families in Co. Kilkenny, running their little lordship through a fusion of English and Gaelic law. In 1585 the head of the family, Walter Walsh, held a manor court at Lettercorbally. For the most part the proceedings, recorded in Latin, followed the usual English customs, except that Walter was announced to the court in the Gaelic manner as *capitalis sui nationis* ('chief of his nation').[280] During the course of the hearing sixteen jurors confirmed that Walter was entitled by hereditary right to demand that all his free tenants assist him 'in making provision for the marriage of his daughters when they come to the age of seven years [the canonical age of marriage]'. Thus rendered, it looked like just another Anglo-Irish feudal exaction, but it was in fact very similar to the practise of a lord raising dowry from his subjects that was then universal across Gaelic Ireland and Scotland.[281]

Evidence of gaelicisation did not end here. More than any other Kilkenny family the Walshes were organised along Gaelic lines, that is, as a corporate patrilineal descent group. Members of the Walsh bloodline owned and occupied almost all of the territory and, as in any Gaelic lordship, many of them performed important legal and political functions on behalf of the Walsh nation. Hence it was stated that once their chief, Walsh of Castlehowell, decided to collect his daughters' dowry, it would only be lawful for him to do so 'according to the discretion of four of the better sort of the inhabitants of the said nation'.[282] The Castlehowell chiefs performed various tasks on the nation's behalf,

277 *COD*, iv, no. 50.   **278** Hore & Graves (ed.), *Social state*, 63, 71, 189.   **279** PRO, SP 63/108/34; NLI, Ms 2181, no. 9. His career is treated in Chapter 4 below.   **280** Carrigan, 'Walsh Mountain history, No. 1', *WSEIAS* 9 (1906), 182.   **281** Ibid., 185; Nicholls, *Gaelic & gaelicised Ireland*, 35–6; 'Irishwomen and property in the 16th Century', in M. MacCurtain & M. O'Dowd (ed.), *Women in early modern Ireland* (Dublin 1990), 20–1.   **282** Carrigan, 'Walsh Mountain history, No. 1', 185.

protecting vulnerable members of the lineage and working to keep the Walsh territory intact.[283] The Castlehowell Walshes also practised partible inheritance, generation by generation setting aside part of their land for the benefit of younger sons, so that by 1640 many thousands of acres had passed from their hands to set up junior branches at Owning, Listerling, Kilcregan, Derrylackagh, Arderny and elsewhere (see Appendix 1).

The chiefs of the nation, the Walshes of Castlehowell, enjoyed great prestige. As lords of the mountain they were famous for their military prowess, and though they never gained a peerage from the crown, they were usually counted among the lesser nobility of Leinster and Munster. Between 1500 and 1640 they married into many of the leading families of the south, becoming kindred to the Butlers, Viscounts Mountgarret, the Mastersons and Devereuxs of Co. Wexford, the Powers and Mandevilles of Co. Waterford, the Fitzgeralds of Cloyne, Co. Cork, and the Sextons of Limerick.[284] In 1625 they confirmed their position as minor Irish lords when they successfully negotiated a marriage with the English noblewoman Magdalen Sheffield, granddaughter of the earl of Mulgrave, formerly Lord President of the North.[285] The Walshes' wealth helped them to maintain this high status. On one occasion towards the middle of the seventeenth century they were able to raise marriage portions amounting to £1,100 from their tenants.[286]

One of the clearest indicators of the Walshes' power is the degree to which they acted as patrons of some of the Co. Kilkenny gentry. Tenants-in-chief on their mountain lands included younger sons of branches of the Graces, Butlers, Bolgers, Tobins and O'Ryans. Early in the reign of James I Walsh of Castlehowell offered his protection to the daughters of a deceased Tipperary landlord, Comyn of Graigelevane, when the girls faced possible disinheritance by their uncle.[287] Still more revealing, some of the servants of the earls of Ormond were offered employment in the Walsh country. Peter Shee, a Kilkenny lawyer and Ormond servant, served as seneschal to Walsh of Castlehowell in the late sixteenth century. Likewise one of Earl Thomas' chaplains, Peter Rothe (another Kilkennyman), was allowed to take up a church post on Walsh land at Owning.[288]

But as in many Gaelic lordships, there was a darker side to the power and wealth of the lords of the Walsh Mountains. The Walshes of Castlehowell were rich and influential because they kept their kinsmen in check. Since the early fifteenth century nearly all of the junior branches that they had established had been assigned what might best be described as marginal land. Only the Walshes of Owning, along the Tipperary border, had good quality ground, capable of

---

283 For an example of this in 1519 see NLI, D 2040, a document about the sept of William Magnus Brenagh. This was poorly calendared in *COD*, iv, no. 50.   **284** Carrigan, *Ossory*, iv, 74–6; *Burke's Landed gentry of Ireland* (10th edn., London 1904), 296, 670; GO, Ms 171: 57–8; NLI, Ms 8315 (9).   **285** Walter Walsh visited Mulgrave in England in 1638: Sheffield City Library, Str. P. 18, no. 187.   **286** *CSPI, 1669–70*, 620.   **287** NA, CP K/184.   **288** Carrigan, 'Walsh Mountain history, No. 1', 182, 187.

arable production, but with an estate of less than 1,000 acres, they never had enough land to become strong.[289] Most of the other junior branches were confined to land that was only suitable for grazing, and even the biggest of them, the Walshes of Listerling – who had almost 2,500 acres – did not have a large enough estate to develop into an independent force. Indeed, far from prospering, several of the lesser Walshes struggled to survive economically. The same was true of some of their non-Walsh neighbours. The Healys (or Howlings) of Derrinahinch were forced to mortgage a third of their estate to a local husbandman, William Lang, during the 1580s.[290] In the meantime, possessing the best land in ample measure, the lords of Castlehowell prospered, imposing extensive feudal dues on the inhabitants of their territory, among other things claiming the right to have common pasture for their cattle 'through all the domain of the Walsh Mountain'.[291]

This remained the case after 1603. Although the economy of the southern uplands began to show signs of improvement, with land values in some places approaching a shilling an acre, nonetheless the Butlers, earls of Ormond, still kept their distance. Admittedly, this may have been due more to the collapse of the earldom than any real disinterest, but whatever the case, the Walsh country remained firmly under Walsh control. Unfortunately for historians this means that it also remained obscure, for without a strong Ormond presence to excite its interest, the royal government made no special effort to collect information about the territory. All that remains on record regarding post-1603 developments is a handful of references to the spread of mining, with a mine established in the Derrinahinch woodlands by 1635, and another, run by Englishmen, opening on the Butler of Duiske estate at Graiguenamanagh in the east before 1641.[292]

SOUTHERN LOWLANDS

South of the Walsh country lay the last distinct geographical zone of Co. Kilkenny, in the lowlands that run from the Walsh Mountains to Waterford harbour. Forming a crescent-shaped area, this region stretches from the parish of Rosbercon in the east to Owning in the west. It is notable for the fact that it is bounded by water on three sides, hemmed in by the banks of the Barrow and the Suir rivers that meet at the Waterford estuary. Its proximity to Waterford, which was probably Ireland's principal port of trade in the sixteenth century, insured that the Butlers of Ormond paid close attention to the south.

The Ormond dynasty was well represented across the region. In Ida, in the north-east of the barony, the earls held Rosbercon – by the sixteenth century a town in terminal decline, but still a place prized for its strategic value, affording easy access to the Barrow and the Co. Wexford river-port of New Ross,

289 For their descent see St Kieran's College, Carrigan MSS, Vol. 21, unpaginated. **290** NA, CP A/188–9. **291** Carrigan, 'Walsh Mountain history, No. 1', 183, 185. **292** NLI, D 3980; TCD, Ms 812, fol. 204v.

of which it was virtually a suburb.[293] In Iverk the earls possessed Norbane, Castletown, Kilmacow and the manor of Grannagh, substantial rural settlements containing what was then some of the best pasture land in the area. Grannagh was especially important.[294] A large medieval fortress on the Kilkenny side of Waterford estuary, it had a commanding view of the boats and barges that plied across the Suir river between Waterford and Kilkenny. The artist Francis Place's depiction of it in 1699 shows how imposing it was, with its large circular and square towers and its great hall. Built originally in the fourteenth century by the Power family, it had passed to the earls of Ormond in 1375. In the 1490s Piers Ruadh and his wife, Countess Margaret, renovated and extended it,[295] and it subsequently became the main administrative centre of the Ormond lordship in south Kilkenny. In the great hall a carving of the Butler coat-of-arms faced a figure of justice, and sessions of the manorial court were regularly held there before the earls' seneschals and their local representatives, the sergeants of the manor. Between them these officials judged a wide range of crimes on the earls' behalf – trespass, assault and battery and, before *c.*1540, possibly even cases of treason.[296]

In other ways too Grannagh Castle and manor had a tight grip over local affairs. Down to Earl Walter's fall in 1619 it controlled one of the main ferries from Kilkenny to Waterford, reckoned to be worth five marks a year in rent to the earls in the early 1500s (but probably worth a lot more to the lessees).[297] And like other Ormond manors elsewhere in the county, Grannagh was a focal point of the feudal power of the earldom. Most of the gentry of Ida and Iverk held part of their lands of the manor by knight's service, as did the viscounts Mountgarret for their estate at Fiddown.[298]

Unlike other parts of Co. Kilkenny, the southern lowlands lacked a major community of gentry. Apart from the Ormond and Mountgarret Butlers there was just a handful of important landlords in the region. Indeed, between 1500 and 1640 only five local families – the Stranges of Dunkitt, the Galls of Gaulskill, the Barron Fitzgeralds of Brownesford, the Freneys of Ballyreddy and the Datons of Kilmodally – achieved any prominence around the shire or wider afield, occasionally serving as Ormond officials or government commissioners.[299] Moreover, of these, only the Stranges of Dunkitt and the Fitzgeralds of Brownesford were a consistent force in local affairs, maintaining a public role across the sixteenth and early seventeenth centuries. Traditionally the Stranges,

293 Documents concerning Rosbercon deposited in the National Library forty years ago as part of the Glascott collection are still unavailable. See NLI, Ainsworth Reports, Vol. 14 (Report 41) 2893. **294** *COD*, vi, Appendix 1, 143–4. **295** Lambeth Ms 626: 124. **296** E.g., *COD*, vi, Appendix 1, 142. **297** D.B. Quinn (ed.), 'Ormond papers, 1480–1535', in COD, iv, Appendix, 344–5. In July 1634 the Grannagh ferry was granted (with many other Irish ferries) to Henry Marwood, Robert Hodges and James Horncastle: NA, Lodge MSS, Rolls, Vol. V, 305–7. **298** *Cal. Carew MSS, 1515–74*, no. 273; *COD*, iv, no. 361. **299** E.g., see Appendix 3 below; *CSPI, 1509–73*, 505; NA, Lodge MSS, Rolls, Vol. I, 217; ibid., RC 9/7, 104–5; G.D. Burtchaell, 'The Geraldines of County Kilkenny, pt. 3: The Barrons of Brownesford', *JRSAI* 23 (1893), 408–20; HMC, *Ormonde MSS, 1543–1711*, 1–4.

closely connected to the Waterford merchant family of the same name,[300] were loyal supporters of the earldom of Ormond, and successive earls pursued their friendship. Thus in 1531 Piers Ruadh entered into a bond with Nicholas Strange, lord of Dunkitt, in which he guaranteed that 'he and his heirs shall be as good and favourable lords to Nicholas and his heirs as the late James, earl of Ormond [probably the fourth earl, d. 1452] was to the ancestors of the said Nicholas'.[301] With the end of the Elizabethan wars, the Stranges were able to move in wider social circles, and by 1619 they had contracted a marriage with a Munster planter family, the Pynes of Mogeley, Co. Cork.[302] The Brownesford Fitzgeralds were not quite so important, but they still carved out a niche in Ida, possessing two strong castles at Clonamery and Brownesford, and dominating large parts of the Barrow and Nore rivers, often to the annoyance of the local fishermen.[303] During the early sixteenth century one of their number, Milo Barron, rose to become bishop of Ossory, and it was in the period of his epis-copacy (1528–50) that they enjoyed their greatest prominence. Though they fell away a little after his death, they remained an important lineage. They con-tinued to prosper as a force in southern affairs in the early seventeenth century, between 1611 and 1614 purchasing land at Ballinabarney for a younger son, Thomas Fitzgerald, who subsequently established a cadet branch there,[304] and they maintained a strong hold on Rosbercon, where they held nearly 400 acres beside the town.[305]

The rest of the principal southern gentry struggled to make their mark. The Freneys made a bid for greater authority in Henry VIII's time, laying claim to the feudal barony of Norragh in Co. Kildare. Had they been successful they might have become one of the principal families in Tudor Leinster. They failed, however,[306] and later slipped back in importance, disappearing from the main records of county affairs. The Datons were much the same. In 1592 the head of the family, William Daton, may have plunged the family into a period of hardship because of his enthusiasm for the new Tridentine Catholicism. Desiring admittance to 'the Holy Company of Heaven' he made a will (witnessed by a priest) in which in accordance with the age-old 'custom of Ireland' he divided his goods and chattels into three equal parts, and bequeathed them as follows: one part to his wife, Margaret Butler, the second part to his children and the third part – that is, 33 per cent – to the Catholic church for the care of his soul.[307] Having inherited a very prosperous estate, accounted the eighth most valuable in the county in 1560, William passed on to Edmund, his son and heir, lands that were heavily encumbered with debts and other financial obligations. Edmund found it hard going, and had twice to mortgage property before his death in 1629. By this time the Datons faced further strain, having also become embroiled in costly legal disputes with wealthy Waterford merchants who seem

---

300 After 1603 the Dunkitt line was named among the remainders to the Strange of Waterford estate: NA, RC 5/4, 36–44. **301** *COD*, iv, no. 166. **302** NA, Thrift Abstracts, no. 2961. **303** Went, 'Short history', 22–3. **304** NA, RC 5/4, 52–69. **305** NLI, Ms 975: 144–5. **306** *COD*, iv, no. 212, and sources cited there. **307** Carrigan, *Ossory*, iv, 221–2.

suddenly to have had claims over their property.[308] In contrast, the O'Dea Fitzgeralds of Gurteen did well to hang on to a position of moderate importance. The lands they possessed in Ida were poorly positioned, forcing them to rely on their neighbours the Stranges for a supply of water diverted from 'the pill of Drumdowney' with which to work their 'mill of the Gurtines'. This dependency on Drumdowney left them economically exposed, as the tenants of the Stranges were able break the millpond, cut off the water supply, and so demand favours from them.[309] Nevertheless, the O'Dea Geraldines participated in local government in the south, in 1608 providing one of four coroners of the county and one of two constables of Ida barony.[310]

Poverty apparently prevented the rest of the southern gentry from attaining high status. As shown earlier in Chart 1.1, much of the southern lowland region was worth relatively little in Elizabethan times, and this despite the fact that it was a place of peace, rarely affected by war. Indeed, some of the land of Ida and Iverk was actually worth less than large parts of the violent borderlands of the north of the shire, rated at a mere 2*d.* per acre *c.*1560. Only at Clonmore in Iverk were conditions much better, with successive owners like John Archdekin, treasurer of Cashel, and Chief Justice Sir Nicholas Walsh, able to profitably mix arable farming with pastoral and so supply the Waterford market with wheat, barley and malt.[311] This may seem strange to modern readers, for the southern lowland zone is now one of the prosperous areas of Co. Kilkenny. However, its wealth is a relatively recent phenomenon, and it is wrong to assume (as some writers have done) that the area was always rich.[312] Ironically, access to the tidal waters of the Barrow and Suir rivers – the basis for its recent prosperity – was probably the cause of its poverty in pre-modern times, for the simple reason that large parts of the region were badly drained. In 1634, when the English traveller William Brereton talked to a gentleman-tenant on the Mountgarret estate at Tibraghny, he was taken aback to learn of the lowness of its rent yield. Despite its proximity to Waterford, Tibraghny was underdeveloped, only producing 'milk, butter and cheese, … [that] was excellent good', but leaving large areas unutilised as swamp ground. Brereton could not comprehend why marshland and moorland, so profitable in England, was left untouched: 'if it were but divided and enclosed, [it] would yield more than the rent of the whole'.[313]

The south Kilkenny countryside seems also to have been underpopulated. According to archaeological evidence proto-clachans, small isolated hamlets of just 3–4 farmsteads, had been typical of southern settlement patterns for a long time prior to the seventeenth century. It is difficult to know why the south lagged so far behind the shire midlands, but whatever the reason it was only much later than the period covered by this study, from the 1690s onwards, that

308 NA, Lodge MSS, Wardships, Vol. I, 256; ibid., CP Z/8; TCD, Ms 2512: 38, 61. **309** *CPRI., Eliz. I,* 12–13. **310** *Cal. Carew MSS, 1603–24,* 27. **311** NLI, Ms 2509, fol. 151. **312** J. Burtchaell, 'The South Kilkenny farm villages', in W.J. Smyth & K. Whelan (ed.), *The common ground* (Dublin 1988), 110–23. **313** Brereton, *Travels,* 161–3.

the southern lowlands witnessed a rise in population and the appearance of some small towns.[314]

Given such underdevelopment the influence of the Butlers of Ormond was enormous. Dominating large parts of Ida and Iverk, they were able to maintain strong patron/client relations with many of the local gentry, especially the minor gentry families, many of whom benefited from Ormond leaseholds. The Bolgers and the lesser Forstalls, Grants and Powers were all occupants of the earls' southern lands, named as tenants on extant rentals and inquisitions.[315]

However, protecting and preserving the existing gentry network was not the sum of the earls' efforts in south Kilkenny between 1515 and 1640. They also played an important role in vetting newcomers to the area, in particular giving their assistance to the various Waterford families that sought to buy land there. Thanks to the earls' backing, the baronies of Ida and Iverk became more and more part of Waterford's hinterland. In medieval times Waterford corporation had gained control of all river commerce in south Kilkenny as far north as Inistioge on the Nore,[316] and long before 1500 some of its main merchant dynasties, such as the Aylwards and Dobbins, had begun colonising the area.[317] After 1550, however, the rate of colonisation increased significantly. In 1551 the Dobbins acquired a mortgage of part of the Walsh of Ballinacowley estate, by 1610 the Waterford Stranges had bought Drumdowney from their Dunkitt kinsmen (and Ballyleogue and Ballycogsoust from unidentified sellers), and sometime in the reign of James I another line of the Dobbins gained Ballyrowragh in Ida (from the Waterford Fitzsimons).[318] None of these encountered difficulties with the earls of Ormond, and the benign hand of Thomas, the tenth earl, can be detected behind the appearance of other Waterfordians. Records of a 1577 court of inquisition giving details of the Kilkenny estate of Alderman James Walsh of Waterford note that some of his lands – in this case, in the Kilkenny midlands – were held of Thomas, earl of Ormond. In 1618 another court of inquisition recorded that Paul Strange – the alderman who bought Drumdowney – held further parcels of south Kilkenny land in fee of the earldom, granted to him by the tenth earl before 1614.[319]

Patronage like this proved invaluable to the house of Ormond. By permitting – and in some cases sponsoring – the expansion of Waterford's merchant elite into south Kilkenny, the earls were able to increase their influence over the great southern port and its powerful corporation. As a result, for much of

---

314 Burtchaell, 'South Kilkenny', passim; L.M. Cullen, 'The social and economic evolution of South Kilkenny in the seventeenth and eighteenth centuries', *Decies* 13 (Jan. 1981), 36–8. **315** NLI, Ms 2506, ff 13r, 39r, 40v. **316** Perhaps this explains why on 9 April 1589 the mayor of Waterford presided over a court of inquisition held at Rathkieran to examine a case concerning concealed lands in Inistioge (NLI, Ms 2181)? **317** J. Walton, 'The merchant community of Waterford in the sixteenth and seventeenth centuries', in P. Butel & L.M. Cullen (ed.), *Cities & merchants* (Dublin 1986), 184. For Dobbin involvement in south Kilkenny c.1483, see NA, Chancery MSS, Catalogue of Deeds in Chancery, no. 52. **318** Ibid., no. 69; ibid., RC 5/4, 36–51; Anon (ed.), 'Old Waterford wills, VIII: William Dobbin', *WSEIAS* 11 (1908), 94. **319** NA, RC 9/7, 96–8; NLI, Ms 11, 053 (3).

the sixteenth and early seventeenth centuries, as most of the major urban centres of southern Ireland wriggled free of aristocratic dominance, two cities, Waterford as well as Kilkenny, remained closely tied to the Ormond lordship. True, the earls of Ormond did not control Waterford to anything like the extent that they controlled Kilkenny, but the port remained partly under their sway. The Waterford civic elite stood by the earldom throughout the reign of Elizabeth I, giving their support to Earl Thomas during the 1569 crisis, for instance, a critical moment in his career. They also supported his bid for Munster plantation land in the parliament of 1585/6.[320]

Waterford's growing contacts with the community of the Ormond lordship in Co. Kilkenny was ultimately of national (even international) importance. It is not usually noted that Waterford's troubles with the royal authorities in James I's reign coincided with the decline of the Ormond earldom. This was not mere happenstance. Had the earldom remained as powerful after 1614 as it had been before, Waterford might not have been so humiliated by the early Stewart government, for it would have had a friendly overlord to intervene on its behalf with the crown. The consequences of the government's simultaneous assault on both city and earldom would eventually prove disastrous for crown interests. In 1642 Waterford threw its weight behind the anti-government conspiracy that had emerged in Kilkenny, thereafter serving as the main seaport of the Kilkenny Confederation.

CONCLUSION: THE NATURE AND EXTENT OF ORMOND RULE

Though it has long been recognised that, based in Kilkenny, the Butlers, earls of Ormond, ran one of the most important aristocratic lordships in Ireland between 1500 and 1640, the nature of their overlordship and the extent of their power on the ground has rarely been examined. The diversity of their behaviour around Co. Kilkenny as outlined in the foregoing pages may therefore seem surprising, as they were aggressively expansionist (while careful to nurture support) in the north and east, voluntarily marginal in the Walsh mountains, well connected but sensitive in the midlands, and often ambivalent towards the towns in the Nore valley, jealous of their corporate independence, though protective of their wealth and trade. Their overlordship was a complex, multifaceted thing, and despite the fact that they held a great deal of land and power in each region of the shire, their authority, like their behaviour, was heavily regionalised, stronger in some places than others (and more beneficial for some places than for others).

Historians have sometimes given the impression that, inside their respective territories, the powers and privileges enjoyed by nobles such as the Ormond Butlers were somehow homogeneous, carrying equal weight in all corners of their lands. This can be highly misleading, especially for older, bigger lordships

320 *COD*, v, no. 157; *CSPI, 1586–8*, 52–3.

like the Ormond lordship, which encompassed a huge amount of land that had been acquired over many generations dating back to the thirteenth century. Each parcel of land that the Butlers and their ancestors had acquired over the centuries had its own status at law, endowing them, as the owners, with often widely diverging legal powers.

In general, Ormond power was greatest wherever the dynasty held manors. However, the fact that by the early seventeenth century the earls were lords of 16 or 17 manors[321] in Co. Kilkenny should not obscure the fact that in some of the places where they owned land in large quantities and were politically very influential they did not possess manorial rights. This was the case, for example, at Jerpoint and Kells in the midlands breadbasket, the wealthiest part of the county. Moreover, even where they did hold manorial jurisdiction, the extent of their rights and privileges differed from one manor to the next: as lords of each of the manors of Kilkenny, Callan, Gowran, Knocktopher, Ballycallan, Rosbercon, Dunfert, Kilmanagh and Glashare, the earls had a formidable hold over the local church, as they were entitled to present clergy to the adjoining rectories and vicarages; yet they did not possess this right in the manors of Pottlerath, Dammagh, Foulkescourt, Ballykeefe, Dunmore, Kilmocar or Grannagh.[322] Similarly, the labour services they demanded seem to have varied from manor to manor, and in some places they controlled large areas of river and road, in others not. In the final analysis, then, the Ormond lordship in Co. Kilkenny was not a streamlined, formal institution. If anything, it was more a multiple or composite lordship than a single unitary one. This had a major impact on the nature of Ormond power. Despite the vastness of its landholdings, the power of the Ormond dynasty was essentially local and personalised.

It was probably much more effective for that. Across the county people faced varying but immediate demands for rent and service from a person, the earl, whom they knew by sight and whose servants and officials invariably lived nearby. In comparison, the royal administration in Dublin was hopelessly distant and impersonal, and it seems clear that after it had decided under James I to strike the house of Ormond low, the government never stood a chance of taking the earldom's place. In later medieval and early modern Ireland local power was everything, and for all the government's efforts, it lacked the resources to supplant such a long-established, deeply embedded, controlling presence. By the early seventeenth century the influence of the earldom was such that it was impracticable to rule Co. Kilkenny without it. Nearly all the major families of the shire, no matter what region they came from – periphery or centre, upland or lowland – were intimately bound to the earldom, so that when it was attacked they felt threatened too.

---

321 In a chancery case held between 1603 and 1608 it was claimed on the tenth earl's behalf that Palmerstown and Earlsgrange together comprised a single manor (NA, CP I/238). To my knowledge no other source bears this out. Rather Palmerstown belonged to Kilkenny manor, while Earlsgrange seems not to have had any manorial affiliation (*COD*, iv, no. 361; ibid., v, no. 293). **322** NLI, Ms 11,064 (10).

The earls had strong ties with the rest of the shire's landowners. Apart from holding land of the earldom, many of the local squires and gentry were part of the earls' affinity, having intermarried quite heavily with younger Ormond children and with various junior branches of the Butlers. For example, between *c.*1500 and 1620, in the space of four generations, the Blanchvilles of Blanchvillestown entered into marriages with a niece of the eighth earl of Ormond, a daughter of the eleventh earl, a daughter of the first viscount Mountgarret and a daughter of Butler of Paulstown.[323] Likewise, in the late sixteenth century Nicholas Shortal of Clara was married to a niece of the tenth earl of Ormond, while in the early seventeenth century the head of the Dens of Grenan was wedded to a niece of the eleventh earl.[324] Because of these unions, the Blanchvilles, Dens and Shortals became part of the Ormonds' extended family, and their own subsequent marriages with the Shortals of Ballylorcaine, the Walshes of Castlehowell, the Sweetmans of Castle Eve, the Lawlesses of Talbot's Inch, the Purcells of Ballyfoyle, the Archdekins of Bawnballinlogh, the Langtons of Kilkenny and the Datons of Kilmodally, to name but a few, stretched the Ormond affinity still further throughout the county. In fact, by late in the reign of James I, as Walter, the eleventh earl, fell foul of the government, the Ormond connection extended so far around Kilkenny that most of the shire's major families were somehow related to him.[325] These all shared his loss of power.

The subsequent failure of the Dublin administration to rule Co. Kilkenny without Earl Walter, his kindred and supporters (discussed in Chapter 5 below) revealed the limitations of the state apparatus. In an area where it had worked so effectively and for so long, the aristocratic lordship of the house of Ormond was hard to replace. The earls had encouraged many of the local gentry to participate in running the county. They had apportioned power relatively evenly among the local landlords, merchants and lawyers, fostering a delegatory, 'in the family' style of government which, because so many of the shire gentry were related to them, was open to approximately 40 local families. The earls rarely tried to override gentry opinion, and only on a few occasions between 1515 and 1614 – chiefly in the 1520s – did they seek to rule without constraint, irrespective of local interests. Their power was usually collaborative, open to checks and balances. In comparison, the New English crown officials who began appearing in the shire with increasing regularity at the time of the earldom's decline misguidedly attempted to force through unpopular crown policies without consulting or recruiting the local gentry; they were rejected by Kilkenny society as a result. To sum up, whereas the earldom of Ormond represented

323 Carrigan, *Ossory*, iii, 414–5, which is inaccurate in places, and should be read with St Peter's College, Wexford, Hore MSS, Vol. 31, 213–4. **324** Carrigan, *Ossory*, iii, 358; ibid., iv, 268. About this time successive heads of the Graces of Ballylinch married daughters of the second viscount Mountgarret and the third baron of Dunboyne: Burke, *Landed gentry* (4th edn., London 1968), 578–9. **325** Lamacraft (ed.), *Ir. funeral entries*, 125; Carrigan, *Ossory*, iii, 471; Prim, 'Family of Langton', 84 facia; Burtchaell, 'Family of Rothe', 504n, 510n; Patrick Den's funeral entry (St Kieran's College, Carrigan MSS, Vol. 21, unpaginated).

familiar 'insider government' to the shire populace, and was highly successful because of it, the royal administration was unable to take over from it because it was colonial 'outsider government' with no local roots. After 1614 the shadow of the Ormonds' achievements hung heavily over the government's agents.

Before that date the earls of Ormond had been remarkably influential in Kilkenny. Between them the eighth, ninth and tenth earls shaped and moulded county society to a degree that is nowadays hard to imagine. As demonstrated above, the earls were largely responsible for defining the modern boundaries of the county, in the north-west driving Upper Ossory out of the shire into Queen's County while simultaneously annexing both Idough in the north-east and the Barrow lands in the mid-east from Co. Carlow. They also played a principal part in advancing the notion of a county community in the shire, bringing the gentry of the various geographical zones together in support of their cause. Service to the earls helped greatly to unite distant families and to merge them into a single community. For instance, during the mid-sixteenth century the earldom's military demands compelled the likes of the Graces and Purcells from the north, the Sweetmans, Blanchvilles and Comerfords from the midlands, branches of the O'Ryans from the east, the Walshes from Walsh country, and the Brownesford Fitzgeralds and Freneys from the southern lowlands to all go campaigning together, side by side under the Ormond banner.[326]

There could not have been a properly integrated Kilkenny county community without the earldom to join things up. Serious local divisions existed that might have split the shire down the middle had not the earls smoothed over the cracks. Politically, for much of the sixteenth century the clannish, partly gaelicised, frontier gentry of the north and east had had an uneasy relationship with the population of the midlands, and especially with the people of the towns, who viewed them with suspicion as a rough lawless element. Though sometimes it taxed them greatly, the earls managed to prevent an unbridgeable gap from emerging, curbing the worst excesses of the northern and eastern captains when occasion demanded, though generally favouring the border gentry (their fellow landlords, and an important military source) more than the townsmen. Related to this, inter-class jealousies occasionally erupted between the merchants of the towns and the landlords of the countryside. From the middle of the sixteenth century onwards the rich merchants of Kilkenny, Callan and Thomastown had acquired a great deal of land throughout the county, becoming landlord-merchants or merchant gentry. The traditional gentry resented this development, as John Archer, a Kilkenny merchant, discovered early in the seventeenth century, and such was the ill-feeling generated by his buying land from the Purcells that he declared 'all the gentlemen of [the county] ... had joined in a faction against such of the gentlemen and merchants of the town of Kilkenny as would venture to purchase ... any land among them'.[327] Here again the Ormond lordship helped to ease the tension, employing both merchants

---

326 NLI, Ms 2507, ff 21v–23v. **327** NA, CP I/6.

and gentry in its service and encouraging them to adopt a common political outlook towards the outside world. Finally, it should be noted that no major inter-familial feuds or vendettas are recorded for Co. Kilkenny before the earl-dom lost its power after 1614. Only in 1625, while Earl Walter was imprisoned in London, did a serious bloodfeud erupt between two of the shire's leading families, the Blanchvilles and the Purcells, when Leonard (alias Lionel) Blanchville attacked Edmund Purcell of Ballyfoyle on the Gowran highway and cleaved his head open with a blow of his sword, fatally wounding him. Had the earl not been in prison, perhaps relations between the two families – both staunch Ormond supporters – might never have got so out of hand. As it tran-spired, Leonard was pardoned four years later, having fled to London to see Earl Walter, and sometime during the early 1630s, after the earl's return to Ireland, a Blanchville-Purcell marriage was arranged, involving the Blanchvilles of Milltown and the Purcells of Foulkesrath.[328]

In the final analysis, the Ormonds' ability to dominate the county provides a startling testimony to the continuing vitality of patriarchal feudalism in six-teenth and early seventeenth century Ireland. By manipulating the feudal exchange of land for service, the new Pottlerath line of earls that took charge of Kilkenny after 1515 enjoyed a century of unparalleled growth, taking more and more families under their wing and stretching out to control previously unreachable parts of the shire. Their capacity to dominate was inextricably linked to the size of their ancestral estate, which grew enormously before the death of the tenth earl, Thomas, in 1614. As their lands had multiplied, so had their power and influence, for they had made sure that many of the local squires and gentry shared in their gains. But their estate was not open to all: it was much too precious to them to be managed laxly. Although they farmed out large parcels on lengthy leases the earls always made sure to keep the bulk of the estate intact, so that their successors would be able to continue to enjoy the financial benefits of feudal power. Because they kept their lands together, no strong oppo-sition ever emerged against them in Co. Kilkenny from among the numerous junior branches of the Butlers. Until well into the reign of James I not even the second most senior Butler lineage, the Butlers, viscounts Mountgarret, could realistically hope to close the gap on the earls, and then this seemed possible only because the earldom had fallen into a sudden decline. Challenges to the earls' dynastic authority were few before 1614, occurring only in 1569 and 1596, and on both of these occasions their main challengers had to look outside Kilkenny for most of their support.[329] Ultimately, then, Co. Kilkenny became more and more 'my lord of Ormond's country' because the earls guarded the succession to the dynastic lands very carefully. It was only when the crown decided to interfere in their inheritance and strip them of their lands that the earls of Ormond finally weakened and fell away.

---

328 *CPRI, Charles I*, 524–5; St Kieran's College, Carrigan MSS, Vol. 3, unpaginated. The murder occurred on 31 Aug. 1625.   **329** See Chapters 3 and 4 below.

But the feudal power of the Ormond Butlers was not just about land; it entailed a whole political culture, a cosmology that embraced principles of lordship, service and mutual protection that could not be easily discarded when the land was taken away. Had the Jacobean monarchy appreciated this, and viewed the Ormond estate as a means by which to strengthen the feudal relationship between the crown and the Kilkenny community, then its attack on the Ormond lordship would not have alienated the community as badly as it did. Alternatively, had the crown not given the earls so much assistance before 1614, helping them to secure the inheritance and add to its size, then the dynasty might never have become so powerful, and such a sudden and dramatic attack as took place shortly afterwards would not have been needed to curb them.

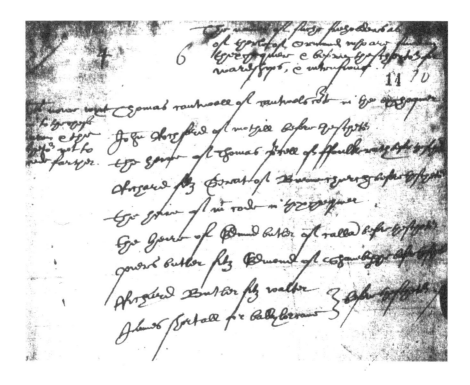

The Ormond feudal clientele in Co. Kilkenny. A document naming nine local gentry who held their estates of the earldom of Ormond c.1590: Cantwell of Cantwell's Court; Rochford of Mothill; Purcell of Foulkesrath; Fitzgerald of Burnchurch; Archdekin (McCody) of Ballybawnmore; Butler of Callan; Butler of Butlerswood; Butler of Paulstown; and Shortal of Ballylorcaine (PRO, London, State Papers, Ireland)

CHAPTER 2

The Ormond inheritance

Difficulties with the Ormond succession lay right at the heart of Co. Kilkenny's history during later medieval and early modern times. Although like most Anglo-Irish dynasties they adhered to the twin principles of primogeniture and male descent, the Butlers, earls of Ormond, twice experienced successional crisis, in 1515 and again in 1614. On both occasions the lack of a son and heir led immediately to long-lasting and far-reaching inheritance disputes involving the claims of heiresses which, when settled, radically altered the earldom's position in both county and country. The resolution of the 1515 succession struggle heralded a major increase in the powers of the earls in Ireland, while that of 1614 signalled a major decline in their fortunes. But before the story of these conflicts can be told, something needs briefly to be said of the peculiarity of the situation, for by the strict terms of inheritance law neither dispute should ever have occurred. Since 1328, when the earldom of Ormond was first created, it had been held in tail male. As such it could not be inherited by an heiress, only by the nearest surviving male relative.[1] What factors, then, allowed these two successional hiccups to become full-scale inheritance crises centred on theoretically ineligible female claimants? Why did the appearance of heiresses cause so much difficulty?[2]

Strange though it may seem, the Ormond inheritance problems were not due to any biological failure in the male line. Unlike some major noble lineages of England and Wales,[3] the Ormond family enjoyed a fairly high reproductive rate during the sixteenth and seventeenth centuries. Infertility did not affect them, and they certainly had no problem producing male heirs. All five Butler earls of Ormond who lived between 1515 and 1642 produced legitimate sons by marriage. In addition, the Butler earls were also productive outside the marriage bed, through their mistresses producing a steady stream of bastard children. Children sired out of wedlock are recorded for five of the seven earls that lived between 1461 and 1633, and for all four between 1515 and 1633. More

1 *Rotuli Parliamentorum*, ii, 90; GEC, *Complete peerage*, x, 117–18n; S. Duffy, *Ireland in the Middle Ages* (Dublin 1997), 145; Nicholls, 'Irishwomen and property', 26–7. 2 In the bigger British context, of course, the Butlers were not that unusual in experiencing two female successions in a century. This was entirely normal among the English and Welsh nobility at this time: M.L. Bush, *The English aristocracy: a comparitive synthesis* (Manchester 1984), 44; B. Coward, 'Disputed inheritances: Some difficulties of the nobility in the late sixteenth and early seventeenth centuries', *BIHR* 44 (1971), 194. 3 Stone & Fawtier Stone, *An open elite?*, 75–6.

remarkable still, however, is the fact that aside from the earls' own offspring, the other senior claimants to the earldom in the sixteenth and seventeenth centuries – the brothers and cousins of the earls, etc. – all managed to produce sons too, and plenty of them. The Mountgarret Butlers, the Dunboyne Butlers, and the Butler lineages of Paulstown, Kilcash, Grantstown, Nodstown, Ballinahinch, Neigham and Annagh all experienced uninterrupted descents in the male line before 1640.[4]

Clearly, the root of the problem was not genetic. Delving deeper, it seems the earls' first successional dilemma, in 1515, hinged on an important legal technicality. Despite producing an abundance of male children the Butler dynasty had failed to secure the Ormond inheritance in the male line before that date, and the entail had lapsed, probably because of their problematical immersion in English politics during the third quarter of the fifteenth century. Throughout the tumult of the Wars of the Roses (1453–85) James, John, and Thomas Butler, the fifth, sixth, and seventh earls of Ormond, had each remained loyal to the Lancastrian cause, and they had suffered the consequences when Yorkist influence was in the ascendant.[5] In 1461–2 acts of attainder had been passed in the London and Dublin parliaments against Earl James (since 1449 earl of Wiltshire in the English peerage),[6] and although the Ormond title was restored in 1475 to his brother John,[7] the entailment, crucially, was *not* restored.[8] It is entirely feasible that the oversight occurred more by accident than design, with the act of restoration based on an assumption made at Whitehall (by crown officials ignorant of Irish inheritance arrangements) that the earldom of Ormond was just like its English counterparts, many of which by this time had abandoned the use of entailments. Whatever the case, the failure to restore the entailment with the restoration of the earldom in 1475 meant that when Thomas Butler, the seventh earl, died in 1515, it was possible to contemplate the earldom's passage to an heiress for the first time in its history.

But what of the appearance of an heiress for a second time a hundred years later? The 1614 inheritance crisis cannot be attributed to any legal deficiency. After 1515 the earls had made sure the lands were entailed and female descent precluded. The emergence of an heiress in the early 1600s was due to an entirely different factor – the crown's dislike of the male heir to the earldom, who as a leading Catholic was deemed a danger to the state. In the crisis that followed

---

4 Details of the descents of these other Butler lineages during the sixteenth and early seventeenth centuries can mainly be found in Lambeth Palace MSS 626 and 635; Dunboyne, 'Carve's Butler families of 1641', *Butler Soc. Jn.* 6 (1975–6), 424–34; and Lamacraft (ed.), *Ir. funeral entries*, 37–8, 42–3, 44–5, 47–8, 62–4, 69, 115, 117, 139, 205. It should be noted that the genealogical data contained in such standard reference works as Carrigan's *Ossory*, Cockayne's *Complete peerage* and Burke's *Landed gentry of Ireland* (especially the latter) are often inaccurate for the period before 1600.   **5** Ellis, *Ireland*, ch. 3; D. Beresford, 'The Butlers in England and Ireland, 1405–1515', PhD thesis, Trinity College, Dublin, 1999, ch. 3–4.   **6** *Rotuli Parliamentorum*, v, 477–8, 480; *Statute Rolls, Ire., Edward IV*, ii, 25.   **7** COD, iii, nos. 242, 248.   **8** It is noteworthy that in his supplication for restitution to the Ormond earldom, made *c.*1477–8, the seventh earl neglected to specify 'his heires' as heirs male (ibid., no. 248).

the government was able to utilise the prerogative powers of the crown to undermine the legal position of the heir and promote the heiress, a Protestant, at his expense. The politics of religion were primarily responsible for the second inheritance crisis.[9]

And so it seems the Ormond succession was beset by two quite different sets of circumstances in 1515 and 1614, and that there was no common cause to explain the emergence of heiresses on both occasions. Yet in a sense the two crises were inextricably linked. It will be shown below that after 1515 and again after 1614 the crown had an inordinate influence on the outcome of the Ormond succession disputes. On both occasions the crown used the claims of heiresses to install candidates of its own choosing on the Ormond estate in Kilkenny and Tipperary. On both occasions the crown created a new earldom to legitimise the position of its preferred nominee, the earldom of Ossory in 1528, the new earldom of Desmond in 1620. Also, it played fast and loose with the law, in 1515 by-passing the entitlements of two English-based Butler heiresses to promote the claims of the male head of the Pottlerath (MacRichard) Butlers in Ireland, while in 1614 promoting the dubious legal claim of an heiress and her Scottish courtier husband to destroy the fortunes of the legally recognised Irish male heir. With the Ormond lordship strategically vital for control of so much of southern and eastern Ireland, the English monarchy made it a priority of state to tie the earldom tightly to its banners. Under its influence the Ormond territories were drawn ever deeper into the world of the royal court. For this reason the following chapter is as much about court politics and intrigue as it is about the workings of inheritance law.

SECURING THE POTTLERATH SUCCESSION, 1515–38

When Thomas Butler, seventh earl of Ormond, died in London in August 1515 it was generally recognised that his passing signalled a turning point in the history of the Butler dynasty in Ireland. Though twice married, he had failed to produce a male heir to keep his property intact. Thus, with the original Ormond entail of 1328 having fallen into abeyance, it appeared that the earl's estate would have to be divided between his two daughters, Margaret and Anne Butler, and the offspring of their marriages to the prominent English knights, Sir William Boleyn and Sir James St Leger respectively – in other words, that Kilkenny Castle and the rest of the Irish lands would pass from Butler control into the custody of absentee English owners.[10] The assumption that the era of Butler lordship in Co. Kilkenny was about to end was strengthened considerably by the fact that at Whitehall the earl's English grandson, Sir Thomas Boleyn (Margaret Butler's son) had emerged as a prominent courtier and intimate of

---

9 Treadwell, *Buckingham*, 114–15 provides an important new general interpretative framework for these events. **10** Ormond's second wife died in 1501. For details of Boleyn and St Leger, see E.W. Ives, *Anne Boleyn* (Oxford, 1986), 3–5.

the king, Henry VIII.[11] In England the carve-up of the extensive Butler patrimony proceeded routinely, the seventh earl's English lands passing automatically to the Boleyns and St Legers.[12]

This, however, was not how events transpired in Ireland. Although Boleyn secured full legal recognition for himself and his fellow heirs-general when he was granted livery of the Ormond lands, it soon became clear that gaining actual possession of the Irish estate would be an uphill task. No matter how well-placed Boleyn and his relatives were in London, they could not prevent a strong challenge being made to their title by a junior member of the Butler dynasty, Piers Ruadh Butler of Pottlerath, a formidable and rather intimidating character whom some onlookers feared would have little trouble persuading the government to accept his pretensions to the earldom of Ormond, despite the rights of others.[13] To properly understand the strength of this rival claim, it will be necessary to review the political circumstances of the Butler lordship in Kilkenny and Tipperary during the later fifteenth century.

Largely because of their immersion in the politics of the Lancastrian affinity, culminating in their involvement in the Wars of the Roses,[14] the earls of Ormond had moved to England by the 1450s. Apart from a brief (and disastrous) visit to the country by the sixth earl in 1462–4, they were absent from their Irish estate for at least sixty years.[15] After 1464 the power and hostility of their ancestral enemies, the Fitzgeralds of Kildare and Desmond, blocked their return to Kilkenny. As time passed the Ormonds settled permanently in England, and considering the high status granted by Henry VII to the ageing seventh earl after 1485,[16] this was hardly surprising. Nonetheless, their desire to remain close to royal power in London caused the earls to forfeit control of their Irish lands.[17]

During their absence the Ormond lordship fell into a long period of internecine feuding between the junior branches of the Butler family, chief amongst who in Tipperary were the rival Butlers of Cahir and Dunboyne, while the principal combatants for mastery in Co. Kilkenny were Piers Ruadh's family, the MacRichard Butlers of Pottlerath.[18] As the struggle intensified, the distrib-

---

11 Ibid., 11–13; H. Miller, *Henry VIII and the English nobility* (Oxford 1986), 80; D. Starkey, *The reign of Henry VIII: personalities and politics* (London 1985), 44–5. **12** For the growth of the Ormond English estates see esp. Beresford, 'The Butlers', ch. 1–2; Bod. Lib., North Ms C.26, no. 42; Cambridgeshire RO (Cambridge), Ms R 52/15/1. **13** *L&P, Henry VIII*, ii, no. 1277; PRO, SP 60/1/7–8. **14** E. Matthew, 'The governing of the Lancastrian lordship of Ireland in the time of James Butler, fourth earl of Ormond, *c.*1420–1452', PhD thesis, University of Durham, 1994. **15** The seventh earl is known to have made England 'his abode all his life', in like manner to his brother, the sixth earl (*COD*, iv, no. 267). Remarkably, his will of July 1515 makes no mention of Ireland whatsoever: Beresford, 'The Butlers', 298–304. **16** Appointed a member of the English council in 1486, the seventh earl also served as English ambassador to Burgundy in 1497, and was chamberlain of the queen's household (GEC, *Complete peerage*, x). **17** The following few paragraphs draw upon Empey & Simms, 'Ordinances', 164–9, Beresford, 'The Butlers', ch. 5, and C.A. Empey, 'From rags to riches: Piers Butler, earl of Ormond, 1515–39', *Butler Soc. Jn.* 2/3 (1984), 299–312. **18** By the later fifteenth century the MacRichard Butlers resided at Pottlerath, not Polestown: G. Butler, 'Saltair of MacRichard, or Laud Misc. 610', ibid., 3/1 (1987), 25–6; *COD*, iii, no. 274.

ution of power within the region fragmented, and the Ormond lordship ceased to fill a central role in Irish politics. For the local gentry and tenantry it was probably a period of great hardship. A generation or so later, in 1542, some of the leading squires and gentlemen of Tipperary recalled how their fathers and grandfathers had suffered 'utter impoverishing and intolerable losses' as a result of the warfare. Conditions in Kilkenny had hardly been any better.[19]

Moreover, the possession of the Ormond estate became itself a matter of violent dispute. Since the 1450s the Pottlerath Butlers had served successive earls of Ormond as deputy governors of their lands, but the longer the earls' absenteeism lasted the more the Pottlerath line came to view the estate as theirs for the keeping.[20] In 1487 the head of the family, James fitz Edmund MacRichard, completely ignored the legal rights of his lord and master when he bequeathed his office as earl's deputy to his son, Piers Ruadh.[21] Although Piers found himself deprived of the office four years later when the seventh earl's illegitimate nephew, Sir James Ormond, was authorised to take his place,[22] the Pottlerath family's hold over the estate was hard to break,[23] and in 1497 Piers Ruadh regained control in a dramatic turn of events. One day, while out riding in the Kilkenny countryside near Dunmore, Piers espied Sir James on the road in front of him. Seeing his opportunity, at full gallop he 'gored the bastard through with his spear'.[24]

Cold-blooded murder though it was, it was one of Piers Ruadh Butler's most important exploits. Enjoying as he did the protection of the lord deputy of Ireland, his foster-father the eighth earl of Kildare,[25] Piers knew he would not be prosecuted for his crime, and so with one blow he laid bare the weakness of the seventh earl of Ormond in Ireland. To add insult to injury, Piers himself informed Ormond of Sir James' bloody end, bragging that he was proud to act as an agent of God's grace in sending a sinner to meet his maker. The fact that he wrote the letter from Kilkenny Castle indicated he had full control of the Ormond estate and that Earl Thomas would receive no revenue from his lands should he try to appoint anyone else as his deputy.[26] The ageing earl tried very hard to ignore his renegade kinsman, but over the next few years he was regularly compelled to write to Piers Ruadh demanding leave for his agents to go quietly about his business in Kilkenny and Tipperary.[27] No matter how authoritative the tone of these letters, the earl could not hide the fact that he was making a request, and his correspondence only served to acknowledge the power that Piers, a usurper and murderer, now held over his lands.

19 Ibid., iv, no. 267. **20** Ibid., iii, nos. 211 and 229. **21** Ibid., iii, no. 329. **22** *Cal. Close Rolls, 1485–1500*, no. 580. **23** E.g., P. Connolly (ed.), *Statute Rolls of the Irish parliament, Richard III–Henry VIII* (Dublin 2002), 95, 135–7. **24** *Cal. Carew MSS, Addenda: The Book of Howth* (London 1871), 177; R. Stanihurst, 'The historie of Ireland', in L. Miller & E. Power (ed.), *Holinshed's Irish Chronicle* (Dublin 1979), 326; R. Butler (ed.), 'The annals of Thady Dowling', *Irish Archaeological Soc.* (1849), 33. **25** Piers had been fostered with Kildare about 1483: Quinn (ed.), 'Ormond papers', no. 53; Beresford, 'The Butlers', 244–5. For the importance of fosterage see esp. F. Fitzsimons, 'Fosterage and gossiprid in late medieval Ireland: Some new evidence', in Duffy, Edwards & FitzPatrick (ed.), *Gaelic Ireland*, 138–49. **26** Quinn (ed.), 'Ormond papers', no. 31. **27** Ibid., nos. 40, 47, 63.

All Ormond could do to retaliate was to refuse to sell or grant away any part of his property to his persecutor, thus denying the head of the Pottlerath Butlers any legal footing on the estate,[28] but this may not have been of great concern to Piers. He for his own part had consolidated his position by 1500, overrunning large parts of the earl's patrimony in Kilkenny, where he seized the manors of Callan, Rosbercon, Grannagh and Dunfert to his own use and garrisoned them with his troops.[29] At about this time he also took control of the manor of Carrickmagriffin (Carrick-on-Suir) in Co. Tipperary, imposing coign and livery on the earl's tenants 'contrary to the old use and custom'.[30] Without a soldier like Sir James Ormond to do his fighting for him, there was little the earl could do to undermine Piers, and eventually he reached an accommodation with his former deputy, in 1505 granting him a lease of some of his Co. Kildare lands.[31] With the benefit of hindsight it is possible to say that after lancing Sir James Ormond, Piers Butler must have fancied his chances of one day succeeding to the earldom itself.

Piers began to publicly press his claim soon afterwards, quickly emerging as the only candidate in Ireland capable of canvassing support, a fact as much due to his rising political influence as it was to his ruthless ability to throttle any opposition. Sometime previously, probably early in the 1490s, he had completed the terms of an agreement originally undertaken in 1485 with his foster-father, Garret Mór, earl of Kildare, to marry the earl's daughter Margaret Fitzgerald (only fourteen years old in 1485).[32] The marriage secured his entry into the network of contacts that formed the basis of the Kildare ascendancy, and made him comfortable in the company of Geraldine-sponsored government officials in Dublin. The other factor that operated in his favour was his military power in Kilkenny and Tipperary, where many of the local community seem reluctantly to have accepted his leadership, partly in the expectation that he would use his family ties to prevent the Geraldines from ravaging the region.

Because his claim to the title did not have a strong basis in law Piers needed all the support he could muster. The fact that the MacRichards of Pottlerath were only one of several Irish branches of the Butler family with a stake in the earldom was not his chief concern. It was relatively easy to demonstrate the superiority of the MacRichard's interest over that held by the Butlers of Cahir and Dunboyne.[33] Rather, the principal weakness in Piers Ruadh's position concerned his standing within the Pottlerath family itself.

Piers was not his father's eldest son and heir. He had two older brothers, Edmund of Neigham and Theobald, both of whom outlived their father and were capable of pursuing their own claims to the title. The fact that they had both been born some time before their parents' marriage at Listerlin parish church was of little benefit to Piers, for Edmund and Theobald had been declared legitimate by an act of the Irish parliament in 1468, and try though he

---

28 PRO, SP 46/130, fol. 23; Quinn (ed.), 'Ormond papers', no. 35.　**29** Ibid., no. 53.　**30** Ibid., no. 48.　**31** Ibid., no. 74.　**32** For the marriage contract of 1485, see esp. Beresford, 'The Butlers', 243–6.　**33** Empey, 'Rags to Riches', 308–9.

did, Piers found it very difficult to persuade the London government to have the act repealed.[34] He was still struggling to suppress the birthright of his brothers and their children as late as 1532, when (possibly prompted by the ninth earl of Kildare, who had become Piers' enemy) the Butlers of Neigham tried to challenge him. Piers responded in what was by then the customary fashion, producing a string of unreliable witnesses to swear before two bishops that, just as the founder of the Neigham line was a bastard, so too was the current head of the family.[35] In the event the Butlers of Neigham never managed to establish their genealogical credentials, and by 1536 Piers' power was such that he was finally able to have the act of 1468 overturned in parliament.[36] Yet perhaps the most remarkable aspect of Piers' victory over his brothers and their descendants is not that he won, but that he won so easily. During the fifty years prior to his succession as earl of Ormond in 1538, the family of Neigham hardly questioned his rights to the inheritance, leaving the distinct impression that it spent most of the period squirming under his boot.[37]

Successful though he was, establishing himself as the principal Irish claimant was only the start of Piers' legal difficulties in his bid for the earldom. He had also to prove that the Irish estate was still entailed, a tricky business to be sure, as it meant manufacturing evidence about the arrangements for the succession that had been made by the fourth (or 'White') earl of Ormond, who had died intestate in 1452. With no documentary proof of an entailment, all Piers could do was call up more supporters as witnesses to say there had been one planned all those years ago – hardly reliable evidence. Despite the dubious nature of their testimonies, Piers made sure that his witnesses – who included John Shortal of Cloghmantagh, Gilbert Blanchville of Kilmidimoge and John Cantwell of Moycarky – were heard, parading them before the archbishop of Dublin in September 1515, and before the bishop of Ossory in November 1516.[38]

It was not enough to prevail. In London the heirs general, led by Sir Thomas Boleyn, persuaded Henry VIII to ignore Piers Ruadh's claim in favour of their own. Unless Piers could sidestep them and have his case brought to the king by someone on whom Henry relied, his claim stood no chance. Thus by early 1516 the question of how to displace the Boleyns and St Legers began to weigh heavily on Piers Ruadh's mind. In the past he had had his claim supported by his in-laws, the Fitzgeralds, earls of Kildare, King Henry's chief governors in Ireland. Now, however, Piers needed someone in England to adopt his cause.

That someone materialised in the person of Thomas Wolsey, the archbishop of York (later a cardinal). Wolsey had his own reasons for involving himself in the Ormond inheritance problem. Concerned that the Fitzgeralds of Kildare were too powerful in Ireland, he was looking for a means to curb them. Piers

---

34 *Statute Rolls, Ire., Edward IV*, i, 487; *LP, Henry VIII*, 1519–23, no. 1926. The reasons for the illigitimacy of Edmund and Theobald are succinctly dealt with in G. Butler, 'Red Piers of Ormond', *Butler Soc. Jn.*1 (1968), 38. **35** *COD*, iv, no. 177. **36** Connoly (ed.), *Statute Rolls*, 173–6; NLI, Ms 2556 (10); PRO, SP 60/3/21. **37** The fact that the Butlers of Neigham felt compelled to surrender their claims to Piers in 1523 only strengthens this impression (NLI, D. 2092–3). These documents are inaccurately calendared in *COD*, iv, no. 90. **38** Ibid., no.33, and Empey, 'Rags to riches', 309.

Butler of Pottlerath was ideal for his needs: a strong regional lord, hitherto a dependent of the Fitzgeralds, but now requiring a new patron to further his ambitions. An understanding was reached, and by 1517 Piers had broken with the Fitzgeralds. For the next twelve years he followed Wolsey's lead and tried to make himself indispensable to Henry VIII by hacking away at the foundations of the Fitzgeralds' authority. As a sign of his good faith he had to allow his eldest son and heir, James Butler, to be taken into Wolsey's care in London during 1520–1. Officially James was described as a 'gentleman retainer' of Wolsey's, but in reality he was more like a hostage for his father, who was made lord deputy of Ireland in place of Kildare in 1522.[39]

Yet Piers was still some distance from securing the earldom of Ormond. There was only so much that Wolsey was willing to do on his behalf. Certainly Wolsey had no intention of suggesting to the king that the vacant earldom be granted to Piers over the heads of the Boleyns; to have done so would have been too risky, especially in the early 1520s when the king took one of Sir Thomas Boleyn's daughters, Mary, as his mistress. Instead of risking a confrontation, in 1521 Wolsey agreed with the suggestion made by the new lord lieutenant of Ireland, Thomas Howard, earl of Surrey, to unite the rival claimants to the earldom by arranging a marriage between Piers' son James and Sir Thomas Boleyn's younger daughter, Anne. Anne was accordingly summoned home to England from France late in 1521, but to no avail. Her proposed union with James soon fell through, getting no further than an engagement, with the Butlers pitching the price too high, demanding the Boleyns surrender their rights to the earldom of Ormond. Sir Thomas Boleyn for his own part was dismissive of the need for a marriage, confident that he could acquire the earldom for himself, through his influence with the king.[40] Eventually, of course, fate would grant Anne a more illustrious (and dangerous) husband than James Butler.

The Ormond succession remained locked in this impasse till early 1528, when Piers Butler and Sir Thomas Boleyn finally reached a compromise. How much cajoling they both received is anyone's guess, but certainly they were both handsomely rewarded for ending the 13-year-long dispute. Egged on by Wolsey, the king made it plain to Boleyn that he did not wish to put the loyalty of the Butlers in Ireland in jeopardy. Consequently, Boleyn became earl of Wiltshire and Ormond, with Piers' consent. In return Piers got an earldom of his own. After many years of struggle, he was at last recognised as a nobleman, and on Sunday 23 February 1528, he was invested as a member of the Irish peerage when Henry VIII created him earl of Ossory in a ceremony at Windsor Castle.

An account of the day's proceedings survives, and it affords a rare glimpse of the ritualised world of the Renaissance prince into which Piers Ruadh had gained admittance. From beginning to end, the entire ceremony was designed as an elaborate spectacle in which the monarchy appeared centre stage as the fountain

---

39 J.G. Nichols (ed.), *The Chronicle of Calais, 1485–1540* (Camden Soc., xxxv, London 1846), 98; D. Edwards, 'James Butler, ninth earl of Ormond (*c.*1496–1546) in *New dictionary of national biography* (forthcoming). **40** Empey, 'Rags to riches', 310.

from whence the aristocracy arose, and Henry's power and munificence was openly displayed. Like any royal occasion, Piers' investiture was a matter of state, and it was deemed important to demonstrate his special position in the social order as one transformed by the bounty of majesty. The performance began as soon as he arrived at court, when a company of royal attendants led Piers for a brief meeting with his liege lord, the king, before Henry went to mass. This introduction served a two-fold purpose. In the first place, it allowed him to offer his obedience to Henry as his lord on Earth before the king in turn paid homage to the ruler of Heaven. Secondly, the fact that Piers Ruadh was honourably received by all of the noblemen who surrounded the monarch was meant to indicate that the peerage recognised him as one of their own. The ceremony reached a climax after mass. As Piers approached the great door of the king's chamber he was joined by the garter king-at-arms and three of the most distinguished noblemen in England, the marquis of Exeter, the earl of Oxford and the earl of Rutland. His arrival was greeted by a fanfare of trumpets, at which the procession halted to allow the crown servants to file past and take up their positions before him. This done, Piers formally entered the royal presence, and with the king sitting under a canopy of estate, the letters patent of his creation were read aloud in Latin by the dean of Windsor College. On the utterance of the words *cincturam gladii*, the earl of Rutland presented Henry with a sword and Piers sank to his knees 'and the king girt the said sword about him baudrewise … which act done, the king commanded the new created earl to rise and stand up'. Following this, Henry VIII departed, his part in the ritual concluded, leaving Piers Butler, first earl of Ossory, to lead his fellow lords back to his palace lodgings, where in a symbolic display of fraternity, they removed their ceremonial robes and went to dine together at a banquet in which Piers sat at the head of the table. Later that night, when the meal was over and the trumpeters and officers of arms had been suitably rewarded, Earl Piers took his leave of the king and the royal family. It is interesting to note, however, that the last thing he did before returning to Ireland was to pay a visit to Wolsey in London. Piers had no doubt that he owed his peerage to the influence of the cardinal.[41]

It is easy to assume that his creation as earl of Ossory signalled the triumph of Piers Butler's ambitions. Although he had been forced to relinquish his claims for the foreseeable future to the earldom of Ormond, he had nonetheless been awarded an earldom of his own, a fitting honour for one apparently destined to spearhead the crown's efforts to reduce the power of the Fitzgeralds. Moreover, the fact that he was re-appointed to the lord deputyship for the second time a few months later adds considerable weight to the interpretation that Piers was on a winning streak in 1528.[42]

But while his elevation to the peerage was certainly a great achievement, it did nothing to increase his hold over the Ormond patrimony. Indeed, the very agreement that had cleared the way for his ennoblement had also quashed his hopes of securing a greater share of the ancient Ormond lands. As well as con-

41 *Cal. Carew MSS, 1515–74*, 37–9.   **42** He received the deputyship on 4 Aug. 1528.

ceding the Ormond title to the heirs general, Piers had been persuaded to become a tenant on what was now designated the Boleyn-St Leger estate. Wolsey and the king arranged that he would receive a lease for 30 years of four-teen of the old Ormond manors in Cos. Kilkenny, Tipperary, Carlow, Wicklow, Kildare, Dublin and Meath. Admittedly, the leasehold came cheap, as the rent was fixed at the decidedly nominal sum of £40 per annum, but this was hardly the point.[43]

For many years Piers had controlled most if not all of the property formerly held by the seventh earl of Ormond in Ireland. It is unlikely that he had ever paid rent for it. Now, however, he only had part of the whole, and a much smaller part than he was accustomed to possessing. In Co. Kilkenny, by the terms of the 1528 settlement he received a valuable lease of the manors of Kilkenny, Gowran and Knocktopher, but the document recording the arrangement makes no mention of the six remaining Ormond manors in the shire, nearly all of which he had seized a long time ago. The only possible explanation for this oversight is that Piers had finally agreed to cede the greater part of the estate to the increas-ingly influential Boleyn and St Leger families, who evidently intended to make a going concern of the property in their own right. Since 1517 Sir Thomas Boleyn had been awaiting the chance to collect rent from his mother Margaret Butler's share of the Ormond lands in Ireland,[44] and in 1528 he employed a lead-ing Palesman, Sir Bartholomew Dillon, to impose his seigneurial rights and com-mence taking in the rent in Tipperary and the Pale.[45]

It would seem, therefore, that the rapid changes in the distribution of power that attended the rise of the Boleyns in England persuaded Piers Butler that the way to political survival lay along the path of compromise. By accepting a lease-hold on the Ormond estate it is true that he received a great deal, not the least of which was a secure legal share of some of its richest parts, but this did little to disguise the fact that his entry into the agreement was essentially a climb-down. Viewed in this light, the earldom of Ossory was an expensive acquisi-tion. Ironically, Piers had not enjoyed his investiture, spending much of the day suffering from incontinence as a result of a chill he had caught on his way to Windsor.[46]

In another sense, however, Piers Butler's promotion to the ranks of the titled nobility was no more than a man of his wealth and power merited. Although some writers have interpreted his life as a rags-to-riches story, there is no evi-dence that he ever experienced poverty. On the contrary, in the 1480s, as the head of the MacRichard Butlers, he had inherited a sizeable estate in the Slieveardagh hills that amounted to at least 4,440 acres, and comprised the manors of Pottlerath and Ballykeefe.[47] Furthermore, ever since the turn of the

---

43 *COD*, iv, no. 136. **44** Berkeley Castle Muniments: Berkeley Ch., General 4611. **45** From 1528 until 1534 Dillon did manage to collect money from some of the Boleyn/St Leger estate. (NLI, Ms 2551, ff 1r–2v; *L&P Henry VIII, Addenda*, i, no. 926). **46** *Cal. Carew MSS, 1515–74*, 37. **47** Piers' father had purchased the lordship of Ballykeefe in 1483 (*COD*, iii, no. 258). Beresford, 'The Butlers', 239, argues for an even larger MacRichard estate, but I am not con-

century Piers had assiduously developed his position, purchasing large tracts of land particularly in the north-west of the shire, so that by the time of his ennoblement his private estate had quadrupled in size, measuring no less than 16,970 acres in February 1527.[48] As the largest secular landowner in Co. Kilkenny the title earl of Ossory made sense. Only the absentee English owners of the Ormond lands, the Boleyns and St Legers, had more than he.

Following Wolsey's fall in 1529 Earl Piers continued to make himself useful to the crown, encouraged by Thomas Cromwell, Wolsey's successor as chief minister, to carry on providing an alternative to Kildare power in Ireland. The story of his challenge to his Geraldine kinsmen is dealt with in Chapter 3 below. Suffice it to say for the present purposes that his efforts to present himself as the principal military lord in southern Ireland were eventually so successful that he helped incite the Kildare revolt of 1534. During the war against the Fitzgeralds he and his family fought well, preventing the insurgents from seizing the south, and when the fighting was over he and the Butlers could anticipate more royal favours. In May 1535 Sir James Butler, already lord treasurer, was appointed high admiral of Ireland and warden of the ports, a largely honorific position which apparently required him to act as the Irish representative of the recently expanded English admiralty.[49] He was promoted to the peerage the following October as Viscount Thurles, a timely grant that enabled him to sit with his father in the house of lords in the next Irish parliament, which opened in Dublin on 1 May 1536.[50]

Attendance at this was of the highest importance, for the crown intended to pass four bills of especial interest to the Butlers. Three pieces of legislation directly concerned the inheritance. The act of absentees (1536) cleared the way towards the Butlers' re-seizure of the earldom of Ormond, as it extinguished the tripartite agreement that Piers had been compelled to enter into in 1528 with the absentee Boleyns and St Legers. Here Piers had Henry VIII's matrimonial problems to thank, for following Anne Boleyn's miscarriage of a child in January 1536 the power of the Boleyns had collapsed, with the king convinced he was damned for marrying with them. In the ensuing months Queen Anne and her entire family were arraigned of treason, leaving Piers without serious rivals for the title.[51] To guarantee his succession to the Ormond earldom another act was introduced, overturning the claims of his supposedly illegitimate relatives from east Kilkenny, the Butlers of Neigham.[52] Finally, late in 1537, Piers attained his Holy Grail when he was recognised in the Irish parliament as the rightful heir-male of the old seventh earl of Ormond. It is interesting to note that the head of the Boleyns, Thomas Boleyn, earl of Wiltshire

vinced by the evidence, a *c.*1500 report by an outside observer (Quinn (ed.), 'Ormond papers', 345). **48** *COD*, iv, no. 127. **49** *CPRI, Henry VIII–Eliz. I*, 15, 24; J.C. Appleby & M. O'Dowd, 'The Irish admiralty: its organisation and development, *c.*1570–1640', *IHS* 24/95 (1985), 300. **50** NA, Ferguson MSS, Exchequer Memoranda Rolls, Henry VIII, 192. **51** Ives, *Anne Boleyn*, 343–408; R.M. Warnicke, 'Sexual heresy at the court of Henry VIII', *Historical Jn.* 30 (1987), 247–68. **52** Connolly (ed.), *Statute Rolls*, 173–6.

and Ormond, formally agreed to Piers being named 'earl of Ormond in Ireland'. In truth, of course, Boleyn had little choice in the matter, being then imprisoned in the Tower of London and facing execution, but the crown still wanted his agreement all the same, so as to give Piers' belated recognition as old Ormond's heir the requisite air of legality. Nothing was left to chance, and in order to have Piers accepted as the new Irish Ormond while the English Ormond, Boleyn, was still alive, the government was careful to give a precedent for this curious division of the title. Piers and Boleyn were to hold their respective Ormond earldoms 'as the two Lord Dacres be named, the one of the south and the other of the north'.[53] On 22 February 1538 Piers Butler was formally 'restored' to the earldom. Henceforth, until the middle years of the seventeenth century, he and his heirs would be known as earls of Ormond and Ossory, possessing one of the few joint earldoms in the British Isles.

By the time the 'Reformation Parliament' of 1536/7 ended, Earl Piers was an old man in his seventies, and his acceptance of the earldom of Ormond in Ireland was one of his last public acts. It is recorded that towards the end of 1538 he was too frail to travel up to Dublin from Kilkenny, and there is no further mention of him in the records until his death in August 1539. Before dying he made his last will and testament, a document which was destined to have a lasting effect on the Ormond inheritance. In order to insure that his successors did not face opposition from heiresses and heirs-general as he had done, he once more entailed the earldom and its estate.[54]

DYNASTIC CONSOLIDATION

Piers' successor as ninth earl of Ormond, his eldest son, James Butler, was one of the most capable aristocratic politicians of the late Henrician period. Though he never emulated Piers in achieving the premier post in Irish government, the lord deputyship, in many ways he was a fitting successor to his father. At a time when royal officials hoped to profit from the destruction of the Kildare lordship by drastically reducing all noble power in Ireland, he greatly consolidated the Butlers' position in Anglo-Irish affairs. His often thorny relations with the English lord deputies, Leonard Grey (1536–40) and Anthony St Leger (1540–7), need not concern us here (they are discussed in detail in Chapter 3), except to note that in the ninth earl of Ormond they found a dangerous adversary. The fact that he failed to become lord deputy was immaterial. After 1534 the English monarchy altered its policy concerning the chief governorship, until well into the following century manning the post exclusively with Englishmen, that is, outsiders who, it was intended, would not use the office to develop an independent power-base in Ireland.[55] That 'James the lame' of Ormond (so called

---

53 *Cal. Carew MSS, 1515–74*, 127; J.H. Round, 'The heirship of the Percies: the earldom of Ormonde', *Notes & Queries*, 6th series, 5 (3 June 1882), 431.   **54** *COD*, iv, nos. 239, 242; J. Graves & J.G.A. Prim, *History and antiquities of St Canice's cathedral* (Dublin 1857), 232–46.   **55** The extent

because of a leg wound he had received as a youth) survived the monarchy's decision to seize greater control of the country, and even managed to add to his family's powers, was no mean achievement. Powerful forces in Dublin and London were opposed to further Ormond expansion after 1534, lest the Butlers recreated the Kildare threat in their own image. Despite constant suspicion Earl James survived and prospered, and in doing so he laid secure foundations for the future of his dynasty.

The ninth earl's achievements have often been overlooked, mainly because he was earl for only a brief period of time after succeeding in 1539, ruling for just seven years until his untimely death in October 1546. Because his career ended so suddenly, while he was still in his prime – he was barely fifty years old when he died[56] – historians have tended to treat it as a brief hiatus between the much longer (and, it has been assumed, much more successful) careers of his father 'Red' Piers and his son and successor 'Black' Thomas. Yet the relatively brief duration of his earldom was one of the most important eras in Ormond Butler history. More than his father he cashed in on the dissolution of the monasteries, becoming arguably the single biggest beneficiary of the ex-monastic land bonanza in Ireland. By the early 1540s the ninth earl had outmanoeuvred his enemies to such an extent that, despite his magnate status, advocates of 'reform' on the king's Irish council accepted him as a steadying influence in the realm. With huge grants of land in the Pale at his disposal, he wasted no time putting his new-found wealth to good use, building up an Ormond party in Dublin by granting leases of parts of his property on very generous terms to influential figures such as Sir Thomas Luttrell, the chief justice of the king's bench, Sir John Travers, the master of the ordnance, and Thomas Howth, a leading legal official.[57] In Co. Kildare he made peace with some of the former subjects of the Fitzgeralds, granting the tenancy of Cloncurry manor to the Keatings and the Wogans in 1543, and in Co. Meath he likewise recruited the Tallons as his clients.[58]

Unlike his father, Earl James was not just strong in Ireland. His years in England had helped him to develop an understanding of court politics. Not only was he aware who the leading figures at the royal court were, he also knew many of them personally (he had known Sir John Dudley, Sir Thomas Heneage and Richard Page since 1521).[59] He counted Thomas Wriothesley, the lord chancellor of England and a leading conservative and Howardite, among his friends,[60] as well as the Cromwellite Sir George Carew, a member of the coun-

---

to which it succeeded is debatable: H. Morgan, '"Overmighty Officers": The Irish lord deputyship in the early modern British state', *History Ireland* 7/4 (Winter 1999), 17–21. **56** He was probably born in 1496, as his mother Margaret Fitzgerald was recorded as pregnant with her first child that year: Stanihurst, 'Historie', 326; *Cal. Carew MSS, Addenda: The Book of Howth*, 177. **57** *COD*, iv, nos. 311, 319, 343 and 349. His befriending of Howth was especially significant. A few years earlier, in 1538, his supporter Walter Cowley had called Howth a Geraldine, and accused him of working against the Butler interest: *SP, Henry VIII*, iii, no.227. Luttrell too had not previously been well inclined towards the Butlers: ibid., no.230. **58** *COD*, iv, nos. 299–300. **59** Nichols (ed.), *Chronicle of Calais*, 98. **60** His ties to Wriothesley can probably be dated as early as 1538:

cil of Calais.[61] Above all, at a time when England was becoming more and more involved in Irish affairs, James, ninth earl of Ormond, found himself in the enviable position of being the only Irish lord who fitted in naturally at the Tudor court. It has been shown that he sat for a portrait by Holbein.[62] When Murrough O'Brien and Ulicke Burke were created earls of Thomond and Clanricard respectively at Greenwich Palace in July 1543, he played a central part in the state pageantry; in doing so, he was given equal status with one of the most powerful English nobles, Edward Stanley, third earl of Derby.[63] Earl James paid careful attention to his court contacts throughout the 1540s. As the decade progressed and King Henry began to fade, English politics became increasingly divisive, with conservative and radical factions jostling for control of the royal succession when the king died.[64] Despite the mounting tension in London Earl James continued to prosper, staying in contact with both the conservatives and the radicals without over-committing himself to either side. He realised that, as the greatest Irish magnate, he had much to gain by remaining neutral, as both groups would need his support to secure Ireland in the event of a *coup d'etat*. The final piece of his court jigsaw involved his son 'Black' Thomas, whom he despatched to London as a twelve- or thirteen-year-old boy in May 1544 so that he would be raised in the company of Henry VIII's heir-apparent, Prince Edward (the future Edward VI).[65] Under the ninth earl's charge, the future looked bright for the Ormond lordship.

At home in Ireland his strong position in London allowed him to carry on his father's work of establishing the Butlers as the most powerful dynasty in the country. He worked hard to prevent other branches breaking free of renewed Ormond dominance, especially in his liberty of Tipperary, where he insured that his most dangerous dynastic rivals, the Butlers of Dunboyne, stayed weak, incapable of opposing his earldom. He prevented Edmund, the young head of the Dunboynes – who had been his father's ward – from succeeding to his estate until 1545, when he was 28 years old; by rights, he should have succeeded in 1537.[66] In 1543 he even tried to have Dunboyne sent to England to serve as one of the king's gentleman pensioners rather than let him take up possession of his lands in Tipperary. Though unsuccessful on this occasion – the government blocked Dunboyne's departure[67] – he persevered, and a year later he had the young baron and his uncle, Piers Butler of Grallagh, sent overseas to serve Henry VIII in an army raised to fight the French.[68] Sometime before 1545 Earl James had even appropriated the Dunboyne estate into his own hands, and he expelled Baron Edmund from the captainship of Treinemanagh in the barony of

PRO, SP 60/7/52. **61** *SP, Henry VIII*, iii, no. 234. **62** D. Starkey, 'Holbein's Irish sitter?', *Burlington Magazine* 123 (1981), 300–3. **63** *SP, Henry VIII*, iii, 472–3; Miller, *Henry VIII & the English nobility*, 154. **64** Starkey, *Reign of Henry VIII*, ch. 7–8; J.J. Scarisbrick, *Henry VIII* (paperback edn., London 1971), ch. 13–14; L.B. Smith, *Henry VIII: the mask of royalty* (London 1973), ch. 10–11; J. Guy, *Tudor England* (Oxford 1989), ch. 7. **65** *LP Henry VIII*, xix, pt. 1, no. 473. **66** NLI, Ms 7409. **67** *SP, Henry VIII*, iii, no. 395. **68** T. Blake Butler, 'King Henry VIII's Irish Army list', *Irish Genealogist* 1/1 (1937), 4–5.

Middlethird, which he claimed was in his gift as earl of Ormond.[69] In the long run his heavy-handed approach succeeded in its objective. While hardly well inclined towards Ormond power, Edmund Butler, baron of Dunboyne, was hopelessly weakened; his family never again posed a serious threat to the house of Ormond, and generally fell into line with its requirements for fear of reprisals. On a similar note, it is worth stressing that during Earl James' period as overlord the two Kilkenny branches of the Butlers who had once opposed his father, the Butlers of Neigham and Annagh, did not dare to raise their heads. Though they never signed anything in his favour, neither did they put their names to anything against him.[70] Both families remained in obscurity for many years to come.

Another of Earl James' lasting contributions to Irish political life was the untroubled rise of his younger brother Richard, who established a new branch of the Ormond tree, the Mountgarret line based at Ballyragget in north Kilkenny, and took charge of Butler interests to the east, in Wexford. All too often in major Irish lineages brothers behaved as rivals, but Earl James and Richard Butler worked in unison, with the earl advocating in 1540 that Richard be made 'great master' of a garrison at Ferns.[71] In 1542, when their mother Countess Margaret died, James did not oppose Richard's emergence as a major landowner in his own right, inheriting Margaret's jointured and personal estates in Kilkenny, Wexford and Tipperary.[72] Apart from Ballyragget, Richard inherited four other manors in Co. Kilkenny, at Baleen and Urlingford in the north, and Fiddown and Tibraghney in the south. After James' death Richard was promoted to the peerage as first Viscount Mountgarret and baron of Kells (1551). In the years ahead the Mountgarrets would ape the senior Ormond line in increasing their hold over large parts of Co. Kilkenny.

James, ninth earl of Ormond, was above all a dynast. In his will of November 1545 he apportioned outlying land in the Ormond lordship to each of his younger sons Edmund, John, Walter, James and Edward – his youngest son Piers was not yet born – while reserving the main bulk of the patrimony (and most of the best land) for his eldest son and eventual successor, 'Black' Thomas.[73] In effect, he arranged things so that Thomas's younger brothers would grow up to be lords of the frontier, vanguards of future Butler expansion, while Thomas himself would have his own lands protected by their satellite lordships. According to the ninth earl's plan, Edmund would represent the dynasty in Carlow, holding the Dullough (Tullow) and other lands; John would be established in south Tipperary at Kilcash and look to expand into west Co. Waterford; Walter would hold the line of Butler power in mid-west Tipperary, at Nodstown, like John facing into the Desmond country beyond; James would provide a bulwark against

69 NLI, Ms 7409. **70** The Annagh Butlers may have come to terms with him and his family. In 1539 Edmund Butler fitz Richard of Annagh recognised the authority of Earl James' mother, the Dowager Countess Margaret Fitzgerald: *COD*, iv, no. 243. **71** *SP, Henry VIII*, iii, nos. 315, 330. **72** Countess Margaret had built up a large estate of her own before 1542, chiefly around Ballyragget: *COD*, iv, 268. **73** Ibid., no. 352; W.F.T. Butler, 'The descendants of James, ninth earl of Ormond', *JRSAI* 59 (1929), 29–44.

the Kavanaghs from his base in east Kilkenny at Graiguenamanagh; and Edward (and eventually Piers) would take up lands wherever was necessary along the frontier of the Ormond lordship that ran in a long semi-circle from New Ross in Wexford past Limerick to the Decies in Waterford. It was a shrewd plan that, if effective, would long maintain the Butlers' hold over much of southern Ireland. It also had the advantage of nipping in the bud the prospect of a successful successional war against his eldest son, the future tenth earl, Thomas – for none of these satellite lordships was large enough or strong enough to support a challenge to the earldom. (This helped to insure the failure of two Butler rebellions in the later sixteenth century.)

SURVIVING WARDSHIP, 1547–54

The period immediately following the ninth earl's death in October 1546 was a difficult one for his family. By dying before Thomas, his heir, was old enough to succeed, Earl James left his lordship exposed to the hostile gaze of his opponents in government, who were suddenly presented with an excellent opportunity to interfere in the Butler territories. Because 'Black' Thomas was a minor – just fifteen years old in 1546 – he was debarred from inheriting the estate until he was twenty-one, the legal age of succession. Instantaneous with his father's death, Thomas became a ward of his feudal overlord, the king, a situation that not only necessitated his being kept in royal custody until he attained his majority, but also entitled the monarchy to seize two-thirds of the profits of his estate so long as the wardship lasted. The crown's authority seemed all the greater as young Thomas was already in royal custody, a companion of Edward VI. With good reason the Ormond family feared that the remit of revenue officials appointed to collect the crown rent from their lands would be extended to embrace rather more than the feudal dues of the king. Occasion might be taken during the six years of young Earl Thomas' wardship to investigate irregularities on the Ormond estate, and it was even possible that the authorities might uncover patches of concealed land among the earl's property and re-appropriate them for the crown. The Ormonds therefore had little option but to try and stall the machinery of government. From 1546 control of the Ormond patrimony became the object of a tug-of-war with the crown, and for a time it was unclear what the outcome would be.

The first signs of the struggle came in March 1547, when Robert St Leger, the brother of the lord deputy, warned the dowager countess of Ormond of his intentions to dismiss the Butlers' military retainers from those parts of the estate that would fall into the hands of the crown during her son's wardship. He received a swift response. Having first written to Protector Somerset to complain of St Leger's behaviour,[74] the countess boarded ship for London, and by

74 PRO, SP 61/1/1.

July she had presented herself at Lambeth Palace where she brought a petition to the notice of the king's privy council.[75] Thereafter she continued to travel widely in her family's cause,[76] and her efforts had the desired effect. The governmental procedures regarding the Butler lands ground to a halt. As late as the end of 1548, some six months after his installation as the new chief governor in place of St Leger, Sir Edward Bellingham had still to receive confirmation of his powers over the Ormond property, an oversight that he found infuriating. Even worse, rumours were abroad that young Earl Thomas was to be sent home from London – presumably through the influence of his mother – news that Bellingham suspected was yet another stalling device aimed at frustrating his intention to demilitarise the Butler patrimony.[77]

As with any wardship, time was of the essence, and already the Butlers had succeeded in subtracting two years from the six available to the crown. But the fact that another two years would elapse before the royal coffers finally benefited from the Ormond wardship was not due to the time-killing skills of the countess or her contacts. In Ireland, the machinery of state was slow at the best of times, and for a variety of reasons the administration of wardships was particularly under-developed.[78] In June 1549 Walter Cowley, a former Butler client but now the surveyor general of Ireland, went to Kilkenny to file a report on the state of the Ormond lands. Although the dowager countess attempted to interfere, there was little she could do to prevent him proceeding, and he made a series of recommendations as to how the king's part of the estate should be managed.[79] Cowley's work completed, the responsibility in the matter next passed through the hands of the lord deputy in Dublin Castle to the royal government in London, business that should not have taken more than a few weeks. It is therefore remarkable that the privy council eventually issued instructions for the Irish government to 'let the lands of the young earl of Ormond which be now in the king's power to lease' on 5 August 1550, more than a year since Cowley had submitted his report, and nearly four years since the Ormond estate had fallen under crown control.[80] The entire process quickened up considerably thereafter. In Michaelmas term, the ninth earl's brother Richard Butler was prosecuted in the court of exchequer for intruding into part of the Kilkenny property (so too was Edmund Blanchville of Blanchvillestown),[81] and on 18 November 1550 the crown at last leased its share of the Butler patrimony in Ireland to Thomas, tenth earl of Ormond, for an annual rent of IR£681 4s. 3d., a considerable sum by any standard.[82] The tardiness of the government's proceedings was inexcusable from a financial perspective. Over a period of four years it had deprived an under-nourished exchequer of potential revenue amounting to IR£2,725.

---

75 Ibid., SP 61/1/4. **76** Ibid., SP 61/1/11. Among those she dined with in London *c.*1548 was Sir Thomas Smith: J. Strype, *The life of the learned Sir Thomas Smith* (Oxford 1820), appendix 3. My thanks to Dr Hiram Morgan for this reference. **77** PRO, SP 61/1/140. **78** V. Treadwell, 'The Irish court of wards under James I', *IHS* 12/45 (1960), 4–6. **79** PRO, SP 61/2/43, 46. **80** *APC , 1550–1552*, 98. **81** NA, Ferguson MSS, Exchequer Memoranda Rolls, Edward VI–Philip & Mary, 130; Essex RO, Ms D/DL Z9. **82** *Ir. Fiants*, Edward VI, no. 625.

This was not the only opportunity squandered by the royal authorities through mismanagement of the Ormond wardship. By leasing all of the property in its possession back to the earl and his family, the crown threw away its chance of increasing control over the lordship before Thomas reached his twenty-first birthday. In particular, it forsook the opportunity to weaken the military might of the earldom by dismissing the troops from tenancies on the estate. Although Lord Deputy Bellingham had challenged the rights claimed by the Butlers to quarter galloglass in Co. Kilkenny, nothing had been done by the London privy council to support him.[83] Doubtless the frequent political about-turns and changes in personnel that afflicted the Irish government in the late 1540s contributed towards this lack of achievement, but so too did other factors.[84] Ultimately, the royal authorities in mid-Tudor England recoiled from interfering in the Ormond estate because it feared the consequences of reducing the Butler's military strength, and this no matter how distasteful it found the concept of private armed force in post-Kildare Ireland. In practice, therefore, the Ormond lordship was the subject of two mutually exclusive government policies, one based in Dublin which advocated an outright assault on its autonomy, the other based in Whitehall which favoured the maintenance of the _status quo_ by doing as little as possible. The Butlers were able to exploit this conflict to escape some of the costs of wardship and preserve their independence of central government.

Strategically, a royal policy of non-interference in the Ormond lordship made sense, if only in the short term. The aggressiveness shown in 1546 by Sir William Brabazon, the lord justice, had provoked a full-scale war in Leinster, as first the O'Connors and then the O'Mores responded badly to his movements, and their subsequent revolt committed the English government towards a more interventionist policy in Ireland which required the support of loyalist marcher lords like the Butlers if it was to succeed.[85] To antagonise the dynasty would have been to court disaster, especially as the Butlers were themselves under attack at the time. In Tipperary, the Ormond family experienced problems in the south and the north simultaneously, as the Butlers of Cahir and the O'Kennedys attempted to break free of the earldom's domination.[86] Meanwhile, the rebellion of the O'Mores meant that once again the Kilkenny-Laois border became the scene of sporadic marchland violence,[87] and the eastern frontiers of Co. Kilkenny were also reduced to a battleground after Richard Butler fell out with Murrough Bacagh and Cahir MacArt Kavanagh in 1548.[88] Viewed in this context, it is not surprising that the monarchy ultimately turned a deaf ear to the entreaties of St Leger and Bellingham for permission to interfere in the running of the Ormond estate. Treated gently, the Butlers could help the crown

---

83 PRO, SP 61/1/140. **84** D.G. White, 'The reign of Edward VI in Ireland', _IHS_ 14/55 (1965), 197–211. **85** Ibid., 198–9. **86** _COD_, v, nos. 5, 13, 22, 28. M. Boland, 'The decline of the O'Kennedys of Ormond', _Tipperary Historical Jn._ (1994), 131–2 overlooks this development, mistakenly concluding that major conflict with the Ormonds was avoided in the 1540s and '50s. **87** PRO, SP 61/2/35. **88** Ibid., SP 61/1/81; Moore, 'English action, Irish reaction', 59–60.

to crush a major uprising along the borders of the Pale; treated harshly, they might join the insurgents.

Another reason for the crown's sensitivity to Ormond interests was because the dynasty was undergoing a period of serious internal instability. The premature death of Earl James had produced a power vacuum in the lordship that nobody was able to fill. In 1548 his widow the dowager countess had tried to boost the Butler's political standing by marrying a prominent English courtier, Sir Francis Bryan, but he was not equal to the challenge. Within months the couple were estranged, the countess accusing her new husband of allowing the Butler's position in Co. Carlow to be trampled underfoot by Bellingham's appointees.[89] The fact that Bryan was also a notorious drunkard did not help matters. According to one probably apocryphal account, when he expired in February 1550, he did so during a prolonged boozing session 'sitting at table leaning on his elbow', and his last request was to be buried among 'the good fellows of Waterford (which were good drinkers)'.[90]

For a time the crown tried to use Richard Butler, the ninth earl's brother, as its delegate in the south, raising him to the peerage as Viscount Mountgarret,[91] but while Edward VI reigned he was by and large an ineffective representative, as he mistrusted the crown officials in Dublin and disliked the religious direction the monarchy was taking towards radical Protestantism. In the end, Edward's ministers in London decided that only young Earl Thomas himself could fill the void at the heart of the Ormond lordship, and on 27 October 1551 it was agreed at Westminster to send the earl home. To facilitate this decision Thomas Butler was made the recipient of a very unusual crown grant, gaining livery of his estates a year early while only twenty years of age.[92]

Thus the Butlers of Ormond survived Thomas' wardship remarkably well. They even managed to add to the estate – something usually impossible during a wardship.[93] Early in 1549 Sir Francis Bryan and the dowager countess, acting on the young earl's behalf, acquired at least 4,870 acres in the barony of Galmoy from Elinor Freney, an impoverished gentlewoman.[94] When eventually Earl Thomas returned home in the autumn of 1554[95] – political troubles affecting

---

89 HMC, *Salisbury MSS*, i, 78. **90** S. Brigden (ed.), 'The letters of Richard Scudamore to Sir Philip Hoby, September 1549–March 1555', *Camden Miscellany* xxx (Camden Soc., London 1990), 121–2. **91** *Ir. Fiants*, Edward VI, no. 579. **92** NA, Lodge MSS, Wardships, i, 55. Most standard authorities suggest that Thomas was born in 1532, but the date of this grant clearly indicates that 1531 is the correct year. The fact that the grant was only processed four months later in Ireland (on 10 Feb., 1552) probably accounts for the error (*Ir. Fiants*, Edward VI, no. 956). **93** Miller, *Henry VIII & the English nobility*, 14, 100, 154. **94** COD, v, nos. 14 (1), 15. **95** Not 1556, as one authority has claimed (Canny, *From Reformation to Restoration*, 58), or 1555, as another has it (Brady, 'Thomas Butler', 51, 54). For confirmation that he returned in 1554, as stated in the Annals of the Four Masters, see esp. C. Giblin (ed.), 'Catalogue of Irish material in the Nunziatura di Fiandra', *Collectanea Hibernica*, 1 (1958), 46, but also J. Kirwan, 'Thomas Butler, 10th earl of Ormond: his early career and rise to prominence, Pt. 1', *Butler Soc. Jn.* 3/4 (1994), 525. Lord Deputy St Leger notified estate officials of the earl's impending return in a letter of 12 April 1554: NLI, Ms 2507, fol. 25v.

the monarchy had delayed his departure from London – he came back to take charge of an inheritance that was larger than that left him by his father.

THE GOLDEN AGE, 1554–1614

The accession of 'Black' Thomas Butler as tenth earl of Ormond marked the beginning of an unprecedented period of growth and prosperity for the earldom. In the course of a long public life Earl Thomas emerged as one of the single most powerful aristocrats in the royal dominions. He held a string of important government appointments, at various times serving as lord treasurer of Ireland, lord admiral of Ireland, lord general of the Irish army, and as an Irish privy councillor.[96] On St George's Day 1588 he was made a knight of the garter, the first 'earl of the Irish' to receive the honour in nearly a century.[97] In 1603, in recognition of his standing, he came closer to the Irish chief governorship than any native lord since the Kildare era when he was made deputy lord deputy (a unique appointment).[98] Throughout the reign of Elizabeth I (1558–1603) he time and again stamped his mark on Anglo-Irish politics, sometimes dominating affairs, crushing the ability of successive chief governors of Ireland to conduct policy as they would have wished.

Had he come home immediately after his father's death in 1546, his life would have followed a markedly different course. He would probably have received a traditional Irish education as a warlord. Instead, he stayed in London to be reared as a courtier, as his father had wished. His subsequent career revealed the value of strong court attachments in a period of increasing crown (and decreasing noble) power in Ireland. Because of his court connections the agents of the English colonial administration in Dublin found it difficult to challenge him. His first marriage, in 1559 to Elizabeth Berkeley, reputed 'the fairest that lived in the courts of Edward VI and Queen Mary', was a court marriage, taking place in London,[99] as was his second marriage, in late 1582 to Elizabeth Sheffield.[100] His closest friends included Thomas Radcliffe, third earl of Sussex, who was chief governor of Ireland from 1556 to 1563 and subsequently lord chamberlain of the queen's household, a position that enabled him to control access to the court.[101] Sir Thomas Heneage was another of Ormond's great friends, and like Sussex he held major office at court, consecutively appointed treasurer of the chamber and vice-chamberlain of the household. Through him

---

96 *Ir. Fiants*, Eliz. I, nos. 133, 6166; NA, Ferguson MSS, Exchequer Memoranda Rolls, 1558–85, 80–1; Appleby & O'Dowd, 'Irish admiralty', 300–1. 97 HMC, *Ancaster MSS* (London 1907), 138. 98 NLI, D 3334. Deputy lords deputy had been common under Kildare rule: Ellis, *Ireland*, 366–7. 99 J. Smyth, *Lives of the Berkeleys* (2 vols., Gloucester 1883), ii, 254–5. 100 T. Birch, *Memoirs of the reign of Queen Elizabeth* (2 vols., London 1754), i, 27; G.J. Armitage (ed.), *Allegations for marriage licenses issued by the bishop of London, 1520–1610* (Harleian Soc., London 1877), 112. 101 *Cal. Carew MSS, 1515–74*, 370–3; *Cal. SP, Spanish, 1558–67*, 564–5; P. Wright, 'A change of direction: The ramifications of a female household, 1558–1603', in D. Starkey (ed.), *The English court* (London 1987), 154.

Ormond could be sure his interests were favourably represented to Elizabeth's premier adviser, the secretary of state and later lord treasurer of England, Sir William Cecil, Lord Burghley, who was Heneage's patron.[102] These aside, Earl Thomas enjoyed good relations with many other Elizabethan nobles and courtiers, including Walter Devereux, first earl of Essex, Edward de Vere, fourteenth earl of Oxford, Gilbert Talbot, seventh earl of Shrewsbury, Philip Howard, earl of Arundel, Sir John Perrot, Sir Thomas Knyvett, Sir George Bourchier and Sir Charles Cavendish.[103] As Wallace MacCaffrey has commented, the 'Black Earl' of Ormond was 'the one Irish nobleman at home in the court'.[104]

Most significantly, however, Ormond was the only Irish lord to enjoy a personal relationship with the queen. According to Secretary Cecil, Elizabeth I had grown fond of Earl Thomas while they were both teenagers, during the reign of her half-brother King Edward.[105] Elizabeth admired Ormond and at times confided in him (he was two years her senior), something which caught the eye of courtiers and foreign ambassadors, and made him a 'point of contact' between the queen and her subjects, as petitioners from England as well as from Ireland sought his patronage.[106] Like other favourites such as Leicester and Hatton, he knew how to influence Elizabeth – or how, as he once said, to put ideas 'into the queen's head'.[107] Unlike Leicester, he never made the mistake of pressing her about marriage or the royal succession, realising that she intended to stay single.[108] Elizabeth for her part occasionally held him up as an example to other lords and courtiers, and according to the chronicler William Camden, before the Butler revolt of 1569, she 'now and then with joy gloried in the untainted nobility of his family'.[109] Even after his brothers' rebellion she held him in high esteem, and in Ireland her officials were forced to accept – often with great reluctance – that they would have to share power with him and respect his interests. Although he had to spend more and more of his time in residence in Ireland after 1569 he endeavoured to return to court once a year or every eighteen months or so, usually spending the Christmas season there, participating in Accession Day tilts and New Years' Day celebrations whenever he could.[110] When in 1593 he left the queen's court for what proved to be the last time, Elizabeth took pains to write one of those intimate personal letters that she reserved for her most valued associates. Addressing the earl as 'Old Lucas' – her pet-name for him – she sought to assure him that, though out of her sight, he would never be out of her mind:

102 Ibid., 163; *Cal. SP, Spanish, 1558–67*, 529. 103 T. Wright, *Queen Elizabeth and her times* (2 vols., London 1838), i, 26–7; HMC, *Bath MSS, v, 73*; J.H. Pollen & W. MacMahon (ed.), *The Venerable Philip Howard, earl of Arundel, 1557–95* (Catholic Record Soc., London 1919), 35–6; Bod. Lib., Carte Ms 57, fol. 259. 104 W.T. MacCaffrey, *Elizabeth I* (London 1993), 421. 105 PRO, SP 63/16/71. 106 Corpus Christi College, Cambridge, Ms 114. 65; *Cal. SP, Dom., 1547–80*, 314; *Cal. SP, Spanish, 1558–67*, 559, 576; HMC, *Pepys MSS*, 79; ibid., *Bath MSS, v*, 144; *Cal. SP, Rome, 1572–78*, 209; *CSPI, 1509–73*, 342, 414, 427; ibid., *1574–85*, 63, 191, 225, 335, 485, 506. 107 Bod. Lib., Carte Ms 1, fol. 22. 108 *Cal. SP, Spanish, 1580–6*, 421. 109 W. Camden, *The history of the most renowned Princess Elizabeth, late queen of England*, ed. W.T. MacCaffrey (London 1970), 125. 110 E.g., R. Strong, *The cult of Elizabeth* (London 1987 edn.), 207–8; J.G. Nichols, *The progresses and palaces of Queen Elizabeth* (3 vols., London 1788), ii, 6, 9, 14–15, 17, 65, 90, 94, 107.

'You have been too long acquainted with the disposition of the writer to expect any spark of ingratitude.'[111] For him Elizabeth was usually as good as her word. Despite his mounting years and failing eyesight, the Black Earl of Ormond remained a potent force in Ireland until 1603, when the queen died.

His high standing with the queen had a direct impact on the Ormond inheritance. In the first place, Elizabeth paid no notice to efforts by one of her leading councillors, Lord Hunsdon, to press his claim to the earldom of Ormond in England in his capacity as heir general of Sir Thomas Boleyn.[112] Secondly, as shown in the previous chapter, while Earl Thomas held the earldom, the Ormond patrimony reached its peak in Co. Kilkenny, by 1600 encompassing almost one-third of all available land in the shire. It peaked elsewhere too. Beginning in the 1570s the earl was the recipient of an extraordinary series of land grants from the queen, obtaining grants of crown property (usually ex-monastic or ex-rebel land) scattered across fourteen counties in three of the four provinces of the country. Consequently, the Ormond patrimony for the first time included estates in Cos. Cork, Kerry and Limerick in Munster, Co. Roscommon in Connaught, and also Co. Clare (alias Thomond).[113] From a purely geographical point of view, these grants gave the earldom a better footing in the west of Ireland than it had previously had, a fact that suitably reflected Earl Thomas' emergence as the most dominant figure in Anglo-Ireland since the days of the Kildare ascendancy. Like the Kildares he also increased his territory in the Pale, between July 1573 and November 1581 gaining possession of a long sequence of grants which greatly strengthened his footing in Cos. Dublin and Meath – adding significantly to his father's gains there during the 1540s, for not only did these bring new lands to the earldom, but they were also granted to him and his heirs for ever in free and common socage.[114] From the 1570s onwards, thanks to Earl Thomas' status as a major Elizabethan courtier, the Butlers of Ormond were able more effectively to merge their interests with the Anglo-Irish community of the Pale; this would have major implications in the early seventeenth century. To cap it all, in the early 1590s the tenth earl became an English landowner also, gaining grants of crown land mainly in Yorkshire, but also in Durham and Gloucestershire.[115]

Royal largesse on such a lavish scale insured that the economic value of the Ormond inheritance increased dramatically. When he was granted legal possession of the earldom and its land in 1552, the estate probably brought in rents amounting to not much more than £1,500–£1,750 per annum.[116] As Chart 2.1 indicates, the rent returns from his lands in Kilkenny, Tipperary, Carlow, Waterford, Wexford, Arklow and Leix Abbey grew steadily in the years that

---

111 Cambridge University Library, Ms Kk.I.15, fol. 48. 112 *Cal. SP, Dom., 1595–7*, 510–11. 113 NA., Lodge MSS, Rolls, Vol. I, 127–31, 176, 284, 396–403; ibid., Vol. II, 33, 55–6. 114 In addition to the foregoing references, see NLI, Ms 2506, ff 22r–23r, and St Peter's College, Wexford, Hore MSS, Vol. 4: 1–5, 8, 12, 26, 29, 39–40. 115 Nottinghamshire RO, Ms DD 4P, 28/27–34; *Cal. SP, Dom., Addenda, 1580–1625*, 587. 116 The dowager countess' jointure realised nearly £500 in 1564.

Chart 2.1 Ormond rent returns, c.1574–1639
(temporal and spiritual rents from the south-east)

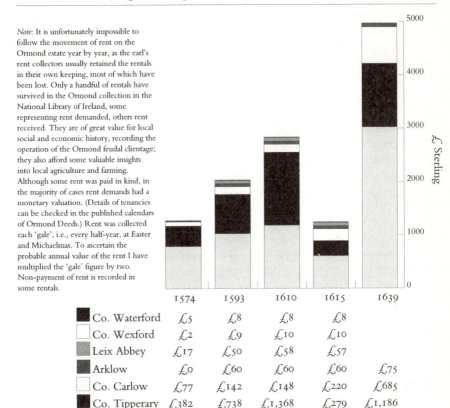

Note: It is unfortunately impossible to follow the movement of rent on the Ormond estate year by year, as the earl's rent collectors usually retained the rentals in their own keeping, most of which have been lost. Only a handful of rentals have survived in the Ormond collection in the National Library of Ireland, some representing rent demanded, others rent received. They are of great value for local social and economic history, recording the operation of the Ormond feudal clientage; they also afford some valuable insights into local agriculture and farming. Although some rent was paid in kind, in the majority of cases rent demands had a monetary valuation. (Details of tenancies can be checked in the published calendars of Ormond Deeds.) Rent was collected each 'gale', i.e., every half-year, at Easter and Michaelmas. To ascertain the probable annual value of the rent I have multiplied the 'gale' figure by two. Non-payment of rent is recorded in some rentals.

	1574	1593	1610	1615	1639
Co. Waterford	£5	£8	£8	£8	
Co. Wexford	£2	£9	£10	£10	
Leix Abbey	£17	£50	£58	£57	
Arklow	£0	£60	£60	£60	£75
Co. Carlow	£77	£142	£148	£220	£685
Co. Tipperary	£382	£738	£1,368	£279	£1,186
Co. Kilkenny	£794	£1,031	£52,285	£614	£3,025

Source: NLI, MSS 2506, 2509

followed, from *c.*£1,300 in 1574 to £2,100 in 1593, before reaching £3,000 in 1610. Unfortunately rentals do not survive for his burgeoning estate in the Pale. In 1576 Earl Thomas was owed approximately £120 by his middleman in the region, Christopher Barnewall, in return for the rights to collect one-third of the profits and issues of the manors of Rush, Balscaddan and Portrane, Co. Dublin, Blackcastle and Donore, Co. Meath, and Castlewaring, Oughterard and Cloncurry, Co. Kildare.[117] I have been unable to discover how much the Pale lands realised beyond this, but it seems certain that the annual value of the Pale estate must have run to several hundreds of pounds. Information is similarly scarce concerning Ormond's lands in Connaught, but the lordship of

117 NLI, Ms 2506, fol. 9r.

Burrishoole, Co. Mayo, and the manors of Coillagh and Aughrim Hy Many, and the Aran Islands, Co. Galway, were worth at least £60 by 1610.[118] The value of the Ormond prisage on wines is also shrouded in mystery. According to a 1564 rental drawn up for Earl Thomas' mother, the Dowager Countess Joan, the prisage was then worth in the region of £360 per annum in the five ports of Waterford, Limerick, Dublin, Drogheda and Dundalk (of which she received £120),[119] but other ports also contributed, such as Carrickfergus and Carlingford, though sometimes only when compelled by Ormond's lawyers.[120] Never as valuable in practice as it should have been (owing to widespread evasion) the prisage nonetheless contributed significantly to Ormond's income, and was probably worth at least £500 a year by the early 1600s.

Whatever rents and prisage he received, Thomas Butler, tenth earl of Ormond was a very rich man. Unlike many of his fellow English and Irish nobles he rarely had to consider selling or mortgaging land to meet his expenses. On the contrary, apart from a few short periods of hardship – after returning to Ireland in 1554, after the 1569 revolt, after the Desmond revolt and after the Nine Years' War – his revenues grew constantly and he was often able to buy land. In rents alone he was probably worth more than £3,500 by the reign of James I, and perhaps as much as £4,000. How much extra he made each year from feudal incidents, or from profits of office in the form of gifts (that is, bribes) and fines is unknown, but it must have been considerable, as must the agricultural and farming profits from his estate. In the final analysis, the Black Earl was probably among the ten or fifteen wealthiest noblemen of the Elizabethan age.[121]

It would be fair to say that the queen's generosity to Ormond was excessive. In so boosting his position she created a major problem for her officials in Dublin, who usually had to direct their energies towards the reduction (not increase) of magnate power in the country. Ormond's high standing made their task more difficult, for native lords such as the Anglo-Irish earl of Desmond resented the fact that they were required to cede power to the crown while Ormond went from strength to strength. Worse, from the mid-1560s Earl Thomas was often capable of destroying government policies that were not to his liking by going over the heads of the Irish chief governors and appealing directly to the queen in London. Successive Elizabethan lord deputies could only deal with the 'Ormond problem' in two opposing but equally unsatisfactory ways, either by following a confrontational approach in the vain hope that he would overstep the mark and disgrace himself (the path chosen by Sir Henry Sidney, Sir William Drury, Arthur, Lord Grey de Wilton and by the earl's one-time friend, Sir John Perrot), or by consciously avoiding conflict with him and allowing him to behave more or less as he wished (the path taken by Sir William Fitzwilliam in his first lord deputyship and later by Sir William Russell). Whatever direction the chief

118 Ibid., ff 19v, 85r; E. Curtis, 'Original documents relating to Aughrim, Burrishoole and Aran', *JGAHS* 17 (1936), 134–9. For Coillagh manor see NA, CP A/53.   119 Ibid., Ms 2507, ff 18v–19r.
120 E.g., NA, CP A/254; ibid., C/129.   121 For English noble incomes at this time, see the appendices to L. Stone, *The crisis of the aristocracy, 1558–1642* (Oxford 1965).

governors chose, they were forced to admit that Ormond's power was potentially greater than their own, and at different times during Elizabeth's reign they
were all made uncomfortably aware that the earl could cut the ground from
under them. Ormond rarely excited the queen's wrath, and he was often able
to undermine government expansionism with relative impunity, offering his
protection to those he saw as the victims of Dublin's misrule, thus making him
an alternative focus of power to the central administration. Through his influence the Munster presidency was almost strangled at birth in the 1560s, the opponents of the government's cess (a new military tax) had their grievances heard
in England in the 1570s, the excesses of official corruption and martial law were
curbed in the 1580s, and dispossessed natives had lands restored to them in the
Munster plantation in the 1590s.[122] In the small world of Irish politics he was a
giant. In the chapters that follow it will be shown that the scale of his influence
produced mixed results for the subjects of his ancestral lordship in Co. Kilkenny.
Although the county community escaped many of the worst developments to
occur in Elizabethan Ireland, so that at times Kilkenny and east Tipperary led a
charmed existence, on other occasions the locals paid heavily for offering
Ormond allegiance, especially under Sidney and Drury. Above all, as the colonial government struggled to contain his power, relations between Kilkenny and
Dublin were characterised by mounting ambivalence. Once the earl lost his grip
on affairs after Elizabeth I's death, royal officials seized the chance to reduce the
Ormond lordship. As his successor would discover, it did not take much to bring
the golden age of Ormond power to a close.

NEW SUCCESSIONAL PROBLEMS

In 1590, for all his success, the tenth earl of Ormond received a shattering blow.
His only son James, Lord Thurles, died unexpectedly in London, aged just six-
and-a-half. Ormond was greatly upset by his son's death, unable to restrain his
grief. As a token of her sympathy Elizabeth I granted her Irish favourite the
honour of having his child buried alongside the kings and queens of England
at Westminster Abbey.[123] The burial ceremony over, the earl had to face the
political impact of his loss. Suddenly the Ormond inheritance was a major issue
of state. Ever since marrying his second wife, Elizabeth Sheffield, in 1582, Earl
Thomas had been able to look to the future with confidence, certain following James's birth in September 1583 that he could pass his lands and title intact
to his heir without fear of a succession dispute breaking out among rival branches
of the Butler dynasty.[124] Indeed, he was not alone in assuming that the future
of his earldom was assured. One of the more interesting aspects of the state

---

122 D. Edwards, 'Thomas Butler, tenth earl of Ormond (1531–1614)', *New dictionary of national
biography* (Oxford, forthcoming). 123 PRO, SP 63/159/46; J.G. Nichols (ed.), *Dingeley's History
from marble* (Camden Soc., 2 vols, London 1867–8), ii, 141. 124 Birch, *Memoirs*, i, 27; Annals of
Kilkenny, 1567–83 (O'Conor Don MSS, Clonalis House Ms 6.4 HN002).

papers of the later 1580s is the fact that they contain little information about the cadet branches of the house of Ormond. Evidently no-one in government expected the Cloghgrenan, Kilcash, Ballinahinch, Leix Abbey or Mountgarret Butlers to lay claim to the greatest earldom in Ireland, and royal officials paid less and less attention to their activities. This confidence evaporated in 1590. At a stroke uncertainty surrounded who would succeed Earl Thomas to the earldom. Just sixty, he was becoming old, and extant evidence hints that his bride the countess was weak, apparently incapable of giving birth again in the years following the arrival of their second child, a daughter, Elizabeth Butler, c.1585.[125]

In theory, the line of succession was obvious: should Earl Thomas fail to produce another son, then the earldom would pass at his death to the Cloghgrenan Butlers, the line founded by his nearest brother, Sir Edmund Butler. Deeds made early in the 1590s relating to the Ormond estate confirmed this, with Sir Edmund and his sons Piers, James and Theobald named at the top of the remainders to the estate.[126] In practice, however, nothing was certain. Twenty years after crushing it the Butler revolt of 1569 came back to haunt the earl. Technically, because of a 1570 act of attainder passed against Sir Edmund for his part in the rebellion, the Cloghgrenan Butlers stood classified as traitors, debarred from inheriting property in the queen's dominions. Earl Thomas had since received repeated assurances that the act would be repealed in a future Irish parliament, but nothing had come of such promises. Were the Cloghgrenan Butlers heirs to the title, or were they not? For Earl Thomas it was imperative that the matter be tidied up as quickly as possible, for he feared the results of a disputed inheritance. Bypassing the Cloghgrenan family in favour of the next most senior line, the Butlers of Kilcash, would be foolish, for the Cloghgrenans could not be expected to acquiesce peaceably. Although he himself mistrusted the Cloghgrenan Butlers – they rebelled for a second time in 1596 in a vain attempt to press their claim (see Chapter 4 below) – Ormond was determined to avoid passing on a dynastic civil war to his successor. Hence his decision after 1596 to nominate Sir Edmund's youngest son, Theobald Butler, as his heir designate. Theobald was untouched by his family's treason, too young to have participated in their revolt. To keep him from rebellion as much as to prevent any harm coming to him Ormond arranged for Theobald to be taken into government custody in 1599. Theobald was sent to Dublin Castle where he was incarcerated at the request of his uncle the earl. He was allowed to take his daily exercise along the castle walks, otherwise remaining under lock and key until such time as Earl Thomas could extract a guarantee from Queen Elizabeth that he would be recognised as heir-apparent.[127]

Securing Theobald as his heir was one of Ormond's last great undertakings, and it required his last great sacrifice: dismissing his idea that one day his daugh-

125 In 1600 Irish government officials described Countess Elizabeth as suffering 'weaknes in body' and being 'nott able to travell' at the time her husband the earl was captured by rebels: J. Graves, 'The taking of the earl of Ormond, 1600', *JKSEIAS*, 2nd series, 3/2 (1860–1), 391.   **126** *COD*, vi, nos. 85, 101.   **127** HMC, *Haliday MSS*, Appendix, 293.

ter, Lady Elizabeth Butler, would marry a great English nobleman. Instead
Ormond took the coldly pragmatic decision that she should marry Theobald.
It did not matter that they were first cousins. Where once marriage within
degrees prohibited by canon law could be achieved through papal dispensation,
now because of the royal supremacy over the church, it could be attained
through the queen's dispensation. The marriage of Elizabeth and Theobald
Butler was doubly attractive to Earl Thomas in that it would consolidate
Theobald's claim to the title and negate the possibility of his daughter ever pressing her claims as his heiress through the offices of a powerful English husband.

To help him realise this marriage of first cousins Earl Thomas recruited the
assistance of his friend and kinsman, Gilbert Talbot, seventh earl of Shrewsbury,
the wealthiest nobleman in Elizabethan England and a prominent member of
the queen's privy council. Through Shrewsbury's influence Elizabeth Butler
was brought over to London following the death of her sickly mother in 1600.
For eighteen months or more she was a regular guest in Shrewsbury's household, preparing for the moment when she would make her court debut.
Shrewsbury and his family took a keen interest in the girl – Earl Gilbert even
advised Ormond to endow her with an estate worth £700 or £800 per annum,
advice Ormond took – but above all the Talbots coached her carefully. During
Christmas 1602 she was summoned to appear in the queen's privy chamber at
Whitehall by her maternal grandmother, the Dowager Lady Sheffield. What
followed was a cynical exercise in manipulation aimed at stroking the ego and
stirring the memories of the ageing monarch, reminding her that this child who
bore her name was worthy of royal protection, for she was Ormond's daughter, and bore his stamp. The strategy worked. Elizabeth's court debut was a great
success. Shrewsbury spoke to her in the privy chamber, joking about her father
Earl Thomas, 'Noble Tom Duff', and she played along, making sure to end her
'discourse' with a show of sorrow about the increasing frailty of the earl in
Ireland. As Shrewsbury wrote, Lady Elizabeth 'hath the queen and all the great
ladies and lords in court on her part'. Touched in all the right places, the last of
the Tudor monarchs recognised that Lady Elizabeth Butler was 'a courtier naturally, even as it were by birth'. Thus the way was cleared for Theobald to present himself. Still a prisoner of the crown, Theobald had arrived in England in
August, accompanied by Ormond's servant Bartholomew Daniel, but he had
had to wait till early December before being freed by royal warrant. Eventually
the queen agreed to interview him, 'out of her favour' to his uncle, Ormond.
Encouraged by Shrewsbury and Sir Robert Cecil, Theobald dedicated a rhetor-
ical exercise in Latin on the judgement of Solomon as a New Year's Day gift
to the queen, the better to convince her of his civility. In return for his help,
Ormond sent Shrewsbury an Irish riding horse, a 'fine hobby'.[128]

Shortly before 22 January 1603 the queen finally informed the privy council of her assent to the marriage. The fact that she agreed to Earl Thomas' plans

---

128 Ibid., *Ormonde MSS, 1572–1660*, 3–7; ibid., *Salisbury MSS*, xii, 301–2, 368–9, 410, 506–7; BL, Royal Ms 12.A.Ll.

was not surprising. What was startling, however, was her claim that it had always been her intention to have Sir Edmund Butler's sons restored in blood by act of parliament in Ireland.[129] If only she had made this known earlier![130] Had she done so there would never have been a second Butler rebellion in 1596 involving Sir Edmund's family, and the tenth earl's search for an eligible heir would not have become so difficult. Certainly if the queen had been less secretive and more encouraging to the elder sons of Sir Edmund, she might have spared Earl Thomas the expense of hiring a team of three lawyers – Robert Rothe, Henry Sherwood and Richard Hadsor – to go to London to advance Theobald's claim as his heir. Moreover, had Elizabeth I not prevaricated so long, Ormond's daughter would not have had to wed Theobald, a marriage that would prove disastrous for the Ormond lordship.

Following the accession of James I, Earl Thomas belatedly retired from public life, having earlier contemplated doing so, and over the course of the next ten years he spent most of his time residing at Carrick in Co. Tipperary, free to enjoy the comforts of the fine Elizabethan manor house he had built there. To some onlookers he must have seemed an eccentric figure. Old and partially blind, according to one source he sported a long grey beard, and he was so proud of his status as one of the knights of the garter that every day he wore the insignia of the order on a chain about his neck, 'whether he sat up in his chair, or lay down upon his bed'.[131] Yet, despite looking like a relic from the past, Thomas was not an entirely spent force; nor was he 'senile', as some historians have claimed.[132] Until the last months of his life the Jacobean establishment treated him with respect and agreed to meet most of his requests concerning the condition of his estate, dispatching a series of handsome land grants to him and his family.[133] Occasionally he was even summoned out of retirement to perform some public duty or other, as in November 1607 when he was empowered during the lord deputy's absence to enforce martial law throughout the realm in the wake of the Flight of the Earls.[134] Most importantly, he retained power over his own dynasty. Largely because most of his Butler kindred were public Catholics, and because he tried to keep his religious inclinations to himself (the habit of a lifetime), the Jacobean authorities bolstered his dynastic powers in his final years. Indeed, it may well be that the power that he continued to exert from his chamber at Carrick did not serve the interests of the Butler dynasty as well as it might have done. Neither the trials of old age nor the ambitions of others could compel him to relinquish his authority over family affairs, a fact which some of his relatives found hard to bear.

This is best illustrated by his handling of his designated male heir, Theobald, since 1605 Viscount Tulleophelim (or Lord Tully, as he was usually called).

---

129 Bod. Lib., Carte Ms 30, fol. 34. **130** It is interesting to note that Lord and Lady Shrewsbury knew of the queen's favourable intentions by 31 Dec. 1602, yet she did not make her feelings plain to the privy council for another three weeks (HMC, *Ormonde MSS, 1572–1660*, 3). **131** Carte, *Ormond*, i, 4. **132** Treadwell, *Buckingham*, 122; J. McCavitt, *Sir Arthur Chichester, lord deputy of Ireland, 1605–16* (Belfast 1998), 84. **133** NA, Lodge MSS, Rolls, ii, 33, 55–6, 100–5; ibid., iii, 129–31. **134** Ibid., Articles with Irish Chiefs, etc., 109.

Although the reasons remain obscure, the earl was openly distrustful of Theobald even while securing him the succession in 1603, and before the arrangements were finalised he not only sought royal permission to 'bridle and correct him', but also made sure he received official confirmation of his power to disinherit Theobald should the need to do so ever arise.[135] Nothing could improve Ormond's low opinion of his heir. Even when the earl of Shrewsbury spoke up in Tully's defence, stating that 'I may boldly affirm he is such a one as you may assuredly take good comfort in', his words had little impact.[136] Relations between Theobald and Earl Thomas showed no sign of improvement, and the viscount found himself in the frustrating situation of being formally recognised as the heir to one of the greatest estates in Ireland while holding next to no real power in his own right. Indeed, what little influence he did achieve he had to create for himself, being made lord lieutenant of Co. Carlow only after complaining to the authorities of his mistreatment by his uncle.[137] But even this proved to be an isolated success. Otherwise the crown did little to comfort him, constantly preferring to place its trust in the wrinkled hands of Earl Thomas instead.

The government's indifference towards Tully is hard to understand. It may well have been that crown officials avoided interfering in Butler family affairs out of respect for the increasingly antique Ormond; yet on the other hand, the Black Earl's advanced age would surely have suggested that it was high time to nurture his successor. Whatever its reasons, the administration did not disregard Lord Tully because it was unaware of his condition. The viscount was desperate for royal favour, assailing Dublin and London with a series of attention-seeking performances. In 1610 alone he notified Lord Deputy Chichester of the whereabouts and movements of a gang of outlaws who were in hiding along the frontier between King's County and Tipperary; informed the earl of Salisbury of wild rumours spread by 'evil-disposed people' to destabilise Kilkenny; and uncovered news of a supposed Spanish fleet destined for Ireland.[138] In spite of such energetic displays of loyalty he failed utterly in his objective to gain crown patronage, and as a result his resentment of his father-in-law grew steadily worse. Eventually the government was forced to intervene.

Events came to a head in 1613. Earl Thomas was taken ill early in the year, but although he felt close to death, he would not speak to his heir about arrangements for the succession, leaving Tully to comment ruefully that 'he will not hear a word from me … with patience'.[139] For a long time the viscount had itched to break free of Ormond. The old earl not only refused to die but would not even allow him to establish his own household, compelling Theobald to live with him either at Carrick or Kilkenny where he could keep an eye on him. These stifling domestic arrangements further fuelled tension. Ormond complained of the low breeding of Tully's servants: they were not true subjects of the crown, quarrelled with his own officers, made too much noise. More

135 Bod. Lib., Carte Ms 30, fol. 34. 136 HMC, *Ormonde MSS, 1572–1660*, 4. 137 Ibid., *Shrewsbury & Talbot papers*, ii, 237, 240; *CPRI, James I*, 71. 138 *CSPI, 1608–10*, 398–9, 522; HMC, *Ormonde MSS, 1572–1660*, 7–10. 139 Ibid., pp 10–11.

seriously, the fact that the earl later claimed he was angered and ashamed by the 'unseemly and dishonourable' conduct of his son-in-law towards his daughter would tend to suggest that Theobald blamed his wife for the intolerable state of his existence, and he may have abused her in his fury.[140] He found he could withstand things no longer in August, when according to a near-contemporary account, 'being a very proud and conceited man', he flung back his chair and stormed out of the dining room at Carrick after Ormond had passed a remark at table that he found offensive. Never one to be upstaged, the earl responded with another insult, venomously barking out that Tully 'is a flower that will soon fade'.[141] If the viscount's word is reliable, Ormond expelled him from the house and would not allow him to return, an action that at last persuaded the government that the 'unnatural separation' between the earl and his heir had gone too far. But although the king himself attempted to mediate, no evidence survives that the two noblemen were reconciled.[142]

As well as being denied authority in the running of the lordship, the viscount found himself unable to make ends meet, a problem he attributed to the earl's meanness towards him.[143] Ormond certainly reacted sternly to Tully's mounting debts, forcing him into an arrangement whereby the profits of his estate would be collected by the earl's servants for the payment of his creditors, an arrangement which made Theobald look incapable of managing his own affairs. Additionally, Earl Thomas expected Lord and Lady Tully to get by on an annual allowance of £500 as long as he lived, not much for people in their position at the head of the Ormond succession list.[144]

From a purely economic viewpoint, only the earl's death could improve Tully's situation. Unexpectedly, however, just as Theobald looked forward to the final collapse of Ormond's health, he himself took ill, and 'after a long sickness and grievous torture therein sustained', he died childless on 29 December 1613, his marriage having been a barren one.[145] Albeit he had achieved very little during his life, his death soon proved to be of major importance. By failing to sire an heir or outlive his uncle, the viscount set in motion a chain of events which ultimately undermined the power of the Ormond lordship in Ireland

CRISIS, 1614–28

The troubles began almost immediately, and revolved around the blow dealt to Earl Thomas' daughter, Elizabeth, Lady Tully, by the demise of her husband. For more than ten years she had been led to expect that her sole consolation for mar-

140 *CSPI, 1611–14*, 422–3. Writing in exile some years later the Catholic cleric Thomas Carve, a native of Tipperary, recorded for posterity Tully's 'supremely happy marriage' to 'Isabelle', the 'truly beautiful daughter' of the Black Earl (Dunboyne, 'Carve's Butler Familes', 426)! **141** J. Graves (ed.), 'Anonymous account of the early life and marriage of James, first duke of Ormonde', *RHAAI*, 2nd series, 4/2 (1863), 279–80. **142** *CSPI, 1611–14*, 412–13. **143** Ibid.; HMC, *Shrewsbury & Talbot papers*, ii, 237. **144** NLI, Ms 2487: 247. **145** R. Dudley Edwards et al. (ed.), 'The Chichester Letter Book', *Anal. Hib.* 8 (1938), 152.

rying Theobald was that one day she would become countess of Ormond and live in great estate. Now her hopes withered. Debarred from the inheritance because the estate was entailed, she was forced to look on as she and the viscount were replaced at the top of the family tree by the Tipperary knight, her cousin Sir Walter Butler of Kilcash, who as the nearest male relative of both Theobald and the earl, was set to inherit the Tully lands as well as the Ormond patrimony.

Walter's clean sweep of the board left Elizabeth facing serious financial problems. Although her father had settled land worth £800 a year upon her (as Shrewsbury had advised) she could not receive it until the old earl died. In the meantime, all she had to her name was her widow's portion of the Tully property, but here too she was confronted by adversity. The estate was heavily encumbered with the cost of her late husband's unpaid bills, obliging her to dig deep into her remaining earnings in order to help pay the debt.

To make matters worse, although her jointure was inadequate for her needs, it seemed an ample and alluring prize to others less favoured by birth and privilege. In particular, her portion of the estate was prey to the rapacious eye of Theobald's bastard brother, Captain Thomas Butler, who hoped to revenge the injustice of his illegitimacy by staking his claim to a share of the Tully lands in Co. Carlow. Elizabeth tried to avert the danger, persuading her elderly mother-in-law, Lady Eustace, to look after Cloghgrenan Castle while she visited her father at Carrick. She advised the old woman to place watchmen on the walls 24 hours a day and enjoined her to be especially suspicious of night-time visitors, but for all her efforts she could not prevent the captain from forcefully occupying first Cloghgrenan and later Tulleophelim, the two principal manors that had been set aside for her maintenance during her widowhood.[146] Elizabeth despaired. Her expectations already in tatters, she was now constrained to commence proceedings to regain her rightful possessions from an impostor whose actions threatened to destroy her solvency completely.

Elizabeth looked in vain to her father for help. A dynast through and through (and always a pragmatist) Earl Thomas was not prepared to place her interests above those of Sir Walter Butler, someone whom he had always favoured, and who as his new male heir he deigned should be given a deciding voice in the management of Ormond family affairs. In effect, Lady Tully could only squeeze concessions from her father if Walter was agreeable. She was not alone in fearing the worst from this situation: even Lord Deputy Chichester reckoned that the tenth earl's fondness for Sir Walter would incapacitate her greatly.[147]

She was soon informed of the new state of play. Immediately after learning of Lord Tully's death, the earl asked her to hand over to Walter 'the Red Book [of Ormond] and all other writings which concern me and my house', before summoning her to Carrick for an important meeting at which the final settlement of the estate was to be made.[148] The principal outcome of the talks proved

146 HMC, *Ormonde MSS, 1572–1660*, 14; *APC, 1613–14*, 462–3; NLI, Ms 2487: 229–32. **147** *CSPI, 1611–14*, 458. **148** HMC, *Ormonde MSS, 1572–1660*, 12–13.

to be Earl Thomas' last will and testament, drawn up on 16 January, in which the earl duly confirmed Walter as his heir by primogeniture. In accordance with the gradual transfer of the reins of power he made no new grants of land to his daughter. For all his hard-headedness, however, the old nobleman wanted to mitigate Elizabeth's circumstances: he ordered that in addition to the property set aside for her ten years before, she was to receive one-third of his silver plate and household utensils when he died.[149]

At first glance, this should have pleased Elizabeth. The silver and utensils were valuable, and although a matter of paradise postponed, she could rest assured that her problems would end after her father's death. But the new legacy was a complicated one. There is reason to believe that her father had only granted her a share of the family silver to ease his own conscience, as the bequest coincided with his efforts to further the greater cause of the house of Ormond by tampering with her finances. Evidently egged on by his male heir, the earl had once again broached the subject of the late Lord Tully's debts, which Walter was adamant should be borne by Elizabeth alone, and this although he himself was the chief beneficiary of the viscount's demise. And so it was, with Walter's interests in mind, that Earl Thomas made one last demand of his daughter, asking her to agree to a cut of £200 in her annual allowance in order to reimburse her husband's creditors more expeditiously.[150]

Elizabeth was enraged by the proposal. Before travelling to Carrick she had hoped that the earl would feel moved by his 'honourable and fatherly care' to assist her, presumably by spreading the cost of Theobald's debts among other members of the family.[151] Instead she discovered that part of her fortune was to be sacrificed, and she recoiled at the suggestion that while her father lived she get by on a mere £300 per annum in order that Walter of Kilcash could prosper more easily at her expense. Henceforth her relationship with the earl and his heir declined. She utterly refused to comply with their wishes, and fearful lest they interfere any further in the running of her affairs, she determined to fight her corner. Her subsequent success sheds a revealing light upon the character of Jacobean politics.

To begin, she shrewdly limited her objectives to securing her rightful inheritance and escaping the more untoward demands of her relatives, things that she readily accomplished by notifying the authorities of her predicament. Because she was the sole daughter and heiress of Ireland's leading peer, Elizabeth's servants had no difficulty gaining access to those in high places to present petitions on her behalf. During the spring and early summer of 1614 her concerns became the subject of a number of routine government orders in Dublin and London,[152] the most important of which would seem entirely unremarkable were it not for the course which her dispute with Sir Walter Butler was about to take. Quite plainly, on 23 March 1614 the lord justice and lord chancellor of Ireland sent their directions to Jacob Newman, one of the clerks of chancery, empowering

---

149 NLI, D 3580. 150 Ibid., Ms 2487: 247. 151 HMC, *Ormonde MSS, 1572–1660*, 12–13. 152 Ibid., 14; *APC, 1613–14*, 345–6, 422–3.

him to enrol a deed of 1603 wherein the estate settled upon Elizabeth by her father was outlined in full. It therefore became a matter of public record that she was only entitled to lands worth £800 a year, and the fact that her portion of the earl's possessions in Co. Kilkenny was largely confined to the four manors of Dunmore, Kilmocar, Ballykeefe and Foulkescourt was also entered on the chancery roll.[153] As events would show, Newman need not have carried out his orders, for the deed was destined to become no more than a minor hindrance to the ambitions of Lady Elizabeth. It was quickly left to gather dust among the state archives in Dublin Castle, conspicuous by its absence in the troubles that were about to unfold.

Elizabeth did not try to patch up her differences with Walter after her father Earl Thomas finally passed away on Tuesday, 22 November 1614.[154] On the contrary, Earl Thomas' death encouraged her to unveil the true extent of her aspirations, as his demise at the advanced age of 83 removed the only member of the Butler dynasty with sufficient pull in government circles to block her path. Indeed, the old lord was barely cold in his grave before it emerged that his daughter intended to overturn completely the final settlement of his property, contriving to disinherit Walter of Kilcash by advancing her claims as her father's heiress to the entire Ormond estate, lock, stock and barrel. From a legal context, it seemed an enormous undertaking, as Elizabeth would surely experience insurmountable problems trying to disprove the fact that the earldom and its lands were entailed in the male line. But this was to underestimate the capacity of court politics to bypass the law. In Jacobean Ireland, to gain the ear of the king was to possess a priceless advantage over your rivals, and this is what Elizabeth Butler attained after making an inspired second marriage to the Scottish peer, Richard Preston, Lord Dingwall, in the latter part of the year.[155]

To suggest that Preston was a good catch may seem misguided. One of the more obscure figures of the Jacobean age, the sole incident for which he has been widely remembered shows him in a mildly ridiculous light. In 1610 he went to considerable trouble to stage a dramatic entry to the Accession Day tilt at Whitehall Palace, and after conferring with Inigo Jones on the matter, he caused a sensation when he appeared in a pageant perched on top of an elaborately decorated elephant. He was unable, however, to make the poor creature perform its part in the spectacle with anything like enough speed, and as a result he ruined the rest of the day's programme, forcing the king's knights to flee from the tilt-yard as the elephant sluggishly trudged about, making any other activity impossible.[156]

It would be wrong to let this event stand as the sole memoir to his career. Far from being a buffoon, Preston was a behind-the-scenes attendant of James

153 NA, Lodge MSS, Rolls, iv, 446–7; *COD*, vi, appendix, 165–7.   **154** Dudley Edwards et al. (ed.), 'Chichester Letter-Book', 173.   **155** The wedding took place some time between 1 Oct. and 24 Nov. 1614, when Preston received a grant of denization (English livery) in Ireland: *CSPI, 1611–14*, 506; *CPRI, James I*, 274–5.   **156** T. Birch, *The court and times of James the first* (2 vols, London 1849), i, 92. The story has since been re-told in G.P.V. Akrigg, *Jacobean pageant: the court of James I* (London 1962), 162, and Strong, *Cult of Elizabeth*, 159.

I who put his adroit diplomatic skills and organisational abilities to good use in the service of his monarch. He was also a self-made man, capable of living by his wits when occasion demanded, a trait which the Butlers of Ormond and his numerous creditors discovered to their cost.

The third son of a minor Scottish laird, he had been sent to serve as a page at Holyrood Palace in Edinburgh in 1591. Gradually his fortunes had improved, receiving a grant of lands in Forfarshire in 1599, the same year in which he was appointed captain over all the officers in the king's household.[157] After James' accession to the English throne in 1603, his career continued to blossom. Never sufficiently important to achieve high public office, even so Preston was assured of his place near the king when he was appointed a gentleman of the privy chamber.[158] Thereafter he established himself among a group of Scottish courtiers in London who were detested by the English for their near-monopolisation of the royal bounty.[159] In 1606 he was granted the right to collect crown debts, a privilege which poured more than £2,300 into his coffers and probably enabled him to purchase the lordship of Dingwall in Scotland the following year.[160] Like many of his fellow Scots, he also benefited from the inflation of honours under James I, raised to the peerage as Baron Dingwall before being sent to Venice as the king's envoy in 1609.[161]

Though not a major player in the Jacobean regime, Preston was a player nonetheless, and he continued to prosper despite many upheavals in political life. Indeed, he was blessed with a keen instinct for survival. When the future duke of Buckingham, Sir George Villiers, emerged to supplant the earl of Somerset as the new royal favourite in 1615, Preston was among the first to desert the ranks of Somerset's supporters for the Villiers camp.[162] Clearly, Richard Preston was no lightweight, and the fact that King James himself arranged his marriage to Elizabeth Butler – possibly through the recommendation of the hapless Somerset – goes to show that he was *persona grata* in the highest circles.[163]

It is hard to tell which of the pair profited most from the marriage. For his own part, the *parvenu* Preston could display the more distinguished coat of arms that his union with Elizabeth gave him. The Butlers of Ormond were highly regarded as an ancient feudal dynasty, and an alliance with them went a long way towards acquiring the sort of social profile he needed to represent the king in diplomatic circles. Preston would surely have been pleased to learn that some of his colleagues in the English foreign service were impressed by the quality of his marriage, the envoy to the United Provinces sending news of it in a bul-

---

157 Balfour Paul, *Scots peerage*, iii, 121–2.   **158** Preston was a member of the privy chamber by October 1608 at the very latest : Notes on transactions, *c*.1623 (Kent AO, Sackville MSS, U 269, uncatalogued Cranfield (Irish) papers).   **159** For anti-Scottish sentiment in London, see Akrigg, *Jacobean pageant*, ch. 5.   **160** Ibid., 162; Balfour Paul, *Scots peerage*, iii, 122.   **161** *Cal. SP, Venetian, 1607–10*, nos. 678, 728, 743–4; GEC, *Complete peerage*, sub 'Dingwall, baron of (1609)' and 'Desmond, earl of (1619)'; Stone, *Crisis*, ch. 2–3.   **162** P.R. Seddon (ed.), *Letters of John Holles, 1587–1637* (2 vols., Thoroton Soc., Nottingham 1975), i, no. 162.   **163** Graves (ed.), 'Anonymous account', 280. The king had even commanded old Earl Thomas not to interfere in the match: *CSPI, 1611–14*, 548–9, 505–6.

letin to his counterpart at Venice. But ultimately, of course, his contemporaries were mainly interested in his wife because she was an heiress with potentially a very large fortune, and this did most to set consular tongues wagging.[164]

Elizabeth Butler, on the other hand, gained a new husband completely at home in the world of high politics, and to someone who had just spent a decade kicking her heels in the claustrophobic environs of her father's house, Preston must have seemed an exotic figure. By marrying him, she would be re-admitted to the company of princes and courtiers she had experienced as a young girl in 1600–2, and Preston's propensity for international relations meant that she could expect to travel abroad in the service of the crown. Less loftily, she could not have failed to notice that even though her Scottish spouse was troubled by creditors, he had easy access to funds in the king's gift, and she had every reason to believe that her own fortunes would be boosted with him by her side. Additionally Elizabeth would have found marrying Preston an attractive proposition because his accomplishments stood in stark contrast to those of her cousin and rival, the eleventh earl of Ormond, Walter Butler.

Walter may have been a complete stranger to the exalted world of the royal court. In all of his fifty-five years[165] he is not known to have visited England before the spring of 1614, just seven months prior to his accession to the earldom. Even then the circumstances of his journey were inauspicious. As a public Catholic – he was known to contemporaries as 'Walter of the Beads and Rosary'[166]– he had given the crown cause to distrust him. Specifically, his behaviour during the opening session of the 1613 parliament had been perfectly designed to excite the wrath of those in power: when the government elected a Protestant, Sir John Davies, as speaker of the house of commons, Walter was identified as the person responsible for the unseemly scuffle that ensued between Catholic and Protestant MPs, when the Catholics tried to place his friend and client, Sir John Everard, in the speaker's chair in place of Davies.[167] Walter's prominence among the Catholic opposition on that and other occasions invited his destruction.

Certainly, the timing of Walter's first confrontation with the king had been most unfortunate, coming as it did just a short while after Tully's death had cleared his path to the Ormond title. As things stood, the government did not lack reasons for seeking to punish him, but his impending succession to one of the largest estates in the country gave an added urgency to official efforts to reduce his power and influence. No sooner had the news reached Dublin that Theobald was dead than Lord Deputy Chichester penned a letter to the king's

164 HMC, *Downshire MSS: the papers of William Trumbell, 1614–16* (London 1988), 84. **165** Although all the standard reference works claim Walter was born in 1569, the correct year of his birth was 1559, as he succeeded to the Kilcash estate at the age of twenty-one during Easter 1580 (*COD*, v, no. 315). **166** E.g., N. French, *The unkinde desertor of loyall men and true friends* (Louvain 1676), reprinted in *The historical works of Nicholas French* (2 vols., Dublin 1846), ii, 26. **167** *Cal. Carew MSS, 1603–24*, 273; *CSPI, 1611–14*, 405.

principal ministers in London suggesting first, that Walter may not be next in line to the earldom, and second, that even if he was he should be stripped of the liberty of Tipperary as and when he did succeed.[168] The hint was not lost, and after the wedding of Preston to Lady Elizabeth the following autumn, Walter faced an uncertain future. Not only had the question of his inheritance become a matter of court intrigue, but his prospects of winning were far from good, as the king by arranging the Preston marriage had intimated what way the wind would blow in the Ormond succession dispute.

The role played by the lord deputy in the subsequent course of events is indicative of the sort of problems Earl Walter encountered. Though careful to preserve the appearance of impartiality, Chichester made sure that Preston was kept well informed of Walter's movements. It was sensible to do so: better to aid the ambitions of a royal favourite than forward the cause of a proven recusant. Thus, in December 1614, when Walter visited him in Dublin seeking confirmation of the Ormond lands, Chichester equivocated, and advised the new earl to have an *inquisition post mortem* held into his predecessor's estate, hardly a helpful recommendation, as one had to be held anyway as a matter of course! His visitor gone, Chichester then dashed off a letter to Preston, 'whom I have ever honoured with my best respects', to tell him that Walter was on his way to court. The message left nothing to chance. Forewarned of the eleventh earl's departure, the Scot gained the initiative, possessing the necessary time to head off his rival.[169]

When the eleventh earl arrived in London, he found progress frustratingly difficult. Preston had prepared his case well, in August 1615 securing the opinion of old Sir Robert Napper as a key witness. A former chief baron of the Irish exchequer, Napper had advised the tenth earl of Ormond on the settlement of his estates before 1603, and the experience had led him to believe (albeit not entirely correctly) that Earl Thomas had intended his daughter to inherit everything when he died. Admittedly, his testimony was not ideal. Writing from his sickbed, 'for I think I cannot live many days', Napper's memory could easily be discounted as that of a weak and dying man. Alternatively, however, his word might be accepted as that of an old and reliable servant of the state who possessed a unique insight into the problem in hand. If this latter viewpoint held firm, then Preston and Lady Elizabeth would be a lot closer to overturning the entail on the Ormond lands.[170]

The second factor to frustrate Earl Walter's progress was Preston's reaction to the latest swing of the factional roundabout at court. By offering his allegiance to Sir George Villiers, Preston made one of those make-or-break choices that periodically arose to determine the success or failure of a courtier's career. In his case, he chose correctly. Villiers had firmly established himself as the new royal favourite by August 1615;[171] later raised to the peerage as marquis of

---

168 Dudley Edwards et al. (ed.), 'Chichester Letter-Book', 152–3; *CSPI, 1611–14*, 458. **169** HMC, *Ormonde MSS, 1572–1660*, 14–15. **170** NLI, Ms 11,058 (1). **171** R. Lockyer, *Buckingham: the life and political career of George Villiers, first duke of Buckingham* (London 1981), 22.

Buckingham, the influence he exercised over the king boded ill for the earl of Ormond. According to an anonymous history of the Butler family written many years later, it was entirely due to Buckingham that Earl Walter suffered so much. But even though the writer certainly exaggerated his story and was highly partisan in his outlook, claiming Villiers cast 'an envious eye upon ye splendour and greatness of ye ancient and noble house of Ormond', he was undoubtedly correct to attribute the cause of Walter's downfall to the power of the royal favourite.[172] It was common knowledge in London that Preston made possession of the Ormond estate the price of his loyalty to Buckingham.[173]

Buckingham's patronage brought access to some of the most influential legal figures in England. Preston could soon count on the advice of the lord keeper, Sir Francis Bacon, and the solicitor-general, Sir Henry Yelverton, both of whom owed their advancement to Buckingham, and each of whom was eager to retain Buckingham's favour by assisting his Scottish sidekick. (Their 'legal opinion' survives among Preston's case papers.)[174]

The dispute with Earl Walter escalated between 1615 and 1617. A series of judicial enquiries came and went, and bonds were signed, sealed and delivered as Preston and Elizabeth Butler, with royal connivance,[175] tried to oust the eleventh earl from his lands. Initially their efforts failed to bear fruit. The crown commissioners could find no solid legal grounds for disinheriting Ormond,[176] and one of the judges in the case, Justice Dodridge, actually went on record to say that nothing could be done to deny Walter his estate.[177] Finally, however, with a seemingly endless succession of expensive court hearings looming on the horizon, Buckingham brought his influence to bear on Preston's behalf. In December 1617 it was ordained that all litigation was to cease, and arrangements were made for both parties to stay in England so that the king himself (advised no doubt by Buckingham) could consider how best to settle the dispute.[178] It was now that Earl Walter's prospects sank without trace. An early indication of the likely outcome of royal intervention soon came, when the king refused Ormond permission to have a copy made of an Elizabethan decree among the state archives confirming the liberty of Tipperary to his predecessor.[179]

The axe fell on 3 October 1618, when the king, supposedly in accordance with his mandate 'to plant and settle the peace and amity betwixt the said parties', made his judgment in favour of Preston and Lady Elizabeth. Openly admit-

---

172 Graves (ed.), 'Anonymous account', 280–1. Using a copy that turned up in southern Ireland in 1850 (presently in the possession of Mr Richard Donovan of Ballymore, Camolin, Co. Wexford), Graves could only assume it was written anonymously late in the seventeenth century when he presented it for publication in 1863. Recently Dr Billy Kelly has identified what seems to be the original version of the document (NLI, Ms 2514), and has suggested it was composed early in the eighteenth century by one Dr Clarke, an Ormond family physician: W.P. Kelly, 'Ormond and Strafford, pupil and mentor?', *Butler Soc. Jn.* 4/1 (1997), 102, n. 6. 173 Seddon (ed.), *Letters of John Holles*, i, no. 162. 174 NLI, Ms 11,046 (11). 175 Treadwell, *Buckingham*, 123. 176 E.g., NLI, D 3586; *Cal. SP, Dom., 1611–18*, 361. 177 NLI, Ms 11,046 (9). 178 CPRI, James I, 343. 179 *Cal. SP, Dom., 1623–25 & Addenda*, 553; S.R. Gardiner (ed.), *The Fortescue papers* (Camden Soc., London 1871), 115.

ting that some of the finest legal minds in the realm had been perplexed by the problems of the case, he stated that nonetheless he could see his way clearly to the fairest outcome. He upheld the interests of Preston's wife on a grand scale. In Co. Kilkenny Lady Elizabeth's holdings jumped from 21,170 to 47,700 acres, and whereas she had only been entitled to the four manors of Dunmore, Foulkescourt, Ballykeefe and Kilmocar by the terms of her father's will, now with a majestic sweep of the king's hand she was possessed of another ten, including the castle and manor of Kilkenny itself. Nor did her reward stop here. In an attempt to ensure she would be able to live in a manner befitting the wife of a courtier, Elizabeth was also given all her father's ex-monastic estates in Co. Kilkenny, situated at Jerpoint, Kells, Callan and Rosbercon respectively, and these in addition to the manors of Roscrea and Nenagh in Tipperary, Rathvilly and Clonmore in Carlow, and the manor and lordship of Arklow in Wicklow.[180]

The scale of her victory stunned Earl Walter. Having succeeded to an estate with a rental income of several thousand pounds in 1615,[181] he now found himself confronting a situation whereby he could expect to receive not much more than £1,000 in rent from his remaining lands.[182] The wound inflicted to his wealth was seen most painfully in Kilkenny, where although he continued to own 19,700 acres, the land was widely dispersed in scattered parcels around the shire, and he only possessed the one manor, at Gowran.

The bitter taste that remained after receiving the king's judgment was exacerbated by some of the reasons given by the monarch to justify his decision. The explanation offered for the bestowal on Elizabeth of the five manors of Kilkenny, Dunfert, Knocktopher, Glashare and Rosbercon, seemed especially far-fetched, as the tenth earl had explicitly entailed them to his male heirs in January 1603.[183] If now these were considered as not entailed, why had the king left him with Gowran manor, which was also mentioned in the 1603 document? Moreover, had not the king confirmed Kilkenny Castle and its manorial privileges to Walter by letters patent in June 1614?[184] A similar puzzle could be raised concerning Walter's loss of Dammagh manor and some other lands in the county, which had been entailed by a deed of 1608.[185]

To these and other possible queries the explanatory preamble to the king's award was most unsatisfying. There James stated that he had overturned Walter's rights because the estate settled on the Lady Elizabeth Butler by Earl Thomas was presently barely worth half of the £800 per annum that it was meant to realise. To this Earl Walter could have presented a number of objections, had he been given the chance. For instance, the low rent value of Elizabeth's portion was caused primarily by those long leases at cheap rents at which the tenth

180 NLI, D.3619; *CPRI, James I*, 455–9; Treadwell, *Buckingham*, 123–4. 181 NLI, Ms 2506, ff 81r–87r, for his rents in the south-east. 182 Ibid., Ms 11,063 (1). This account of the revenue culled by the crown from Earl Walter's estate also includes notice of a few rents collected from the lands of the Lady Elizabeth. I have subtracted these from the overall figure. 183 *COD*, vi, appendix, 163. The manors of Roscrea, Nenagh, Rathvilly, Clonmore and Arklow were also affected by the entail. 184 *CPRI, James I*, 312. 185 *COD*, vi, appendix, 164–5.

earl had usually set his lands. As already shown in Chapter 1, the Black Earl of Ormond used the leasing of his property as a basis for the patronage of his friends and supporters. Walter, like Elizabeth, could only hope to improve the rent return on his portion of the estate when the terms of these old leases expired. Given that they both suffered from the same problem, why should Earl Walter suffer for the temporary shortfall on Lady Elizabeth's land? It was not as though he had refused to help her overcome her financial difficulties. As he now tried to tell the king, since her wedding to Preston in 1614 he had paid her handsomely for her losses, giving her £399 per annum out of his own money.[186]

The eleventh earl wrote to the king in vain. Overcome by the manifest injustice of it all, he adamantly refused to accept the royal settlement. In doing so he courted disaster. King James wanted his award ratified as quickly as possible, intending to have it passed into statute form at a proposed new Irish parliament (one which, in fact, was destined never to meet); in the meantime, in accordance with his tendency towards absolute monarchical rule, James also wanted the award enrolled in Ireland as an act of the royal prerogative or 'act of state', enough to make it enforceable. However, by demanding these things the king overstepped the mark: Walter, in agreeing to the award, had never intended anything so binding to come of it.[187] More and more convinced that he had been double-crossed, the earl decided to stand his ground, withholding his cooperation so as to make the award unworkable, invoking the common law as his defence. It proved quite the wrong approach to take (though, given the circumstances, it is difficult to know what else Walter could have done to save his inheritance).

Under an absolute monarch as James I aspired to be,[188] the common law afforded little protection to those who intended to question the actions of the monarchy. Firstly, the principal 'guardians' of the law, the judges, were carefully chosen royal employees, and often they used their exalted positions to extend the range of powers enjoyed by the king.[189] Secondly, the king himself did not readily tolerate legal challenges to his decisions, especially if they came from Irish recusants like Earl Walter of Ormond. In his own eyes, James I was nothing less than 'the linchpin of justice', the foundation of the law; as for the Ormond inheritance, his arbitration and award must not be questioned, for as one scholar has put it, he as king embodied 'the [very] idea of enforceable arbitration'.[190] By this precept, Walter should not have dared to cast doubt upon the king's award, as it insinuated that the 'linchpin of justice' had acted illegally.

---

186 NLI, Ms 11,046 (30). **187** Ibid. (34). **188** It has become the fashion among English historians to no longer classify James' government as an 'absolutist' one, on the grounds that he never acted 'without restraint': S.J. Houston, *James I* (London 1973), 38; J.P. Kenyon, *The Stuart Constitution* (London 1966), 48. Suffice it to say that I disagree, finding in the treatment of the eleventh earl of Ormond a classic instance of absolutist government, that is, of government unrestrained by the niceties of law. See J. Somerville, 'Ideology, Property and the Constitution', in R. Cust & A. Hughes (ed.), *Conflict in early Stuart England* (London 1989), 67 n. 2. **189** W.J. Jones, 'The crown and the courts in England, 1603–25', in A.G.R. Smith (ed.), *The reign of James VI and I* (London 1973), 177 and 182–3. This was particularly true in Ireland: H. Pawlisch, *Sir John Davies and the conquest of Ireland: a study in legal imperialism* (Cambridge 1985). **190** Jones, 'The crown', 183.

But dare Walter did. Having been assured by his lawyers that the king had no right to dispossess him of any part of his estate by virtue of arbitration (in other words that the king *had* acted contrary to law),[191] Walter once again put pen to paper to plead his case. A copy of one of his pleas survives, and it allows a fascinating insight into the rather delicate situation in which the earl found himself. Trying hard to disguise his outrage, Ormond first of all praised King James as 'the fountain of justice' before getting to the point, indicating the legal failings of the king's actions and asking him to admit his error and make a new award.[192]

It was a pointless exercise. The king, infuriated by the earl's insolence, determined to chastise him for his 'scandalous speeches' about the arbitration. On 11 November 1618, six weeks after the award, Earl Walter was summoned to appear in star chamber at Westminster, where he was greeted by Preston and Lady Elizabeth. The lords of the privy council curtly reminded him that neither he nor anyone else was fit to judge the king. Ormond, they said, should rejoice that he had been left 'so fair a portion' of his inheritance, and they ordered him to stop pestering the monarch. Again he was required to submit to the award, as Preston and his lady had done. In reply, the earl said he would lay all his lands at the king's feet, 'but made no other direct answer', unable to agree to the terms of the proposed settlement, even though it was the king's doing and under the broad seal.[193]

In the end, still refusing to bow down, it was announced on 11 June 1619 that Ormond was to be sent to the Fleet Prison, London, where he was to remain until willing to end his stubborn opposition. At once his incarceration became a major talking point, all the more interesting for the fact that he was joined in prison by Lord Haughton, an English nobleman who, like him, had been jailed for opposing the terms of a royal award made in a dispute over property.[194]

The fate of the two men was of particular interest to the landowning classes and, more generally, to anyone interested in the new relationship between the law and the constitution as it was developing under James I. Both lords were in effect victims of purely royal authority, for the king's use of the arbitration process had no standing in common law. This had serious potential implications for future cases of contested inheritance. The monarchy had found in arbitration a means of insuring the victory of the candidate most to its liking. It did not matter what the common lawyers said about this (and they said little). Because arbitration awards had no established legal status, they did not have to go before the courts. This was precisely what made them so attractive to King James, who saw them as a useful extension of his royal prerogative. After 1619 the precedent was set that the crown could interfere without restraint in succession disputes.[195]

---

191 NLI, Ms 11,046 (29), which plainly states 'I know no law that an arbitration hath any power to give any possession unto any of the parties'.   192 Ibid. (28).   193 *APC, 1618–19*, 301–2; *Cal. SP, Dom., 1611–18*, 595.   194 Ibid., *1619–23*, 53; *APC, 1618–19*, 467.   195 It was part of a trend. Sommerville ('Ideology') has shown that both James I and Charles I claimed the ability to impose tax without consent.

Earl Walter needed no convincing that his constitutional rights were being trampled underfoot. Having been denied a trial because of the king's insistence on arbitration he was imprisoned without trial[196] for defying the king's award (and by implication the prerogative). Worse, no sooner was he under lock and key than Preston and Elizabeth Butler were made earl and countess of Desmond in the Irish peerage in July 1619,[197] and at once they threatened to make away with more of his land. Because of his imprisonment Ormond was unable to defend himself against them at law – 'which liberty and freedom the meanest subject in your Majesty's dominions claimeth to be his birthright', he wailed.[198] Despite his protestations, the king would not allow him to answer the Desmonds' charges in court, a decision which ultimately cleared the way for Ormond's almost total destruction.[199] But before describing this it will first be necessary to take a closer look at the eleventh earl's predicament, as well as at some of the problems agitating his foes. After years of legal combat both parties were financially vulnerable, Earl Walter especially so, as he was an ageing patriarch with a large family to protect.

THE PRISON YEARS, 1619–27

After June 1619 Ormond was destined to spend the next eight years under restraint. During this time everything – his family life included – continued to go against him. A few months after being imprisoned he learned of the death at sea of his eldest son, Thomas Butler, Viscount Thurles, news which reduced him to despair.[200] For some time Thomas had been the main source of Earl Walter's hopes as he tried to drum up support for his father's cause in Ireland.[201] Once he was reported drowned on 29 November 1619[202] the fire died out of the campaign to have Ormond restored to his inheritance.

It was from this date that Earl Walter's health began to decline. In his own words, he had 'grown aged and … subject to sickness and infirmities'.[203] Fearing the worst, he made ready for death, resolved to put his affairs in order in case the end came. During the next eighteen months he dedicated most of his energy to the depressing matter of Ormond family finance, compelled by reduced circumstances to scrimp and save for the sake of his kindred.

---

196 Professor Kenyon, a leading proponent of the view that James I was not an absolute monarch, must have been unaware of Ormond's case, wrongly claiming that the king 'never imprisoned anyone without trial' (Kenyon, *Stuart Constitution*, 8).   **197** Balfour Paul, *Scots peerage*, iii, 122.   **198** NLI, Ms 11,046 (28).   **199** By common law, had he been permitted to appear as a defendant at trial he might have enjoyed 'a virtually unrestricted freedom' to challenge his accusers: C.B. Herrup, *A house in gross disorder: sex, law and the 2nd earl of Castlehaven* (Oxford 1999), 55–6.   **200** *CSPI, 1615–25*, 270.   **201** Chapter 5 below.   **202** Not 19 Dec., as claimed by other authorities (Graves (ed.), 'Anonymous account', 280 n. 1; Carte, *Life*, i, lxvii); for the correct date see TCD, Ms F.3.27. Nor was he drowned near Skerries in Dublin bay. Rather his ship is known to have been cast away in a storm somewhere off the Welsh coast, near Anglesea (*APC, July 1619–June 1621*, 128).   **203** NLI, D.3629.

The truncated estate that the king had left him, consisting of property in ten counties, should have given Walter a total income of approximately £2,500 per annum,[204] admittedly a significant sum, but nowhere near enough to cover the full range of his commitments, not least as a father. Earl Walter had had many children by his countess, Lady Ellen – twelve offspring in all, three sons and nine daughters – but of these four of the girls were still maidens,[205] remaining at home in their mother's care until suitable husbands could be found for them. It would not be an easy task to furnish each of them with adequate marriage dowries. Summoning his servants to London, Ormond instructed them to set aside a section of his estate solely for his daughter's use.[206]

By itself this should have been enough to fulfil the earl's paternal duty, but events conspired to insure it was not. In particular, the sudden death of Viscount Thurles placed an enormous extra burden on Ormond's finances, for the viscount had failed to provide his wife, Elizabeth Pointz, Lady Thurles, with a jointure for her support and the support of their children. Overnight, as grandfather, Earl Walter became responsible for the maintenance of the viscount's progeny, which included three very young girls. These also would need a share of the earl's money, immediately for their clothing and education as well as eventually for their marriages. In order to meet this unexpected expense, the earl set about a major reorganisation of his estate. Overturning the arrangements for his own daughters, on 20 May 1620 he put in place a new trusteeship for all the Butler females dependent upon him: his four daughters and three granddaughters, and his son's widow, the dowager Lady Thurles. A much larger portion of his estate was set aside for the use of the womenfolk, comprising of property in Leinster, Munster and Connaught, and the new trustees – Sir Piers Butler of Lismalin (future Viscount Ikerrin), James Butler of Bealaborrow and George Bagenal of Dunleckny – were given special instructions for the guardianship of Earl Walter's grandchildren, those 'tender, poor and friendless orphans'.[207]

Clearly, the eleventh earl, confined to the Fleet, would be compelled to support himself there on a shoestring budget for the foreseeable future. He could take comfort, however, in the knowledge that his family was properly provided for. Besides, with careful management, there was reason to believe that those parts of his estate that still remained to his own use, untouched by the trusteeship, could yield a far better return for his countess and himself. Even as he was perfecting his agreement with the three trustees he already had matters in hand to force a high rent from his residual property in Co. Kilkenny. On 26 March 1620 he had leased the tithes and alterages of Oldtown to a local gentleman, Richard Purcell, for a much shorter term than was usual on the Ormond estate, 7 years (rather than 21 years).[208] This was sensible for someone in the earl's position, no longer able to continue with the giveaway leases his predecessors had favoured.

204 His potential income broke down as follows: £1,188 from rent; at least £173 from the Ormond prisage on wines; and £1,068 from spiritualities (ibid., Ms 11,063 (1)). 205 Mary, Elizabeth, Elinor and Ellice. 206 NLI, D 3629. 207 Ibid., D 3641. 208 Ibid., D 3638.

Yet he did not get the opportunity to reap the reward of this belated short lease/high rent initiative. Before he had made so much as a second lease Desmond and the royal administration had again intervened in his affairs, undoing everything he had accomplished since entering the Fleet. This fresh assault was worse than what had gone before, as it threatened to reduce him to utter penury by stripping him of everything he still possessed.

The severity of this second phase of the battle for the Ormond estate owed its origins to the technical failings of the first. Ever since it had been made Lord and Lady Desmond had found the king's award of October 1618 unworkable. No sooner had they tried to take possession of the lands granted to them than they discovered that much of the property was not theirs to have. Because of the incompetence of government officials in Ireland they had been awarded a considerable amount of land that should never have been included in the king's order, as it did not belong to Earl Walter. For instance, King James had mistakenly awarded them lands in Queen's County that rightfully pertained to the MacGiollapadraigs;[209] likewise the manor of Dromineer, Co. Tipperary, which lawfully belonged to John Cantwell, an old Butler servant.[210] Secondly, and more seriously, the Desmonds were infuriated to discover that no less than seven of the ten manors that the king had passed to them in Co. Kilkenny were technically beyond their reach, having been placed in trust by Earl Walter for the maintenance of his wife, the countess of Ormond.[211]

In desperation they sought legal advice, but even the attorney-general of England, Sir William Reeves, was forced to admit that 'by strict course of common law', as it then ran in Ireland, there was little they could do to possess themselves of the seven manors and overturn the trust (or *use*, as a trust was then called).[212] There was as yet no Irish equivalent to the English statute of uses,[213] and consequently it looked as though the Desmonds would not be able to avail of the Kilkenny manors until such time as the countess of Ormond died.

Thus the king's award had turned into a major disappointment for the earl and countess of Desmond. Long before being granted the greater part of the Ormond estate on his wife's behalf, the Scottish nobleman had accumulated heavy debts in London, principally to various members of the royal court,[214] including the king, to whom Desmond owed an undisclosed 'great sum of money'.[215] To a certain extent, awarding Desmond the Ormond lands may have been the only way that James I could be at all certain of retrieving his own money. There is no doubt that the Scot's insolvency was a matter of grave concern to the king. James went out of his way to insure that he alone would be

---

209 *COD*, vi, appendix 4, 179–80. The lands at Sraghenarowe, Sragheliegh, Graigedrislin, Clonboran, Kilgortryan, Ballykenna, Aghary, Killenure and Corbally had been sold to the Fitzpatricks by the Black Earl sometime after 1596 (NLI, D 3242). 210 Ibid., Ms 11,061; *COD*, vi, appendix 4, 180. 211 NLI, D 3669. 212 Ibid., D 3661. 213 27 Henry VIII, c.10 (England). There was no Irish statute of uses till 1634. 214 His borrowings from Richard Croshawe and the earl of Middlesex are treated in M. Prestwich, *Cranfield: business and politics under the early Stuarts* (Oxford 1966). 215 NLI, Ms 11,046 (34).

the first to profit from any windfall that came Desmond's way from the Ormond estate. Commencing in December 1618 and continuing for over a year, the monarch set his seal to a series of royal protections designed to keep Desmond's many other creditors at bay; not until June 1620 were any demands to be made of him, unless, that is, they were made by the king.[216]

Ultimately, so concerned was King James to recoup his money – the amount due must have been very large – that he required Desmond to provide categorical assurance of repayment. He got it on 6 July 1619, when Desmond rearranged things so that his debts to the king would be collected instead from the earl of Ormond, whom, he observed, was technically liable to pay him £100,000 for breaking a bond (given in May 1617) to abide by the terms of the king's award.[217]

By handing over Earl Walter's bond to the king, Desmond achieved a great deal, both directly and indirectly. First, the assignment of Ormond's broken bond enabled him to wipe out his royal debts: the £100,000 that was theoretically due from the eleventh earl was more than adequate for that. Second, he paved the way for what amounted to a royal annexation of the Ormond lordship, the final stripping away of all that remained of Earl Walter's wealth and power in Ireland. The crucial factor in this process was that, following the assignment of 6 July, Walter owed £100,000 not to Desmond, but to the king. As such, he faced prosecution for debt by the king, who as we shall see, lost no time in using his authority to collect what was due to him. Additionally, the monarch also took the opportunity to abolish Ormond's liberty in Tipperary and seize his grandson and heir, James, Lord Thurles, as a royal ward. Desmond benefited immediately from this increase in crown control, as lands previously unobtainable to him now became available.

Of all the steps that James I took against Earl Walter after 6 July 1619, his use of the earl's forfeited bond to collect what was due to him from Desmond was far and away the least controversial one by law. The king had only a limited need of extra-legal measures to enforce collection. As monarch, he had well-defined rights for the realisation of debts, not to mention a string of officials attached to the exchequer whose task it was to pursue his money. Accordingly, his enforcement of the bond took the form of almost routine government business. On 17 July, eleven days after the bond had been assigned to him, the king had two of Desmond's servants in Ireland, Patrick Esmond and Henry Sherwood, bring the assignment to the attention of the Dublin exchequer.[218] Then, after a lull of eighteen months, the government lurched into action. In February 1621 the king's right to the £100,000 owed to Desmond by Ormond was publicly asserted,[219] and shortly afterwards the exchequer issued a commission of sequestration whereby all lands remaining to the earl of Ormond since July 1619 were to be placed under an injunction and seized into the crown's hands to pay for what was due to the king. By 24 June the seques-

---

216 PRO, C 66/2136, 2170, 2174. **217** *COD*, vi, appendix 4, 177–8. **218** Ibid., 178; TCD, Ms 10,724. **219** NLI, D 3661.

tration commissioners, headed by Sir Lawrence Esmond, had journeyed down to Kilkenny and begun the process of drawing up a series of one-year leases between the crown and all of Ormond's tenants.[220] They moved on to Carlow in October.[221] The better to expedite the forfeiture, and prevent resistance by the tenants, Ormond's two main estate officials, Sir John Everard and Robert Rothe, were imprisoned (without trial) during 1620–1.[222]

To Earl Walter, imprisoned in London, the sequestration was a crushing blow. It meant that, until Desmond's debts to the king had been realised, he would receive nothing whatsoever from his truncated estate. Unsurprisingly, he experienced the worst poverty of his life following the sequestration. With no money of his own he was forced to go into debt with his own servants as well as with London merchants; according to one source, the earl had no choice but to accept 'a charitable pension of five shillings per day allowed him by an old servant, who in gratitude for his lordship's former bounty to him, straitened himself to support his noble benefactor'.[223] This embarrassing situation continued for six years until early 1627, when the royal injunction on Ormond's lands was finally lifted, Desmond's debts to the king having been realised.[224] Only then was Ormond free to resume the exploitation of his own estate, and even so he still had to pay back the borrowings that its loss had compelled him to make.

The king's decision of June 1620 to divest Ormond of the liberty of Tipperary[225] was full of dubious omens. Although it was abolished by relatively normal legal means – by a writ of *quo warranto* out of the king's bench[226] – its legality was only paper thin. A few years earlier, in 1615, the Irish government had held an inquiry into Ormond's palatine powers in Tipperary and had come to the conclusion that, with a few minor alterations, the eleventh earl should be allowed to retain his liberty there.[227] Then the king had accepted their advice; now it was conveniently forgotten, and they were instructed to produce a different finding, more in line with the king's new attitude to Ormond. They had no difficulty doing so. Ever eager to please the monarch they performed a striking about-turn, agreeing with James I's stated opinion that the earl's status in Tipperary was 'exorbitant', somewhat 'troublesome and chargeable' to the state.[228] Between 17 April and 5 May 1621 – while Everard and Rothe, Ormond's officials, remained in jail – the necessary information was gathered and indictments laid against Earl Walter as a 'usurper' of the king's authority in Co. Tipperary. Without further ado his liberty was dissolved.[229] What made these proceedings illegal rather than just high-handed was the glaring fact that the earl was unable to defend himself. Under royal restraint in the Fleet, he was again refused permission to answer the charges against him.[230]

220 Ibid., Ms 11,063 (1). Desmond's agent, Henry Staines, helped to draw up the leases. Earlier Ormond's estate had been identified by a jury of the Kilkenny gentry: ibid., D 3633. **221** Ibid., D 3649. **222** TCD, Ms 10,724. **223** Graves (ed.), 'Anonymous account', 281–2. **224** *CSPI, 1647–60 & Addenda Charles I*, 78. Desmond's royal debts had probably been collected from Ormond's lands by Jan. 1623: NLI, Ms 11,044 (61). **225** Ibid. (57). **226** Ibid. (60). **227** Ibid. (43–4). **228** Ibid. (57). **229** Ibid., D 3664. **230** Walter continued denouncing the royal gov-

More alarming still was the manner in which the king deprived him in 1621 of the custody of his eleven-year-old grandson and heir, James Butler, Viscount Thurles. Legally the monarch had no right to the boy, who was not a ward of the crown because the Thurles estate was not held in chief of the crown and his lawful guardian – his grandfather, Walter – was still alive. Nonetheless by liberally applying his royal prerogative the king was able to have the young lord declared a ward in December 1621.[231] Officials in Dublin and London accepted that it was in the crown's interest that the boy be taken away from his insolent Catholic grandfather and raised as a good Protestant in England. In February 1622 Lord Deputy Grandison urged the duke of Buckingham to seize the young nobleman as quickly as possible.[232] A month later Ormond's heir was placed under the care of the archbishop of Canterbury, George Abbot, a fervent anti-Catholic, who was to see to it that the boy was 'bred in conformity in religion'.[233] A plan to have him educated at Eton[234] came to naught, so that James took his schooling at the archbishop's table.

The Scottish earl of Desmond profited considerably from these proceedings. He it was whom James I honoured with the Thurles wardship, a grant which bestowed on him the right to arrange the marriage of Ormond's young heir (or else to sell it to the highest bidder).[235] He was also granted the castle and manor of Kilcash in Tipperary – Earl Walter's family home – thanks to a technical flaw that was discovered in the earl's title dating back more than forty years, another finding which Ormond could not challenge due to his ongoing incarceration.[236] Last but by no means least, in June 1621 the king brought his prerogative powers to bear on Desmond's behalf in the Irish court of chancery, where a decree was issued overturning the trusteeship that Earl Walter had earlier established for his wife, the countess of Ormond. As a result of this action – which again had no basis in common law – Desmond got his hands on Kilkenny Castle and the seven Co. Kilkenny manors of Knocktopher, Glashare, Dammagh, Rosbercon, Callan, Pottlerath and Grannagh.[237]

Within the Ormond territories this last-mentioned decision in Desmond's favour was not well received. Three of Earl Walter's closest supporters – Sir Piers Butler of Lismalin, Walter Lawless of Talbot's Inch and James Bryan of Bawnmore – refused to accept that because of the extra-legal powers of the royal prerogative the countess of Ormond no longer had any property specifically set aside for her maintenance. Irate, they decided to obstruct the chancery's decree. By November 1623 all three had been gaoled in the Marshalsea in

ernment for blocking his defence (in the Latin legal terminology of the time, nihil dicit) for many years to come: ibid., Ms 11,044 (79), ibid. (75). **231** NA, Lodge MSS, Wardships, Vol. I, 25; Beckett, *Cavalier Duke*, 8. **232** O. Ogle & W.H. Bliss (ed.), *Clarendon state papers in the Bodleian Library, i: 1523–1649* (Oxford 1872), 20. **233** *APC, 1621–3*, 159–60; *CSPI, 1647–60 & Addenda Charles I*, 45, where James is incorrectly identified as Earl Walter's son. **234** *APC, 1621–3*, 204. **235** Desmond formally received the grant by patent on 26 May 1623 'without fine or account' (NA, Lodge MSS, Wardships, Vol. I, 25). **236** Ibid. **237** NLI, D 3669. The king often exercised his prerogative through Chancery: A.K.R. Kiralfy (ed.), *Potter's Historical introduction to the English law* (4th ed, London 1962), 159–60.

Dublin.[238] In the meantime the countess of Desmond, Elizabeth Butler, took possession of Kilkenny Castle and the seven aforementioned manors.[239]

Despite these reverses, the Ormond family did not collapse in the 1620s. If anything, the government's attack brought them closer together. Wishing to be nearer her husband, the countess of Ormond headed for London and by 1625 had taken up permanent residence there. She came to share some of the dangers previously experienced by the earl on his own: for example, some of her private correspondence with Edmund Canon, a Catholic priest in the city, was intercepted by the state, probably because she was suspected (like Earl Walter) of harbouring pro-Spanish sentiments.[240]

Not that an attachment to Spain was entirely damaging. For a brief period in the mid-1620s contact with Madrid proved beneficial for prominent Catholics in England. In 1624 Ormond had shrewdly taken the trouble to write to the Spanish sovereign, Philip IV, and as a result Philip's envoys in London had persuaded King James to go a little easier on him.[241] In January 1625 he was even allowed temporary leave from his cell in the Fleet, 'until the return of the earl of Desmond' from Ireland.[242]

Somewhat grimly, then, the family managed to limp along in reduced circumstances, waiting for the moment when the royal injunction on Walter's estate would be lifted and they could begin repaying what they had had to borrow in order to survive. Intense family pride helped to see them through. When the countess of Ormond discovered that some of her London neighbours were wondering aloud how she managed to meet the cost of her maidservants, she responded indignantly, boasting that 'I entertain no servant without allowing them what is fit for my service'.[243] Outward appearances were also maintained through the support of some important noble families back home in Ireland: it was at precisely this time, while Earl Walter was imprisoned, that the Burkes of Clanricard and the Mc Briens of Arra (and probably the Purcells of Loughmoe) stepped forward to open successful marriage negotiations concerning some of the earl's daughters.[244] Unions with families like these confirmed that, though the Ormonds were down on their luck, their stock was still high among Ireland's provincial dynasties.

RECOVERY, 1625–33

In 1625 their fortunes began to improve. Desmond had over-reached himself in the preceding few months and, in doing so, reduced his prospects for con-

---

238 NLI, Ms 11,046 (50).   **239** HMC, *Ormonde MSS, 1572–1660*, 15–16.   **240** *Cal. SP, Dom., 1580–1625*, 680. For Canon's alleged pro-Spanish speeches see ibid., *1619–23*, 363.   **241** BL, Egerton Ms 2618, fol. 15; *Cal. SP, Dom., 1623–5 & Addenda*, 202. An earlier Spanish attempt at mediation had been unsuccessful: *Cal. SP, Venetian, 1621–3*, 426.   **242** *APC, 1623–5*, 420. He would have got out a few weeks earlier, in December 1624, had it not been for rumours of disturbances in Ireland (*Cal. SP, Dom., 1623–5 & Addenda*, 401).   **243** Ibid., *Addenda 1580–1625*, 680.   **244** Lambeth Ms 635; B.P. Horan, 'Butler-Purcell connections', *Butler Soc. Jn.* 2/4 (1985), 418.

tinued royal favour. Not content with stripping Walter of all his inheritance and inducing his bankruptcy, he tried to divest his adversary of the title 'earl of Ormond'. In an extraordinary episode he and his patron Buckingham attempted to have the title bestowed on a minor gentleman from Connaught who called himself 'Pierce Butler', only for 'Butler' to be revealed by Mountgarret and other Irish lords as an impostor whose real name was Pierce Lennon. The affair reflected badly on Desmond, and Buckingham dropped him for a time.[245] Simultaneously, the Scot was unable to capitalise fully on the Ormonds' recent run of setbacks: most importantly, he had failed to sell his rights to the Thurles wardship. Despite repeated efforts to unload the young nobleman, he could not find a willing purchaser, apparently because many suspected that the Thurles wardship was illegal and feared that it might eventually be traversed in the courts.[246] This gave Ormond an opportunity, inviting the prospect that one day he might be able to influence his heir's marriage. In the event, this was what transpired. Desmond's failure to marry off Thurles allowed Earl Walter to salvage Ormond fortunes by finding an ideal bride for the viscount. But all that lay a few years ahead.

The death of James I in March 1625 boosted Walter's chances of improving his relations with the Stewart monarchy. For some time previously the earl had been considering ending the royal injunction on his estate by accepting the award that he had opposed for so long.[247] On 18 March he swallowed his pride and submitted.[248] There is no doubt that the king's impending demise helped Walter to reach this decision. By taking to his deathbed, James – who died nine days later, on 27 March – freed Ormond to surrender to his successor, Charles I, a new monarch whom the earl anticipated might treat him better. Accordingly, it was with high hopes that Earl Walter wrote at about this time to his cousin and erstwhile enemy, the countess of Desmond, to inform her that he was finally content to perform his part of King James' award and accept its division of his inheritance.[249]

It was some time before Ormond reaped the rewards of his obedience. Charles I, like any other monarch commencing his reign, had many matters to attend to that were more important than the Ormond-Desmond succession dispute, but eventually, towards the end of 1626, he found time to give his attention to the affair. From the start he showed himself more willing to listen to Ormond than his father James had been. Moreover, Charles seems not to have liked Desmond: the Scot left the royal dominions immediately after his accession, reportedly fearful that the new king was ill disposed towards him, probably because of his involvement in the Pierce Lennon imposture scandal.[250] Later,

245 NLI, Ms 2302, ff 197, 231–2; *APC, 1625–6*, 450.   **246** Kent AO, Sackville MSS, Hi 85, ON 9265; see also Lady Desmond to Esmond, 7 Aug. 1624 (ibid., uncatalogued Cranfield Irish Papers). **247** Why else did Secretary of State Conway write of sequestering certain lands 'for the earl of Ormond' on 4 March unless Ormond had meant to obey the award? (*Cal. SP, Dom., 1623–5 & Addenda*, 491).   **248** TCD, Ms 10,724.   **249** NLI, Ms 11,046 (51).   **250** B. Jennings (ed.), *Wadding Papers, 1614–38* (Dublin 1953), 103. For discussion of Desmond's disgrace, see Chapter 5 below.

having learned that Desmond, on his return to Ireland, had entered into Ormond's castle at Carrick and removed two trunks of documents from the evidence chamber there – as well as many other things, including 44 pictures from the gallery – the king ordered the Scot to return everything forthwith.[251] At about the same time a law case that Desmond had instigated against Ormond in the Irish chancery was put on hold through the king's intervention.[252]

By March 1627 Earl Walter's ordeal was almost over. The royal injunction on his lands was ready to be lifted, and new arrangements were being made for him to receive £1,000 per annum while the details of James I's award were finalised by King Charles' administration.[253] Within months he was released from the Fleet, freed to confront Desmond before the king at Whitehall,[254] and by the spring of 1628 he was busy preparing for his return to Ireland.[255] His intentions were clear: to fight Desmond in the Irish courts over each and every parcel of his inheritance that had been mishandled or misappropriated under the terms of the 1618 award.[256]

Surprisingly, Ormond did not experience much of a battle once he got home. Instead, providence intervened to destroy his rivals for him. First the earl's cousin, the countess of Desmond, passed away suddenly on 10 October 1628 while travelling through Wales *en route* to Ireland. Just two weeks later, 'about the 28th day of the same month' her Scottish husband followed her to the grave, drowned in the Irish Sea while hurriedly sailing to Wales during bad weather to attend to her funeral.[257]

These deaths marked the end of the Ormond inheritance crisis. By simply outliving the Desmonds, Earl Walter had won an unexpected and fortuitous victory. His prospects improved at once, for now only the small figure of Desmond's thirteen-year-old daughter, Elizabeth Preston, separated him from the principal goal of his unhappy career, that is, to regain all the lands that had been taken from him while her parents were alive. He did not have long to wait before she, sole heiress to all he had lost, fell into his grasp. By December 1629 little Elizabeth Preston was Walter's granddaughter-in-law, married in London to his grandson and heir, James Butler, Viscount Thurles. The vast estate that Earl Walter had inherited in 1614 was thereby reunited under his direct control as head of the Butlers. In little more than a year he had master-minded the definitive marriage of convenience for his family.

Some remarkable tales have been told about the Preston-Thurles marriage of 1629, usually involving James, Lord Thurles, a pedlar's costume, and clan-destine activities in the grounds of Kensington House, but written as they were long after the event they have been generally dismissed as unreliable by serious historians.[258] Probably the most unsatisfactory aspect of the tales is the extent to which they depict the 19-year-old James Butler as solely responsible for the

251 *CSPI, 1647–60 & Addenda Charles I*, 77–8. **252** *APC, 1627*, 34. **253** *CSPI, 1647–60 & Addenda Charles I*, 78. **254** Ibid., 100. **255** Kent AO, Sackville MSS, Hi 56, ON8509. **256** NLI, Ms 2302: 311–18, 347–8. **257** Balfour Paul, *Scots peerage*, iii, 125; NLI, Ms 11,044 (86). **258** See esp. Graves (ed.), 'Anonymous account', 286–7; Beckett, *Cavalier duke*, 10.

marriage, entirely overlooking Earl Walter's part in the union. The earl's responsibility is a matter of record. Fearing that Elizabeth Preston's guardian, and the
owner of Kensington, the earl of Holland, intended to sell her in marriage to
more illustrious (and richer) suitors, he encouraged his kinswoman, Baroness
Esmond, to write to Elizabeth to forward his grandson's suit in March 1629.[259]
Two months later the earl attempted to get closer to the girl, offering a 99-year
lease of a thousand acres at Aghnemolt, Co. Kilkenny, to her servants Patrick
Wemyss and Anne Tindall to secure their support for the Butler cause.[260] Even
Isabella Rich, Holland's daughter, was recruited to help out,[261] and early in
August, just to be on the safe side, Ormond granted the manor of Dunfert to
Richard Christie, Elizabeth's cousin, at a knockdown rent.[262] Small wonder that
on 29 August 1629 Holland finally capitulated to the mounting pressure and
agreed terms with the Earl Walter for Elizabeth's hand in marriage. His asking
price was £15,000, a huge sum, but one that might have been far greater had
the eleventh earl behaved more passively.[263]

DEBT AND DECLINE, 1629–42

A veritable mountain of debt confronted Ormond and his grandson after 1629.
Aside from the £15,000 due to Holland for the Preston-Thurles marriage, they
had to repay the borrowings Earl Walter had made between 1619 and 1627
while his estate was sequestered. Altogether the eleventh earl owed at least
£6,000, and perhaps as much as £10,000,[264] principally to London merchants
such as Abraham Ricksie, Richard Millar and Robert Parkhurst. He made things
worse in 1629 when, largely for political reasons – he needed allies badly – he
joined with three other Irish lords, the earl of Antrim, O'Connor Sligo and the
earl of Clanricard, to act as co-guarantor for a debt of £4,000 due to the countess of Abercorn.[265] Given his circumstances, it was a high price to pay for friendship, especially when it is noted how many other debts he was expected to
honour. For instance, because he had inherited the late Lord Tully's estate in
1614, Earl Walter was supposed to pay off all Tully's remaining debts, one of
which was still outstanding in 1629, in the sum of £2,600 (stg) owed to the
assignees of Walter Kennedy of Dublin.[266] Worst of all, having concluded the
marriage with Elizabeth Preston, the earl and his grandson inherited all the debts
of her late father, the earl of Desmond. These were very extensive (Chart 2.2).
When he died in 1628 Desmond is known to have owed in the region of

---

259 HMC, *Ormonde MSS, 1572–1660*, 21. **260** NLI, D 3724. **261** Beckett, *Cavalier duke*, 10–11.
262 NLI, D 3729. **263** NA, Lodge MSS, Rolls, v, 291. By September, Walter was able to visit
Elizabeth in person at court (NLI, Ms 2485: 85–9). **264** In the early 1630s Walter's steward John
Shee laid out more than £6,600 in payment of his master's debts (ibid., Ms 2549, ff 34v–35v);
unfortunately, there is no adequate record of how much was paid out either before 1630 or after
1633. **265** The money – and Earl Walter's commitment – was still outstanding in 1634: *CSPI,
1633–47*, 44. **266** NLI, D 3974.

Chart 2.2 *The earl of Desmond's debts at the time of his death, October 1628*

Creditor	£(stg)
To Lionel, earl of Middlesex & Richard Croshawe of London	8,099
To Sarah Wale	4,218
To Sir William Smith of London	1,550
To Patrick Black	975
To Lady Judith May	750
To Robert Parkhurst of London	365
To John Carpenter, army clerk	c.300
To Francis Blondeau, servant of Anne of Denmark	unknown
To Thomas Kitchinman of London	unknown

Sources: NLI, Ms 11,058 (1); ibid., Ms 11,044 (66, 86)); Bod. Lib., Carte Ms 1: .99; NA, CP K/53; ibid., CP L/59; TCD, Ms 10,724 (50); *APC, 1626* , 104; *CSPI, 1633–47*, 96; ibid., *1647–60 & Addenda Charles I*, 98, 141

£15,000–£20,000, at the very least, to a variety of creditors, headed by the former lord treasurer of England, the earl of Middlesex. Unfortunately for the Ormonds, Desmond's creditors – especially Middlesex – had to be paid. Several of them were prominent at the royal court, and King Charles put it about that he expected the Ormond family to treat them honourably. The king's insistence on swift repayment was reinforced by the actions of the creditors, many of whom had suffered badly at Desmond's hands and were desperate to make the house of Ormond pay them their due. Consequently, Earl Walter and his heir James were destined to spend much of the 1630s struggling to reduce a terrible financial burden. In total, when all of these commitments (and the interest rates charged on some of them)[267] were added to the cost of the Thurles/Preston wedding, the Butlers of Ormond owed approximately £50,000 to various parties after the reunification of the estate in 1629.

As soon as the 1629 marriage was contracted it was immediately apparent that things were probably going to get worse before they got better. Straight away the Ormonds' main creditors began pressing the king and the privy council to make arrangements for the transfer of rents from the reunified Ormond inheritance into their hands. In December 1629 Middlesex persuaded the Irish chief justice, Sir George Shirley, to sanction the appointment of John Dobbin, a local man from the Kilkenny/Waterford area, to act on his behalf 'to collect the rents for the three gales last past' that were due to him from some assigned lands on the Ormond estate.[268] The interests of Lady May, the widow of Sir

---

267 The interest on the Middlesex debt was between 8 and 10 per cent. I am unaware of the rate of interest demanded by other creditors. 268 Middlesex to Shirley, 29 Dec. 1629 (Kent AO,

Chart 2.3 Ormond household expenses for 12 months, October, 1630–1

Domestic provisions	£240	19s.	6d.
Legal & political affairs	£180	0s.	8d.
Servants' expenses	£79	15s.	2d.
Horses & stables	£69	12s.	3d.
Buildings: construction & maintenance	£41	7s.	4d.
Clothes	£31	9s.	6d.
Miscellaneous	£55	7s.	10d.
Total expenditure	£698	12s.	10d.

Source: NLI, Ms 2549, ff 2r–17v (25 Feb. 1630–22 Feb. 1631)

Humphrey May, were upheld by a special royal committee that recommended that she should receive £150 per annum from the Butlers over a five-year period until the whole debt was repaid.[269]

To compound matters, the Ormond family's legal costs were set to soar. After 1629 interested parties raised queries over the extent and status of the estate. Earl Walter was forced to spend long periods in Dublin and London and disburse great sums of money on legal fees to contest various claims. Among other things, he had to defend his rights as lord of the manor of Kilcash in the court of wards, and the status of Thurles manor was also called into question in Dublin.[270] Defending Kilcash proved to be particularly expensive, ultimately entailing the payment of IR£460 into the exchequer as a livery fine in June 1632.[271] In addition, as one government official gloatingly noted, the earl was also charged with 'two fines for alienation of all the main estate, both of Ormond, Desmond and the Countess Dowager's, and the wardship of the young Lady [Elizabeth Preston], besides some [feudal] reliefs'.[272]

The growing financial crisis necessitated stringent budgeting. Earl Walter's struggle to keep his own expenses down can be seen in his household accounts, which have survived for the years 1630–1.[273] Though similar accounts were probably kept earlier, it is unlikely that they were handled as meticulously as these. The earl's steward, John Shee of Kilkenny, was in charge of the account book, and he kept entries on an almost daily basis. Every penny that he spent had to be accounted for when the book was audited at the end of his period in office, a serious business, as he would be held responsible for any missing sums.[274] Despite

Sackville MSS, Cranfield Irish Papers). See also NLI, Ms 11,044 (72). **269** Ibid. (66). **270** HMC, *Egmont MSS*, i, 66; Northants RO, Ms OK 445; NLI, Ms 2549, fol. 34v and passim for his movements. **271** NA, Lodge MSS, Wardships, i, 90. **272** HMC, *Egmont MSS*, i, 66. **273** NLI, Ms 2549. **274** In 1633 Shee was accused of maladministration by the twelfth earl's auditors (NLI, Ms

this, however, the Ormond family could not keep their costs down, largely because of their legal and political expenses and the size of their debts. Chart 2.3 shows the seriousness of their predicament. For all their efforts they were living beyond their means, with their legal troubles costing them six times what they spent on clothes, more than five times what they spent on maintaining and renovating their houses, and twice what they spent on servants. And this was only the money that came out of the ordinary daily budget, or petty cash. A separate account of 'Greate sums disbursed' was kept at the back of the account-book for all the major payments made to lawyers and court officials. This put the everyday outlay in the shade. According to Shee's careful little account, no less than £5,333 was spent on 'affaires' in 1630–1, a true measure of the dynasty's enormous financial problems in the last years of Earl Walter's life.[275]

The escalation in debt eventually had a profound impact on the management of the Ormond estate. To help pacify his creditors Earl Walter had to relinquish part of one of his chief sources of revenue, the Ormond prisage on Irish wine imports. Shortly after his return home Walter mortgaged his rights to the prisage in several eastern and north-eastern ports – principally Dublin, Drogheda, Carrickfergus and Londonderry – for £2,000 (a decision later regretted by his grandson James).[276] Earl Walter also had to take tough decisions on the ancestral estate in Co. Kilkenny, needing to be stricter with his tenants if he was to repay his creditors. Like many noblemen across the British Isles in the early seventeenth century (if a little later than most),[277] the eleventh earl had to consider reducing the generous leasing policy that for generations his family had adopted towards the local squires and gentry. However, although it appears from surviving documents that Earl Walter did at least give some thought to the eviction of tenants and the increase of rent, it is clear that he was unable to put such ideas into practice. Following his return to Ireland in 1628 his options were limited by the condition of the estate.

As soon as he had reached Kilkenny Ormond had discovered that for several years Desmond had been trying to make the tenants pay two rents – one to him and one to his creditors – and a number of tenants had already been threatened with eviction, especially those with the lowest rents to pay. Thus the treatment of tenants was already a highly charged matter, one that might explode in Earl Walter's face should he fail to handle it tactfully. Moreover, the fact that as soon as he returned most of the tenants on Desmond's portion of his lands had rushed to pay their rent to him, and this even before Desmond had died, meant that they accepted him, not Desmond, as their overlord. Given these circumstances, Earl Walter would have been foolish to proceed with any evictions. Had he done so, he would have lost the backing of a large gentry tenantry, something he decided he could not afford to do. Impoverished though

2505: 13–14). **275** Ibid., Ms 2549, ff 34v–35v. **276** Ibid., D 4023. **277** Stone *Crisis*, passim; *Family and fortune* (Oxford 1973); K. Brown, 'Noble indebtedness in Scotland between the Reformation and the Revolution', *Historical Research* 62 (1989); 'Aristocratic finances and the origins of the Scottish Revolution', *EHR* 104 (1989).

he was, 'Walter of the beads and rosary' accepted that the payment of rent from his estates was a political as well as an economic matter, reasoning that so long as the majority of the tenants supported him the future of his dynasty would be fairly secure.[278]

Even after the deaths of the earl and countess of Desmond and the subsequent marriage of James Butler and Elizabeth Preston, this remained the case. Earl Walter was most reluctant to make enemies of his tenants. This lenient attitude even stretched to the handful of Scottish and English tenants who had been loyal to the Desmonds in the 1620s. The eleventh earl was determined to first of all re-establish himself in the Kilkenny-Tipperary region as a beneficent, forgiving overlord before attempting to initiate any radical changes in the management of his property. His grandson's teenage wife, Elizabeth Preston, insured his protection of the English and Scottish tenants. In May 1630, while residing with friends in England a few months after her wedding, she heard rumours that in Ireland Earl Walter, 'through the instigations of some malicious persons', had been persuaded to expel from the estate some of her father Desmond's staunchest supporters, in particular some Scots and English settled at Bennettsbridge. Taking pen in hand, she chastised the earl for being so easily swayed: 'I am right sorry to see your Lordship should fall in controversy … about so poor a thing.' She was indignant because Earl Walter had earlier expressly promised not to move against her father's friends.[279] In the event, notwithstanding her youth, her intervention had some success. Although some of the Desmond tenants were almost certainly removed,[280] others such as Henry Staines and William Frisby were left unmolested on their leaseholds.[281]

All of this changed, however, in the final months of Earl Walter's life during 1632/3 – he passed away on 24 February 1633 – as his place was taken by his grandson James, succeeding him as twelfth earl of Ormond. Perhaps because he had spent his teenage years in England, James Butler did not have the same strong attachment as Walter to the traditions of the Ormond lordship. Certainly he had little patience for posing as the county's feudal protector. Primarily concerned with the mountain of debt he had inherited, and greatly attracted by the prospect of obtaining reward from the Protestant government, Earl James soon set about transforming the network of economic relationships that had tied so many of the local gentry to the earldom for so long. Even before Walter died, James had made enquiries to Chief Justice Shirley about the possibility of evicting 'obstinate' tenants, who 'without any right … withhold the possession of my lands, to my exceeding prejudice'.[282] His young countess, Elizabeth Preston, may have been similarly unsympathetic to tradition; according to later evidence

---

278 Dongan to Middlesex, 31 Jan. 1627, 21 Oct. 1628 (Kent AO, Sackville MSS, Cranfield Irish Papers). 279 NLI, Ms 2486: 195. 280 Richard Stanley, Richard Ewart and Robert Johnrell, all tenants in 1628, do not feature on subsequent Ormond estate documents (ibid., D 3699). 281 In Nov. 1629 Staines had petitioned Lady Preston to save his farm in Co. Kilkenny, convinced that 'the earl of Ormond will be against my being so near': HMC, *Ormonde MSS, 1572–1660*, 23–4, where he is misnamed as 'Slanes'. 282 Ibid., 25.

she viewed the local gentry as 'mean and little people'.[283] The Ormond estate was about to experience a major shake-up, one in which ready cash counted for far more than outmoded concepts like fealty, kinship and clientage.

At once the twelfth earl sought legal advice to see if he could recover some of his predecessors' more outlandish gifts to the gentry of Kilkenny and Tipperary. In the mid 1630s his eyes fell on the manor of Dromineer in Co. Tipperary, granted to the Cantwells by his great-great-uncle the Black Earl. The Dromineer case provides a clear indication of Earl James' financial desperation. His lawyer – unfortunately anonymous, but probably an outsider from Dublin – told him what he wanted to hear, claiming that the Cantwells' title to the manor was a forgery, indefensible at law, and he encouraged the young earl to press on with a trial.[284] The advice was nonsense. The Cantwells' right to Dromineer was well established, and a glance through previous Ormond rentals would have shown James that since Elizabethan times they had been recognised as its possessors and had regularly paid their rent. Understandably, the enquiry got no further than this preparatory stage, as the twelfth earl realised he did not have a case, but even so in trying to disinherit the Cantwells he sent out a warning signal to the local gentry that a new era in Ormond/community relations had arrived.

It was not his only action against his family's supporters. At about the same time, the earl's lawyers instigated proceedings in the exchequer against a long-standing client family from Co. Kilkenny, the Crokes of Keappahedin, who had been tenants and supporters of the house of Ormond since the late Middle Ages. From beginning to end the Keappahedin trial was a sordid business. Commencing in July 1633, right after Earl James' succession, the Crokes were threatened with eviction from their leasehold, evidently on trumped up charges, for when the earl was finally able to have them ousted from the land by a decree of 3 February 1635, the sole basis for eviction was that the Crokes had not paid their rent for two years, that is, since 1633, when the proceedings to oust them had begun![285] Nor were local Anglo-Irish gentry tenants the only ones targeted for removal by the new earl. In Michaelmas 1634, in the court of common pleas, Earl James succeeded in gaining possession of lands at Aghnemolt from an Englishwoman and her servants.[286] The woman in question was one of the Christies of London, the same family who, as mentioned above, had helped to bring about James' marriage to Elizabeth Preston in 1629 in face of the opposition of Elizabeth's then guardian, the earl of Holland. The twelfth earl had no time for gratitude if it limited his income.

There was a purely financial purpose to each eviction. With the Crokes and the Christies gone, Earl James was able to put their leaseholds back on the market at a higher rent. From his point of view, overthrowing cheap tenancies was

283 T. Barnard, 'Introduction: the dukes of Ormonde', in Barnard & Fenlon (ed.), *Dukes*, 31. **284** NLI, Ms 11,061. **285** NA, Exchequer Decrees, 1609–67, fol. 50. **286** TCD, Ms 2512: 78. Confirmation of her eviction comes from the fact that after 1634 she completely disappears from Ormond estate documents.

exactly what he had to do in order to put the finances of his house back in order. The same was true of other changes that he introduced in the management of the Ormond estate. In 1635 the young earl compelled John Tobyn of Cahirlesky to vacate his Co. Kilkenny leasehold at Coillaghmore. An eviction was not required on this occasion. Instead, Ormond agreed to pay 'disturbance money' to Tobyn to cover his moving expenses. Not that the earl gave Tobyn much choice in the matter: Tobyn would have forfeited a bond of £2,000 had he not vacated the premises.[287] Once again, a parcel of the estate was made available for new tenants at a higher rent.

The earl also embarked on a new leasing policy which likewise shed the custom of centuries and threw the Ormond estate open to the forces of the marketplace. Some shorter tenancies were introduced. Two of the surviving Ormond deeds from 1635 in Co. Kilkenny record leases made for 13 years and 18 years respectively.[288] But these were the exception rather than the norm. By and large the efforts to bring about an increase in the earl's landed revenue owed more to longer leases than shorter ones. Rather than commit himself to a fast turnover in tenants through short-term leases, Ormond adopted an alternative approach, seeking out the 'better sort' of tenant, well-moneyed types who could meet his higher rent demands. In return for agreeing to pay him more in ready money (more than any earl before him had received) Earl James granted leases of at least 21 years duration to these rich incomers.[289] As the 1630s advanced he began offering 31- and 41-year tenancies as well.[290]

He was perhaps fortunate to be able to behave as he did. As already noted, historians now believe that the 1630s was a period of strain in the Irish economy. There would not have been a large number of local squires or gentry with much money to hand to spend on increasingly expensive Ormond land. It seems this did not matter. In the place of locals Earl James was able to attract new tenants from the ranks of the growing number of New English settlers who were still arriving in Ireland even on the eve of the 1641 revolt. Thus people such as Sir John Temple, Ambrose Aungier, Thomas Hume, William Smyth, William Alfrey, and the three brothers Oliver, Joseph and Christopher Wheeler, came onto the estate in Kilkenny,[291] invariably at the expense of Catholic Anglo-Irish gentry like the Cantwells, Forstalls, Raggets, Crokes, Bolgers, Powers, and Flemings, local families that had disappeared off the Ormond rent rolls by 1641/2, unable in the tough economic climate to meet the earl's rising demands.[292]

---

287 NLI, D 3991. 288 Ibid., D 3879–80. 289 Ibid., D 3957, 3960, 3985, 3987, 3990, 3994–5, 3998, 4013–4, 4032, 4037. 290 Ibid., D 4002, 4009, 4026, 4031, 4044, 4089, 4106–7, 4111. 291 Ibid., Ms 2506, ff 185r–188r gives a list of most of the earl's Co. Kilkenny tenants before Easter 1642. Hume, not mentioned in the list, was a servant of the earl's, and was probably in Dublin with his master when the list was compiled (ibid., D 4107). A similar explanation can be offered for Sir John Temple's omission from the list. For his leasehold see HMC, *Ormonde MSS, 1572–1660*, 45, and TCD, Ms 812, fol. 23. 292 In the 1590s there were four of the Flemings, two each of the Cantwells, Forstalls, Raggets and Crokes, and one each of the Bolgers and Powers on the Ormond estate in Kilkenny: NLI, Ms 2506, ff 10v–15r.

Chart 2.4 Mortgages of land by the twelfth earl of Ormond in Co. Kilkenny
(New English mortgagees in italics)

Date	Mortgagee	Sum	Lands involved
1634	Michael Cowley of Radestown	£320	Brownestown Waring (2/3rd pt)
1634	James Butler of Danginspidoge	£500	Lands in the Rower
1635	Sir Edward Butler of Duiske	£300	Drumroe, Powerstown, Garran & Gurtin
1636	Marcus Knaresborough of Waterford	£450	Inistioge Priory
1636	*Sir Cyprian Horsfall of Inishnag*	£500	Woollengrange, Stanesland & Moorhouse
1636	Marcus Shee of Washeshayes	£300	Jennerstown & Dunvill
1636	Henry Archer of Kilkenny	£330	The Earl's Island & 3 watermills at Kilkenny
1638	*Henry Staines of Kilkenny*	£500	Jenkinstown
1638	Nicholas Knaresborough of Kilkenny	£200	Ballycallan manor
1638	Richard Fitzgerald of Owenstown	£140	Owenstown
1638	*The bishop of Meath (Richard Anthony)*	£3,500	Gowran manor
1638	*Oliver Wheeler of Dunmore*	£1,000	Foulkescourt manor
1638	Richard & John Butler of Knocktopher	£1,000	Knocktopher manor
1639	*Sir John Temple*	£2,200	Kilderry and lands in Carlow
1639	*Oliver Wheeler of Dunmore*	£500	Coneshye
1640	Dr John Purcell of Oldtown	–	Clonfilly & Clonfunsion
1640/1	Robert Tobin of Kilkenny	£100	Coolshillbeg
1640/1	James Purcell	£700	Clone, Rathbeagh & Acragarrad
1640/1	*Oliver Wheeler of Dunmore*	£600	Ballyloskill

Sources: NLI, D 3955, 3975–7, 3992, 4025, 4027, 4038–40, 4074, 4078, 4091, 4100, 4104, 4126, 4132; ibid., Ms 2506, fol. 185v; ibid., Ms 2560, 40, 42, 44, 47; HMC, *Ormonde MSS, 1572–1660*, 44–5

As will be shown in Chapter 5 below, politically this was a mistake, helping to confirm the notion – increasingly prevalent in Co. Kilkenny – that Earl James was not a good overlord to the local community, a development that would have dire consequences for him (and the Protestant government he represented) as rebellion spread across the countryside in 1641. However, in financial terms too, the introduction of new tenants was not a great success. True, as demonstrated in Chart 2.2, the earl's rental income leaped ahead in the 1630s, bringing him an anticipated return of approximately £5,000 per annum from his lands across the south-east of Ireland,[293] and of this Kilkenny produced slightly

293 Later in the seventeenth century Sir William Petty estimated that Ormond had enjoyed rents

more than £3,000, altogether a major advance on the sums raised by his predecessors. Yet this was only a short-term improvement. Because of the long
leases of 21 years and more that he had agreed since 1633, it would be the middle
of the 1650s at the earliest before Ormond could hope to hike up the rents again.
(Looking ahead, as things transpired, his 1630s predilection for long leases caught
up with him after the Restoration, when he was still up to his neck in debt and
the descendants of those he had brought onto the estate were still in place with
many years remaining on their leaseholds.)[294]

Plainly, after 1633 his management of the estate was politically and financially short-sighted. By hiking up the rents at a time of economic hardship and
expelling some of his family's oldest clients, he alienated many of the Kilkenny
community. Surrendering to the ready money of New English colonists need
not have been a mistake had he extracted a lot more money from them, or else
granted them much shorter leases. He soon found his rental income too small
to pay his bills, and up to 1641 he was repeatedly forced to mortgage or sell
large parts of the ancestral estate. Between 1633 and 1641 Earl James is known
to have entered into 19 separate mortgage agreements in Co. Kilkenny alone,
transactions that raised in excess of £13,000 (Chart 2.4). Although most of the
mortgagees were natives of the shire, he made the most money by mortgaging
to New English arrivals. The local Anglo-Irish did not have enough spare capital to meet the demands of his creditors, and seem never to have had more than
£500 available for investment. This was not the case with New English speculators – each one of Earl James' New English mortgagees paid him £500 or
more for an interest in his estate. Oliver Wheeler of Dunmore paid him £2,200,
as did Sir John Temple, and highest of all, the bishop of Meath, Richard
Anthony, paid him £3,500. Men such as these seemed to ooze wealth and they
were eager to do business with Ormond. Wheeler negotiated three separate
mortgages with the earl, while Temple advertised the fact that he was looking
for more land: 'I doubt not but that I shall be able (if you have hereafter occasion) to help your lordship with more money on the same terms'. The hard-
pressed earl found their offers irresistible, and was even willing to cede them
temporary possession of some of his best outlying lands in the north and east of
the shire, at Foulkescourt and Gowran, as well as part of the lucrative Jerpoint
Abbey estate in Kilkenny's prosperous central plain. Nor did the local Anglo-
Irish do all that badly in their dealings with him. Although he tried to mortgage land in marginal areas such as the Rower and boggy Clone and Rathbeagh
in Galmoy, he also allowed some of his highly prized midlands possessions to
pass in mortgage, such as Ballycallan manor and Inistioge Priory. In his desire
for quick money, Earl James relinquished control of some of his most valuable
property, and to make matters worse, he often let it go for far less than it was

of about £8,000 per annum in 1641; but scholars have recently revealed his estimates as highly
unreliable: Barnard, 'Introduction', 22. **294** T. Barnard, 'The Protestant interest, 1641–60', in J.
Ohlmeyer (ed.), *Ireland from independence to occupation* (Cambridge 1995), 223.

worth. And yet to be fair he may not have had much choice. Extant travellers' accounts testify to the fact that landowners all across the country were looking to sell or mortgage land at this time. On the eve of 1641 the Irish mortgage market was a buyers' market.[295]

The need to satisfy his creditors forced Ormond to sell land as well as mortgage it. In Co. Kilkenny little was sold, but this was not the case elsewhere. In Tipperary the potentially very prosperous Kilcooley Abbey estate on Kilkenny's western border was sold in 1637 to Sir Jerome Alexander, a servant of the earl of Arundel, for £3,000.[296] The territory of Farren Kavanagh, Co. Limerick, was likewise sold to another English colonist, the notorious John Anktill, for £1,000.[297] In both deals it is probably fair to say that the purchasers did rather better than the seller, for given time and proper management these lands might have yielded Ormond a healthy return. His problem, of course, was he could not afford to wait.

Daunting financial pressure compelled Earl James to take political risks. It will later be shown in Chapter 5 that he bound himself too closely to the Irish administration of Charles I, becoming a leading ally of the unpopular chief governor, Sir Thomas Wentworth, successively lord deputy and lord lieutenant of Ireland, 1633–41. James expected that loyalty to Wentworth – irrespective of the governor's policies – would help him to recover his dynasty's fortunes. It was a dangerous alliance to make. Under Wentworth's influence,[298] Ormond behaved as though he was beyond the reach of the inhabitants of his lordship. He implicated himself in highly controversial transfers of territory: the 1635/6 sale of Idough to Christopher Wandesford for £2,000, a transaction that alienated many landowners in north Co. Kilkenny (and the Howards of Arundel too); and the 1637 scheme for the plantation of the baronies of Upper and Lower Ormond in north Co. Tipperary, an undertaking that led to the disinheritance of native Gaelic Irish and Anglo-Irish families long associated with the earldom.[299] At first glance, the third major land transfer with which he was involved during Wentworth's administration, the sale of Leix Abbey to the king, was not in the least bit controversial, as the estate belonged to him, and the sale was conducted with the assistance of senior officers of the crown, the vice-treasurer of Ireland, Sir Adam Loftus, and the chancellor of the exchequer, Sir Robert Meredith. However, on closer inspection there is not much doubt that Ormond came out of the deal much better than the king, who was led to believe by Wentworth that Leix Abbey was a worthwhile acquisition. Ormond received the astonishing sum of £10,568 (stg) for the estate, a figure that represented more than 100

---

295 E.g., Brereton, *Travels*, 123–69; R. Gillespie, 'The end of an era: Ulster and the outbreak of the 1641 rising', in Brady & Gillespie (ed.), *Natives & newcomers*, 195–6. 296 NLI, D 4056; *CSPI, 1633–47*, 165. 297 NLI, D 3953–4. Anktill had been implicated in the Castlehaven scandal of 1631: Herrup, *House*, 18–9, 60–1. 298 Kelly, 'Ormond and Strafford', greatly improves our knowledge of their relationship, but perhaps underestimates the governor's influence over the young earl. See Edwards, 'Poisoned chalice', 75–82. 299 Knowler (ed.), *Strafford letters*, ii, 93; Bod. Lib., Carte Ms 1, fol. 163.

times its annual value to the earl (Wentworth had told the king it would cost just ten years purchase).[300] Considering the low prices for Irish land during the 1630s, a price of 100 years' purchase for Leix Abbey was exorbitant. In effect Wentworth helped the earl to clear part of his debt by plundering the king's coffers. Although there was only a small risk of being caught – between them Ormond and Wentworth controlled the valuation of the estate – it was a dangerous transaction to oversee, potentially disastrous to both men should the king ever become suspicious of the management of his Irish revenues.[301]

For all his pains, however, James Butler, twelfth earl of Ormond was still enormously in debt by the beginning of the 1640s,[302] still owing in the region of £40–50,000 to a variety of creditors. Despite Wentworth's protection he had been overwhelmed by the problems of his inheritance. He had fought a losing battle against several of his chief creditors (all Englishmen) in the Irish courts. Richard Millar, the wealthy London merchant, had relentlessly pursued Earl James for the repayment of two debts, £2,500 due to himself, and £11,000 originally due to the earl of Holland. That Millar had royal backing insured Ormond could not escape his demands. Other London merchants had also proved hard to shake off – in 1634 the lord mayor of London, Sir Robert Parkhurst, brought his influence to bear over a debt of £2,700 long due to him, having his grievance with Ormond heard before the court of castle chamber in Dublin. The earl of Middlesex had similarly pressed his claims for repayment, eventually (by 1635) recouping every penny of the £8,100 he was due, before pressing on to demand more in interest. Ormond had tried to frustrate him by suggesting that Wentworth and the Irish Council should decide the matter, but Middlesex was able to persuade King Charles to have the debt examined by a four-man crown committee that included Ormond's principal English adversary, the earl of Arundel.[303] Roger Nott of London had likewise collected a debt of £1,600 from Ormond after 1635, and the colonist Arthur Annesley secured £410 that he was owed in 1638.[304] Having to pay out so much so quickly did not ease Earl James' burden. If anything, it made his task more difficult, forcing him to avoid many other lesser creditors, something that, in turn, added to his expenses for his junior creditors were forced to pursue him with increasing desperation. His credit was poor, irreparably damaged. In late 1642 a cloth merchant wrote demanding that the earl should honour his promise of August 1641 to pay his bills, amounting to £226. A money order for £100 signed by Ormond had proved worthless, causing the merchant to bemoan his fate: 'this promise from your lordship I took as good as any security whatsoever'.[305]

300 Edwards, 'Poisoned chalice', 74, n.113. **301** Knowler (ed.), *Strafford letters*, ii, 82, 90, 103; NA, Lodge MSS, Rolls, v, 401(2); *CSPI, 1633–47*, 175. **302** Carte, *Ormond*, v, 358. **303** *CSPI, 1633–47*, 176, 191–2; NLI, D 3974, 4063; ibid., Ms 11,058 (1); Sheffield City Library, Str p17, nos. 168, 185; TCD, Ms 10,726 (1)–(2); ibid., Ms 2512: 116 **304** For Nott, Representative Church Body Library, St Werburgh's Muniments; for Annesley, Oxfordshire AO, Valentia Collection, Bundle 33/1. My thanks to Dr James Murray for the St Werburgh's reference. **305** HMC, *Ormonde MSS, 1572–1660*, 53–4.

To all intents and purposes, Earl James was a bankrupt. In a sense, he was fortunate that the 1641 rebellion occurred when it did. Had the war broken out later it is hard to know how much of the enormous patrimony that had descended to him would have remained in his possession when the mid-century troubles ended. The rebellion brought to a halt the pattern of dispersal and dissipation from which there had seemed no escape. It is all the more ironic, therefore, that when Kilkenny rose in revolt, the shire community intended to add political bankruptcy to his financial embarrassments, for they rebelled as much against him as the central government. They were not to know, of course, that by doing so and losing they would lay the foundations for his political and financial salvation after the Restoration.

CONCLUSION

It is perhaps remarkable that the 1641 rebellion in Co. Kilkenny can be traced back to so mundane a matter as the death in infancy of the only son of the tenth earl of Ormond in 1590. But as A.J.P. Taylor once argued of the origins of World War One, great events do not require great beginnings. The demise of the Black Earl's heir set in motion a chain of events as momentous for the Ormond lordship as the failure of his namesake the seventh earl to sire a male heir a century earlier. In the end the fortunes of the Butlers of Ormond rose (after 1515) and fell (after 1614) because two earls failed to father enough male offspring to outlive them and so succeed unopposed to the earldom and its lands. Both succession crises left the gate open for protracted crown interference in the Ormond lordship. On both occasions the crown got its way, rearranging the succession to further its own power in the south of Ireland. The only difference was that after 1515, by allowing the earldom to grow in power and using it as a vanguard of royal government, the crown succeeded in expanding in its wake, whereas after 1614, by allowing the earldom to decline, the crown found it lacked the strength to replace it and so lost its tentative grip on the south.

PART II

The Rise and Fall of the Ormond Lordship:
A Political Narrative, 1515–1642

CHAPTER 3

Revival and rift: the politics of coign and livery, 1515–69

The year 1515 was significant not just for heralding a change in the Ormond succession. The death in August of Thomas Butler, the seventh earl of Ormond, marked a turning point in the history of Co. Kilkenny (and the south of Ireland also). By facilitating the rise of Piers Ruadh Butler of Pottlerath the earl's demise ushered in an era of profound change when Kilkenny again assumed a central role in Irish political life. Hitherto, for fifty years, with the Ormond family absent in England, Kilkenny had lain under the sway of the Fitzgeralds, earls of Kildare, and the strongest family in the county, the Butlers of Pottlerath, had consolidated their standing through service to the Kildare cause.[1] Ormond's death shattered the Fitzgeralds' local ascendancy. Almost immediately Piers Butler broke with Kildare, negotiated an understanding with the Kilkenny gentry, and set about rebuilding the Ormond country as a strong military lordship, no longer a subjugate region, but an assertive, expansionist one. In time Kilkenny's re-emergence would contribute to the collapse of Fitzgerald power nationally, and historians are agreed that following the disastrous Kildare revolt of 1534 the Butlers replaced the Fitzgeralds as the greatest dynasty in Anglo-Ireland. The following chapter is designed to tell this story in detail, and also to demonstrate the wider social and political effects of prolonged militarisation on a sixteenth century lordship.

It has not been generally recognised that the foundations of Kilkenny's renascence were unstable, resting largely on the military might of an enlarged Butler army, a body of men prone to violence and not easily controlled. When Piers Ruadh set about transforming Co. Kilkenny into an anti-Fitzgerald fortress after 1515, various representatives of the Butler dynasty became used to unfettered military authority. Those holding estates in frontier regions came to depend on larger retinues, and for obvious reasons would not risk forsaking their troops. The army, it transpired, had an inner vitality of its own. Once forces were in place, it proved very difficult to get rid of them: Piers' son James, the ninth earl of Ormond, did not live long enough for the limited reforms he had introduced in the 1540s to bear fruit. During the minority of James' successor, Thomas, the Black Earl, several commanders of the Butler

---

1 The ramifications of the Kildare/Pottlerath alliance are treated in D. Edwards, 'The Ormond lordship in County Kilkenny, 1515–1642', PhD thesis, Trinity College, Dublin 1998, 129–33. See also Beresford, 'The Butlers', 244–7.

army broke free of the earldom. Their independence was guaranteed by their abuse of coign and livery, the military supply system, which when left in their hands, allowed them enormous scope for local racketeering and intimidation.[2] The fragmentation of the army and growing military lawlessness inflicted damage on Butler/community relations and eventually posed a threat to the local authority of the earldom. Indeed, early in the reign of Elizabeth I it threatened to destroy the Ormond lordship in the county: in 1569, in deliberate defiance of the Black Earl's wishes, senior members of the Butler family chose to rebel rather than relinquish control of their bands of troops. And so it was that Kilkenny's political rejuvenation under a new line of Butler earls after 1515 rested on a paradox: externally what was perceived as the earls' greatest source of strength – the enormous Butler army – became internally their greatest source of weakness.[3]

Perhaps the most surprising aspect of the post-1515 revival of Ormond power in Co. Kilkenny is the insight it affords of the reality of government policy in Tudor Ireland. Correctly, historians have emphasised the outright hostility of the Tudor monarchy to the exercise of private military power by Irish lords; certainly, the need to demilitarise the country was a constant refrain of government documents of the time. However, many of these documents took the form of proposals for a future long-term 'reform' or remodelling of Irish society. As recent research has revealed, often the documents had little to do with ordinary day-to-day government behaviour;[4] moreover, if implemented the proposals they contained usually failed because they were not grounded in the realities of Irish political power and were overtaken by events.[5] The following chapter demonstrates the extent to which Tudor rule in Ireland was more short-term and tactical than long-term and strategic, for the overbearing military might that the Butlers enjoyed before 1569, and for which they were loudly condemned by government officials, was partly the government's creation. In the years immediately after 1515 the crown had wanted a large local army in Kilkenny, and this no matter how heavy a burden it placed on the people of the shire. The fact that it later denounced the Butler army as an instrument of repression and began exerting pressure for demilitarisation in the county merely reveals its reaction to a change in political circumstances. Prior to the fall of the Kildare Fitzgeralds a strong Butler army had been a royal *desideratum*; following their fall, and as government power began to spread out from Dublin, it was not. To understand how the maintenance of troops became the single biggest issue in local affairs, it is necessary to examine the reasons why the Tudor monarchy first became involved in the county after 1515.

---

2 For coign and livery see esp. Empey & Simms, 'Ordinances', 162–83.   **3** Edwards, 'Butler revolt', passim.   **4** Edwards, 'Collaboration', treats of the double standard of government objectives and government practice.   **5** For the crown's ill-fated pursuit of ambitious reform projects see esp. Brady, *Chief Governors*, passim; idem, 'Court, castle and country: the framework of government in Tudor Ireland', in Brady & Gillespie (ed.), *Natives & Newcomers*, 22–49.

THE MOTIVES FOR ENGLISH INTERVENTION

At its most basic, the crown renewed its interest in Co. Kilkenny because of growing fears over English security in Ireland. In 1515 King Henry VIII was an ambitious young monarch eager for fresh territory and military glory.[6] Two years earlier he had signalled these intentions by entering into conflict with France and Scotland, and although his armies had enjoyed success, the decision to go to war had necessitated an immediate improvement of the crown's defence of its Irish colony. The king's ministers feared Ireland might be a backdoor to England, and the threat of foreign intervention there, especially by the French, seemed real enough.[7] If the danger of further Franco-Scottish interference was to be minimised, King Henry would need to seize greater control of all areas of the country, Co. Kilkenny included.

The internal situation in Ireland also demanded immediate attention, for it was recognised that the English colony in the country had shrivelled. Outside the Pale the majority of the local lords and chieftains failed to offer even lip service to the king's authority. Certain parts of the country that had long been loyalist strongholds, among them Co. Kilkenny, were now not nearly so accessible to crown influence as they had once been.[8] For three centuries the crown had been accustomed to view Kilkenny as the heart of a 'Second Pale' in the south, a region stretching from southern Wexford to eastern Limerick where contact with England was so close as to be almost taken for granted.[9] Strategically, it was vital to keep it closely bound to the monarchy, for otherwise the First Pale around Dublin might be isolated and large parts of the southern seaboard become exposed to foreign ambition.

There were two courses open to King Henry. The first, instant reconquest, he considered too expensive, much preferring the second course, a gradual expansion of royal power from Dublin outwards, whereby the crown could build up a new network of relationships with sympathetic regional rulers willing to do his bidding. It was in this context that Piers Butler fitted in. As an experienced swordsman hungry for greater status, he was a suitable candidate to baptise the policy in the Second Pale, especially since his desire for recognition as the next earl of Ormond gave Henry a carrot and stick with which to manipulate him. As stated in the previous chapter, Wolsey more than anyone else was responsible for persuading Henry to view Piers Ruadh in this light.

The fact that Piers was the one person in Leinster capable of undermining the Kildare Fitzgeralds acted greatly in his favour.[10] Although the Fitzgeralds had

---

6 J.J. Scarisbrick, *Henry VIII*, 40–4; R.B. Wernham, *Before the Armada: the growth of English foreign policy, 1485–1588* (London 1966), ch. 6–8, S. Doran, *England and Europe, 1485–1603* (London 1986), 23–32. **7** W. Palmer, *The problem of Ireland in Tudor foreign policy* (Woodbridge 1994), 26, 29, 31. **8** E.g., since the 1440s Kilkenny had rarely contributed to the subsidy: D.B. Quinn, 'The Irish parliamentary subsidy in the 15th and 16th centuries', *PRIA*, 42 C (1934–5), 228–9. **9** Empey, 'Butler lordship', 174–87. **10** For Fitzgerald power see McCorristine, *Revolt*; D.B. Quinn, 'The hegemony of the earls of Kildare, 1494–1520', *NHI* ii (Oxford 1987); Lennon, *Sixteenth-century*

long been the monarchy's principal Irish agents, the king lacked faith in them, and he chose Piers as the messenger of his dissatisfaction. It proved a momentous decision. By attempting to reduce the 'Geraldines' King Henry was not just seeking to alter the pecking order among the country's ruling families; rather, his action signalled an essential change in the composition of Irish political life. Under his auspices, it came to pass that England was once again ready to assume a direct interventionist role in Ireland, chiefly by unsettling the *status quo*, blatantly tampering with the regional balance of power. Some areas suffered more than others under this new policy. Because of its strategic position Co. Kilkenny fared better than most. In the following years Piers Butler received extensive royal protection for his Kilkenny/Tipperary lordship while, in contrast, the Fitzgeralds had their autonomy in Co. Kildare regularly challenged by the crown.

Henry VIII's decision to knock the Geraldines off their perch requires some explanation, not least because it has been argued in recent years that the crown had grown stronger in Ireland since the late fifteenth century because of Kildare support.[11] Suffice it to say that, whatever about Kildare service before 1515, after that date Henry VIII and Wolsey were no longer convinced of the Fitzgeralds' dependability. Rather, as reports on the state of Ireland were commissioned, it seemed that the extraordinary level of power enjoyed by Kildare clashed all too visibly with English security interests. To contradict the assertions of one historian, King Henry had cause to doubt that the ninth earl of Kildare was an 'effectual' chief governor of Ireland.[12] Far from perceiving the Fitzgeralds as agents of royal influence, contemporary critics observed that the earl and his family did much as they liked, making peace and war in Ireland without the consent of the king's council,[13] and it was noted that their dynastic policies had contributed directly to the gaelicisation or de-anglicisation of large parts of the country. This included Co. Kilkenny.[14]

Conditions in Kilkenny suggest that fears of a decline of 'the Englishry of Ireland' were well founded. Over the previous century the shire had been gradually transformed into a region where Gaelic customs were in common use. From the 1420s, under the direction of the then earl of Ormond, the White Earl, a series of local ordinances had been introduced that edged Kilkenny towards what Nicholls has termed 'a purely Gaelic system of government'.[15] A little later, with successive earls of Ormond absent in England, the gaelicisation of the county had accelerated due to the efforts of the Pottlerath Butlers: the statutes of Kilcash, by which large parts of Kilkenny and Tipperary were placed under a Gaelic system of criminal law, had been put together in 1478 by James Mac Edmund Butler, Piers Ruadh's father.[16]

Ireland, 68–77; M. Lyons, *Gearóid Óg Fitzgerald* (Dublin 1998).   **11** Ellis, *Tudor Ireland*, 66; Idem, 'Tudor policy', 240, 249; idem, *Tudor frontiers & noble power: the making of the British state* (Oxford 1995), 143.   **12** Ellis, 'Tudor policy', 249.   **13** Ellis, *Tudor Ireland*, 100–2. I further disagree with Professor Ellis' suggestion that Henry was not greatly suspicious of overmighty subjects like the Fitzgeralds (ibid., 101).   **14** *SP, Henry VIII*, ii, 8–9.   **15** K.W. Nicholls, 'Anglo-French Ireland and after', *Peritia* 1 (1982), 401.   **16** NLI, Ms 2551, fol. 2v.

The Kildare Fitzgeralds, the patrons of the Pottlerath Butlers, were responsible for continuance of the trend. Having headed the royal government in Ireland since 1496, they had the capacity to recover Kilkenny for the crown, but had attempted no such thing, preferring to let it drift free of royal control under a friendly puppet regime of their own choosing. By 1515 there was genuine concern that Kilkenny would cease to serve the crown as part of the Second Pale.[17] As the anglophile inhabitants of the midlands breadbasket later complained, English-style assize sessions were no longer held in the county, leaving the administration of justice to the sheriffs, who were invariably Kildare nominees and as such were seemingly not required to make returns (known as proffers) to the royal exchequer in Dublin.[18] Crown observers were further alarmed by reported gaelicisation of the shrievalty, learning that the sheriffs worked closely with the native Gaelic judges, the brehons, and used 'none other law' but the statutes of Kilcash.[19] Not only was Kilkenny adrift of English government in Dublin, it no longer adhered to English law.

A NEW DIRECTION

Disenchantment among the local gentry or 'Englishry' of the shire midlands played no small part in facilitating the emergence of Piers Ruadh Butler as the new overlord, despite his past record under Kildare. By 1515 (omitting Upper Ossory) there were two Co. Kilkennys, an uphill Gaelic one and a lowland English one.[20] Piers already had a steady grip of the gaelicised areas through his allies and clients among the Grace, Walsh, Purcell, Den and Kavanagh lineages, but he needed the support of the anglophile central plain if his bid for the earldom of Ormond was to have a solid basis. This presented him with a dilemma, the resolution of which was destined to determine the success or failure of his career.

To obtain midlands support Piers had to appear to reject his Gaelic past by pinning his banners to an English standard, for the ties that bound the midlands of the county to the crown were still very strong. In 1517, for instance, Kilkenny corporation passed a bye-law requiring all future elected sovereigns to take an oath of loyalty to the king of England.[21] Fortunately for Piers, making such a commitment to the English connection was not difficult. He needed to improve his standing with the monarchy so that his claims to the Ormond title would not be ignored at Whitehall, where his dynastic rivals, the Boleyns and St Legers, were presently doing their best to insure his exclusion from the earldom.

But this was to reckon without the Fitzgeralds of Kildare. Piers Butler's pledge to uphold English ways was not enough to satisfy the gentry and merchants of the central Nore valley of his reliability. Traditional Ormondists, hostile to the house of Kildare, they expected him to remove the Fitzgeralds from

---

17 Canny, *Reformation to Restoration*, 12.   **18** Hore & Graves (ed.), *Social state*, 78; D.B. Quinn, 'Anglo-Irish local government, 1485–1534', *IHS* I (1939), 356.   **19** Hore & Graves (ed.), *Social state*, 99–100, 112.   **20** Chaper 1 above.   **21** Neely, 'Kilkenny city', 43.

a dominant position in the shire. Like the crown, to encourage him they were willing for the moment to put up with his worst excesses in order to wrest control of the area back into non-Geraldine hands. But for Piers, breaking with the Fitzgeralds – his wife Margaret's family, and his own foster-kin – did not come easily. They had protected him for more than thirty years. He could hardly be expected to disown them in an instant, especially as he could not yet be certain of the strength of crown support. In the months immediately following the seventh earl of Ormond's death, there was a noticeable hesitancy about Piers Ruadh's actions as he gradually accustomed himself to the idea that his bid for the vacant Ormond earldom would require a dramatic and thoroughgoing break with the past.

In the event, Piers Ruadh did not dare jump from the safety of the Fitzgerald political structure until he was pushed. At a crucial moment in his career his former protectors let him (and his wife) down; had they not done so, the history of sixteenth-century Kilkenny might have been much different. In the late summer of 1515 the ninth earl of Kildare, Garret Óg Fitzgerald, delayed giving recognition to Piers, his brother-in-law, as the new earl of Ormond, only doing so in April 1516,[22] many months after old Earl Thomas' demise. For Piers the delay was a severe blow, and not just because of the insult of having his previous service to the Geraldines overlooked. In the meantime his English rivals for the earldom had stolen a march on him, gaining the king's ear to press their claim. Kildare had allowed this to happen, more concerned with keeping up with the rising star of the Boleyn family at court than furthering the ambitions of Red Piers Butler of Pottlerath, a man who was still only a minor character on the political map. Indeed, by his failure to offer speedy recognition Kildare probably intended to sabotage Piers' plans to succeed to the title. From a Geraldine perspective, it made little sense to connive at the resurgence of the Ormond lordship under a resident earl. Instead it seemed best to keep Piers as he was, small but manageable in Kilkenny, while welcoming the prospect of a Boleyn–St Leger succession, which would continue the tradition of absenteeism in the earldom of Ormond, a key foundation of the Kildare ascendancy.

The snub proved to be a bad miscalculation, immediately arousing Piers Butler's enmity, and producing the first major chink in the network of alliances around which the Fitzgeralds had developed their countrywide supremacy. Piers' wife, Margaret Fitzgerald, was also angered. Her brother Kildare had blocked her path to becoming a countess. From this date onwards she seems to have broken from her family and dedicated herself entirely to the Butlers' cause. Later evidence suggests she played a key role in steering Piers towards that policy of reanglicisation which allowed him to reach an accommodation with the Englishry of the shire midlands. Years afterwards she was remembered as '[the]

---

22 In his treatment of the Ormond inheritance dispute, Professor Ellis fails to take note of the long delay before Kildare declared his support for Piers, an oversight that leads him to assume Kildare was always steadfast behind his brother-in-law. If this was so, then why did Piers Ruadh break away? (Ellis, *Tudor Ireland*, 103–4; idem, *Reform & revival*, 157–8).

mean at those days whereby her husband's country was reclaimed from the slut-
tish and unclean Irish custom to English keeping and civility'.[23]

Piers Ruadh probably concluded his new deal with the midlands Englishry
by November 1516. With the assistance of the bishop of Ossory, Oliver
Cantwell, a number of ageing Ormond servants were brought variously to
Jerpoint Abbey, Callan Priory and other church centres to swear that Piers was
the rightful heir to the Ormond title. Others who came forward to substanti-
ate his claim included some of the more powerful landlords in Tipperary, and
the depositions were later collated and proclaimed before James Shortal of
Ballylorcaine 'and numberless other persons' convened for the occasion at
Fennell Hill in a 'public assembly of the county of Kilkenny'.[24]

Over the following twelve months Piers expanded his foothold in Tipperary,
bringing the baron of Dunboyne to heel with a show of force in the area. By
this time his representatives included the southern Kilkenny landowner David
Fitzgerald (alias Baron) of Brownesford, who probably commanded some of his
forces.[25] Those who put themselves forward to act as *slanys* – guarantors of the
peace after the Gaelic fashion – included the sovereigns of the towns of Kilkenny
and Callan. By acting as *slanys* they were seen to co-operate for the moment
with Piers' use of Gaelic customs in order to advance his cause. In return, as
part of his treaty with the vanquished Dunboyne, Piers made a point of paying
lip service to the principles of English law, forcing the baron to agree in future
to obey the award of the local assize court.[26]

As yet Piers had not openly declared his opposition to Kildare. Rather, he
had maintained an outward show of friendship, biding his time until his strength
had reached a level appropriate to his ambition. Significantly, Kildare had been
completely taken in by the act, so much so, in fact, that he had actually helped
Piers in 1517, offering him his assistance against Dunboyne, and putting himself forward as one of the *slanys* of the treaty. It was to be Kildare's last act of
friendship towards his brother-in-law. After 1517 Piers struck forth on his own,
no longer content with second place in the Butler territories. Ironically,
Dunboyne's defeat was probably the deciding factor in the breakaway. Previously
the baron had been the one Butler lord capable of barring Piers Ruadh's path.
With him beaten, Piers had most of Tipperary as well as Kilkenny at his feet.
At once he ceased paying Kildare the sum of 100 marks per annum that the earl
charged him for protection. Likewise he prevented his foe from continuing to
collect the two-thirds share of the revenues of the Ormond estate that had fallen
into Kildare's hands while the absentee seventh earl of Ormond was alive.[27]
Nevertheless, the situation confronting Piers when he eventually turned his
army against Kildare was a daunting one.

23 Miller & Power (ed.), *Holinshed's Irish Chronicle*, 256. **24** *COD*, iv, no. 33 (4). **25** Alias 'David
de Geraldinis, Baron of Haliabiron'; he acted as one of Piers' negotiators in the subsequent settlement of the conflict with Dunboyne (ibid., no. 40). **26** Ibid. The gaelicisation of Tipperary
under the Dunboynes is noted in Beresford, 'The Butlers', 236–8. **27** *SP, Henry VIII*, ii, 106;
Quinn, 'Hegemony', 659–60.

PREPARING FOR WAR, 1515–28

Kildare's forces were uncomfortably close. Over previous decades Geraldine troops had been free to infiltrate the Ormond lordship, and they had established themselves in strong positions all around the borders of Kilkenny. In neighbouring Co. Wexford the Fitzgeralds had moved into Roche's country and the Fassagh Bantry, and they also had an important garrison at Old Ross.[28] In Carlow their power was greater still. They had assured themselves of a string of castles in the county, among them Cloghgrenan, which guarded the road from Kilkenny to Carlow town.[29] The Kildare family enjoyed excellent relations with Carlow's Anglo-Irish gentry at this time, having their garrisons housed and fed with the consent of local landowners.[30] In Tipperary too the Kildare Fitzgeralds were ready to answer Piers' challenge. Already possessed of the manor of Knockgraffon,[31] after 1500 they had secured further lands there from the Salls, Uniacks and Ballykelly Butlers.[32]

Worst of all, however, the Geraldines also had a toehold in Co. Kilkenny. In the north-east of the shire they retained the friendship of some of the O'Brennans of Idough, who were anxious to keep the Butlers and the rest of the Kilkenny community out of their mountain territory. In October 1515 Kildare agreed terms with Geoffrey O'Brennan, who was to occupy a castle that the earl owned at Moynleat.[33] Moynleat (the present-day Moyne) was of major strategic significance, standing on high ground near Kilmocar – Piers Butler's main outpost in the area – and guarding one of the principal southern avenues into O'Brennan country.[34] Equally worrying to Piers, Kildare had other friends in the county. In the town of Kilkenny his interests were ably represented by one of the merchant elite, Thomas Langton, a former sovereign of the town, who was granted a lease of part of Kildare's estate in the shire in 1518 or 1519.[35] Further afield, Kildare also had an agent at Callan, Thomas Grace, whose task was probably to administer the earl's nearby lordship of Ballycallan.[36] Clearly, the late fifteenth and early sixteenth centuries had been a period of mounting Geraldine recruitment in Co. Kilkenny.

It had also been a period of Geraldine fortification. By 1515 the earl of Kildare had two major strongholds in the shire. The first of these, in the east at Drumroe – the present Mount Loftus – was another recent acquisition, purchased in April

---

28 Details of the Kildare presence in Wexford can be found in the Duke of Leinster papers in Belfast (PRONI, D 3078/1/18/9–22); for a useful brief discussion, see Ellis, *Tudor frontiers*, 119–23. **29** They acquired it *c*.1500 from 'Arthur, son of Arthur Kavanagh' (PRONI, D 3078/1/1/3, fol. 157). My thanks to Kenneth Nicholls for lending me his notes on this source. The Kildares also held Clonmore and Tulleophelim (NLI, Ms 2506, fol. 1r). **30** Hore & Graves (ed.), *Social state*, 160. **31** NLI, Ms 2506, fol. 1r; Mac Niocaill (ed.), *Crown surveys*, 308–9. **32** PRONI, D 3078/1/22/1–5. **33** Mac Niocaill (ed.), *Crown surveys*, 245. **34** Sadly nothing now remains of Moynleat Castle; perhaps it was destroyed by the Butlers? **35** The precise date is uncertain: Mac Niocaill (ed.), *Crown surveys*, 248. Langton was still on good terms with Kildare in May 1524: ibid., 255. He had been portreeve of Kilkenny in 1511 (Prim, 'Memorials', 69). **36** MacNiocaill, *Crown surveys*, 330; St Kieran's College, Carrigan MSS, Vol. 18, unpaginated; NLI, Ms 2506, fol. 1r.

1509 from Theobald Butler fitz Robert.[37] Its military features were fairly obvious. Built on a steep hill near the banks of the River Barrow, it had a commanding view of the countryside between Graiguenamanagh and Leighlinbridge on the Kilkenny/Carlow border, and also offered a wide prospect of the movement of traffic between Gowran and Thomastown. As such it was one of the more important castles in the Ormond territories. Not only the eastern Kilkenny Butlers, but also the MacMurrough Kavanaghs of Borris in Carlow, lay within its range, and its potential to control the Barrow was confirmed by the acquisition of land at Powerstown, Paulstown and Shankill.[38] Kildare made shrewd use of the fort. Continuing the theme of recruitment, he had handed it over on an annual lease to Theobald fitz Edmund Butler of Neigham, Piers Ruadh's rival for the earldom of Ormond in Co. Kilkenny. It was a classic piece of Geraldine statecraft, strengthening one Ormond claimant against another so as to keep the two divided. The grant seriously reduced Piers' room for manoeuvre. Any future attempt to dislodge the Neigham line from Drumroe Castle would have to depend on speed and surprise, for the Neigham Butlers might receive reinforcements from the Fitzgerald garrison at Old Ross in Wexford.

Piers Ruadh faced a similar problem with Kildare's second stronghold in Kilkenny, at Glashare in the north-west. Like Drumroe, Glashare Castle occupied a key sight, defending one of the main avenues linking Kilkenny to the MacGiollapadraigs' country in Upper Ossory. It also stood within striking distance of Thurles and Templemore in Tipperary, two of Piers's outlying manors. Glashare had been Kildare property since the 1300s,[39] and probably in the mid-fifteenth century the dynasty had rebuilt it into the 5-storey tower house which stands there today. The improvements continued into Piers' time, with cross-shaped gun-holes cut into its walls early in the sixteenth century, signalling the introduction of firearms to the garrison there.[40] Attempts to invest the castle would meet stiff resistance, especially if Kildare summoned the help of his nearby ally, MacGiollapadraig.

It was Kildare's capacity to raise reinforcements that tested Piers Butler most. The Geraldine military machine was based on delegation, for an earl of Kildare depended less on the size of his own army than on the willingness of his relatives, allies and clients to lend him additional forces.[41] Through his network of supporters he could assemble a large army at relatively short notice. At the battle of Knockdoe in 1504, for example, the eighth earl of Kildare, Garret Mór, had led an army against the Clanricard Burkes that included soldiers from most parts of the country, as segments of the O'Neills and O'Donnells from Ulster, the MacDermotts and O'Connors Roe from Connaught, and the O'Farrells and O'Connors Faly from Leinster all answered his call to arms.[42] Piers Butler had himself been part of the Knockdoe force, so now that he intended to break from Kildare he knew that to be successful he had to construct a rival system of alliances.

37 PRONI, D 3078/1/1/3, fol. 156.   38 As note 29 above.   39 St John Brooks (ed.), *Knights' fees*, 181–2.   40 For gun-holes see C. Cairns, 'Guns and Castles in Tipperary', *Irish Sword*, 16/63 (1985), 112–14.   41 Ellis, *Tudor frontiers*, 128, 132–5.   42 Lennon, *Sixteenth-century Ireland*, 65–7.

It proved possible to do so. Although the Kildare dynasty could boast of a countrywide chain of political associates and sympathisers, they had not befriended everyone on the map; far from it. The manner in which they had built up their power had alienated as many lords and chieftains as it had secured to their cause. In a militarised society like Ireland, where neighbouring rulers squabbled frequently over territory, the price of friendship with one lord was enmity with another. Kildare's list of adopted foes was extensive: though he had the largest network of friends, he also had more enemies than any other Irish lord. As Piers Butler soon proved, support for Kildare was noticeably slim in the south of the country, around the borders of Cos. Kilkenny and Tipperary.

Arguably Kildare's most stubborn opponents in Leinster (and Piers' most useful source of support) were to be found among the O'Mores of Laois.⁴³ Led by capable soldier-chieftains such as Connell Mac David and Melaghlin Mac Owney, for many years they had irritated the Geraldines, turning the Kildare/Laois border at Fassagh Reban into a military wasteland.⁴⁴ In 1513 it was at their hands that Garret Mór, eighth earl of Kildare, had met his end, shot by an O'More assassin when out watering his horse in the River Greese near Kilkee Castle.⁴⁵ Thereafter the O'Mores' war with the Fitzgeralds had intensified. Early in 1514 the new earl of Kildare, Garret Óg, had come to Laois seeking revenge, and his campaign on that occasion helped to create the climate whereby many O'Mores were subsequently willing to accept Piers Butler's overtures for an anti-Kildare alliance. The Geraldine army had destroyed their fortress at Cullenagh; moreover, the great wood separating them from Co. Kildare had been cut down.⁴⁶

The O'Carrolls of Ely also considered a link-up with Piers. Like the O'Mores they had long resisted Fitzgerald dominance. Hence their appearance at Knockdoe, when they had sided with the Burkes of Clanricard and O'Briens of Thomond against Kildare and his host of allies. On the losing side then, they had continued to fight on regardless, but gradually the Fitzgeralds had closed in on them. At the time of his assassination in 1513, the eighth earl of Kildare had been attempting a full-scale siege of the O'Carrolls' principal fortress, Leap Castle in southern Offaly. Had it not been for the dramatic intervention of the O'More assassin, the earl would probably have lived to take the castle and crush the O'Carrolls in the region. As it was, his successor Garret Óg was able to seize Leap in 1516, an event that signalled a crisis for the O'Carrolls that not even Piers Butler's friendship could ease.⁴⁷

---

43 It is difficult to accept Professor Ellis's claim (Ellis, *Tudor frontiers*, 228) that the Kildares' close ties to 'Gaelic chiefs like … O'More' had helped to stabilise the Pale frontier in the period before 1534. To which O'More chief is he referring? As argued here, good O'More/Kildare relations only commenced in the mid-1520s, and even then it was only a section of the O'Mores that supported Kildare power. **44** D.B. Quinn, 'Irish Ireland, English Ireland', *NHI*, ii, 634; W. Fitzgerald, 'The O'Mores and their territory of Leix', *Kildare Arch. Soc. Jn.* 6 (1909–11), 6. **45** J. Canon O'Leary & E. O'Leary, *History of the Queen's County* (2 vols., Dublin 1907), i, 421. **46** W.M. Hennessy & B. MacCarthy (ed.), *Annals of Ulster* (4 vols., Dublin 1893), s.a. 1514. **47** Venning, 'O'Carrolls of Offaly', 182–3.

The growth of Geraldine power in Ely had produced a split in the O'Carroll dynastic structure. Though some members of the dynasty continued to resist the Fitzgeralds, after Leap Castle fell others reckoned it was time to yield to the inevitable and seek an understanding with Kildare. For these, the pro-Fitzgerald O'Carrolls, cooperation with Piers Butler was undesirable, as it would antago-nise Kildare and invite further punitive actions by his followers. They could justify their opposition to Piers on the grounds that the O'Carrolls' greatest ene-mies were not the Fitzgeralds but the Butlers, who laid claim to the territory of Ely O'Carroll as part of Tipperary in right of the earldom of Ormond. This anti-Butler viewpoint was destined to gain the upper hand over the course of the next few years, as more and more of the O'Carrolls came to suspect Piers Butler's motives; for the moment, however, he was able to persuade many of his friendship, enough to cause concern for Kildare. The O'Carrolls divided along factional lines, with opposition to Piers revolving around 'Mulroney the Great' and his son Feargananym O'Carroll, whilst Donough and Owney O'Carroll probably led those opposed to Kildare.[48]

A comparable situation evolved in Piers's relations with the MacMurrough Kavanagh lordship to the east of Co. Kilkenny. At the start of the sixteenth cen-tury the 'king of Leinster', Murrough Ballagh Kavanagh, was earnestly opposed to the ongoing aggrandisement of his Carlow lands by the earl of Kildare. Resolved to preserve the boundaries of his little realm in the Barrow valley he too had fought on the losing side against Kildare at Knockdoe in 1504.[49] Following the battle the expansion of the Fitzgeralds into Kavanagh country seemed irre-versible. With Murrough's death in 1511 the lineage split into pro-Geraldine and anti-Geraldine factions.[50] By the early 1520s Piers Butler had negotiated a deal with Maurice Kavanagh, one of three rival candidates for the Leinster kingship. In return for surrendering the Wicklow manor of Arklow to Piers, Maurice was promised half its rents and profits for the rest of his life.[51] Although Kildare undoubtedly had the upper hand with most of the Kavanagh lineage, Piers Butler was ready to force him out of Kilkenny with the help of his own Kavanagh allies.

In early Tudor Ireland most alliances between territorial neighbours were short-term expedients,[52] and those made by Piers Butler with Connell Mac Melaghlin O'More, Donough and Owney O'Carroll, and Maurice Kavanagh, were entirely typical. Based solely on mutual hostility to the Fitzgeralds, it was implicitly understood by all parties concerned that, should the threat from Kildare decline significantly, and Piers's own power grow too great, each of the alliances would dissolve overnight.

The negotiation of the agreements vastly improved Butler's military posi-tion. According to contemporary estimates, more than 5 per cent of all soldiers

48 Ibid., 184–5. 49 R. Butler (ed.), *The annals of Thady Dowling* (Dublin 1849), 33, s.a. 1504. 50 Ibid., s.a. 1512 (*sic*); K.W. Nicholls, 'Late medieval Irish annals: two fragments', *Peritia* 2 (1983), 100. 51 L. Price, 'The Byrnes' Country in the 16th century and the manor of Arklow', *JRSAI* 62 (1932), 55–6. 52 P.J. Duffy, D. Edwards & E. FitzPatrick, 'Salvaging Gaelic Ireland, *c.*1250–*c.*1650', in Duffy, Edwards & FitzPatrick (ed.), *Gaelic Ireland*, 45.

Chart 3.1   Gaelic armies on the Kilkenny frontier, c.1500

Chieftain	Horse	Galloglass	Kerne	Total
MacMurrough-Kavanagh	200	60	300	560
O'More of Laois	60	60	200	320
O'Carroll of Ely	80	60	140	280
MacGiollapadraig of Upper Ossory	40	60	60	160
O'Brennan of Idough	0	0	40	40
O'Ryan of Farren O'Ryan	12	0	24	36
O'Nolan of Forth O'Nolan	12	0	20	32

Source: Liam Price, 'Armed forces of the Irish chiefs in the early sixteenth century', *JRSAI* 62 (1932), 203–4

in Ireland were situated along Kilkenny's northern and eastern borders, with nearly 1,450 men based there, hired by the seven main Gaelic dynasties of the region. By befriending some of the claimants to the chieftaincies Piers was able to avail of at least part of his neighbours' armed strength. But before tackling Kildare he had to increase his own private army.

At the turn of the century the entire Butler dynasty in Kilkenny, divided between the rival elements of Pottlerath, Paulstown, Neigham and Annagh, could field just 280 men in the county, an insufficient force to challenge the Kildare Fitzgeralds, even if united.[53] Consequently it was in the area of military recruitment that Piers Ruadh scored one of the most important breakthroughs of his career. In 1517 he persuaded the rulers of Kilkenny town to lend him additional forces for his campaign against Kildare's satellites, the MacGiolla-padraigs. The expedition was successful, and when Piers returned with the army he presented the town councillors with an iron gate taken from the MacGiollapadraig fortress at Culahill; this was later displayed at the Tholsel (the town customs house) by order of the corporation.[54]

Piers Butler also succeeded in attracting support in some of the shire's other urban centres. At the beginning of the sixteenth century Gowran was experiencing difficulty defending itself against the Kavanaghs, who exacted protection money from it on a regular basis.[55] This threat receded following the death of the seventh earl of Ormond, when Piers Ruadh and his wife Margaret Fitzgerald established their presence there. Gowran Castle was re-edified and the town became the focus point of Piers and Margaret's policy of eastern consolidation and expansion.

53 Price, 'Armed forces', 203. Conditions were similar in Tipperary, where the Butlers of Pottlerath, Dunboyne and Cahir commanded 380 soldiers between them.   54 McNeill (ed.), *Liber Primus Kilkenniensis*, 139.   55 Hore & Graves (ed.), *Social state*, 78.

Critically, Piers Butler had little difficulty gaining the support of the Kilkenny gentry, especially the traditional feudal clients of the earldom of Ormond who dominated the frontier regions and lusted after a renewal of the Ormond lordship. Though the borderlands had been relatively peaceful for some time, lineages like of the Graces, St Legers, Shortals, Purcells, and Dens, were suspicious of the basis of the peace, which they recognised as a manifestation of Kildare dominance. None of the major gentry families of Co. Kilkenny had benefited much from a generation or more of indirect Geraldine rule – on the contrary, they had been excluded from national power – and some feared they would go into decline if the Kildare ascendancy continued.

Significantly, Piers Ruadh began his military build-up in Co. Kilkenny with the consent of the local gentry. What followed was not simply a case of an ambitious warlord forcing his will upon a county community. Rather, ambitious and ruthless though he undoubtedly was, for a decade after 1517 Piers Ruadh was beholden to the Kilkenny gentry for (i) supporting his claims to the vacant earldom of Ormond, and (ii) allowing him to increase his army till it was powerful enough to challenge the Kildares. The gentry, moreover, made sure to define the terms of their alliance with him. As Empey has noted, Piers's demands for the military tax known as coign and livery were very carefully proscribed: the local landowners only agreed to pay an acceptable rate, and this after the customary fashion.[56] They were willing to sustain high coign and livery charges, and impose it on their tenants, only if he acknowledged their right to refuse him. At times during the 1520s Piers Butler became frustrated with this arrangement. In 1526 he sought – and received – royal approval to impose coign and livery more freely in Kilkenny; specifically, he was given authority to quarter troops on recalcitrant landowners who refused to pay him what he demanded. Yet even with crown backing Butler found it hard to free himself from local restraint. An assembly of the county landowners was called and a manifesto drafted in which the gentry reiterated their willingness to maintain Piers's army only if he sought their approval 'by bill' (that is, by petition) and charged and assessed them in the usual way. Signed by nine of the principal gentlemen-freeholders of the shire – Walter Walsh, John Grace, James Shortal, Patrick Purcell, James Sweetman, Edmund St Leger, Roland Fitzgerald (alias Baron), Fulk Den and Edmund Blanchville – the 1526 manifesto made it clear that the main county families were not prepared to be bullied by their new overlord.[57] There was, moreover, a veiled threat underpinning the manifesto. Should Piers fail to impose coign and livery as agreed, the gentry would cease supporting him in his bid for the earldom of Ormond. Because of this Piers was uncomfortably dependent on the Kilkenny gentry until 1528, when his place in the Ormond succession was formalised with his creation as earl of Ossory.[58] Only after 1528 did he dare seriously to infringe his agreement with the local landowners. Until that date the

56 Empey & Simms, 'Ordinances', 176–7.   **57** *COD*, iv, no. 125.   **58** Dr Empey instead represents Piers as seeking to restore the principle of consent to local politics (Empey & Simms, 'Ordinances', 177).

new Butler army that he was able to field against the Kildares and their allies was as much the creation of the Kilkenny elite as it was his own.

With gentry assistance the Butler army in Co. Kilkenny almost trebled in size after 1517. Where once there had been 280 soldiers there gradually emerged a force of 750 men or more. The most important section of the army was the galloglasses, Scots-Irish mercenaries led principally by the Donegal MacSweeneys, whose force numbered 340 ('seventeen score') men organised as two 'battles' or great companies. An additional battle of 100 galloglasses subsequently appeared in the south of the shire under David Fitzgerald of Brownesford, elder brother of the bishop of Ossory.[59] It would appear from these figures that the Kilkenny population was burdened with one of the largest gatherings of *galloglaigh* anywhere in Ireland. Piers Butler 'levied their wages', or bonaght (*buannacht*), 'upon all the whole country' of Kilkenny, maintaining them 'continually', all year round, whether campaigning season or not.[60]. As indicated by the case of the Fitzgerald of Brownesford galloglasses, the gentry of the county participated in the build-up to a great extent, passing the costs of Butler military expansion onto the shoulders of the tenant and peasant classes. Below Piers Ruadh and his sons the gentry dominated the army's command structure. The Purcells of Foulkesrath and the Archdekins of Ballybawnmore served as hereditary captains of the Butler *kernetighe*, or household troops, each taking charge of a company of 'three score kerne in the county of Kilkenny'. In the north-west the Graces of Courtstown were responsible for 10 swordsmen based in their country.[61] Responsibility for cavalry (an especially expensive element) devolved mainly on other Kilkenny landowners, who raised small detachments of an overall force of 80–100 horse, with many fitting out just one or two horsemen from their estates; to help spread costs they were supplied with armour by the Butlers. Additional foot soldiers, or kerne, to the number of 100 or more, were raised by similar means.[62] According to an extant list of Butler sub-commanders drawn up a decade or so after Piers Ruadh's death, the Walshes, Comerfords, Dens, Shortals, Blanchvilles, Fitzgeralds, and Galls formed the backbone of the new Butler military machine.[63]

In London the crown did more than turn a blind eye to Piers Ruadh's growing strength; it actively supported him. In 1521/2, acting on the advice of Wolsey and the earl of Surrey, Henry VIII agreed to offer Piers the Irish lord deputyship.[64] Had he not been strong militarily, appearing capable of bringing a privately-funded army to the defence of the Pale, he could not have been con-

59 Hore & Graves (ed.), *Social state*, 109, 121.   **60** Ibid., 98.   **61** Ibid.; NLI, Ms 2507, fol. 65.   **62** Often an impression of the numbers of retainers kept by the gentry can be reconstructed from the pardons among the government fiants. During the early Elizabethan period, Kilkenny gentlemen usually had at least two soldiers, and sometimes as many as seven or eight, living with them in their castles and tower houses: *Ir. Fiants*, Eliz. I, nos. 1068, 1915 [Garryhiggin Castle troops]; ibid., nos. 924, 927, 950 [Cloghlea Castle]: ibid., nos. 90, 2064 [Butlerswood]; ibid., nos. 1065, 1903, 2031, 2058 [Glashare Castle]; ibid., nos. 950, 1919, 1929 [Ballyfoyle Castle]; ibid., no. 1184 [Lismaine Castle].   **63** NLI, Ms 2507, ff 21v–23v.   **64** The original patent for Piers' appointment was drafted by Wolsey: *Cal. Carew MSS, 1515–74*, 23; *SP, Henry VIII*, ii, 92; ibid., i, 73.

sidered for the post. In Surrey's words, Piers was ' the man of most experience of the feats of war of this country'.[65] Even when his first period as lord deputy ended in failure in 1524 his capacity to raise soldiers remained his single greatest political asset, one which the crown was determined to safeguard. In 1525 the king and his advisers ignored Kildare's searing denunciation of Piers' lawless and blatantly oppressive conduct in Leinster and Munster. As noted above, in 1526 the king sanctioned Piers' request that he be allowed to impose coign and livery in his territories by force, though this was contrary both to law and to the terms of a royal commission of 1523. The crown continued to nurture his aggressive behaviour for several years to come. In 1528 it even encouraged him to acquire land by conquest, a decision which necessarily envisaged his going to war against his neighbours. In a document drawn up just three days after his investiture as earl of Ossory, he was awarded the right to hold *in capite* by knight's service any lands 'which he might conquer, acquire or recover in the whole lordship or county of Kilkenny then in possession of the Irish'.[66] Also in 1528 Surrey, by now duke of Norfolk, added to Ossory's potential, ceding Piers a controlling interest in the Norfolk Irish inheritance in Carlow and Wexford, provided he could recover the lands from 'Irish enemies'.[67]

While Earl Piers was emerging from the shadows to become an increasingly dominant figure in Irish affairs, his rival Kildare was experiencing constant frustration with the crown. In 1519 Kildare was summoned to court to answer directly to the king for his abuse of the royal government in Ireland. A series of charges had been laid against him, probably penned by Robert Cowley of Kilkenny,[68] and as a result of the subsequent investigation Kildare had lost the lord deputyship. The earl's power would never be the same again. During the five years in which the office remained out of Kildare's hands, the crown substantially increased its hold over the Dublin administration in general, and over the deputyship in particular.[69] Nor did Kildare's reappointment as lord deputy in 1524 in place of Piers Butler signal a rebirth of Geraldine supremacy, for it was conceived as a temporary measure only. In 1526 he was again summoned to London to answer more charges of misgovernment, this time with crippling results, as the king consented to Wolsey's request to detain him indefinitely.[70] He was compelled to spend the next four years away, only returning home in 1530, by which time his position was further diminished, and in 1528 Piers of Ossory had again replaced him as lord deputy. For the duration of the 1520s, even when Kildare held high office, the momentum in Irish politics remained with the Butlers.

CONFRONTING KILDARE, 1518–34

But what of the actual fighting that took place between Earl Piers and the Fitzgeralds? Arguably the most interesting aspect of the Butler-Fitzgerald mili-

65 Ibid., ii, 57; *Cal. Carew MSS, 1515–74*, 16.   66 NA, Lodge MSS, Rolls, Vol. I, 58.   67 NLI, D 2158.   68 P. Gwyn, *The king's cardinal: the rise and fall of Thomas Wolsey* (London 1992), 242. 69 Ellis, *Reform & revival*, 20–1; Lyons, *Gearóid Óg*, 39–40.   70 Ibid., 42–3, 44.

tary conflict before 1534 was its intermittent nature. Though it raged for nearly twenty years, the war between Piers Ruadh and his brother-in-law Kildare was essentially a very limited business, breaking out sporadically once or twice a year across the south and east of the country, before returning to a state of uneasy ceasefire. There were no protracted campaigns before the 1534 Kildare revolt, just ambushes, skirmishes, raids and counter-raids.

Kildare was reluctant to confront Butler in open battle, presumably afraid of provoking King Henry by again participating in a major private war in Ireland (as he had done in 1515/16, thereby instigating his troubles with the monarch). The king's treatment of some of his leading nobles in England and Wales, especially his execution in 1521 of the last of the great lords of the Welsh march, Edward Stafford, third duke of Buckingham, can only have impressed upon Earl Garret that no-one, no matter how exalted, was safe from Henry VIII once they fell under suspicion. Buckingham's destruction must have worried Kildare all the more as the two were closely connected, his young half-brother, Thomas Fitzgerald, having been contracted in 1520 to marry the duke's bastard daughter, an arrangement which briefly endangered Geraldine interests when the crown moved against the duke and his allies.[71] Equally important, however, was Kildare's fear of fighting Piers Butler on disadvantageous terms and losing. His own personal army was not as strong as it might have been, for he had a permanent military force of just 160 galloglasses and 160 kerne, more than his predecessor, but still too few to risk in combat against Piers' growing horde.[72] Nor could Kildare depend any longer on superior firepower. For many years before 1515 the Geraldines had had a near monopoly of guns and artillery in the country;[73] this was no longer the case. By the 1520s the Butlers also had artillery pieces and firearms experts: in 1528 four Butler gunners, led by Piers Clinton of Graigerawe, were loaned by Piers of Ossory to his O'Carroll allies to fight Kildare's forces.[74]

The Butlers' growing threat was already apparent by 1518, when Piers Ruadh led his army across the Barrow to attack the Geraldine garrison at Mountgarret Castle in Co. Wexford. Piers probably had the support of some of his kinsmen among the Kavanaghs, because the commander of the garrison, Walter Meyler (a Wexford gentleman), had for some time been hostile towards elements of the Gaelic dynasty. The Butlers took the castle without major difficulty. In doing so they reduced the usefulness of the east Kilkenny stronghold of Drumroe to Kildare, as Mountgarret Castle had been one of Drumroe's main sources of reinforcement.[75] The seizure of Mountgarret also opened up western Wexford to future Butler interference. In later years Piers Ruadh's men regularly extended their activities into the area, and it is possible that he intended imposing coign and livery on as many Wexford people as possible in order to lighten the burden of the demand in Kilkenny and Tipperary.[76]

71 *LP Henry VIII*, iii, Pt. 1, no. 1070. See also Gwyn, *The king's cardinal*, 212–37, 253–64.   **72** McCorristine, *Revolt*, 26; Ellis, *Tudor frontiers*, 128.   **73** Lennon, *Sixteenth-century Ireland*, 72–3.   **74** *SP, Henry VIII*, ii, 121.   **75** Hore & Graves (ed.), *Social state*, 39–40.   **76** Ibid., 47.

Continued awareness of his political vulnerability in London and his mili-
tary weakness in Ireland compelled Kildare to fight an indirect war against the
Butlers. For most of the period before 1534 he opposed Earl Piers only through
his allies in the Leinster and Munster marchlands, calling on the Desmond
Fitzgeralds in the west, the MacGiollapadraigs, O'Connors, and some of the
O'Carrolls in the southern midlands, and pro-Geraldine segments of the
Kavanaghs in the east, to do his fighting for him along the borders of Kilkenny
and Tipperary. During the 1520s members of Kildare's immediate family only
attacked the Butlers directly on a handful of occasions. In December 1523 the
sheriff of Dublin was murdered by the earl of Kildare's brother, James Fitzgerald,
while riding to Kilkenny to spend Christmas with Piers.[77] Two years later, in
1525, another James Fitzgerald – possibly the same man – kidnapped another
of Piers' friends from the Pale.[78] More typically, in 1526, after Earl Garret's
second summons to London, his ally Cahir MacArt Kavanagh invaded Co.
Kilkenny and laid waste his rival Charles Kavanagh, one of Piers's staunchest
supporters, who lived at Drumroe. In a lightning attack, Cahir set fire to the
castle, and his enemy was burnt alive with his soldiers.[79] Likewise, when Piers
was re-installed as lord deputy in 1528, he was reluctant to take up the post,
knowing full well that Desmond and others would attack his lands. In the event
he was proved correct. No sooner had he left for Dublin than disturbances were
reported along the Kilkenny/Tipperary frontier.[80]

It should not be assumed, as some authorities have maintained, that Kildare's
strategy of indirect confrontation was enough to keep Piers Butler 'on the defensive'.[81] The Butler army proved strong enough to slug it out with Kildare, giving
as good as they received. In the mid-1520s, for instance, Butler forces raided Co.
Kildare to attack Earl Garret's estate at Levitstown. According to Kildare's own
testimony, they 'murdered and burned 17 men and women' before heading back
to Kilkenny with spoils valued at IR£200. Kildare also faced a serious challenge
to his authority in Co. Wexford, where Piers of Ossory imposed a fine on the
seneschal for giving aid to Kildare, and pro-Butler forces attacked Kildare's 'nigh
kinsman', Thomas fitz Maurice Fitzgerald, in the Fassagh Bantry and took him
prisoner. Piers and his followers also carried the fight to Kildare in the lordship
of Ely O'Carroll, in 1528 sending reinforcements (including the four aforementioned gunners) when a friendly O'Carroll leader was under Geraldine attack.[82]

Historians have tended to overestimate Kildare's strength in the decade before
1534, reckoning that despite his troubles with King Henry, he remained indispensable to the crown largely because of the military threat that his allies posed
to the Pale. His family's rebellion has even been reassessed as a bold declaration
of confidence in the future.[83] This interpretation requires modification. The
continued rise of Piers Ruadh Butler, earl of Ossory, shattered Kildare's alliance
network. As Quinn and Fitzsimons have noted, when Piers dined at Kilmainham

---

77 Ellis, *Tudor Ireland*, 116.   78 Butler (ed.), *Annals of Thady Dowling*, 34.   79 Ibid., 35.   80 *SP,
Henry VIII*, ii, 126–8.   81 Ellis, 'Tudor policy', 241.   82 *SP, Henry VIII*, ii, 120–4.   83 Brady,
Chief governors, 1; Canny, *Reformation to Restoration*, 18.

Castle as lord deputy in 1528 he brought an important new Gaelic ally to sit with him along with his customary supporters, O'More and O'Carroll – Cahir Ruadh O'Connor, the designated heir (*tánaiste*) of the O'Connors Faly, a lineage otherwise tied to the Geraldine affinity.[84] Worse followed for Kildare in the next few years, when his most dependable midlands allies the MacGiollapadraigs of Upper Ossory split into pro- and anti-Butler factions. The split originated with the decision of the chieftain, Brian MacGiollapadraig, to improve his relations with Earl Piers, and in 1532 Brian took Piers' daughter, Margaret Butler, as his wife.[85] After this the Butlers had allies among all the major Gaelic dynasties whose territories lay to the north and east of Kilkenny and who separated them from Kildare.

Kildare finally decided to confront Ossory more directly early in the 1530s. It is possible, as McCorristine has argued, that Henry VIII's execution in 1531 of the Welsh magnate Sir Rhys Ap Griffith on trumped-up charges of conspiracy was the main factor that persuaded Kildare to become more aggressive.[86] However, concern over the extent of the Butler advance was probably at least as important, especially as Thomas Cromwell, who had succeeded Wolsey as the king's principal minister, quickly showed himself ready to continue the cardinal's policy of curtailing Geraldine power while championing their rivals. Following his return to Ireland in 1530 Kildare threw himself into the task of reclaiming some of the ground he had lost. In 1531 he installed his ally Cahir Kavanagh as chieftain of Idrone over the head of Earl Piers' man Dunlarg,[87] a move that promised to re-establish a strong ring of anti-Butler forces around the borders of Co. Kilkenny. To underline Kildare's new direction late in 1531 Piers' client Roland Fitzgerald of Burnchurch was taken prisoner near Earl Garret's manor of Castledermot, Co. Kildare, while travelling to Dublin to attend parliament. When the parliament ended Moriertagh McOwny, a Kildare servant, seized the two MPs for Kilkenny town at Athy on their way home.[88]

Politically Kildare gained little from this policy. Piers of Ossory was sufficiently strong to weather the storm, and the increase in Geraldine violence encouraged Cromwell and the new English lord deputy of Ireland, Sir William Skeffington, to continue supporting the Butlers. The absentees bill introduced by the crown in the 1531 parliament was designed to further weaken the Kildare interest, revoking the right of the earls of Kildare to hold lands belonging to absentee English lords in south Leinster. Earl Garret's attempted intimidation of pro-Butler MPs backfired badly, for the act of absentees was subsequently passed into law, to Ossory's immediate benefit.[89] Documents surviving at Berkeley Castle show that by May 1534, on the eve of the Kildare revolt, Thomas, Lord Berkeley, had granted Piers a 60-year lease of Carlow and Wexford land formerly possessed by Kildare.[90]

84 D.B. Quinn, 'The reemergence of English policy as a major factor in Irish affairs, 1520–34', *NHI*, ii, 676; Fitzsimons, 'Lordship of O'Connor Faly', 211–2. 85 Edwards, 'MacGiollapadraigs', 327–32. 86 McCorristine, *Revolt*, 48–50. 87 Quinn, 'Irish Ireland, English Ireland', 636. 88 *Cal. Carew MSS, 1515–74*, no. 36. 89 Lennon, *Sixteenth-century Ireland*, 102–3. 90 Berkeley

Ultimately, his refusal to accept the re-emergence of the Butler lordship as much as his general reluctance to share power cost Kildare his political career and forced his family into revolt.[91] Towards the end of 1532 Thomas Butler, Ossory's youngest son, was killed near Ballykealy in Upper Ossory by Kildare's ally Dermot MacGiollapadraig, *tánaiste* of the MacGiollapadraigs. In the subsequent inquiry Earl Piers was able to show the extent of Kildare's involvement in the murder, thanks mainly to the testimony of his son-in-law, the MacGiollapadraig chief, Brian (Dermot's brother). In September 1533 evidence was heard at Waterford before the mayor of the city and the bishops of Ossory and Lismore. Following Brian MacGiollapadraig's statement, Lord James Butler and three Kilkenny gentlemen (Grace of Courtstown, Fitzgerald of Brownesford, and Clinton of Graigerawe) added their own comments against Kildare who, it emerged, had been seen near the place where the killing took place and met up with Dermot after it was done. Evidently Earl Garret had procured the murder. The comments of Brian MacGiollapadraig probably did the most damage. He stated on oath that when told of the killing Kildare 'rejoiced in the murder, and rebuked [the murderers] … because they had not done more vengeance' upon Ossory's family.[92] The statements of all the witnesses were duly taken down and despatched to London for the attention of the royal government. Events moved quickly thereafter. Kildare, who had recently been reinstated as lord deputy, found himself deep in disgrace. In response to the charges against him he was summoned to court for the last time. He himself seems to have expected the worst: prior to his departure he fortified his strongholds with royal ordnance removed without license from Dublin Castle.[93]

In May 1534 Skeffington, Cromwell and Henry VIII formulated a wide-ranging agreement with the earl of Ossory. Piers was permitted to attack those border lords whom Kildare had supported against him, and his influence regarding the selection of government officials was recognised. Clearly a contract of the highest significance, it was concluded despite loud denunciations of Butler military power by the Irish Council, and it appears to have signalled a thoroughgoing break with the Fitzgeralds in favour of the Butlers.[94] With plans in train to restore Skeffington to office at Kildare's expense it proved hugely provocative. Weeks later Robert Cowley was reporting the 'seditious, predatorious rebellion' of the Kildare family and the destruction of the Pale.[95]

In June the Kildare forces swept across large parts of the country, seemingly on the verge of forcing the crown out of Ireland.[96] Apart from Dublin, only the Second Pale of Waterford and the Ormond territories held out for the king.[97] Rebel attacks next concentrated along Kilkenny's northern frontier, with hos-

Castle, Berkeley Ch General 4685–6. **91** Lyons, *Gearóid Óg*, 47, 53. **92** J.G. Prim & J. Graves, *The history, architecture & antiquities of St Canice's cathedral* (Dublin 1857), pp 239–41, summarised by Curtis in *COD*, iv, no. 191; Edwards, 'MacGiollapadraigs', 330. **93** Lyons, *Gearóid Óg*, 56–8. **94** *SP, Henry VIII*, ii, no. 72. Skeffington and Piers Ruadh had earlier discussed details of the agreement with Cromwell (ibid., no. 71). **95** Ibid., no. 73. **96** McCorristine, *Revolt*, 63–6. **97** *SP, Henry VIII*, ii, no.73.

tile neighbours – probably segments of the MacGiollapadraigs – raiding the Ballybawnmore estate of Richard Archdekin, 'chief of his nation', one of Earl Piers's captains.[98] Throughout July the Butlers were able to rally their forces against the Geraldines, attacking them in Carlow and Kildare. John Grace of Courtstown distinguished himself when he invaded the lands of the baron of Offaly, Silken Thomas – Kildare's son and heir – and laid siege to several of his castles and took a large prey of his cattle.[99] But the boot was on the other foot early in August when Offaly returned to the south-east with a large army. After detaching a force to besiege Kilkenny Castle, he led a combined force around the county where, although they lost a skirmish with Lord James Butler at Jerpoint, they still laid waste much of Ossory's estate.[100] The region about Gowran suffered especially, after which Offaly suggested that Earl Piers should support the revolt unless he wanted more of the same.[101] The earl refused but, recognising the Geraldines' superior strength, he agreed to a truce. This enabled him to turn to the defence of Tipperary, which Desmond was threatening to overrun while he was preoccupied in Kilkenny. Soon the Butlers were forced to fight on two fronts, for Offaly broke the truce after only a couple of weeks, returning to Co. Kilkenny shortly before the end of August to defeat them in a battle near Thomastown.

This marked the high point of the rebel campaign in the shire. The Fitzgeralds were unable to capitalise on their victory by taking Kilkenny town, which was guarded by a garrison commanded by James Butler. Had it been taken, the Fitzgeralds would probably have controlled all of southern Ireland before the arrival of royal reinforcements from England. As it was, their second Kilkenny campaign effectively put the Butlers out of the war, for it took Earl Piers a full two months to rebuild his position. He was finally able to move north to Dublin – now the main object of the struggle – in the middle of November.[102]

Yet, limited though it was, the resistance put up by the Butlers played a key role in wrecking the Fitzgeralds' plans. As Sir John Alen informed Cromwell on St Stephen's Day, the Pale and the English presence itself would have been lost 'if the earl of Ossory and the castle of Dublin had given over'.[103] Following Skeffington's return to Ireland in late October with a relief army of over 2,000 men levied in England and Wales, it was clear that the revolt had failed. The renewed availability of the Butler forces from Kilkenny and Tipperary forced Offaly to call a truce with the crown forces before Christmas, in the vain hope that a large Imperial armada would arrive to support the rising in the new year. No foreign reinforcements arrived and the Geraldine insurgents were scattered. The Butlers assisted the mopping up of rebel resistance in the south of the coun-

---

98 *COD*, iv, no.197. **99** Grace, *Memorials*, i, 12–13. **100** Ibid.; Ellis, 'Tudor policy', 261. **101** The principal sources for the rebel campaign in Kilkenny are *SP, Henry VIII*, ii, 250–1; Stanihurst, 'History', 79–81; Butler (ed.), *Annals of Thady Dowling*, 35–6 s.a. 1534; and a copy of Robert Reyly's 1536 account in Lambeth Palace Ms 602: 138. **102** *SP, Henry VIII*, ii, no. 79. **103** Ibid., no. 82.

try in 1535–6. Earl Piers and his heir, James, participated in the siege of Dungarvan Castle, Co. Waterford, in October 1535, and took the fortress into their safekeeping after it had fallen.[104] In January 1536 Piers arbitrated with the chiefs of both the O'Connors and the O'Byrnes to persuade them to surrender on terms to the crown.[105] The influence of Piers and James Butler was apparently crucial in bringing the Kavanaghs back into the king's peace. In May 1536 Cahir MacInnyCross Kavanagh, a strong Geraldine, only agreed to lay down his arms if the Butlers would mediate should the terms imposed on him by the crown prove not to his liking.[106] A few weeks later, in July, Gerald Sutton Kavanagh surrendered and allowed his son, Arthur, to be placed as a hostage with Lord James Butler as a guarantee of his good behaviour.[107]

In most histories of later medieval and early modern Ireland the period following the defeat of the Kildare rebellion is seen as a time of triumph for their factional rivals, the Butlers, and to a large extent it was. As already shown in Chapters 1 and 2, the 1530s and 1540s saw the Butlers gain major new titles, grants and privileges. Piers Ruadh at last attained his lifetime goal when he was recognised as eighth earl of Ormond by the crown early in 1538, and he and his son James, the ninth earl, reaped major benefits from the dissolution of the monasteries, receiving enormous tracts of land around Kilkenny, Tipperary and the south. They also faced difficulties, however. To paraphrase a leading authority, the year 1534 deserves to be recognised as a watershed in Irish history because the fall of the Geraldines let loose a series of new problems between the central government and the native lordships, problems which were impossible to resolve without mutual alienation, even rejection.[108] For all that the resurgent Butler lordship was essentially loyal and pro-English, its relations with the crown underwent a series of crises, major and minor, after 1534.

DUBLIN AND THE ORMOND LORDSHIP AFTER 1534

The destruction of the Kildare Fitzgeralds transformed the Butlers' relationship with the Tudor government. At a stroke Earl Piers and his family stepped into the Geraldines' shoes as the dominant lineage in Anglo-Irish affairs. They soon discovered the disadvantages of pre-eminence. Crown advisers, especially officials of the colonial government in Dublin, were forced to adopt a more critical attitude towards the Butler lordship. Not all royal administrators were convinced the crown needed them as badly as before. Having withstood the challenge of one overmighty dynasty, many of Henry VIII's officials were wary of creating another. Thus the Butlers were in danger of becoming victims of

---

104 *Cal. Carew MSS, 1515–74*, 79. **105** Ibid., 86, 88–9. **106** Ibid., 93; for this agreement, and another of a few months later, see D. Moore, 'English action, Irish reaction: The MacMurrough Kavanaghs, 1530–1630' (unpublished M.A. thesis, St Patrick's College, Maynooth, 1987), 43–6. **107** *Cal. Carew MSS, 1515–74*, 96; NA, Lodge MSS, Articles with Irish chiefs, etc., 2. **108** Brady, *Chief governors*, 1.

their own success. Yet simultaneously a strong pro-Ormond lobby could also be found in Dublin and London, which maintained that the continuance of Butler hegemony in southern Ireland, along the lines sanctioned in the crown's treaty of May 1534, was still a necessary evil.[109] Relations between Dublin and Kilkenny blew hot and cold. They would remain ambivalent for most of the sixteenth century.

It was probably fortunate for Piers Ruadh and his successors that the Dublin administration suffered severe financial constraints after 1534. Like all Tudor monarchs, Henry VIII was unwilling to commit himself to a major spending policy in Ireland; his chief minister, Cromwell, was of a like mind. As a result accommodation with native dynasties was a prerequisite of government.[110] For many years after the Kildare revolt the cheapest way for Dublin and London to control the south of Ireland, from Waterford to Cork and beyond, was to delegate royal authority to the Butlers and other noble houses. In many respects it was a policy that appealed to the monarchy at Westminster rather more than it did to the crown's direct representatives at Dublin Castle, the lord deputies, who sometimes found their ability to command the Butlers and other nobles greatly weakened as a direct result of royal parsimony. It was, for instance, Thomas Cromwell's agent, William Saintloo, and not Lord Deputy Grey, who recommended in March 1537 that Piers Ruadh's younger son, Richard Butler, be granted certain castles in Co. Wexford so that the Butlers could better counter the might of the MacMurrough Kavanaghs there.[111] Henceforth always of English birth, the lord deputies of post-Kildare Ireland struggled to run the colonial government as they would have liked, without fear of the Butlers of Ormond unseating them by appealing directly to London.

The introduction of the Henrician Reformation to Ireland increased the crown's dependence on the Butlers and their supporters. During the 1534 revolt the Kildare rebels had played the religious card against Henry VIII following his breach with Rome, and they had actively sought aid from the pope and the Holy Roman emperor, representing their struggle as a crusade against a schismatic ruler.[112] Fear of a papalist backlash insured that Henry VIII held the Butlers in high regard, despite having doubts over the extent of their power, for Earl Piers had agreed to resist the pope and uphold the king's supremacy over the church.[113] Following the Reformation Parliament of 1536/7 Piers' heir, James Butler, by now Viscount Thurles, gained added influence with the crown through his willingness to continue his family's acceptance of religious change. Although there was little opposition to the early stages of the Reformation in south-eastern Ireland, King Henry faced a serious challenge to his position in England with the Pilgrimage of Grace in 1536, and in the late 1530s a new Irish rebel confederacy known as the Geraldine League erupted, which threatened

---

109 See ibid., 3–4 for a slightly different analysis, which underestimates the pro-Butler lobby, especially in London. **110** Ibid., 15; Ellis, *Tudor Ireland*, 132–3. **111** *Cal. Carew MSS, 1515–74*, no. 97. **112** McCorristine, *Revolt*, 67–78; Lennon, *Sixteenth-century Ireland*, 107–8. **113** SP, *Henry VIII*, ii, no. 72.

once again to make political capital from the king's religious policies.[114] Viewed in this light the constant support Henry received from the Ormond lordship was a major boon to Tudor rule in Ireland. Through James Butler's encouragement Kilkenny became the first area outside Dublin to embrace the Reformation. Early in 1538, 'as one professed of Christ's religion', James wrote to the king praising the sermons of George Browne, the archbishop of Dublin,[115] and within a year he had helped to insure Browne encountered a favourable congregation when he preached at St Canice's Cathedral.

James' religious leanings have attracted considerable attention among historians, and it has generally been accepted that 'he belonged to the advanced party in the schism'.[116] At one stage he expressed his desire to extirpate the 'detestable abusions of the papistical sect' in Ireland, language indicating genuine disdain for at least some Roman practices. He was, moreover, on good terms with Hugh Latimer, the overtly Protestant bishop of Worcester, even asking the prelate to send him religious books.[117] In the early 1540s when conservative crypto-Catholics had charge of the English royal court, James continued to plough an anti-papal line in Ireland, reporting opponents of the king's supremacy to the authorities. In the final period of his life he seems to have moved closer to the proto-Protestant group led by the Dudleys and Seymours.[118] Irrespective of the king's private thoughts on Protestantism, he could be confident that Lord James Butler would not engage in intrigue with pro-papal forces. Increasingly after 1536 James replaced his ageing father as the leader of the Butler interest in Ireland.

The emergence of James Butler had adverse implications for the king's new lord deputy in Dublin, Leonard Grey, Viscount Grane. Having served alongside the Butlers in 1534–5 Grey feared they would annex control of the government and diminish his status. Against his wishes, the earldom of Ormond was bestowed on Piers Ruadh, and James Butler, already lord treasurer, was made lord admiral of Ireland and warden of the ports.[119] Likewise, the Cowleys, Ormond mouthpieces, were promoted to high office in chancery and the Irish council. At once Robert Cowley journeyed to court to advocate that the Butlers lead a thorough military reduction of all Geraldine sympathisers – a policy that, if adopted, would have greatly subordinated Grey's position as head of the royal forces in Ireland. For Grey there was but one solution: to undermine the Butlers before they rendered his office meaningless.[120] The stage was thus set for the first trial of strength between the occupants of Dublin Castle and Kilkenny Castle in post-Kildare Ireland.

---

114 B. Bradshaw, *The Irish constitutional revolution of the sixteenth century* (Cambridge 1979), 174–80. 115 *SP, Henry VIII*, ii, 563. 116 R. Dudley Edwards, *Church & state in Tudor Ireland* (Dublin 1935), pp 33–5; G.V. Jourdan, *The Reformation in Ireland in the 16th century* (Dublin 1932), ii, 209. 117 He also asked Walter Cowley to get him a new book dealing with religious abuses in Rome: *SP, Henry VIII*, iii, 34–5. 118 Ibid., 32; Lennon, *Sixteenth-century Ireland*, 136; PRO, SP 60/11/39. James' relations with Sir John Dudley are discussed in D. Edwards 'Further comments on the strange death of the 9th earl of Ormond', *Butler Soc. Jn.* 4/1 (1997), 58–63. 119 *CPRI, Henry VIII–Eliz. I*, 15. 120 Brady, *Chief governors*, 17.

Playing on the king's paranoia Grey noted that supposed 'true men' like the Butlers of Ormond and Ossory were in fact unreformed military thugs, and further observed that the chief castles and strongholds of these loyalists were manned 'either with men of Irish nation, or else with such as be combined by gossipred or fostering with Irishmen nigh to the borders.'[121] The warning was heeded. In the autumn of 1537 four royal commissioners, headed by Sir Anthony St Leger, arrived to investigate military misrule in Ireland, and they were mandated to pay special attention to abuses in the Butler territories. In October the commissioners travelled to Kilkenny to hear the 'presentments' of local (mostly urban-based) juries regarding political and economic conditions in the county. Though the presentments did not really amount to a damning indictment of Butler rule, they did reveal the widespread resentment felt by many of the county's merchants and traders at the high level of military taxation demanded by the Butlers for the maintenance of their army. The juries of Kilkenny and Irishtown, and a jury of 'the commoners of the county' incorporating spokesmen from the other main towns in the shire – Callan, Thomastown, Inistioge and Knocktopher, though *not* Gowran – all agreed that Piers Butler, earl of Ormond and Ossory, Lord James Butler, his son, and most of the principal gentry, imposed coign and livery in every area of the shire, contrary to a statute of Henry VII. They complained of various instances of extortion and racketeering that had occurred in the county in recent years, since Piers had increased his army, and they also informed the commissioners that outside the towns English law and custom had fallen into disuse.[122]

Grey had reason to be pleased with this outcome, yet before the crown commissioners returned to England in April 1538 his plans to isolate the Butlers were undone. Unlike the Kildares, the Butlers showed themselves adaptable to changing crown demands. In March they declared their willingness to accept political reform of their lordship when Earl Piers reached a private agreement with the commissioners. He would, he said, endeavour to 'plant good civility' and promote the use of English law in the regions under his rule, and he undertook to alleviate the 'enormities and abuses' perpetrated by his family and followers.[123]

Thus Grey was out-manoeuvred. In response, he adopted a new approach. He would drop all pretence of neutrality, hoping that by befriending the Butlers' enemies and insulting their allies he might root them out of their Kilkenny lair and incite them to rebel. In theory it seemed a viable approach; in practice, it quickly became undone, for it entailed the lord deputy behaving like an earl of Kildare. The fact that Grey himself was related to the Kildares gave his new direction an added edge, for befriending anti-Butler forces meant befriending ex-Geraldines and ex-rebels. Undaunted by criticism from Irish council members, he proceeded against the Butlers in 1538 in a lengthy campaign of indirect provocation. In Laois, Grey sided with Kedagh Roe, Rory

121 Wilson, *Beginnings*, 66, 70 n13.   **122** Hore & Graves (ed.), *Social state*, 97–136.   **123** Ibid., 83–4; SP 60/6/16, 27.

Caech and Gilpatrick O'More in their dispute with the pro–Butler O'More chief, Piers Mac Kedagh, despite the fact that they had participated in the 1534 revolt, and Piers Mac Kedagh had been loyal. Piers Mac Kedagh was arrested and Grey hired the ex-rebel O'Mores as his midlands agents, using his servant, Edmund Archbold of Maynooth, as intermediary. The O'Mores subsequently destroyed the Butler estates in Cos. Kildare and Carlow.[124] In Ely, Grey sinisterly told the dying O'Carroll chief that he could expect no favours in Dublin if he continued to aid the Butlers, and to encourage O'Carroll to change sides he allegedly stated that Earl Piers and James Butler were both in prison on suspicion of treason.[125] When the chieftain died and was replaced by another former Geraldine, Feargananym, Grey quickly undertook to help the new leader regain land on the Tipperary/Offaly border previously seized by the Butlers. Within weeks O'Carroll forces were harassing Ormond tenants and servants in north Tipperary. He likewise reactivated Cahir MacArt Kavanagh as an anti-Butler agent in north Wexford. In Munster, following lengthy negotiations involving Feargananym O'Carroll he briefly secured the confidence of James fitz John Fitzgerald of Desmond, before fitz John again recoiled in favour of the Geraldine League conspiracy.[126]

Caught by surprise, the Butlers were forced to spend much of 1538 defending the frontiers of their lordship. Lord James Butler patrolled the Munster border zones where Tipperary ran into Desmond country in west Waterford and east Limerick, while in Leinster his brother, Richard, went to Ferns in north Wexford, and his father, Earl Piers, was for a time based at Carlow Castle. In the event, the Butlers overcame their difficulties with relative ease. There was little open warfare, and at no point did the Butlers consider challenging Grey directly. Instead they observed his presence near their borders and awaited attack from hostile Kavanaghs, O'Mores, O'Carrolls and Desmond Fitzgeralds that invariably erupted after he had moved on.

By failing to take the bait the dynasty gained sympathy on the Irish Council, where New English officials such as the vice-treasurer, William Brabazon, and the master of the rolls, John Allen, condemned what they saw as Grey's increasingly high-handed rule. Speaking of Grey's imprisonment of the pro–Butler O'More, Brabazon said 'I have never seen like handling', and Archbishop Browne of Dublin, no lover of the Butlers, spoke out against Grey regarding his maintenance of the ex-rebel Feargananym O'Carroll.[127] Accordingly, by the end of 1538 the Butlers and some of the council joined forces to plot the deputy's overthrow. Alen and the chief justice, Gerald Aylmer, composed a lengthy list of charges against Grey's government, reporting how he had endangered the security of the Pale by succouring ex-rebels.[128] At first the conspiracy failed to make progress, for in London Cromwell moved to protect Grey, insuring that

---

124 Fitzgerald, 'The O'Mores', 24; Carey, 'End of the Gaelic political order', 217–8; PRO, SP 60/6/55; *SP, Henry VIII*, iii, 17–8. **125** Ibid., 22–3. **126** Ibid., 27–9, 31, 44–6; Venning, 'O'Carrolls', 186–7. **127** *SP, Henry VIII*, iii, 18, 35. **128** Ibid., 36–43.

the charges against the deputy were shelved without reaching the king.[129] For much of 1539 the anti-Grey conspirators laid low, biding their time, but after Grey and the Butlers had combined successfully against the Geraldine League rebellion, and brought about its collapse, the scheming recommenced. Again Grey was isolated. In February 1540, despite his continued high standing with Cromwell, he was unable to prevent the Irish council from thumbing its nose at his authority, defending John Alen against him, and among other things accusing Grey of still hankering after the Butlers' reduction.[130] During 1540 James Butler – since August 1539 ninth earl of Ormond – emerged from the shadows as one of the chief architects of the attempted coup, travelling to London to support the charges against Grey with a personal plea to the king's advisers.

Conditions were fast changing at the royal court. Since late 1539 Henry VIII had been reconsidering the religious and foreign policy pursued by Cromwell; a conservative faction led by the duke of Norfolk pounced to unseat the great minister and his supporters, who included Grey. On 10 June Cromwell was accused of treason and arrested. Two days later, following a flood of indictments against his behaviour in Ireland, Grey too was accused, and sent to the Tower. Less than two weeks passed before Sir Anthony St Leger, one of Norfolk's allies, replaced him as lord deputy. The fact that St Leger had previously served in Ireland and enjoyed good relations with the Butlers of Ormond is highly significant. St Leger was the conduit between Grey's Irish opponents and Norfolk, and there is no doubt that he used the complaints of the Butlers and their allies on the Irish council to have Grey sacked so that he could succeed him. Grey was beheaded on 28 July 1541, the first of several high-ranking officers to fall foul of the Butlers' conspiratorial talents during the sixteenth century.

Their participation in the intrigues against Grey was doubly advantageous to the Ormond Butlers: as well as ridding them of an unfriendly lord deputy, it enabled them to forge closer ties with the Howards and the new conservative faction that came to dominate Henry VIII's court in the early 1540s. Though hardly a religious conservative James Butler, ninth earl of Ormond, was nonetheless able to work with the Howards on a strictly political basis. It is not usually noted that St Leger, the Howards' nominee for the chief governorship, had drawn up a programme of government for Ireland which suited the Butlers well enough. Indeed, Earl James and his younger brother, Richard Butler, must surely have encouraged St Leger to enact a programme that included the new deputy (i) leading a government army against some of their border enemies among the Kavanaghs, O'Carrolls and O'Connors in the autumn of 1540,[131] and (ii) continuing the giveaway of cheap ex-monastic land as a result of the dissolution. The fact that they fell out later should not obscure the fact that, during the early part of his deputyship, St Leger and the Butlers got on famously.[132] In return for his help the Butlers committed themselves to the task

---

129 For an important new evaluation of Grey's destruction, see Brady, *Chief governors*, 23–5. **130** *SP, Henry VIII*, iii, nos. 263–4. **131** Lennon, *Sixteenth-century Ireland*, 152–6; *Cal. Carew MSS, 1515–74*, no. 155. **132** Failing to recognise the good relations that existed between the two par-

of making St Leger's government a success. Having defeated the rebel earl of Desmond, the ninth earl of Ormond persuaded him to submit to the new governor and to enter into a treaty of surrender and regrant with the crown.[133] Desmond's subsequent concord with the government turned out to be a watershed in St Leger's career, his submission allowing the deputy to parade him around the country as a talisman for his policy of assimilation of the regional lords through surrender and regrant. Desmond's participation convinced other lords and chieftains to embrace St Leger's 'liberal revolution', and in 1541 at the Irish parliament a bill was passed with native consent declaring the king of England to be king of Ireland. Everyone living in Ireland would be hereafter a subject of the crown, answerable to the laws and statutes of the kingdom.[134] Notably James Butler, earl of Ormond, played a prominent role in the promotion and dissemination of this legislation. It was he who in the house of lords announced and explained the 'Act for the Kingdom of Ireland' to a group of Irish lords who were present as guests of the house, addressing them in Gaelic, their native language, 'greatly to their contentation'.[135] Ormond was apparently the only senior member of St Leger's government who could speak the Irish language. As such, he played a greater role in advancing the policy of assimilation than has generally been accredited to him, for he is known to have mediated with Gaelic lords on St Leger's behalf on other occasions also.

If the attempt to reconcile the Irish to English rule owed as much to Ormond (and others on the Dublin council) as to Lord Deputy St Leger, then the subsequent falling out between St Leger and the Butler dynasty can no longer be attributed to the earl's conservative intransigence. Ormond was no feudal dinosaur, inflexibly opposed to the political and legal transformation of Anglo-Irish relations; he was instead an active participant in the implementation of the programme, and perhaps in its formulation. When he and his followers began quarrelling with St Leger late in 1541, it was not because they wished to prevent St Leger's policies succeeding; rather they wanted to take control of the programme away from the deputy, the better to turn it to their advantage. For the Ormond party these political changes offered a unique opportunity for aggrandisement. Moreover, as steadfast crown loyalists, Earl James, his family and clients sought influence in government as theirs by right. The problem, in their eyes, was St Leger, who expected to rule as viceroy irrespective of Ormond interests.

St Leger felt threatened by the Butlers. In 1540 the king had warned him to be wary of their power;[136] by the autumn of 1541 these words seemed prophetic. The deputy's recent efforts to develop a viceregal party in Dublin had excited

ties before late 1541, some historians have assumed that one of the main reasons why St Leger and the Butlers subsequently fell out was because St Leger had a claim over, or interest in, the earldom of Ormond. This tradition, maintained most recently by Dr Brady and Professor Canny, is a fallacy (Canny, *From Reformation to Restoration*, 36; Brady, *Chief governors*, 42). Not a shred of evidence exists to show that St Leger ever advanced a claim to the earldom. **133** Edwards, 'Malice aforethought?', 33. **134** Bradshaw, *Irish constitutional revolution*, passim **135** *SP, Henry VIII*, iii, 304; A. Bliss, 'Language and literature', in J. Lydon (ed.), *The English in medieval Ireland* (Dublin 1984), 30. **136** *LP Henry VIII*, xvi, 1540–1, 23.

the suspicion of Robert Cowley, who somewhat hastily tabled a series of allegations, among other things accusing St Leger of defrauding the crown in the
valuation and distribution of ex-monastic land in Ireland. As Ormond, his
master, was among those profiting most from St Leger's financial chicanery,
Cowley might have chosen a different line of attack. Ormond remained quiet,
and with no support in government circles (everyone of importance was on the
take) Cowley was dismissed as a crank by the defrauded king, and died in disgrace in London.[137] Yet Cowley's downfall did not mean the deputy was safe,
for the ninth earl soon began to challenge him directly. The earl was greatly
concerned by St Leger's choice of friends. In June 1542 he granted royal protection to an ex-Geraldine rebel, James Gernon of Gernonstown.[138] At about
the same time he decided to promote the earl of Desmond's position in Munster
at Ormond's expense, a decision that entailed going back on the terms of the
1534 agreement between the king and the Butlers in which the Butlers had been
promised a pre-eminent role in the government of the south. To Ormond it
seemed St Leger was pursuing the same path as his predecessor, Grey: 'traitorous' Geraldines were returning to power to keep the loyal Butlers in check.[139]

Earl James was not the only leading figure concerned by the emergence of
a viceregal group. The lord chancellor, Sir John Alen, was also suspicious of St
Leger's manoeuvres. One of the most forceful personalities on the Irish council, Alen believed it was part of the deputy's duty to heed the advice of his council. Already sympathetic to Ormond, he moved closer to the earl as St Leger's
challenge progressed. Continuing till 1546 a struggle ensued for control of the
Irish government.

At first glance, Ormond's decision to take on the lord deputy after 1542
might seem foolhardy. St Leger was a more dangerous opponent than Grey,
not least because (historians are agreed) St Leger was no ordinary chief governor, but a trusted confidant of King Henry himself. On closer inspection, however, it seems that Ormond had prepared the ground for his challenge well
enough. Having forged an alliance with disaffected Irish councillors the earl
extended his contacts with the dominant conservative faction at the king's court,
befriending Thomas Wriothesley, the English lord chancellor, and seeking a
better understanding with Norfolk, the main leader of the faction and St Leger's
chief patron. Norfolk did not reject Ormond's overtures, but in a letter to St
Leger supported a proposal Ormond had made to him to save the king money
in the reform of southern Leinster.[140] One reason why Earl James was able to
inveigle his way into the conservatives' ranks was because their grip on power
was not as tight as it had been in 1540. Henry VIII was growing dissatisfied with

---

137 Brady's account of Cowley's downfall is the best by far (*Chief governors*, 41), easily surpassing
my own earlier comments on the episode (Edwards, 'Malice aforethought?', 34). **138** *CPRI,
Henry VIII–Eliz. I*, 71–2; *SP, Henry VIII*, iii, no. 373. **139** Ibid., nos. 368, 394. **140** Ibid., no.
392. In February 1545 St Leger tried in vain to convince Wriothesley that he had nothing 'but
love' for the earl of Ormond, whom he claimed had wrongfully accused him of seeking his reduction: ibid., no. 410.

Norfolk and the Howards, and increasingly sickly, he lusted after military glory before his death. The royal military cravings played into Ormond's hands. The greatest commander in Ireland, the earl's help would be needed for the king's projected invasions of Scotland and France. More sinisterly, because the king's health was so poor, his ministers and courtiers were laying plans to secure their futures after his death. Any successful *coup d'etat* would need to secure Ireland, where Ormond was the single most powerful lord, capable of securing it until conditions in England stabilised. As a result, by 1543 Earl James found the doors to influence in London opening towards him as Henry VIII's advisers, conservative and non-conservative, courted his support.

St Leger responded to Ormond's growing authority in the only way he could – by interfering in the frontiers of the Ormond territories. Unlike Grey before him, he shrewdly intended to avoid a head-on collision with his adversary, and consequently he put the earldom under much greater pressure than Grey had done. He infuriated Ormond by questioning the earl's rights to the prisage on wine imports and to palatine jurisdiction in the liberty of Tipperary.[141] Furthermore, instead of passing it to Ormond, he gave possession of Dungarvan Castle in Co. Waterford to his brother, Robert St Leger, who also received important posts in Carlow against the earl's wishes.[142]

Eventually St Leger over-reached himself. On 26 June 1543, while Earl James was absent in England, the deputy and his officers rode south to Kilkenny hoping to collect information about the earl's misgovernment of his territories and to gather evidence of the Butlers' use of coign and livery and other unlawful military exactions. The project failed. The ninth earl, it emerged, was not a traditional warlord like his late father. The only complaint of substance that the local community proffered against him was that 'he should take and levy of them against their wills a great sum of money for an aid towards his charges [in] repairing [to the king in London]'. Worse for the deputy, the local elite signed their names to a qualified declaration of support for Earl James' overlordship, with the bishops of Ossory, Cashel and Waterford, the sovereigns of Kilkenny, Clonmel and Callan, and more than thirty local squires and gentlemen praising him as a champion of reform in the south of Ireland. Contrasting him with his father and previous earls they noted how James 'diminished their burden … after a better sort than any of his predecessors'. Through his influence, they claimed, many local gentlemen and border lords had begun to reduce the exaction of coign and livery. Ormond, moreover, had placed himself in debt in order to serve the king and advance the crown interest in the south. The 'Address' ended with a criticism of St Leger and his government, observing that things might be made 'more firm and permanent' if the deputy desisted from criticising the earl.[143] The Ormond lordship supported its overlord.

Henry VIII's return to an aggressive foreign policy undermined St Leger. When in 1544 the king required a military levy from Ireland to fight in Scotland

---

141 *SP, Henry VIII*, iii, no. 400.   **142** Ibid., nos. 398–9.   **143** HMC, *Ormonde MSS, 1543–1711*, 1–3.

and France, the deputy discovered that many of his 'friends' among the native Irish nobility were unwilling to deprive themselves of soldiers for the benefit of the king of England. The chief of the MacGiollapadraigs, for instance, sent just one soldier from his lands, and this despite being ennobled as baron of Upper Ossory by St Leger in 1541 and having had an audience with the king in 1543. Desmond performed much better, supplying 120 soldiers for the king's army, but this paled when compared with Ormond's procurements, fitting out the 100 troops demanded of him before sending another 100 to make up for the shortfall in other native levies. To rub it in, Earl James declared his willingness to raise yet another 100 men if asked. The earl's value to the crown was further enhanced by the fact he agreed to provide gunners for the army. No other Irish lord was willing or able to equip soldiers with guns for the king's service. Eventually just 200 of Ormond's men, including 36 gunners, were called upon, destined to serve in France at the sieges of Montreiul and Boulogne. Commanded by two Tipperary captains (Piers Butler of Grallagh and Edmund Purcell of Templemore) and three Kilkenny petty captains (James fitz Robenet Purcell of Foulkesrath, Patrick Archdekin and Patrick Fitzgerald), they distinguished themselves; Butler of Grallagh was knighted by the king for his valour, and another member of the force, Piers Walsh, was appointed a royal pensioner.[144] By dominating the royal war effort in Ireland Ormond greatly embarrassed his critics. From mid-1544 St Leger was forced repeatedly to sing his praises, when otherwise trying to snipe at him, in his letters to London.

Late in 1545 Ormond was given an opportunity to become one of the king's principal commanders, being asked to take joint charge of an attack on western Scotland with the king's Scottish kinsman, the earl of Lennox. St Leger was alarmed. In response he planted a double agent in Ormond's territories, William Cantwell, whose task it was to provoke Ormond into challenging the deputy. Cantwell proved a good choice. In October 1545, as Ormond was making his final preparations in Kilkenny for the Scottish expedition, Cantwell forged a letter from an anonymous friend of the earl warning of a plot against the earl's life: 'Right honourable Lord Earl of Ormond, If you were the man that some men writeth you to be, I would not write this letter for any good in the world; but I doubt not you will prove a true man, and all they in Ireland that do think with craft to cast you away, will prove false.'

Going on, Cantwell's little forgery told of a plot hatched by St Leger to kill Ormond in Scotland, and to add substance to the charge the document claimed that the lord deputy's servants were boasting their master would spend Christmas in Ormond's 'strongest houses'. Leaving it to be discovered in the chamber of Gowran Castle, and another similar note at New Ross, Cantwell succeeded in escalating the tension between Kilkenny and Dublin. Ormond took the threat seriously, and before embarking for Scotland he sent a copy of the Gowran letter to one of his friends on the English privy council, the lord privy seal, Lord

144 T. Blake Butler, 'Henry VIII's Irish Army List', 4–7; *LP Henry VIII*, xxi, Pt. 2, 189.

Russell.[145] When he returned to Ireland from the Western Isles early in the new year the controversy continued, so that by Easter 1546 the king was forced to intervene. Both parties were summoned to London, the charges that they had presented against each other to be investigated there.

St Leger's chance to strike down his foe had finally arrived. By the time he and Ormond reached Whitehall the king's need for Ormond's military aid had declined as peace negotiations commenced with the French. The royal inquiry soon boosted the deputy's recovery. A number of witnesses were called to testify on St Leger's relations with Ormond, and on examination it emerged that, encouraged by the *agent provocateur* Cantwell, Chancellor Alen and Walter Cowley had plotted to turn the earl of Ormond against the deputy. When Cowley owned up to the charges St Leger manipulated his confession to reveal Alen as a liar to the king and his officers. Ormond responded to these revelations in the only way that he could: falling to his knees at the royal court he begged the king's forgiveness for having heeded evil counsel. His feud with St Leger was over. The deputy emerged much strengthened from the showdown, and shortly afterwards – sometime in September – he and the earl entered into formal negotiations in London in which most of the main issues between them were settled. Principally, Ormond would be permitted to retain his palatine status in Tipperary if it were deemed 'convenient for the commonwealth'; though the earl lost nothing tangible, St Leger had won.[146]

Within weeks, however, everything was again uncertain. On 17 October 1546 Earl James and 50 of his servants were invited to a banquet at the Limehouse hosted by Sir John Dudley, Lord Lisle. During the meal Ormond and 35 of his men sickened; although 18 eventually recovered, the earl was not among them. On 28 October he died, cut down in his prime by one of the worst instances of accidental food poisoning in the history of sixteenth-century London.[147] His sudden death precipitated a crisis in Ireland, where St Leger had cause to regret his passing. The two men had been reconciled in London – if only for the time being – with Ormond prepared to follow his directions regarding the reformation of Leinster and Munster. With Ormond dead, St Leger faced the prospect of having to control the south without a dominant regional representative. Desmond was not an adequate replacement for Ormond, having precious little leverage over the likes of the O'Mores or Kavanaghs. By late 1546 large parts of the south and east were in chaos, partly as a result of recent government policy, and partly because the unexpected demise of the ninth earl of Ormond created a power vacuum. In the ensuing period St Leger's administration in Dublin lost control of events, as a new proto-Protestant clique headed by the deputy's foes, the Seymours and Dudleys, seized power in London and St Leger himself was recalled.

145 *SP, Henry VIII*, iii, 539; *LP Henry VIII*, xx, Pt. 1, 545–6; ibid., xxi, Pt. 1, 450–3; D.G. White, 'Henry VIII's Irish kerne in France and Scotland, 1544–5', *Irish Sword* 3 (1957–8), 213–25. **146** *SP, Henry VIII*, iii, no. 448. **147** Edwards, 'Malice aforethought?', 35–8; idem, 'Further comments', 61–3.

In Kilkenny the ninth earl's death came at a bad time for the county community. The government's recent policy towards the Gaelic Irish of the midlands and south Leinster had gone terribly wrong, leaving pro-English areas partly surrounded by belligerent forces. In particular the failure of the Dublin administration to mollify the O'Mores following the death in 1545 of Rory Caech threw Kilkenny and its neighbours off balance.[148] The prospect that the crown might crush the O'Mores caused not only the Butlers, but also the Keatings, MacGiollapadraigs and some of the MacMurrough Kavanaghs, to try to capitalise on the situation and create a new pecking order in the region. For instance, knowing that the O'Mores were divided and otherwise preoccupied, a branch of the northern Kavanaghs – probably the Idrone sept – invaded Idough in an effort to bring the O'Brennans under their sway, and so take them away from the Butlers and O'Mores, their usual masters. Up to 100 of the O'Brennans were killed in the ensuing war.[149] In response Ormond's brother, Richard Butler, pushed deep into the heart of O'More territory in southern Laois around Slievemargy, where he built a castle, and his men struck out in all directions, preying on his rivals and taking hostages.[150] The MacGiollapadraigs, meanwhile, hoped to prevent major Butler penetration of Upper Ossory. By 1548 Lord Upper Ossory, the MacGiollapadraig chief, had had a new stronghold built on the bishop of Ossory's land at Durrow, within shooting distance of the Butler's followers who occupied the episcopal house there.[151]

The situation quickly deteriorated. The renewal of Butler/MacGiollapadraig hostilities necessitated the involvement of the Graces of Courtstown and St Legers of Tullaghanbroge, and the north of the county was plunged into a decline that lasted fifty years.[152] Conditions were equally grim in the Rower and the Barrow borderlands. By the late 1540s one of the principal northern branches of the Kavanaghs, the *Sliocht Airt Buidhe* sept headed by Cahir MacArt, was at open war with other members of the lineage, led by Art Boy Kavanagh. With the Butlers siding with Art, Kilkenny became embroiled.[153] Cattle raids proliferated, and as late as 1552 some of the Kavanaghs continued to cause problems in the Rower at Grangekill, stealing food from farmers there.[154]

The sense of dislocation was further exacerbated by aggressive new initiatives from Dublin. St Leger's replacement as lord deputy, Sir Edward Bellingham, was a military man first and foremost, and he intended to secure the Pale and southern Ireland through the creation of a network of royal garrisons at strategic points around the country. To his soldier's mind, the Ormond lordship, at the centre of the Second Pale, was too important strategically to be controlled by a major noble family. After six months in office, towards Christmas 1548, he advocated that Kilkenny Castle be taken from the Ormonds during the young tenth earl's minority and given to him, the chief governor, to serve

148 White, 'Reign of Edward VI', 197–211.   **149** Butler (ed.), *Annals of Thady Dowling*, 38.   **150** SP 61/1/16; SP 61/2/35.   **151** White (ed.), *Ir. mon & ep deeds*, 218.   **152** Chapter 1 above.   **153** Moore, 'English action, Irish reaction', 59–60.   **154** *Ir. Fiants*, Edward VI, no. 935.

as a viceregal seat.[155] It has already been discussed in Chapter 2 how his attempts to get control of the Ormond estate during Earl Thomas' wardship were undone by the machinations of Ormond's mother, the Dowager Countess Joan. However, this does not mean that Bellingham's plans never posed the Butlers a threat. The dynasty came close to a head-on collision with the crown over the matter, for in January 1549 Bellingham received a patent from the London privy council granting him the necessary powers to rid the Ormond castles in Cos. Kilkenny, Carlow and Tipperary of their Butler-appointed constables.[156] In the event, the patent was never used – it was not even enrolled on the patent rolls – but the fact that it was drawn up at all suggests that some at least of the royal ministers in England were prepared to go along with undermining the Butlers in Ireland in the interests of state security. Only court intrigue saved the dynasty from having to face a major challenge from Dublin.

Ultimately, Bellingham and his successor as chief governor, Sir James Croft, achieved little in the Ormond lordship other than to make conditions worse. Far from seizing the area for the crown they were forced against their better judgement to allow it to drift further away from central control, as Ireland was threatened with invasion by England's continental enemies and the Pale's frontiers were overrun by rebels. Kilkenny experienced a crisis. The absence of a strong overlord combined with the enforced withdrawal of royal authority encouraged hostile neighbours to attack and local landowners to take the law into their own hands in retaliation. As border warfare escalated military racketeering was given free rein, the limited reforms imposed by Earl James quickly forgotten. It was at this time that coign and livery lost its allure as a method of county defence, revealed as an instrument of oppression by which to sustain gangs of soldier-brigands who roamed the shire seemingly out of control. Though aware of the deterioration of law and order in the Ormond country, the Dublin government hoped to press the local troops into service against growing rebel forces, and so turned a blind eye to their misdemeanours, issuing pardons rather than prosecute them in the courts. Only when England's security concerns receded would the government respond to the problem of the military in Kilkenny. In the meantime coign and livery, and those who imposed it, caused turmoil in the region.

THE COIGN AND LIVERY PROBLEM

Coign and livery could only work effectively when political conditions were stable. In the past the Kilkenny community had agreed to provide food and lodging for soldiers and stabling for horses when the force required for local defence was fixed with their consent. From the late 1540s, however, attempts by military commanders to raise the number of troops in response to changing

---

155 SP 61/1/140.   **156** SP 61/2/3.

circumstances threw the system into disarray. In an instant what was set and established was overthrown, and captains took on extra men despite local disapproval, so that coign and livery became a subject of scandal. Hitherto a private defence tax negotiable between the head of the Butlers and the local gentry and freeholders, it was now transformed into a non-negotiable tax levied by individual military commanders on as many unfortunates as possible.[157]

The wave of pardons issued by the government between 1547 and 1552 allow us to identify the geographical nature of the coign and livery problem.[158] Hundreds of soldiers from the northern and eastern borders received general pardons so that they could evade prosecution for their offences, while comparatively few from the midland breadbasket were pardoned. Decoded, this suggests it was the landlords of the borderlands who lay behind the crisis, hiring more and more soldiers to protect or extend their lands and letting them forage far and wide for their maintenance money. It was entirely understandable that they did this. Soldiers were expensive, particularly specialist soldiers such as gunners, costing as much as 4*d.* per day. To adequately feed and equip a force large enough to do battle with hostile O'Mores, MacGiollapadraigs or Kavanaghs was probably well beyond the pockets of most borderlords, whose lands often yielded a low income. To pay for a large garrison of a dozen men at Ballyragget or Gaulskill would cost at least £75 a year, an enormous sum, and given that there were at least twenty castles of strategic significance in the Kilkenny borderlands, the tax necessary to support large garrisons in each would never be acceptable to the majority of the county population who lived in the midland bowl. Thus the local borderlords had recourse to illegitimate means of military maintenance, and they bastardised coign and livery, employing a whole range of illegal and repressive methods to pay for their forces.

The cheapest option was to let the soldiers forage for themselves. A number of commanders encouraged their men to boost their earnings through protection rackets, intimidation, theft and murder. In 1552/3 a woman refugee fleeing the Laois plantation was caught on the highway leading into Co. Kilkenny and 'spoiled of all, [stripped] to her very petticoat' by her assailants, kerne employed by Viscount Mountgarret and the baron of Upper Ossory.[159] It is significant that her attackers put her four servants to the sword. Despite the high level of incipient violence along the northern and eastern marchlands, murder had been a relatively rare occurrence. As noted earlier, even in the early 1530s little blood had been spilled between the Butlers and their then enemies, the Geraldines. The level of bloodshed – murders and 'accidental killings' – that occurred in the mid-Tudor period was quite unprecedented. Among those slain as tensions mounted was the horseman Richard Archdekin, hacked down by a group of kerne that included one of the O'Brennans.[160] It could be said that, as

157 Edwards, 'Butler revolt', 235–7. **158** *CPRI, Henry VIII–Eliz. I,* 172–3, 175–6, 179, 182–3, 185–8, 199–201, 236, 241–3, 245–7, 249–50, 272–80, 285, 294–6. **159** Parke (ed.), *Vocacyon of Johan Bale,* 415. **160** *Ir. Fiants,* Edward VI, no. 454. Archdekin was probably one of a band of soldiers commanded by Robennet Purcell of Foulkesrath active at this time (ibid., no. 384).

a professional soldier, he was bound to run the risk of a bloody death – but not so the gentry. The killing of one of their number, Thomas Purcell of Derrileigh, must have come as a shock to the county community, indicating that those responsible for the upsurge of violence had scant regard for social boundaries.[161]

The most serious murder of the period involved one of the county's leading landlords, John Fitzgerald of Burnchurch, who in 1552 was ambushed and killed at Mallardstown, three miles from his home, by a gang of soldier-outlaws led by Edmund More O'Clery. Significantly, at the time of his death he was the serving sheriff of the shire, engaged in the revitalisation of the English judicial system in Kilkenny. As a government agent put it, Fitzgerald was slain 'only for doing justice'.[162] Irrespective of the wishes of many powerful groups in the shire – the merchants, the midlands gentry, even the earls of Ormond – other sections of local society, chiefly borderers, soldiers and their relatives, dreaded the replacement of mixed law and brehon law with the English common law, which carried the death penalty for so many offences. This became clear in the career of Piers Grace. Grace was among Fitzgerald's killers, and although hated by many of the county elite, he successfully evaded punishment for his part in the murder and became a bandit.[163] For more than forty years thereafter he played cat-and-mouse with the county authorities, sure of the support and protection of local groups who shared his distaste of the law courts.[164]

The Kilkenny gentry were confronted by a serious loss of social control, and their estates were plundered. Sir John Grace of Courtstown was one of the principal victims of the local troops. Late in the reign of Edward VI one of his own kinsmen, Adam Grace, joined with some northern Archdekin soldiers to rob his stud in the Slieveardagh hills.[165] This attack must have come as a great surprise, for hitherto Sir John had counted the Archdekin troops among his subordinates in his capacity as a senior commander of the Ormond army. It seemed the Butler lordship was coming apart. For possibly the first time in the sixteenth century, Tipperary-based bandits were constantly active in the heart of the county. In 1551 Shane Bane Tobyn MacThomas, a kern from Polcapple, robbed Oliver Grace's estate at Ballylinch in the Kilkenny midlands.[166] A subject of the Ormond liberty, Tobyn knew the risks of stealing from someone like Grace, another leading servant of the earldom, but clearly fancied his chances now that disorder reigned.[167] The true nature of what was occurring is perhaps best illustrated by the Cantwells of Killeen, a Tipperary gang found guilty of stealing cattle from a rival gang of rustlers operating along the Kilkenny-Laois border.[168]

Cattle-raiding was widespread. In the east the frontier had become porous, so that a gang from Co. Carlow led by William McFirr O'Byrne was able to raid into the heartland of Kilkenny almost at will. According to official records,

---

161 NA, Lodge MSS, Articles with Irish chiefs, etc, 42. **162** SP 61/4/72. **163** *Ir. Fiants*, Philip & Mary, no. 162. **164** For some of Grace's post-1552 deeds see SP 63/15/15; SP 63/22/24; SP 63/72/46. **165** *Ir. Fiants*, Edward VI, no. 1024. **166** *COD*, v, no. 1. **167** For Oliver Grace's connections with the earls, see ibid., iv, nos. 264, 317 (2); ibid., v, nos. 47 (1), 59, 80, 101, 138. **168** *Ir. Fiants,* Edward VI, no. 996.

O'Byrne had stolen four horses from Oliver Grace's estate in the dead centre of the county at Ballylinch; five cows from Robert Oge Shortal at Clara near Kilkenny town; three cows from Edmund Blanchville at Blanchvillestown beside Gowran; and ten sows from Dermot Bolger along the frontier at Shankill.[169]

THE FRAGMENTATION OF BUTLER POWER

It was no coincidence that the breakdown of authority occurred during an inter-regnum in the Ormond lordship. Following Earl James' death in 1546 the Butler dynasty was suddenly without a proper head, as his London-based son Thomas was as yet too young to succeed him. Consequently, the dynastic unity that the ninth earl had imposed on the cadet branches of the Butlers quickly eroded. In Co. Tipperary the baron of Dunboyne cut loose of Ormond control and began redeveloping an autonomous lordship of his own. Further west, the Butler baron of Cahir again allied himself with Desmond. Large parts of Tipperary were soon overrun. For a time the ninth earl's widow, the Dowager Countess Joan, was recognised by the crown as the co-governor of her late husband's territories along with her brother-in-law Viscount Mountgarret. She remained *in situ* until 1549, but following the death of her second husband, Sir Francis Bryan, she decided to leave Kilkenny and return to the south-west. There she once more married, taking her cousin Garret Fitzgerald, the heir to the earldom of Desmond, and many years her junior, as her third and final husband.

Though he managed to do his duty to his deceased brother by keeping the Ormond estate intact, Richard Butler, first Viscount Mountgarret, was an ineffective head of the Butler family. Most of the lands that had been settled on him were frontier lands in the north of the county at Ballyragget and in the east bordering Wexford. His main concern was to develop a strong base for himself independent of the earldom. From the 1530s onwards, following his return from Liege in the Low Countries, where he had lived for a number of years,[170] he had made Wexford (especially the territory known as the Fassagh Bantry) the main focus of his interests. Inevitably his heavy involvement in Wexford diverted his attention from Kilkenny, something that compounded the spread of law-lessness there.

The early stages of Mountgarret's local leadership were marked by poor relations with Dublin. Unlike his dead brother, the viscount was a strident Catholic. Though he had benefited from Henry VIII's religious policies, receiving a crown lease of an ex-monastic estate at Inistioge, he became uncomfortable under Edward VI, when the established religion lurched from a form of Catholicism without the pope to open Protestant heresy. The appearance of John Bale, a zealous Protestant bishop, at Kilkenny in 1552 drove the viscount into a conspiracy with his neighbour, the MacGiollapadraig baron of Upper Ossory, to drive the

169 Ibid., no. 946. **170** *Cal. SP, Spanish, 1553*, 412.

1 Seal of Piers Ruadh Butler, 8th earl of Ormond, 1539

2 Kilkenny Castle, overlooking the Nore. Nineteenth-century drawing

3 Gannagh Castle, on the banks of the Suir, by Francis Place, 1699

4 James 'the lame' Butler, 9th earl of Ormond. Sketch by Holbein, *c*.1540

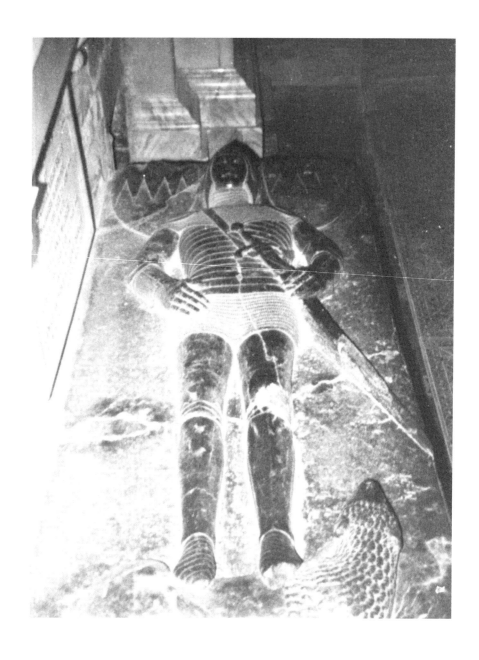

5 Tomb of James Butler, 9th earl of Ormond (d. 1546), St Canice's
Cathedral, Kilkenny

6 'Black' Thomas Butler, 10th earl of Ormond. Probable wedding portrait of 1559; artist unknown

7 Kilkenny city street scene, 19th century drawing

8 Burnchurch Castle

9 James Butler, 12th earl of Ormond, c.1635

10 Christopher Wandesford, master of the rolls and lord deputy of Ireland,
c.1640

prelate out. Previously Mountgarret and Upper Ossory had been at war. Bale's strident advocacy of Protestantism alienated Mountgarret from the Edwardian government; so too did other factors. The promotion of his main adversary on the Kilkenny/Wexford border, the ex-rebel Cahir MacArt Kavanagh, to the Irish peerage as baron of Ballianne in 1552 outraged Mountgarret, who took it as a deliberate affront to his long record of loyal service. By 1553 the ties binding the Butler lordship to Dublin and London had been temporarily sundered. Though it is impossible to be certain, Mountgarret may have been behind a rumour circulating in Co. Kilkenny that in England the Protestant government had ordered the killing of his nephew, young Earl Thomas. Bishop Bale suspected this was the case. If so, then Mountgarret and the Butlers may have been on the brink of rebellion prior to King Edward's death on 6 July 1553.[171]

Queen Mary's accession was announced to general celebration in Kilkenny town square on 20 August 1553, and in the presence of the shire gentry there was a Catholic procession through the streets. Similar festivities took place shortly afterwards at Thomastown. At once Mountgarret and Upper Ossory despatched their men to eke out Bishop Bale and his servants. On 8 September five of Bale's episcopal tenants, including three Englishmen, were ambushed and killed in a hayfield by an armed gang of 20 soldiers, who 'leaped out of their lurking bushes, with swords and with darts'. Bale was convinced that his life was in danger from 'the furious family of Mountgarret', and about a week later the frightened bishop stole away and fled the country. Following his exit Kilkenny was a more staunchly Catholic place than it had been before his arrival.[172]

The reign of Queen Mary witnessed a pronounced improvement in Mountgarret's relations with the Dublin administration, and by 1556 he was busy helping the government to establish the new English colony in Laois and Offaly. Among other things he attained a degree of notoriety for his part in the 1557 capture and execution of the dispossessed O'More chieftain, Connill Oge.[173] Following Queen Mary's death, however, and the accession of her Protestant half-sister, Elizabeth I, the viscount began experiencing fresh difficulties with the government. Although his position seemed safe and secure in the summer of 1559, with Lord Deputy Sussex agreeing to forward his suits for the renewal of certain crown leases,[174] by Easter 1562 the renewals had still not materialised. Despite testimonials on his behalf by the earls of Clanricard and Thomond, he never in fact received the lands that he wanted from Elizabeth.[175] Perhaps the Protestant queen was unwilling to forgive his earlier rough treatment of Bishop Bale, now installed as one of her chaplains at Whitehall?

Mountgarret's greatest shortcoming was his failure to reverse the ongoing fragmentation of Butler power. Without a resident earl of Ormond, the Butler

171 S.G. Ellis, 'John Bale, Bishop of Ossory, 1552–3', *Butler Soc. Jn.* 2/3 (1984), 287–91. 172 Ibid.; Parke (ed.), *Vocacyon of Johan Bale*, 415–7. 173 Mountgarret's involvement in Connill Oge's death was recalled years later: Anon (ed.), 'The complaints of Shane O'Neill', *UJA* 2 (1854), 222. 174 *Cal. Carew MSS, 1515–74*, 283; SP 63/1/56; *Ir. Fiants*, Eliz. I, nos. 54, 56, 64. 175 SP 63/5/68, 74.

dynasty was splintering into an increasing number of rival groups. Where once everything had been centralised at Kilkenny Castle, now rival Butler branches vied with each other for control of their respective areas, and it had become customary for them to reject the larger dynastic interest and follow an independent line aimed at self-aggrandisement.[176]. Indeed, the decline of central control was speeding up as the 1550s progressed, for towards the end of the decade several new players appeared on the stage, three of them younger brothers of 'Black' Thomas, the absent tenth earl. Beginning with Sir Edmund Butler of Cloghgrenan *c*.1556, followed by Edward Butler and Piers Butler shortly afterwards, the earl's siblings announced their arrival on the scene like typical Gaelic warlords, in a rites-of-passage orgy of cattle stealing and violence. Unconcerned by the interests of Mountgarret and Ormond, Edmund, Edward and Piers Butler looked to break free of their elders. It remained to be seen if the long-delayed return from London of the young tenth earl would succeed in re-establishing order.

EARL THOMAS AND REFORM, 1556–65

Since going to England in 1544 Earl Thomas had grown apart from his younger brothers and from other representatives of his dynasty. Unlike them, he was not a border warlord. He was instead a thoroughly anglicised courtier, just what his father, the ninth earl, had intended him to be. Having spent a decade in London attending upon three Tudor monarchs – Henry VIII, Edward VI and Mary I – Thomas was more accustomed to the pomp and circumstance of English royal ceremony than the raids and counter-raids of Irish frontier life. His brothers' military activities must have seemed alien to one who had participated in the coronation of Edward VI in 1547 and gone on embassy to France a few years later.[177] At the time of his return to Ireland in 1554 his friends and associates were young English lords. The distance between him and his family was perhaps best revealed by his cautious response to the restoration of the Fitzgerald earldom of Kildare. In 1556 he became embroiled in a squabble with the eleventh earl of Kildare, Garret Fitzgerald, over the correct order of precedence to be followed at state ceremonies in Ireland, disputing Kildare's right to walk before him. Otherwise Earl Thomas refrained from competition, preferring if possible to seek common cause with Kildare – like him a prominent Irish courtier – in defending the role of the great feudal magnates in the government of the country. (Limited rivalry with Kildare in Leinster had the added benefit of preventing Kildare from drawing too close to the Fitzgeralds of Desmond, Ormond's great foes in Munster). His caution contrasted with the behaviour of his brother Sir Edmund Butler, who repeatedly came to blows with Kildare over Shillelagh in Wicklow.[178] Despite Sir Edmund's desire to carve out a large

---

176 Edwards, 'Butler revolt', 235–7.   **177** *APC, 1547–50*, 85; ibid., *1550–2*, 271.   **178** E.g., SP

private fief in the area, Ormond stood back, refusing to sanction further Butler aggression there if it meant antagonising Kildare. The young tenth earl saw the land of his birth through a courtier's eyes. Arousing the enmity of Kildare would mean risking the wrath of the monarchy itself, a chance he was not willing to take. Throughout his life Ormond remained convinced that the interests of his dynasty were best served by close identification with the Tudor monarchy.

Earl Thomas understood the underlying principles of crown policy and realised that noble power could only survive and prosper by adapting to royal authority. Before his homecoming he had already twice distinguished himself as a loyal subject of the Tudors. In 1547, barely sixteen years old, he had fought in Edward VI's English army that had invaded Scotland. More recently, early in 1554 he had served in the defence of King Edward's successor, Queen Mary, campaigning outside London against the Wyatt rebels. By acting as he did Ormond not only helped to secure the throne for Mary, thus gaining her lasting gratitude; equally important, he had earned a reputation as a loyal Irish nobleman 'of outstanding power and lineage'.[179]

For more than a decade after his return to Ireland Earl Thomas attempted to bridge the English and Irish worlds, determined to stay in touch with the royal court from his seat at Kilkenny Castle. At times his eagerness to return to London had to be restrained, as in January 1558, when Queen Mary wrote a note urging him to stay at home and 'perform the part of a nobleman' in Kilkenny while the lord deputy, his friend the earl of Sussex, was away at court on government business.[180] His marriage in London in 1559 to Elizabeth Berkeley marked his entry into the powerful Howard/Radcliffe faction of conservative nobles at court, for his bride was a kinswoman of Thomas Howard, fourth duke of Norfolk, and the greatest magnate in England.[181] Yet Ormond remained his own man, and factional loyalties did not prevent him from having good relations with Norfolk's opponents, chiefly the secretary of state, Sir William Cecil,[182] and the master of the royal horse, Robert Dudley, who was created earl of Leicester in 1564. It is not usually recognised that Ormond actually maintained friendly contact with Leicester before 1566, at one stage even trusting Leicester to present his grievances directly to Elizabeth I.[183] During the 1560s, as he matured it became increasingly clear that Ormond had already managed to carve out a niche for himself at the Tudor court, and was regarded by royal officials as a model Irish subject, one who could blend in with 'English majesty'. The accession of Elizabeth I in 1558 greatly improved his position, and gave him the edge over the earl of Kildare.[184] In August 1559 Elizabeth appointed him lord treasurer of Ireland, on the recommendation of Sussex, a development that concerned Kildare only a little but greatly alarmed the earl of

63/26/19. **179** *Cal. SP, Spanish, 1554*, p.86; D. MacCulloch (ed.), 'The *Vita Mariae Angliae Reginae* of Robert Wingfield of Brantham', *Camden Miscellany* 28 (1984), 284. **180** HMC, *Ormonde MSS, 1543–1711*, 4–5. **181** Smyth, *Lives of the Berkeleys*, ii, 252–5. **182** E.g., SP 63/8/1. **183** HMC, *Pepys MSS* (London 1911), 34; D. Wilson, *Sweet Robin: a biography of Robert Dudley, earl of Leicester, 1533–88* (London 1981), 99. **184** Chapter 2 above.

Desmond, whose father had held the post previously.[185] The treasurership was just the beginning of a long period of royal favour for Ormond. Following a lengthy sojourn at Elizabeth's court in 1562 the number of grants and commissions that came his way began to multiply.[186] Desmond, increasingly anxious, hoped that by forcing Earl Thomas into open warfare in Munster he could check his advancement; Ormond, however, was reluctant to play this game and hoped to overcome Desmond more by political intrigue at Whitehall and Greenwich than by wholesale confrontation on the murky frontiers of Munster. As many historians have noted, the Black Earl found it impossible not to be drawn into conflict, and authorised a series of attacks against Desmond, yet it is often overlooked that his inclinations were against the military option.

The distance separating Ormond from his kinsmen was not immediately apparent after his return, as one of the first things he did was to join them on a campaign against rebels who also happened to be their enemies. Once the crown required more of him than simple frontier soldiering, however, the gulf between him and his brothers became manifest. Mary reminded him of the need to look not just to military glory, but also to the 'maintenance of justice, peace and tranquillity'.[187] The crown insisted there be no private feuds, no harbouring of bandits, no repression or racketeering, in his territories. His errant siblings must cease being warlords and conform to English law and custom. Writing in 1560 Lord Deputy Sussex insisted that coign and livery be thoroughly abolished in all Irish lordships, Ormond's included; the Ormond lands could only be brought into line with English conditions through systematic demilitarisation.[188] Earl Thomas soon indicated his willingness to comply with the crown's wishes, irrespective of his brothers' interests.

One of the first things the Black Earl did was to bring Kilkenny back into the government's tax net. The subsidy, a problem in Kilkenny/Dublin relations earlier in the century, was no longer a major issue. In 1559 the earl's servant Oliver Grace helped the government prepare its assessment,[189] and following the 1560 parliament the subsidy was raised without apparent difficulty, the crown aiding its acceptance by agreeing to levy one third of the overall sum on the inhabitants of Upper Ossory. The assessment was based on a royal valuation of the wealth of all the gentry and freeholders of the county who held land by knight's service, and encountered no local opposition.[190] The tax continued being paid as late as 1565, when four local gents, Oliver Grace, John Rochford, Edmund Fitzgerald and Walter Gall, were appointed collectors of the levy by writ out of the exchequer.[191]

The tenth earl showed his eagerness to embrace more far-reaching reforms by allowing a new military tax known as the cess (that is, assessment) to be col-

---

185 *Ir. Fiants*, Eliz. I, no. 133. 186 He received at least eight royal grants in the two-year period from Dec. 1562 to Nov. 1564: ibid., nos. 469, 497, 504, 542, 563, 666, 682, 685. 187 HMC, *Ormonde MSS, 1543–1711*, 4. 188 *Cal. Carew MSS, 1515–74*, no. 227. 189 SP 63/1/81. 190 Lambeth Ms 611, fol. 87. 191 St Peter's College, Wexford, Hore MSS, Vol. 70: Exchequer Memoranda Rolls, 1563–1614: 30.

Chart 3.2 *Government cess demands in Co. Kilkenny, 1556–9*

Year	Money	Labour service	Wheat	Malt	Value
1556	IIR£38	—	1,000 pecks	1,000 pecks	IR£198 8s. 0d.
1557	—	400 men	200 pecks	—	IR£106 6s. 4d.
1558	—	—	200 pecks	—	IR£16 6s. 6d.
1559	IR£38	—	200 pecks	—	IR£54 6s. 6d.

Sources: HMC, *De L'Isle & Dudley MSS*, i, 366, 373; HMC, *Haliday MSS*, 22–3, 32, 67, 73–4

lected in his territories. This was a significant concession. In theory, the cess was designed to gradually undermine the need for coign and livery and local private armies by facilitating the emergence of a larger, more active, royal army in the country. Following on the policies of Bellingham and Croft in Edward VI's time, it was decided *c.*1556 that two new government garrisons, Leighlinbridge in Carlow and Fort Protector in Queen's County, should be partly financed by the Kilkenny population. In addition the county community was asked to contribute to the costs of viceregal expeditions. Accordingly, between 1556 and 1559 contributions worth nearly £100 a year were paid over as cess to the government (Chart 3.2). The successful introduction of cess may have signalled the young earl of Ormond's desire to curb the private armies in his country. No other explanation seems feasible, for had he allowed private force and coign and livery to remain, his acceptance of cess would have meant asking the county to pay two defence taxes instead of one, something he would have been unwise to attempt, especially so early in his overlordship. Evidently, from the very beginning of his career 'Black' Earl Thomas was suspicious of the Butler forces and was inclined towards the erosion of their military power and independence through reform and re-anglicisation.

The earl's commitment to military reform was genuine insofar as it was entirely self-interested. By accepting the cess he could eventually replace coign and livery with a new charge of which both he and the government approved – and for a courtier like him, crown approval was no minor matter. So long as he remained on good terms with the Tudor monarchy, he knew that in practice he (and men of his own choosing) would be allowed to oversee the collection of the cess. This would pay for a 'shire force' such as operated across England and Wales, ostensibly to the crown's benefit, but in reality to his too, for he would gain a new local army more answerable to his command. Ormond, in other words, intended to use the abandonment of coign and livery and the acceptance of cess to take greater control of the local soldiery. It was a clever analysis of the possibilities of state expansion, a piece of opportunism that could simultaneously enhance the earldom in Kilkenny and London. His brothers

might be persuaded to accept this new arrangement if they were given commissions as commanders of the local force on the government payroll. As early
as 6 May 1558 Ormond showed himself ready to oversee the introduction of
government musters in Co. Tipperary.[192] Within a year this had spread to
Kilkenny when, in May 1559, he and thirteen others – including his brother
Sir Edmund and the sovereigns of Kilkenny, Callan and Thomastown – received
a combined commission of muster and array. This enabled them to assess the
inhabitants of the shire 'according to the quantity of their lands and chattels ...
and to muster all the inhabitants of every barony or hundred, according the
tenor of a proclamation annexed to the commission'.[193]

The establishment of musters was central to Ormond's plans. In theory, an
annual gathering of the serviceable population of the county (adult males
between 16 and 60) would provide yearly confirmation of the earl's authority.
Like everyone else, his brothers' men would have to present themselves for
inspection by his representatives. The system was operative before July 1560,
when the government was able to announce that the provincial muster-point
for the men of Kilkenny was Lyons Hill, Co. Kildare.[194]

The earl's acceptance of the re-emergence of the common law would have
further concerned his brothers and kinsmen. Though impossible to be certain
– too few court records survive – the Kilkenny assize courts had apparently
struggled into life in the late 1540s and early 1550s.[195] Earl Thomas did not
oppose their continuance. Extant documents among the Ormond papers, and
lists of long-lost government records, indicate that shortly after Sussex's appointment as deputy in 1556 sessions of the peace and pleas of the crown were held
regularly in Co. Kilkenny as part of a twice yearly assize circuit. In January 1557,
for instance, pleas of the crown were held at Thomastown before the vice-treasurer, Sir Henry Sidney,[196] and sessions were apparently held in Kilkenny town
every year after 1558.[197]

The proceedings of these courts ran immediately counter to the interests of
the junior Butlers and their retainers. At the 1557 Thomastown pleas several
local soldiers were indicted of various crimes, principally theft, but also of major
offences such as conspiracy and treason. Thus one Maurice fitz Morish and some
border gentlemen were accused of assembling their forces unlawfully at
Dammagh – one of Ormond's manors – on 10 October 1556, where they were

---

192 *Eighth Report of the Irish Record Commission* (Dublin 1819), 519.   193 NA, Lodge MSS, Articles,
etc., no page number.   194 HMC, *Haliday MSS*, 81–2.   195 There may have been court sessions
around the county in 1550 following a commission of oyer and terminer and gaol delivery granted
to members of the Irish council, Lord Mountgarret, and others (NA, Lodge MSS, Articles, etc.,
87). Sir Thomas Howth, chief justice of the king's bench, almost certainly held sessions during his
prolonged visit to Kilkenny in August 1553 (Ellis, 'John Bale', 288–90). Another sign that the
county court was operative by the end of Henry VIII's reign is the increasing number of royal
pardons that were granted to local lawbreakers between *c*.1545 and 1552 (see note 158 above).
Pardons had to be produced in a shire court to prevent an indictment proceeding.   196 NLI, D
2626. Sidney received a commission of oyer and terminer on 12 February following (NA, Lodge
MSS, Articles, etc., 91).   197 *Eighth Report of the Irish Record Commission*, 117–21.

said to have entered into an alliance (probably with Conill O'More) 'to make war on the English subjects ... within the county of Kilkenny and elsewhere'. The jurors in the case, Anglo-Irishmen from the shire midlands, stated on oath that in the event of the accused failing to prove their innocence, they would be 'adjudged traitors', attainted of high treason in accordance with a statute of the Irish parliament of 10 Henry VII, and so face the death penalty.[198] Should the common law continue in this manner, it would only be a matter of time before the followers of the Butlers faced similar verdicts.

The legal reforms gathered speed around March 1560 when, following the closure of parliament, the winter assize was held in Kilkenny. Ormond's hench-man, Oliver Grace, and Grace's grandson, Philip, appeared before the court, to answer charges of having committed theft, arson and accidental manslaughter at Garryhiggin while hunting rebel O'Fogartys. They confessed their guilt and were subsequently pardoned.[199] Another of those brought before the court was Richard O'Morghoe of Thomastown, who was found guilty of conveying stolen sows across the River Barrow to New Ross. The government also pardoned him. William Grace, however, was not so fortunate. A kern, he had stolen some clothes and household effects, just the sort of behaviour that made soldiers a major nuisance. On the orders of the court – which may have been presided over by Ormond, who was in residence in Ireland – he was hanged for felony.[200]

Ormond was aware that these changes would have seemed meaningless to his government critics if he allowed coign and livery, the basis of his brothers' military independence, to remain in place. Yet he remained cautious about its abolition. Though his family was an embarrassment, the speed with which they could put a force in the field was entirely the product of coign, which (in its bastardised form) enabled troops to be hired almost at will. Moreover, the fact that Earl Thomas expected raids into Tipperary by the Desmond Fitzgeralds delayed its abrogation. In 1561 he began to remove coign from his own lands in Co. Kilkenny, leaving it to his brothers to decide whether to continue its use in the frontier territories under their control. In 1564 Ormond's problems with Desmond seemed to have ended, which at last freed him to act. Further distancing himself from his brothers and kinsmen, on 1 July he issued a procla-mation in the liberty of Tipperary that definitively eliminated the levying of coign and livery there 'to God's mercy, the honour of the queen's majesty and the advancement of the commonwealth'. Coign, the earl argued, was a 'horri-ble devouring monster' that had outlived its usefulness and caused much unnec-essary suffering among his subjects, who had been plunged into 'poverty, misery and calamity ... by the licentious multitudes of Irish rascals' that the levy main-tained. His words represented a rebuke of the conduct of his kinsmen (partic-ularly the baron of Dunboyne). Henceforth, these would again be under Ormond's thumb, with coign and livery banned from all parts 'of the Butlers' lands and possessions ... in any part of the county and liberty'.[201]

198 *COD*, v, no. 67.   199 *Ir. Fiants*, Eliz. I, no. 232.   200 Ibid., no. 255.   201 Edwards, 'Butler

Ormond had little choice in the matter. He had to take the military back into his own hands for fear that the outlying areas of the Butler lordship would achieve autonomy. Like Dunboyne in Tipperary, his brother Sir Edmund Butler of Cloghgrenan was in the process of establishing a large power-base of his own in Carlow, and his actions there increasingly conflicted with Earl Thomas' interests. By the beginning of Queen Elizabeth's reign Sir Edmund had annexed the O'Doran territories in Idrone along Kilkenny's north-eastern frontier, thus fulfilling a policy initiated by his father, the ninth earl,[202] but this was not the limit of his ambitions. He began meddling further to the east, in Wicklow, defying Earl Thomas by challenging the Kildare Fitzgeralds in the region.[203] Of still greater concern to Ormond was Sir Edmund's behaviour in Co. Kilkenny, where he had made inroads into Idough and the O'Brennans' country, apparently dominating the Clan Wickelow sept, able to lead his troops through their lands without encountering any opposition. Indeed, a considerable number of the O'Brennans had fallen under his sway, for according to one source up to a quarter of his soldiers were members of the lineage.[204] This might have suited Earl Thomas had it led the O'Brennans to recognise his claims over their lands, but nothing of the sort was forthcoming, probably because Sir Edmund's gains in Idough were made in a private capacity, not on the earldom's behalf. What better way, then, for Ormond to keep Sir Edmund's expansionism in check than to call a halt to coign and livery, the basis of his military might?

The abolition of coign and livery in Tipperary should have been mirrored in Kilkenny shortly afterwards, and so brought Ormond's reform efforts to completion, but this was not to be. The abolition policy had been greatly facilitated by a negotiated settlement with Desmond in the first half of 1564. The peace did not last, and in November Desmond's men raided one of Ormond's richest farms in Tipperary, rounded up his cattle and put several of his tenants to the sword. Ormond reacted violently and, vowing swift and bloody vengeance, he rallied his family, and sanctioned the continuance of coign in Kilkenny and its re-imposition in Tipperary.[205] By February 1565 it was as though he had never attempted change. Accompanied by three of his brothers, Sir Edmund, James and Edward Butler, he led an army of about 500 men – 100 horsemen, 300 gallowglasses and kerne, and an unspecified number of stragglers – south from Clonmel to encounter his enemy near Affane Cross in Co. Waterford. In the ensuing battle, the Butlers prevailed, and Desmond became Ormond's prisoner having been wounded by a shot from Sir Edmund Butler's pistol.[206]

---

revolt', 237–8; *COD*, v, no. 102; SP 63/11/39 (ii).   **202** Moore, 'English action, Irish reaction', 62, 66; *COD*, v, nos.109–10, 112, 125, 153.   **203** HMC, *Haliday MSS*, 152–3.   **204** SP 63/11/4; N. Murphy, 'The O'Brennans and the ancient territory of Hy-Duach', *Ossory Arch. Soc. Jn.* i (1874–9), 399, where Cloneen is given as 'Cloyne'.   **205** SP 63/11/108.   **206** G. Butler, 'The Battle of Affane', *Irish Sword* 8 (1967/8), 33–47, remains the standard account of the confrontation, although his suggestion (43) that Ormond may have had up to 4,000 men in his army is untenable. As shown above, at their peak in the 1530s the Butlers of Ormond had 800–1,000 soldiers only. The tenth earl's Affane force would have been smaller still, as both Mountgarret and Dunboyne were not present with their detachments.

Traditionally, Irish historians have portrayed the battle of Affane as a major (and entirely positive) turning point in the career of the tenth earl of Ormond. Instead of being punished for fighting a private war, he managed to win the queen's favour and emerge as one of her leading courtiers by early 1566, while Desmond, in contrast, found himself under lock and key in the Tower of London. However, as I have argued elsewhere, Ormond's rapid elevation should not obscure the fact that immediately after Affane he was in serious trouble with the royal government. During the summer of 1565 he discovered that his involvement in the battle had been a serious miscalculation, for Elizabeth was furious, and authorised a full-scale inquiry that was empowered to look into his conduct as much as Desmond's. The fact that Earl Thomas's call to arms had been supported by his brothers suddenly came back to haunt him, putting him on the same level as them, and sustaining his government critics who suspected his hand behind every Butler transgression. For more than six months his fate hung in the balance, until Christmas Eve 1565, when the queen finally made her award. Even then, he did not escape lightly. Though he avoided imprisonment, he was made sign a recognisance of £20,000 promising to abide by the terms of the royal decree and keep the peace forever with his enemy. Should he, or his family, be seen to break this promise in the future, then he would face bankruptcy.[207]

The increased prominence that Ormond enjoyed in the queen's circle from 1566 brought added political vulnerability. His sudden high status at Whitehall earned him the jealousy of other, more established figures. His chief opponent, of course, was Robert Dudley, earl of Leicester, who for several years had been Elizabeth's main favourite, and who greatly resented Ormond's intrusion onto what he perceived as his rightful place. Ormond did not help matters by letting it be known that he was among those who thought, of all her suitors, English and foreign, the queen should marry the archduke of Austria, the half-brother of Philip II.[208] In doing so he invited the hostility not only of Leicester, but of the entire Protestant party at court, a group that ranged from the church of England bishops to lay peers such as the Puritan earl of Bedford. All of these feared that marriage to the archduke, a leading Catholic prince, would greatly undermine their religion.[209] One of the first to criticise Ormond during 1566 was Dr Thomas Young, the archbishop of York.[210] With adversaries like these the earl's position was precarious, especially as he had recently been in disgrace for his recourse to arms in Ireland. At a stroke his family's military strength had become Ormond's weakest point, and the maintenance of the queen's good opinion the main key to his political security. If the earl was to survive the scrutiny of so many envious and suspicious onlookers, it followed that he could not afford to be associated with any more acts of violence. Once again he would have to distance himself from his brothers and their soldiers, otherwise their

207 Edwards, 'Butler revolt', 240–2. 208 *Cal. SP, Spanish, 1558–67*, 529. 209 The Protestant party's misgivings are discussed in N. Jones, *The birth of the Elizabethan age: England in the 1560s* (Oxford 1993), ch. 4. 210 *Cal. SP, Spanish*, 1558–67, 553.

conduct might ruin his prospects of becoming one of the great figures of the Elizabethan court.

Ormond's concern over the military issue was compounded by the appearance in Ireland of a new chief governor, Sir Henry Sidney. Sidney was appointed to the lord deputyship in October 1565, following the conclusion of the royal inquiry into the battle of Affane. Worryingly for Ormond, he was already ill disposed towards the Butler family. Sidney had served in the Irish administration in the late 1550s, first as vice-treasurer, then as lord justice, and during that time he had taken a dim view of conditions inside the Butler territories, which he had seen at first hand. A partisan politician, as early as 1558 he had befriended the earl of Desmond,[211] whom naively he was convinced needed protection from Butler aggression. Most recently he had defended Desmond's cause during the Affane inquiry.[212] Sir Henry's intervention was effective insofar as it helped to force Earl Thomas into accepting his share of the blame for the battle. He was undoubtedly the last person Ormond would have wanted installed in Dublin Castle once the inquiry was over.[213]

Even had Sidney been better inclined towards the Butlers he would have had to tackle the military problem in Kilkenny and Tipperary as soon as he arrived in office, for the local soldiery had continued to run amuck after Affane. In one incident they achieved widespread notoriety across southern Ireland, for it was reported that the Marian bishop of Ossory, John O'Thonery, had died as a result of their villainy. Sometime in 1565 O'Thonery had sold some of his see lands to local gentry, including Ormond's agent, Richard Shee. Shortly after he had been paid for the lands, brigands stole the sums he had received. The robbery was apparently a violent one, and the bishop fell ill and died soon afterwards, reputedly of shock.[214] The local armed gangs were as out of control as ever. Although those responsible for the prelate's death were eventually tracked down, brought to trial at Kilkenny, and executed, by the time Sidney set sail for Ireland there was growing agitation in the Kilkenny area for stern steps to be taken against the military as a group. Immediately before his crossing to Ireland Sidney gained firsthand experience of the problem when one of his own servants was robbed at Liverpool by a follower of the Butlers, the cut-purse Patrick Fyn, a 'lackey late in the earl of Ormond's livery, now out of service', who divested Sidney's man of jewels and gold worth £5. In deference to Sidney the Liverpool authorities had Fyn 'nailed to a post by the ear and ... whipped out of the town naked from the middle upwards'.[215]

211 In Feb. 1557 Sidney entertained Desmond's father at Kilkee Castle, Co. Kildare: Kent AO, Ms U1475 025/1, fol. 77v. 212 SP 63/14/38. 213 Sussex's hostility towards him also explains his anti-Butler stance: Brady, *Chief governors*, 115. 214 Moran, 'Bishops', 252. 215 D.B. Quinn, *The Elizabethan and the Irish* (Ithaca, New York 1966), 149.

With the commencement of the Sidney administration in Dublin the fate of Fyn and his ilk was sealed. By the middle of 1566 combating the soldiers of Kilkenny and Tipperary had become doubly important to the new lord deputy, for he suddenly discovered that it was his only viable tactic against the Ormond and Butler interest. While Sidney had been readying his plans for government, Earl Thomas had been working on Queen Elizabeth, colouring her views on Irish affairs, so that through her he could wreck almost all of Sir Henry's projects one by one. Such was the impact of Ormond's manoeuvring that Sidney soon despaired of the fate of his deputyship. Principally, his plan to reduce Butler influence in Munster by initiating a lord presidency in the province was killed off by Ormond just as it got going. The earl cast doubts over the neutrality of Sir Warham St Leger, the proposed first lord president, persuading Elizabeth that St Leger (the son of the former chief governor, Sir Anthony St Leger) was prejudiced against the Butler family.[216] Apoplectic with frustration, Sidney was powerless to prevent St Leger's withdrawal. Other equally vexing reversals piled up as the queen warmed to the charms of her new favourite. Sidney, she ordered, must restore Ormond to land in Tipperary previously awarded to Dunboyne, give royal ordnance to Ormond to help him recover territory from the native Burkes and O'Mulryans, and levy money due to Ormond on the inhabitants of Cos. Limerick and Waterford. Above all, he must favour Ormond in all his causes, especially against Desmond, or face the queen's wrath.[217] It is hardly surprising that, faced with this barrage of unsolicited instructions from London, Sidney balked at the very notion of aiding the tenth earl of Ormond, whose power in his view was already much too extensive. It was therefore largely to save his deputyship and protect his reputation as a strong man of government that Sidney focused his gaze on the military racketeering of the earl's brothers and their followers. Hopefully he might embarrass Earl Thomas and persuade the queen to send him home to tend to his 'disordered country' before Ormond was able to undermine him completely.[218]

In April 1566 Sir Henry travelled south to Kilkenny, 'the most disordered of all the English counties', and began proceedings against the Butler army in the county court.[219] Aided by Nicholas White of Knocktopher, an ex-client of Ormond who now worked in Dublin, Sidney gathered charges of robbery and extortion against Sir Edmund Butler and 88 of his men. He prosecuted them forthwith, his charge sheet including 15 O'Bryns from Carlow and Wicklow, and 12 Purcells and 20 O'Brennans from north Kilkenny. The case was a watershed in Kilkenny history. Never before had the Butlers of Ormond been taken to task in the local courts, and Sidney let it be known that more prosecutions

216 SP 63/16/67. St Leger was formally withdrawn later in the year: Brady, 'Faction', 295.   **217** HMC, *De L'Isle & Dudley MSS*, ii, 2; SP 63/17/49, 54, 62; SP 63/16/6–8, 70.   **218** Sidney's repeated calls for the earl's return are treated in J. Curtis, 'The Butler revolt of 1569', unpublished MA thesis, St Patrick's College, Maynooth (1983), 50–6.   **219** SP 63/17/13. Considering this and other evidence noted below it is difficult to accept the view of one scholar that Sidney was unable to take 'corrective action' against the Butlers in the period 1565–9 (Curtis, 'Butler revolt', 60).

would follow unless they obeyed the queen's laws. In addition, he asked James Grace of Kilkenny to hand over his stone castle in the town, known as Grace's Castle, for use as a new county jail; evidently, the shire had not had a proper prison for many years. For co-operating Grace was appointed hereditary constable of the jail.[220]

Sidney's victory was short-lived.[221] When he tried to bring the indictments to trial in Dublin he found the way blocked, in June receiving a stern warning from Cecil that the queen was displeased and wanted him to drop the case.[222] Still he tried to press on. In July he asked Sir Edmund Butler to appear before him, only for Sir Edmund to point out that this was impossible, as the queen had ordered the charges to be stayed. The following day, 10 July, with no alternative course available, he offered Sir Edmund and his retainers a full royal pardon for their misdemeanours, which was accepted.[223] A month later, utterly fed up, he sought the comfort of Leicester, his brother-in-law: 'So innocent a mind as I bear … you may judge whether my severity or lenity [with the Butlers] hath been my greater fault.'[224] It is difficult not to feel sorry for Sidney. Unbeknownst to him, even his Dudley connection was gone, for Leicester and Ormond had recently settled their differences in London. As a result Leicester told Ormond much of what he knew about Sir Henry's plans to damage him.[225]

Again Earl Thomas had outwitted Sidney. Objecting to the irregular manner in which Sidney had initiated proceedings against his family – proposing to settle the case outside the confines of the common law, by using his prerogative powers in a specially convened deputy's court – Ormond persuaded Elizabeth to chastise the governor. Unfortunately the letter that the queen wrote to the deputy on the matter has not survived; all we know is that Cecil saw it and tried to moderate its harshness by writing separately to Sidney to assure him his service in Ireland was worthwhile.[226] Something else to which the queen apparently alluded was the curious fact that Sidney had accused the Butlers of imposing coign and livery unlawfully, yet he had failed to announce its abolition, as she had authorised him to do, with Ormond's blessing.[227] Stung by the criticism, Sidney returned to Kilkenny early in August, and immediately issued a government proclamation formally outlawing coign and livery and similar exactions in the county. Thomas Masterson, an English official in Kilkenny,[228] wrote to his patron at court, the queen's cousin, Sir Francis Knollys, reporting how there was 'universal joy' among the ordinary people that at last the authorities had acted against their oppressors. Unaware of the intricate politicking that lay behind the proclamation, he beseeched Knollys not to let Elizabeth be persuaded by Ormond to restore the levy.[229] Earl Thomas did not want anything

---

220 *CPRI, Henry VIII–Eliz. I*, 522; *Ir. Fiants*, Edward VI, no. 1238. 221 Sidney's rather skewed version of what ensued is in HMC, *De L'Isle & Dudley MSS*, ii, 4. 222 SP 63/18/19. 223 *Ir. Fiants*, Eliz. I, no.911. 224 HMC, *De L'Isle & Dudley MSS*, ii, 4. 225 Edwards, 'Butler revolt', 242–3. What follows is a revision of that article's analysis of Sidney's August proclamation (ibid., 243). 226 SP 63/18/19. 227 The queen had authorised the general abolition of coign and livery in a letter to the deputy of 14 May 1566 (SP 63/17/49). 228 *Ir. Fiants*, Eliz. I, no. 682. 229 SP

of the sort. Through his influence with the queen, he had managed to get his enemy, the lord deputy, to do his work for him, abolishing an exaction favoured by his brothers that caused him nothing but discomfort.

However, the Black Earl had for once miscalculated. By allowing Sidney to spearhead the assault on military abuses he had given his foe a chance of revenge. As well as outlawing coign, when the deputy went to Kilkenny in August 1566 he had also outlawed the professional Gaelic poets who wrote verses in praise of the Butlers' military prowess. In doing this Sidney was on safe legal ground. An act of the Irish parliament had ordained that 'no rhymer nor other person whatsoever shall make verses ... to anyone after God on Earth except the [English] king, under penalty of the forfeiture of his goods'.[230]

Accordingly, all the Irish poets in the vicinity of Kilkenny – there were several – were arrested, divested of their belongings by Sidney's officials, whipped, and ordered to leave the region.[231] Coincidentally, as required by the terms of the pardon of 10 July, he summoned Sir Edmund Butler and all his followers to appear before him for a second time in the Kilkenny shire court, to demonstrate that they were still under bond to keep the peace.[232] The fact that at about this time he granted powers of martial law in Kilkenny to relative outsiders such as Masterson, Nicholas Heron, and John Sanky (all New English) is surely significant. Absolute discretionary authority – including power of summary execution – was suddenly no longer the preserve of the Butlers, as it had been since martial law had first appeared in the county in the 1550s.[233] As a deliberate act of provocation, this was serious, especially when combined with the punishment of the rhymers, and it soon set the Butlers on edge. After Sidney returned to Dublin, Sir Edmund's forces went on the rampage, and the new sheriff, Masterson, was attacked and forced to leave the shire. As he was later reported to have testified, he had 'his goods stolen, his lands wasted ... [and] hardly escaped with his life'.[234]

The Butlers had other targets also. Plainly aware that the earl of Ormond approved of the abolition of coign and livery – for the earl's agent, Richard Shee, was aiding Sidney[235] – they broke openly from the earl's authority. According to his own later testimony Edward Butler seized control of Upper and Lower Ormond in north Tipperary at about this time, and this although his brother the earl had excluded him from any official position in his territories, keeping him confined to his estates around Ballinahinch.[236] At the end of 1566 the Black Earl's hopes of extracting compensation from Desmond over Affane were scuttled when Sir Edmund Butler refused to travel to Dublin to

63/18/78. According to the queen Ormond's only reservation about the abolition of coign was that it be first removed from disloyal elements (that is, his enemies) before loyal families like his own had to relinquish it: SP 63/17/49. **230** Hore & Graves (ed.), *Social state*, 84. **231** Thomas Churchyard, *Churchyarde his choice* (London 1579), sig. D2v. **232** *Ir. Fiants*, Eliz. I, no. 911. **233** Ibid., no. 953; for earlier commissions of martial law in Co. Kilkenny, which were always to Ormond and his family, and to people of the earl's choosing, see ibid., nos. 56, 64, 182, 469, 682, 724. **234** SP 63/115/10. **235** *Ir. Fiants*, Eliz. I, no. 1030. **236** SP 63/26/4 xiii; SP 63/19/68 to

present the evidence that the earl's servants had meticulously compiled against the Munster Fitzgeralds.[237] By behaving thus he gave succour to Sidney, who had no wish to see Desmond further punished by Ormond.[238] More worrying still for Earl Thomas was his siblings' behaviour in the new year. In January 1567, just as everything was falling into place for Ormond, with Sidney at last deciding to sacrifice Desmond to please the queen, Edward and Piers Butler commenced a new war in Munster. At a stroke Ormond's hopes of compensation collapsed, and his £20,000 bond of 1565 – his very solvency – was placed in jeopardy.

Presented with his best opportunity yet to break Ormond's hold over him, the deputy made haste for Kilkenny. At last able to swipe out at the Butlers without fear of royal obstruction, he held sessions in the county at the end of January. On his orders, certain 'malefactors' were executed, but the main object of his interest was Piers Butler, Ormond's youngest brother. Sometime late in 1566 Piers had shown his contempt for the English legal system by organising an attack on the new county jail, enabling 'prisoners convicted of felony' to effect their escape. Sidney had Piers brought to him and proceeded to humiliate the young nobleman, forcing him, on his knees, to submit to the crown in open court and confess his guilt, before releasing him in a highly contrived demonstration of royal clemency.[239] The deputy acted similarly in Tipperary, hearing indictments against Edward Butler, the baron of Dunboyne, and Piers Butler of Grallagh, recording all the charges against them in a journal of his proceedings composed specially for the queen. The journal was easily as important as the events it purported to record. Sidney was a skilled propagandist, and he made sure that it gave a lasting impression of 'the excessive trains of horsemen and footmen led and kept by the younger brothers of the earl of Ormond, who rather consumed than defended the goods of the poor country'.[240]

In writing the journal Sir Henry hoped to undercut Ormond, claiming that though conditions in Kilkenny–Tipperary had improved under his deputyship, they were bound to deteriorate when he returned to England, as Earl Thomas had failed to appoint officers of 'good reliability' to govern the region.[241] Like many of Sidney's words, these latter comments were a fiction, purposely designed to mask the deteriorating situation in the Ormond territories, where the Butlers were proving themselves no longer answerable to the Black Earl's authority and scornful of his officials. Ignoring their independence, Sidney advised the queen that the earl of Ormond would have to strip his kinsmen of their power, and replace them as rulers of his territories with men of his, the deputy's, choosing. In doing this Sir Henry helped to accelerate the fragmentation of the Butler dynasty and push the earl's brothers further along the road to revolt, for by the end of the year Ormond had partly complied with his

---

237 SP 63/19/72. In September Ormond's officer Patrick Sherlock had brought evidence against Desmond to Cecil in London: SP 63/19/17. **238** Brady, 'Faction', 301–2. **239** J. Buckley (ed.), 'A viceregal progress through the south and west of Ireland in 1567', *WSEIAS*, xii (1909), 66. **240** Ibid., 69–70. **241** Ibid., 66, 70–1.

wishes. Rather than cede power to Sidney's nominees (people such as John Sanky, the new under-marshal of the army) the earl dropped his brother Sir Edmund and recruited Viscount Mountgarret and Sir John Grace of Courtstown to serve as his senior representatives in Ireland.[242]

The tenth earl, it seems, had come to a turning point in his career. By now firmly embedded at court,[243] he was nonetheless concerned that Sidney's version of events in Kilkenny and Tipperary was gaining the queen's sympathy.[244] Previously overlooked private notes and memoranda made by Ormond's servant, Oliver Grace, indicate how the earl was thinking in the years 1567–8.[245] If his brothers could not be relied upon to conform to the crown's wishes and drop coign and livery – described in the memoranda as 'the occasion of the misery of Ireland' – then he would have to distance himself further from them and look to others to act on his behalf. Moreover, now that Sidney had had Desmond imprisoned, Ormond was confident he no longer needed coign, the risk of serious attack from the west having abated.[246] Hence his decision before the end of 1567 to appoint Mountgarret and Sir John Grace to negotiate the full-scale removal of coign and other exactions from all his lands in Ireland with Sidney's agents, Sir Warham St Leger and Henry Davells. The talks were tense, hinging on the amount of compensation that Ormond should receive in order to put in place an alternative method of local defence, but eventually agreement was reached. By the latter part of 1568 it was public knowledge that coign and livery, the basis of the Butlers' military power, was to be abandoned.[247]

The earl's brothers reacted badly to this development. By the autumn of 1568 it was reported how Sir Edmund and Edward Butler were in open defiance of the changes, refusing to abandon coign, and in the earl's continued absence from his territories they spread a rumour that Kilkenny and Tipperary had become exempt from the government's authority.[248] Taking to arms, Sir Edmund attacked Shillelagh in Wicklow, his forces killing women and children there in the absence of the local menfolk.[249] Elsewhere Edward Butler openly fraternised with the bandit Piers Grace, who had regularly attacked Ormond's lands in the past, and whose arrest and execution the earl often desired.[250] Without seeking the earl's permission, Edward hired a large number of extra troops, perhaps doubling the size of the local army, intending to suppress opposition to Butler power across the south. The Ormond lordship became occupied territory. The Butler threat even extended into Wexford, where Edward paraded an army of 1,400 men before 12 November – 400 galloglasses, 200 horsemen, 200 gunners and 600 kerne – by far the biggest force the family had had during the sixteenth century.[251] Government officials in Dublin were greatly

242 Grace, *Memorials*, 11.   **243** A. Strickland, *Lives of the queens of England* (London 1851), iv, 267; *Cal. SP, Spanish, 1558–67*, 627, 630.   **244** E.g., SP 63/21/10.   **245** NLI, Ms 2507, ff 57v, 60r. **246** The manuscript contains a note that Desmond and his brother were imprisoned in the Tower of London for treason on 27 Dec. 1567 (ibid., fol. 60).   **247** Grace, *Memorials*, 11.   **248** SP 63/26/12, 47.   **249** Bod. Lib., Carte Ms 131, fol. 83.   **250** SP 63/26/4, inclosure ii; BL, Cotton Ms Titus B XII, fol 153; ibid., Cotton Ms Vespac. F XII, fol. 1.   **251** His following had increased

alarmed by this show of force. The archbishop of Armagh, Thomas Lancaster, was convinced that Kilkenny and Tipperary were in a state of insurrection because of Edward Butler's activities: 'what he intends, God knoweth, [but] the example is evil'. The prelate was further alarmed by news that Edward had taken forceful possession of 'at least twelve' of Earl Thomas' castles.[252] Lord Deputy Sidney was less surprised. On returning to Ireland in September he felt that the Butlers' resort to arms had been staged for his benefit, to demonstrate that the Ormond country was 'exempted from my authority'. To his eyes, the Butlers were merely posturing.[253]

Instead of seeking an accommodation, Sir Henry tried to brush the Butlers aside, intending to recommence his drive against them with a new strategy – land forfeiture. For some months now he had been encouraging an English Protestant adventurer from Devon, Sir Peter Carew,[254] to pursue his claims to an estate in Leinster and Munster that his ancestors, the de Carrewes, had lost to the Irish in the late fourteenth century.[255] Some of the lands involved were situated in the territory of Idrone, Co. Carlow, where Sir Edmund Butler had his main seat, at Cloghgrenan Castle. The MacMurrough Kavanaghs held much of the rest of the territory. In order to secure Carew's claim, Sidney took an unusual step, and one that caused leading judges in Ireland some unease. He decided to award the lands to Carew by government decree, rather than permit the Butlers and Kavanaghs to challenge Sir Peter in chancery or common pleas, the appropriate courts for such a case. The Dublin council issued the decree in Sidney's absence on 7 December 1568, formally granting Idrone to Carew by act of state, and it received the deputy's signature fifteen days later. And so it was that Sir Edmund Butler and the Kavanaghs were disinherited with neither promise of compensation nor prospect of appeal. Carew received possession of the territory from the sheriff of Carlow before Christmas.[256] Simultaneously, Sidney arrived in Kilkenny for the fourth time in his deputyship, resolved to confront Butler opposition. In a demonstration of unyielding state force, and possibly by power of martial law, he pronounced sentence of execution on 'a great number of Edward Butler's followers'.[257]

During the ensuing months the Butlers sought redress for their plight, but failed to get satisfaction. In London Queen Elizabeth and her ministers were

since September, when O'Carroll reported his forces as 100 horsemen, 200 galloglasses, 100 gunners and 500 kerne: Bod. Lib., Carte Ms 131, fol. 80. See also SP 63/26/4 iii. Carew's claim that in Nov. 1568 the Butler army totalled 2,500 men was surely exaggerated (SP 63/26/12). **252** SP 63/26/20. Lancaster did not name the castles, 'for lack of time'. **253** HMC, *De L'Isle & Dudley MSS*, ii, 9. **254** Sidney signalled his approval of Carew at least as early as the summer of 1568 (SP 63/25/11, 15). **255** The latest account of the Carew land claim, J. Wagner, *The Devon gentleman: a life of Sir Peter Carew* (Hull 1998), ch. 10, provides a careful reconstruction of Carew's side of the case. However, it is often unreliable as a guide to Carew's impact in Elizabethan Leinster, having been written without consulting recent Irish historical scholarship. **256** NA, Lodge MSS, Rolls, Vol. I, 163–4; Moore, 'English action, Irish reaction', 86–7; J. Hughes, 'Sir Edmund Butler of the Dullough', *RHAAI*, i (1870), 267–72. **257** Carew's denial that Sidney had used martial law in Kilkenny suggests others claimed he had (SP 63/26/124).

supportive of Carew's land claim, and the question of revoking the abolition of coign and livery was simply not up for discussion. In the opening session of the 1569 Irish parliament Sir Edmund Butler tried to obstruct the progress of several of the government's bills, including a bill to suppress native Irish captaincies and, it must be assumed, that for the banning of private military taxes such as coign.[258] His objections were ignored. Disillusioned of constitutional opposition, he returned to tried and trusted means when the second session ended in March 1569. The chronicle of Sir Peter Carew's life, by his lawyer John Hooker, mentions that in the spring of 1569, on his way home to Leighlin from Waterford, Carew was attacked at Thomastown by Sir Edmund's forces. If Hooker can be believed – often he cannot – his master was in mortal danger of assassination because of the Butlers' daily conspiracies against him.[259] Worse was to follow when the deputy sent three prominent officials to Kilkenny and Tipperary in April to hold the Easter assizes.

Sidney's three representatives (the attorney-general, Luke Dillon, the chief remembrancer, John Thomas, and the chief justice of Wexford, Edward Fitzsimon) rode into an area on the brink of revolt. Although things were relatively quiet in Kilkenny, where the sheriff, John Cantwell, was using martial law to keep the peace,[260] Tipperary was teeming with military activity, with the Butlers standing out in defiance against the new anti-captaincy legislation that Sidney had sponsored in parliament. In yet another display of force, the Butlers arrived to meet the three commissioners at Carrick-on-Suir accompanied by 40–50 horsemen and 200 kerne. Their subsequent actions made their intentions plain. At Annagh-O'Fogarty, as the commissioners looked on in amazement, Edward Butler departed to make war on the O'Carrolls; on his return he boasted of how he had killed two men. At Roscrea, Edward ignored the commissioners' request to produce witnesses in defence of his actions. Further afield, the commissioners' investigation into the spoiling of the Dunboyne estate was obstructed by the alleged spoiler, Sir Edmund Butler, who promised that he would give his side of the story before an assembly of the gentlemen and freeholders of Tipperary. Yet no such gathering occurred, as Sir Edmund neglected to ask Ormond's liberty officials to summon one. This all amounted to much more than posturing. Edmund Power of Mothill, a major landlord and a kinsman and ally of Ormond, alleged that Piers Butler had tried to ambush him and his followers in a church in Tipperary. More shocking still, the burgesses of Clonmel further charged that Piers had recently raided the town, the capital of the Ormond liberty, rounded up some livestock and killed 'seven or eight honest burgesses' who resisted them. When the Butlers rested at Loughmoe their soldiers 'pilfered and spoiled the poor people' of the village there, a clear message to Purcell, the local lord, that he better not give succour to Sidney's commissioners. The Ormond lordship was in a state of civil war.[261]

---

258 V. Treadwell, 'The Irish Parliament of 1569–71', *PRIA*, 65, C, 67–9, 73–4. **259** Hooker's life of Carew is printed at the front of *Cal. Carew MSS, 1515–74*; see esp. cii–civ. **260** *Ir. Fiants*, Eliz. I, no. 1261. **261** SP 63/28/31 (= Hughes, 'Sir Edmund Butler', 158–64).

Based on a report of their experiences by Dillon, Fitzsimon and Thomas, and with more news of disturbances reaching him from the south, Sidney convened an emergency meeting of the Irish council at Dublin Castle on 16 June 1569. There was a high turnout for the meeting, with the earl of Kildare, the baron of Louth, and Sir Peter Carew present together with the usual senior government officers. Together they drafted a proclamation declaring the Butlers outlaws. 'That Sir Edmund Butler, Edward Butler and Piers Butler, brethren unto the earl of Ormond, should for their disloyalty and disobedience, contemptuously refusing to come in to the lord deputy and council and to answer to justice … be from henceforth denounced and published as rebels and traitors unto the queen's most excellent majesty'.

It was a precipitate step typical of Sidney, offering the Butlers no prospect of compromise or negotiation. Yet it was not unjustified. The proclamation was not irrevocable, allowing the Butlers 14 days grace to 'come in' before becoming fully operative.[262] But the Butlers had no intention of submitting to Sidney. During June it suddenly emerged why they had dared to go so far. They were not acting alone, but were part of a countrywide conspiracy against Sidney's government. Traditionally described by historians as an anti-English rebellion, the Butler revolt was anti-English in a deeper, more complex way than usually claimed. The rebels were not just opposed to the English colonial administration. They also intended to overthrow the Ormond lordship in Kilkenny and Tipperary because Earl Thomas had co-operated so eagerly with the re-anglicisation process that threatened to destroy their tradition of military autonomy. As Edward put it when approached by a government messenger, he could anticipate 'no favour' or fortune in the Tipperary borderlands because of 'the hatred of his brother, the earl, toward him'.[263] The Butler revolt was an anti-Ormond revolt.

REVOLT

For local peasants and ordinary people, the Butlers and their allies could hardly have chosen a worse time to go out on campaign. Cold and stormy weather had meant that the previous year's harvest had been a poor one in many parts of Ireland,[264] and by Easter 1569 the food supply was running low in the Ormond territories. Government agents riding through Kilkenny and Tipperary in April were struck by the 'miserable estate of the country' and the 'poverty of the poor people'.[265] On Good Friday the mayor and aldermen of Waterford, moved with pity by the sight of 1,100 hungry and wretched people huddled outside the city walls, ordered that the gates be opened to let them in; they had fled to the city from the surrounding region in hope of relief, some of them from southern Co. Kilkenny.[266] A growing fear of famine turned to panic when

262 HMC, *Haliday MSS*, 228–9.   **263** Collins (ed.), *Sidney letters*, pp 37–8.   **264** W.M. Hennessy (ed.), *Annals of Loch Cé* (2 vols., London, 1871), ii, s.a. 1568; HMC, *Salisbury MSS*, i, 404–5.   **265** Hughes, 'Sir Edmund Butler', 159.   **266** SP 63/28/6.

the Butlers rebelled in June.[267] Wherever the Butlers went, they burned crops and seized livestock, and it is fair to assume that their campaign caused general suffering and increased peasant mortality. However, such was the nature of the political order in Elizabethan Ireland that the extent of peasant hardship went largely unreported and was soon forgotten.

Having spent months planning, Sir Edmund and his advisers had concocted a revolt that encompassed the length and breadth of the country. Their principal Leinster allies were the Kavanaghs of Idrone, who shared the Butlers' resentment of Sidney over the Carew land claim. In Munster they could count on the support of the new captain of the Desmond army, James Fitzmaurice, who joined them on campaign once he had received assurances that help was imminent from Spain. Finally, the Butlers were also linked to Turlough Luineach O'Neill, who was rapidly emerging as the government's principal enemy in Ulster. In 1569 the Butler brothers were part of the largest rebel conspiracy to develop against English rule in Ireland since the 1530s.

But therein lay their problem. In order to honour their commitments to their allies, the Butlers had to take their forces out of Kilkenny and Tipperary to fight elsewhere, principally in Cork and Wicklow. Furthermore, although they chose some of the most powerful lords in Ireland as their allies, these had little in common with the Kilkenny/Tipperary community. At first glance, it might be said that Sir Edmund did well to team up with Turlough Luineach O'Neill; from a military perspective the arrangement they reached seemed very promising. The Butlers were to attack the Pale if Sidney took the government army north, while Turlough was to come down from Ulster if the royal forces went south. Yet the anglophile gentry of the Ormond lordship were alarmed by the O'Neill connection and Sir Edmund could not persuade them to join the confederacy. The Fitzmaurice alliance was even more problematic. A leading Kilkenny landlord, William Sweetman of Castle Eve, was disgusted with the Butlers for linking their cause to the Desmond lord. At the start of the rebellion he had been required by Sidney to apprehend Piers Butler over 'divers heinous complaints exhibited against him'.[268] In the course of trying to track Piers down, on 25 July Sweetman travelled to Killough Castle in Tipperary, where he had a heated exchange with Sir Edmund Butler when the latter bragged about his friendship with Fitzmaurice. Hoping to sow seeds of doubt in Sir Edmund's mind and so foreshorten the revolt, Sweetman denounced the conspiracy in forthright terms. 'I do marvel what enterprise is this ye have begun: it is the most unreasonable and outrageous that may be, for ye … distain your lineage, whereof surely you are not rightly sprung, for you are [become] rather a Desmond than a Butler.' More than any of their actions, the Butlers' link-up with the detested Desmond Fitzgeralds confounded their prospects of mobilising gentry support in the Ormond country.[269]

When their campaign reached its climax in July 1569, the Butlers commanded a force of more than 3,000 men, but at least two-thirds of these were

---

267 SP 63/29/5.   **268** Hughes, 'Sir Edmund Butler', 175, n. 1.   **269** SP 63/29/24.

not their own followers, belonging instead to their allies from Munster. It can thus be estimated that Sir Edmund and his Leinster partners the Kavanaghs raised approximately 1,000 soldiers from the area under their sway in Cos. Kilkenny, Tipperary, Carlow and Wexford, a considerable force it is true, but hardly the stuff of a popular revolt. Indeed, if the figures are reliable, their following may actually have dwindled since late 1568, when Edward Butler was reported as leading 1,400 men around the south-east. The only people who are known to have openly participated in the rebellion were those whom the Butlers had relied on from the very beginning, namely their own retainers and their closest friends and confidants. From Kilkenny their confederates were Thomas Comerford of Ballymack and some sons of Lord Mountgarret and Walter Butler of Paulstown; from Tipperary they were aided by the MacSweeney galloglasses and by Cantwell of Moycarkey, but Purcell of Loughmoe was an unwilling and unreliable follower.[270] Their utter failure to excite more widespread support is of crucial significance, firstly because it prepared the ground for their eventual defeat, and secondly because it demonstrates how much the local community of the Ormond lordship had lost faith in the Butler family.[271]

Sir Edmund and his brothers went to extreme lengths to gain wider sympathy. At the start of their campaign they put it about that Earl Thomas was dead. As a ruse it was entirely ineffective. Within weeks, by the start of July, it was confirmed that Ormond was alive and well in London, and furious with his family for committing treason and besmirching his good name. Ormond's servant, Oliver Grace, sailed to Waterford from England to challenge Sir Edmund and to ask him to obey his brother the earl's orders to lay down his arms, but to no avail. Sir Edmund rode off with his troops, for appearances' sake claiming he did not believe Grace's statement that Ormond was still living. To deny the prospect of a gentry counter-attack in defence of Ormond and the crown, the Butler brothers commenced their revolt with a trick, disarming the local community by stealing all the weapons that had been collected for a muster of the shire force set for 15 July. It was only because of this that civil war between rebels and loyalists did not erupt in the Kilkenny region in the summer of 1569.[272]

The rebellion peaked on 16 July when the Butlers laid siege to Kilkenny town. Outside its walls Sir Edmund, Edward, and Piers Butler were joined by Fitzmaurice and Donal MacCarthy Mór. Inside, in addition to the townsmen, there was gathered many of the local gentry, Ormond's officials and servants, and a sizeable number of New English refugees from Munster, including the wife of Sir Warham St Leger, Fitzmaurice's great enemy. For probably the first time in its history, Kilkenny had to thank royal troops for its survival. Just before the rebels began the siege, a company of soldiers arrived led by Captain William

---

270 The size of the rebel army is outlined in SP 63/29/22. **271** It has been recently claimed, without any corroborative evidence, that Sir Edmund Butler enjoyed more support than Fitzmaurice (Ellis, *Ireland*, 296). **272** Edwards, 'Butler revolt', 248.

Collier, an officer who had spent much of the preceding year in command of the isolated royal garrison at Newry. He was ideally suited for the task in hand, being a stranger neither to Irish sieges nor Scots-Irish galloglasses. Together with Ormond's servants and some local dignitaries, including the bishop of Ossory, the dean of Cashel, Edmund Butler of Callan, and Richard Shee, he was able to convince the townspeople to continue their resistance. After a sortie to round up a few sheep that the rebels had not seized, the sovereign, Walter Archer, ordered that the town gates be closed and the walls reinforced with earth. Confident that the town would surrender, after five days the Butlers agreed to the townsmen's request that they remove themselves a couple of miles away and cease burning the 'suburbs and granges' outside the walls. Collier saw his chance. Seeing that MacCarthy was taking 800 men away in search of food, the captain and his soldiers sallied forth and beat off the more adventurous of the besiegers. In less than a week the siege was over.[273]

In the ensuing fortnight the rebels were reduced to harrying 'the country round about', burning and destroying crops in the shire midlands. Fitzmaurice and MacCarthy Mór departed, shortly before the appearance of Sir Peter Carew and Captain Humphrey Gilbert in the vanguard of Sidney's government army. Believing that Sir Edmund Butler's forces were a few miles north of Kilkenny, Carew set forth and according to his own account, routed a large force of rebels at Kilmocar, killing 200 (in fact, he killed only 80).[274] The trouble was those he killed might not actually have been rebels! According to other, more reliable, sources it is recorded that most of the Kilmocar troops, all galloglasses, were unarmed when Carew's men attacked, and none of the Butler brothers were with them. More revealing still, Sir Edmund Butler later acknowledged that those slain were the tenth earl's men, *not* his own. Finally, Ormond himself, on learning of the slaughter, was greatly upset by the news, noting that the dead included two of his captains of galloglass, 'that were tall fellows', that is, loyal and trustworthy men, not rebels.[275]

By this time the Butler revolt had collapsed in Kilkenny and Tipperary. The Butlers retreated into Idough and then left the area altogether, drawing away into north Wexford and Wicklow. In most histories of the period it is assumed that the Butler brothers finally agreed to surrender when their eldest brother arrived to parley with them outside Kilkenny Castle on 1 September. As I have shown elsewhere, this is a dangerous assumption to make, for it draws a veil over one of the most significant aspects of the rebellion. From the very start the rebels had striven to destroy Earl Thomas' power. At Callan Piers Butler had attacked Ormond's manor and robbed his treasurer, Fulk Comerford, of nearly £2,000 of the earl's money and plate. Outside Clonmel the rebels seized cattle worth £300 belonging to the wife of Ormond's steward, John Aylward. When William Sweetman had chastised Sir Edmund for betraying his noble brother,

---

273 Camden, *History*, 125; *Statutes at large, Ire.*, 370; SP 63/29/22. **274** *Cal. Carew MSS, 1515–74*, cvi–cvii. **275** SP 63/29/47, 80. Discrepancies between Carew's version of events and other accounts are discussed in Wagner, *Devon gentleman*, 322–6.

Ormond, Sir Edmund had scoffed at him, declaring that Ormond would not control him again if the rebellion went to plan. Time and again during the rising the rebels targeted Ormond's property for destruction. When he returned to Ireland on 14 August they paid him no heed, but carried on in revolt until all hope of O'Neill's support disappeared. Repeatedly the earl's messengers were spurned and at the end of August, just days before they surrendered to him outside Kilkenny, Sir Edmund, Edward and Piers Butler performed their final exploit, attacking Ormond's manor at Arklow, leaving it waste.[276]

CONCLUSION

For the Black Earl of Ormond the audit of war was grim indeed. Although he had retained the trust of Elizabeth I – in itself a remarkable achievement – the profile of his dynasty was tarnished. His brothers had danced on the Butlers' reputation for steadfastness to the crown. Sir Edmund's comments to William Sweetman that Sidney's administration was bent on the extirpation of the Irish – 'I do it [rebel] to make war against those that banish Ireland and mean conquest' – revealed the chasm that separated him from Earl Thomas.[277] Sir Edmund and his fellows felt more in common with those Ormond termed 'Irish rascals' than with the English governmental system. And yet Sir Edmund's claims could not easily be ignored. Ormond himself had been alarmed by Sidney's penchant for high-handed arbitrary rule, for government that operated outside the common law and drew heavily on the use (and abuse) of the royal prerogative. Commenting on Sidney's handling of the Carew land claim Ormond castigated 'these rash dealings in matters of land'.[278] Of equal concern to him was the prospect of future disaffection. Though the great majority of the Kilkenny gentry had stayed loyal, refusing to go along with the rebels, Ormond reckoned that further trouble was almost inevitable. In particular the aggressive behaviour of colonialist adventurers like Carew was threatening to sour the county's relations with the royal authorities. When Carew and Gilbert had arrived in Kilkenny town in July they had squabbled with the local people, accusing them of collusion with the rebels. As long as adventurers like these received encouragement from Dublin Ormond felt he would be unable to rest. Thus the Butler revolt transformed Ormond's career, forcing to turn his back on the prospect of greatness in England. Henceforth he must become an Irish lord and adapt himself to his native land in a manner he had thus far avoided. From 1569 he had to reinvent himself and become in a very real sense a lord of two worlds, Irish and English, at home in both without relinquishing his contact with Queen Elizabeth. It was a tall order.

---

276 Edwards, 'Butler revolt', 246–50. **277** SP 63/29/24. **278** Hughes, 'Sir Edmund Butler', 172, 215.

CHAPTER 4

The encroachment of central government, 1569–1603

Surmounting the crisis of his brothers' rebellion was not the only challenge to face the Black Earl after 1569. His need to reassert his authority in his ancestral territories was greatly complicated by the increasingly confrontational attitude of the Dublin government towards the autonomous Irish lordships. Since his first return to Ireland in 1554 the Tudor monarchy had been turning more towards a military solution in the provinces, determined to force local lords and lineages into compliance with its demand for political reform. New forts had been established around the south-eastern borderlands, uncomfortably close to Kilkenny, at Philipstown in Offaly, Maryborough in Laois, Leighlinbridge in Carlow, Ferns in Wexford, and Dungarvan in Waterford. At each stronghold garrisons had been assembled, under the command of constables and seneschals, English officials responsible for the military reduction of the native rulers and their followers. Often these commanders had behaved as colonialist adventurers, intimidating local leaders and landowners, provoking them to the point of revolt in the pursuit of greater personal wealth and power. The introduction of a new pre-emptive form of martial law to Ireland after 1556, enabling commissioners to execute suspected offenders *before* they had committed an offence, added enormously to the threat posed to the regional lordships by the crown.[1] So too did the pursuit of land for colonisation. The forced dispossession of the O'Mores and O'Connors to make way for the Laois/Offaly plantation[2] and the subsequent seizure of territory belonging to the O'Morroghs, O'Dorans, and Kavanaghs (and later the Butlers) in Wexford and Carlow,[3] eventually served to radicalise politics, with the rights to ownership of Irish land called into question by agents of the crown and private speculators. As long as Ormond's friend, the earl of Sussex, had been chief governor (1556–63) Earl Thomas had not expressed concern over these developments, his welfare assured and even strengthened in return for service; indeed historians are right to state that he had actively supported Sussex's military and colonial exploits.[4] However, following Sussex's replacement by Sir Henry Sidney, the Black Earl was at length

---

1 Edwards, 'Beyond reform', 16–18; Donovan, 'Tudor rule', 119–21; Lennon, *Sixteenth-century Ireland*, 164–75; Ellis, *Ireland*, 186–7. Canny, *Elizabethan conquest*, ch. 2–5 provides the most extended discussion to date of the hardening of government policy in the mid-sixteenth century. 2 Carey, 'End', 218–31; Fitzsimons, 'Lordship', 218–22. 3 Donovan, 'Tudor rule', 122 n.11. 4 Brady, 'Thomas Butler', 52.

forced to think again about how best to balance his interests as an Irish overlord with his need to co-operate closely with the crown.

Though it angered him greatly, it was not just Sidney's deliberate targeting
of the previously loyal Butler territories that gave Ormond cause for alarm, or
even the fact that the deputy had effectively driven his brothers into revolt.
Rather, he came to realise that the whole drift of government conduct since
the days of the Sussex regime was now, years later, threatening to engulf his
Kilkenny-Tipperary lordship in a storm of unrest derived from surrounding
areas. As well as Ormond's brothers, other disenchanted lords and leaders were
growing belligerent. As the 1570s commenced the government excited violent
reactions from entirely new opponents such as Connor O'Brien, earl of
Thomond, the Clanricard Burkes of Galway, the Furlongs of Wexford, and the
hitherto quiet Mac Rory Mac Conall sept of the O'Mores of Laois.[5] All of these,
significantly, could usually be identified as political affiliates of the Butler affinity.[6] Their growing resistance to Tudor rule revealed the limitations of the Black
Earl's influence in Ireland, and called his usefulness into question. Accordingly,
in order to reverse this trend and preserve the strategic importance of his territories in the south, the tenth earl sought a reorientation of crown policy as it
was implemented back towards the ideas of conciliation and co-operation with
the 'well affected' autonomous lordships that had been in vogue in his youth.
To Ormond's mind, far from seeking to undermine or abolish the lordships
(something which Sidney in particular seemed determined to effect), the crown
should instead nurture the autonomous powers of the regional lords as the best
guarantee of its authority in Ireland.

Ormond therefore resumed his involvement in southern Ireland after 1569
ready to oppose the actions of senior government officials to a far greater extent
than he had attempted before, willing if necessary to pose as a leader of loyalist
dissent. If the Dublin administration had seemed hostile to his Kilkenny overlordship before 1569, his new direction as self-appointed interferer-in-chief
insured that further hostility would often prove unavoidable. In the years to
come it would transpire that Sidney was by no means the only chief governor
to view the autonomous status of the Ormond lordship with suspicion, or to see
the extent of Earl Thomas' power in the south as antipathetic to strong English
government in Ireland – and this despite the earl's continuing record of loyal
service to the crown. Several of Sidney's successors, principally Sir William Drury
(1578–9), Lord Grey de Wilton (1580–2), Sir Henry Wallop (1582–4), and Sir
John Perrot (1584–8), were anxious to reduce his authority, and even less overtly
hostile governors like Sir William Fitzwilliam (1571–5, 1588–94) proved unwilling to curtail policies that he was known to oppose. Indeed, the more Ormond
stood out against the colonial government in Dublin in order to defend the principles of aristocratic delegation and devolution, the more the chief governors
were inclined to interfere in the running of his territory in order to reveal it as

5 Lennon, *Sixteenth-century Ireland*, 240–4; Donovan, 'Tudor rule', 123–7; Carey, 'End', 237–8.
6 Brady, *Chief governors*, 184–6.

a place where forces hostile to the crown lurked and plotted under the earl's nose. Thus the history of Co. Kilkenny between 1569 and 1603 is best presented as a story of the Black Earl's struggle to preserve an independent power-base in the shire in the face of constant encroachment from Dublin.

It is one of the more peculiar features of political developments in Elizabethan Ireland that Earl Thomas could not have countered the policies of successive chief governors and other leading crown officials without the sympathy and support of Queen Elizabeth I and members of her court. Although the Butler revolt of 1569 required him to spend more time in Ireland than he might have wanted, crucially he did not relinquish his position as Elizabeth's premier Irish courtier. When circumstances allowed he returned to Whitehall, often for the Christmas season, but sometimes for prolonged periods, most notably in the years 1576–9 and 1586–93. During his absences from London his friends there lobbied for him and defended his reputation. Sir Thomas Heneage appears to have been particularly helpful in this context, receiving and keeping copies of some of Ormond's most important bulletins for circulation among a carefully chosen audience.[7] The earl's other great support was Sussex, a member of the English privy council from 1570 and lord chamberlain of the royal court. Less partisan, but equally important, was Sir William Cecil, Lord Burghley, the queen's principal minister, who usually held the earl in high regard. Partly through their efforts, the rebellion of Ormond's brothers failed to shake the queen's belief in him. On the contrary – and notwithstanding the contention of one historian[8] – the unreliability of the Butlers only emphasised the earl's importance to the Elizabethan regime.

Yet lobbying the court was only part of his political strategy after 1569. The viability of Ormond's opposition to the encroachment of the Dublin authorities into his (and others') territories also depended on his capacity to re-establish order in his troubled lordship

The Butler rebellion cast a long shadow over his affairs, causing him to monitor developments in Kilkenny and Tipperary more carefully than before. If he was to succeed in altering government policy by blaming the 1569 rising and

---

7 E.g., SP 63/30/68. The enclosure with this item was ideal for Heneage's purposes, providing a listing of castles in Co. Clare that Ormond had recently secured for the crown. For other evidence of Heneage taking copies of Ormond's correspondence, see HMC, *Finch MSS*, i, 7.   8 A recent study has continued to cling to the idea that to some extent Ormond was 'guilty of serious collusion' with his brothers at the time of their rebellion, and that, furthermore, his loyalty was 'seriously in doubt' in 1569 (Brady, *Chief governors*, 171), a view that ignores compelling evidence to the contrary. On 9 July 1569, immediately after news of the revolt reached court, Elizabeth I wrote to Sidney in praise of the Black Earl, urging the governor to 'trust him [Ormond], howsoever his brethren do err'. She further informed the deputy that she wished to accede to the earl's request to be allowed to serve against the insurgents, for she and some of her privy council, chiefly Cecil and Leicester, felt confident that Ormond was 'a principal nobleman and officer of that our realm [of Ireland] in whom we have ever found fealty towards us and our crown, and whom we also think worthy of as much trust for his loyalty and service as any person of any degree born within that realm': O'Laidhin (ed.), *Sidney state papers*, no. 69. She wrote in similar style on 15 October, after Ormond had received his brothers' submission: ibid,, no. 72.

other disturbances on the activities of excessively aggressive officials, he needed to bring local unrest to an end as quickly as possible. Should his troubles with his family and their private retainers remain unchecked, and new uprisings materialise, Ormond might lose face in the eyes of the queen and forfeit the support of the local community who had borne the brunt of the rebels' depredations. Unthinkably, the coercive tactics of Sidney and his ilk might even be vindicated. If, on the other hand, the sources of insurrection melted away after his return, the earl would demonstrate that he, not the lord deputy, was best qualified to govern his territories for the crown; and should he secure the principle of autonomous rule, perhaps then the queen might be persuaded to restrain her chief governors elsewhere in the country and allow him and his supporters greater influence over the formulation and implementation of royal policy. But first he had to pacify his brothers.

CONTINUING UNREST

Perhaps the simplest way for Ormond to have dealt with the problem of his three errant brothers would have been to hand them over to the authorities for execution. However, though they had flagrantly defied his authority and attacked his servants and supporters he needed to keep Sir Edmund, Edward and Piers Butler alive. Only by saving them could he hope to retain a large independent power-base in Kilkenny and Tipperary. Were they to be attainted and executed, their land would be seized by the government, and Earl Thomas knew that Sidney and his supporters would be quick to advocate that it be granted to persons opposed to him. As such, the earl set out to take personal responsibility for his brothers' punishment, resolved not to treat them leniently, while at the same time criticising the Dublin government as much as possible in order to save their skins.

Until November 1569 things went Ormond's way. News of his return was warmly received by the Kilkenny community. Some of the principal gentry rode forth to offer him their services, and with their help he soon reimposed his rule over the region. According to a 'certificate' in praise of Ormond that was addressed to the queen on 3 November and signed by 75 gentlemen of Kilkenny and Tipperary, normal life had resumed in the earl's country. The rural refugees who had fled to the 'walled towns and other places of strength' to escape his brothers returned to their cabins in the countryside, in time to gather up what corn and hay was left on the land. Those who had been taken prisoner by the Butlers were set free on Ormond's orders 'as complaints came unto him', and some of the goods and cattle stolen by the rebels were identified and restored to their rightful owners. For the moment at least, the document claimed, 'good order, tranquillity and peace' had returned to south-eastern Ireland.[9] It did not last much longer.

9 *COD*, v, no. 157.

Although the gentry who petitioned the queen insisted that the earl's brothers had 'lived in quiet and dutiful manner since ... coming to him' on 1
September, their confidence in the Butler family was ill-founded. When Sir
Edmund, Edward and Piers had surrendered to Ormond, they had spoken
angrily of Sidney's 'cruel and ill usages' towards them, and with the benefit of
hindsight it is possible to discern that they were uneasy at the prospect of having
to render formal submission to the deputy. Their subsequent actions cut right
across Ormond's efforts to save them and made him look foolish, forcing him
among other things to offer some rather lame excuses for their behaviour, on
more than one occasion even claiming that Sir Edmund Butler was out of his
mind, 'distracted', 'not his own man', 'bewitched'.[10]

Signs of their intransigence had emerged in September, when Piers Butler
feigned illness, taking to his bed at Kilkenny Castle to avoid meeting Sidney at
Limerick.[11] A month or so later, on 16 October, Sir Edmund and Piers fell into
a violent argument with the deputy at Dublin over the latter's right to constrain
them while they were under Ormond's protection. The Black Earl was unable
to silence Sir Edmund, and could only look on while his brother, probably fearing for his life, flung insults at the chief governor in the presence of the Irish
council. Hardly a fitting way for an ex-rebel to behave, Sir Edmund's outburst
created entirely the wrong atmosphere for the furtherance of Ormond's policy
of winning sympathy against Sidney in official circles. One bystander who greatly
admired the earl was astonished at the conduct of his family, and quickly formed
the opinion that Sir Edmund and Piers Butler did not deserve to be descended
from 'that noble house of Ormond'. Earl Thomas was unable to object to the
decision of the lord deputy and council that Sir Edmund be gaoled in Dublin
Castle for his obstinacy.[12] Nor could he prevent his youngest sibling, Piers, from
slipping out of his private lodging in the capital later that same night while in
his keeping, an occurrence that inevitably aroused Sidney's darkest suspicions.[13]

The earl's embarrassment deepened later in November when Sir Edmund
Butler escaped from Dublin Castle, plunging into the moat before making his
way along the River Dodder to the safety of the Wicklow hills, where he
received succour from the rebel O'Byrnes.[14] It is perhaps significant that when
he next appeared in the Ormond territories Sir Edmund was reported as having
made a public show of Catholic piety at Holy Cross Abbey in Co. Tipperary,
'making an offering' there for his escape. Sidney believed he was in communication with the exiled 'Romish bishop' of Cashel, Maurice Fitzgibbon.[15] For
the next few months he remained at large in the south, and if the somewhat
garbled reports that reached the ears of the Spanish ambassador in London are
reliable, it would seem that early in the new year Sir Edmund rejoined Edward
and Piers in an effort to re-establish their power. In the event, their initiative
amounted to little more than a brief campaign of 'routing and robbing on the

---

10 SP 63/30/68, 96.   **11** SP 63/29/61.   **12** SP 63/29/77.   **13** SP 63/29/70.   **14** Hore (ed.),
'Sidney's memoir', *UJA*, v (1857), 305.   **15** SP 63/29/86.

roads'.[16] Finally, by the end of February 1570, unable to assemble a suitably large body of troops to assert their independence, Sir Edmund and Piers decided to follow Ormond's advice to surrender themselves immediately to the lord deputy and admit they had 'swerved ... from [their] allegiance to her highness' and committed 'sundry offences and treasons'.[17] They were led off as prisoners to Dublin.

Their belated receptivity to the earl's messages should not hide the principal point to be gleaned from their adventures, namely Ormond's inability to control them. Despite appearances, his influence had not been enough to convince them of the wisdom of capitulation; far more compelling was the decision of their erstwhile allies the Kavanaghs to cast themselves on Sidney's mercy earlier in January.[18] Most disturbing of all from Ormond's standpoint was the behaviour of Edward Butler. Having been committed on Sidney's orders to the custody of Marshal Bagenal, Ormond had managed to secure his release on promise of good behaviour,[19] only for Edward later to flee into Munster in order to reunite with the rebels led by James Fitzmaurice Fitzgerald.

Edward's antics played straight into the hands of the deputy. As Sidney stated in a letter to Carew in May 1570, 'Edward Butler will yield to no obedience. I think God hath ordained him for a sacrifice for the rest.' Yet Sir Henry could not order the killing. Because of the queen's sensitivity towards Ormond, he had to be content with her desire that the earl should 'bring in [Edward's] ... head with his own hands'.[20] In the meantime the governor proceeded with his plans to introduce an act of attainder against all three Butler brothers in the next session of the Irish parliament. When eventually the bill appeared Ormond was away campaigning for the crown in Thomond, as Sidney had required, so that he could not oppose its introduction.[21] It was quickly passed and took its place on the Irish statute rolls.[22]

Despite appearances, however, Sir Henry had failed to triumph over his rival Ormond. Like many other events associated with Sidney's rule, the attainder of the Butlers was an artificial achievement that promised much but delivered little.[23] For all his threats and feisty rumblings the deputy was unable to punish the Butlers as he wanted. Following the queen's intervention even the act itself lacked bite. Before giving her approval to its enactment, Elizabeth instructed Sidney that under no circumstances was he to proceed with the execution of the Butlers or the forfeiture of their property, provided they admitted their treason and surrendered themselves to her mercy.[24]

16 *Cal. SP, Spanish, 1568–79*, 236. **17** SP 63/30/19, 27 i. **18** HMC, *Haliday MSS*, 238–9. **19** SP 63/29/66. **20** SP 63/30/52. **21** SP 63/30/50 i, 56 iii. **22** *Statutes at large, Ire., 1310–1612*, 369–73; Treadwell, 'Irish parliament', 81–2. **23** Sidney frequently exaggerated the importance of his actions, and occasionally hired writers to glorify them: D.B. Quinn, 'Government printing and the publication of the Irish statutes in the sixteenth century', *PRIA*, 49 C (1943), 55, 66. **24** O'Laidhin (ed.), *Sidney state papers*, no. 75. Her requirement that the Butlers admit their guilt indicates that the deputy may not have forwarded to her the text of Sir Edmund and Piers' submission of 28 February (SP 63/30/19).

Hence, although the act besmirched his family's reputation and 'nippeth [him] at the heart'[25] the earl of Ormond lost surprisingly little when it was passed by parliament. The fact that it laid the foundations for future successional problems – its one great blow to Ormond's position – was an accident due essentially to the earl's failure to father a legitimate male heir. Besides, at the time the act received the royal signet it was clearly understood that it would be repealed in a future parliament. It just so happened that parliaments were rarely convened in Tudor Ireland, and were rarest under Elizabeth I. When one was planned for 1578, Ormond had a bill for his brothers' restoration in blood brought forward for consideration by the London privy council;[26] but the parliament never sat, and as shown in Chapter 2, the Black Earl had to wait until 1603 before ironing out the successional difficulties caused by his brothers' treason. The length of this delay should not disguise what had actually transpired. The junior Butlers should have been dead and buried as a political force after 1569. Thanks to Ormond they were still alive. It is hard to think of another example of a Tudor nobleman who, with royal approval, was able to overcome an act of attainder in order to save the traitors in his family. Certainly Sir Henry Sidney must have wondered how it had been done.

At the time it was passed the act against his brothers seemed a decidedly dull measure. Sidney did not even have the satisfaction of having the act included in the first printed book of Irish statutes, published in 1572. Ormond objected to its wording, which described in lurid prose the events of the 1569 rebellion, and also to its flawed legal logic, which implied that former rebels now at peace with the crown could nonetheless stand attainted of treason for crimes they had not yet perpetrated. It was omitted from the book as a result.[27] Nor did Ormond's achievements stop here. Following an extended sojourn at court in 1572–3[28] he persuaded the queen that the land claims of Sir Peter Carew were odious to many people in Ireland, and the ageing adventurer was quietly discouraged from pursuing them any further, forced to make do with Idrone.[29] Finally, on 12 March 1574[30] the earl procured the queen's official pardon for his brothers, a measure that negated the prospect of their lands being confiscated, as Sidney had wished, and instead allowed them to retain their estates for the duration of their lives.[31]

His ongoing influence at Whitehall is only one explanation for his success. The other principal reason why Ormond retained his monarch's favour was his ruthless performance against the rebels in Ireland. As soon as he had set foot on home turf in August 1569 he had begun gathering information against those who had supported his brothers' disloyalty. Through his efforts, the next few years were exceedingly bloody ones in the Co. Kilkenny area.

---

25 SP 63/30/68. **26** SP 63/60/31. **27** Curtis, 'Butler revolt', 213–4; SP 63/36/50. **28** Ormond was at court from Oct. 1572 to July 1573: SP 63/38/22; Bod. Lib., Carte Ms 56, fol. 178. **29** SP 63/41/17. **30** Not 1573, as some authors have claimed. Issued in March in the 16th year of Elizabeth's reign (17 Nov. 1573–16 Nov. 1574) the pardon must belong to 1574: *CPRI, Henry VIII–Eliz. I*, 555. **31** HMC, *Ormonde MSS, 1543–1711*, 72–3 (1).

ORMOND'S PURGE

The figures tell their own story. Between 15 August 1569 and 23 September 1571 no less than 165 of the 'notorious traitors and malefactors of the last rebellion' were either killed or captured on his orders. Even those who surrendered did not live long, led away under armed escort to Kilkenny gaol to await public execution. The majority of those who died came from the lands under Ormond's control in Kilkenny, Tipperary and Carlow. Although he took his revenge on nearly fifty of the Munster Geraldines,[32] Earl Thomas was primarily concerned to reassert his power by purging his own lands, and he left nothing to chance. The fact that he lacked a commission of martial law – Sidney had not given him one, despite the queen's instructions[33] – did not prevent him from passing the death sentence against the rebels wherever he encountered them. Indeed, it was only in September 1571 (after Sidney's departure) that he petitioned the government for proper martial powers. His urgency in carrying out the executions before this date was largely due to his uncertainty over the behaviour of his brothers. He showed no mercy to their soldiers, insuring that Sir Edmund and the rest could not start another rebellion.[34]

The earliest fighting occurred in Co. Kilkenny, where Ormond was assisted by some of the leading shire landowners, most notably Thomas Den, Gerald Blanchville, Walter Gall, and the new sheriff, Oliver Grace. Seven Butler retainers met their end at Cottrellsboley, and there was a pitched battle at the earl's manor house at Dunfert, where thirteen Butler rebels were slain and five fatally wounded, stumbling away 'sore hurt' to die in the fields. For the earl, the clash at Dunfert was all the more satisfying as one of those killed was Geoffrey Carragh Purcell, a local swordsman who had achieved notoriety by murdering the former sheriff of the county, John Cantwell of Cantwell's Court.[35] In dispatching Purcell the earl and his men gained widespread gentry approval.

The ferocity of his campaign enabled Ormond to push the rump of the rebel forces from Kilkenny into the western reaches of his lordship, so that by July 1570 they had fled to the banks of Lough Derg in northernmost Tipperary, where Edward Butler apparently attempted to rally them. The earl allowed them no time to respond, arriving soon afterwards to secure Annagh Castle, the home of the O'Fogartys and the principal stronghold in the area. Maintaining the hunt for Edward for another seven months, he eventually forced the most unmanageable of his brothers to begin negotiations with the government for his surrender. This occurred early in 1571; over the previous year Ormond had accounted for thirty of Edward's troops, a telling commentary on Butler family relations.[36]

---

32 Given this and other evidence it is difficult to accept the assertion that Ormond 'did much to encourage the rebels in Munster' (Brady, *Chief governors*, 172). **33** O'Laidhin (ed.), *Sidney state papers*, no. 69. **34** Bod. Lib., Carte Ms 57, fol. 148. The ensuing two paragraphs are based on this source. **35** Purcell murdered Cantwell shortly after 3 November 1569 (*COD*, v, no. 157). **36** Ibid.; *COD*, v, no. 167. Sidney, predictably, was unimpressed, wondering why Ormond failed to kill Edward: SP 63/30/56.

With Edward's capitulation the Butler revolt finally ended, eighteen months after it had first erupted. Yet Ormond still faced serious problems in his lordship. Political conditions in Co. Kilkenny in the wake of the rising were anything but normal. Although defeated, some rebel groups were still restless, especially the ordinary soldiers. It was they who had suffered most from the earl's onslaught. Now that their former leaders, the Butler brothers, had fixed up personal terms with the earl and the government, they found themselves out in the cold. None of the local loyalist gentry were willing to 'book' (or employ) them, so that legally they sank to the level of 'masterless men', people without rights, subject to summary execution by martial law.[37] Already decimated by Ormond's brutal efficiency, there was no prospect of respite. Though beginning to become uncomfortable with the government's use of martial law elsewhere in Ireland, Earl Thomas was eager to use it against unwanted soldiers in Co. Kilkenny. He accepted commissions in September 1571 and July 1574 that authorised him 'to search out, after the order of martial law, all disorders committed in the county, and on finding any persons to be felons, rebels, or notorious evil-doers, to punish them by death'.[38]

From the earl's perspective, those of the local soldiery who had continued to support his brothers after his return to Ireland were a dangerous group, one that must be extirpated if his authority was to prevail. This remained the case even *after* Sidney had been replaced as chief governor by Sir William Fitzwilliam in April 1571.[39] The stamping out of untrustworthy elements was no mere subsidiary to the tenth earl's relationship with Dublin Castle; it was part of his private agenda, a policy he would have needed to pursue even without government approval.

The purge was not indiscriminate. Rather, it was aimed at those local swordsmen who would neither subordinate themselves to Ormond's officers nor abandon the criminal aspects of their activities. The soldiers' refusal to comply with the earl's wishes is not hard to explain: many of them probably mistrusted him after witnessing his recent treatment of their colleagues. A concerted effort was made to drive them out of Kilkenny before they could form an organised resistance. In 1573 the earl's new captain, Piers Butler of Butlerswood, took his men to Ballymack, where some of the ex-rebels were holed up. There he killed Shane McOwen McHugh, a horseman, and he also captured Moriertagh MacArt Boy, 'a notorious traitor and leader of kern', whom he sent to Lord Deputy Fitzwilliam, who had him executed.[40] It is interesting that the attack took place at Ballymack, the home of the late Thomas Comerford, one of the principal conspirators of 1569 and the subject of a posthumous act of attainder in 1570.[41] In theory, Comerford's estate should have been occupied by a royal grantee, but because of the inefficiency that often beset the government's management of

37 For the penalties facing unbooked soldiers see Donovan, 'Tudor rule', 120, n.4. **38** *Ir. Fiants, Eliz. I*, nos. 1831, 2430. **39** E.g., SP 63/34/14. **40** *CSPI, 1588–92*, 285–6. **41** *Statutes at large, Ire., 1310–1612*, 374–5. The royal warrant for the passage of the bill of attainder against Comerford was given to Lord Keeper Bacon on 2 May 1570: Glasgow University Library, Ms Hunter 3, no. 58 (5).

forfeited property in Ireland it was not until 1575 that it was finally made the subject of a crown lease.[42] In the meantime, the Ballymack lands had been illicitly occupied by members of the Comerford lineage who ignored the queen's rights to the property. With the aid of a few soldiers they had maintained their interest there until hounded out by Ormond's men.[43]

It is impossible to know if the hideout at Ballymack was unusual; it probably was. Later evidence confirms the suspicion that by the mid-1570s Ormond and his supporters had largely succeeded in forcing many rebel soldiers to vacate the county. According to a 1577 report by Sir William Gerrard, bands of unbooked soldiers were then to be seen wandering through the borderlands of Kilkenny and other south Leinster shires. They had been there for some time, and Gerrard suggested that in all there were 'commonly 200 or 300 in a county'. His comments probably indicate the extent of Ormond's achievements, as well as pointing to the bloated presence of the local military before the purge.[44]

Once rid of the most rebellious military elements – those whom Gerrard called 'coignists' – Earl Thomas was at last able to proceed with the final abolition of coign and livery, a crucial development in the Second Pale region that has hitherto been overlooked by historians.[45] He had taken tentative steps in this direction in October 1571, when ordering that in return for an increase in rent, the collection of coign and 'divers other impositions' should cease on his outlying estate at Arklow in Wicklow.[46] A more general cancellation was deferred for the time being due to continuing uncertainty over the reaction of the troops permitted to remain in his lordship; only when their cooperation was assured could the changes go ahead. Accordingly it was another four years before the Black Earl was confident that his purge of the local military had attained its objective, instilling fear and obedience among a normally fearless and disobedient group. The soldiers who survived his assault were ideal for his needs, a core of loyal and pliable swordsmen, his to command and no-one else's. In 1575 he was finally able to announce the abolition of coign and livery from the main bulk of his territories in Kilkenny, Tipperary and Carlow.[47]

In organisational terms, although the ensuing changes in Co. Kilkenny were significant, they were not particularly extensive, insofar as they affected only a few people. An English-style shire force, revolving round the muster of all able-bodied men, was already in place in the county. Ormond had no desire to tamper with this, primarily because those who served in it were only part-time soldiers, and offered no great threat to order in the area. Rather, he aimed his reforms at the minority of fighting men, those who were professional and independent, and hence a potential source of trouble. With coign and livery out-

---

42 *Ir. Fiants*, Eliz. I, no. 3012.   43 In addition to the three previous references, see SP 63/19/39, incorrectly dated 1566 in *CSPI, 1509–73*, 317.   44 C. McNeill (ed.), 'Lord Chancellor Gerrard's notes of his report on Ireland', *Anal. Hib.* 2 (1931), 115.   45 Brady, *Chief governors*, 184, states Ormond was 'unable to suppress … coign and livery'.   46 *COD*, v, no. 192.   47 Butler (ed.), 'Annals of Thady Dowling', 41. The fact that the earl of Desmond had finally agreed to the abolition of coign in his country in 1574 may also explain Ormond's delay.

lawed, these full-time soldiers were removed from the pay-rolls of the local landlords, and placed more directly under the rule of the earl himself.

Their function changed from being part of a small private gang working exclusively for a local family into something more acceptable to the government. On Ormond's prompting, the kerne and horsemen who stayed in Kilkenny adopted a similar role to that filled in England by the trained bands, that is, they now formed a permanent basis for the shire force.[48] To further facilitate this change, in 1575 the earl had John Sweetman of Castle Eve appointed the marshal of the county.[49] The choice of title is interesting, suggesting Sweetman was assigned to fill a role normally associated with the provosts-marshal in England. If so, then he not only assumed command of the trained band, maintaining discipline among its troops – in itself a novel development – but he also took responsibility for the enforcement of martial law against those officially identified as outcasts, the 'unbooked' soldiers or masterless men.[50]

Ormond was fortunate that Sir William Fitzwilliam was in charge of the Irish government as he was overseeing the implementation of these decidedly draconian reforms. A more hostile lord deputy might have manipulated the need to purge the Kilkenny area of unreliable soldiers in order to undermine the Ormond lordship. In particular, it would have been difficult to resist the temptation to grant sweeping powers of martial law to English officers suspicious of the earl and his followers (as was happening elsewhere, in other lordships). Fitzwilliam, however, saw nothing wrong with consolidating the tenth earl's position, seeing a strong Ormond presence as a useful expedient that tended towards the greater security of southern Ireland. Had he helped the Fitzwillian regime to last longer the Black Earl might have experienced less anxiety in his struggle with government policy.

AUTONOMY WITH CONSENT, 1571–5

Throughout the four years of his first deputyship (1571–5), Fitzwilliam rarely interfered in the Ormond country. He allowed local men acceptable to Earl Thomas to carry out the day-to-day business of government. Indeed, while Fitzwilliam remained chief governor, the traditional leaders of the county community enjoyed a level of control over the shire and its affairs they were not to experience again. Through Ormond and the new deputy they became for the last time the sole agents of the crown in the county, acting as its social partners in the maintenance of order. The list of those named as commissioners for muster and array in 1573 reads like a contemporary who's-who of the Kilkenny elite, embracing as it did members of the Butler, Blanchville, Shortal, Cantwell, Grace, and Shee families.[51]

48 Boynton, *Elizabethan militia*, 90–8. **49** HMC, *De L'Isle & Dudley MSS*, ii, 30. **50** Williams, *Tudor regime*, 202–3. **51** *Ir. Fiants*, Eliz. I, no. 2345.

Fitzwilliam was content to leave well alone, relying on the tenth earl to deal with most problems as and when they arose. Initially, the policy paid dividends – for the deputy as well as for the earl and his supporters. Having gained Ormond as a temporary ally, Fitzwilliam was able to extend his reach into some of the outlying parts of the country, simply by pressing the earl into service. He gained access to Earl Thomas' personal network of allies and kindred in the south. Although Ormond was a court noble, his authority partly determined by the strength of his relationship with the English monarch, he was still unavoidably bound up in the web-like world of the native Irish lordships. At the highest level, via his late mother the dowager countess, his late uncle the first Viscount Mountgarret, his cousin Edmund, the second viscount, and his three dead and three surviving brothers, Earl Thomas was related to the earl of Desmond, the earl of Clanricard, Viscount Baltinglass, Viscount Decies, the baron of Upper Ossory, and Lord Power of Curraghmore, all noblemen like him, most of them loyal to the crown, but some not greatly so.[52] As a matter of course Ormond knew a lot about their affairs, more than the government did. Equally enticing for Fitzwilliam, the Black Earl also possessed a string of contacts with the Gaelic lords of southern Leinster and Munster. One of the earl's mistresses at about this time was the daughter of a former O'More chieftain, a potentially invaluable link now that the O'Mores were again in revolt in Laois.[53] Moreover, not just Ormond, but some of his servants, were well informed regarding the movements of the local Gaelic families. Richard Shee, Ormond's seneschal, enjoyed close personal ties with the O'Bryns of Carlow-Wicklow and the Scots-Irish galloglass family, the McDonells of Crostybeg, with both of whom he fostered children; significantly, the new O'More leader, Rory Oge, was described as Shee's 'gossip'.[54] Fitzwilliam put these contacts to use, collecting information on the south and encouraging Ormond and Shee to put out feelers to the disaffected.[55]

The advantages accruing to the Dublin executive through this arrangement were best demonstrated during the first rebellion of Rory Oge O'More. Fitzwilliam had noticed that Ormond was evolving into a skilful military commander, and in the summer of 1572 he insisted on using Earl Thomas (and the earl of Kildare also) instead of the royal army to combat the O'More threat to the Pale.[56] This of course gelled perfectly with Ormond's desire to impede the growing threat of the English garrison commanders in the regions, and to attach Fitzwilliam more firmly to his side he undertook to enter the field at his own expense.[57] After a brief campaign to track Rory down, Earl Thomas persuaded the rebel leader to submit to the lord deputy at New Ross.[58] Although we can

---

52 GEC, *Complete peerage*, sub 'Ormond' and 'Mountgarret'.   53 Lambeth Palace Ms 626, ff 173v–174r.   54 SP 63/115/10. For the importance of such affinity ties see Fitzsimons, 'Fosterage and Gossiprid', 138–49.   55 *CSPI, 1509–73*, 446, 460, 466, 471, 477, 480–1; Bod. Lib., Carte Ms 57, ff 97, 335.   56 E.g., SP 63/37/26.   57 SP 63/37/35. The earl also made over a large loan of money (£700) to Fitzwilliam on at least one occasion: Bod. Lib., Carte Ms 131, fol. 121.   58 O'Hanlon & O'Leary, *History of Queen's county*, ii, 452; *Cal. Carew MSS, 1575–88*, no. 593.

only surmise, it seems likely that Ormond's mistress and Shee's foster-kin helped to bring about the cessation of hostilities,[59] for previously Rory had proved most reluctant to negotiate with government military officials, fearing capture or assassination.[60]

Ormond derived considerable personal benefit from his accord with Fitzwilliam. For one thing, in 1572 it was partly due to Fitzwilliam's special pleading that the earl's brothers, hitherto 'tied to abide within the county of Kilkenny', were freed by Queen Elizabeth to fight for the crown, an important step in their political rehabilitation;[61] for another, Fitzwilliam bowed to the earl's request that he be allowed to offer protections to local outlaws in order to prevent them destabilising the Kilkenny/Tipperary frontier.[62] Yet Lord Deputy Fitzwilliam was never Ormond's creature. Though often glad to indulge the earl's whims, there were limits to what he was prepared to do. Early in 1573, much to Ormond's exasperation, he decided to resume Sidney's chosen method of dealing with the main Gaelic lordships of Leinster – state terror and military conquest. He granted extended powers of martial law to the seneschals of the garrisons at Ferns, Leighlinbridge, and Maryborough, who were authorised to escalate the assault on the disaffected lineages that lived along Kilkenny's northern and eastern borders, chiefly the O'Mores and Kavanaghs, and also the O'Byrnes.[63] The danger was equally serious to the west, in Munster. When Earl Thomas's officers, Richard Shee and James Tobyn, tried to oppose Lord President Perrot's intrusion into the liberty of Tipperary in 1573, Fitzwilliam turned a blind eye to Perrot's behaviour, which included a threat to impose martial law on the liberty in order to get his way.[64] In this instance, Ormond yielded, willing to allow Perrot in provided his palatine rights were not directly challenged, but he resented the fact that Fitzwilliam had not defended his independence. Subsequently, when he complained of MacGiollapadraig provocation along the Kilkenny/Ossory frontier in 1573–4, only for Fitzwilliam to again refuse to respond, his patience snapped. Relations between the two men soured, the earl adding the deputy to his list of government foes and seeking his dismissal.[65]

Ormond failed to recognise that the MacGiollapadraig troubles betrayed one of the main practical difficulties of a royal policy of conciliation in the provinces – the problem of taking sides between rival loyalist lordships. Had the MacGiollapadraigs been rebels Ormond might realistically have expected support from Dublin; however, as strategic allies of the crown in the southern midlands no lord deputy was willing to give serious consideration to the earl's

59 Shee's involvement is further suggested by his receipt of some unusual privileges from the government in 1573: *CPRI, Eliz. I*, 460–1. **60** Carey, 'End', 238–9. **61** Bod. Lib., Carte Ms 57, fol. 476. **62** Ibid., Ms 55, fol. 136; ibid., Ms 131, ff 154, 158; NA, M 2041. **63** Donovan, 'Tudor rule', 125, 128–9; Carey, 'End', 239–40; D. Edwards, 'Ideology and experience: Spenser's *View* and martial law in Ireland', in H. Morgan (ed.), *Political ideology in Ireland, 1541–1641* (Dublin 1999), 132–3. **64** D. Kennedy, 'The presidency of Munster, 1570–1625', unpublished MA thesis, University College, Cork (1973), 71–5. **65** I can find no evidence to support the assertion that Ormond and his family wished to maintain Fitzwilliam in power in 1574–5 (Brady, *Chief governors*, 188).

demand that they be punished for violating his frontiers. Since the 1530s the MacGiollapadraigs had aped the Butlers step for step, like them welcoming English reintervention in Ireland in order to profit from it, but whereas the Butlers expected the crown's blessing for territorial expansion, the MacGiollapadraigs desired royal protection of their territories from outside aggressors, principally the Butlers.[66] Furthermore, whether Earl Thomas accepted it or not, the incumbents of Dublin Castle were usually grateful to the MacGiollapadraigs for providing a means by which to restrict Butler power in the south. Given a choice between rival lords in Ireland the Tudor government preferred to prop up the weaker the better to hold back the stronger, perceiving the politics of conciliation to be fundamentally about limiting noble power in the regions.

Since first assuming the deputyship in April 1571 Fitzwilliam had manfully ignored a flood of complaints by Ormond alleging all manner of transgression by the MacGiollapadraigs, even turning a blind eye to the fact that, despite repeated promises to the contrary, they had yet to expose their territories to English law or administration. To appear balanced Fitzwilliam had likewise overlooked depredations committed against the MacGiollapadraig leader, Sir Barnaby Fitzpatrick, by Ormond's clients among the Grace family of north Kilkenny. When in May 1573 the Graces ransacked Sir Barnaby's house at Culahill and kidnapped his wife and daughter, Fitzwilliam had intervened only minimally, travelling to Kilkenny to take personal control of the inquiry into the 'miserable captivity' of the two ladies before commissioning Ormond's brother, Edward Butler, to locate the kidnappers and secure the women's freedom.[67] Remarkably, rather than antagonise Ormond he even let the Graces go unpunished, a decision that hardly endeared him to Sir Barnaby Fitzpatrick. Despite this, however, the Black Earl of Ormond was unwilling to forgive Fitzwilliam for refusing to punish the MacGiollapadraigs when they forced an entry into Foulkescourt Castle in November 1573 and rescued a prisoner he had committed there 'for felony'. What particularly angered Earl Thomas was what he perceived as Fitzwilliam's hypocrisy over the matter of legal and military reform. Striving as he was to abandon coign and livery and nurture the development of the English legal system in his territories, Ormond felt that the deputy's sensitivity towards the MacGiollapadraigs had enabled the troublesome rulers of Ossory to infringe every government directive on military power and law and order with impunity. Hence his demand that Sir Barnaby Fitzpatrick be imprisoned for waging private war, contrary to statute, and his irate letter of 28 November berating Fitzwilliam for having consciously allowed the MacGiollapadraigs to flout the laws of the realm. His cooperation with the chief governor was over.[68]

---

66 Edwards, 'MacGiollapadraigs', 330–1. 67 SP 63/40/27, 31, 48; SP 63/42/13. See also *COD*, vi, Appendix 1, 133–4, where a document drawn up twenty years after the event suggests that MacGiollapadraig attacks on John Grace of Glashare contributed to the tension in the early 1570s. 68 Bod. Lib., Carte Ms 56, ff 216, 546.

In the summer of 1574 the earl brought his influence at Whitehall to bear against Fitzwilliam, whom he charged with failing to honour his legal obligations. Soon the deputy became the subject of a corrosive whispering campaign at the highest levels of the royal court. Both Sussex and Heneage penned letters warning him of the advisability of supporting Ormond's position in Ireland. The Black Earl, said Sussex, was 'the surest pillar of that state', and just as he had been a good friend to Fitzwilliam in the past, so, it was hinted, he might prove a fearsome enemy in the future.[69] Burghley then pitched in, reminding the deputy of 'the honourable good service' that Ormond had performed for the crown,[70] and when Elizabeth I learned of Ormond's grievance she left Fitzwilliam in no doubt of her inclination to take the earl's side.[71] For the sake of his viceregal office Fitzwilliam could hardly afford to heed such advice. His authority in the south quickly declined. His ongoing refusal to punish the MacGiollapadraigs only encouraged the lineage to escalate their campaign against Ormond's authority in Kilkenny, assaulting his tenants, stealing his livestock, burning two of his borderland castles, and finally, before February 1575, temporarily occupying his newly acquired manor house at Durrow.[72] Accordingly, it came as no surprise that when the idea was mooted that Fitzwilliam be replaced, Ormond made no attempt to defend him. Perhaps the earl should have been more forgiving. Rather than appoint Ormond's friend the first earl of Essex, Walter Devereux,[73] to the lord deputyship, as many had expected she might, in August 1575 the queen again handed the charge of her Irish kingdom to Sir Henry Sidney. It is indicative of Ormond's reaction to this news that within weeks he was writing to Burghley in praise of Fitzwilliam's recent good government.[74]

AUTONOMY CHALLENGED, 1575–8

Earl Thomas' unease at the conduct of crown policy under Fitzwilliam paled into insignificance compared to his misgivings over Sidney's return to Dublin Castle. The new governor's attitude to Butler power had not softened since his last term of duty, and he had not forgotten the reversals he had suffered at Ormond's hands before 1571. Still smarting from the criticism he had received for his part in provoking the 1569 rising, Sir Henry was determined to impose his authority on the Butlers and their allies now that he had the chance. Understandably, he felt that they had not been punished adequately for their past crimes – where he had been required to relinquish his post following their rebellion, it seemed they had barely suffered at all. Animated by a deep-seated resentment of Ormond and his family Sidney made the reduction of the Butler

---

69 Ibid., ff 398, 420. 70 Ibid., fol. 364. 71 SP 63/46/21. 72 Bod. Lib., Carte Ms 56, fol. 599; SP 63/47/1, 16; *COD*, v, nos. 252–3. 73 T. Wright, *Queen Elizabeth and her times* (2 vols, London 1838), ii, 26–7, 35. 74 SP 63/53/53.

country around Kilkenny one of the primary objectives of his second period of rule in Ireland (1575–8). For Earl Thomas and the Co. Kilkenny gentry this meant that what Fitzwilliam had done to cause tension in the region Sidney immediately intensified. Fitzwilliam's partiality for martial law and military government in the native lordships situated near the Kilkenny frontier was adapted by Sidney for use in Kilkenny itself. Similarly, Fitzwilliam's unwillingness to curb MacGiollapadraig incursions on Kilkenny shire ground was transformed by Sidney into outright encouragement of MacGiollapadraig aggression. But to begin his challenge to the autonomous standing of the Ormond lordship, Sidney gave his attention to the position of Earl Thomas' brothers, apparently certain that Sir Edmund, Edward and Piers Butler were still rebels at heart. As before, he intended to bait them to reveal their true natures to the queen, and in so doing weaken the Black Earl and tighten his own control over the conduct of government policy in the south of Ireland.

No sooner was Sidney back in Dublin than Sir Edmund Butler found himself accused of planning raids and 'stealths' into Wexford with his former confederates in treason, the Kavanaghs, and Sidney also reported that, as a result, Co. Kilkenny had become 'the sink and receptacle of innumerable cattle and goods' stolen out of neighbouring areas.[75] It was an astonishing assertion to make, for, if true, it implied that Ormond and Fitzwilliam must have colluded in covering up a renewal of Butler misdemeanours. Adding colour to such suspicions were the MacGiollapadraigs' allegations against Edward Butler, initially advanced in August 1575 (shortly after Sidney's appointment). These charged that in 1574 Edward had refused to meet with Fitzwilliam, only for the latter to ignore this rebuff to the dignity of his office.[76] Taken together, such apparent revelations about Sir Edmund and Edward Butler cast serious doubt on the wisdom of the Butlers' royal pardon of 1574.

On balance, the charges advanced against Earl Thomas' brothers following the return of Sir Henry Sidney to office should be treated with the utmost caution. The Fitzwilliam lord deputyship of 1571–5 had witnessed the gradual resumption of Butler military service on behalf of the crown, not the re-emergence of Butler complicity in revolt. For instance, it is a matter of record that in the months immediately prior to gaining their royal pardon, both Edward Butler and Piers Butler had been applauded in Dublin for their role in the prosecution of rebel groups across Leinster, Munster and Connaught.[77] It is, then, interesting to note that Sidney's charges against the Butler brothers failed to elicit alarm at Whitehall; evidently nobody believed his allegations. Sidney quietly dropped the most serious of the charges (that about Sir Edmund Butler's supposedly criminal ventures with the Kavanaghs) for lack of corroboration, and the story of Edward Butler's reputed slighting of Lord Deputy Fitzwilliam was contradicted by no less an authority than Fitzwilliam himself.[78] Yet the alle-

---

75 *Cal. Carew MSS, 1575–88*, no. 33; SP 63/54/17. 76 SP 63/53/7. 77 SP 63/39/65; SP 63/42, un-numbered item after no. 84; SP 63/43/14. 78 SP 63/53/2.

gations served a useful purpose all the same. While Sir Edmund briefly evaded the new governor's clutches, Edward Butler had to spend the latter part of 1575 and the early months of 1576 under prolonged investigation as Sidney and his officials dragged things out.[79] To judge by later developments (treated below), both brothers were unnerved by the experience and began once again to waver in their loyalty to the earl, Edward especially.

As the pressure mounted on the Butler brothers fresh troubles erupted on the Kilkenny/Ossory frontier that threatened to undermine the recent military reforms introduced by Ormond. Sometime between 9 January and 14 April 1576 Durrow Castle was attacked and recaptured by forces commanded by Tirlagh MacGiollapadraig. Having placed a garrison there, Tirlagh led a detachment of troops deep into Fassadinin, where for the second time in three months the MacGiollapadraig troops laid siege to the Black Earl's tower house at Kilmocar. Apparently the first attack, which had occurred in January, had been repulsed thanks to a spirited defence by Ormond's tenant, Donill MacShane, a pro-Butler MacGiollapadraig, but on this occasion the MacGiollapadraig forces were better organised, and were able to occupy the fort. The seizure marked a significant moment in the history of the struggle between the MacGiollapadraigs and the Kilkenny community. Previously the Ossory lineage had largely confined their raids to the north-western limits of the county; now, by grabbing Kilmocar, their soldiers had stretched out to encompass part of the north-east as well. A second detachment, led by Tirlagh's brother Callough MacGiollapadraig, ravaged large parts of the northern Nore valley, attacking Aghoure, the estate of Richard Shee, and taking a large prey of cattle in the glens of Ballyfoyle that belonged to the Purcell family.[80] Caught off guard, Ormond's new arrangements for county defence had proved hopelessly inadequate.

Earl Thomas was quick to identify Sidney as the architect of the MacGiollapadraig invasion. Writing to the governor he commented: 'Truly if my lord [Barnaby] of Upper Ossory did not presume so much upon your favour, he would not deal in this sort with me.'[81] Sidney did little to disprove the allegation. Feigning outrage at the earl's suggestion that he, the queen's representative, 'should deal one way in appearance and another way in secret', he nonetheless failed utterly to take action against the MacGiollapadraigs despite giving repeated assurances that he would.[82] Although messengers came and went between Kilkenny, Dublin and London over the matter, the forces of Baron Barnaby Fitzpatrick were allowed to remain in possession of Durrow Castle throughout the entire summer of 1576. The extent of the deputy's trickery was revealed to Ormond on 13 August, the date agreed with the government for the formal return of Durrow into the earl's hands. Having ridden forth to the castle to receive the

---

79 SP 63/53/59; SP 63/55/16.   **80** BL, Add. Ms 15,914, fol. 33; HMC, *De L'Isle & Dudley MSS*, ii, 33. For Aghoure, NA, M 2816: 3–4.   **81** HMC, *De L'Isle & Dudley MSS*, ii, 38.   **82** Ibid., 38–9.

keys from Baron Barnaby's men, as he had been led to believe he could, Ormond was told to go away again by the baron's 'base born' servants, who informed him that their master the baron had just reached a new arrangement with Sidney, wherein the deputy had agreed to place the matter on hold until such time as the earl had established his proper legal title to the premises. This was the first Ormond had heard of any new arrangement, Sidney not having told him of the change of plan. As a stalling device, it was poorly disguised, but as a slight to the earl's honour, it was faultless.[83] It was also deliciously provocative, enabling the MacGiollapadraigs to retain possession of the castle for another year.[84]

Sidney's most serious challenge, however, was still to come. On 6 November 1576, a few weeks after the Black Earl had departed for court to bring his grievances against the governor to the queen's attention,[85] Sir Henry appointed Francis Lovell, a personal servant, as the new commissioner of martial law for Co. Kilkenny.[86] At a stroke Ormond's efforts to keep the shire free of what he saw as the worst excesses of government behaviour were overthrown. Shortly before his departure for England the tenth earl had made his cousin Edmund Butler, second Viscount Mountgarret, deputy governor of the 'eight quarters' (or baronies) of Co. Kilkenny during his absence.[87] Through the earl's influence Mountgarret had obtained a martial law commission for himself, the better to sustain the privileged autonomous standing of the Butler dynasty in the county. This had been issued just two days previously, on 4 November.[88] Lovell's patent of 6 November effectively nullified Mountgarret's, and insured that the power to execute without trial suspected offenders in the shire was no longer the preserve of the earl and his representatives. Within hours of the Lovell appointment, Kilkenny was placed under the military rule of Captain Henry Harrington, Sidney's nephew, who had become the *de facto* martial governor of Leinster.[89] Simultaneously the earl's liberty of Tipperary was threatened by the appearance of a new lord president of Munster, Sir William Drury, another Sidney associate. On assuming office, Drury made no secret of his hostility to Tipperary's ongoing (if rather limited) exemption from the jurisdiction of the presidency.[90]

Lovell, Harrington, and Drury each served a dual function in the Ormond country. As soldiers they were directly responsible for hunting down those identified as the government's enemies in the region, and killing them; equally significant, as policemen they gathered intelligence that Sidney hoped would prove damaging to Earl Thomas and his family. Their endeavours proved rather more successful in Tipperary than Kilkenny.

---

83 Ibid., 42; SP 63/56/17. 84 On 22 Sept. 1576, as Ormond was about to leave for court, Sidney wrote to Baron Barnaby to reprimand him for his 'nightly' attacks on the earl's tenants, but after Ormond's departure he let the matter rest (HMC, *De L'Isle & Dudley MSS*, ii, 47). 85 *COD*, v, no. 288. 86 Lovell first served Sidney in Ireland in the late 1550s: Kent AO, Ms Ui 475 021, ff 2b, 10a, 12a, 17a; HMC, *De L'Isle & Dudley MSS*, i, 257, 387; *Ir. Fiants*, Eliz. I, no. 2918. 87 A. Collins (ed.), *Letters & memorials of state of Sir Henry Sidney* (2 vols, London 1746), i, 134–5, 147. 88 *Ir. Fiants*, Eliz. I, no. 2916. 89 Ibid., no. 2921. 90 Kennedy, 'The presidency', 89–90.

The fruits of their inquiries were immediately apparent in the liberty of Tipperary, where power was fragmented between competing branches of the Butler lineage and Sidney's encouragement of O'Carroll independence added to the tension. When Drury arrived to convene court sessions at Clonmel in November 1576, two local gentlemen, Edmund Comyn of Kilconnell and Jacob Fleming of Cashel, came forward to present allegations against the earl's brothers Sir Edmund and Edward Butler, as well as against the Butlers of Grallagh and Lismalin. Among other things they testified that since 30 October coign and livery had been reimposed in parts of Tipperary by Sir Edmund and Edward and their followers, who included a number of Kilkenny-based soldiers.[91] This was damning evidence, and its veracity seems indisputable. To take just Comyn: not only was he a former sheriff of Tipperary, but he was also a tenant on part of the Ormond estate, and was counted among the earl's main clients.[92] It was as if Ormond's reforms of military practices had never occurred. With the earl absent at court, Sidney had once again managed to coerce Sir Edmund and Edward Butler into a rash reaction that ran contrary to the interests of their eldest brother.

Sir Edmund was subsequently indicted by the lord president,[93] but Edward, strangely, escaped prosecution. In a letter written late in 1576 or early in 1577, only a draft of which survives, Sidney sought to inform the Black Earl that Edward had decided to abandon the protection of the house of Ormond to become his 'servant' and 'such a one as I like and esteem', an extraordinary statement considering his previous desire to have Edward beheaded. Going on, he chided the earl for not taking better care of Edward, who 'regarding he is your lordship's brother [wishes] he may be esteemed'. Sidney advised Earl Thomas to settle a permanent estate on Edward in Kilkenny or Tipperary, something Ormond had thus far refused to do in order to control his most errant sibling and punish him for his past wrongs. Decoded, Sidney's message was a stark one: through a mixture of intimidation and friendly promises he had managed to recruit Edward Butler to use as he wanted in the earl's lordship. As long as Edward proved useful to the deputy, he might avoid prosecution for breaking the law.[94]

Investigations were far less effective in Co. Kilkenny, where power was centralised in the earl of Ormond's hands and coign and livery remained inoperative. On 30 September 1576, prior to his 'going into England', Ormond had issued orders for the government of Kilkenny during his absence. His arrangements afforded Sidney little prospect of advancement. Beneath Mountgarret, his deputy governor, Ormond placed the eight baronies of the shire under the command of 16 gentlemen commissioners, nearly all clients of proven loyalty to both the crown and the earldom, men such as Walter Walsh of Castlehowell, James Shortall of Ballylorcaine, Gerald Blanchville of Blanchvillestown, and

91 Hore & Graves (ed.), *Social state*, 238–42. **92** *COD*, v, nos. 16, 99, 157, 225. **93** Canny, *Elizabethan conquest*, 106. **94** Kent AO, Ms U1475, no. 015/29

John Sweetman of Castle Eve. The earl's arrangements represented something of a fusion of English and Gaelic structures. While his gentlemen commissioners resembled the constables of the shire hundred that operated in England, the police force that Ormond appointed to serve under them was of purely Irish origin, the *kethern tighe*, organised into units of six horsemen and twelve footmen per barony. Unlike similar orders made by other Irish lords, however, Ormond's instructions of September 1576 anticipated the unfettered operation of English law and administration. Vagabonds and idlemen were to be apprehended and committed to the county gaol to await trial before a government judge at the next court sessions. The Black Earl even insisted that his officials take further directions from the lord deputy when necessary, and allow Sidney's man, Francis Lovell, to operate beside them in the baronies of Knocktopher and Kells.[95] His orders were carried out to the letter. No military attack was launched against the MacGiollapadraig occupation of Durrow, enabling Ormond, on his arrival at Whitehall, to play the role of injured party with conviction. By following a policy of restraint, relying on the law instead of force, Earl Thomas' men placed Sir Henry Sidney in a delicate situation. The earl, for his own part, hoped to emasculate Sidney by reasserting his influence at Whitehall as the queen's principal Irish courtier. As he explained to a servant: '[because] the lord deputy and I should never agree, … I had rather be absent [at court] where I may seek remedy'.[96] How far would the deputy go to challenge Ormond's power?

Far from undermining the earl, Sidney's interference in Kilkenny was counterproductive, binding the county community and Ormond's representatives closer together. This proved inevitable when it was discovered that Sidney's appointees had attempted to manufacture evidence against senior members of the Butler dynasty when none could be found legitimately. Suspicions were first aroused by another of the deputy's new officials in the Kilkenny area, Francis Cosby. As seneschal of the Queen's County, Cosby asked Lord Mountgarret to serve under his command against Rory Oge O'More, an insulting suggestion to a social superior. The viscount refused. In doing so, however, Mountgarret was mindful of Ormond's requirement that he maintain a loyal profile towards the crown while serving as the earl's deputy, and he offerred to 'do good service … under some other', eventually placing himself under the command of Henry Harrington, the son of an English lord.[97] Mountgarret did not get the chance to fulfil his promise of service. In May 1577 Cosby had him arrested on charges of aiding and abetting the O'More rebels, and the viscount was imprisoned in Dublin Castle.[98] It is interesting that both the secretary of state of England, Sir Francis Walsingham,

95 Collins (ed.), *Letters & memorials*, i, 134–5. **96** Bod. Lib., Carte Ms 1, fol. 22. **97** MacNeill (ed.), 'Lord Chancellor Gerrard's notes', 117–8. **98** Collins (ed.), *Letters and memorials*, i, 185–9. This is not to say that nobody from the shire helped the rebels. On or about 10 May 1577 Rory Oge O'More set up camp at 'the Nesker' along the Kilkenny-Laois frontier, where he received succour from William O'Loughlin, and his daughter Ellen, who lived nearby at Clontubbrid in Shortal country (*Ir. Fiants,* Eliz. I, no. 3219).

and the lord chancellor of Ireland, Sir William Gerrard, seem to have sympathised with Mountgarret's complaint that his committal was the result of a government conspiracy.[99] Few in the south of Ireland believed the charges against him. He was later released, for lack of evidence.

Other 'revelations' of collusion in Co. Kilkenny proved equally misleading. Having travelled to the shire for the Lenten assizes in 1577, Lord Deputy Sidney urged his officials to turn the screw tighter on the Butlers and their associates, his intention being to 'work hangings' on suspected troublemakers. In particular he required them to look to the frontier areas of the Ormond country, where a military underworld still lingered, and to 'banish all mountain meetings'.[100] Surprisingly little evidence of serious wrongdoing was uncovered, but eventually, on or about Christmas Eve 1577, Sidney moved against Ferdorrough McEdmund Purcell, one of the captains of Ormond's 'kernety', or police, and constable of the earl's manor of Pottlerath. Probably based on information supplied by Lovell,[101] the deputy attempted to portray Purcell as Cosby had earlier failed to portray Mountgarret, as a senior Ormond official who supported the O'More rebels. His evidence was entirely circumstantial, Purcell's sole misdemeanour having been to act as foster-father to a child of Rory Oge O'More. It will be recalled that a few years earlier Sir William Fitzwilliam had viewed the bonds of affinity that existed between some of Ormond's servants and the embattled O'More leader as a means by which to influence the rebel chieftain, and persuade him to lay down his arms; Sidney viewed the situation differently. Representing Purcell's fosterage relationship as an anti-English practice common among rebels, he used it to launch one of his strongest denunciations of the inhabitants of the earl of Ormond's country. Writing to the privy council, he depicted Kilkenny as a place where his presence was resented while rebels received hospitality, and where the influence of the Butler family ran contrary to English law and custom.[102] His simultaneous attempt to prosecute three more of Ormond's agents in December 1577 ended in high farce in the county court, when three juries comprised of local gentlemen, freeholders, merchants and artisans refused to recognise his charges, returning bills of ignoramus to each indictment, to his utter fury.[103]

The increasing wildness of Sidney's assertions betrayed his desperation. Having first compelled, and then 'uncovered', the Butlers' re-imposition of coign and livery in Tipperary in late 1576, by the beginning of 1578 the deputy and his agents had been unable to produce anything else that could be used to damage Ormond. This might not have mattered had the methods they employed not caused eyebrows to be raised in other sections of government. In Dublin Lord Chancellor Gerrard was concerned by what he saw as Sidney's

99 HMC, *De L'Isle & Dudley MSS*, ii, 57. **100** *Cal. Carew MSS, 1575–88*, nos. 48, 80 (2). **101** In a report of 1585 recalling his past experiences in Kilkenny Lovell laid stress on the covert fosterage relationships he had uncovered in the area: SP 63/115/10. **102** *Cal. Carew MSS, 1575–88*, no. 83. **103** The indicted Ormondists were James Shortal of Ballylorcaine, John Rochford of Killary and Donill MacShane of Kilmocar (Ibid.; HMC, *Egmont MSS*, i, 10).

arbitrary and partisan conduct towards the Ormond territories. Gerrard's observations over conditions in Co. Kilkenny did much to discredit Sidney in
London, where Earl Thomas' influence was in the ascendant, with the queen
increasingly mindful of his grievances, showering him with grants of land and
revenue in aid of his supposedly 'poor estate'.[104]

In response to Sidney's command, Gerrard had visited Kilkenny in July 1577.
Expecting widespread opposition to English law and government, he encountered an altogether different scenario and was soon rejecting Sidney's contention
that Ormond's servants and the local gentry presided over a militarised bandit
society. In his subsequent report to the privy council the chancellor declared 'I
liked better of the civility within the county of Kilkenny than in any other …
of the counties [of Leinster]'. He especially approved of the local acceptance of
the common law. Having held a general sessions in the county courthouse he
noted 'a better form of justice observed; better persons of the jury; and a more
indifferent [that is, unpartisan] trial'.[105] This was not to say that he was entirely
satisfied with local conditions. Ormond's reforms had still a long way to go
before Co. Kilkenny was fully anglicised, and although Sidney had greatly exaggerated its shortcomings, the shire's legal apparatus required serious attention.
Crucially, Gerrard encountered no resistance to his proposed changes to local
administration. Rather, he received the active support of Ormond's seneschal,
Richard Shee, in promulgating his 'Orders for the County of Kilkenny', which
were proclaimed in the shire sometime after 9 July. The result of detailed examination of local social and political circumstances, these paid surprisingly little
attention to military matters. Indeed, they largely reiterated Earl Thomas'
arrangements of September 1576, offering just one refinement, a guarantee that
the 'holding kerne' of 300 foot soldiers who comprised the professional core of
the shire force could be maintained at their full complement. Otherwise Gerrard
turned his gaze to eradicating the black market trade in stolen cattle that per-
meated parts of the county, and he also attempted to limit the capacity of the
sheriff of the shire for corruption and racketeering, which he identified as the
only serious defect in Ormond's local administrative arrangements.

Instead of advancing Sidney's policy of intrusion and disruption Gerrard was
greatly concerned by the government's handling of the county and its overlord.
His investigation of the Black Earl's complaints against the lord deputy over the
activities of the MacGiollapadraigs around Durrow led him to believe that only
the earl had proper legal title to the property, and he found Sidney's refusal to
demand the MacGiollapadraigs' withdrawal hard to credit.[106] He was equally
bewildered by Sidney's treatment of Edward Butler, who roamed about
Kilkenny and Tipperary with 29 followers threatening the earl's lands and tenants. When Ormond had complained that the lord deputy was protecting
Edward from prosecution, Gerrard had not believed him, and 'marvelled it

---

104 E.g., NA, Lodge MSS, Rolls, Vol. I, 400–1.   **105** MacNeill (ed.), 'Lord Chancellor Gerrard's
notes', 118.   **106** Ibid., 162, 164–8.

should be so'. On further investigation, however, he found the allegation to be true, with Edward himself asking him to honour the lord deputy's promise 'that he might be exempted' from indictment in the local courts by Ormond's officials.[107] The final paragraph of Gerrard's 'Orders' reveals the extent of his anxiety over government policy in Kilkenny. Conscious that the exercise of martial law in the area was presently in the hands of the lord deputy's agent, Lovell, the chancellor felt compelled to insist that no gentleman or freeholder suffer summary execution, but should have the charges against them brought to 'trial of common law'. To his lawyer's mind it appeared as though Sidney preferred terror to due process, arbitrary rule to the rule of law.[108] When he finally returned to England in March 1578 to present his report on the government of Ireland to the queen and her advisers, Gerrard presented a damning picture of Sidney's administration in which the deputy's severity towards the Ormond lordship in Co. Kilkenny figured prominently.

Through his relentless assault on Ormond's position Sidney had sown the seeds of his own destruction. As his allegations against his enemy collapsed, unsubstantiated, one by one, Earl Thomas grew in strength. Long before Gerrard had arrived at court to present his report, it had been the talk of the royal palace that Sidney was discredited and would soon be removed from office. As long ago as November 1576 Sidney had received a message from England advising him to stay on good terms with Ormond, for the sake of his career.[109] He had received further warnings to the same effect during 1577, from Leicester and Walsingham,[110] but understandably (and like Fitzwilliam before him) he found it impossible to compromise with Ormond without losing face, all the more so as he had made the curtailment of the earl's authority such an obvious policy objective. His hold on the deputyship had begun to loosen in September 1577, when at court his son the poet Philip Sidney had offered what Walsingham described as 'little discourtesies' to the Black Earl in response to the earl's criticism of the Irish administration.[111] Thereafter, and thanks largely to Ormond, complaints of Sir Henry's severity found easy expression around Whitehall. As Sidney was later to recall, at court the tenth earl, 'my professed foe', 'sometime with clamour, but oftener with whispering, did bitterly backbite me'.[112] Earl Thomas managed to turn the queen against him. Having formed a combination with the earl of Kildare, another Sidney adversary, and brought his kinsman, the earl of Thomond, in from the political wilderness,[113] Ormond was able to make representations on behalf of the lords and gentry of the southern, eastern and western lordships to demand immediate change in Ireland. In a private message sent from London he told his servant the Kilkenny merchant, Thomas Archer, that though he longed to return home he had decided to remain at

107 Ibid., 169–70. **108** Ibid., 174–80. **109** SP 63/56/48. **110** HMC, *De L'Isle & Dudley MSS*, ii, 51, 53, 57. **111** Ibid., 69. **112** Hore (ed.), 'Sidney's memoir', *UJA* 5 (1857), 308. **113** SP 63/58/21; SP 63/59/77; SP 63/60/14; Collins (ed.), *Letters and memorials*, i, 211. For Kildare's role, see V.P. Carey, *Surviving the Tudors: the 'Wizard' earl of Kildare and English rule in Ireland, 1537–1586* (Dublin 2002), 185–6.

court 'till it please[d] God to put [it] into the queen's head to reform [the government of Ireland]'.[114] Eventually, with the cost of the Irish administration spiralling out of control, Gerrard's report delivered the knockout blow to Sidney's tottering reputation. By March 1578 the decision had been taken to recall him as governor.

Significantly, despite yielding to the demand for Sidney's dismissal early in the new year, Elizabeth I did not inform Earl Thomas of her decision until the beginning of summer. A letter dated 24 June 1578 indicates that Ormond had only recently learned that his enemy had been sacked and would be returning to court.[115] Evidently, although the queen favoured the earl hugely, and was prepared to maintain him even against her most senior officer in Ireland, she wished to conceal the full extent of his influence. Accordingly she allowed Sidney to delay his departure from office for several months, so that he might save face as her representative.[116] For some of the Co. Kilkenny gentry it proved an unfortunate decision, especially those who had served on the local juries that frustrated Sidney's prosecution of Ormond's officials in December 1577. Examining them in the court of castle chamber on 8 May and 3 July 1578, Sidney was able to impose fines ranging in size from £3 to 12s. 6d. on all 42 members of the three juries, before moving against the men who had acted as their ringleaders, namely Thomas Cantwell of Cantwell's Court, Thomas Den of Grenan and Robert Forstal of Kilferagh. For these he reserved the special punishment of imprisonment in Dublin Castle 'until further notice'.[117] Although records are not extant they probably remained incarcerated until Sidney's final departure from Ireland, on 12 September 1578.

Historians have rightly noted his role in orchestrating Sidney's downfall as one of the main political achievements of 'Black' Thomas Butler, tenth earl of Ormond.[118] At a stroke the earl had demonstrated that his mastery of court intrigue had not deserted him, and that, to a much greater extent than any other Irish lord, he derived his power as much from Whitehall and Greenwich as he did from his 'country' and followers. However, his success in ridding himself of Sidney did not diminish the earl's problems in dealing with government encroachment in Leinster and Munster. If anything it made his problems more acute. Having provided such an explicit demonstration of his influence, Ormond marked himself out as someone to be feared, a shark in the water of Anglo-Irish relations. In his campaign to oust the deputy he had helped to create something altogether new in Tudor Ireland, a united loyalist opposition.[119] His alliance with Kildare appalled certain English officials, who hitherto had capitalised on

---

114 Bod. Lib., Carte Ms 1, fol. 22.   **115** Ibid., fol. 24.   **116** Possibly she did so in response to Sidney's plea of 1 May: HMC, *De L'Isle & Dudley MSS*, ii, 80.   **117** HMC, *Egmont MSS*, i, 10, which overlooks the fact, recorded in the original castle chamber entry book (BL, Add. Ms 47,172, ff 33v–35v), that the Kilkenny city jury were tried separately from the county grand jurors, on 3 July.   **118** E.g., Canny, *From Reformation to Restoration*, 96–7; Brady, 'Thomas Butler', 55; Cyril Falls, *Elizabeth's Irish wars* (London 1950), 121–2.   **119** I will discuss Ormond's contribution to the politics of loyalist dissent in a forthcoming paper.

ancient factional divisions among the Irish ruling lineages to increase crown control over the provinces through a policy of divide and rule, certain that the local lords and chieftains were incapable of effective, unified opposition. Ormond's leadership of the loyalist lords, and their combined critique of the military and fiscal programmes of the government, was as unwelcome as it was unexpected. Therefore, while it has been argued that after 1578 'only the most rash of administrators dared openly to attack Ormond's status',[120] nevertheless many leading crown officials were compelled to oppose him covertly and to continue to nibble away at his high standing. Ormond, indeed, expected as much. Conscious that Sidney for all his failings remained a much admired figure in government circles, the earl knew that after the deputy's departure he would not be able to escape 'the malice of any that shall join with [Sir Henry] against me', 'wheresoever I am', in England or Ireland.[121] After 1578 the earl and his officers continued to confront unsolicited government advances.

RELIGIOUS REFORM AND THE HANGING JUDGE

Ormond's fears of further attrition were soon confirmed. Rather than gain a new chief governor willing to respect the autonomous position of his territories, he was confronted by Sir William Drury, a man who had spearheaded Sidney's challenge to the Ormond lordship in Tipperary, and who was notorious for his use of martial law and the hangman's rope in Munster.[122] Although Earl Thomas's success against Sidney necessitated the scaling-down of martial law in the Kilkenny area, Drury was most unwilling to leave the county to the rule of its overlord. To carry on Sidney's assault by other means Drury adapted the policy advocated by Chancellor Gerrard (and which Ormond himself supported) of making 'justices the soldiers', applying the common law rigorously against all suspect groups in the autonomous lordships. What made Drury's efforts dangerous to Ormond was his interest in religion, for in matters of faith the earl occupied a precarious position. Drury wore his Protestantism very much on his sleeve, but the Black Earl, though a Protestant, was anxious to avoid having to impose the new religion on his subjects, and was prepared merely to uphold the queen as head of the church in place of the pope. The great majority of his family, servants and subjects were Catholics, and public about it. Even before his promotion to the chief governorship Drury had expressed his alarm at the level of influence enjoyed in Co. Kilkenny by Catholic clergymen returning from the Continent, 'arrogant enemies to the gospel' and 'breeders of treachery'.[123] His insistence on confessional conformity threatened to undermine Ormond far more effectively than anything Sidney had attempted, introducing religious tension into the earl's territories.

120 Brady, 'Thomas Butler', 55.   **121** Bod. Lib., Carte Ms 1, fol. 24.   **122** Canny, *Elizabethan conquest*, 106–8.   **123** W.M. Brady (ed.), *State papers relating to the Irish Church in the reign of Elizabeth* (London 1868), 22–3.

At the behest of Nicholas Walsh, the new Protestant bishop of Ossory, the religious issue came to the fore immediately on Drury's appointment to the chief governorship. In November 1578 Walsh informed Drury of the dire state of his diocese. Across Co. Kilkenny parish churches were 'utterly ruined and decayed', and the bishop could find no-one among his flock willing to repair them. Conditions were particularly displeasing in Kilkenny town. All but a mere handful of the burgesses and merchants treated his arrival in St Canice's Cathedral with scornful disregard, making no effort to disguise the fact that they were 'bent on popery'. On Sundays the zealous new prelate had the bells of the cathedral rung long and loud, only for the townsmen to go deaf, refusing his demand that they bring their families 'to hear the divine service … as by her majesty's injunctions they are bound to do'.[124]

The extent of the local attachment to Rome was indeed striking. The Catholics of Co. Kilkenny were still without a bishop, as the papacy had yet to nominate a successor to John O'Thonery (d. 1565), but Counter-Reformation clergy such as John White and the Jesuit James Archer had enjoyed considerable success since their arrival from Europe.[125] The co-founder of the Irish seminary at Douai, White was the acknowledged leader, 'worshipped like a god between Kilkenny and Waterford and Clonmel'.[126]

Bishop Walsh was better equipped than his predecessor, Christopher Gaffney, to further the Protestant cause. Able to preach in Gaelic as well as English, he took a leading part in attempts to translate the New Testament into the native tongue.[127] On its own, however, it seemed 'the Word' was not enough to insure success, and Walsh wished to have resistance to his episcopacy weakened in order to achieve general conformity to 'true religion' in the shire. At Walsh's behest, Lord Justice Drury was encouraged to take the loyalist rulers of Kilkenny town to task for their failure to attend Protestant service, contrary to the terms of the statute 2° Elizabeth.

A royal commission was issued empowering the bishop to enforce church attendance. Those who failed to comply were to be fined, the money raised to go towards the renovation of local church buildings. To be certain the commission was taken seriously Drury had the chief men of the town enter into bonds worth £40 each to guarantee their good behaviour. The governor and his companion, Sir Edward Fitton, later reported that 'since our coming thence [from Kilkenny] we hear from the bishop of the good conformity of some'.[128]

The Catholic merchants and tradesmen were not the only ones to experience government intervention in November 1578. Drury also set his sights on the frontiers of the shire, where low level violence continued to prevail. As usual, things were worst in the north, where the recent killing of the rebel chieftain, Rory Oge O'More, had not improved relations between the Butlers and

124 *Cal. Carew MSS, 1575–88*, no. 109.   125 Anon (ed.), 'Miscellano Vaticano-Hibernica', *Archivium Hibernicum* 5 (1916), 180.   126 W.M. Brady (ed.), *State papers*, 22–3.   127 C. Quinn, 'Nicholas Walsh and his friends: a forgotten chapter in the Irish Reformation', *Butler Soc. Jn.* 2/3 (1984), 294–8.   128 *Cal. Carew MSS, 1575–88*, no. 109.

the MacGiollapadraigs.[129] Rather, with Rory dead, the two dynasties at once set about competing for control of southern Laois. The conflict was rendered more acrimonious by the Butlers' exploitation of a family quarrel between the second baron of Upper Ossory and his younger brother, Geoffrey MacGiollapadraig of Ballyowley. By the time Drury decided to intervene, Geoffrey had joined the Butlers in return for their aid against Baron Barnaby.[130]

For the government this was an undesirable development. Because Barnaby had no son, the Butlers' wooing of Geoffrey threatened to provoke a successional war among the MacGiollapadraig lineage and produce a significant growth in the regional dominance of the house of Ormond. To prevent this, Drury had to induce a reconciliation between Baron Barnaby and Geoffrey MacGiollapadraig.

A meeting was set for Kilkenny early in November amid an atmosphere of mutual recrimination between Drury and the Ormond group. Several of the tenth earl's closest supporters were called before Drury to answer for their actions. John Grace, brother of Fulk Grace of Roscrea, sensibly submitted to the governor and repented for his 'former life' of skulduggery in the Kilkenny-Tipperary marchlands. Had he not submitted, he would have been outlawed and faced the threat of martial law.[131] Sir Edmund Butler, Donill MacShane, and Nicholas Shortal of Clara were each also required to appear before Drury, who compelled them to enter a joint recognisance of £500 to guarantee the future dutiful conduct of Geoffrey MacGiollapadraig, whom they were sheltering.[132] Although trying to appear impartial – letting Walter Gall go unpunished for failing to answer his summons and treating the baron of Upper Ossory in much the same fashion as he treated the Butlers[133] – the leaders of the Kilkenny county community were angered by what they perceived as Drury's meddling in matters of local security. As they saw it, the MacGiollapadraigs' difficulty was their opportunity to buttress the north. Because of his intervention the chance was gone.

Drury's handling of the southern frontier gave the Kilkenny gentry further cause of complaint. In October he had been made aware of Shane Brenagh fitz Robert, 'a mean gentleman of the surname of the Walshes', who was responsible for a series of raids into Co. Waterford. Refusing to accept Shane's submission in Waterford city 'unless I saw him come with a rope about his neck, which the poor fellow was willing to do', he ordered Shane to remain in the custody of Henry Davells, the captain of Dungarvan,[134] on pain of forfeiting £500, an enormous sum for such a small landholder. A month later, having been brought to Kilkenny by the sheriff, Shane's liability was raised to £1,200 and permission was given for the pursuit of members of his gang.[135]

129 SP 63/61/29, 31. **130** SP 63/63/17. **131** SP 63/63/16. **132** SP 63/63/20. John (alias Ferdorrogh McEdmund) Purcell entered a separate bond at Waterford: SP 63/63/5. **133** SP 63/63/21. Callough MacGiollapadraig was imprisoned in Dublin Castle shortly before 20 November 'for hurts lately done' (*Cal. Carew MSS, 1575–88*, no. 109). **134** *Ir. Fiants*, Eliz. I, no. 2517. **135** *Cal. Carew MSS, 1575–88*, no. 109; SP 63/63/7.

Though Shane was guilty, it is likely that some of the local landlords felt for him. A year earlier the estate of his brother, Richard Walsh (alias Brenagh) of Ballinacowley, had been ransacked by a group of men armed with swords and clubs;[136] to some it may have seemed that Shane was only recovering his losses by robbing in Waterford the sort of things that had been stolen from his family in Kilkenny. Whether this was so or not, many locals would have been concerned by the fate of one of his accomplices, James Walsh, who was hunted down by Drury's guide, Francis Colby. Having caught him, Colby had Walsh executed following a trial at a 'private sessions' in Waterford.[137] There was no such thing at English law as a private sessions. Walsh had been the victim of a kangaroo court.

Under Drury government policy towards Kilkenny had remained severe. Greatly feared already, Drury resolved to frighten the inhabitants of the Ormond lordship into direct obedience to the state. The court hearings in Kilkenny over which he presided in November 1578 were perfectly designed to spread terror in the area. The harshest in the shire since the end of the Butler revolt, the sessions left the town gaol empty, with 36 people hanged. Drury enjoyed the occasion. A week or so later, he and Fitton referred to it jokingly in a letter to the privy council, reminiscing that there had been 'some good ones' among those they sentenced to die, including 'a black Moor and two witches'.[138] Yet his meddling with religion proved his most dangerous legacy. By the time Ormond had returned from the royal court to Kilkenny in September 1579 sections of the local community had become excited by news of a major religious uprising in Munster instigated by the earl's old adversary, James Fitzmaurice Fitzgerald.

THE MUNSTER REVOLT

When Fitzmaurice and a small band of Spanish and Italian soldiers had landed at Smerwick harbour on 17 July 1579, they had come accompanied by an envoy from the pope, the English Catholic clergyman, Dr Nicholas Sander. With Sander's help Fitzmaurice hoped to inspire a crusade against Protestantism in Ireland. As he told one of his military followers, 'we are Catholic Christians, and they are heretics; justice is with us, and injustice with them',[139] precisely the sort of language Ormond dreaded.

Ormond's worries were exacerbated by his continued mistrust of his brother, Edward Butler. Several times now Edward had demonstrated an abiding attachment to Catholicism. In 1571 he had broken into the house of the archbishop of Cashel, Miler McGrath, and set at liberty two friars imprisoned there for preaching against the queen's supremacy in the church. Like many Catholics,

---

136 NA, CP E/60.   **137** *Cal. Carew MSS, 1575–88*, no. 109.   **138** Ibid.; Fitzgerald, 'Historical notes', 40; E. Ledwich, *Collectanea De Rebus Hibernica* (Dublin 1786), ii, 389.   **139** J. O'Donovan, 'The Irish correspondence of James Fitzmaurice of Desmond', *KSEIAS Jn.*, 2nd series, 2 (1858–9), 363.

Edward hated McGrath, a papal appointee who had secured his position in the Irish church by renouncing the pope and embracing Protestantism. He had once referred to the wily prelate as a 'traitorly devil … [and] perjured turncoat', and the pair had regularly come to blows in Tipperary. The most recent flare-up between them had occurred in 1578, when Governor Drury had intervened in McGrath's favour.[140]

By 1579 Edward found it difficult to look dispassionately at events unfolding in the west. Sympathising with the pro-papal stance of his former ally Fitzmaurice, he recognised that the rough treatment dished out to the earl of Desmond in the autumn bore more than a passing resemblance to the abrasive handling he himself had recently received from the government. He was especially incensed by the behaviour of Sir Nicholas Malby, the man mainly responsible for pushing Desmond into rebellion. On Malby's orders, royal troops destroyed the tomb of the former dowager countess of Ormond, Lady Joan Butler, Edward's mother and Desmond's ex-wife, who had been buried at Askeaton in 1565.[141] The fact that Edward shared a bed with Desmond's sister, his wife since 1573,[142] may also have played on his loyalties.

Watched by the government and mistrusted by Ormond, Edward bided his time before declaring for the rebels,[143] but eventually in August 1580 he headed west to join Desmond's army with a force of 100 men.[144] Several members of the Kilkenny gentry supported his cause. Chief amongst these was the minor landowner George Sweetman, the ever-troublesome Shane Brenagh, one John Grace, and the Callan merchant, George Comerford, who probably helped to maintain an open line of communication with the Munster rebels through his trading contacts.[145] But by far the most active conspirator from Kilkenny to come out in support of the Geraldines was the gentleman James Gall, alias James Gankagh, who joined the earl of Desmond's army in Aherlow and 'served with Desmond all the time of his rebellion'.[146]

ORMOND'S RESPONSE AND GOVERNMENT INTERFERENCE

In response to these troubles, and probably with the active connivance of Chancellor Gerrard, in October 1579 Ormond persuaded the Irish council to allow him to take command of the prosecution of the the war against the Geraldines of Desmond. To secure the council's agreement he undertook to provide the queen with part of the necessary force, 'a companie', from the ranks of his freeholders and tenants in Kilkenny and Tipperary, at minimum cost to crown coffers. With Drury having died, the council yielded, praising the earl as an example 'to all the

---

140 Marron (ed.), 'Documents', 80–1, 86–7, 89. **141** SP 63/69/50; Brady, 'Faction', 311. **142** SP 63/42/45. **143** In February 1580 the government thought it had patched things up between the earl and Edward, who was described as 'a little wavering' (*Cal. Carew MSS, 1575–88* no. 322). **144** SP 63/75/82. **145** *CPRI, Eliz. I*, 70. **146** So did his kinsman Redmund Gall: SP 63/108/34.

nobles and subjects of Ireland',[147] and he was named lord general of the army in Munster,[148] the highest military position granted to a native noble in Ireland for 35 years.[149] Elizabeth I confirmed him as general after Gerrard sailed to England to secure her approval, and the Black Earl was assigned a force of 1,700 men.[150] Gathering victuals in Kilkenny while awaiting artillery and ammunition, he prepared to secure his growing influence in Irish affairs, and silence his critics once and for all, by bringing a speedy conclusion to the Desmond conspiracy.

Significantly, however, on 29 December 1579 the new chief governor of Ireland, Drury's successor as lord justice, Sir William Pelham, was required to justify Ormond's appointment as general to the earl of Leicester, who disapproved.[151] As Earl Thomas was about to discover, news that the papal standard had been raised in the south of Ireland, practically on his doorstep, had caused a hardening of attitudes at Whitehall against him and his ally the earl of Kildare. Conscious of the strength of Catholicism in the Ormond and Kildare lordships, leaders of the advanced Protestant party at court (principally Leicester and Walsingham)[152] feared that sympathy for the Munster rebels might cause the supposedly loyalist Anglo-Irish lordships to waver.[153] In this new and increasingly sectarian environment any contact between the great loyalist lords and Catholic rebels would be viewed with the utmost suspicion. Lacking a strong personal relationship with the queen, Kildare was unable to withstand the scrutiny, and fell under suspicion of collusion with his kinsman Viscount Baltinglass, a Catholic zealot, who rose in revolt in support of the Munster Geraldines in the summer of 1580. A new lord deputy was despatched to Ireland, the militant Protestant Arthur, Lord Grey de Wilton. A friend of Sir Henry Sidney, who advised him on how to govern and who to trust in Ireland,[154] Grey immediately abandoned the politics of aristocratic delegation advanced by Chancellor Gerrard and personified by Ormond and Kildare. By December 1580 Kildare was the subject of so much suspicion that he was arrested, partly at the behest of Gerrard, who was anxious to distance himself from the earl, and thereafter the chancellor's influence went into sharp decline.[155] Suddenly Ormond seemed vulnerable.

Ormond's greatest problem was the ease with which his enemies in government were able to portray him as not entirely reliable. His great friend at

147 SP 63/69/56; Hogan & McNeill O'Farrell (ed.), *Walsingham Letter Bk*, 218. Curiously, as early as April 1579 Lord Justice Drury had been informed of the queen's willingness to avail of Ormond's military services in the south and west, yet on the outbreak of the Geraldine revolt he had ignored the earl: C. MacNeill (ed.), 'Report on MSS in the Bodleian Library, Oxford: Rawlinson MSS (Class C)', *Anal. Hib.* 2 (1931), 4. 148 SP 63/70/87. 149 Since his father's command of the Irish forces sent into western Scotland in 1545. 150 SP 63/70/41. 151 BL, Cotton Ms Titus B XIII, fol. 141. 152 Guy, *Tudor England*, 279–81; 'Tudor monarchy and its critiques', in J. Guy (ed.), *The Tudor monarchy* (London 1997), 97–9; R.B. Wernham, *Before the Armada* (London 1966), 324–5; S. Adams, 'Eliza enthroned? The court and its politics', in C. Haigh (ed.), *The reign of Elizabeth I* (London 1984), 65–7. 153 *Cal. SP, Spanish, 1580–6*, 89. 154 HMC, *De L'Isle & Didley MSS*, ii, 93–4. 155 Carey, *Surviving the Tudors*, 186–211; Lennon, *Sixteenth-century Ireland*, 202–3; Ellis, *Ireland*, 314–5.

the royal court, the lord chamberlain, Sussex, was periodically absent from Whitehall in 1580–1 due to personal and family illness,[156] so that for a time Elizabeth received mainly negative assessments of his military ability and the dependability of his followers. As he was later to discover too late, Lord Deputy Grey did not forward to London the news he had sent of his successes against the rebels, so that 'her majesty' received only 'false reports … of my slackness in service'.[157] Increasingly his actions were viewed in a sinister light. When Kildare fell under suspicion, one of the main grounds for moving against him was the fact that Baltinglass had invited his support. Unfortunately for Ormond, the viscount had also approached him, and though he had immediately informed Walsingham of the overture (and passed on Baltinglass' 'traitorous' letter), the episode raised doubts about his sympathies that he found difficult to dismiss so far from court.[158]

The last thing the Black Earl needed in this darkening environment was a fresh eruption of unrest inside his ancestral territories. Clearly the revolt in August 1580 of Edward Butler, noted above, was inauspicious. So too was that of another of the Butlers, Richard Butler, an illegitimate son of Sir Edmund Butler, who rode off at the head of a small force to join Baltinglass and Feagh McHugh O'Byrne in Wicklow at about the same time.[159] In the ensuing months the O'Dowills of Wicklow, followers of Feagh McHugh, were discovered mingling with dissident military elements in the north and east of Kilkenny.[160] Soon the entire Ormond frontier was ablaze with insurrection. In Tipperary, the dissident Burkes were joined by Piers Grace, John Wale, Piers Tobyn and Shane Butler,[161] while in Carlow and Wexford, to Earl Thomas' utter rage, the Kavanaghs under Donal Spaniagh also took to arms after the government seneschal, Thomas Masterson, executed forty of their number whom Ormond had earlier taken into his protection.[162]

It did not help that this explosion of rebel activity in and around the Ormond country was orchestrated by the Fitzgeralds of Desmond. Ormond's great fear as lord general of Munster was being forced to fight Desmond on more than one front. Because of the favourable reception of Desmond's messengers in some of the territories bordering the Kilkenny marchlands, this fear was realised within less than a year of his assuming command of the royal war effort.[163] In August 1580 Sir John of Desmond was guided by Piers Grace and Moriertagh Roe O'Heffernane on a daring journey along Kilkenny's northern border, attacking Ormond's brother Piers Butler at Leix Abbey and plundering Maryborough before riding on to team up with Baltinglass and the O'Byrnes for a raid on the Pale.[164] As historians have shown, Sir John Fitzgerald's Leinster journey gave a

156 S. Doran, 'The finances of an Elizabethan nobleman and royal servant: Thomas Radcliffe, 3rd earl of Sussex', *BIHR* (1988) 297–8; C. Read, *Lord Burghley and Queen Elizabeth*, 226 n.67. 157 SP 63/84/19. 158 SP 63/74/64. 159 SP 63/75/82. 160 SP 63/108/34. 161 *Cal. Carew MSS*, *1575–88*, no. 373; SP 63/72/46; SP 63/86/3i. 162 Donovan, 'Tudor rule', 135–7. 163 O'Hanlon & O'Leary, *Queen's County*, ii, 461; Hogan & McNeill (ed.), *Walsingham letter bk*, 260. 164 Fitzgerald, 'Historical notes', 40–1.

new lease of life to the Desmond rebellion in Munster. Just as his older brother the earl of Desmond was thinking of surrender he had cut a hole through Ormond's net.[165] Henceforth Earl Thomas could expect the infiltration of Geraldine forces behind his back whenever he left Kilkenny for Munster.

Instead of increasing their support for him, prominent members of the queen's government heaped criticism on the tenth earl for allowing conditions in the south to get out of hand. The vice-treasurer of Ireland, Sir Henry Wallop, a close confidant of Walsingham, questioned Ormond's worth as a commander, as did the new secretary of state for Ireland, Sir Geoffrey Fenton, a client of Leicester. Following Lord Grey's arrival Wallop observed pointedly that Ormond's expenses as general were higher than those of the new governor;[166] simultaneously, Fenton dismissed the earl's services as bad value for money, remarking how Desmond was still at large, and the Catholic insurrection, far from being contained, was spreading.[167] In a joint letter from Dublin Wallop and Edward Waterhouse (another Walsingham agent) went so far as to wonder if the Black Earl was secretly plotting with Kildare to deliver Ireland over to the forces of international Catholicism in return for viceregal authority from the pope.[168]

Unable to pursue an all-out war against Desmond because of chronic shortages of men, munitions and victuals from England,[169] Ormond was forced to adopt a different military strategy than that originally envisaged by the government. His war of attack became a war of defence, a development which only compounded his political problems. In order to insure Co. Kilkenny and the liberty of Tipperary was protected from rebel strikes (and so preserved as a springboard for future royal campaigns) the earl decided to spend most of the summer of 1580 in his own country, using detachments of the royal army to guard the area until the danger posed by Sir John of Desmond had passed.[170] Immediately he faced a mutiny. While the stationing of government troops at Kilkenny, Callan and Clonmel eased the concerns of the loyalist gentry of the region, it exasperated the earl's English critics, who did not share his concern for the security of his territories, and expected him to wage total war in Munster. Why else had the queen appointed him lord general? Was he not guilty of putting his own causes before those of the state? Unease at his behaviour was compounded by his use of protections as a ploy to coax the rebels away from Desmond. His detractors could not understand how he had agreed to spare the lives of proven traitors in exchange for a mere promise not to rebel again.

---

165 Falls, *Elizabeth's Irish wars*, 134–5; Lennon, *Sixteenth-century Ireland*, 225. 166 SP 63/82/9i.
167 SP 63/79/3. 168 SP 63/78/6. 169 For his supply problems, see Falls, *Elizabeth's Irish Wars*, 131–2, 142. 170 Ormond's movements can easily be followed in the state papers, through the addresses given on correspondence: after attacking Desmond in Kerry in June, he spent his time in Waterford and Kilkenny during July, rode to Limerick early in August, but returned promptly to Kilkenny within a few days and remained there for the rest of the month, before news of the arrival of foreign reinforcements at Smerwick compelled him to go back to Kerry in September (*CSPI, 1574–85*, 229, 236, 241, 243, 246, 254).

Heatedly arguing that once a traitor, always a traitor, Wallop and the captains convinced Walsingham and others on the English privy council that Ormond had placed the realm in peril by leaving too many Desmondites alive.[171] The ensuing flood of complaints contributed to one of the greatest reversals of his career, when reportedly at the insistence of Leicester and Walsingham, he lost command of the Munster army in 1581.[172]

It is important to realise that Ormond suffered this setback less because of his pursuit of a risky and unnecessarily expensive military strategy in Munster – the main accusation against him – but more because he was unable to demonstrate the efficacy of his strategy adequately to the queen and Lord Burghley. One of the more remarkable features of the state papers for 1580–1 is the paucity of reliable information they contain about the earl's soldiering activities. Indeed, for the period between August 1580, following the arrival of Lord Deputy Grey, and June 1581, when Ormond was finally required to relinquish the generalship, the state papers contain not a single report of the casualties inflicted by the earl and his officers on the rebels.[173] Small wonder, then, that the Black Earl failed to persuade Elizabeth of the military logic of a campaign against southern Irish rebels that put his ancestral territories at its heart. Using Kilkenny Castle as his command headquarters, he had intended to contain the spread of Catholic insurrection by frustrating the Fitzgeralds' plans to link the Munster and Leinster rebellions. When at last he realised how his military reports had been suppressed, Earl Thomas had his servants compile a four-page list of 'such traitors and rebels as were slain and executed by the earl of Ormond and the companies under his leading during his charge in Munster', copies of which he then despatched (by different routes) to Burghley at Whitehall. The list reveals the brutal efficiency of his campaigns. Far from killing just three traitors, as Secretary Walsingham had been claiming at court, the Black Earl revealed that he had been responsible for the deaths of more than 5,650 rebels and their followers in the south before being relieved of command.[174] If his figures are accurate – and there seems no serious reason to doubt them, save that they may represent Pelham's efforts as much as his own – then Ormond had far more rebel blood on his hands than Lord Deputy Grey, the self-styled chief executioner of Ireland, who managed to kill barely 800 of the Munster rebels during his deputyship.[175] But again it seems the earl's correspondence was tampered with. His list of rebel casualties was temporarily lost or misdirected, for several months later, early in 1582, he had to compile an almost identical one for Burghley when finally he arrived at court to defend his reputation.[176]

---

171 SP 63/102/17; *Cal. Carew MSS, 1575–88*, no. 494; Sir J. Pope Hennessy, *Sir Walter Ralegh in Ireland* (London 1883), 29–30, 59, 95–6.   **172** *Cal. Carew MSS, 1575–88*, no. 317; SP 63/75/34, 37; *Cal. SP, Spanish, 1580–6*, 86.   **173** SP 63/75–83. Likewise the other main collection of papers relating to the Munster war, BL Cotton Ms Titus B XII–III.   **174** Three lists survive: SP 63/86/2, 3 i, 4.   **175** In all Grey claimed the lives of 797 enemy soldiers in Munster, 500 of whom died at Smerwick harbour, and this out of a total of 1,485 rebels 'of greater sort' killed all across Ireland during his rule, 1580–2 (SP 63/106/62).   **176** SP 63/91/55–6. Ormond arrived in London shortly

The Black Earl was assured of a favorable reception from the queen long before he set sail for England. By July 1581, within weeks of his losing the generalship, an Irish visitor to London (probably Sir Nicholas White) had arrived bearing news of Grey's misrule as deputy and spread a story that helped to undermine his allegation that Earl Thomas was 'soft' towards rebels.[177] By August Lord Burghley (White's protector) had been moved to intervene on Ormond's behalf in the presence of Elizabeth and contradict Walsingham's 'bad reports' of his services. Almost immediately Walsingham backed off, criticism of Ormond ceased, and as if by magic the earl's correspondence began reaching the royal palace. The arrival of Ormond's letters proved ominous for Lord Deputy Grey. Sometime before 2 November Queen Elizabeth had received the earl's complaints about how Grey had treated him dishonourably. The deputy, he claimed, had not only misrepresented his military conduct, but had also encouraged his subordinates in Munster, the English captains, to defy him and sabotage his efforts to prosecute the war.[178] At the earl's request, all inquiries into events in Munster were put on hold until he was able to travel to court, where he promised to deal with his defamers, 'such Machiavellis', 'face to face'.[179] Crucially, by delaying his journey till March 1582 Ormond gave White and other opponents of Grey's regime adequate time in which to produce a series of allegations about the deputy's indiscriminate use of martial law and misappropriation of royal revenues. Burghley, as lord treasurer of England, was probably most concerned by Grey's financial mistakes, but the queen, while sharing his anxiety over the high cost of Grey's government, was also agitated by the damage the deputy's fondness for summary executions was doing to her reputation for justice.[180] After a protracted investigation at Whitehall during the spring and early summer of 1582 Ormond emerged triumphant, his conduct while lord general of Munster vindicated.[181] Grey, in contrast, fell into disgrace and was sacked, making him the third chief governor of Ireland in just over a decade to suffer dismissal partly as a result of having excited Ormond's hostility. In recognition of his loyal service, and finally convinced that of all her servants he was the one best qualified to end the Desmond rebellion, on 8 November 1582 Elizabeth made Earl Thomas 'lord general and governor of Munster', a post which gave him control of the civil as well as the military affairs of the province.[182]

Months before Ormond's political recovery the only information about his activities to reach London concerned his charges against Baron Barnaby Fitzpatrick over the the latter's entertainment of the rebel leader Sir John of

---

after 19 March 1582: *Cal. SP, Spanish, 1580–6*, 319.   **177** The story suggested that Grey only accused Ormond of being soft in order to deflect attention from his having authorised the killing of former rebels who had surrendered and were under the earl's protection: ibid., 140. On White, see N. Canny, 'Identity formation in Ireland: the emergence of the Anglo-Irish', in N. Canny & A. Pagden (ed.), *Colonial identity in the Atlantic world, 1500–1800* (Princeton 1987), 166–7.   **178** SP 63/87/29.   **179** SP 63/86/63.   **180** BL, Add Ms 37,536, fol. 1.   **181** SP 63/90/67; SP 63/91/55–6; SP 63/106/56.   **182** *COD*, v, no.359.

Desmond at Culahill Castle in August 1580.[183] To the earl's critics his relentless legal pursuit of the baron seemed like nothing more than a personal vendetta, yet another example of his capacity to confuse a private grudge with public service, but there was more to it than that. It is not usually noted that soon after he had secured Baron Barnaby's imprisonment in Dublin Castle in January 1581 his efforts to prevent a fusion of the Munster and Leinster rebellions began to take effect.

Having intimidated other senior members of the MacGiollapadraig lineage into reluctant submission,[184] Ormond was able gradually to resume the offensive and regain control of the key strategic corridor between the two provinces running through Laois and Offaly along the northern borders of Kilkenny and Tipperary. The earl's efforts helped to change the course of the war. During the summer of 1581 (immediately after his dismissal as lord general) he was responsible for killing 159 rebels in the region, a devastating blow to their strength.[185] Among his principal victims was 'the son of Edmund Eustace, uncle to Baltinglass ye traitor', who was also a near kinsman of Baron Barnaby Fitzpatrick. Deprived of MacGiollapadraig protection, Eustace was easy prey, and Ormond had him captured and delivered to the lord deputy; for the record, Grey failed to acknowledge the earl's assistance in this arrest. Another important participant in the Baltinglass conspiracy to fall into his clutches was Edmund O'Doran, who delivered letters to the Eustaces and Feagh McHugh from Baltinglass in France after the viscount's flight into exile. On O'Doran's information Ormond had several natives of Wexford arrested and sent to Grey in Dublin for aiding and abetting the Leinster rebellion (this too the deputy concealed). Turning closer to home, the earl destroyed the rebel party in Cos. Kilkenny, Carlow and Tipperary, putting to death various minor members of the Grace, Archdekin, O'Brennan, O'Ryan and Walsh lineages who had gone into revolt.[186] Piers Butler of Butlerswood, his principal lieutenant, pursued Piers Grace through the northern marchlands, and by the autumn of 1581 had slain seven of Grace's followers, a striking instance of the sudden helplessness of local outlaws once the mantle of MacGiollapadraig protection was removed from them. Soon the northern borders of the Ormond country from Ikerrin in Tipperary to the Dullough in Carlow became a no-go area for rebels,[187] and the Munster Geraldines failed in their efforts to break out of the south-west and re-open the corridor around north Kilkenny into Wicklow. In April 1582 a major expedition towards Laois led by Desmond himself was intercepted in north Tipperary by Earl Thomas' forces and repulsed; another expedition into Tipperary later in the year met a similar fate, but only after Desmond had won his last ever victory, defeating Ormond's brother, Sir Edmund Butler, at Knockgraffon in August. Reinforced, Sir Edmund quickly recovered, and

---

183 SP 63/73/30; SP 63/75/73; SP 63/76/25 i; SP 63/80/12; *Cal. Carew MSS, 1575–88*, no. 489. Baron Barnaby's reasons for entertaining Sir John are discussed in Edwards, 'MacGiollapadraigs', 348–9. **184** SP 63/86/51. **185** SP 63/86/3 i. **186** Ibid. **187** Over the next two years, Piers ambushed a further 14 rebel soldiers in the north: *CSPI, 1588–92*, 285–7.

Desmond beat a hasty retreat to the south-west, where he remained, boxed in, thereafter.[188]

When Ormond returned to Ireland on 22 January 1583, putting ashore at Dunmore East, Co. Waterford,[189] he was able finally to proceed against Desmond as he had always intended. With the rebel earl confined to the mountains and woodlands of west Cork and Kerry, and all traces of resistance in Leinster having collapsed, Ormond could use Kilkenny as a secure base from which to concentrate on isolating his foe and hunting him down. Elizabeth had given him permission to abandon the indiscriminate terror preferred by Grey in favour of his own methods of stern and forceful moderation.[190] Accordingly he relied on native intermediaries as well as English soldiers to finish the war in Munster, recruiting friendly Irish lords to inform the remaining rebels that they must surrender and be pardoned, or face the consequences. As before, the English captains who had supported Grey doubted the wisdom of Ormond's approach, detecting too much carrot and not enough stick, but at length his policy prevailed. By June 1583, despite having killed only 200 rebels since his arrival in January, more than 2,100 had come in to him on promise of protection, and received pardons.[191] In all of this his greatest ally was famine. Having suffered four years of constant warfare in which crops and livestock were routinely destroyed, the people of Munster were starving. In contrast, thanks to regular shipments of provisions through Waterford that were supplied to Ormond as provincial governor,[192] the earl's power-base in Kilkenny and east Tipperary seemed like a land of plenty, and the lords and gentry of Munster and their followers were quick to accept his offer of protection and hospitality. Desmond, deserted, was left to inhabit a desolate landscape. Though he managed to evade capture during the summer and autumn, by the beginning of winter it was becoming increasingly difficult for him to hide in the woods and live off the land. Eventually, on 11 November 1583, he was discovered in a mountain cabin near Tralee by a band of Kerry swordsmen in Ormond's employ. Drawing their swords they promptly killed the earl and cut off his head, for fear the reward money for capturing him would be claimed by the English constable of Castlemaine.[193] Ormond had won the grimmest of struggles.

The war against Desmond had been the biggest test of Earl Thomas's career. He rejoiced unreservedly: 'So … is this traitor come to the end I have long looked for, appointed by God to die by the sword to end his rebellion.'[194] On 21 November, ten days after his death, Desmond's severed head arrived in Kilkenny, where Ormond had it displayed for a week before sending it overseas in a box to the queen in London. As the anonymous annalist of Kilkenny

---

188 SP 63/95/90. For the battle at Knockgraffon see Clonalis House, O'Conor Don Ms 6.4HN002. 189 Ibid. 190 BL, Cotton Ms Titus F V, fol. 5. 191 Ibid., ff 15r–16v, 20v–21r; SP 63/102/47, 86, 123. 192 Ormond's food shipments are recorded in the Bristol port books for 1583: PRO, E190 1130/4, ff 4v, 7r, 8v, 17v; ibid., E190 1130/5, ff 12r, 25r–v; ibid., E190 1130/6, ff 3r, 18v. 193 A.J. Sheehan, 'The killing of the earl of Desmond, November 1583', *JCHAS* 88 (1983), 106–10. 194 SP 63/105/67.

quietly put it, 'a great triumph had the earl'.[195] He had won a terrible war which, had he not, might have ruined his credit at court and called into question his status as an autonomous feudal lord in the south of Ireland.

IMPAIRING ORMOND'S ADVANCE

Anger with his government enemies made victory a bittersweet experience. Ormond could not resist the temptation to taunt his former accusers, those 'lying malicious knaves' among the Dublin executive and the Munster army who had dared to doubt his loyalty.[196] The sheer vitriol of some of his comments reveals the extent to which the royalist cause in Ireland had become polarised, primarily over issues of ethnicity and religion. Ormond greatly resented that many of the queen's New English officers drew a pejorative distiction between themselves, 'English by birth', and the Anglo-Irish lords and gentry, 'English by blood only'. He was equally agitated by the growing intolerance of English Protestant officials, whose insensitive handling of the queen's Catholic subjects struck him as wilfully provocative. Even more than in 1569–70, when he had criticised the buccaneering adventurism of the Carew land claim, Ormond was convinced that many New English officials had come to Ireland with the sole intention of achieving rapid social and material advancement, hoping to get rich quick through the confiscation and plunder of as much native property as possible. To his mind the Anglo-Irish community should be rewarded for the loyalty exhibited by most of its members during the Munster and Leinster uprisings, not punished for the treason of a few. Accordingly he not only demanded that native loyalists receive a share of any projected redistribution of ex-rebel land in the two provinces, but he also set himself the task of wresting greater control of the royal government back into Anglo-Irish hands. Although the eleventh earl of Kildare had survived the official inquiry into his conduct, he was damaged by the experience and suffered increasing bad health (he died in 1585),[197] leaving Ormond as the undisputed leader of the native loyalists in Ireland. Having managed to kill Desmond and end the Munster rebellion, Earl Thomas and his allies among the southern lineages had demonstrated that the Anglo-Irish nobility were at least as well qualified as New English colonialists to govern the country on behalf of the crown. In the wake of Desmond's death the Black Earl emerged as the dominant personage in Irish politics. Positioning himself at the front of the disgruntled loyalist community, he became what his detractors in government had always feared he might, an effective scourge of New English interests in the country. Recognising that the earl was uniquely well-placed to exact revenge for past wrongs, and aware that he was actively seeking a showdown with officialdom, a rumour spread that he might soon be named lord deputy of Ireland.[198]

---

195 SP 63/105/83; Clonalis House, O'Conor Don Ms 6.4HN002, sub 1583.   **196** SP 63/105/71 i.   **197** Carey, *Surviving the Tudors*, 212–13.   **198** SP 63/94/64; *Cal. SP, Spanish, 1580–86*, 413.

Ormond's tussle with the New English executive in Dublin began even before the Desmond war finished. Despite the earl's high standing with Elizabeth and Burghley, the new lord justice of Ireland, Sir Henry Wallop, had maintained a steady barrage of criticism attacking his position. Writing mainly to Secretary-of-state Walsingham, Wallop repeatedly stressed that Earl Thomas had become much too powerful, and that unless something was done to curb his vaunting ambition, he would succeed in his apparent desire to wreck English policy in Ireland.[199] His entreaties had some effect. Walsingham was not prepared to let Ormond's military success metamorphose into a counter-revolution in Ireland in which power over the localities was removed from English hands and returned to the control of the (predominantly Catholic) Anglo-Irish. Moreover, further complaints about the earl's military tactics in Munster, and especially his liberal use of pardons and protections, may have convinced the secretary that the Ormond territories were a potential security risk.

At Walsingham's special request,[200] on 1 December 1582 Sidney's former servant Francis Lovell, now the secretary's man, was sworn in in Dublin as the new sheriff of Co. Kilkenny. By this date, as we have seen, most rebel sympathisers in the shire had been dealt with severely by Ormond. Nevertheless, in the course of the next several months – and while Ormond was absent in Munster finishing the war against Desmond – Lovell committed wholesale butchery in the county, authorising the execution by martial law of approximately 240 locals, including 22 women.[201] His victims included some important rebels who had managed to evade capture by Earl Thomas's officers. One such was Desmond's lieutenant, James Gankagh Gall, who Lovell discovered lurking 'in the woods of Rochestown' and ordered to be taken away for public execution in Kilkenny town; another was George Sweetman, a junior member of the Castle Eve family, who was attainted of conspiracy, and executed, on information supplied by Lovell. Nonetheless, of many of the rest who died, Lovell seems to have found little in the way of evidence to justify his having them hanged, save that somehow they knew rebels, or were related to rebels.[202] In consequence, his actions caused a local outcry, and it was widely reported that he had killed indiscriminately, hanging the innocent as well as the guilty in order to provoke the disaffected into a reaction. On learning of Lovell's behaviour Ormond wished to have him prosecuted for murder, only to discover to his great frustration that the sheriff and his followers had been granted a royal pardon by the lords justice in Dublin, so that no trial could take place.[203] Once again, it seemed to him that the Dublin authorities preferred arbitrary methods to the rule of law when meddling in his territories; significantly, he was as yet ignorant of Secretary Walsingham's patronage of Lovell. To insure

199 SP 63/99/56; SP 63/101/28; SP 63/111/89.   **200** SP 63/108/33; SP 63/111/21.   **201** In an earlier publication the present writer carelessly attributed the figure of 'nearly 400' dead to Lovell in 1582–3, having failed to identify the 160 or so executed by Ormond before June 1581 for whom Lovell, falsely, claimed credit: Edwards, 'Ideology and experience', 141.   **202** SP 63/108/34.   **203** SP 63/106/32; *Ir. Fiants*, Eliz. I, no. 4225.

Burghley appreciated the loyalty of the Kilkenny gentry the earl sent Edmund Walsh to London as the bearer of his correspondence. Walsh had lost his brother in service, and might enlighten the lord treasurer of the activities of Lovell, who had treated the inhabitants of the Walsh mountains with especial brutality in the course of his recent operations.[204]

Instead of withdrawing Lovell from Kilkenny, the government granted him a 21-year lease of the estate of the Comerfords of Ballymack.[205] His continued presence in the shire was soon justified by events. In September 1583 the new Roman Catholic archbishop of Cashel, Dr Dermot O'Hurley, had arrived in the Ormond country from Dublin, having been led south by 'Black' Piers Butler of Duiske, Earl Thomas' illegitimate son, a young man of 24 who was a leading recusant. O'Hurley's appearance caused a flurry of activity in the colonial capital, and among the measures then taken by the authorities Lovell was re-selected as sheriff of Kilkenny. To judge by his subsequent actions he had been instructed to broaden his policing to take heed of the religious question, for within weeks he had begun to reveal Kilkenny and Tipperary as a well-spring of Catholic sympathy and to cast doubt on the Protestant credentials of the Black Earl himself. With Ormond believed to be in contention for the vacant post of lord deputy, Lovell's progress was followed with interest in Dublin and London. Although difficult to be certain, there is a strong possibility that the queen was moved to disregard Earl Thomas and choose Sir John Perrot as her next deputy because of the nature of the information coming out of southern Ireland during the winter of 1583–4.

Ormond was enormously discomforted by O'Hurley's presence. As the local overlord of Kilkenny and Tipperary he was anxious not to add to the growing sectarian tension by handing the archbishop over to the government, yet with Lovell on O'Hurley's trail neither could he afford to turn a blind eye to the prelate. Should the archbishop be allowed to rove about without restraint the earl feared he might bring the full weight of government suspicion down on his clients among the local Cathlic gentry.[206] Accordingly, he agreed to a private meeting with O'Hurley at his Carrick mansion in which he promised to grant the papal appointee his protection provided he confined himself to the boundaries of Tipperary and refrained from making overtures to rebel elements. Subsequently, at the request of his Catholic kinsman the baron of Slane, who had himself fallen under suspicion of Catholic plotting and was anxious to demonstate his reliability, the earl allowed O'Hurley to be arrested and led away in chains to Dublin – but too late, the damage was done. On his arrival in Dublin O'Hurley revealed little to his interrogators, so that officials were prompted to assume he must have reached a secret deal with Ormond (and Slane), who they reckoned had 'schooled' him to keep his mouth shut.[207]

---

204 SP 63/104/60.   **205** *Ir. Fiants,* Eliz. I, no. 4267.   **206** W. Hayes, 'Dermot O'Hurley's last visit to Tipperary', *Tipperary Historical Journal* (1992), 163–73.   **207** W.M. Brady (ed.), *State papers,* pp 70–1.

Efforts intensified to reveal the earl as a closet papist and protector of rebels. As a direct result of Lovell's policing, a second Catholic prelate who had appeared in the area late in 1583, the new papal bishop of Ossory, Dr Thomas Strong, was forced to return to the Continent in fear of his life.[208] Archbishop O'Hurley was not so fortunate. On 10 December 1583, having received instructions from Walsingham that the queen wished to put O'Hurley to torture 'to gain his knowledge of all foreign practices against Her Majesty's states', Lords Justice Wallop and Loftus interpreted this to include questions about 'such as hosted and entertained him after his landing', that is, Ormond and Slane, and Ormond's bastard son, Piers Butler. Although reluctant to carry out the torture themselves (insisting it could be done most effectively in the Tower of London), they approved of it in principle, and reiterated their suspicion of O'Hurley's 'Irish patrons and favourers', who 'at the time of his apprehension' had schooled him 'to be silent in all matters of weight'.[209] Eventually, following further instructions from Walsingham, O'Hurley was put to torture in Dublin Castle at the beginning of March 1584. Despite suffering the most gruesome treatment he revealed nothing about Earl Thomas or his other protectors among the Irish lords and gentry, 'retaining his former obstinacy', something which instead of reassuring his persecutors, only increased their anxiety.[210] On 1 March a major gathering had taken place at Kilkenny, where many of the lords and gentry of the south had convened to sign a petition to Queen Elizabeth praising Ormond for his conduct of the war in Munster.[211] Plainly the earl was ready to launch his long-awaited counter-attack against English officialdom in Ireland. O'Hurley's agony having produced nothing that might be used to damage him, the lords justice were in fear of the earl's imminent departure for court. A search of O'Hurley's cell on 7 or 8 March had uncovered a letter written to Earl Thomas by the archbishop 'since his torture', causing Wallop and Loftus to panic. What if the prelate had managed to smuggle out other, earlier, messages to the earl that revealed the truth about their line of questioning? Turning once more to Walsingham, they beseeched him to intercede with the queen to persuade her 'what favour these Romish runnagates have' with Ormond, 'our great potentate here'. Above all they wanted permission to kill O'Hurley as quickly as possible, before Ormond got confirmation of his torture.[212]

Their entreaties were heeded. Ormond's return to court in the spring of 1584 was a serious political setback. Prior to his embarkation Elizabeth I had sent a letter requiring him to remain in Ireland, but he had landed in England before learning of it.[213] Refused admittance to the royal presence he returned

208 Moran, 'Bishops', 259–61. **209** W.M. Brady (ed.), *State papers*, 72–3. **210** Ibid., 74. **211** J. Gilbert, *Facsimilies of the national MSS of Ireland*, iv (pt 1), plate 19. **212** W.M. Brady (ed.), *State papers*, 76–7. **213** SP 63 110/59. The suspicion remains that Ormond's correspondence was subject to interference. An earlier letter by the queen, written on 31 January 1584, congratulating him on his victory over Desmond and asking him to come to court at his earliest convenience to receive his reward, did not reach the earl until 29 May – and this although he was usually resident at either Kilkenny or Carrick during the spring (Bod. Lib., Carte Ms 30, fol. 22).

home in June, sailing to Dublin, his plans to repudiate his government enemies frustrated. Worse, just as he put ashore news spread that O'Hurley had been hanged at Hoggen's Green outside the city walls. In recent weeks, with Walsingham's assistance, Wallop and Loftus had received the tacit permission of the queen to do away with the archbishop by martial law, but they had delayed doing so, evidently preferring to pass responsibility for the execution onto the incoming lord deputy, Perrot, who approved of the killing. Significantly, it was only on their discovery that Ormond had set sail for Dublin in order to be present at Perrot's swearing in on 21 June that Wallop and Loftus were suddenly moved to rid themselves of the troublesome churchman.[214]

The failure of Ormond's court mission of May–June 1584 was doubly upsetting for the earl in that it meant his Kilkenny subjects would have to continue to withstand the scrutiny of Francis Lovell. Like Wallop and Loftus in Dublin, Lovell had been unnerved by the prospect of the Black Earl re-establishing his presence near the queen. Aware that Ormond intended to bring Shane Brenagh (alias John Walsh) to Whitehall, Lovell had gone across before the earl, arriving at Whaddon Hall, the home of Arthur, Lord Grey de Wilton, on 21 March.[215] Anticipating difficulties over his indiscriminate use of the death penalty, he compiled a list to be presented to Walsingham. Designed to justify his ruthlessness, it named all his purported victims as 'traitors and thieves' that he had executed at his own charge 'in her majesty's County of Kilkenny' – and this although many of them had never been traitors, and some, possibly, not even thieves. Having gained admittance to Whitehall Palace on the recommendation of Lord Grey, Sir Henry and Sir Philip Sidney, Lovell remained there throughout the summer. Ormond's inability to secure court access meant that Lovell was able to throw mud at the earl's reputation without obstruction; he made the most of his opportunity. Posing as a model sheriff intent on his duty, he drew particular attention to Richard Shee, Earl Thomas' chief officer, who had constantly obstructed his inquiries in Kilkenny so that he could discover little about the earl's dealings. As well as being corrupt, Shee was, Lovell claimed, 'a secret maintainer of papistry'. He was shrewd in his choice of target, for Perrot, the new lord deputy, hated Shee, having found him to be a mulish opponent and 'perilous fellow' when he had last served in Ireland, during the early 1570s.[216] Moreover, like any other chief governor before him, Perrot went to Ireland in 1584 determined to rule the country free of the political menace posed by the overmighty Black Earl of Ormond. Like Sidney, Drury, Grey and Wallop, he recognised Lovell as a valuable agent of government power in the Ormond country, the status of which as an autonomous noble lordship remained intact, and seemed irritatingly vibrant after the earl's great victory over Desmond. Lovell returned to Kilkenny certain of the government's continued support.

The growing awareness that Lovell's attack on Richard Shee enjoyed high-level support spread a ripple of fear across Co. Kilkenny, not least because, for

---

214 W.M. Brady (ed.), *State papers*, 79–80, 84–5. **215** SP 63/108/33. **216** SP 63/40/35.

once, it was well directed. Not only Shee, but others of Ormond's officers, were at this time busily engaged in the secret maintenance of priests. On 2 June 1584, while Earl Thomas was out of the country, Shee had joined with another prominent servant of the earl, Robert Rothe, and with the earl's chaplain, Robert Gaffney, in admitting a leading Catholic priest, Laurence Reneghan, to the parsonage of Callan, which was in Ormond's gift as lay patron.[217] It is not recorded whether or not the earl knew of this arrangement. Whatever the case, suspicion of Ormond mounted following Lovell's next piece of service – his hunting down and execution of John O'Phelan of Callan, a Kilkennyman who had been one of the servants of Dr Nicholas Sander, the late papal representative to the Desmond rebels. Ormond's enemies in Dublin were jubilant. Despite all the earl's comments about the dependability of the people of his lordship, sections of the Kilkenny and Tipperary populace had permitted an agent of Rome to live in their midst.[218]

The killing of Sander's man heralded what the earl knew his adverseraries in officialdom most desired, a Catholic retaliation in Kilkenny and Tipperary. On the night of 7 November 1584 Francis Lovell was attacked at his house at Lismacteige, near Knocktopher. The attack was led by Shane Brenagh fitz Robert, who could not contain his animosity towards Lovell, having twice before experienced rough treatment at his hands.[219] He paid a heavy price for his action. Called upon to honour a forfeited bond of £300, Shane refused to pay, having earlier received a pardon for his offences, since lodged in the office of Peter Dormer, the clerk of the crown for Co. Kilkenny. Lovell, however, was unconcerned by the pardon and even turned down the chance to buy it from one of Dormer's servants. He had no need of corruption. The pardon applied only to crimes committed by Shane in Kilkenny; it said nothing of crimes in Waterford or Tipperary. Thus Lovell had Shane arrested and brought to trial in Co. Waterford, where 'by verdict of twelve men' Shane was condemned and executed early in 1585.[220]

Lovell felt vindicated, telling his patron Walsingham that Shane's behaviour corroborated his contention that Ormond's country was still full of 'Robin Hoods', just as his old master Sidney had once stated.[221] But the events surrounding the demise of one of the most dangerous outlaws of them all, Thomas Grace of the Mill, soon gave the lie to Lovell's aspersions. It was revealed that he was more concerned with ruining the career of Ormond's new deputy governor, Richard Shee, than with ridding Kilkenny and Tipperary of one of its worst lawbreakers.

Thomas of the Mill was a notorious bandit in the region, described as 'the first [that is, greatest] ringleader … of villainy and rebellion within man's

---

217 *COD*, vi, no. 11.   218 SP 63/112/86. For more details of O'Phelan's death, see SP 63/115/10. Ormond's fears were further exacerbated by the execution at Knocktopher of Cahir O'Ryan of Gurteen on 13 Oct. 1584: NLI, Ms 2181, unpaginated inquisition held at Gowran, 1589.   219 Ibid.; *CPRI, Eliz. I*, 68–70, 81.   220 The inquisition into his estate is dated 15 May (NA, Lodge MSS, Rolls, I, 216–7), but he was dead by the beginning of April: SP 63/116/3. See also SP 63/113/8, and NA, CP U78. Lovell could have had the pardon for £10.   221 SP 63/112/86.

memory'. The son of Piers Grace, his infamy was such that in December 1584 Lovell had been able to assume the high moral ground upon discovering that he had received a protection from the earl of Ormond. Early in the new year Lovell stayed noticeably silent when the earl's servants, organised by Shee, galloped off in pursuit of Grace, who had broken the terms of the earl's protection by resuming his criminal career. In February 1585 he was fatally surprised at Painestown, Co. Carlow, by Piers Butler of Butlerswood, a deed which would normally have been considered worthy of praise and reward. Lovell, however, turned the ambush to his own advantage.

Having consulted Piers Grace, Thomas's outlaw father, Lovell condemned the killing. Thomas of the Mill, he said, had been shamefully murdered; he had been harmlessly travelling to Dublin under a royal protection to confer with Lord Deputy Perrot when he met his death; the attack was the work of the vilest vigilantes, and he accused Richard Shee of 'heinous treason' for masterminding it. The double standard was clear for all to see: here was Lovell proclaiming the innocence of a known rebel, the sort of man whom he himself had often stated should be afforded no mercy. Nonetheless, Shee was gaoled in Dublin Castle at the beginning of March. He was taken before the chief governor in June and forced to render his submission, and in September he had to enter a bond for the crippling sum of £2,000 (stg) before being allowed home in disgrace to Kilkenny.[222] Shee's accomplices, Piers of Butlerswood and his brother Thomas Butler, were also incarcerated for a time in Dublin. It was only with great reluctance that Perrot bowed to Ormond's protests in London and authorised their release in January 1586.[223]

By this time the Black Earl was beginning to regain admittance to the queen's circle, and was clawing his way back into favour. Following the outbreak of war between England and Spain in 1585, and with no tangible evidence of 'secret practices' uncovered against him, Secretary Walsingham and others were forced to again accept Ormond's value to the state. Although the earl's ancestral territories were undeniably infested with 'popery', and an increasing number of his kinsmen and followers had become open recusants, it seemed Ormond himself had remained steadfast to the Protestant religion. Through his influence the people of Kilkenny, Tipperary, and much of southern Ireland, were more likely to support the crown against Catholic Spain than *vice versa*. Ironically, considering the allegations of underperformance that had been made about his command of the Munster forces just a few years earlier, Earl Thomas was now lauded as arguably the queen's greatest soldier. Encouraged by Burghley (who repeatedly played host to the earl and his countess at this time), it was recognised that Ormond more than anyone else had been responsible for Desmond's defeat, and it was said that such was Earl Thomas's standing among the natives that his presence in Ireland was worth 1,000 men to the queen.[224] Moreover,

---

222 Quinn (ed.), 'Cal. Irish council bk', 172; *CSPI, 1588–92*, 287; SP 63/114/78; SP 63/115/9; SP 63/118/19 i. **223** *CSPI, 1586–8*, 2–3; C. McNeill (ed.), 'The Perrot papers', *Anal. Hib.* 12 (1943), 34. **224** For Ormond staying with Burghley, see *Cal. SP, Foreign, 1584–5*, 37; HMC, *Bath*

as England prepared to resist an anticipated Spanish onslaught, Elizabeth I needed
the counsel of experienced military commanders. Of all her courtiers none was
more experienced in military matters than her Irish cousin, who by 1585 had
completed more than 30 years of service to the Tudor monarchs. To compensate for the recent cool treatment that he had received from members of her
government in London and Dublin, the queen invited Ormond to participate
as a 'principal' in the ceremonies of the exclusive Order of the Garter at Windsor
Palace.[225] Surviving documents also indicate that from this time forward,
prompted by the earl, Elizabeth began to express serious reservations about the
nature of government conduct in Ireland, in particular the excessive use of martial law and executions without trial.[226]

The full rehabilitation of Ormond worried Lord Deputy Perrot, who had
much to lose by the queen's interference in Irish policy. Having singled out the
Ormond territories for special treatment since his arrival in 1584 – not least by
his enthusiastic support of Francis Lovell – the deputy was anxious to insure
that details of Lovell's behaviour could not be brought to Elizabeth's attention.
Accordingly, when in 1587 the Black Earl's servants draw up charges against
Lovell, accusing him of murder and abuse of position while sheriff and martial
law commissioner in 1582–3, 'executing divers persons … for his own private
gain than upon any just cause', Perrot attempted to undermine the proceedings
by a pretence of administrative incompetence. Making a farce of the legal
process, he demanded that the Kilkenny justices of the peace (all Ormond's
men) deliver the evidence against Lovell into his hands in Dublin by Monday
24 April 1587; but he did not send his order for convening the county court on
Saturday 22 down to Kilkenny until Thursday 20. Consequently Henry Shee,
Ormond's secretary, did not have enough time to summon his witnesses or
empanel a jury to try Lovell, while in contrast Lovell had been tipped off by
Perrot and was able to appear at the shire court with all his witnesses. The trial
was duly abandoned, and Perrot was able to carry on pleading Lovell's innocence of the allegations laid against him and defending him as the 'fittest man'
for the position of sheriff of Co. Kilkenny.[227]

Unfortunately for Lovell, Perrot's efforts were in vain. Increasingly determined to pursue a more moderate line in Ireland, Queen Elizabeth decided to
recall Perrot as lord deputy and replace him with Sir William Fitzwilliam. With
the Spanish Armada preparing to set sail it was necessary to place the government of Ireland in the hands of someone who was less likely to excite opposition to English rule than Perrot, who in four years in charge had managed to
antagonise not just Ormond, but most interest groups – including, fatally, and
for reasons that remain a mystery, the lord treasurer of England (and Ormond's
ally), Burghley.[228] Within weeks of the new deputy's appointment, Lovell was

MSS, v: Talbot, Dudley & Devereux Papers, 71, 73. **225** BL, Harleian Ms 304, fol. 147v. **226** Ibid.,
Add Ms 4786, ff 37–8; Edwards, 'Ideology and experience', 137–9. **227** *CSPI, 1586–88*, 294–5,
325–30. **228** H. Morgan, 'The fall of Sir John Perrot', in J. Guy (ed.), *The reign of Elizabeth I:
court and culture in the last decade* (Cambridge 1996), 109–25.

officially in disgrace, replaced as sheriff of Co. Kilkenny by Richard Shee, and Ormond insured he spent the remainder of his life in the shadows.[229] Earl Thomas had managed to overcome yet another high level combination against him, and regain full autonomy over his territories.

AUTONOMY PRESERVED

Despite the fact that Sir William Fitzwilliam had been badly stung by Earl Thomas in the past, his approach to government had not altered greatly since the early 1570s, and as before he intended to leave Kilkenny and Tipperary in Ormond's hands. Not that he had much choice. For the next several years, although a few New English officials continued to express the view that the earl was much too powerful, the queen was manifestly of a different view. During the Armada crisis she had turned to Earl Thomas as a key adviser on English as well as Irish security policy. Ormond was one of the select 'inner circle' who remained close to Elizabeth at St James's Palace in July and August 1588. The earl helped Leicester to organise the main army camp in southern England, at Tilbury in Essex, and when the queen arrived there to review the troops after the Armada had passed he carried the English sword of state before her when she proceeded through the ranks. In 1589 he sat on the committee for war strategy that met at Whitehall to work out England's best course for carrying the war forward.[230] Elizabeth turned a deaf ear to Fitzwilliam's repeated requests that Ormond be sent home to help pacify restless Irish lords, determined to keep him close now that she had grown accustomed to his input.

Sometime late in 1590 or early in 1591, following the death of the sixth earl of Shrewsbury, Ormond was granted the highest office he would receive, when Elizabeth appointed him to the post of earl marshal of England, 'one of the five historic Great Offices of State'. For about a year-and-a-half, the earl presided over the College of Arms and the high court of chivalry in London, and had power to vet claims to grants of arms or titles by the English and Welsh nobility and gentry. In theory, he was also entitled to deputise for the monarch as supreme commander of the royal forces in England, and had authority to summon the English parliament in an emergency. In time, however, the earl tired of the position, which required him to reside permanently in London, at great personal expense, and in 1592 he resigned the post and (to Fitzwilliam's relief) returned home to Ireland, wishing not to become 'a stranger to his country'.[231] Because of his age – he had just entered his sixties – and temporary ill-

---

229 See Appendix 3.   **230** HMC, *Twelth Report, Appendix 9: Miscellaneous MSS*, 166; A.J. Kempe (ed.), *Loseley MSS* (London 1836), 285–6; *APC, 1588*, 263; SP 63/136/46. For a detailed discussion of the earl's growing status after 1585, see my forthcoming article 'Elizabeth I's Irish favourite: "Black" Thomas Butler, 10th earl of Ormond'.   **231** TCD, Ms 842, ff 160v–161r; S. Gunn, 'The Earl Marshal', in D. Starkey (ed.), *Rivals in power: lives and letters of the great Tudor dynasties* (London 1990), 74.

health, he was allowed to live in semi-retirement in Kilkenny and Carrick, only venturing to Dublin for important government business, occasionally returning to London to spend a 'season' attending upon the court.

At home in Kilkenny he enjoyed absolute control over the selection of the county sheriffs until the end of Elizabeth's reign. As such, all of those who are known to have filled the position between 1588 and 1603 were close affiliates of the earldom, ranging from Earl Thomas' bastard son, 'Black' Piers Butler of Duiske (sheriff 1589, 1595), to long-established feudal clients such as Sweetman of Castle Eve (1591) and Fitzgerald of Burnchurch (1592).[232]

Outwardly at least, it seemed all was well in the shire. Fewer and fewer officials were willing to criticise the earl, fearing the consequences of challenging someone so highly prized by the queen. Compared with other areas, Ormond's territories appeared well ordered, accessible to English law and order, so that local conditions could no longer be used against him. However, the tranquillity was increasingly disturbed by two issues that the earl was unable to becalm, religion and taxation, so that for all that he appeared to have seen off his government enemies, his overlordship was confronted by a new difficulty – the growth of internal dissent among the local gentry.

Religion was the thorniest problem. In the months immediately following the Spanish Armada, the Protestant authorities in Dublin had decided to step up the surveillance of the Catholic population, fearing they might secretly be preparing to offer aid to the Spanish king, Philip II. The number of government spies multiplied, and by the early 1590s the Fitzwilliam administration was well informed of the movements of a small group of priests who were roaming around Kilkenny, Tipperary and Waterford in an attempt to minister to their co-religionists. It was even discovered who was sheltering these 'earnest preachers of popery'. For example, John Ley, the sixth son of the Kilkenny merchant, Nicholas Ley, kept a cleric under his roof in Waterford, and a priest named Patrick O'Hoen lived in Kilkenny with the earl of Ormond's servant, Robert Rothe.[233] In fairness, Ormond was powerless to prevent these investigations. To have done so would have been to heap suspicion on himself, and considering the problems he had received over his protection of the Catholic archbishop, O'Hurley, in 1583–4, it is hardly surprising that the earl tried now to keep a safe distance from religious questions.

However, thanks largely to the activities of his principal servant, Sir Richard Shee, in the eyes of some local Catholics Earl Thomas became associated with the politics of Protestant enforcement. In 1589, during the earl's prolonged residence at court, Shee seized the opportunity to profit from the powers bestowed on him by Ormond and the government by initating a protection racket on the Catholic inhabitants of Kilkenny and Tipperary. His behaviour caused an outcry and the government held an inquiry, but although Ormond eventually punished Shee, sacking him as deputy governor of his territories, he was slow to do

---

232 See Appendix 3.   **233** Bod. Lib., Rawlinson Ms C.98, ff 26r–29v.

so, only removing Sir Richard about October 1591, a full two years after complaints of extortion had first been made.[234]

No matter how much the Black Earl tried to ignore the fact, he was part of a system of government which increasingly excluded Catholics from positions of power and viewed their religion with suspicion. By the 1590s, only those who conformed by recognising Elizabeth as head of the church could rise in the state service, and aside from the earl, there were just two men from Kilkenny who were able to do so, Gerald Comerford of Inchyhologhan and Sir Nicholas Walsh of Clonmore. Both accepted the royal supremacy and were handsomely rewarded, Comerford being made the attorney for the province of Connaught, and Walsh rising to become justice of the court of queen's bench and a member of the Irish privy council.[235] Their success set them apart from the rest of the shire community, which by this time was beginning to wince under the impact of the government's programme. Catholics returning from abroad were closely watched by Ormond's agents, and if they were found to have had dealings with the Spaniards or the Jesuits, the earl did not hesitate to order their arrest and interrogation.[236] As a result, his own popularity and that of his associates slipped a little. Sir Nicholas Walsh was physically threatened, and thought of leaving Ireland for good 'in respect of his own safety'.[237] To some it may have seemed that the Ormond lordship in Co. Kilkenny might be undone by gathering religious tension.

Less problematic, but a growing cause of discontent all the same, was the question of taxation. As a reward for his services, the Black Earl was granted freedom from the new government levy known as 'the composition in lieu of cess'. As a result, the Ormond estate in Kilkenny, comprising approximately one-third of all available land, became a tax-free zone, something which would not have become controversial had the Fitzwilliam government reduced the overall sum to be demanded of the county. The government would not budge, however, and as a result the local gentry in effect were required to pay extra to compensate for Ormond's exemption. In 1592 the earl intervened in the controversy, and managed to deflect criticism from himself by blaming crown officials for failing to reach an adequate compromise with representatives of the local community.

In the final analysis, however, despite these stresses and strains, neither religious discord nor opposition to the new taxation arrangements were sufficient to provoke many of the shire gentry into revolt when the Ulster and Leinster rebellions erupted in 1594. No matter how great their distrust of Dublin, the Kilkenny gentry judged it to be in their best interest to stay loyal to Ormond and Elizabeth I. Accordingly, the previous year, when the government convened a general hosting at the hill of Tara for the defence of the Pale against attack, John Grace of Courtstown rode forth, accompanied by several archers

234 *CSPI, 1588–92*, 425–7. **235** *Ir. Fiants*, Eliz. I, nos. 4607, 4625, 5096, 5583. **236** E.g., *CSPI, 1592–6*, 246. **237** SP 63/142/41; N. Canny, 'Why the Reformation failed in Ireland: *une question mal posée*', *Jn. of Ecclesiastical History* 30 (1979), 430–1.

on horseback, fully furnished at his own expense.[238] When the rebellion finally broke out, the gentry of the shire followed the lead of Earl Thomas, the ex-earl marshal, and took part in a loyalist cavalcade at Kilkenny as part of the St George's Day celebrations.[239]

The government responded favourably to this. Content to leave Kilkenny to its own devices as the threat from Ulster grew, it appointed Ormond as 'the general and chief leader of the army and forces' residing within the six shires of Kilkenny, Wexford, Carlow, Queen's County, Kildare and Dublin, commissioned to defend the region against the O'Byrnes, the O'Mores and the followers of the old outlaw Piers Grace, who was still alive.[240] It was to be the first of a series of similar appointments whereby the state acknowledged that the earl had a special interest in the south-east, and was the one person capable of controlling the region from his Kilkenny base. Moreover, in 1595–6 it transpired that there were pressing family reasons for confirming and extending the earl's authority over the region. Excited by the prospect of dynastic advancement, senior elements of the Butler lineage decided to rebel.

A SUCCESSIONAL WAR: THE SECOND BUTLER REVOLT

Having failed to produce a living legitimate male heir, the Black Earl was experiencing increasingly strained relations with his kinsmen, several of whom had a claim to the earldom when he died. The fact that he was an old man – he was sixty-three in 1594 – added to the growing confidence felt by some of the junior Butlers that, by dabbling in treason, they might force the state to recognise their respective claims in the succession. Their subsequent decision to rebel was pure opportunism. As they saw it, Ormond had monopolised royal favour for far too long, while they had been ignored.

The most important of their number was Edmund, second Viscount Mountgarret, after Ormond the most senior Butler lord in the country. According to a speech he made at the close of the century, he felt badly treated by the earl, especially since the latter's return from court in 1593. Ormond, he complained, had scorned his standing as a nobleman, constantly choosing to ignore his counsel in favour of that of upstarts like the Rothes and the Shees. The viscount was convinced he had been frozen out of the local political process. When the justices of assize came to Kilkenny, he was made to sit among commoners, a smarting wound to his pride.[241] Of course, this was not all: acutely conscious of his lineage, the viscount was preoccupied with the opportunities presented by the death of Ormond's young son in 1590. Quite apart from being a grandson of the eighth earl, Piers Ruadh, Mountgarret was also descended through his mother from the Butlers of Neigham, a branch of the Ormond

238 Grace, *Memorials*, i, 13. 239 Ledwich, 'Antiquities', p. 391. 240 NA, Lodge MSS, Articles, etc., p.101. 241 *CSPI, 1599–1600*, 53–4.

dynasty that had once possessed a superior claim to the earldom.[242] Mountgarret made no attempt to hide his ambitions, and in 1600 the government's agents in Co. Kilkenny informed the privy council that the viscount 'thinks … he ought to be earl of Ormond'.[243]

The question of the succession also agitated Ormond's nephews, James and Piers Butler, the sons of Sir Edmund Butler of Cloghgrenan. Since 1590 they had ranked high on government lists of 'doubtful men' in the south,[244] making no secret of the fact that they resented the crown's failure to repeal the act of attainder passed against their father in the parliament of 1569–71. Ormond was always nervous of them. They held him partially responsible for their predicament, despite the fact that he had tried to have the act overturned in 1578 only to see the proposed new parliament cancelled, and its legislative programme abandoned. In September 1596 Piers, the eldest of the two brothers, openly denounced the old earl for not making a greater effort to clear a path for them in the succession, stating that out of malice he did not wish to see them restored in blood.[245] Ormond could not persuade them to secure their place in the succession through loyalty, and admitted that the only sure way to prevent them rebelling was to capture them and have them hanged.[246]

It is difficult to pinpoint how much Mountgarret and the sons of Sir Edmund Butler cooperated during the subsequent course of events. They definitely had an arrangement of some description, for in 1595 or 1596 (the date is uncertain) Piers Butler was married to one of the viscount's daughters, a union which went much against Ormond's will.[247] However, if the marriage precluded them from fighting *against* each other, it cannot be said that it greatly facilitated them fighting *for* each other. Mountgarret and the sons of Sir Edmund were rival claimants to the earldom: to cooperate fully would have been unusual. It is hardly surprising that next to no evidence survives of them presenting a united front against the state. Over the next few years their rivalry weakened their plans, and did much to insure their defeat.

The movements of Sir Edmund's sons were largely confined to the east, as Piers and James linked up with the O'Mores in Laois, the Kavanaghs in Carlow and the O'Byrnes in Wicklow. The brothers tried using another marriage to secure an alliance. In May 1596 it was reported that James Butler was to take to wife one of the sisters of the new O'More leader, Owney MacRory.[248] But even so there were signs that the Butlers' association with the south Leinster Gaelic lineages was brittle. The Gaelic Irish found it difficult to trust them, aware that the brothers might change sides if the government offered to reinstate them at the top of the Ormond succession list by repealing the 1570 act of attainder against their father. To offset the risk of them receiving such an offer, Feagh McHugh O'Byrne required them to demonstrate their

---

242 See Chapter 2 above.   **243** J. Graves, 'The taking of the earl of Ormond, 1600', *JKSEIAS* 3/2 (1860–1), 403.   **244** SP 63/149/32.   **245** *CSPI, 1596–7*, 101.   **246** SP 63/192/31, i; SP 63/193/20, v.   **247** SP 63/193/37.   **248** SP 63/189/46, xi.

dependability as true rebels by doing his bidding before he accepted them as allies. Only after they had performed the necessary service did Feagh ride beside them.[249]

Owney MacRory O'More treated them likewise. Before agreeing to campaign with them he too needed a token of their good faith. Thus the brothers agreed to carry out the murder of 'some special man' in the Laois area. Although they never had the chance to kill anyone of note there – it was hard to catch local loyalists out of doors unprotected[250] – they eventually passed the test, accompanying Feagh and Owney on a combined assault of Ballinacor, a new government stronghold in Wicklow. Their acceptance was assured when James laid a trap for some of the members of the Ballinacor garrison, hanging six of them after they had surrendered to his men.[251]

But still Piers and James made unconvincing rebels. Crucially, they dithered over closing the door on the prospect of a future reconciliation with the crown. They continued to send messages to Lord Deputy Russell in Dublin, saying that if only they had been treated better, they would never have breached the peace.[252] It was only in November (more than two months after the assault on Ballinacor) that they rejoined forces with the O'Byrnes and O'Mores to issue an appeal to the gentry of Laois to rise up in defence of the Catholic religion.[253] Even then they moved too late, for winter was closing in and their soldiers began to go home, bringing an end to the campaigning season.[254] More seriously, they failed to secure their own forts. Ormond had been able to take the castles of Cloghgrenan and Tullow from their men during September, thereby insuring that much of their time was wasted trying to secure other bases. Lastly, they were not equal to the demands of their own soldiers. When Ormond had grabbed their castles he discovered that several of their chief followers wanted to leave the brothers' employment, reckoning they were inept as military commanders and that their conspiracy was doomed to failure.[255] In the end, the sons of Sir Edmund Butler gave Kilkenny little cause for worry.

Mountgarret posed a much greater threat. Gradually after the outbreak of war in 1594 he moved closer to the Ulster rebels, carefully biding his time before openly declaring himself. He finally decided to act sometime after the summer of 1595 when it was discovered that Hugh O'Neill, earl of Tyrone, had definitely thrown in his lot with O'Donnell and the rest of the native chieftains in a Catholic crusade against English rule in Ireland. Before O'Neill joined in, Mountgarret had kept a low profile, so much so that Ormond had felt able to delegate the command of some of his companies to the viscount while he himself was too sick to participate in the campaigns against the rebels.[256] The earl's trust was soon spurned, Mountgarret revealing his intentions after October 1595 when he arranged the marriage of his son and heir, Richard Butler, with

249 SP 63/ 192/7, ix; SP 63/192/11, ii. 250 SP 63/193/9; SP 63/ 193/9, iv. 251 SP 63/192/7, ix; SP 63/192/11, ii. 252 SP 63/193/20, vii; SP 63/193/32. 253 SP 63/195/7, v. 254 SP 63/195/25. 255 SP 63/193/32, ii. 256 SP 63/180/26.

Margaret O'Neill, daughter of 'the arch-traitor Tyrone'.[257] As a reward, Mountgarret was made 'lieutenant to Tyrone of all his forces',[258] and over the next few years he invited members of the O'Neill lineage to stay in his castle at Seskin on the Ballyragget road, where they helped to coordinate the southern end of Tyrone's grand strategy.[259] Because of Mountgarret's O'Neill alliance, over the next few years parts of Co. Kilkenny occasionally came close to falling into rebel hands.

The danger to the shire should not be overrated. The overall size of the rebel forces in the Kilkenny area remained small throughout the Nine Years War, significantly less than the number of men who had been attracted to the Desmond banner in the early 1580s, and a mere fraction of the army that the Butlers had taken into the field in 1569. Indeed, at their peak, the rebels of the 1590s could depend on barely 200 armed men from the shire; normally they had less. A report drawn up for the government in April 1599 noted with relief that between them, Mountgarret and the rest of the rebel Butlers could only muster 20 horsemen and 130 kerne; even with outside help from the O'Carrolls and 'the strangers' (that is, the O'Neills) they only received an extra 30 foot soldiers, giving them a total force of 180 when at their strongest.[260] The viscount aside, there was no-one of prominence among their ranks. A few minor gentlemen enlisted, like Richard Walsh of Ballinacowley, Robert Drilling fitz Piers, Teige Walsh and John Shortal,[261] but for the most part their captains were made up of Mountgarret's sons and brothers, his nephews and in-laws, such as Walter Tobyn of Killaghy and Theobald Butler of Neigham, and his Gaelic clients among the O'Ryans.[262] The rebellion in Kilkenny was largely a family affair, exciting the involvement of a handful of disaffected Butlers with an eye on the earldom of Ormond.

This point was not lost on the government, and until October 1597, when he was appointed lieutenant-general of the royal army in Ireland, Earl Thomas was permitted to deal with the problem in his own way. As far as chief governors like Russell and Lord Burgh were concerned, if Ormond could reduce the level of rebel activity in Leinster by putting his house in order, he should be encouraged to do so; it would allow the crown to concentrate its resources more effectively against Tyrone and O'Donnell in Ulster and Feagh McHugh in Wicklow. The fact that he was willing to augment the royal army with an auxilary force raised from his territories and fitted out at his own expense added appreciably to his value. Hence Ormond's free rein in the mid-south and south-east of the country.[263]

257 The marriage took place in the early months of 1596, as a son Edmund – the future fourth viscount – was born before the year was out (Dunboyne, 'Carve's Butler families', 433). **258** HMC, *Kenyon MSS*, 610. **259** *Ir. Fiants.*, Eliz. I, no. 6484. **260** Northants RO, Ms FH 127, ff 3r, 8r; SP 63/205/31. **261** NA, RC 9/7, 126–7; Ibid., Ferguson MSS, Exchequer Memoranda Rolls, Eliz. I, 1586–1603, 383–4; Stafford, *Pacata Hibernica*, ii, 67; SP 63/198/60. **262** Blake Butler, 'Seneschals', 110; SP 63/205/74. **263** Carte, *Life*, i, p. cvi–cvii; for a reassessment of Russell's campaign in Wicklow, see Edwards, 'In Tyrone's shadow', 229–42.

The tactics he used were unremarkable. Those of his kinsmen who were reliable he promoted, and the baron of Dunboyne, Walter Butler of Kilcash, Piers Butler of Butlerswood, and Ormond's 'dearest nephew', James Butler – the eldest son of his troublesome brother Edward – each rose to take charge of detachments of his forces. The less dependable members of his house he punished. In October 1596 he arrested Mountgarret, Mountgarret's son Richard, and Sir Edmund Butler of Cloghgrenan, his intention being to have them all imprisoned in Dublin Castle.[264] He later arrested Redmund Butler fitz Theobald of Neigham.[265] When the perilous state of the roads prevented their immediate despatch to the capital, the earl insured that they were kept under lock and key, placing them in the custody of the sovereign of Kilkenny, Geoffrey Rothe, until conditions improved.[266] Mountgarret found the experience frightening. He subsequently recalled that when he was eventually taken to Dublin under armed guard in February 1597, he was in fear of his life. He had heard it said that the earl's horsemen were going to kill him along the way.[267]

The viscount's anxiety was well founded. Earl Thomas was determined to stamp out all trace of treason within his family, and was quite prepared to kill his relatives in order to get his way. The subsequent fate of Sir Edmund Butler's sons removed any doubts about the seriousness of his intentions. Having learned through his spies that they intended to disguise themselves in "poor man's weeds" in order to escape into Ulster,[268] he set out in pursuit. The 'chief man of action', James fitz Edmund, was the first to be apprehended, tracked down and killed in March 1597.[269] His brother Piers did not survive much longer. At the end of May he fell into the earl's clutches along the banks of the Shannon on his way north. He was taken to Thurles and beheaded with Walter Butler, Mountgarret's bastard son.[270] According to later reports, Piers refused to admit he had done wrong to Ormond. And so, to quote Ormond, he 'died desperately, as he had lived wickedly'.[271]

With his Cloghgrenan nephews dead, the earl found it easy to isolate and destroy the rump of their followers. As in 1569–71, he dispatched the local rebel soldiers with clinical efficiency. On 5 May 1597 he sent the heads of 24 traitors to the lord deputy in Dublin; two weeks later, on 19 May, he delivered 12 more, thereby accounting for his enemies at the rate of more than two a day.[272] A little earlier, five rebels had been executed by martial law at Pottlerath.[273] The killing continued intermittently between the autumn of 1597 and June 1598. The most notable fight to occur during this period was at Mountgarret's castle of Ballyragget early in 1598. For three days the royal army maintained the attack until they forced their way into the fort, and once the breech was made Ormond ordered that all the survivors – numbering 15 in all

264 *CSPI, 1596–7*, 138. 265 SP 63/198/60. 266 NLI, Ms 11,048 (2), item (j); KCA, Ms CR/J 22. 267 *CSPI, 1599–1600*, 54; *Cal. Carew MSS, 1589–1600*, no. 270. 268 SP 63/196/31, iv. 269 *Cal. Carew MSS, 1589–1600*, no. 270; *CSPI, 1596–7*, 257, 294–6, 309–10. 270 Ibid., pp 294–6. 271 Ormond presented Piers' head to the lord deputy early in June (ibid., 309–10). 272 *Cal. Carew MSS, 1589–1600*, no. 270. 273 SP 63/198/60.

– be hanged nearby as an example to the local populace.[274] The number of rebel dead was mounting steadily.

By the beginning of 1598 the earl had cause to be satisfied by the recent course of events. Charged by the queen with defending the whole of Leinster and the Pale, up to this point he had managed to hold onto Kilkenny and its surrounding area – strategically a key region – without making any special effort. Enough members of his family had stayed loyal to render the policing of Kilkenny's northern borderlands a relatively simple task. His seizure of Ballyragget meant that, with few exceptions, the rebels were forced to keep their distance behind a long line of Butler and government forts stretching from Thurles and Templemore in Tipperary to Rathvilly and Clonmore in Carlow. Controlling these points, he knew the heart of his lordship would be safe.

His self-assurance was borne out by subsequent occurrences. Though 1598 was a dreadful year for the English monarchy in most parts of the country, under Ormond's leadership Co. Kilkenny remained steadfast in its support of Elizabeth. Kilkenny town, the capital of his lordship, stood out as a bastion of loyalty, receiving refugees from the surrounding counties, and expending considerable sums of corporation money on building up the town defences: for instance, in January 1597 the town ordnance was safely re-housed in a renovated building, in June 1598 the tower near St Francis' Well was rebuilt, and the following July an entirely new tower – costing £3 0s. 10d. – was built along the town wall. The shire capital was preparing to withstand a siege, should one materialise.[275]

The sole cause for alarm was Mountgarret's recapture of Ballyragget before the end of the year; otherwise, the rebels failed to capitalise on the advances made by Tyrone and his followers elsewhere. Even after Tyrone's great victory at the Yellow Ford in August 1598, there was little chance of the rebellion igniting in Co. Kilkenny. Barely three weeks after the royal forces in Ulster had been decimated, Ormond reassured the English officers under his command that some of the extra men that were now needed to defend Dublin and the Pale could be raised from his lands in Kilkenny and Tipperary.[276]

His confidence was boosted by the precarious state of the local rebel alliance, where things were not going well for Mountgarret. In recent months the viscount had sought the assistance of some dissident members of the MacGiollapadraig dynasty, but found it impossible to trust them. When camping in the hills to the north-west of Kilkenny with Phelim MacGiollapadraig, his companion refused to forgive him for his actions against the MacGiollapadraigs in the past. Looking down from a hill-top on the Butler territories below, Phelim declared that the lands 'were once my ancestors', and I mean to have them back … Now is the time that we [the MacGiollapadraigs] shall be righted of the wrongs heretofore done unto us.' Mountgarret withdrew and sent a messenger to Dublin exploring the possibility of receiving a royal

274 Wood (ed.), *Perrot's chronicle*, 144–5.　**275** KCA, MSS CR/J 23, 28–9.　**276** HMC, *Hodgkin MSS*, 35.

protection in return for his promise to keep the peace.[277] It is unlikely that the viscount was genuinely interested in ending his rebellion – he had too much to gain if Tyrone won – but nonetheless his discomfort with his southern Gaelic allies did much to reduce the threat that he posed to Kilkenny. This fact was not lost on Tyrone's son, Con O'Neill, who visited Mountgarret and the southern rebel lords after Christmas 1598, and was provoked to a 'great rage' by the evidence of petty rivalries among them.[278]

Growing mistrust in rebel ranks insured that Ormond and the local loyalists had little to fear when the Munster Irish rose in revolt later in the year. Taking only 700 men with him the earl reinforced all the major towns in the province in October, after which the rebels fell out among themselves and failed to make any further progress against his forces. Significantly, none of the reinforcements that he used came from his own lands. Determined to protect his lordship now that danger was at hand, he capitalised on his position as general of the royal army to place companies previously stationed in the Pale in some of the principal forts and walled towns in the south. By doing so he went back on his promise (given in August) to make more men from his territories available for the government's needs, and within days some at court began whispering that Ormond would fight only when his own freehold was put at risk.[279] They were catty remarks to be sure, an obvious reflection of England's growing crisis in Ireland, but – as with the Desmond war ten years before – the murmurings did Earl Thomas no lasting harm. His prompt response to the Munster uprising in 1598 had probably saved the province (and parts of Leinster too) from falling completely into rebel hands, and this although his motives for saving it were unavoidably self-serving.[280]

At home in Kilkenny he had no need to excuse himself for his actions in Munster. By seeing to it that outside forces were brought in to safeguard the frontiers of his lordship, especially in neighbouring Tipperary, he received widespread local approval.[281] Clearly, had Tipperary been overrun by the rebels, Kilkenny would have been next in the line of assault. The bad faith that had recently marred the earl's relations with sections of the shire elite began to subside. Tellingly, there was no adverse reaction when he chased the papal nuncio, Dr Derby McCragh, out of Kilkenny into the baron of Cahir's country in west Tipperary in December 1598. While the counties all around it were becoming battle-zones, Co. Kilkenny continued to escape the full effects of the war.

It remained a safe haven throughout most of 1599. In a fresh attempt to safeguard it, Earl Thomas enticed the new lord lieutenant, Robert Devereux, second earl of Essex, to bring a detachment of the royal army south during the summer. This also was a controversial arrangement, and news of it was badly received at court, where the general consensus was that Essex, the queen's greatest noble-

---

277 Wood (ed.), *Perrot's chronicle*, 150–1. **278** SP 63/205/74. **279** N.E. McClure (ed.), *The letters of John Chamberlain* (2 vols., Philadelphia 1939), i, 50–2. **280** A.J. Sheehan, 'The overthrow of the Munster plantation, 1598', *Irish Sword*, 15 (1982–3). **281** As early as 1596 extra forces had been introduced in Kilkenny (HMC, *Salisbury MSS, 1596*, 543).

man, should have stayed in the Pale until the time was right to campaign against Tyrone in the north. Yet Essex's movements around Kilkenny made sense.

Essex was an accomplished military commander,[282] and to his soldier's mind, Ormond's suggestion that he spend some time away from Dublin was an attractive one. Why waste months waiting for the chance to fight his most dangerous adversary, Tyrone, when he could immediately deliver a telling blow to smaller fry elsewhere? In the words of an English onlooker: 'having once beaten or brought in the weaker ones, the stronger would the sooner yield or be the easier subdued.'[283] Whatever one makes in retrospect of his wisdom as a politician, his military presence in the south succeeded in temporarily restoring the crown's control over the region. The problem was not Essex's tactics, but the briefness of his stay in Ireland, which was dramatically cut short when he returned to England in September in order to defend himself against his detractors.[284]

While Essex remained in office, the scale of the rebel activity in Cos. Kilkenny, Tipperary and Wexford declined significantly, and Ormond's position was strengthened. The old earl had intercepted Essex at Athy at the start of his southern journey, bringing Mountgarret and the baron of Cahir with him to beg the lieutenant's pardon for their recent record of treachery. Going through the motions the two noblemen went down 'upon their knees, [and] submitted themselves without condition', but no-one was fooled by their display of remorse.[285] As one chronicler noted, their families and followers still remained 'out against the prince', and Essex promptly marched the royal army into Mountgarret's country, determined to secure it for Elizabeth while he had the chance.

As soon as Essex's troops entered the area on 17 May 1599 they were attacked by the viscount's sons and Owney MacRory O'More, and two of their captains were slain in the ensuing skirmish. After a time, however, the rebels were forced to retreat in the face of superior opposition, and the following morning, when the battle was over, Essex arranged for a garrison of 100 men to be placed in Ballyragget Castle. As commander he selected Captain Henry Folliott, who had 'behaved himself very valiantly', receiving a wound in the foregoing struggle;[286] later events would show that Folliott was well chosen.

The occupation of Ballyragget was of vital importance locally. Built as it was on raised ground, the fort was easily defensible, and it dominated the principal route between Kilkenny and Laois. Its seizure was a major setback for the insurgents. Even when their prospects improved, they were unable to re-take it from Folliott, and their subsequent movements lacked penetration; they were primarily confined to the border fastnesses for the duration of the war.[287] Indeed, having lost Ballyragget they only had one remaining fortress in Kilkenny, at

282 L.W. Henry, 'Essex as a strategist and military organiser, 1596–7', *EHR* 68 (1953), 363–93; Williams, *Tudor regime*, 134. **283** Wood (ed.), *Perrot's chronicle*, 162. **284** Falls, *Elizabeth's Irish wars* (London 1950), ch. 16–17; L.W. Henry, 'The earl of Essex and Ireland 1599', *BIHR* 32 (1959), 1–23. **285** HMC, *Kenyon MSS*, 610. **286** Ibid., 610–11; Wood (ed.), *Perrot's chronicle*, p.164; C.L. Falkiner (ed.), 'William Farmer's chronicle of Ireland, 1594–1613', *EHR* 22 (1907), 112. **287** *CSPI, 1599–1600*, 40.

Coulhill in the Rower, a situation which later compelled them to switch their attention to Co. Wexford, where conditions seemed more promising. In the meantime, expulsion from their principal stronghold in northern Kilkenny persuaded some of the rebels to lay down their arms. On 20 June 1599 two of Mountgarret's brothers surrendered to Essex at Waterford. Others might have followed had he stayed on as governor.[288]

Following Essex's departure, the rebels again flooded into the north of the county. In January 1600 they received a major boost when Tyrone came down out of Ulster to Tipperary to rendezvous with the pretender to the earldom of Desmond, James fitz Thomas Fitzgerald, and other southern rebels. His appearance signalled a crisis in Kilkenny. At last it seemed that Mountgarret's plan to overrun the region by bringing in outside help was about to be realised.

Militarily, there was little Earl Thomas or his junior officers could do to prevent Tyrone's appearance in Tipperary, for he came accompanied by more than 2000 soldiers.[289] On the way his men plundered Ormond's land near Roscrea, and eager to display his religious credentials, Tyrone saw to it that a fragment of the true cross 'was brought out to shelter and protect him' when he reached his destination, Holy Cross Abbey, just a few miles from Callan and the western borders of Kilkenny.[290] Tyrone stayed at Holy Cross for a few days, visited by Catholic priests and southern chieftains in full view of Ormond's followers. The Black Earl was exasperated by whate he perceived as Tyrone's mockery of his power in the region, but try as he did, he could not bring the arch-traitor to close quarters. Twice in the space of a few weeks Tyrone evaded his grasp, on the first occasion remaining on the western side of the River Suir out of Ormond's reach, on the second sneaking past the earl's camp before he was seen.

It should be stressed that Tyrone tried to escape Ormond, not the other way round. Ormond and his kinsmen the baron of Dunboyne and Walter Butler of Kilcash had their army out in force, and Tyrone was anxious not to confront them so far from his Ulster base. Hence, when he saw his chance to make for home, he dashed for it. According to Farmer, once Tyrone caught sight of Ormond's camp on the Kilkenny-Tipperary frontier, he and his men 'marched [away] so fast that they travelled in one day about 33 or 34 miles with bag and baggage'.[291]

Tyrone's flight from the south in the spring of 1600 should have been one of the highlights of Earl Thomas' overlordship in Co. Kilkenny. Once more it seemed he had guaranteed the area's safety, and although it is true he had failed to trap his enemy, the local population was probably relieved that a major battle had not ensued so close to the shire. With Tyrone gone, it was possible to look forward to another period of relative calm.

The peace was short lived. On Thursday 9 April 1600, at the age of 69, Ormond was asked to attend a parley the next day with the Laois rebel, Owney

---

288 Falkiner (ed.), 'Farmer's chronicle', 113. 289 McClure (ed.), *Letters*, i, 86–8. 290 Graves, 'The taking of Ormond', 388. 291 Falkiner (ed.), 'Farmer's chronicle', 116. The march must have lasted nearly 14 hours: for sixteenth-century march rates, see R. Hassig, *Mexico & the Spanish conquest* (London 1994), 16.

MacRory O'More. The invitation was a hoax. When the earl turned up at the appointed meeting place – Corranduff on the borders of Idough – he was surrounded by O'More's troops, dragged off his horse and led away into captivity. Suddenly Kilkenny was leaderless, its vulnerability exposed. After six years the 'Nine Years War' had finally arrived in earnest.[292]

From the rebel viewpoint, Ormond's seizure was a potential masterstroke. The rising in the south, seemingly dead after Tyrone's departure, was reborn, and the O'Byrnes, Kavanaghs and Mountgarret Butlers all became active again. The government was forced to divide its army, sending a large detachment south despite fears of another assault on the Pale by Tyrone. Moreover, in Dublin and London the circumstances of the capture shed doubt on Ormond's competence. The new lord deputy, Mountjoy, could not understand why the earl had gone to talk with proven rebels in the company of no more than a handful of his servants and two other high-ranking officers, the earl of Thomond and Sir George Carew. Only after Thomond and Carew had written a detailed account of the incident did Mountjoy accept that Ormond had acted in the interests of the crown, and that the rebels had tricked him.

The seizure had been planned long in advance of the meeting. Owney MacRory had assembled a large force for the occasion, bringing over 500 men with him 'whereof 300 were bonnaughts [galloglass paid for by a forced levy]', a special hosting for a special task. The appearance of James Archer, the Kilkenny-born Jesuit, by Owney's side was also a sign of thoughtful planning. Ormond detested Archer as a born troublemaker, and so when they met, the Jesuit was able to keep him occupied in hot disputation, allowing Owney's men time to edge closer to their prey.[293] By the time Ormond realised what was happening, it was too late. In the ensuing scuffle his longstanding servant, Piers Butler of Butlerswood, was wounded, and one of his attorneys, the Oxford graduate Philip Comerford, was killed.[294]

Yet Ormond's capture brought the rebels little success. Possibly taken aback by the speed of the crown's response they secured none of the major access points along Kilkenny's borders. For example, a few days after the earl's seizure, Mountgarret's sons attempted to regain Ballyragget Castle, surrounding it in the hope of starving its garrison into submission. The siege was a failure. No attempt was made to block the main road leading to the fort from Kilkenny town, so Carew was able to take 'a strong convoy of horse and foot' with him to clear the rebels away, and the castle was thereby reinforced with 30 men and revictualled with six weeks' supply of food. Elsewhere in the county the rebels also lost their chance. Sir George Bourchier, one of Ormond's English relatives, was despatched to the shire in order to take command of the royal forces there, and by 18 April the number of government troops patrolling the

292 The ensuing paragraphs are based on Graves, 'The taking of Ormond', passim.   **293** Archer's career is admirably analysed in T. Morrissey, *James Archer of Kilkenny* (Dublin 1979).   **294** A. Clark (ed.). *Register of Oxford University, 1571–1622* (2 pts., Oxford 1887), pt. 2, 98.

countryside had been increased to 400 foot and 85 horse. The local rebel forces were no match for this.

Ultimately, the manner of Ormond's capture did the rebels more harm than good. The fact that he had gone in good faith to parley with them only to be kidnapped earned him much sympathy. Forced by his captors to live in rough conditions, it was feared he would die, clearing the way for Mountgarret or Sir Edmund Butler to claim the earldom. Several of the Catholic clergy residing in the county were agitated by the earl's predicament, concerned that one of their number, Archer, had been party to his deception. Although Archer intended to attempt the earl's conversion, he was denounced. The papal nuncio Derby McCragh came forward to declare 'that as the earl was treacherously taken, so it is not lawful [for a Catholic] … to keep him prisoner'. Patrick O'Hoen, Archer's fellow Jesuit, echoed this statement, and demanded Ormond be set free. It seemed not to matter that Earl Thomas was a heretic.

It was important for the Catholic church that the local hierarchy denounce the kidnapping, lest the Kilkenny and Tipperary gentry turn to Protestantism in protest. Anger at the perceived underhandedness of Archer and O'More had galvanised public opinion against the very notion of Catholic revolt, culminating in an outpouring of loyalty towards Ormond. Once the earl's whereabouts was known, 'sundry of Kilkenny' sought permission from his captors to visit him, bringing him food and drink and other comforts. By early May he was able to sit out his captivity in relative luxury. As the government learned, though cooped up in the woodlands of Laois 'the earl hath his own cook and butler, and sitteth at a table by himself.' He even slept in his own bed, carried up from Kilkenny Castle by his servants.

Not since 1582–3 had the earl been so popular. His handling of the war had scored a high approval rating from the local gentry, especially the ruthless manner in which he had sanctioned the execution of the treasonous members of his family. To prevent him coming to harm, the Kilkenny elite set out to obtain his freedom.

The principal actors in this unusual turn of events were Sir Richard Shee and Thomas Cantwell. Shee was determined regain the earl's trust, something he had not enjoyed for nearly ten years. He acted as the chief coordinator in the ensuing negotiations with Ormond's captors. In doing so, he risked being called a traitor by suspicious government officials – among them Lord Deputy Mountjoy – who feared that Earl Thomas would join the rebellion to save his life. But it was Cantwell who took the greatest risk for Ormond's sake. Unable to persuade Owney O'More of the advantages of releasing the earl, he departed for Ulster in the middle of May in order to bargain for Ormond's freedom directly with Tyrone.

Cantwell was successful. Tyrone was anxious to end the business, having realised that the kidnapping was a tactical mistake: Kilkenny and Tipperary had not capitulated, and the possibility of Ormond being rescued by his followers was increasing. Worse, Ormond might die while still in O'More's keeping and thus become a martyr for the crown. Better, then, to hand him over graciously and on beneficial terms than have the southern loyalists claim a victory when he was found.

The deal that Cantwell brokered with Tyrone was, actually, far less beneficial to the rebels' cause than either Tyrone or Owney O'More had intended. Before agreeing to let Ormond go, O'More had concocted a fresh scheme to line his pockets and make the earl appear a traitor by having him sign a treasonable document. He envisaged a formal declaration wherein Ormond would promisee to fight alongside Morgan MacBrian Kavanagh and Redmund MacFeagh O'Byrne against the crown forces on a future campaign. Should Ormond break his word – as O'More expected – then O'More would receive £3,000 in compensation for granting him his freedom. It was a clever idea, for had Ormond committed his signature to such a declaration, his reputation as Ireland's leading loyalist would have been greatly damaged. But in the event the scheme backfired, for O'More's men made a mess of the declaration and Earl Thomas was able to capitalise on their mistake.

The earl's captors, it transpired, had left no-one with him who understood English. Consequently, as the earl later stated, the drafting of the would-be treasonous declaration fell to someone – possibly a spy – who was secretly well disposed towards him. What was issued was not very treasonous at all, merely stating that 'I, Thomas, earl of Ormond, being captive in the hands of Owney MacRory, and being not to be redeemed otherwise, am compelled to be sworn to take part with the said Owney in his rebellious actions' – that is, the earl had only signed his name under duress, and had *not* agreed to rebel. Whoever composed the declaration also played a trick on the rebels, insinuating that Morgan Kavanagh and Redmund O'Byrne were actually loyal subjects of the queen, something they were not, viz 'Morgan Mac Brian and Redmund MacFeagh to win my liberty hath promised to join with me'. In a statement originally conceived to weaken the crown, Ormond and his secret helper had produced one that could be used instead to weaken the Irish rebellion. The declaration was dated 12 June 1600. Four days later, after two months in captivity, the earl of Ormond was allowed to go free.

He returned to Kilkenny Castle a hero. As far away as Edinburgh, and even on the Continent, the news of his release was relayed by crown officials and professional letter writers,[295] where it was perceived as a turning point in a war of increasing international significance. The Spanish were disappointed, convinced that an opportunity to undermine the queen's position and enhance the power of 'the Catholic party' by converting the earl had been lost.[296] Whether he liked it or not, his freedom was seen as a victory for the Protestant as well as the English interest in Ireland.

In Co. Kilkenny his release was welcomed by most of the shire community. His captivity had had a major impact on the local landlords, forcing them to examine their attitudes towards a range of issues, from the advantages and dis-

---

295 E.g., HMC, *Shrewsbury & Talbot papers*, ii, 221; ibid., *Salisbury MSS, 1600*, 127. **296** Ibid., 242–3.

advantages of the English connection to the destiny of the earldom of Ormond. Peeking out at conditions in the rest of the country, they adopted a conservative loyalist position, preferring to be governed by an English monarch and have Earl Thomas (a courtier) to protect them than risk all under a new political regime dominated by Tyrone and Ormond's enemy Mountgarret. Despite its shortcomings in certain matters, the Ormond lordship should continue in the county, the earldom to be occupied by Earl Thomas or, in the event of his death, by someone who would maintain the English connection and preserve the *status quo*.

What ensued when the tenth earl regained his freedom was unparalleled in the history of sixteenth century Ireland. In order to secure his release, 17 of the most important figures in the county voluntarily gave themselves up as hostages to Owney MacRory O'More, among them Sir Richard Shee, Thomas Cantwell, Robert Rothe, Lucas Shee and Ormond's bastard son, Piers Butler of Duiske Abbey. Even William Lovell, Francis Lovell's son and heir, handed himself over. More remarkably, perhaps, the local community was prepared to pay Owney O'More the £3,000 he had demanded for the earl's release. A list has survived of approximately 300 individuals, nearly half of them from Co. Kilkenny, with the rest from Carlow and Tipperary, who 'engaged in the redemption of the earl of Ormond from captivity'.[297] The sum of money that each paid towards Earl Thomas's freedom is not recorded, but the list does mention the domicile and social standing of most of the contributors. The earl enjoyed widespread support. No less than 30 of the squires and gentry of Co. Kilkenny paid a share of the sum that was due, and donations were also forthcoming from more than eighty yeomen and husbandmen. In geographical terms, financial assistance was equally distributed, with money arriving from almost every zone, especially from the northern uplands and the eastern borderlands, areas that the earl had tried so hard to pacify and secure ever since assuming the earldom in the 1550s.

Possibly the most interesting aspect of the list is what it reveals about Ormond's standing in the context of inter-ethnic relations and Elizabethan colonialism in southern Leinster. The minor Gaelic families of Co. Kilkenny also contributed towards the cost of his release, the O'Hedians, MacCraghs, O'Ryans and O'Bryns joining with the Anglo-Irish as avowed supporters of the earl and his cause. Moreover, the O'Kellys, MacEvoys and O'Lawlors, three of the 'seven septs' of Laois who had lost their lands in the Laois-Offaly plantation and had since come to live in Kilkenny, did likewise, helping to pay off the earl's ransom in return for the shelter he had given them since the late 1570s.[298] Evidently Earl Thomas was held in high regard by many of the Gaelic Irish, who viewed him as the acceptable face of English rule, someone who over the years had tried to temper the severity of crown policy. In Kilkenny,

297 *Ir. Fiants*, Eliz. I, no. 6565.   **298** I will discuss his treatment of the Laois septs in detail in a future paper.

of course, it had always been easy for Ormond to treat the native Irish fairly because he had no large Gaelic lordship threatening him inside the county; his relations with the more powerful Gaelic lineages of Tipperary were not so benign. Nonetheless, in the excitement surrounding his release in June 1600 his capacity to unite different ethnic and social groups behind the royal banner in Ireland was loudly advertised.

He did not have long to recuperate following his release. The war was now reaching its peak, with the Ulster rebels expecting the imminent arrival of help from Spain,[299] and in August Earl Thomas was once again out in the field. With his Pale kinsman Sir Christopher St Lawrence he led a detachment of royal troops into Idough in Kilkenny's north-eastern hill country, the object being to secure the O'Brennans' territory and drive out Owney MacRory O'More's forces that were hiding there. The expedition was successful, and shortly afterwards, with Co. Kilkenny almost completely rebel-free, the crown was able to ruthlessly obliterate the remaining rebels in Laois and Carlow.[300] On 17 August 1600 Owney MacRory O'More was killed in a border skirmish.[301]

Owney's death marked the end of the Nine Years War in Kilkenny and the surrounding Ormond lands. There was no longer an effective military leader to represent the local rebel interest, and the tenth earl and his captains, Sir Walter Butler of Kilcash and Lawrence Esmond, threw a blanket of government control across the area.[302] The remaining dissidents were routinely hunted down and punished. A group of the rebel Burkes was ambushed and defeated in Co. Kilkenny by Sir Walter Butler,[303] and Mountgarret's nephew, Walter Tobyn, was executed in Kilkenny town for treason.[304] Such was the onslaught that in July 1601 Mountgarret's third son, Edward, Sir Edmund Butler's illegitimate son, Thomas, and some of the outlaw Graces fled to the borders of Ikerrin in Tipperary, where they were sheltered for a time by Kedagh O'Meagher.[305] The arrival of the Spanish expeditionary force at Kinsale later in the year excited little response, and the government made Kilkenny its base of operations against the invaders.[306] The final significant act of the war came in September 1602, after more than a year of rebel inactivity, when Richard Walsh of Ballinacowley was killed by government troops acting under Ormond's command.[307]

The Ormond successional problems that had prompted the outbreak of the second Butler revolt in 1596 were also settled (temporarily) at this time. Although Earl Thomas had no legitimate son, as shown in Chapter 2, with crown approval he was able to arrange for the earldom to pass to his nephew Theobald Butler, the youngest of the Cloghgrenan line who was untainted by the treason of his brothers. The earl's machinations were greatly assisted by the death of the two senior claimants to the earldom, Theobald's father, Sir Edmund of Cloghgrenan, and Edmund, second Viscount Mountgarret, both of whom

299 E.g., Graves, 'Taking of Ormond', 429.   **300** *Cal. Carew MSS, 1589–1600*, no. 442.   **301** *AFM.*, vi, 2179, s.a. 1600.   **302** HMC, *Ormonde MSS, 1572–1660*, 2–3.   **303** Ledwich, 'Antiquities', 402.   **304** Blake Butler, 'Seneschals', 110.   **305** Lambeth Ms 624, ff 81–2.   **306** *CSPI, 1601–3*, 66, 86–7, 201.   **307** He had been proclaimed a traitor on 24 Sept. 1597 (NA, RC 9/7, 126–7).

passed away late in 1602.[308] With them gone, and Sir Edmund's eldest sons executed, Earl Thomas could proceed with his twin objectives of confirming his successor and restoring the image of the Butlers of Ormond as a dynasty loyal to the crown.

The second Butler revolt had not posed as serious a threat to the personal authority of the Black Earl as the first one in 1569. It had excited little support within the Ormond lordship, only stretching Earl Thomas in October 1598 and January 1600, times when the prospect of outside help materialising from Munster and Ulster had loomed largest. Had Ormond been a younger man, or his successor better established, he might have been able to enjoy the fruits of his victory. However, already showing signs of ill health in the early 1590s, his ordeal in captivity, the death of his second wife, and old age, all began to take their toll. Just as the war turned its final corner he slipped from the limelight, authorised on the instructions of Elizabeth I 'to repose himself more than he hath done, he being a nobleman so well deserving of us as we would have all the world know that we make extraordinary estimation of him'.[309]

CONCLUSION

If Earl Thomas had seemed unassailable in the final years of the Nine Years War, his position as the lord and master of Kilkenny and Tipperary apparently assured, his retirement after 1601 brought him little peace of mind. Although the main bulk of his territories had been an island of peace during the conflict, the eventual defeat of the rebels in 1602/3 left him exposed to an altogether more familiar threat – the power of the royal government. Suddenly, with Tyrone defeated and the whole country subjugated, the Ormond lordship no longer occupied a position of major strategic significance in national affairs. Those policies that he had opposed since 1569 were still operative, as the Dublin government resumed its remorseless drive towards the 'reform' of Ireland and the reduction of regional power. Following the death of Elizabeth I in March 1603 a new age was dawning, one in which the writ of the lord deputy and council was enforceable everywhere, and autonomous noble lordships seemed increasingly anachronistic and dispensable. To make matters worse, as crown officials prepared to take over, religion, an issue Ormond had long avoided, moved to centre-stage.

---

308 Sir Edmund died shortly before 4 Dec. (HMC, *Salisbury MSS, 1602*, 507), following Mountgarret, who had died on 24 Nov. (GEC, *Complete peerage*, sub 'Mountgarret').	**309** Lambeth Ms 632, fol. 208.

CHAPTER 5

Lordship redundant:
religion, land and power, 1603–42

Although mindful of the fact that it was not immediately apparent to those who lived at the time, historians – blessed with the benefit of hindsight – are agreed that the victory of the crown forces at the battle of Kinsale signalled the end of aristocratic autonomy in Ireland.[1] With Tyrone and his confederates defeated and forced to sue for peace, all the inhabitants of the country were for the first time made subject to one authority, the English colonial government in Dublin. Loyalist elements among the native population rejoiced at the victory of the crown. They expected to benefit from the establishment of full royal sovereignty and anticipated that, as punishment, the ex-rebel lordships would be reduced and neutered. Of course, within a few years of Kinsale many of the ex-rebel territories were indeed subdued, their lands confiscated and granted to new colonists from England and Scotland under the various plantation schemes for Ulster, North Wexford, Longford, Leitrim and elsewhere. However, it was not only ex-rebels who saw their position diminished by the newly dominant central government. Irish society experienced a political revolution in the early seventeenth century in which the power and authority of all the traditional lords and ruling lineages was systematically subdued by the crown. Loyalist lords and lordships were as much affected by this change as their ex-rebel counterparts. Hence the rather curious fact that the new plantations that spread across the country after 1609 witnessed the partial, and sometimes total, forfeiture of the lands of native rulers who had fought for the crown before 1603; likewise, the government's banning of private lordly exactions and the taking of tributes was aimed not at specific local rulers, but at all Irish lords. If Ireland was to be made more like England – the ultimate objective of English policy in the country – then local autonomy must cease, with central government enjoying absolute, unrivalled supremacy. If, for the sake of expediency, the crown had tolerated limited aristocratic devolution before its great victory at Kinsale, it was not prepared to do so anymore. To quote an expert in the period: 'once centralised administration from Dublin became feasible', loyalist lineages that had long acted as satellites of the crown in Ireland were now 'merely instruments to be discarded'.[2]

1 G.A. Hayes-McCoy, 'The completion of the Tudor conquest and the advance of the Counter-Reformation, 1571–1603', *NHI*, iii, 140–1; Canny, *From Reformation to Restoration*, ch. 6; D. Edwards, 'Legacy of defeat: the reduction of Gaelic Ireland after Kinsale', in H. Morgan (ed.) *The battle of Kinsale* (forthcoming). 2 K. Nicholls, 'Celtic contrasts: Ireland and Scotland', *History*

No other lordship demonstrates this development as effectively as the earldom of Ormond. It is true that, in the immediate aftermath of the Nine Years War, the tenth earl of Ormond, 'Black' Thomas, was 'above criticism because of the prominent role he had played' in helping to secure English victory.[3] On a personal level, Earl Thomas continued to enjoy royal favour after the death of Queen Elizabeth in March 1603. The new monarch, the first of the Stewart kings, James VI & I, viewed the earl as an exemplar for other Irish nobles, praising him for 'his faithful service, valour, wisdom and provident circumspection, [both] to the late queen and himself'.[4] Nevertheless, as regards the earl's position as traditional overlord of Co. Kilkenny, the crown was determined to impose greater control over the shire (and over Tipperary also). The Ormond lordship would continue to exist for as long as the ageing lord lived; as soon as he was dead, reduction would begin.

There were two reasons for this. First, in strategic terms, Co. Kilkenny and the Ormond country was no longer vital to the crown, which had effectively re-conquered the entire island after Kinsale. The remorseless militarisation of the state that Earl Thomas had tried in vain to curtail in Elizabethan times had culminated by the time of King James' accession with no part of Ireland beyond the reach of a royal garrison. Second, for all the trust it placed in Earl Thomas the government was increasingly uncertain of the loyalty and dependability of the local population, whose preference for Counter-Reformation Catholicism made them ideologically suspect. In 1604 the crown was dismayed to learn that there were at least 30 'Romish priests' working in the county; within less than ten years this figure had risen to almost 50, making Kilkenny the Irish county that was probably most under the control of Rome.[5] To Protestant officials in Dublin and London the notion of Catholic loyalism seemed utterly illogical, a contradiction in terms. If Catholics insisted the pope was the head of the Christian church and followed his teachings, then they must also believe that all Protestants, from the king down, were schismatics and heretics. And given that Tyrone's rebellion had enjoyed papal backing, how much store could be set by the promise of 'loyalist' Catholics that they would obey the king in all secular matters?

Religion became the defining issue in crown/community relations from the very beginning of King James' reign. In April 1603 the urban elite of Kilkenny, supported by Ormond's nephew (and potential successor), Sir Walter Butler of Kilcash, overthrew the Protestant establishment in the town and permitted a Jesuit from Clonmel, Dr James White, to reconsecrate St Mary's and St Patrick's parish churches as Catholic places of worship. According to a government account of this, the so-called 'recusancy revolt', 'the said Dr White ran into the throng of the people with a crucifix in his hand, crying out "This is the God that you must fight for", with many suchlike seditious speeches'. Earl Thomas

---

Ireland 7/3 (Autumn 1999), 26. **3** Canny, *From Reformation to Restoration*, 150. **4** NA, Lodge MSS, Articles etc., 109. **5** Moran, 'Bishops', 254, 266–71; F. O'Fearghaill, 'The Catholic Church in County Kilkenny, 1600–1800', in Nolan & Whelan (ed.), *Kilkenny*, 197–202.

had attempted to intervene, persuading the Kilkenny town councillors and merchants to submit to Lord Deputy Mountjoy and beg his forgiveness, but after what was only a token demonstration of remorse, the townsmen resumed their previous activities, to the fury of the deputy.[6] Later in the year Mountjoy had Martin Archer, the new sovereign of Kilkenny, imprisoned for failing to restore Blackfriars Abbey as the county courthouse. Archer subsequently fled the country and died in exile in 1604. His incarceration was destined to be the first of a series of punitive measures that the government would find necessary to force Kilkenny's Catholics to respect Protestant rule.

Much more than during the Elizabethan period, the central government was determined to protestantise as well as anglicise local power structures in the area, a development that necessarily threatened the long-term future of the Ormond lordship. Unless Earl Thomas and his successors could be relied upon to stop patronising the Catholic recusant gentry of the shire, the government would have to intervene directly in the selection of local administrative personnel in order to consolidate and extend Protestant power. Likewise, when occasion arose, the crown was prepared to support the creation of a new Protestant elite by forfeiting Catholic property in the shire.

Crucially, in pursuit of its goals the government was more than ever prepared to meddle in both local administration and landowning arrangements irrespective of the interests of the house of Ormond. Even before Earl Thomas died, the earldom lost its capacity to serve as a check on government authority in Co. Kilkenny. For the local community, this change from aristocratic rule to direct crown rule was traumatic. The various points of contact that had formed the framework for the county's relationship with the monarchy were worn thin, with the gentry and merchants of the shire increasingly dissatisfied with their lot: land held of the English king was suddenly the cause of insecurity for the local landlords, and the towns, often havens of loyalty in the past, lost their freedom from outside interference. Growing unease led, gradually, to alienation and opposition, so that eventually the Dublin administration was compelled to govern the shire without hope of consent. During the 1630s the rapid promotion to high office of the Protestant twelfth earl of Ormond, James Butler, failed to bridge the gap between government and governed. Raised in London, Earl James had no memory of the workings of traditional lordship, and seems to have had little regard for the concerns of the local gentry. Far from being a buffer or filter between the Kilkenny community and the state, James tried to profit from his promotion by helping to advance the Protestant interest in the shire. In 1641 disenchantment with what many locals saw as his betrayal of the Butler family and its traditions, as well as hatred of the land-grabbing regime in which he served, made rebels of Kilkenny's Catholic loyalists, and the county became the centre of an alternative, Catholic, government.

---

6 Falkiner (ed.), 'Farmer's chronicle', 532; *CSPI, 1603–6*, 32–3; Moran 'Bishops', 262.

PROTESTANT POWER

The appointment of the militant Protestant Sir Arthur Chichester as lord deputy in 1605, followed soon afterwards by the uncovering at Whitehall of the Gunpowder Plot, served to insure that across much of Ireland the threat of local disempowerment as a punishment for religious non-conformity was realised. Even in the state capital the government was prepared to impose a new Protestant order by challenging the power and privileges of the Catholic families that had dominated Dublin city and corporation for generations.[7] Elsewhere, the lord president of Munster, Sir Henry Brouncker, and the vice-president of Connaught, Sir Robert Remington, were authorised to confront the Catholic elite through an extension of the prerogative powers of the crown, by royal order, or 'mandate', requiring leading Catholic gentry and merchants to attend Sunday service in the Church of Ireland, or (literally) pay the consequences.[8] Such was the scale of the fines levied on recusants that it contributed to the dramatic rise in Irish government revenues after 1605.[9]

Events in Co. Kilkenny have been largely overlooked in historical discussion of the policies of Chichester, largely because the shire was not drawn into the mandates initiative during the years 1605–7. The county was not unaffected, however. For one thing, many of the merchants and gentry of Cos. Tipperary and Waterford who suffered fines and imprisonment as a result of mandates were near relatives and friends of leading Kilkenny families; for another, something as important as mandates was implemented in Co. Kilkenny in the period after Chichester's assumption of the deputyship. Essentially a policy of selective repression, it entailed the crown administration creating a new local order in which, whenever possible, Protestants replaced Catholics in positions of local authority.

Traditionally, of course, the nomination of local government personnel in Co. Kilkenny had been the preserve of the earls of Ormond. Throughout the sixteenth century shire officials such as the sheriff, the provost marshal, the clerk of the crown and peace, and the various commissioners of martial law and muster and array had nearly all been affiliates or clients of the earldom. Apart from a period of sustained anxiety between 1576 and 1587,[10] Thomas, the Black Earl, had managed to maintain a strong measure of control over the selection and appointment of local office-holders. At first glance, it might seem that this remained the case early in the seventeenth century. A well-known document recording the names of officials in the county, barony by barony, as they existed

7 Lennon, *Lords of Dublin*, 170–1. **8** H. Pawlisch, *Sir John Davies and the conquest of Ireland: a study in legal imperialism* (Cambridge 1985), ch. 6; J. McCavitt, *Sir Arthur Chichester, lord deputy of Ireland, 1605–16* (Belfast 1998), ch. 7. **9** Castle chamber fines, which were mostly recusancy fines, may have accounted for almost a quarter of the post-1605 increase in government revenue (A.J. Sheehan, 'Irish revenues and English subventions, 1559–1622', *PRIA* 90C (1990), 58; J.M. McLaughlin, 'The making of the Irish Leviathan: statebuilding in Ireland during the reign of James VI and I', PhD thesis, NUI Galway (1999), 129). Additional revenues were raised in the provinces through the presidency courts and the assize commissioners, but reliable figures for the sums realised are not extant. **10** See Chapter 4 above.

on 9 July 1608, reveals that beneath Earl Thomas, lords Mountgarret and Tully, and the Protestant bishop of Ossory, the county was administered by more than 40 local gentlemen, comprising 21 justices of the peace, four coroners and 17 constables of baronies. The great majority belonged to Ormond's feudal clientele, holding part of their lands directly of the earl by knight's service, and several held other properties by lease from Ormond.[11] In addition, the provost marshal of the county, an official not mentioned in the list, was another Ormond associate, David Serment of Lismacteige; likewise the clerk of the crown, John St Leger, tenant-in-chief of Ormond's manor of Dammagh.[12]

Besides their ties to the earldom, the most striking characteristic of the local government officers as they existed circa 1608 was their attachment to Catholicism. Indeed, just seven were Protestants – Ormond himself, albeit there was growing uncertainty about his true religious leanings; his heir, Lord Tully; Bishop Horsfall; the deacon of Ossory, Richard Deane; the rector of Callan, John Butler; Henry Mainwaring; and the Kilkenny city lawyer, Walter Archer fitz Walter. The commissioner of the peace Sir Richard Shee, for many years identified as a Protestant, is known to have converted to Catholicism at this time through the efforts of Brian O'Kearney, a Tipperary-born Jesuit who probably was invited into Shee's mansion in Kilkenny High Street by the old knight's second wife, Margaret Fagan, the daughter of a leading Dublin recusant.[13] O'Kearney's involvement with Sir Richard marked a trend among local officers. As Chart 5.1 below illustrates, of all the local government personnel named as serving in 1608 no less than 12 justices of the peace, three coroners, and four constables of baronies were so closely committed to the Catholic cause as to harbour 22 priests and clerics in their castles and townhouses, in direct contravention of the government's orders. In other words, the very persons who were expected to oversee the banishment of Catholic clergy from Co. Kilkenny provided shelter for almost half the priests in the shire.

The importance of this paradox should not be underestimated. In the first place, it had a direct bearing on the future of the Ormond lordship. The government realised that the Catholic grip on power in the county was the result of many years toleration by old Earl Thomas; a less sympathetic view of the earl emerged. Eventually this would result in radical intervention in the affairs of the earldom. In the second place, the existence of so many Catholic officers helps to explain the success of the Counter-Reformation in the south-east of Ireland. Among those living under the roofs of the Kilkenny officials were Catholic clergy from six dioceses (Cashel, Ossory, Leighlin, Ferns, Waterford

---

11 *Cal. Carew MSS, 1603–24*, 27–9. Extant Ormond deeds and the rentals of Michaelmas 1593 and Easter 1610 indicate that in the period immediately before and after 1608 the following local officials were Ormond tenants: Sir Richard Shee, James Butler, Lucas Shee, Robert Rothe, Gerald Grace, Walter Archer, Henry Shee, Helias Shee, commissioners; Thomas Shortal, coroner; Robert Walsh, Geoffrey Power, constables (see esp. NLI, Ms 2506, ff 10r–20r, 36r–48r). **12** Ibid., fol. 38r; 'Michaelmas & Easter Rent 1621 and 1622' (ibid., Ms 11,063 (1): 5); McLaughlin, 'The making', 349. **13** P. Moran (ed.), *Spicilegium Ossoriense*, i, 116–17. For Margaret's father, Alderman Christopher Fagan, see Lennon, *Lords of Dublin*, 246–7.

Chart 5.1   Priests harboured by local officials, c.1608

Justices of the Peace	Catholic clergy under their protection
Richard Butler, Viscount Mountgarret	Dr David Rothe, vice-primate of Ireland and vicar-general of Ossory; John Coppinger, priest; Donnell O'Gunney, priest
Sir Richard Shee of Kilkenny and Upper Court	Brian O'Kearney, Jesuit, harboured by Sir Richard's wife in Kilkenny city
Sir Richard Butler of Paulstown	Edmund Seix, priest
Robert Grace of Courtstown	Teige O'Duigean, Jesuit
Robert Rothe	William Lawless, priest
James Butler, esq., brother of Lord Mountgarret	Richard Marob, Jesuit; also Matthew Roche, vicar apostolic of Leighlin
Henry Shee of Kilkenny	Dr James White, his brother-in-law; also Thomas Morough, a preacher
Thomas Den of Grenan	Lucas Archer, priest
Thomas Strange of Dunkitt	Piers Strange, priest
Lucas Shee of Upper Court	David Kearney, titular archbishop of Cashel
Walter Walsh of Castlehowell	Teige O'Hely and Donnogh O'Hely, priests
Patrick Archer of Kilkenny	Lucas Archer, priest, his brother
Coroners	
John Walsh of Kilcregan	William McMahon, priest
Fitzgerald of Gurtines	Thomas Woodlock
Constables of baronies	
William Fitzgerald of Burnchurch	Edward Archer, priest
Edmund Daton of Kilmodally	Thomas Daton, priest
Richard Archdekin of Ballybawnmore	Donnell O'Howley, priest
John Walsh of Kilcregan	As above, under Coroners

Source: *Cal. Carew MSS, 1603–24*, 27–9; TCD, Ms 567, ff 37v–39r, printed in Moran, 'Bishops', 267–70

and Lismore), including the archbishop of Cashel, David O'Kearney, and the vicars apostolic of Leighlin, Waterford and Ossory.[14] Nor was this all. Elsewhere in the county one of the most senior Catholic churchmen in Ireland, the 'general vicar from the pope', Laurence Reneghan, enjoyed a special stipend col-

---

14 Matthew Roche, Dr James White, and Dr David Rothe respectively.

lected on his behalf by the officials of Kilkenny corporation. Presumably this stipend was transferred to Dr David Rothe after 1609, when he replaced Reneghan as vicar general and became the chief representative of the Catholic primate of Ireland, the absentee archbishop of Armagh, Peter Lombard.[15]

It was not long before Lord Deputy Chichester was made aware of this situation. Knowledge of the local Catholic clergy and their protectors is chiefly derived from two manuscripts, both held in the library of Trinity College, Dublin, and both composed for the eyes of Chichester and his government. The first, entitled 'The names of sundry priests and friars within some dioceses and counties in Ireland',[16] was written about 1609 or 1610. Relatively short, it had been drawn up merely to indicate 'what number of priests were come over' from the Continent and to help the government determine 'whether it were not time' to move against them. The second document,[17] written a little later,[18] was far more detailed, and concentrated almost exclusively on Co. Kilkenny. As well as listing 'the priests, commissaries, friars and Jesuits' that resided in the shire, its author – a local informer[19] – went to considerable lengths to identify 'their relievers and maintainers' and so establish where they might be discovered. Implicitly, this second document anticipated action against the Kilkenny Catholic elite. Its author was not to be disappointed.

Changes were already under way. In autumn 1605 Chichester had signalled his desire to take greater control of the government of Kilkenny by naming his servant, Denis O'Daly, as sheriff of the county.[20] Two years later, determined to insure that those who presided over the county sessions were good Protestants, the lord deputy compelled Ormond's choice of justice of the liberty of Tipperary, the Catholic legalist Sir John Everard, to resign from the Kilkenny assize circuit, thus clearing a path for English Protestant officers such as Sir James Ley, Sir John Elliott and Peter Palmer, amongst others, to control the bench in the county courthouse.[21] Temporarily, the crisis caused by the flight of the northern earls in September 1607 forced the deputy to curb his desire to meddle in the shire, not least because, following the flight, he had to

15 TCD, Ms 567, fol. 37v. The 'viccarse annuity' mentioned in the Irishtown book under 1610 may be a reference to this stipend (Ainsworth (ed.), 'Irishtown corporation bk', 63). **16** TCD, Ms 567, ff 32r–35v (see 34v–35r for Kilkenny). **17** Ibid., ff 37v–39r. **18** Probably about 1610, not 1613, as is usually claimed. Although the document contains a reference to 'this year 1613', the phrase is not actually part of the original text, but rather belongs to a note written in the margin in a different hand that, clearly, was added later. Internal evidence provides the best clue to when it was composed, in particular a reference to the vicar general, Laurence Reneghan, as being still active, something which indicates that, at the very latest, the document dates to the period soon after David Rothe's arrival in 1610 and before it was generally recognised that he had superseded Reneghan (O'Fearghaill, 'Catholic Church', 199). More compelling still is the mention made of Lady Shee as Sir Richard Shee's wife, and not his widow, although Sir Richard had died in August 1608. **19** Perhaps Cyprian Horsfall, or the native Protestant lawyer, Walter Archer fitz Walter? **20** Appendix 3 below. **21** C. Kenny, 'The exclusion of Catholics from the legal profession in Ireland, 1537–1829', *IHS* 25/100 (1987), 339; McCavitt, *Sir Arthur Chichester*, 98; idem, '"Good planets in their several spheares": the establishment of the assize circuits in early 17th century Ireland', *Irish Jurist* 24 (1989), 267–78.

call upon the old and blind earl of Ormond to come out of retirement and take charge of crown security for the duration of his absence in Ulster.[22] However, once conditions had settled, and Ormond was no longer needed, Chichester began interfering in the county with renewed vigour. In 1608 John St Leger was removed as clerk of the crown, replaced by the Cork-based English Protestant, Randall Clayton, who in turn made way for another Englishman, William Bradley.[23] St Leger's removal was vital to the Protestant interest. As an associate of Edward Rothe, elder brother of the Catholic vicar-apostolic Dr David Rothe, his reliability in keeping accurate records of those who were tried for religious offences at the county sessions was doubtful to say the least.[24]

In Ireland, unlike in England, the office of sheriff was still of major importance in local government, and retained a judicial function through the holding of barony tourn courts well into the seventeenth century.[25] Accordingly, the fact that a leading recusant such as Lucas Shee filled the post in Co. Kilkenny in 1608 cannot have gone unnoticed in Dublin. In Michaelmas term 1609 Chichester found an ideal candidate to serve as the new county sheriff – the Englishman Cyprian Horsfall, the son and heir of the local Protestant bishop.[26] To many of the Kilkenny elite news of Horsfall's promotion to the shrievalty must have caused surprise, for he had never previously figured in the shire administration in any capacity, save perhaps as an aid to his father.[27] Unfortunately, records of the sheriffs of the county are incomplete for the first half of King James' reign, but enough information has survived to pinpoint the most important thing about Horsfall's appointment: he was the first of a series of Protestants to obtain the position. After 1609 Protestants served as sheriff of Co. Kilkenny on at least seven occasions before 1622 – in 1613, 1614, 1616, 1618 and 1619–21 – with Horsfall followed by Thomas and Clement Daniel, John Butler fitz John, and another English newcomer, Henry Staines.[28]

The emergence of these men altered the nature of the county shrievalty. Hitherto, only the most prominent of the shire gentry had served as sheriff, so much so that holding the post was synonymous with wealth and status. This could not be said of the Protestant appointees, none of who were the equal of the Catholics they displaced. Besides their religion, their only qualifications for office was that four of the five lived locally and were closely related to senior Protestant churchmen, Horsfall to the bishop of Ossory, Thomas and Clement

---

22 NA, Lodge MSS, Articles etc., 109; *CSPI, 1608–10*, 104–5.   23 NA, Index to Fiants, James I, loose page entitled 'File 38. 6 James I'; ibid., Ferguson MSS, Equity Exchequer Orders, 1604–18, 184. For Clayton, see M. Curtis, 'The Claytons and their circle: new English arrivals in early seventeenth-century Cork', MA thesis, University College Cork (1998).   24 Burtchaell, 'Family of Rothe', 529. His removal may have been related to the theft of a roll of fines from the Lenten assizes of 1608: NA, Ferguson MSS, Revenue Exchequer Orders, 1592–1657, 101.   25 Quinn & Nicholls, 'Ireland in 1534', 23; Ellis, *Reform & revival*, 90–5, 189, 191–3.   26 Appendix 3 below. 27 His only recorded involvement in local affairs prior to 1609 was when he sued his mother-in-law, Alison Dalton of Knocknamona, Co. Waterford, over an unpaid marriage portion for his late wife, Anne, in the court of exchequer in Nov. 1603: Donovan & Edwards, *British sources*, 298; NA, RC 6/1, 271.   28 Appendix 3.

Daniel to the Kilkenny-born archbishop of Tuam, William Daniel, and John Butler fitz John to (his father) the vicar of Callan. Of them all, only Horsfall enjoyed a large estate, having secured a cheap lease of the episcopal manor of Inishnag and parcels of Bishopslough manor 'for a long term of years' before his father's death in 1610.[29]

The local Catholic elite soon had cause to be alarmed by the promotion of their social inferiors to office, for immediately the crown government attempted to get tough in the county. During 1610 two Catholic officials of the newly created city of Kilkenny, Walter Ryan and Thomas Pembroke, appeared in the Dublin exchequer on foot of summonses served by Sheriff Horsfall, to answer various charges of maladministration that were presented against them. From the moment that King James had approved its new charter in April 1609 Chichester had been uneasy at the range of privileges procured by the aldermen and merchants of Kilkenny, especially those regarding the authority of the city officials to collect all fines due to the crown by the citizens. Given the strength of Catholicism in Kilkenny the deputy was concerned that recusancy fines would not be collected in the city courts. Hence the appearances of Ryan and Pembroke in the exchequer in 1610 and 1611, where they were asked to account for various sources of revenue.[30]

Meddling with the county sheriffs was clearly contrary to the Ormond interest; however, meddling with civic officials signalled no obvious threat to Earl Thomas, given his objections to the 'great charter' of 1609, and for a time Chichester was able to advance his attack on the city by defending the earl's traditional privileges there.[31] Yet in time his campaign against the city alarmed Ormond greatly. In January 1612 Chichester authorised the justices of assize, Sir John Elliott and Sir John Denham, to take the civic leaders to task over religion. Accordingly the mayor, Thomas Archer – one of Ormond's longest-serving estate officials[32] – and the two city sheriffs, John Rothe (an Ormond tenant)[33] and John Murphy, were asked to prove their conformity by taking the oath of supremacy recognising the king instead of the pope as head of the church. The crown had been aware of Archer's recusant disposition for some time, having earlier learned that he had sheltered the vicar-general from Rome, Reneghan,[34] but the religious leanings of Rothe and Murphy were not so well known. On being challenged by the justices, all three refused to take the oath, and resigned their positions.[35]

The government maintained pressure on the local Catholic elite throughout these months. During the autumn Thomas Archer, the deposed mayor, was required to answer charges brought against him in a Dublin court;[36] in February

29 Carrigan, *Ossory*, iv, 394–6. **30** NA, Ferguson MSS, Revenue Exchequer Orders, 1592–1657, 105, 116, 118–9. The case of the city charter and its revenues was still rumbling in Michaelmas 1612: KCA, CR/J 36–7. **31** Chapter 1 above. **32** By 1612 Archer had worked for Earl Thomas for at least 35 years (e.g., Bod. Lib., Carte Ms 1, fol. 22; *COD*, vi, passim). **33** He leased Jerpoint mill from the earl (NLI, Ms 2506, fol. 40r). **34** TCD, Ms 567, fol. 11v. **35** NLI, Ms 2531, 100–1. **36** KCA, CR/J 36.

1613 John Tobyn of Killaghy, a gentleman whose land straddled both sides of the Kilkenny/Tipperary border, and a one-time ward of Earl Thomas, was fined the enormous sum of £200 for refusing to cooperate with anti-Catholic measures at the Clonmel assizes;[37] and on 30 March 1613 Justices Elliott and Denham returned to Kilkenny to test the conformity of the city officials. Again they asked the mayor (Edward Rothe) and the city sheriffs (James Langton and Patrick Murphy) to take the oath of supremacy, only for the officials to again refuse, and resign their posts.[38]

That the government adopted such an aggressive position on the eve of Irish parliamentary elections reveals how important the suppression of Catholic office-holders had become. In 1611, as the erosion of Catholic power was beginning to bite, an assessment had been made of the probable return of MPs from elections. It was reckoned that even Gowran and Inistioge, urban constituencies under the sway of Ormond's Protestant heir, Theobald, Lord Tully, would send recusants to the house of commons.[39] Two years later the crown's hopes had improved. Having tightened its control of local administration and demonstrated its will in Kilkenny city, the government expected that the Catholic grip over both Gowran and Inistioge must have been loosened, with each town predicted to return Protestants to parliament at the forthcoming polls.[40]

Such confidence was misplaced. For all its efforts towards the protestantisation of authority, the government had not cowed the Catholic elite of Co. Kilkenny into docility. If anything, its heavy-handed approach was counter-productive, strengthening rather than weakening the power and influence of the papal party in the shire. It is commonly recognised that the trial and execution in Dublin of the Catholic bishop of Down, Conor O'Devanny, on trumped-up charges of treason in January 1612, failed utterly in its purpose to secure the election of Protestant MPs in the greater Dublin area in the 1613 elections, with O'Devanny, a Gaelic Ulsterman, proclaimed a martyr and 'adored' as a saint within days of his death.[41] Similarly aggressive tactics proved equally unsuccessful in and around Kilkenny. In 1611 Protestant officials in Tipperary had attacked and jeered pilgrims going to the Catholic shrine at Monahincha near the border with Kilkenny. About the same time one of the new Protestant sheriffs of Co. Kilkenny (possibly Cyprian Horsfall) was responsible for an outbreak of anti-Catholic iconoclasm in the shire. At three separate places, each an established venue for the sheriffs' tourn court – at Knocktopher, Dunfert, and Dunmore – searches were carried out for old statues and images of saints, which were then either publicly burnt or smashed. There was also confrontation at Thomastown.[42] The quartering of government soldiers in

---

37 HMC, *Egmont MSS*, i, 42; *COD*, vi, nos. 15–16.   **38** NLI, Ms 2531, 100–1.   **39** *Cal. Carew MSS, 1603–24*, 169.   **40** As Davies put it, 'the lo: viscount Butler will govern the choice in those towns wherein are divers Protestants' (Carte Ms 61, fol. 92r).   **41** Lennon, *Lords of Dublin*, 197–8; McCavitt, *Sir Arthur Chichester*, 175–7; C. Tait, 'Adored for saints: Catholic martyrdom in Ireland, c.1550–1655', *Jn of Early Modern History* 5/2 (2001), 141; P.J. Corish, *The Irish Catholic experience: a historical survey* (Dublin 1985), 97–9.   **42** Rothe, *Analecta*, 527. For tourn court venues, see e.g., NLI, D 4052.

Gowran in January 1613, right on the eve of parliamentary elections, failed to justify the assumption that coercion would produce moderate MPs.[43] At the hustings a few weeks later every MP elected for Co. Kilkenny was a recusant. On arriving at parliament, together with their Tipperary colleagues the Kilkenny members played a primary role in the opposition to Chichester and his government that erupted in the opening session.[44] As previously discussed in Chapter 2, in doing this they followed the lead of one of the most influential members of the commons, Sir Walter Butler of Kilcash, future eleventh earl of Ormond.

The extent to which Sir Walter's oppositionist actions enjoyed the blessing of his uncle, Earl Thomas, remains a mystery, for Ormond was increasingly infirm and was absent, bedridden at Carrick, throughout the parliament. However, if a Jesuit source is to be believed, the tenth earl was on Sir Walter's side, as it claims that the old nobleman was reconciled to Rome at about this time.[45] Less partisan sources show that, at the very least, the old earl did not wish to obstruct the Catholic opposition. For instance, it is known that he gave his proxy to a Catholic lord, and not to Lord Tully, his Protestant heir apparent.[46] However, probably the best indication of the earl's opinion on the developments in parliament is provided by his subsequent warm approval of Sir Walter of Kilcash as his heir following Tully's sudden death in December 1613. By then Sir Walter was deep in trouble with Chichester and the king. If Ormond had not sympathised with his nephew's assertion of the customary rights of the Irish Catholic elite, he would hardly have favoured him as much as he did in his arrangements for the succession.[47]

Alarmed that he had not sought to silence Sir Walter, the government assumed that Ormond had either lost his reason, 'scant know[ing] what he doeth', or, more sinisterly, had fallen under a spell cast by 'the lewd and dishonest practices' of his Catholic servants and 'evil ministers' in Carrick.[48] Thus, although the likes of Chichester in Dublin and Archbishop Abbott in London readily acknowledged that the tenth earl was 'ever true to the crown', a decision was nonetheless taken to interfere in Butler family affairs in order to diminish Sir Walter Butler's leadership of the southern Irish Catholics. It has already been seen how, in the course of 1614, Chichester and King James threw the full weight of the state behind the claims of Elizabeth Butler, Dowager Lady Tully, to a greater personal share of the Ormond estate, while simultaneously summoning Sir Walter to court for a royal ticking off.[49] Other measures were also taken, simultaneously broadening the scope of government reprisal to embrace more of the Butlers and their followers, and signalling the extent to which Catholic power and privilege was to be downtrodden having dared to

43 KCA, Ms CR/J 35. For a rather different assessment, see Clarke, 'Pacification', 213–14.   **44** Edwards, 'Ormond lordship', 270–4; B. McGrath, 'The membership of the Irish house of commons, 1613–15', M Litt thesis, Trinity College, Dublin (1986).   **45** Moran (ed.), *Spiciligium Ossoriense*, ii, 43–7.   **46** T.W. Moody, 'The Irish parliament under Elizabeth and James I', *PRIA* 45 C (1938–40), 55.   **47** Chapter 2 above.   **48** HMC, *Downshire MSS*, iv, 378; *CSPI, 1611–14*, 412; *APC, 1613–14*, 543–4.   **49** Chapter 2 above.

raise its head. On 18 August 1614 three of Ormond's gentlemen servants, and two of Viscount Mountgarret's, were arraigned and tried at the Co. Kilkenny sessions by the commissioners of assize, Sir John Denham, Sir John Blennerhasset, and Peter Palmer. Despite pleading exemption from prosecution on the grounds that 'no servants of lords in parliament can be brought to trial during parliament' – a longstanding noble privilege – the commissioners pressed ahead with the trial and passed sentence on all five, who were fined between £10 and £20 apiece. Given that the defence of parliamentary privilege had become a major political issue in England in recent years, and caused considerable embarrassment to the king, it seems inconceivable that the commissioners were unaware of the possible legal and constitutional implications of proceeding with the trial. Presumably, therefore, reservations about provoking a reaction in the Irish parliament were outweighed by the opportunity the trial presented to unnerve the Butlers just as the question of the Ormond succession was moving up the political agenda. Significantly, among those they tried and fined in Kilkenny was Thomas Butler fitz Walter, esquire – the eldest son and heir of Ormond's new heir apparent, Sir Walter of Kilcash.[50]

Reprisals against the Butlers had only begun. For several years to come the government would give special attention to conditions in Kilkenny, Tipperary and the south-east. It did so partly, of course, to reduce Sir Walter's authority as eleventh earl of Ormond after he succeeded Earl Thomas in November 1614. In addition, however, having witnessed the strength of Walter's local Catholic following in the house of commons, the government was determined to proceed with the disempowerment of the recusant gentry that formed the core of the Ormond Butler clientele. The protestantisation of the local administration was set to continue in much the same way as before, with one exception: henceforth it would run parallel with a direct assault on the Ormond inheritance.

REPRESSION AND DISPOSSESSION

For four years prior to the fateful royal award of October 1618 that divided the Ormond estate, crown policy towards Co. Kilkenny was persistently confrontational. The county sessions house in Kilkenny city was again the main focus of events, with the justices of assize and the sheriffs of the shire acting as the chief agents of government disapproval; however, increasingly important was the court of castle chamber in Dublin, an equity court where members of the privy council and the Irish bench enjoyed prerogative powers to deal with religious and 'political' offences as they saw fit.[51] Thus, for instance, at the county assize in August 1615, on the orders of Justices Sir William Methwold and Peter

---

50 Objections were made, and the fines imposed on the five were later 'discharged' by special order of the Irish privy council (NA, Ferguson MSS, Abstracts of Revenue Exchequer Orders, 1592–1657, 200–1). See also McCavitt, 'Good planets', 277; Lockyer, *The early Stuarts*, ch. 3, ch. 7. **51** Pawlisch, *Sir John Davies*, 38, 47, 109.

Palmer, a jury of 14 gentlemen and artisans of the city was asked 'to present recusants', that is, to bring to trial those of their fellow citizens who were accused of practicing the Catholic religion, contrary to the laws of the realm. Without exception, they refused to present, after which a warrant was issued to the sheriff (the local Protestant, Thomas Daniel) for their appearance in castle chamber in November following. There, in accordance with the usual practice of the court, they were fined and imprisoned for an indeterminate period, 'during the lord deputy's pleasure'.[52]

The use of castle chamber against Catholicism greatly unsettled the local order. In Kilkenny city the citizens were compelled to elect five mayors in less than six months during 1616, as Lucas Shee (5 April), John Rothe fitz Piers (28 June), David Rothe (12 July) and Clement Ragget (21 August) were each made to resign the mayoralty after refusing to take the oath of supremacy when required by government commissioners. The resignations only ended when the corporation elected a Protestant, the recently knighted Sir Cyprian Horsfall, as mayor.[53] Enforcement of the oath caused similar disruption in other towns. In Gowran William Nash was removed as sovereign, as was Patrick Dobbin in Thomastown, while in Inistioge first James Dulan, then James Archdekin, was ousted as portreeve, and in Irishtown Portreeve William Shee, 'fearing he might be put to the oath, did make suit to the lord bishop [of Ossory] and the burgesses to dismiss him of that office, to what end God He knoweth'.[54] After dismissal came trial and punishment. John Rothe fitz Piers was fined the most (either £50 or £66 13s. 4d.)[55] on his appearance in castle chamber, but evaded imprisonment; in contrast, Dobbin, Nash, Dulan, Archdekin and Lucas Shee were all jailed as well as fined.[56]

At the king's suggestion Kilkenny city was singled out for special treatment in Ireland while Earl Walter was in London to attend upon the first commission of inquiry into his case.[57] In July 1616 Lord Deputy St John and the Irish privy council received instructions from Whitehall regarding 'his majesty's pleasure' that they proceed with 'some severer course of justice' towards such Irish towns and cities that, through 'perverseness', carried on electing Catholic magistrates. Having found that 'neither admonition nor moderate correction doth work the ends which he aimeth at', King James now wished to instigate a policy first mooted by Chichester in 1614, namely, the 'overthrow' of the urban charters 'of one or two principal cities', beginning with Kilkenny and Limerick.[58] Subsequently, of course, the king changed his mind about where best to introduce the new policy, switching his attention to the city of Waterford, which lost its charter in 1618, but even so Kilkenny's city status remained under threat

52 HMC, *Egmont MSS*, i, 44. **53** NLI, Ms 2531: 100–1. **54** Notes of cases in 'Star Chamber', 1616 (Birr Castle, Earl of Rosse MSS); HMC, *Egmont MSS*, i, 49; Ainsworth (ed.), 'Irishtown Corporation Bk', 67. **55** The two sources for his trial give different figures for the fine he received (BL, Sloane Ms 3827, fol. 21v; HMC, *Egmont MSS*, i, 47). **56** Ibid., 45; Notes of cases, 1616 (Birr Castle, Earl of Rosse MSS). **57** *Cal. SP, Dom, 1611–18*, 361; HMC, *Rutland MSS*, iv, 511; NLI, Ms 11,046 (10), (15), (18–19). **58** *APC, 1615–16*, 689–90.

for a year or more.[59] Indeed, as a result of another spat with the assize commissioners in 1617, and another castle chamber trial, several city jurors served unusually long prison sentences in Dublin, and one of their number, John Troy, seems actually to have died in prison.[60]

The rural gentry, from whom Earl Walter derived so much of his power, were also subjected to punishment. At castle chamber in November 1616 sentence was passed on ten members of the county grand jury, several of them Ormond clients, including the head of the O'Ryans, Pierce MacEdmund of Stakally. Six of the jurors received fines of £10 apiece, with the remaining four getting £20 fines and imprisonment at the lord deputy's pleasure.[61] An interesting coincidence is that, just a few months before King James' long-awaited arbitration of the Ormond inheritance case, the scale of fines imposed by castle chamber on recusant gentry from the Ormond country increased dramatically. Thus in May 1618 young William Sweetman of Castle Eve (head of one of the most prominent Ormond client families), his uncle William Sweetman of Kilcross, and William Drilling of Kilbraghan, were brought to castle chamber for refusing to present recusants at the recent assizes. They were each fined the enormous sum of £100, imprisoned, and required to 'acknowledge their offence in writing'.[62] The fines threatened to cripple them. Even Sweetman of Castle Eve, the richest of the three, would have struggled to raise £100, having been a ward of the crown for nearly eleven years before 1616, and his estate was burdened with debt.[63] Increased financial difficulties after 1618 may explain why he disappears from local records for the rest of his life.[64] As for Drilling, it is recorded in a government account that to avoid paying his fine he conformed, and took the oath of supremacy.[65]

For the gentry the threat of fines and imprisonment for jury service was accompanied by growing dread of the land policies of the crown. It was disconcerting enough that the government had allowed Lady Elizabeth Butler and her well-connected Scottish husband to continue to advance their claim to the Ormond estate, irrespective of the Ormond entail and Earl Walter's legal rights – a decision that clearly jeopardised the future of all those lucrative tenancies of Ormond land enjoyed by many local families. Far harder to bear was the emerging threat to the gentry's own lands. Throughout the 1610s, besides the vari-

---

59 Ibid., *1616–1617*, 91–2. For events in Waterford, see esp. N.J. Byrne, 'Jacobean Waterford: religion and politics, 1603–1625', PhD thesis, University College, Cork (2001), ch.6. 60 HMC, *Egmont MSS*, i, 51. Troy was described as *mortusi* in William Marwood's account of castle chamber fines of Feb. 1623 (BL, Sloane Ms 3827, fol. 21v). 61 HMC, *Egmont MSS*, i, 48. Pierce O'Ryan was related to Earl Walter through the marriage of his kinsman Donal O'Ryan to Elinor Shortal of Clara, the earl's niece (Carrigan, *Ossory*, iii, 358). Other Ormond clients included Edmund Dobbin of Lisnetane and Thomas Purcell of Garryduff (*COD*, v, no. 89; NLI, D 3826; Healy, *History*, 178). 62 HMC, *Egmont MSS*, I, 55. 63 NLI, D 3376. I hope to publish a brief study of the Sweetman estate in a future article. 64 All that is known of his later years is that his estate shrank to 1,200 acres by 1641 and he was transplanted to Connaught in 1653. 65 BL, Sloane Ms 3827, fol. 21v. Consequently, his fine was reduced to a mere 20 shillings (NA, Ferguson MSS, Equity Exchequer Orders, 1618–38, 11).

ous plantations that were proceeding in predominantly Gaelic regions of Ireland (Ulster, north Wexford, Ely O'Carroll, etc.), the landowning arrangements in Anglo-Irish parts of the country were turned topsy-turvy by government agents holding warrants authorising the discovery and disposal of land the title to which was deemed 'defective' at English law.[66] Hitherto Co. Kilkenny had remained one of the few places in Ireland where property could pass from one relative to another without serious risk of official interference. Now, suddenly, it seemed that nothing could protect either the Anglo-Irish or Gaelic gentry of the shire from the threat of dispossession. Many Kilkenny families had imperfect title to their estates, most obviously those inhabiting the former marchlands in the north and east, where Gaelic and English inheritance practices had long intermingled.[67] Equally unsettling, however, shortcomings in the government apparatus as it had existed before the early seventeenth century meant that the majority of landowners in other parts of the county were also vulnerable to dispossession. In particular landowners who held their lands *in capite* by knight's service suddenly faced forfeiture on the technicality that they had not sued for livery or honoured other crown entitlements (especially wardships, and homage and alienation fines) for generations, although really it had not been possible for them to do so, given the absence of crown feodaries before 1616 and a properly designated court of wards and liveries before 1622.[68]

To their great alarm the gentry discovered that, contrary to conditions that had applied as recently as 1611,[69] willingness to have defective title remedied by process of surrender and re-grant no longer offset the threat of dispossession. In February 1618, in order to secure proper English title through a re-grant, Michael Cowley surrendered his estate at Radestown to the government, but it was not in fact returned to him. Instead four months later the property was granted to Sir Henry Holcroft, an entrepreneurial crown official holding as his passport to riches an interest in a warrant for 'concealed lands' granted to Thomas, Lord Kerry, in 1616. Under cover of the same warrant Holcroft also managed to lay hold of estates belonging to the Graces at Ballylinch, the Purcells at Purcellsrath, and the Walshes at Clonmore, that had not been surrendered, but rather had been identified as 'concealed' by a crown informer – almost certainly someone with privileged access to central administrative and legal records who was able to discover that these families had failed to sue for livery or pay outstanding alienations fines that had fallen due sometime during the previous sixty or seventy years.[70] Fortunately for the dispossessed, Holcroft was more

66 Treadwell, *Buckingham*, ch. 3, esp. 130–5. **67** Chapter 1 above. **68** V. Treadwell, 'The Irish court of wards under James I', *IHS* 12/45 (March 1960), 1–27. Fines for homage appear to have been vigorously pursued from Michaelmas 1611: NA, Ferguson MSS, Revenue Exchequer Orders, 1592–1657, 143, 160, 173, 175–6. **69** In May 1611 Richard Archdekin of Ballybawnmore had completed a successful surrender and re-grant of his entire Co. Kilkenny estate (NA, Lodge MSS, Rolls, III, 72–3; Erck (ed.), *Reportory*, 145, 201; M. O'Dowd, 'Irish concealed lands papers', *Anal. Hib.* 31 (1984), 88, 91). **70** NA, Lodge MSS, Rolls, IV, 139–40, 462–4. For Holcroft, see Treadwell, *Buckingham*, 49, 131; see also O'Dowd, 'Irish concealed lands papers', 69–173.

interested in making easy money than estate building: the Cowleys, Graces, Purcells and Walshes all managed to regain their lands from him on payment of some unrecorded fee.[71]

It fell to the O'Brennans of Idough to suffer the largest single land seizure to occur in the county before the division and sequestration of the Ormond estate in 1618. In September 1611, in fulfilment of the Carew Commission of that year, senior members of the Irish government had recommended that the O'Brennans' homeland be considered for plantation, on the grounds that the old Gaelic family had no proper title to the territory, which in medieval times had pertained to the dukes of Norfolk, but now belonged to the crown as a result of the Act of Absentees of 1536.[72] In an attempt to avoid colonisation the leaders of the old Gaelic lineage had turned to the tenth earl, Thomas, for protection. Signing an agreement with him, they engaged to surrender their land to the crown provided it would be re-granted to them and their heirs, to be held forever of the house of Ormond after the English fashion of tenure, in free and common socage at a rent of 6s. 8d. per townland per annum.[73] Nothing came of this proposal – it is not clear why – and Idough remained in the crown's gift. Eventually, sometime after the tenth earl's death in November 1614, a government clerk named Francis Edgeworth[74] again identified the area as available for forfeiture. Like Holcroft, Edgeworth was an official on the make, being the Dublin agent of Sir John Eyres, a gentleman of the king's privy chamber, who had received a license from the king for £100 worth of crown land in Ireland. On 3 November 1615 Edgeworth entered into a tripartite indenture with Walter Archer fitz Walter of Kilkenny and Chichester's former secretary, Sir Henry Pierce, promising to convey Idough to them as soon as it had been formally seized.[75] The forfeiture took place two years later, in August 1617, when the entire territory was granted to Edgeworth as Eyres' assignee;[76] immediately, as agreed, he sold a two-thirds interest to Archer, and a third to Pierce.[77] Formal dispossession was delayed until a few years later, when a protest led by Donogh McFirr O'Brennan and his son Teige was overcome by the Protestant sheriff, John Butler fitz John, who imprisoned them in the county jail.[78] All resistance ceased in 1622 when another member of the lineage, Melaghlin O'Brennan, was publicly executed for felony.[79]

In this fashion, under a rising tide of forfeitures, fines and jail sentences, the local community was softened up prior to the royal division of the Ormond

---

71 In 1622 the clerk of the pells noted that John Bowen of Ballyadams, Queen's County, held Ballylinch as Holcroft's assignee (John Ryland's Library, Ms 246, fol. 34v), but given that Bowen was a kinsman of the Graces, and his father had acted as a trustee for the family, it is likely that he received the estate from Holcroft on their behalf. In a separate forfeiture the Ballylinch Graces also lost Moorhouse, which was granted to Edward Southworth, but they had regained it by 1622 through Southworth's assignation (ibid., fol. 8r). **72** *Cal. Carew MSS, 1603–24*, 105. **73** Graves, 'Ancient tribes', 239–40. **74** He was neither a knight nor a privy councillor, as has been claimed (Nolan, *Fassadinin*, 33). **75** Deed of sale, 6 Dec. 1622 (NLI, Prior-Wandesford MSS, Irish material). **76** NA, Lodge MSS, Rolls, III, 472–3. **77** As Note 75 above. **78** NA, Ferguson MSS, Abstracts of Exchequer Orders, 1592–1657, 281. **79** Ibid., 302.

estate in October 1618. Other seizures of property were authorised, most notably of the lands of the Butlers of Paulstown, granted to Lawrence, Lord Esmond, after a dormant act of attainder that had been passed against a member of the family decades earlier, and not acted upon, was discovered.[80] On payment of an undisclosed sum Esmond immediately conveyed the estate back to the current head of the Paulstown line, Edmund Butler. At least this forfeiture was done regularly, in accordance with usual practice, and for all that it reeked of official opportunism, it helped the Butlers to overcome a serious obstacle to their title to Paulstown. Far more worrying was the treatment of the Butlers of Annagh, who had their lands declared for the crown because of the unscrupulous conduct of Nicholas Kenny, the feodary of Leinster. On the death of the head of the family he held an inquisition into their estate in such haste that the widow and children 'had not their evidences in hand to present before the jury'. Their subsequent complaints against Kenny went unheeded in the exchequer, and for some time afterwards the family struggled to raise the funds necessary to re-secure possession.[81] Also curbed was the ideological leadership hitherto provided by senior Catholic clergy. The vicar apostolic, Dr David Rothe, and other clerics were driven into hiding after 1616 following the apprehension and imprisonment of a regular priest sometime that year,[82] and some, including Rothe, went into temporary exile abroad.[83] Finally, around October 1618, right on the eve of the royal award in the Ormond inheritance case, Lord Deputy St John named the Essexman Henry Staines as the new sheriff of Co. Kilkenny. It was hardly a neutral choice. The senior servant in Ireland of Lady Elizabeth Butler and her Scottish husband, Lord Dingwall, Staines was named to the shrievalty the better to facilitate the efforts of his master and mistress to lay hold of the Ormond lands.[84]

When the royal award against Earl Walter was announced it encountered little opposition in the Ormond territories. Yet the government expected trouble in Kilkenny and Tipperary all the same, and the movements of Earl Walter's son and heir, Thomas Butler, Viscount Thurles, were closely monitored. A few weeks after the award, Thurles convened an assembly of 'friends and followers' to decide on a response. Reports soon reached Dublin that the viscount was riding the length and breadth of the Ormond country 'accompanied with many gentlemen', that he had ordered the occupation and fortification of the earl's

---

80 Owing to the loss of local court records it is not possible to date this attainder, still less identify the cause, but the Elizabethan head of the Paulstowns was pardoned twice, in Sept. 1575 and Nov. 1576: *Ir. Fiants*, Eliz. I, nos. 2700, 2940.   81 NA, Ferguson MSS, Equity Exchequer Orders, 1604–18, 219, 240, 255; *CPRI James I*, 453–4.   82 The priest had been discovered disguised as a layman, but having 'the sacred vestments' in his possession (Moran, 'Bishops', 276–7).   83 W. O'Sullivan, 'The correspondence of David Rothe and James Ussher, 1619–23', *Collectanea Hibernica* 36–7 (1994–5), 7–8.   84 NA, Ferguson MSS, Revenue Echequer Orders, 1592–1657, 241. Staines had been present in the county barely a year, since Easter 1617: NLI, Ms 2506, ff 110v–111v. He was almost certainly responsible for procuring lodgings near the gates of Kilkenny Castle for those servants of Lord Dingwall whose presence caused Viscount Thurles such concern: *CSPI, 1615–25*, 237.

main castles and manor houses, and that he had issued an invitation to all the wandering 'idle people' and masterless men of the region to enlist as soldiers under his pay.[85] In London Earl Walter's appearance in star chamber on 11 November added to the crown's concern, as he refused to submit to the award.[86] By the middle of December the authorities were worried by the prospect of an imminent Butler revolt, and letters about local conditions were exchanged between the lord deputy, the English privy council, the archbishop of Canterbury, Secretary Blundell, and Sir John Everard, amongst others.[87] It was only in January 1619, when Thurles arrived unbidden in Dublin to talk with St John that the government accepted that a revolt was unlikely, at least in the short term.

It is possible from St John's account of his interview with Thurles to discern some of the main features of the Butlers' strategy at this time of profound family crisis. According to the deputy, Thurles declared that he had no intention of arming himself against the king and promised that he would be 'always ready to obey whatever his majesty should command'. However, he did not deny offering hospitality to strangers and idlemen who resorted to his houses, entertaining them according to 'the custom of the country', and he admitted that he had placed men in Kilkenny Castle in order to prevent the estate records that were kept there from falling into the possession of Lord Dingwall's servants. He also admitted requiring the tenants and custodians of various Ormond castles 'not to deliver the voluntary possession of those places' until ordered to do so by him. Thus, for all his promises of conformity, one thing seemed clear: Thurles might not resist the king, but he was certainly prepared to resist the beneficiaries of the king's award, Lord Dingwall and Lady Elizabeth Butler.[88]

St John and the Irish council accepted his assurances, but tightened its grip on Kilkenny and Tipperary as a precaution. In December St John despatched assize commissioners to Kilkenny with authority to deal severely with 'the malefactors which formerly did declare themselves in numbers' – a frustratingly vague form of words, referring either to the local recusant agitators of recent years, or else to the quasi-military followers of Viscount Thurles.[89] Whichever group was meant, the commissioners were confident Co. Kilkenny had been 'much pacified' by their proceedings. Sheriff Staines had been busy making arrests prior to their arrival in the city on 18 December, filling the shire jail. The following day the commissioners had decided to adjourn the jail delivery hearings until 15 January 1619, explaining in a subsequent letter to St John that this would work to 'the greater terror' of the families and sympathisers of the prisoners, who would be condemned to spend a full month (including the Christmas holidays) in the wretched little jail before learning their fate when the sessions resumed.[90] Though apparently stopping short of using martial law in Co. Kilkenny, the government was not so shy of its use in Co. Tipperary – Lord Thurles' main abode – where a special provost marshal, Francis Ackland, was confirmed in office, empowered

---

85 *CSPI, 1615–25*, 236. 86 *APC, 1618–19*, 301–2. 87 *CSPI, 1615–25*, 236. None of these letters seem to have survived. 88 Ibid., 236–7. 89 KCA, Ms CR/K 23a. 90 Ibid., CR/K 23b.

to hunt down and execute such 'idlemen' as were found wandering about the area.[91] A sense of how strong the government's grip had grown over the Ormond territories can be gathered from the movements of David Rothe, the Catholic churchman. Having been made bishop of Ossory while exiled in Paris in 1618, on his return home early in 1619 he left practically at once, joining the Franciscan mission to Scotland in order to evade capture in Kilkenny.[92] Likewise Rothe's protectors, Lord and Lady Mountgarret: in May 1619 they were followed to Chester by a government spy, and had one of their servants arrested and imprisoned on suspicion of being a priest in disguise.[93]

In July 1619 the local gentry were required formally to participate in the transfer of Ormond property to Dingwall and Lady Elizabeth Butler. On 11 June Earl Walter had been confined to the Fleet for continuing his objections to the king's award. A month later, on 6 July, a jury of twelve gentlemen-freeholders, headed by Edmund Butler of Paulstown, Roland Fitzgerald of Burnchurch and Richard Comerford of Ballybur, obeyed a summons to meet in Kilkenny to serve on an inquisition into the earl's Co. Kilkenny estate.[94] Having previously witnessed the government's treatment of uncooperative juries it is not surprising that they complied, especially as, at this stage, and despite his imprisonment, Ormond and his advisers still hoped to persuade the king to reconsider aspects of the award. Yet resistance was not entirely stamped out. Rather than defy the crown directly, some local gentry chose other methods to express their discontent, intimidating Dingwall's representatives. For instance, it is recorded that by late summer the local Protestant lawyer and crown agent, Walter Archer fitz Walter, was being boycotted, and that he feared for his safety in Kilkenny city. As well as colluding in the state's prosecution of recusants, Archer had played an important background role in the Ormond estate proceedings,[95] and it was reported to the English privy council that he had 'drawn upon himself the hatred of his countrymen and the heavy displeasure of his nearest kinsmen … to his great prejudice in his practice, the weakening of his estate and danger of his person'.[96]

It is interesting to observe that, in the face of continuing local unrest, the sequestration of the Ormond estate was pushed through during the shrievalty of a native Kilkennyman, and a Butler too, the Protestant John Butler fitz John, who was retained as sheriff of Co. Kilkenny for three years consecutively by Lord Deputy St John, from Easter 1619 until Michaelmas 1622. Late in 1619 or early the next year – the source is not precise – Sheriff Butler took Ormond's rent receiver, Thomas Comerford, into close custody, until the earl's arrears were paid into the exchequer.[97] The sudden death of Thomas, Lord Thurles, in October 1620 slowed proceedings somewhat,[98] but in August 1621 the ser-

91 McLaughlin, 'The making', 349. **92** O'Sullivan, 'Correspondence', 8. **93** Chester City RO, Ms M/L/6/138; *Cal. SP Dom., 1619–23*, 46, 76. **94** NLI, D 3633. **95** E.g., NLI, Ms 11,046 (25), Archer's abstract of the lands to be awarded to Dingwall; ibid., un-numbered item after (34), Archer's note of Dingwall's debts to various parties and how they might be satisfied. **96** *APC, 1619–21*, 26. **97** NA, Ferguson MSS, Revenue Exchequer Orders, 1592–1657, 246. **98** Thurles

vices of Sheriff Butler and his counterpart in Tipperary, the Englishman Robert Carew,[99] were called upon once more. Following a letter to the Irish executive by the king, a writ was issued for the arrest of Sir John Everard and Robert Rothe, Earl Walter's principal legal representatives, after they had refused to obey an order regarding the sequestration of the earl's estate and demanded a proper legal hearing to examine the basis for the government's action. Everard and Rothe were duly seized and placed 'in restraint'. Subsequently sent to London, they were held there for some time, obliged to ponder 'what it [was] to disobey a decree ... grounded upon [the king's] just award'.[100] Their removal ended Earl Walter's recourse to law, and made it possible for crown officials and the servants of the earl and countess of Desmond (as Dingwall and the Lady Elizabeth were now known) to begin collecting rents from the Ormond lands.[101]

It seemed that by 1622 the crown had Kilkenny under control. Following the Ormond sequestration, more than a third of all available land in the county was forfeited, the local overlord was in prison, as were several of his most important servants and advisers, and his eldest son and heir was dead. In fact, royal authority had grown all across the mid-south. In Tipperary the Ormond liberty was abolished, with the crown at last able to appoint all officials there, and (as in Co. Carlow) up to a quarter of the total shire territory was seized through the sequestration. Elsewhere, through separate initiatives, Waterford city remained unincorporated, reduced to 'the nature of [a] village, without power of government'; opponents of plantation in north Co. Wexford had been transported to Virginia; and in Upper Ossory the lordship of Earl Walter's allies, the MacGiollapadraigs, was assigned for a new plantation.[102]

It is hardly surprising, therefore, that instead of rebelling the Kilkenny community accepted the new order as best it could, anxious to avoid further punishment. Ever since 1618 the grand jury of the shire had been markedly less obstructive of the government's anti-recusancy drive, with the result that gentlemen such as Robert Walsh of Ballinacowley were successfully indicted for recusancy before the county court (probably in 1619), and subsequently tried and fined.[103] In the towns Protestants were now commonly elected to urban office. In Irishtown, for instance, Paul Johnson, John Lawless and John Barry occupied the position of sovereign after 1616 'because none could serve but a comfortable man',[104] and in Kilkenny city the mayoralty was filled successively by Sir Cyprian Horsfall (1620) and the unpopular Walter Archer fitz Walter (1621).[105] With the government so clearly in the ascendant, perhaps the time had come for a new beginning in crown/community relations?

had been actively involved in disputing the crown's rights to various parcels of Ormond land before his death (NLI, Ms 11,046 (35)), and important legal papers probably disappeared with him when he was drowned.   **99** Blake Butler, 'Sheriffs', 160.   **100** TCD, Ms 10,724 (30).   **101** NLI, Ms 11,046 (38–40, 42–4).   **102** Edwards, 'MacGiollapadraigs', 360–2; Byrne, 'Jacobean Waterford', ch. 7; Clarke & Dudley Edwards, 'Pacification', 219.   **103** Carrigan, 'Walsh Mountain history', *JWSEIAS* 16 (1913), 132.   **104** Ainsworth (ed.), 'Irishtown', 67.   **105** NLI, Ms 2531: 100–1.

THE NEGATION OF COMPROMISE, 1622–33

Owing to new developments in foreign policy and at the royal court the arrival of Henry Carey, Viscount Falkland, as the new lord deputy in September 1622 signalled a gradual shift in government behaviour in Ireland. The search for a continental bride for Prince Charles precipitated change, as marriage negotiations with the Catholic powers Spain and France forced the crown to review the expediency of the various anti-Catholic measures in force in England, Wales, Scotland and Ireland. At first a more relaxed attitude towards its Catholic subjects seemed advisable merely to advance the marriage talks, but when negotiations turned sour, leading to the outbreak of hostilities with both Spain and France, the monarchy was anxious to secure Catholic political and financial support for the war effort.[106]

It is important to realise that for the Kilkenny Catholic community this did not mean that the crown was willing to reverse its recent actions. Earl Walter would remain incarcerated for the foreseeable future, until he accepted the terms of the royal award of 1618; his teenage grandson and heir would continue in the care of the archbishop of Canterbury, to be reared as a Protestant; and the government would continue to favour Protestantism as the religion of power. Nevertheless, after years of repression, the Stewart monarchy was ready to offer an olive branch to those of the Kilkenny elite who were willing to pledge their loyalty to the crown and do its bidding.

The new direction of government thinking is indicated in an undated manuscript that most likely was written in the latter part of 1623 (shortly after the knighting of Edmund Blanchville of Blanchvillestown).[107] A list of the names of those who were under consideration for inclusion on a local government commission, it shows that the crown was hoping to temper Chichester and St John's policy of positive discrimination towards New English Protestants by reaching out to at least a few senior Catholic figures. Consequently, major Catholic landowners such as Richard Butler, third Viscount Mountgarret, Sir Oliver Shortal of Ballylorcaine, Sir Edward Butler of Duiske, and Sir Edmund Blanchville were 'thought fit' to serve on the commission alongside new Protestant establishment figures like Sir Cyprian Horsfall and Henry Mainwaring. But any movement towards greater Catholic inclusion was unlikely. According to the anonymous compiler of the list, no less than eleven leading local gentlemen were deemed 'unfit' for inclusion on the commission, either because of their prominent attachment to Ormond or their pronounced recusant disposition (Chart 5.2). It remained to be seen if their exclusion would help diminish local tension, or if a reputed Catholic moderate like Sir Oliver Shortal, appointed

---

106 A. Clarke, 'Selling royal favours, 1624–32', *NHI*, iii, 232–42; Lockyer, *Buckingham*, ch. 5–8; T. Cogswell, 'England and the Spanish match', in Cust & Hughes (ed.), *Conflict*, 107–30. 107 Sir Edmund Blanchville was knighted by Lord Deputy Falkland on 23 October 1623 (Carrigan, *Ossory*, iii, 415). The fact that the list includes Lucas Shee (d. 27 July 1622) suggests it cannot have been compiled much later than Blanchville's dubbing.

Chart 5.2 The government's choice of Co. Kilkenny commissioners, c.1623

Those thought fit for insertion in the commission	Those thought unfit
Richard, Viscount Mountgarret	Walter Walsh of Castlehowell
The Mayor of Kilkenny	Thomas Cantwell of Cantwellscourt
Sir Oliver Shortal of Ballylorcaine	Edmund Butler of Paulstown
Sir Edward Butler of Duiske	Patrick Den of Grenan
Sir Edmund Blanchville of Blanchvillestown	Roland Fitzgerald of Burnchurch
Sir Nicholas Walsh of Clonmore	Piers Butler of Callan
Henry Mainwaring of Kilkenny	Walter Lawless of Talbot's Inch
John Tobyn of Killaghy	Lucas Shee of Upper Court
Sir Cyprian Horsfall of Inishnag	David Rothe of Tullaghmaine
William Shee of Kilkenny	James Bryan of Bawnmore
Thomas Shortal of Rathardmore	Michael Cowley of Radestown

Source: TCD, Ms 672, fol. 362

sheriff in Michaelmas 1622, was willing to bend as much as the government wanted.

In order to fill the vacuum left by Ormond's imprisonment and the late Lord Thurles' death, the crown looked to Richard Preston, earl of Desmond, to step forward as the new overlord of Kilkenny. He seemed suited to the task: as a Scottish Protestant and a close confidant of both King James and the duke of Buckingham, his political and religious credentials were impeccable. Moreover, with Lady Elizabeth Butler as his countess, it was possible to make his grab for the Ormond estate seem more principled than it was. In particular, the case could be made that in attacking Earl Walter he had only been defending the rights of his wife, the daughter of the late great overlord, the Black Earl. It also helped that Desmond was not a Protestant zealot, and counted Catholics such as Lewis Bryan of Kilkenny among his servants.[108] Unhappily for both crown and community, however, Desmond was not willing to fulfil his obvious potential, and showed little interest in assuming the responsibilities of protection and representation performed by his wife's family for generations. A creature of the court, and a near bankrupt, his primary object was to extract money from the Ormond lands to subsidise his expensive lifestyle; little else mattered.

Extant evidence indicates that Desmond had a poor relationship with the people of Kilkenny. He never sought to soothe local grievances, allowing his aggressive seizure of Earl Walter's estate to make him the sworn enemy of everyone associated with the Ormond dynasty in the county. Indeed, rather than

108 NLI, Ms 8360; BL, Add Ms 11,033, fol. 37.

trying to mollify Ormondist sentiment, his attempt to promote Pierce Lennon, the impostor from Galway, to the Ormond title only galvanised local opinion against him and his patron, Buckingham.[109] The wrath of the Butlers presented him with an almost insurmountable obstacle in the years ahead. Even with full crown support, it was not until the early-to-mid 1620s that he was able at last to overcome their obstruction and take control of all the Ormond lands. Late in 1623 he had two of the new ringleaders of the local Ormondist resistance, Walter Lawless of Talbot's Inch, and James Bryan of Bawnmore, imprisoned in the Marshalsea in Dublin without trial, the better to get at the tenants and lay hold of the rents.[110] It was probably also because of his influence that both men had been excluded from the aforementioned government commission, described as 'unfit' for inclusion (Chart 5.2).

With the Ormond country still restless, on 7 July 1624 Desmond was appointed governor of Kilkenny and Carlow with command of a company of foot and 'power of life and death ... according to the martial law', in the process becoming the only Scottish official in early Stewart Ireland permitted to use martial law against civilians.[111] Yet still the friends of Ormond managed to frustrate him. Rents due in May 1624 were only partly collected by August, when Desmond returned to court;[112] the following year rents supposed to be paid to Desmond's receivers were instead taken up by William Cantwell, an Ormond client who had to be sued for restitution in the exchequer.[113] An interested English observer later reckoned that the threat of Desmond's military retainers probably improved the collection of his rents, but only by oppressing the tenants, who were 'much troubled' and would 'all turn from him' at the first opportunity. The same commentator also noted that the people of Co. Kilkenny, while retaining some affection for Desmond's countess, Elizabeth Butler, were 'for the most part obstinate' towards Desmond himself and would do him no honour.[114]

Desmond was not the only cause of local resentment. No sooner had the crown begun toying with the idea of relaxing anti-Catholic policy than Protestant officials in Ireland had responded by pointing to the dangers of leniency. On his arrival in Dublin in 1622, Lord Deputy Falkland had had to sit through a sermon by Archbishop Ussher urging the unrestricted enforcement of 'those laws that were made for the furtherance of God's service', that is, the anti-Catholic laws. As Alan Ford has shown, events in Kilkenny city had provided the catalyst for Ussher's demand, the archbishop having learned that

109 Chapter 2 above.   **110** NLI, Ms 11,046 (50). Nearly £300 of the rents due to Desmond and his assignees at Easter 1623 were still in the tenants' hands the following Michaelmas, with an even larger sum retained on Earl Walter's behalf by Lawless, Bryan and Pierce Butler of Lismalin, Co. Tipperary: Esmond to Cranfield, 12 Sept. 1623 (Kent AO, Cranfield Irish Papers).   **111** *CPRI, James I*, p.574; see also D. Edwards, 'Scottish officials and secular government in early Stewart Ireland', in J. Young (ed.), *Scotland & Ulster, 1585–1750* (forthcoming).   **112** Desmond to de Renzi, 6 Aug. 1624; Lady Desmond to same, 7 Aug. 1624 (Kent AO, Cranfield Irish Papers).   **113** NA, Ferguson MSS, Equity Exchequer orders, 1618–38, 45–6.   **114** Dongan to Middlesex, 30 Jan. and 31 Jan. 1627 (Kent AO, Cranfield Irish Papers).

a Protestant minister there had been denied entry to his church while a Catholic priest held mass.[115] Subsequently the refusal of Sir Oliver Shortal, the supposedly pliable sheriff, to collect a recusancy fine imposed at the county sessions on Walter Walsh of Castlehowell added to the Protestant clamour for 'proper' severity.[116] The Dublin administration was compelled to revert to the earlier policy of penalisation. Hope of compromise faded in 1624 when the local community began to doubt the good faith of the lord deputy. It is well known that in February that year Falkland had received orders from Whitehall expressly ordering him to suspend the operation of anti-recusant measures; less familiar is the fact that he failed to apply the suspension fully to Co. Kilkenny, where partly because of the ongoing Ormond troubles, but also because of the recent return of the Catholic bishop and papal vice-primate, David Rothe, the deputy was convinced special circumstances existed for pursuing a tougher line. Apparently aware of the inter-provincial synod held by Rothe at Kilkenny, the government placed the movement of priests under close surveillance. William O'Shee, a local friar travelling dressed as a layman, but carrying a cache of letters about Catholic church affairs, was arrested at Birr in King's County in October 1624 and sent to Falkland in Dublin Castle, where he was jailed and interrogated.[117] Somewhat ironically, the Kilkenny synod had approved the need for clergy to behave in such a way as to ease Protestant suspicion, requiring priests to avoid involvement in confrontation or subversion.[118]

Falkland's actions were largely a reaction to the crown's worsening relations with Spain. When recommending, as a security measure, that Viscount Mountgarret be summoned to London in April 1624, he identified the Butler lord as a pro-Spanish agent of major standing in southern Ireland who had been formerly married to an O'Neill and participated in Tyrone's rebellion in his youth.[119] The fact that the viscount had long since severed his O'Neill ties and in more recent years had twice remarried, on both occasions to prominent English heiresses, was disregarded. Also overlooked was his association with the Howards at court, and his attempt to mediate in the parliamentary troubles in 1613–15.[120] When circumstances required, Falkland was as unforgiving of the king's Catholic subjects as his predecessors. Having Mountgarret removed to England allowed him to strike the viscount's name from the Kilkenny local government commission and so consolidate the Protestant grip on power in the shire. In furtherance of this policy, in Kilkenny city Walter Archer fitz Walter was reinstalled as mayor (replacing Thomas Shee, a Catholic).[121]

Fresh hopes for an accommodation between the crown and the county community following the accession of Charles I in 1625 fared no better. Although

---

115 A. Ford, 'James Ussher and the Godly Prince in early seventeenth-century Ireland', in Morgan (ed.), *Political ideology*, 216–7. 116 St Peter's College, Wexford, Hore MSS, Vol. 71: Exchequer Memoranda Rolls, 1614–66: 64; BL, Sloane Ms 3827, fol. 21v. 117 BL, Add Ms 11,033, ff 32–7. 118 A. Forrestall, *Catholic synods in Ireland, 1600–1690* (Dublin 1998), 45. 119 *CSPI, 1615–25*, 478. 120 E.g., BL, Stowe Ms 755, fol. 1; *Cal. SP Dom, James I, 1611–18*, 519. 121 NLI, Ms 2531: 100–1.

the new king promised to consider a reduction of Irish Catholic grievances in return for a grant of money towards the cost of war with France, the only substantial reform to materialise was the replacement of the oath of supremacy with an oath of allegiance, and the Catholic population was left feeling tricked and betrayed after raising huge sums for the war.[122] The Kilkenny population had more reason to feel wronged than most. In an expression of enthusiasm for the war and the opportunity it afforded for a demonstration of loyalty, a large detachment of military volunteers was raised in the county and the surrounding area, recruited by Mountgarret's brother, Captain John Butler, and Earl Walter's near kinsman, Captain Oliver Shortal of Clara. Marched to the southern coast to await shipping, the volunteers embarked with their commander-in-chief, Colonel Sir Piers Crosby, on the invasion of the Isle of Ré (near La Rochelle), and earned great praise for their bravery when the royal army had to withdraw.[123] Local optimism that such loyal service would produce major improvements in domestic political conditions proved ill-founded. Although the volunteers' participation in the expedition suggested that the crown was willing to allow loyal Catholics the right to bear arms in state service, the government never confirmed that this was so, and when the war ended those who had served were swiftly decommissioned, the crown having no further use for them. In the case of John Butler, far from securing a place on the military establishment, he and his followers had to leave Ireland on their return from Ré, and spent much of the next ten years fighting for Catholic rulers in Europe.[124]

One of the biggest grievances brought to the king's attention in the negotiations of 1626–8 was the behaviour of the regular crown forces around the country, with soldiers and their captains frequently accused of flouting the law, committing acts of intimidation, racketeering and theft. In Co. Kilkenny people had been complaining about royal troops since 1624,[125] when Desmond, as military governor, had quartered a company of foot on the shire. Besides wondering why, in a time of peace, the company was necessary (other than to serve as an occupying force on Desmond's behalf), the local community objected to having to pay the soldiers' expenses, known as 'entertainment money', while its commander, Desmond, was usually absent, living either in London or at Donington House in Berkshire.[126] The longer the entertainment money had remained unpaid the troops had become increasingly violent, taking free quarter wherever they could, but the government's solution – the return of Desmond – was counter-productive. In 1628, at the earl's direct order, the troops kidnapped the commander of the Kilkenny civic watch, John Seix, and brought him, struggling, to the dungeons of Kilkenny Castle for some special treatment

122 A. Clarke, *The Graces, 1625–41* (Dublin 1966). **123** Lambeth Ms 250, ff 431v, 433r; Sheffield City Library, WWM Str. P. 24–25/253; NA, CP H/150; G. Bennett, *The history of Bandon* (Cork 1869), 76; A. Clarke, 'Wentworth's "tawney ribbon": Sir Piers Crosby, 1590–1646', *IHS* 26/102 (Nov. 1988), 152–3. **124** *APC, 1628–9*, 303; Dunboyne, 'Carve's Butler families'. **125** E.g., Ainsworth (ed.), 'Irishtown corporation bk.', 75. **126** Desmond's petition, 12 July 1628 (NLI, Ms 11,062); for his Donington House residence, see ibid., Ms 2552, ff 1r–3r.

for having earlier arrested and jailed one of their colleagues. 'About eleven o'clock at night', they deposited Seix 'prostrate upon the street' in front of the mayor's house, before discharging 'two great volleys of shot … to the great terror of His Majesty's subjects'. It was said that for some time afterwards Kilkenny's civic officials were wary of doing their duty 'for fear [of being] imprisoned and questioned at his honour [Desmond]'s will'.[127] Unease at the troops' presence was also expressed in Callan, Thomastown, Gowran, and Inistioge, but Falkland swept the reservations aside.[128] The local royal garrison continued to fester as a grievance for several years more.

The long awaited return to the shire of Walter, eleventh earl of Ormond, in July 1628,[129] should have heralded a significant improvement in crown/community relations. Since the accession of Charles I in 1625 the earl's circumstances had gradually improved, with the new king seemingly embarrassed by some of Desmond's actions (especially the attempted imposture of 1624) and ready to make amends to Ormond provided the earl confirmed his willingness to accept the terms of the royal award of 1618, which he did. Accordingly, in addition to setting Earl Walter at liberty and consenting to the earl's request to have the activities of the court of wards and liveries temporarily suspended in Co. Tipperary,[130] King Charles had encouraged Ormond to re-enter politics. There were sound reasons for doing so: Charles and his advisers realised that the government's chances of securing Irish Catholic aid in the war against France would be greatly boosted through Ormond's influence. In all probability, the levy of troops raised in Kilkenny and Tipperary for the Isle of Ré expedition in 1627 was a direct consequence of Earl Walter's rehabilitation, for according to a memorandum in the state papers the commander of the expedition, Buckingham, was advised to call upon Ormond as well as the earl of Cork for the provision of his Irish military support.[131] However, following Buckingham's assassination in August 1628 the heart went out of the French war, and the king decided to withdraw from his engagement with Irish affairs, leaving Ormond and other Catholic leaders high and dry.

Earl Walter was unable to regain his former hold over Co. Kilkenny and his other lands. On first returning home he was shocked to find that he, the earl, could no longer bend local officials to his will, with all executive power in the area now concentrated in the hands of a small Protestant clique. As the earl of Middlesex's man, Thomas Dongan, put it, on his arrival in the shire Ormond

127 HMC, *Ormonde MSS, 1572–1660*, 17–18.   **128** KCA Ms CR/K 29–31.   **129** He travelled to Ireland shortly after 22 July 1628, having appeared before the English council (*APC, 1628–9*, 49). **130** The withdrawal of the court was intended merely to allow Walter enough time to produce a number of documents defending his rights over various lands in the county, a fact that is misconstrued by A. McClintock ('The earls of Ormond and Tipperary's role in the governing of Ireland, 1603–41', *Tipperary Historical Jn.* 1 (1988), 165), who incorrectly assumes that the court of wards was permanently suspended. The king's reasons for a short-term suspension are given in Northants RO, Ormonde (Kilkenny) Papers, Ms OK 437.   **131** *CSPI, 1647–60 & Addenda Charles I*, 107.

'discovered … his greatness and power … [was] foiled'.[132] His subsequent efforts to reverse this trend enjoyed some success during the years 1630–1, a period when the crown proved eager to grant him concessions in the belief that, with just a little stroking, he would cooperate with the planned plantation of north Tipperary. Hence the Co. Kilkenny shrievalty was granted to two leading pro-Ormond recusants, John Tobyn of Killaghy and Walter Walsh of Castlehowell, a significant concession,[133] and in August 1629, as a personal honour, he and his grandson James, Lord Thurles, were admitted to Gray's Inn.[134] But as soon as he indicated that he found the projected plantation scheme repugnant, and would not go along with it,[135] all concessions ceased. In 1632 the Kilkenny shrievalty reverted to Protestant control; in Tipperary Earl Walter's request for a re-grant of the Ormond liberty was ignored, and for the final months of his life the earl was confronted by fresh legal problems relating to his estate.[136]

With the appointment of Richard Boyle, earl of Cork, and Adam Loftus, Viscount Ely, as co-governors (or lords justices) of Ireland on the departure of Viscount Falkland in 1629, political conditions in Co. Kilkenny had slowly reverted to their pre-1622 state. Once again priests were banished by proclamation, and anti-recusancy laws were implemented by a central administration that was inclined to equate Catholicism with subversion. In Kilkenny city and elsewhere across the county a number of chapels and 'mass houses' were closed, and their contents confiscated.[137] In a related initiative the recusant gentleman George St Leger was summoned to appear in the exchequer to explain why his family had failed to pay for necessary repairs to the Church of Ireland parish church at Tullaghanbroge,[138] but it was over the organisation of funerals that local passions became most inflamed. New rules requiring gentry families to place the burial of their dead under the supervision of the heralds' office in Dublin caused many to fear that the government was intending to have Catholics buried as Protestants.[139] Those affected by the new regulations included the families of Sir Oliver Shortal (d. 1630) and Alderman Nicholas Langton (d. 1632), who resorted to elaborate arrangements to insure Catholic services for the deceased.[140] As so often before, the government's measures backfired. The chief beneficiaries of the funerals controversy were the local Catholic clergy, who greatly strengthened their position among the local gentry by providing a growing range of alternative methods of commemoration for families whose traditional burial places – major churches such as St Canice's Cathedral, St Mary's parish church in

132 Dongan to Middlesex, 21 Oct. 1628 (Kent AO, Sackville MSS, uncatalogued Irish papers). 133 See Appendix 3. 134 J. Foster (ed.), *The register of admissions to Gray's Inn, 1521–1889* (London 1889), 188. 135 Bod. Lib., Carte Ms 30, fol. 259; *CSPI, 1625–32*, 597. 136 Ibid., *1647–60 & Addenda Charles I*, 160; Grosart (ed.), *Lismore papers*, 1st series, iii, 30; see also Chapter 2. 137 P. Corish, 'Two seventeenth-century proclamations against the Catholic clergy', *Archiv. Hib.* 39 (1984), 54–5. 138 NA, Ferguson MSS, Equity Exchequer Orders, 1618–38, 162, 172. 139 E.g., A. Walsh, 'A memorial presented to the king of Spain on behalf of the Irish Catholics AD 1619', *Arch. Hib.* 6 (1917). See also C. Tait, 'Harnessing corpses: death, burial and commemoration in Ireland, *c.*1550–1655', PhD thesis, University College, Cork 1999, ch. 3. 140 Jennings (ed.),

Kilkenny, and St Mary's in Callan – were now controlled by the Protestant state. The fact that the heralds expected payment for interfering in local funerals was seen as especially provocative, and families such as the Blanchvilles and Shees registered their dissent by refusing to pay what was demanded.[141]

And so it was that when Earl Walter died in February 1633 his Protestant grandson and heir, James Butler, succeeded to a lordship where the forces of religious discord were increasingly sharply defined. Having spent several years as a royal ward in the household of the Calvinistic archbishop of Canterbury, George Abbott,[142] it was not long before the new earl became himself a major focus of tension.

IMPERFECT APOLLO

Recent historical research has transformed our understanding of James Butler, twelfth earl (and future duke) of Ormond.[143] Whereas once the earl was portrayed in an entirely positive light as a worthy hero who managed to keep his honour intact while steering his family through a prolonged period of political and financial crisis,[144] scholars no longer emphasise either his virtue or success to such a great extent. In place of 'the Cavalier Duke' of later seventeenth-century propaganda, James of Ormond is now seen as a more typical representative of the Stewart era, a pragmatic political operator who was no stranger to craft or dissimulation, and was often guilty of pursuing short-term advantage without a thought for its long-term implications. The following account of James' pre-1641 overlordship in Co. Kilkenny corroborates this more critical view of James's behaviour. Far from exhibiting concern for the traditional clients of his house, the local Catholic gentry, the twelfth earl elected to leave them to their fate in order the better to improve his standing in Dublin and London. In doing so he forfeited the respect and trust of many, with dire results for the state he served: when a Catholic uprising swept across the country in 1641 it was Kilkenny that emerged as its centre.

Wadding papers, 448–9; Prim, 'Family of Langton', 86. **141** GO, Ms 2, ff 11, 23. **142** Carte, *Ormond*, i, 7–9. **143** E.g., Edwards, 'The poisoned chalice', 55–82; P. Little, 'The marquess of Ormond and the English parliament, 1645–7', in Barnard & Fenlon, *The Dukes*, 83–99; É. Ó Ciardha, '"The unkinde deserter" and "The bright duke": contrasting views of the dukes of Ormonde in the Irish royalist tradition', in ibid., 177–93; M. Ó Siochrú, *Confederate Ireland, 1642–9: a constitutional and political analysis* (Dublin 1999), passim. The work of William Kelly deserves special mention: W. Kelly, 'The early career of James Butler, 12th earl and 1st duke of Ormond, 1610–43', PhD thesis, Cambridge University (1995), passim; '"Most illustrious cavalier" or "unkinde desertor"? James Butler, 1st duke of Ormond, 1610–88', *History Ireland*, 1/2 (Summer 1993), 18–22; 'James Butler, 12th earl of Ormond, the Irish government and the Bishops' Wars, 1638–40', in J.R. Young (ed.), *Celtic dimensions of the British civil wars* (Edinburgh 1997), 35–47; 'Ormond and Strafford', 88–102. **144** This line of interpretation began with Carte, *Ormond*, passim, and has featured in Lady Burghclere, *Life of James, first duke of Ormond* (2 vols., London 1912), and J.C. Beckett, *The cavalier duke: a life of James Butler, first duke of Ormond* (Belfast 1990).

The crux of the twelfth earl's problems as county overlord was his unwillingness to share his success outside the shire with the Catholic community
within it. The local landlords and merchants were left to look on from the side-
lines as he steadily went about developing his contacts in government. In particular, in 1633 he entered into a mutually beneficial relationship with Sir
Thomas Wentworth, the new lord deputy of Ireland.[145] Thanks mainly to
Wentworth's influence James attained high public office in Dublin with astonishing speed. In 1635, aged just 24, he was made an Irish privy councillor.[146]
Three years later, despite possessing no military training whatsoever, he was
appointed lieutenant general of the new royal army that Wentworth was busy
fashioning in Ireland, and became its acting supreme commander in 1640.[147] In
just a few years he had regained much of the ground lost by his predecessors.

This contrasted enormously with the experience of the Kilkenny gentry,
who continued to be excluded from office during the 1630s, and this although
the Protestant clique that had dominated local government since *c.*1609 had
begun to decline. In 1623 the only son and heir of Henry Mainwaring, Thomas,
had unexpectedly died at Trinity College, Dublin, so that when Henry too
passed away in 1634 no one inherited his position in local affairs.[148] Likewise,
Walter Archer fitz Walter had died in January 1626.[149] The local Protestant community was not big enough to replace either of these men, and when two more,
Edward Deane and Henry Staines, passed away in the late 1630s,[150] the state was
visibly short of Protestant officials.

If the recusants of the county expected the twelfth earl to draft them in to
fill the gap, they were soon disillusioned. Instead of nominating local Catholics
for office, Earl James cooperated with the Protestant monopoly of power. He
supported Lord Esmond's pre-eminence across the Barrow, especially as Esmond
had served his young wife, Countess Elizabeth, steadfastly,[151] and he counted
Sir Cyprian Horsfall as a close friend and adviser.[152] Likewise the earl's Scottish
relative Patrick Wemyss was appointed sheriff of Co. Kilkenny in 1632, and
with his help the Scot (who had only settled in the shire in 1629) retained the
shrievalty as virtually a private fiefdom for several years.[153] It should be noted
that Wemyss owed his promotion as much to the earl of Cork as to Ormond's
patronage. An ardent Protestant, he had earlier helped Cork to undermine the
moderate Lord Mountnorris, one of the late Earl Walter's few friends in government circles.[154] (Wemyss' links to Cork and the Irish Puritans would prove
helpful to Ormond in the 1640s.)

---

145 Carte, *Ormond*, v, 201. **146** *CSPI, 1633–47*, 93. **147** T.D. Whitaker (ed.), *The life & correspondence of Sir George Radcliffe* (London 1810), 248. **148** Lamacraft (ed.), *Ir. Funeral Entries*, 111.
149 NLI, Ms 2531, 100–1; *Inq. Lagenia*, Co. Kilkenny, Charles I (8). **150** Deane was dead by
August 1638 (Sheffield City Library, Wentworth Irish Deeds, WWM Add., brown parcel 2, bundle
3, no. 18); Staines died on 16 Jan. 1639: 'Note of Staines' funeral certificate', 8 May 1639 (St
Kieran's College, Kilkenny, Carrigan MSS, Vol. 21, un-paginated). **151** For Esmond and Ormond
see esp. the transcripts of Esmond's correspondence at NA, Accession 981; see also Sheffeld City
Library, Str. P. 14/190. **152** NLI, Ms 2486: 201. **153** See Appendix 3. **154** NA, M 2445: 128.

Religion quickly became central to James's relations with the shire community. An eager convert to Protestantism, he distanced himself from his Catholic parents and kinsmen and counted Protestants as his principal associates. As he said in later years: 'My father and my mother lived and died Papists, and bred their children so, and only I, by God's merciful providence, was educated in the true Protestant religion, from which I never swerved.'[155] His known disdain for the Catholic religion opened the door to political advancement. As his patron Wentworth told Archbishop Laud, Ormond was a model Protestant who, had he been left to the care of his grandfather Walter, would certainly have become 'as mere Irish and Papist as the best of them [that is, the Butler family]; whereas now he is a very good Protestant, and consequently will, I am confident, make not only a faithful, but a very affectionate servant to the crown of England'.[156]

Wentworth's faith in Ormond was well founded.[157] After 1633 James threw his full weight behind the Church of Ireland, becoming the most publicly committed Protestant among the native nobility. To counter advances recently made in the field of education by the local Catholic church, which had opened several schools in the shire, Ormond became the patron of a rival Protestant school that was established in Kilkenny city in 1634 under the guardianship of its headmaster, John Wyttar.[158] It seems to have been relatively successful, for it was still operating in 1641, by which time two more teachers named Hughes and Lemon (the latter a Scot), had been taken on.[159] The earl paid for the school out of his impropriated church livings.

It was Ormond's attitude to church property that first provoked local Catholic discontent towards him. A key objective of the Wentworth administration was its intention to enhance the power of the Church of Ireland by bringing about the restoration to the Protestant clergy of many of those church livings that had passed, or 'impropriated', into the hands of the laity during the sixteenth century. In Kilkenny Wentworth's resolve to follow this through would have been hardened by the knowledge that the county's recusants held a variety of church livings there on long leases. He and the church hierarchy were therefore delighted – and the Catholic gentry correspondingly concerned – when in December 1634 Ormond let it be known that he, alone of all the Anglo-Irish lords of the realm, was willing to bargain with the state over the future of the church revenues in his possession. His cooperation allowed the crown to pursue a policy that it hoped would weaken the economic might of Catholic landlords while bolstering the finances of the Church of Ireland.[160]

---

155 B.M. Mansfield, 'Elizabeth, Lady Thurles (1588–1673)', *Butler Soc. Jn.* 3/1 (1986–7), 42–4; R. Gillespie 'The religion of the first duke of Ormond', in Barnard & Fenlon (ed.), *The dukes*, 101–13. 156 Knowler (ed.), *Strafford letters*, i, 378. 157 Kelly, 'Ormond and Strafford', 89,while accepting the importance to Wentworth of the earl's religious conformity, casts doubt on Ormond's 'potential as a missionary'. 158 NLI, Ms 11,064 (7). Ormond negotiated the costs of the school with Bishop Jonas Wheeler (NA, Graves Papers, M. 594). 159 TCD, Ms 812, ff 202v, 213r. 160 SP 63/254/185.

Ormond's concession to the Protestant hierarchy came at a crucial moment in Wentworth's deputyship. Before summer 1634 many of the recusants had been willing to negotiate with Wentworth in the expectation that he would have such concessions as were discussed with the crown during the late 1620s passed as statute law in the upcoming Irish parliament. Profoundly as it proved for Ormond, the deputy was entirely insincere in the negotiations, only dangling the prospect of concessions before the Catholics' eyes in order to extract a large sum of money from them. Late in November, having achieved his goal – parliamentary subsidies amounting to £120,000 – he broke off talks, abruptly reversing the promises he had made earlier. For this Wentworth was 'esteemed no better than a mountebank' by the Catholics, who henceforth set themselves against him and his followers, the young earl of Ormond included.[161]

The earl's perceived involvement in Wentworth's duplicity immediately bore bitter fruit. From 1635 onwards Co. Kilkenny became increasingly difficult to manage. As soon as the government set about gathering in the parliamentary subsidy it encountered widespread obstruction, so much so that surviving sources indicate that the county was at the forefront of opposition to the charge in Leinster. The identity of some of the defaulters is instructive. At least five were Ormond tenants.[162] Of the rest, easily the most prominent was the 1634–5 MP Robert Grace of Courtstown. Fifty-five years old, Grace had twice represented the county in parliament, having earlier joined the late Earl Walter and Sir John Everard in the doomed defence of Catholic power in 1613. He had been remarkably quiet in the interval between the two parliaments. Perhaps feeling that there was nothing to be gained by conflict, he had quietly gone about building bridges with the Protestant establishment, becoming friendly with Sir Roger Jones, the Vice-President of Connaught, and negotiating an important local marriage alliance with the Horsfalls of Inishnag. Grace was clearly a moderate, and his re-election in 1634 should not have caused the government any concern. If his attitude towards Wentworth's subsidy is anything to go by, the depth of feeling against the levy must have been enormous.[163] Moreover, none of the others who defied the subsidy could be described as firebrands either. Patrick Purcell of Glanmagow and Edward Langton of Kilkenny had no previous record of political activity. The same was true of Charles Greene and Arthur Wright, two of a growing group of English Catholics who had come to Kilkenny in order to practice their faith in an environment where 'popery' was unexceptional.[164] Significantly, defaulting on the subsidy was the first step that Greene the Englishman and Purcell the Anglo-Irishman are known to have taken on the path that led them both to join the rebellion in 1641.[165]

161 Clarke, *Old English*, pp 75–89.   **162** NA, Ferguson MSS, Equity Exhequer Orders, 1618–38, 305, 308, 316, 343.   **163** *CSPI, 1633–47*, 64; Grace, *Memorials*, i, un-paginated genealogical table; NA, Lodge MSS, Rolls, Vol. V, 474–5; ibid., Wardships, Vol. I, 146.   **164** For another, Henry Norton of Westham in Sussex, who died at Freshford in 1637, see East Sussex RO, Ms SAU 1321. **165** TCD, Ms 812, ff 173r, 181r. As late as Feb. 1638 there were still many defaulters in Kilkenny city (KCA, Ms CR/K 40).

Mistakenly, Wentworth expected Earl James to suppress opposition in Kilkenny, and to control local society, just as his ancestors had done. To be fair to the deputy, Ormond never admitted that he was beginning to lose mastery of the area. Rather than lose face, the young earl tried to deceive his patron that all was as it should be in his ancestral territories. Hence, when Wentworth stopped at Kilkenny on his way to Munster in August 1637, Ormond made sure to avert his eyes from local troubles by organising a suitably convincing official welcome. Nothing was left to chance. Kilkenny corporation had to submit its plans for a civic reception to Ormond and Esmond for approval, and to discourage any spontaneous displays of disaffection Earl James brought a troop of his horse to the city, where they remained for much of the summer. He also persuaded the corporation to allow one of his men, Corporal Birch, an Englishman, to train 200 citizens in basic military drill so that they could be paraded before the deputy as loyal yeomanry. The whole event was stage-managed to resemble an English public reception, with Kilkenny not just meant to appear English, but Protestant too. The city's Church of Ireland congregation were encouraged to participate in the celebrations. The Protestant clergyman Peter Fitzgerald was hired to write special orations for the occasion, and James Kyvan, the vicar of Castlecomer, agreed to sing one of his own compositions. In the event Wentworth, usually so sceptical, was delighted by what he saw. It was his first time in Kilkenny, and though he returned for a second visit later that September, he did not stay long enough to form a more realistic impression of the place. For him Kilkenny seemed a safe haven for English culture, true religion and loyalty to the crown. As he told his wife in a letter penned at Kilkenny Castle, 'I have not seen anything so noble since my coming into this kingdom as is this place'.[166] Had he but stayed a little longer! The good behaviour shown throughout his sojourn was meaningless. Once he was gone, conditions returned to normal, with the citizens of Kilkenny embroiled in a row with the crown subsidy commissioners, while the city council argued heatedly with Ormond over the latter's abuse of his military authority.

Indeed, the controversy that raged over Ormond's use of soldiers became so intense that it transformed the deputy's visit into a public relations fiasco. During Wentworth's stay, the earl had expected the city to pay for housing and feeding his horsemen without any assistance from the other towns in the shire. Unfortunately for the deputy, it was not the first time Ormond had treated the city in this way. There had been trouble there over his use of royal soldiers as early as 1633,[167] and in 1636, when opposition to the subsidy had been at its peak, Ormond had sought Wentworth's permission to increase the Kilkenny garrison, plainly hoping that the threat of force would keep the city and the county quiet until things calmed down.[168] Unwisely, Wentworth had agreed to

---

166 P. Watters (ed.), 'Entries in the Kilkenny Corporation records regarding Wentworth's visit in 1637', *JRSAI*, 4th series, 6/2 (1884), 242–9; M. Phelan, 'Sir Thomas Wentworth's visit to Kilkenny, August 1637', *Butler Soc. Jn.* 2/2 (1982), 190–2. **167** KCA, Ms CR/K 35; see also Bod. Lib., Carte Ms 1, fol. 56. **168** Knowler (ed.), *Strafford letters*, ii, 15.

his request then; his tolerance now of the continued use of troops was equally imprudent. The question of the unlawful use of military force in Co. Kilkenny would later trouble the deputy; in the meantime the continuance of tension in the shire was guaranteed.[169]

Local disenchantment with the *status quo* was manifest. Almost every shire official encountered hostility. The sheriff, for instance, was no longer able to impose order as he had once done. By the beginning of 1637 his commands were flagrantly disregarded by gentry and husbandry alike. A little while earlier, on 1 December 1636, his bailiff had been refused admittance to Dunbill Castle by Walter Walsh, its proprietor; likewise his officers experienced difficulty retaining possession of cattle that they had seized in distraint from recalcitrant farmers who had refused to pay the fines demanded of them. On seven separate occasions between January and April 1637 the sheriff's bailiffs were waylaid by those whom they had just dispossessed, and the cattle that they had taken were retrieved.[170]

The subsidy commissioners had an equally hard time of it. At Ballycurran in 1637 the collector, William Croke, was beaten up by two of the inhabitants there, and the horse that he had seized towards the payment of the levy was taken off him. Another of the collectors was run aground at Nicholastown by its owner, irate that he should be forced to pay Wentworth's cursed subsidy. All around the shire, whether it was at Killary near Kilkenny city or Foulkscourt in the north-west, Catholic parishioners refused to maintain pen-folds designed to contain cattle seized from local defaulters by the authorities.

Religion, of course, played its part in the disturbances. When the petty constable of Freshford parish was jeered and insulted in 1637 by Philip Walsh, the fact that he served the Protestant bishop – the lord of Freshford manor – was probably not far from the mind of his detractor. The same considerations may have influenced John Duigin, a Catholic arrested for abusing and 'scandalising' the jury empanelled by the sheriff at Freshford 'for His Majesty's service'.[171] In the far south of the shire, at Whitechurch, Church of Ireland officials attached to the diocese of Lismore encountered widespread obstruction and evasion, and growing contempt for their authority,[172] while nearby another sign of religious tension was the failure of the parishioners of Rathkieran to keep their churchyard in a presentable state.[173] Incidents of explicitly sectarian conflict are recorded in the county, with English Protestants victimised in some areas. For instance, in the foothills near Clara, Edmund Cole and John Byrd were attacked 'in most rebellious manner' by Captain Oliver Shortal,[174] and in Callan the English-born Church of Ireland cleric, Francis Kettleby, was confronted by some of the leading Catholics of the town, who promised to deprive him of his tithes when they fell due.[175]

169 KCA, Ms CR/K 39, 41.   **170** At Raheen, Cruitt, Courtneboly, Killaghy, Burnchurch, Dirren and Garrinduff respectively (NLI, D 4052).   **171** Ibid.   **172** Court book of the archdeacon of Lismore, 1639, a stray manuscript from the Christ Church Cathedral Muniments, Waterford, that is currently in safe keeping at University College. Cork.   **173** NLI, D 4052.   **174** NA, M 2448: 12.   **175** Ibid.: 177. Two years earlier, in March 1636, four locals – James Blanchville, John Butler,

Yet, whatever the popular attitude to English-born Protestants, by the late 1630s the principal target of abuse was the twelfth earl of Ormond. Documents show that Earl James was unpopular in most parts of the county. After 1635, in response to a spate of evictions on his estate (discussed in Chapter 2 above) some of his tenants refused to obey his orders. His estate officials were ignored, insulted, even attacked, when going about his business. In 1637, for example, his principal rent collector, Nicholas Comerford, encountered violent opposition from the earl's sub-tenants at Ballyspellane, Foulkscourt and Comfilla, and when he rode to Aghtubbrid he was assaulted by two of its inhabitants, who, reportedly, beat him badly enough to draw blood.[176]

Two years later, in January 1640, another of Ormond's men – a soldier named Richard Shee – was subjected to similar treatment a little further afield, across the Barrow in New Ross, where the constable, bailiffs 'and a dozen more' of the town arrested him for defending himself when he was attacked by a local wine merchant. Shee soon attributed his experience to the fact that he worked for Ormond, later complaining to the earl that 'every one of them knew that I have been an old servant of your lordship'.[177] He had gone to the town on his master's business at a bad time. Since 1638 the twelfth earl had become a very unpopular figure with the New Ross merchants, attempting to reclaim his rights to the prisage charged on wine imports, a detrimental development for leading members of the town elite.[178] Moreover, by 1640 the earl had also commenced proceedings against important local families such as the Fitzharrises, Duffes and Comerfords for detaining certain properties in the town from him.[179] It is revealing that on the night that Richard Shee was jailed Earl James was in New Ross dealing with some of these matters. Indeed, when Shee threatened his aggressors that he would give their names to the earl, they jeered him, stating that in New Ross they did not care much for Ormond's authority. Shee's imprisonment was a deliberate slight to his master.[180]

By this time the balance of power within Co. Kilkenny and the mid-south had shifted away from Earl James and his Protestant associates in favour of his Catholic granduncle, Richard Butler, Viscount Mountgarret. In particular, events in the north-east of the shire, in Idough, had driven a wedge between the two noblemen, persuading the viscount to mount a direct challenge to the earl and his protector, Wentworth. Rarely mentioned in standard historical accounts of the period,[181] the Idough controversy was of major importance in Anglo-Irish politics. It placed Kilkenny and the Ormond lordship near the centre of events as the Stewart monarchy began to collapse and the spectre of religious civil war first loomed over Britain and Ireland.

John Bryan and Peter Walsh – were convicted and imprisoned for the manslaughter of an Englishman named James Swinnerton (*Cal. SP Dom., Charles I*, 1635–6, 330).   **176** NLI, D 4052.   **177** Shee to Ormond, 18 Jan. 1640 (ibid., Ms 2505, 17–18).   **178** Ibid., Ms 11,045 (31).   **179** Ibid., Ms 11,044 (103).   **180** As note 177 above.   **181** The principal previous account, Nolan, *Fassadinin*, 29–33, 53–6, gives a geographer's perspective, focusing on settlement rather than politics.

IDOUGH

Idough distilled into a single potent mixture several of those features of early Stewart government that most antagonised the Co. Kilkenny community – land-grabbing adventurism and corruption among crown officials; the arbitrary use of law, the courts and the royal prerogative; and the government's illegitimate, even illegal, use of force in a time of peace. The fact that occurrences in the territory involved what many saw as the arrant treachery of the local overlord, Ormond, only added to its potency.

Ormond's involvement in events was directly due to his late father-in-law, the Scottish earl of Desmond. It will be recalled that when Idough was granted to Sir John Eyres and Francis Edgeworth in 1617, the lands involved were immediately sold, in accordance with an earlier agreement, to Desmond's local agent, Walter Archer fitz Walter, and also to Sir Henry Pierce. Five years later, in December 1622, Archer had conveyed his two-thirds share of the area to Desmond;[182] it was this interest in Idough that passed to Ormond following his marriage in 1629 to Lady Elizabeth Preston, Desmond's daughter and heiress.[183]

Inheriting as he did the unpaid debts of three noblemen – Desmond, Earl Walter, and the long dead Viscount Tully – and having accumulated new debts of his own since succeeding to the Ormond title in 1633, there was little prospect of Earl James renewing the promise of protection once made to the O'Brennans by the Black Earl, Thomas, c.1611. From James's perspective Idough had nothing to offer other than its sale price. The slightest perusal of his family estate papers would have shown that, despite their repeated claims to overlordship, his ancestors had made hardly anything out of Idough during the previous hundred years, and the O'Brennans had never exactly been willing subjects of the earldom. The fact that the lineage had eventually embraced the authority of the Black Earl seemed singularly unimpressive, given that right up until the royal forfeiture of August 1617 they had failed to pay rent to either Earl Thomas or Earl Walter.[184] Yet Ormond's desire to sell his rights in Idough to the highest bidder was far from straightforward. Long before 1617 several client families of the house of Ormond had acquired a stake in the territory, most notably the Butlers, viscounts Mountgarret, and the Butlers of Castlecomer, and since then other lineages such as the Purcells, Shortals and Comerfords had seized on the O'Brennans' economic frailty to purchase lands in the area.[185] If Ormond was to

---

182 Deed of sale, 1622 (NLI, Prior-Wandesford MSS, Irish Material).   183 Ormond did not purchase his share of Idough from Francis Edgeworth, as one scholar has claimed (Nolan, *Fassadinin*, 33).   184 Ibid., Ms 2506, ff 36v, 81r.   185 Nolan, *Fassadinin*, 29–32, 42–9; *Inq. Lagenia*, Co. Kilkenny, Charles I (64). Statement of Melaghlin and Donogh McFirr O'Brennan, 10 Dec. 1617; Bargain and sale by same, 4 March 1618; Quitclaim of Richard Tobin fitz Edmund, 20 Feb. 1625; Indenture of Donell O'Crokeran and Honor O'Brennan, 10 Oct. 1628; Assignment by Nicholas Comerford; Agreement of Donogh McFirr O'Brennan and Teige McDonogh, 26 July 1628; Indenture of Owen McEdmund O'Brennan, 20 Oct. 1630 (ibid., Prior-Wandesford MSS, Irish Material).

proceed with cashing in his two-thirds' share of the territory, he would utterly alienate these families, leaving them angry that he, their traditional overlord, had sold them out. Remarkably, the young earl considered this a risk worth taking.

Barely a year after his succession he set about establishing the legal basis for a sale. In 1634 his representatives, and those of Robert Ridgeway, second earl of Londonderry (who had acquired Sir Henry Pierces' portion), entered Idough to assert the rights of the two noblemen as co-owners of the entire territory by royal letters patent. The O'Brennans, Mountgarret, Richard Butler of Castlecomer, and the rest were required to 'show cause why the king should not be entitled to ye lands', but when the case was subsequently heard in chancery all objections were dismissed, with the court recognising 'no cause … to stay the king's entitlement'.[186] In May 1635 a royal commission, headed by Ormond's friend and kinsman, Lord Esmond, and including the master of the rolls, Christopher Wandesford, arrived in Kilkenny to formally secure Idough for the crown and, by association, the two earls. The O'Brennans, and all who claimed title through them, whether by purchase, mortgage, inheritance or otherwise, were dispossessed, on the grounds that the old Gaelic lineage were intruders who three hundred years earlier had unlawfully seized the area from the descendants of Richard de Clare, earl of Pembroke (alias Strongbow), and occupied it ever since 'by the strong hand'.[187]

In a number of important respects the proceedings of the court of inquisition seemed flawed. For instance, the fact that Lord Mountgarret had held his lands in Idough by royal letters patent since 1619 was overlooked.[188] It proved likewise with Richard Butler: in 1623 he had been confirmed as heir to his father's Castlecomer estate, which was held directly of the crown in capite; yet this too was suppressed by the inquiry.[189] The suspicion that these oversights were part of a pattern of official corruption emanating from Dublin Castle was not dispelled by subsequent government decisions. When Mountgarret complained of injustice to the lord deputy, Wentworth had him submit his lands under the commission for defective titles, which promptly encumbered the viscount with a £300 fine while confirming the confiscation of all his Idough property.[190] Most revealing of all, however, was the identity of the chief beneficiary of the seizure – none other than the judge who had presided over the inquisition, Christopher Wandesford. As Wentworth later admitted in his private correspondence, the holding of the court of inquisition had merely been a ploy to expedite Ormond and Londonderry's sale of Idough to the master of the rolls, who was 'both judge and party' at the Kilkenny hearing.[191] Following a royal grant to the notorious military adventurer Sir Charles Coote (Ormond and Londonderry's assignee), erecting the entire territory into the manor of Castlecomer on 24 May 1636, the way was at last cleared for the sale to take

186 Sheffield City Library, Ms WWM Str. P 17/269. **187** W.J. Smyth (ed.), *Herbert correspondence* (Dublin 1963), 90; *Inq. Lagenia*, Co. Kilkenny, Charles I (64). **188** NA, Lodge MSS, Rolls, Vol. IV, 281–2. **189** *Inq. Lagenia*, Co. Kilkenny, James I (37). **190** Clarke, *Old English*, 109. **191** Carte, *Ormond*, v, 204–5.

place. Ormond gained the most, receiving £2,000 from Wandesford in July 1637, with Londonderry getting £300.[192] Wentworth also profited, albeit secretly – according to a hitherto unnoticed document among his personal estate papers, Wandesford gave him £1,000 as a consideration for his help, money that the deputy immediately concealed in a trust established for his brother, Sir George Wentworth.[193] A Wandesford memorandum confirms the covert nature of the payment. Headed 'An estimate what I am to pay for Edough', it records the payment due to the deputy, but even in this most private of documents, little more than a jotting, Wentworth is not named, with the payment referred to as being due 'To another'.[194]

Wandesford's generosity to Wentworth is understandable, for the deputy had not merely acquiesced in his acquisition of Idough, but had actively conspired to make it possible, not least by authorising the use of coercive measures in the area in order to intimidate the local population into silence. Government troops were first deployed in Idough in May 1635, when Wentworth authorised Lord Esmond to quarter a detachment of men from his Duncannon garrison in the area. Immediately the soldiers encountered difficulties. Despite disarming 'the native Irish [O'Brennans] near the mountain [that is, the Castlecomer ridge]', Esmond complained that gentry from all across northern and central Co. Kilkenny had provided shelter and relief to those facing dispossession.[195] Once the territory had been reassigned to the new manor of Castlecomer in 1636, in readiness for its purchase by Wandesford, a fresh show of force was deemed necessary, with the O'Brennans and some of the other local families reported as having entered into a 'combination' to resist the transfer.[196] Again Wentworth issued the necessary instructions, in July 1636 signing a government order approving 'the settling of a company of foot [in Idough] if there be cause', and as later sources noted, the whole area was for a time placed under martial law.[197]

It was at this point that the earl of Ormond became involved in the military operations. With his position as a garrison commander in Leinster confirmed,[198] and Wentworth, as noted above, willing to increase the number of 'horse troopes' under his command at Kilkenny Castle, it was Earl James, not Esmond, who now took charge of the reduction and occupation of Idough. Thus were the O'Brennans 'pacified' and dispossessed by the chief financial beneficiary of their dispossession. Moreover, when one of Wandesford's servants was attacked when entering the territory to seize a portion of the corn crop at harvest time, the offender, a woman, was punished by Ormond's servant, Walter Evers, the

192 BL, Harleian Ms 430, ff 204v–206r; An estimate, 29 Oct. 1636, Ormond's indenture to Coote, 25 July 1637, and Articles of Agreement, 29 July 1637 (NLI, Prior-Wandesford MSS, Irish material). 193 Sheffield City Library, Ms WWM Add., Wentworth Irish Deeds, Brown parcel 5, Box 3, Bundle 2, no. 2 (8). 194 An estimate, 29 Oct. 1636 (NLI, Prior-Wandesford MSS, Irish material). 195 Ibid., Ms WWM Str. P 15/86. 196 HMC, *Ormonde MSS, 1572–1660*, 32. 197 Ibid., 34; Grosart (ed.), *Lismore papers*, 2nd series, iv, 181. 198 Sheffield City Library, Ms WWM Str. P. 24–25/242.

newly appointed constable of the area.[199] Before Christmas, following an injunction out of chancery – Wandesford's court – 'sundry of ye natives, about ye
number of 25 or 30 persons', were arrested by Ormond's troops and sent to the
Marshalsea prison in Dublin, ostensibly to await trial for obstructing the efforts
of the sheriff to uphold Wandesford's title to the territory. Trial was repeatedly
deferred. Left in their cells for months, Wandesford occasionally visited the prisoners holding out promises of freedom provided they accepted him as their
landlord. When eventually a trial was set (nearly a year after their arrests) for
October 1637, it was held in the *coram deputato*, or lord deputy's court, presided
over by Wentworth, who true to form upheld Wandesford's case against them.
Meanwhile the government took the opportunity to again avail of its military
might in Idough, and 'my lord of Ormond's troop … came to attack and dispossess' those of the O'Brennans who remained in the area.[200] It was only after
this, the third show of force, that Wandesford finally gained full possession, and
Ormond, Londonderry, Wentworth, and other interested parties such as Oliver
Wheeler and Sir Cyprian Horsfall were paid.[201]

Had it merely been a matter of overcoming the O'Brennans and some of
the lesser Anglo-Irish gentry the confiscation of Idough would soon have been
completed. However, as early as March 1636 opposition to the forfeiture had
been growing from a singularly powerful source – Thomas Howard, earl of
Arundel & Surrey, magnate, courtier, premier privy councillor, lord lieutenant
of Norfolk, and earl marshal of England.[202] For some time he and his son, Henry,
Lord Maltravers, had been looking to reclaim the huge Leinster estate held by
their ancestors during the medieval period. Arundel was a descendant of
Strongbow, and if the inquisition of May 1635 was correct in ascribing Idough
as part of the old De Clare lands, he presumed he must be its rightful owner.
Moreover, King Charles had agreed to support his quest for his medieval inheritance in Ireland, towards this end naming Arundel and Maltravers as members
of the Irish council in 1634, a development that had compelled Wentworth to
offer his 'continual favour and care' in protecting Arundel's Irish interests
throughout the duration of his lord deputyship.[203] Unhappily for Arundel, he
had taken Wentworth at his word, allowing the deputy to take charge of his
affairs in Ireland, and 'to mould my business as you thought best'. Consequently,
the news of Idough's fate had not only disappointed the great nobleman; worse,
it had insulted him too, with the earl irate that he had been treated like a fool
and made to appear 'to others [as if] fallen from your lordship [Wentworth]'s

---

199 For Evers' links to Ormond, see NLI, D 4023.   **200** Sheffield City Library, Ms WWM, Str.
P. 17/269; BL, Harleian Ms 430, ff 204v–206r; Case to answer against Richard Butler, n.d., c.1641
(NLI, Prior-Wandesford MSS, Irish material).   **201** James Purcell's assignment, 2 May 1637, and
Oliver Wheeler's release, 26 May 1637 (ibid.).   **202** For Arundel's career, see esp. Sharpe, *The
personal rule*, 163–4; 'The earl of Arundel, his circle and the opposition to the duke of Buckingham,
1618–1628', in K. Sharpe (ed.), *Faction & parliament: essays on early Stuart history* (London 1978),
209–44; D. Howarth, *Lord Arundel and his circle* (Yale 1985).   **203** Knowler (ed.), *Strafford letters*,
i, 232, 276.

respect'.[204] Ormond, who had made similar assurances of support and friendship in January 1635, also incurred Arundel's wrath.[205] Determined to have his revenge, the earl marshal set about stirring things up in Idough. He sent three agents to the area to inquire into the government's proceedings there and to make contact with those who had suffered dispossession.[206]

By August 1636 Arundel's men had achieved enough to scupper the chances of compromise. In particular their arrival in Kilkenny had encouraged Viscount Mountgarret to abandon his pursuit of compensation from Wandesford in order to join Arundel in overturning the findings of the 1635 court of inquisition, the basis for Wandesford's title. By October the master of the rolls was complaining that the viscount had become mulish in his desire 'not to submit himself to the justice' of the court's findings;[207] the following year the O'Brennan leaders (incarcerated in Dublin) sneered at the 21-year tenancies offered by Wandesford, dismissing his overtures with violent language that offended his reputedly Puritan sensibilities.[208] The government's third recourse to military force, noted above, seemingly made no difference. As Wandesford put it in April 1638: 'these obstinate people expect such favours from the other side [that is, Arundel in England] that they will hearken to no reason', believing that their deliverance was imminent.[209]

Growing confidence in Arundel's ability to turn things around encouraged Richard Butler of Castlecomer to offer his services to the earl marshal, and in 1638 the government could only look on as he went about north Co. Killkenny collecting testimonies and documentary evidence that Arundel required for his legal team in England.[210] Mountgarret's heir, Edmund Butler of Baleen, also became involved. By August 1638 he had acquired a London base from whence to coordinate the Idough campaign with Arundel, leasing a house in High Holborn.[211] Plainly, had it not been for the outbreak of the First Bishops' (Anglo-Scottish) War later that year, Wandesford's ownership of Idough, and the manner in which he had obtained it, would have been the subject of both legal measures in London and Dublin and political intrigue at the royal court.

The war brought a temporary halt to proceedings. From late 1638 until midsummer 1639 Arundel was occupied with much weightier matters, as he was granted command of the royal army to confront the Scots. Partly as a result of his failure to organise his forces effectively, the king had to sign a ceasefire with the Scots at Berwick in June 1639, and Arundel's star dimmed as a result.[212] The fact that Wentworth, his loudest critic, subsequently replaced him as comman-

204 Ibid., ii, 3. **205** HMC, *Ormonde MSS, 1572–1660*, 29. **206** Knowler (ed.), *Strafford letters*, ii, 29–30. **207** HMC, *Ormonde MSS, 1572–1660*, 38; Bod. Lib., Oxford, Ms Add. C. 286, ff 17–18. **208** BL, Harleian Ms 430, ff 204v–206r; HMC, *Ormonde MSS, 1572–1660*, 43. **209** Sheffield City Library, Ms WWM, Str. P. 18/11. **210** YAS, Ms DD5/38/2, no. 37. **211** *Cal. SP Dom, Charles I, 1637–8*, 587. **212** C. Russell, *The fall of the British monarchies, 1637–1642* (Oxford 1991), ch. 3; P. Donald, *An uncounselled king: Charles I and the Scottish troubles, 1637–1641* (Cambridge 1990), ch. 4; M. Perceval-Maxwell, 'Ulster 1641 in the context of political developments in the Three Kingdoms', in B. Mac Cuarta (ed.), *Ulster 1641: aspects of the rising* (Belfast 1993).

der only compounded the earl's loss of face and insured that he was discouraged to pursue his interest in Idough, at least for the time being. Hence for two years Christopher Wandesford was left undisturbed to get on with developing his private colony around Castlecomer, at great expense improving and extending the local mining operations, stocking the manorial parkland with game, building a new village, and bringing in tenants from England.[213] However, by August 1640, following the eruption of the Second Bishops' War and a successful Scottish invasion of northern England, Wandesford's title became vulnerable again as the enemies of Wentworth (recently created earl of Strafford and appointed lord lieutenant of Ireland) gathered for the kill. Strafford, always so confident, had left himself dangerously exposed after the king accepted his ill-judged advice to summon both the English and Irish parliaments in order to raise the funds needed to finance renewed military operations. Parliaments, he was certain, could be managed. Events proved him wrong.

CRISIS, 1640–1

The work of Michael Perceval-Maxwell has revealed the extent to which disgruntled elements of the Protestant colonial classes in Ireland contributed to Lord Lieutenant Strafford's downfall and execution, and the collapse of his government,[214] and has noted that one of the ways in which they brought their foe down was by linking up with the earl of Arundel in London.[215] However, as I have contended elsewhere, while accepting the importance of the Protestant plotters, it is important not to overlook the role played by the Irish Catholic lords and gentry in the anti-Strafford conspiracy, especially those from Co. Kilkenny, who with Arundel's support used the Idough controversy against Strafford with devastating effect in early 1641.[216]

That the Kilkenny Catholic community was able to make such a telling contribution to larger British as well as Irish affairs was a consequence of the decline of Ormond influence in the county. Although the twelfth earl, James, threw himself into the task of managing the local parliamentary elections, and succeeded in having a high number of government men returned as MPs, it is important not to over-estimate his achievement, as some historians have tended to do.[217] As many anti- as pro-government MPs were elected from Kilkenny in 1640–1, with the influence of Viscount Mountgarret as discernible as that of Ormond in determining the outcome. Thus, where Earl James had seven candidates returned to support Strafford (five English Protestants, one Scottish Protestant and one

---

213 Articles of agreement, 10 Aug. 1637; Richard Foster's observations, 20 Oct. 1639; The case concerning the territory of Idough, n.d., *c.*1653 (NLI, Prior-Wandesford MSS, Irish material). **214** M. Perceval-Maxwell, *The outbreak of the Irish rebellion of 1641* (Dublin 1994). **215** Idem, 'Ireland and Scotland, 1638–1648', in J. Morrill (ed.), *The Scottish National Covenant in its British context, 1637–51* (Edinburgh 1990), 201–2. **216** Edwards, 'Poisoned chalice', 77–80. **217** E.g., Kelly, 'Ormond and Strafford', 92–4.

pro-government Catholic),[218] Viscount Richard could rely on five who were willing to undermine the lieutenant, including his cousin Walter Walsh of Castlehowell, and his feoffee Peter Rothe fitz John.[219] Moreover, after November 1640 Ormond's hold over the Kilkenny electorate slipped badly and Mountgarret's correspondingly increased when the viscount's kinsman the Knight of Kerry, John Fitzgerald,[220] and another Catholic candidate, Walter Den, replaced the two Protestant members that had been previously returned for Inistioge. Later still, in March 1641, Mountgarret's son-in-law, the Palesman Richard Bellings, took the place of the Protestant MP for Callan.[221]

Already in the first session of the Dublin parliament the prospect of disaffected Protestant and Catholic members forming a united front against Strafford's regime had reduced Christopher Wandesford, the new lord deputy, to panic. Aware that the lord lieutenant was too busy in England preparing to fight the Scots and managing the English house of commons to give his full attention to developments in Ireland, where 'we have no small trouble with the parliament', on 24 June Wandesford pleaded with Strafford's agent in London 'for God's sake bring us clear directions about all things'.[222] Ormond likewise betrayed signs of uneasiness. As William Kelly has shown, Earl James availed of the pregnancy of his wife, Countess Elizabeth, to stay away from Dublin throughout the summer of 1640, anxious to disassociate himself from Strafford's military and political policies, which he had begun to realise might not prove successful.[223] Such reservations were soon justified. In the wake of the Scots' routing of the English army at Newburn in Northumberland in August the coalition of Strafford's enemies that Wandesford had dreaded all summer finally came to pass. Even before the impeachment of Strafford by the English commons on 11 November Kilkenny's Catholic MPs had begun to participate in anti-government initiatives in the Irish parliament;[224] following the impeachment their activities became increasingly visible. Moreover, encouraged by Arundel in England, Mountgarret and Richard Butler of Castlecomer made ready to re-ignite the dispute over Idough.

Wandesford had been aware for some time that a new case against his ownership of the territory was being prepared. With this in mind, he had made pro-

---

218 Sir Thomas Wharton (MP for Callan), Sir Robert Loftus (Inistioge), Seafoule Gibson (Thomastown), John Wandesford (Inistioge), Michael Wandesford (Thomastown), all English; the Scot Patrick Wemyss (Gowran); and the local Catholic Edward Comerford (Callan). **219** Walsh's grandmother, Lady Ellice Butler, was Viscount Richard's aunt (Carrigan, *Ossory*, iv, 74–5); Rothe was a trustee for Mountgarret's manor of Kells (NA, Lodge MSS, Wardships, Vol. I, 254). **220** Fitzgerald had a shared affinity with Mountgarret through the Tuchets, earls of Castlehaven. **221** For Bellings' background, see R. Gillespie, 'The social thought of Richard Bellings', in M. Ó Siochrú (ed.), *Kingdoms in crisis: Ireland in the 1640s* (Dublin 2001), 217–20. **222** Bod. Lib., Carte Ms 1, ff 210–11; ibid., Ms Add C 286, fol. 29. **223** Kelly, 'James Butler', 44–6; 'Ormond & Strafford', 96–102. **224** On 12 October three Kilkenny gentlemen had staged a protest over rising government fees from the public gallery of the commons; their case was subsequently taken up by their local MPs; also in October, four Kilkenny MPs joined a commons committee investigating government behaviour in Carlow: *Journals of the Irish house of commons, 1613–66* (Dublin 1796), 147, 156–7, 160.

vision in his will of 2 October 1640 for his trustees to pay some limited compensation to 'all of those who shall be found to have been the reputed possessors of the land' prior to the court of inquisition of May 1635.²²⁵ However, once
Strafford was impeached, it became clear that a little compensation was never
going to be enough for those who had suffered dispossession. As his brother
William acknowledged shortly afterwards, by the time of his death in December
Wandesford knew that his title to the territory was once more in doubt and that
his name had been linked to 'the troubles and molestations wherewith his best
friends [that is, Strafford] stand charg'd'.²²⁶ Early in 1641 Richard Butler sailed
to England with revelations about the behaviour of the Irish government in
Idough during the mid-to-late 1630s. At first William Wandesford was confident that Butler's agitation would 'soon cease'.²²⁷ He was hopelessly misin-
formed. The impeachment proceedings against Strafford at Westminster were
presided over by the earl of Arundel by virtue of his office as lord high steward
of England. Almost certainly through his influence Butler's allegations about
the unlawful and arbitrary nature of the Idough forfeiture became part of the
final list of charges against Strafford, forming the centrepiece of Article 15, which
one leading historian has suggested was the most damaging of all the Irish articles in the impeachment.²²⁸

Sadly no copy of Richard Butler's 'petition to the Commons house of parliament in England' seems to be extant. However, it is possible to identify key
aspects of the petition from other documents, principally Article 15 of Strafford's
impeachment and the 'Answer' to Butler's case that was prepared in London
by the Wandesford family's legal counsel.²²⁹ Utilising these, it emerges that
having outlined Arundel's claim to the territory through descent from the De
Clares and the Mortimers, Butler focussed on certain irregularities perpetrated
by agents of the Irish government in Idough after May 1635, acting under
Strafford's direction. Thus, Butler claimed that, as judge, Christopher
Wandesford had issued an injunction from chancery against the local inhabitants in May 1636, entirely for the advancement of his own land claim, and that
Strafford had authorised the use of force against peaceful subjects in the area in
order to secure Wandesford's interest. In defence, the Wandesfords' counsel
argued that Arundel's claims to ownership were spurious, and that the crown's
entitlement to the territory had been repeatedly confirmed. However, it was
the use of royal troops that quickly became the main issue. Although the
Wandesfords' counsel asserted that such soldiers as were despatched into Idough
after 1635 'were there not as soldiers but as assistants to the sheriff' of Co.
Kilkenny, the English commons dismissed his contention. Strafford's parliamentary enemies seized upon Butler's revelations about government 'tyranny'
in Ireland to nail their foe. Citing an English statute of 1352, it was alleged that

225 McCall, *Family of Wandesford*, 283. 226 C.H. Firth (ed.), 'Letters of William Wandesford to
Sir Rowland Wandesford', *EHR* 9 (1894), 551. 227 YAS, Ms DD5/38/2, no. 35. 228 Russell,
The fall, 282–3. 229 Case to Answer, n.d., *c*.Feb. 1641 (NLI, Prior–Wandesford MSS 756 (4)/10).

Strafford's authorisation of military repression in Idough was an act of high treason, as to wage war on the king's peaceful subjects was to wage war on the king.
Thereafter the impeachment proceedings were replaced by a bill of attainder,
which passed the house of lords on 7 May, under the terms of which Strafford
was pronounced guilty and sentenced to death. On 9 May, the king conferred
with his privy council regarding Strafford's fate, and according to historians'
best estimations, it is likely that a majority of the council advised him to sign
the bill.[230] Strafford was beheaded three days later.

While all this was happening in London, Kilkenny's Catholic MPs were
increasingly prominent in the attempt spearheaded by their disgruntled Protestant
colleagues to inflict as much damage as possible on members of Strafford's
administration in Dublin. The first to make an impact was John Fitzgerald, the
Knight of Kerry, who, on 2 December 1640 – just days after Mountgarret had
had him elected as the new member for Inistioge – was brought to trial in castle
chamber, sentenced and imprisoned, a development which impinged on his
constitutional rights as a MP. The Irish commons adopted his case, and when
the government attempted to overturn his election in February 1641, the house
defied the order and instigated proceedings to identify those in authority that
were responsible for his unlawful imprisonment. By 4 March this had metamorphosed into a report on the Irish government's misuse of castle chamber
that was to be sent to the English house of commons to further its attack on the
prerogative courts of the crown.[231]

Significantly, the March 4 resolution in the case of John Fitzgerald ran
counter to the recommendations of the earl of Ormond. On or about 22
February Ormond had become involved in the case, evidently hoping to kill
the scandal surrounding Fitzgerald's treatment by stirring up aristocratic resentment in the house of lords against the privileges claimed for a member of the
commons.[232] His efforts were ineffective. Moreover, the March 4 decision was
doubly unwelcome to Earl James because the previous day he had tried to head
off the despatch to England by asking the lords to reconsider the case itself.[233]
The lords' refusal to do so, and its preference to work with the commons rather
than against it, indicated clearly that Ormond and the rest of Strafford's men
had lost control of parliament in Dublin. Other simultaneous developments
confirmed this impression.

The second Kilkenny member to participate in the attack on the administration was Walter Walsh of Castlehowell, who on 15 February 1641 was elected
to a committee charged with uncovering abuses in the management of the tobacco
monopoly that had occurred since Strafford had come to office. This committee
enjoyed extensive powers of inquiry, being able to search for account books and
other documents that might help them link Strafford and his servants to alleged
acts of fraud, 'and, if occasion be, to break open any chests, trunks, desks, cham-

230 Russell, *The fall*, 299 n.107.   **231** *Ir. Lords Journal, 1634–98*, 146, 154; *Ir. Commons Journal,
1613–66*, 177–8, 179, 184, 194–6.   **232** *Ir. Lords Journal,1634–98*, 158, 165.   **233** Ibid., 174.

bers or closets' in the course of the search. Within a week, Walsh and the rest of the committee members had uncovered enough information to be able to identify two of Strafford's associates as suspects, Thomas Little and James Peisley, and proceeded immediately to seize all the money and tobacco in their possession.[234]

At about the same time a third local MP, Peter Rothe fitz John, entered the fray. In fact, it fell to Rothe to help bring the crisis to its head. On 27 February 1641 he became a member of the commons' committee that was required to draw up charges against Strafford's agent, Sir George Radcliffe, the lord chancellor, Sir Richard Bolton, the bishop of Derry, George Bramhall, and the chief justice of the common pleas, Sir Gerald Lowther, 'and therein impeach them of high treason'. Three months later, on 18 May, Rothe was still busy with this assignment, helping to collect more information against Bishop Bramhall and Justice Lowther. His Co. Kilkenny colleague, the knight of Kerry, John Fitzgerald, joined him in this latter task.[235]

The Wandesford family did not escape scrutiny. In London 'the business of Idough', as it was called, refused to die down, even after the adoption of the bill of attainder against Strafford. In May the English parliament had issued a warrant sequestering Idough, so that 'nothing [could] be received … [from] the plantation' by Christopher Wandesford's widow, Alice, or his brother, William.[236] By midsummer Arundel and Mountgarret were exerting pressure over both the English and Irish parliaments simultaneously: on 26 June Alice Wandesford reported from Dublin that 'here is a petition preferred in parliament' about Idough, an occurrence that had happened 'already', that is, rather quicker than she had anticipated; a month later, in London, one of her relatives was informed that Richard Butler of Castlecomer was preparing to bring the matter before the Irish committee of the English house of commons.[237] Subsequent developments are a little obscure, owing to the adjournment of the Irish parliament until November at the special request of the Dublin government. Nevertheless during the Irish recess (probably in August) plans were made to transfer the case back to Ireland, where Richard Boyle, earl of Cork, was probably responsible for encouraging Arundel to seek redress in the parliament there as soon as it reconvened. A document providing detailed advice on how to proceed with the recovery of Idough, endorsed 'Lands in Kilkenny County: A memorial for the earl of Arundel', exists among Cork's papers.[238] Tipped off, William Wandesford calculated that, thanks to Poynings' Law, the threat posed to the family estate could easily be run to ground through the influence of Irish

---

234 *Ir. Commons Journal, 1613–66*, 173, 175, 179. Had the committee but gained access to the accounts of Sir George Radcliffe, it would have discovered that Christopher Wandesford had been a secret investor in the tobacco trade, having given Radcliffe £1,500 in cash to invest privately on his behalf: YAS, Ms DD5/38/2, no. 1.   **235** *Ir. Commons Journal, 1613–66*, 184–5, 203–4, 208.   **236** YAS, Ms DD5/38/2, no. 39.   **237** Ibid., Ms DD5/38/2, nos. 2, 32.   **238** BL, Egerton Ms 80: 83–4. For the obscurity of Cork's role in the proceedings of 1640–1, see P. Little, 'The earl of Cork and the fall of the earl of Strafford, 1638–41', *HJ* 39/3 (1996), 619–35; Perceval-Maxwell, 'Protestant faction', 245–6, 254; idem, 'Ulster 1641', 98.

privy councillors such as the earl of Ormond and Lord Chancellor Bolton, men who, he noted, had a special interest in the case, and would want to prevent the details of how they had organised the seizure of the territory from coming before both houses. However, by August 1641 there was in fact very little that these pro-Wandesford councillors could do to prevent Idough coming before the Irish parliament. It was far from certain that a majority of the Irish council would have agreed to block a bill about Idough; as William Wandesford himself acknowledged, some of the other councillors, most notably Viscount Ranelagh (a supporter of the earl of Cork), but also Sir William Parsons and Sir John Borlase, had nothing to lose and a lot to gain if further disrepute attached itself to Ormond, Bolton and the Wandesford family.[239]

As things stood going into September 1641, the growing scandals over Idough, the tobacco monopoly and other issues insured that the remnants of Strafford's Irish clique could anticipate a further erosion of their position. William Wandesford had learned that Arundel and Richard Butler had indeed by-passed the Irish council and were getting ready to have their grievances brought before the Dublin parliament, with a special recommendation from the king. He wrote to his kinsman Sir Edward Osborne: 'Now I begin to suspect … they may presume upon some advantage to themselves.'[240] By 24 September the prospects for the Wandesfords and their friends surviving a proper discussion of their acquisition of Idough had deteriorated so much that William asked Osborne to try to get the king to 'countermand' the transfer of the case from England. Incredibly he hoped that provided the matter remained in London, the English privy council might be relied upon to confirm his family's ownership of the territory – manifestly a calculation born of desperation, as it overlooked the thorny little matter of the influence of the premier privy councillor, Arundel.[241] Provided that the alliance of opposites in the Irish parliament (Catholic and Protestant, native and colonist) managed to hold firm during the recess, it seemed that the game was up and the Wandesfords would lose Idough.

The earl of Ormond shared the Wandesfords' fears.[242] The storm that had engulfed Strafford had left him exposed. The prospect of further parliamentary investigations into the seizure of Idough was a troubling one, primarily because he, not Christopher Wandesford, had been responsible for the unlawful use of royal soldiers in the area during 1636–7, an offence that the English commons had deemed worthy of treason. Recognition of his role in the seizure had already cost him advancement, in December 1640, with his proposed promotion to the office of lord deputy of Ireland following Wandesford's death quashed by Arundel's objections.[243] Since Strafford's execution Earl James had begun to become the focus of growing criticism, on one occasion being told he should pay back what had been misappropriated on his behalf while Strafford was

---

239 YAS, Ms DD5/38/2, no. 37. **240** Ibid., no. 42. **241** Ibid., no. 36. **242** The following paragraph provides a slight modification of the discussion in Edwards, 'The poisoned chalice', 81. **243** Carte, *Ormond*, v, 245.

alive.[244] The success of Arundel and Richard Butler in having the Idough case transferred from London to Dublin threatened to end his political career. The longer the controversy dragged on, the more likely it seemed that he would be denied further access to royal favour; indeed, it was even possible that the king would find it expedient to sacrifice him. Clearly dreading the reconvening of parliament in November, Ormond again withdrew from public life and returned to Kilkenny, where he remained throughout the summer and autumn of 1641, attending to private business.[245]

And so it was that on the eve of the Ulster rebellion of 23 October 1641, James Butler, twelfth earl of Ormond, appeared to be a spent force in Irish affairs, and the regime in which he had served stood on the brink of collapse – and this partly because of his involvement in the forfeiture of Idough. The rising in the north, when it came, spared both him and the Wandesford family from the ignominy of defeat in parliament at the hands of Arundel, Mountgarret and the rest of their enemies. Parliamentary proceedings dissolved in chaos amid a torrent of recriminations and accusations between the Protestant and Catholic members of both houses, and as Catholic rebellion spread southwards it was no longer possible for Arundel in England to continue his close relationship with Mountgarret, an Irish Catholic lord who had been a rebel in his youth.

In a sense, the insurrection saved Ormond's career. Prior to 23 October the earl had reason to suspect that Strafford's replacement as lord lieutenant, Robert Sidney, earl of Leicester, was ill disposed towards him and would probably replace him as commander-in-chief of the Irish government forces, a position earlier granted him by Strafford. However, given the state of emergency across the country after the eruption of the Ulster rising, Leicester had little choice but to confirm Ormond as commander-in-chief.[246] As a result, for all his recent reverses, Ormond found he was guaranteed a leading role in subsequent events.

It remained to be seen how this confirmation of his military role would be received in his ancestral territories. Would the Catholic community of Co. Kilkenny and the mid-south, having supported Arundel and Mountgarret's campaign of constitutional opposition to Ormond and his hated patron, Strafford, continue to defy Earl James, or bow down to his orders now that unconstitutional opposition to the government he served was growing? The answer to this question was of major importance. If the traditionally loyalist Catholics of Co. Kilkenny were prepared to reject the command of Ormond, their traditional ruler, they were also ready to throw off the Dublin Protestant government too, and the Catholic rebellion that had begun in Ulster would have a realistic chance of evolving into a genuinely countrywide phenomenon. It is a telling comment on the state of Ormond's reputation in Kilkenny that the key personality in determining the answer to this matter was not the earl, but his principal adversary, Mountgarret.

244 *CSPI, 1647–60 & Addenda Charles I*, 256.   245 HMC, *Egmont MSS*, i, 139–40; Bod. Lib., Carte Ms 2, fol. 1.   246 HMC, *Ormonde MSS*, ii, 13.

THE GREAT CATHOLIC REBELLION

Richard Butler, third Viscount Mountgarret, felt he had little choice when, in the closing weeks of 1641, he took command of a Catholic insurrection in Co. Kilkenny. For as long as he could remember, he had been excluded from power because of his religion. Even in October 1641, as the rebel Ulster army surged south towards the capital, this was still the case. Despite his association with Arundel he was again deemed untrustworthy of holding provincial office and had to wait several weeks before, begrudgingly, 'lest they should complain', he and other Catholic figures were granted commissions to 'resist the conspirators' and raise local forces for the defence of the crown.[247] His commission, when it came, was hardly satisfactory. Firstly, it did not give him power of martial law, something that had been granted to other, apparently more trusted, Catholic lords elsewhere.[248] Secondly, it may have arrived too late, for already by 22–25 November a general rebellion had been provoked in neighbouring Tipperary[249] after the inhabitants of Goldenbridge, Ardmoyle, Ballyowen and other villages were summarily executed by martial law by government troops commanded by the lord president of Munster, Sir William St Leger, a close friend of Ormond.[250] When challenged by senior Butler lords at Clonmel about the injustice of his actions, the president responded angrily, denouncing the Catholic members of the lineage and their gentry supporters as 'all rebels' at heart because of their religion, and as persons who deserved to be hanged.[251] St Leger's behaviour caused panic and outrage in Kilkenny and surrounding areas, as news spread of the 'merciless' cruelty of his company, who allegedly 'ripped up' 'a woman great with child', and 'caused honest men and women', at peace with the crown, 'to be most execrably executed'. In the words of Mountgarret's near kinsman, the baron of Upper Ossory, Lord President St Leger's pre-emptive use of terror against law-abiding subjects 'put many in a sort of desperation'.[252] As late as 29 November Mountgarret was apparently still undecided as to what course to follow, writing to Ormond in Dublin for authority to act in Tipperary against the rebels who had begun to break out there.[253] However, when news reached him that St Leger had commenced a new and equally savage campaign in Co. Waterford and, without consulting him, was looking for rebels from Co. Kilkenny, the viscount's mind was made up. Suspecting the complicity of Dublin Castle in St Leger's action, and fearing that a general slaughter of southern

247 Rushworth, *Historical Collections IV*, 169; Clarke, *Old English*, 168.   **248** E. Borlase, *The History of the execrable Irish rebellion* (London 1680), 28.   **249** For Tipperary, see R.S., *A collection of some of the massacres and murthers committed on the Irish since the 23rd of October 1641* (London 1662), 19; R. Cox, *Hibernia Anglicana* (London 1689), 93–4; M. Hickson (ed.), *Ireland in the Seventeenth Century* (2 vols, London 1884), ii, 37–46, 240–8; N. Canny, *Making Ireland British, 1580–1650* (Oxford 2001), 525–8.   **250** St Leger was godfather to one of Ormond's sons, and in regular correspondence with the earl in 1641 (Carte, *Ormond*, v, 259–61, 263–8).   **251** Hickson (ed.), *Ireland*, ii, 241–2.   **252** Carte, *Ormond*, v, 279. Later Protestant writers did not deny the provocative nature of St Leger's conduct, but rather lauded it as necessarily hard: Cox, *Hibernia*, 93–4.   **253** D. Coffey, *O'Neill and Ormond: a chapter in Irish history* (Dublin 1914), 101.

Catholics was intended, he employed his commission 'against those from whom he had it', ordering the forces he had raised out into the field against the government.[254] The onset of Mountgarret's revolt can be dated with a fair degree of accuracy to 30 November.[255]

The viscount's men made swift progress, overpowering every English Protestant 'worth a groat' within a day or two,[256] for there was no one in Kilkenny capable of blocking his orders or securing the area for the state. His immediate superior, and the usual commander of the local forces, the twelfth earl of Ormond, was absent. On 28 October Ormond had been advised by Sir John Temple to leave his territories for Dublin as quickly as possible;[257] he arrived in the capital on or after 7 November.[258] Crucially, Ormond did not travel to Dublin on his own: acting on Temple's advice (and in response to more recent government entreaties) he brought his troop of horse with him.[259] Because of this, there was no government cavalry in Co. Kilkenny to resist Mountgarret's hastily assembled companies of horse and foot. Such forces as existed were foot-based, relatively immobile, tied to particular spots, and small in number. A company of 20 musketeers under Captain John Farrell was based at Castlecomer,[260] and in Callan Ormond's clients Ambrose Aungier and Edward Comerford ensured that a militia of 30 musketeers and 40 pikemen was levied 'against all rebels and disloyal people', though it seems the musketeers had no muskets or bandoleers.[261] These, together with a small number of footmen in Kilkenny Castle under Captain Warren, seem to have comprised the core of the Ormond/government force in the shire.

Leadership problems compounded their weakness. Other commanders besides Ormond were absent during October and November. Patrick Wemyss, recently knighted and appointed a captain, and Ormond's *de facto* second-in-command in Kilkenny, was in Edinburgh attending upon King Charles at the beginning of November, and only joined Earl James in the Pale a few weeks later.[262] Thus the Protestant sheriff of the county, Ormond's other chief side-kick, Sir Cyprian Horsfall, was without military support to disperse the gatherings of increasingly hostile Catholic volunteers assembling around the county in response to Mountgarret's summons; Horsfall subsequently disappeared from the shire, to be replaced as sheriff by Redmund Purcell (probably one of the Purcells of Esker and Rosconnill), a Catholic landowner and Mountgarret client.[263] Likewise, the only remaining person capable of taking charge on behalf

---

254 TCD, Ms 812, fol. 271r. **255** Carte, *Ormond*, v, 267. **256** HMC, *Egmont MSS*, i, 153. **257** Bod. Lib., Carte Ms 2, fol. 2. **258** Ibid., ff 9, 18. **259** Ibid., fol. 7. **260** TCD, Ms 812, ff 190r–192r. **261** The pikemen, however, did have halberds and brownbills (Bod. Lib., Carte Ms 2, fol. 32). **262** Carte, *Ormond*, v, 257, 267–8. Contemporaries referred to him as 'captain lieutenant to the earl of Ormond': Sir J. Temple, *The history of the general rebellion in Ireland* (London 1646; 7th edn., Cork 1766), 338; Borlase, *History*, 60. **263** TCD, Ms 812, fol. 208r. Redmund Purcell of Rosconnill, Co. Kilkenny, married Margaret, daughter of Thomas Butler of Widdingstown, Co. Tipperary – a close relative of the baron of Dunboyne – before 1641 He was probably the second son of William Purcell of Esker (d. 1632); if so, he would have inherited Rosconnill from his uncle, Geoffrey Purcell, sometime after July 1632 (St Kieran's College, Carrigan

of Ormond and the central government, the moderate Catholic Sir Edward Butler of Duiske, had no authority to act, and with his son and heir, Pierce of Barrowmount, and his second son, John, both gone to join Mountgarret, he decided to sit things out as a neutral.[264]

Though poorly armed and attired – several witnesses refer to them as a 'rabble' – the Catholic army that Mountgarret raised was at least as numerous as anything that his Butler ancestors had commanded in the previous century. Most of the Butler lineage rose with him, revealing the extent to which he (and not the earl of Ormond) was now recognised as the dynasty's real figurehead. The three Butler peers in Tipperary, Viscount Ikerrin and the barons of Dunboyne and Cahir, gave Mountgarret their undivided support, with Ikerrin to the fore in military matters, eager to serve in Leinster as well as his native Munster.[265] Among the senior officers serving under Mountgarret in Kilkenny were his eldest son and heir Edmund Butler of Baleen (a colonel), his second son Edward Butler of Urlingford (a captain), his son-in-law Walter Butler of Paulstown, Pierce Butler of Barrowmount, John Butler of Duiske, and Thomas Butler of Aghtubbrid (all captains).[266] A later claim, made in Cromwellian times, that Mountgarret's brother James Butler of Tinnahinch, Co. Carlow, was not a captain under the viscount is cast into doubt by other evidence that shows James clearly had command of a company at Tinnahinch, and was in regular consultation with senior commanders throughout the rebellion.[267] In 1642 these would be joined by two other important members of the dynasty: a son of Sir Richard Butler of Knocktopher;[268] and, more significant, the earl of Ormond's brother, Richard Butler of Kilcash, a devout Catholic who resented Earl James's rejection of his parents' religion, and teamed up with Mountgarret's army some-time before the end of January 1642.[269] For political as much as military reasons, Richard was given the post of general in the rebel army, taking command of southern Tipperary.[270]

Additionally, it was hoped that Mountgarret's brother, Colonel John Butler, a professional soldier with experience of the continental religious wars, would return to Ireland to take charge of a regiment of horse in Kilkenny.[271] In the event he did not arrive, in January 1642 arrested at Holyhead on his way home by order of the English parliament.[272] His failure to appear was important in the

MSS, Vol. 3: 76, 83; Lamacraft (ed.), *Ir. funeral entries*, 45–6). **264** J. Hughes, 'The Butlers of Duiske Abbey', *RHAAI Jn.*, 3rd series 1/1 (1868), 69–70. **265** J.T. Gilbert (ed.), *A contemporary history of affairs in Ireland, 1641–52* (Dublin 1879), i, pt. 1, 29–30. One of Ikerrin's pikemen was a Kilkennyman, Richard Costello of Durrow (TCD, Ms 829, fol173r). **266** Ibid., Ms 812, ff 166r–168v. **267** Ibid., ff 251r, 259r, 261r. **268** Ibid., fol. 166r. **269** BL, Egerton Ms 80, ff 85–6. Richard was a friend of Mountgarret's son and heir, Edmund Butler of Baleen (HMC, *Ormonde MSS, 1572–1660*, 31). The religious virtue of his household at Kilcash is celebrated in the Catholic devotional tract written by the Carmelite Paul Browne, *The soul's delight* (Antwerp 1654). **270** Grosart (ed.), *Lismore papers*, 2nd series, v, 33–4, 56–7. **271** Gilbert (ed.), *Contemporary history*, i, pt. 1, 41. **272** Rushworth, *Historical collections*, IV, 259–61; Chester City RO, Ms ML/6/179; Cheshire County RO, Ms DCC 14/6. Having been detained for more than a week at Chester gaol, Butler was subsequently despatched under armed guard across England to London, 'deliv-

long term, for although the rebels got by without him in late 1641, the absence of such an experienced officer eventually took effect, compounding the army's chronic shortage of guns and gunpowder,[273] and it helps to explain why Mountgarret's forces met with such limited success outside Kilkenny and the south-east in the critical year of 1642.

Mountgarret's army was not just a Butler monopoly. Many of Co. Kilkenny's leading squires and gentlemen also enlisted as senior officers. By 1642 the provost marshal of the army was Thomas Cantwell of Cantwell's Court; on him devolved the twin duties of disciplining the soldiers and rounding up and restraining Protestant stragglers around the county. The head of the local Purcells, Philip Purcell of Ballyfoyle, was a captain, as was the acting head of the Blanchvilles, Garret Blanchville of Blanchvillestown (his father, Sir Edmund, was reputedly a madman by this date), the brothers John and Richard Comerford of Ballyburr, Thomas Fitzgerald, 'the eldest son of Mr Fitzgerald of Brownesford', John Bryan of Bawnmore, Patrick Forstall of Kilmanehine, and at least one of the Shortals.[274] Elsewhere in the ranks, commands also went to John, Lewis and Edward O'Brennan (all captains) and John MacWilliam O'Brennan (a lieutenant).[275]

Two things must be said regarding the composition of this large rebel army. It contained members of most of the traditional pro-Ormond families of Kilkenny, showing that little support remained for Earl James around the county. And the Idough dispossession had clearly boosted recruitment to the army's ranks, making it a genuinely inter-ethnic cross-county affair. Fighting alongside the Gaelic O'Brennans of the north, for instance, were the Anglo-Irish Stranges of the south. The army also contained local New English Catholics among its ranks, such as George Derrett of Smithstown and 'James Carlton of Idough, late servant to Richard Harrison', the Wandesfords' park-keeper at Castlecomer.[276] The inclusion of English Catholics in Mountgarret's army confirms what the most recent research on the 1640s conflict in Ireland has suggested, namely that religion more than ethnicity was the key factor in hostilities.[277]

Odd as it might seem, the Kilkenny 'rebellion' was in large part a loyalist one. Many who rallied to Mountgarret's banner viewed themselves as loyal subjects of the king. What they were rebelling against was not the monarch, but rather the corrupt officials of his government in Dublin, men who had penalised Catholicism and undermined local land titles, in the process doing the king a

ered from sheriff to sheriff (ibid., Ms DCC 47/19). **273** For the Confederate munitions problem, see P. Lenihan, 'Celtic warfare in the 1640s', in Young (ed.), *Celtic dimension*, 120–1; D. Edwards (ed.), 'The ships' journal of Captain Thomas Powell, 1642', *Anal. Hib.* 37 (1998), 254. **274** TCD, Ms 812, ff 166r, 169v, 181r; Carrigan, *Ossory*, iii, 415. Pierce Shortal of Kilbline & Rathardmore, Edmund Shortal of Killary and Robert Oge Shortal all supported the uprising, but it is not clear which of them was the 'Captain Shortal' referred to in the depositions. **275** TCD, Ms 812, ff 167r–v. **276** Ibid., ff 169v, 170r, 173r. **277** Canny, *Making Ireland British*, ch. 8; Tait, 'Harnessing corpses', ch. 12; A. Clarke, 'The 1641 rebellion and anti-popery in Ireland', in B. Mac Cuarta (ed.), *Ulster 1641: aspects of the rising* (Belfast 1993), 139–58. I will examine the role of English Catholics in the events of 1641 in a forthcoming paper.

disservice and insulting the religion of his queen, Henrietta Maria.[278] It seemed entirely logical to Viscount Richard and his followers to require Protestant officials, holding positions of authority directly from King Charles by royal letters patent, to surrender those very same positions into Catholic hands as 'unto us who stand for his majesty'. In rising up what they most wished to demonstrate was that they, the disempowered Catholics, were better monarchists than the Protestants who controlled the Dublin government. As Mountgarret put it in 1642, a 'traitorous faction … of the Puritan party' had subverted royal power in England as well as in Ireland; it was time to call them to account.[279]

The insurgent campaign in the county was a short one, lasting about three weeks in all places except Castlecomer (where by far the longest struggle occurred, from 'All hallows … to Shrovetide following' according to one witness, or 'about 15 weeks', according to another).[280] The sectarian character of the insurrection found expression in a number of sometimes brutal attacks on local Protestants, though in comparison to what happened in parts of Ulster the Kilkenny rising was relatively un-bloody.[281] As we shall see, the fact that a general massacre of Protestants was avoided in Kilkenny had much to do with the preventive hand of Mountgarret; had other voices prevailed, more blood might have been shed.

No more than during the sixteenth century possession of the northern borders was central to military security in Co. Kilkenny. Viscount Richard and his advisers were careful to deploy sufficient resources to the siege of Castlecomer until Lieutenant Farrell's garrison there (joined by up to 100 local Protestant settlers) had fallen. There had been much activity in the area even before Mountgarret had decided to rebel, with elements of the dispossessed O'Brennans combining with the Kavanaghs on cattle-raids and other incursions from a joint-base on the Carlow/Wexford frontier after 21 November. The parish church of Castlecomer, the spiritual heart of the Wandesford plantation, was 'stormed' and ransacked. The Revd Carpenter, a minister living at nearby Skehanagh, was beaten and robbed, as was the parson, John Watkinson.[282] Within four or five days, as the raiding and plundering spread, English colonists began fleeing 'in frost and snow' towards Castlecomer garrison.[283] About 30 November or 1 December Mountgarret authorised the commencement of a siege, anxious that a more coordinated attack be attempted before the arrival of government reinforcements.[284]

Surviving descriptions of the encounter, even the most exaggerated, indicate that fighting was minimal, with few casualties, perhaps four or five on either

---

278 See esp. the 'Humble appollogie' of the Pale lords to the king and queen: Carte, *Ormond*, v, 273–7; for rebel attitudes in general, see Ó Siochrú, *Confederate Ireland*, 11–54.   279 J. Hogan (ed.), *Letters and papers relating to the Irish rebellion, 1642–6* (Dublin 1936), 91.   280 Graves, 'Ancient tribes', 244; TCD, Ms 812, fol. 224r.   281 H. Simms, 'Violence in County Armagh, 1641', in MacCuarta (ed.), *Ulster 1641*, 123–38; Canny, *Making Ireland British*, 469–92.   282 TCD, Ms 812, ff 193r, 291r. 283 Carte, *Ormond*, ii, 146; TCD, Ms 812, fol. 224r.   284 Simultaneously, 'a great number of the Brennans and Butlers of Idough' entered Queen's County and occupied Leix Abbey (ibid., Ms 815, fol. 61v).

side. Presumably this was because a fully fledged culture of dispossession such as was to be found among the natives of Ulster (dispossessed in 1610) had not yet taken root among the O'Brennans (dispossessed in 1635), many of whom still harboured hopes of regaining their homeland by legal means. The ugliest incident occurred when Captain Lewis O'Brennan discovered a 'young English lad', the teenager Richard Barnard, hiding in a house in the town, having slipped out of the castle on an errand for Lieutenant Farrell or his father, the clothier Alexander Barnard. O'Brennan at once 'struck him in the head with his sword', a blow which almost killed him, and then hanged him in front of the castle, in full view of the besieged, 'upon his father's tenters till he were dead'.[285] On another occasion an Englishwoman, the wife of a collier, being a prisoner of the rebels, was sent by her captors to the castle bearing a message for Farrell, only to be shot by mistake 'before the gate' by other rebels unaware of her mission.[286] The garrison held out until 2 March 1642, when it surrendered on terms to forces commanded by Captains John Bryan, Philip Purcell and Edward O'Brennan. Immediately 'the custody and keeping of the castle and fort' was granted to its former owner, Richard Butler of Castlecomer, by a warrant of Viscount Mountgarret.[287] No massacre ensued. As one of the besieged, Ralph Fenton, testified ten years later, formal articles of surrender were signed in which the defeated were granted 'fair quarter' and the choice of remaining disarmed in Co. Kilkenny or else being escorted away under safe conduct towards Ballylemon, a government fort in Queen's County.[288]

One episode set the tone for the local insurrection, and guaranteed its success – the defection of Kilkenny city on 18 December. Here there is reason to suspect that even before Mountgarret formed his army at the end of November, the civic elite had for some time been preparing a Catholic coup d'etat. Late in October Alderman Thomas Ley, a native Protestant who had been reared as a ward of Henry Staines,[289] decided to stand down as the new portreeve of Irishtown. It is quite clear why. Griffith Williams, the new Protestant bishop of Ossory, had left the city in a hurry upon hearing of the Ulster revolt and the outbreak of disturbances in Tipperary.[290] Without Williams' backing, it was impossible for Ley to govern the town, especially as the supporters of the Catholic bishop, David Rothe, were itching to install their man in the episcopal palace. Accordingly, on 6 November Bishop Rothe's kinsman Oliver Rothe was sworn in as portreeve in Ley's stead.[291] With no Protestant in power anywhere in the city, the only remaining obstacle to a Catholic takeover was the local trained band, or civic militia, a force of 300 male citizens, 'mixed of Protestants and Papists', which was called out sometime after 23 October for Kilkenny's defence. Through rumour and intimidation it was soon an exclusively Catholic force, its Protestant members withdrawing to protect their homes,

285 Ibid., Ms 812, ff 298–302. **286** Ibid., ff 298–9. **287** Ibid., fol. 311. **288** Ibid., fol. 296. **289** NA, Lodge MSS, Wardships, etc., Vol. I, 33 and 99. **290** He had only arrived: F.R. Bolton, 'Griffith Williams, bishop of Ossory (1641–72)', *Butler Soc. Jn.*, 2/3 (1984), 325. **291** KCA, Irishtown Corporation Book, 1538–1661, fol. 110r.

'fearing to be surprised by the Papists'.[292] It was at this point that the greatest 'Papist' of all, Bishop Rothe, appeared centre-stage in the city. Almost certainly Kilkenny's decision to make common cause with Mountgarret was taken after consultation with the bishop, Viscount Richard's friend and adviser. When in mid-December the viscount paraded his army outside the city walls, the person who actually opened the gates to the troops was the bishop's kinsman, the city sheriff, Richard Murphy.[293]

As at Castlecomer no massacre of Protestants occurred, largely because there was no need of one: Mountgarret and his men had marched into the city unopposed. Instead, though one woman was smothered to death in her house,[294] the citizens turned their 'implacable fury' towards robbing all the Protestants living in the city. The tailor William Lucas was attacked and divested of all he possessed by neighbours.[295] Another victim of robbery was the English shoemaker James Benn. According to his testimony, when the viscount entered the city intruders saw their chance to break into his shop. Significantly, Benn and his family were not harmed. Greed mostly animated his assailants, who made off with his stock of leather and some 'household stuff'. He was not raided again, but it was several weeks before he and others felt safe. Henry Robinson, a Protestant brought as a prisoner to Kilkenny from Castlecomer, later recalled that the 'common people' of the city were baying for the blood of English Protestants on his appearance there. Granted open access to the city jail, they 'often' visited him in his cell to insult him and 'in a joyful manner' tell him that soon they expected to see him hanged – presumably from the scaffold 'of newly framed timber' mentioned by another witness that had been erected outside. To add to his anxiety, Robinson learned that a petition had been presented to Kilkenny city council, prompted by the Catholic archbishop of Cashel, Thomas Walsh, and an important arrival out of the north, Turlough Oge O'Neill (brother of the Ulster rebel leader, Sir Phelim O'Neill): 'that all English Protestants [in the city] be speedily executed'. The petition was heard and debated sometime about 19–22 December 1641, but after much arguing the local Catholics were 'diverted from this bloody device' and the motion was defeated. Robinson, a prisoner, reckoned he owed his delivery to the Kilkenny alderman, Richard Lawless of Talbot's Inch, but Shoemaker Benn, being at liberty in the city, was more knowledgeable of what had transpired in the council chamber. As he later testified in Dublin, the motion to kill all Protestants had been opposed not only by Lawless, but also by the most senior commanders of the local Catholic army, Viscount Mountgarret, his son Edmund Butler of Baleen, and Philip Purcell of Ballyfoyle.[296] And so it was that many Protestants

292 Cox, *Hibernia Anglicana*, 73; T. Fitzpatrick, *Waterford during the Civil War, 1641–53* (Waterford 1912), 100. Orders for the civic watch survive, dated 27 November 1641: KCA, Ms CR/K 57. **293** TCD, Ms 812, ff 200r–201r. Richard was married to Ellice, daughter of the bishop's nephew Richard Rothe fitz Edward. **294** R.S., *A collection*, 11. **295** TCD, Ms 812, fol. 220. **296** For Benn and Robinson, see ibid., ff 213r–214v, 223r. The new scaffold is noted in Ann Mawdsley's deposition (ibid., fol. 221v). See also Fitzpatrick, *Waterford*, 100.

were able to live on in Kilkenny city after Christmas 1641 – until the summer of 1643, in fact, when a truce with Ormond and the Protestant government in Dublin was in the process of being negotiated and conditions were finally safe for them to leave.

Yet, though the threat of being slaughtered was averted, conditions for Protestants inside the city were far from comfortable. In the wake of the Catholic uprising hundreds of Protestants had poured into Kilkenny from the surrounding countryside, coming from places as far apart as Freshford, Callan, Castlecomer, Ballyburr, Gowran and Clonmore. Some like Peter Pynchory of Glanmagow in Fassadinin came as refugees, abandoning their cottages and fleeing the land to seek temporary refuge with the countess of Ormond and her children at Kilkenny Castle.[297] Many others, however, arrived as prisoners under armed escort, having been rounded up, dispossessed and sent to the city either by one of Mountgarret's captains or by authority of Provost Marshal Cantwell.[298] For the most part they arrived in a pitiful state, 'some of them naked, others hiding their nakedness … with old rags which the Irish in derision had thrown at them', having stripped them of their best clothes, which were valuable.[299]

Conditions became chronic at Kilkenny Castle. By 23 December Countess Elizabeth was providing food, warm clothing and accommodation for 'near 300 Protestants',[300] with space so cramped in the Ormond ancestral seat that her servant Richard Comerford of Danginmore reckoned there were not two rooms left for herself and her own, all the rest being 'full of English families and Englishmen's goods'.[301] Reckoning she would have to start turning away refugees unless some of those already in her care could be moved elsewhere, the countess sought Mountgarret's leave to evacuate 'five score of the said Protestants into Waterford'.[302] She was pushing, literally, at an open door. Like her servants she would have known that during the recent debate before Kilkenny city council the viscount had quietened demands for a massacre by insisting that less drastic ways of ridding the area of Protestants should be explored, reportedly saying that 'such English [Protestants] as were left would soon enough go away and leave the country'.[303] By offering to arrange the flight of 100 Protestants out of the shire the countess was helping him maintain order in Kilkenny. He consented immediately, evidently encouraging more to leave, as subsequently a group of up to 160 assembled by the castle gates for departure.[304]

The evacuees' experience sheds a stark light on the new political order that was dawning in the Ormond territories. For all that Mountgarret wished the countess' followers gone, some of his fellow Butlers were unwilling to ease their departure, at least not before some profit in the form of extortion, and a little bitter amusement in the form of humiliation, had been exacted. The countess persuaded Mountgarret's second son, Edward Butler of Urlingford, to convey

---

297 Ibid., ff 200r–201r.   **298** Ibid., ff 197r–199r, 202r, 211r, 221v, 223r, 293.   **299** HMC, *Ormonde MSS*, 2nd series, ii, 371.   **300** This is the estimate given ten years later by one who had been there, Captain Warren (TCD, Ms 812, fol. 271r).   **301** HMC, *Ormonde MSS*, 2nd series, ii, 369.   **302** Ibid., 367.   **303** TCD, Ms 812, fol. 221v.   **304** Ibid., fol. 198r.

the Protestants south to the waterside, but only after she had agreed to meet the price he demanded for the service (£60), with the money paid up front, 'for the said Edward Butler would not stir without it'. Edward then extracted an additional sum from her followers (£25). The haggling done, the party set out at once, and reached Knocktopher by dark, where, at the countess's request, Sir Richard Butler provided them with shelter overnight. The next morning, Christmas Eve, Edward Butler abandoned them. Feigning toothache, he left, as he later admitted, 'carried in a horse litter', leaving the party defenceless without a guard; needless to say, he kept every penny he had received. Sir Richard Butler later claimed to have sent an armed escort with the evacuees to Waterford, which task he said he performed to 'the uttermost' of his power, but the truth of his assertion is thrown into doubt by the testimony of survivors of the march, who state that after leaving Knocktopher there was no protection to be had. As they marched further south, and as evening closed in, Catholic soldiers waylaid them, some of whom they recognised as having been previously among Edward Butler's company of guards. When one of their number, an Englishman, was killed by the soldiers, apparently as a warning, all thought of resistance subsided, and the company was 'robbed of their monies', divested of some of their clothes, and left 'stripped naked' to struggle on to their destination in 'very frosty' weather, in constant fear of another attack.[305] It was only after this that Sir Richard Butler's escort appeared, led by his younger son, William, and including two other gentlemen, Theobald Butler and 'Mr Sweetman' (probably one of the Sweetmans of Hodsgrove), with the overall responsibility for the operation falling to their superior officer, Pierce Butler of Barrowmount. With these to guard them the party made it to within sight of Waterford city.[306]

Still their ordeal was not over. On reaching the banks of the Suir, hope of a quick escape dissolved, for the party arrived just as a rebel force was gathering outside Waterford, eager to occupy the port city which, so far, had refused to commit to a Catholic revolt. Reckoning they had done enough, William and Theobald Butler, Sweetman, and the rest of the Knocktopher escort bid the evacuees farewell; before going, however, they insisted on being paid for the service they had performed, searching some of the party for 'what poor monies was left', doling out the proceeds among themselves. The evacuees were likewise beset by Pierce Butler of Barrowmount, who turned up promising to keep whatever money or valuables they still possessed safe overnight, and swearing to make full restitution next morning: 'But as soon as he had gotten it, he kept it, and made no restitution of any man's money'. Once more defenceless, the Protestants 'went over the river by boat unto Waterford', armed only with a letter from Lady Ormond to the mayor and aldermen requesting the provision of shipping as quickly as possible. Fearing a siege, and anxious not to antagonise the Catholic army nearby, there was little the city authorities could do.

305 TCD, Ms 812, ff 271–2. **306** Ibid., ff 198, 200–1.

Keeping the gates shut, they offered the evacuees food, which was thrown down from the walls, and advised them to seek transportation elsewhere. With this the party of 160 separated, some going to Passage to await shipping there, the rest staying put, hoping for further aid from the countess.[307]

Apprised of the situation, in Kilkenny Countess Elizabeth secured Mountgarret's consent that the remaining evacuees retreat to Carrick and the protection of her brother-in-law, Richard Butler of Kilcash, until shipping could be had for them.[308] It took three months to arrange transport. In the meantime, shortly after 9 January 1642 (and following Mountgarret's departure on campaign into Munster), the countess grew increasingly fearful of the rebels in Kilkenny, where again there was loud talk of bloodshed. By now desperate to reach her husband in Dublin and avoid being held as a hostage by the insurgents, but 'not daring to adventure herself by land', she was compelled to follow her former charges to Carrick. The situation was perilous there also. Despite being under the protection of Kilcash, other Catholic commanders threatened to attack, all the more so as the countess encouraged more 'distressed Protestants' to join her at Carrick, to the number of another 100 or more.[309] Late in March, expecting a raid by the Tipperary commander Colonel Wale, she 'sent to Edmund Butler [of Baleen], the governor of Waterford', entreating his help to escape.[310] Soon afterwards she and all her followers were ferried across the Suir towards Waterford by Pierce of Barrowmount.[311] However, just as freedom was within reach, it retracted, and the Catholic military leadership made the release of the countess, her children and followers conditional on the setting free of Captain Oliver Keating, a rebel officer held prisoner by Lord Esmond at Duncannon. On 30 March Esmond released Keating and immediately wrote to Ormond in Dublin to report that Countess Elizabeth and 'the little ones' were 'out of the lion's mouth'.[312] They almost were, but not before they had been forced to spend their last night in the south of Ireland huddled up in the 'waste houses without the gates' of Waterford, which (again) were closed in their faces, this time because the city had recently embraced the rebellion.[313] About one o'clock in the afternoon on 31 March they at last sailed out of Waterford harbour in two ships bound for Dublin, one vessel not being sufficient for their numbers. Typical of their experiences, the voyage was 'troublesome', taking them five days to reach the capital and safety.[314]

Later in the seventeenth century, many years after his death in 1651, certain Protestant writers claimed that Richard, third Viscount Mountgarret, had autho-

---

307 Ibid. **308** The following account is derived mainly from the 'letters and attestations' about the countess' conduct made in 1652 by Oliver Wheeler and others (HMC, *Ormonde MSS*, 2nd series, ii, 367–75). **309** Aware of her predicament, on 1 March 1642 Lord President St Leger assembled a force at Youghal to go 'towards the Carrick to bring the Countess of Ormond and her children away': Grosart (ed.), *Lismore MSS*, 1st series, v, 207. **310** HMC, *Ormonde MSS*, 2nd series, ii, 370. **311** TCD, Ms 812, fol. 200. **312** Bod. Lib., Carte Ms 3, fol. 28. **313** TCD, Ms 812, ff 200v–201r. **314** Edwards (ed.), 'Ship's Journal', 264; HMC, *Ormonde MSS*, 2nd series, ii, 372. A child died on the voyage.

rised a terrible slaughter of English Protestants in Co. Kilkenny in 1641–2. Writing in 1680, one author went so far as to suggest that Mountgarret 'proved rather more violent against the Protestants than the first [that is, the Ulster] rebels'.[315] Outrages were laid at his feet: generally, most of the murders committed in the south in 1641–2, while he had overall command of the Catholic forces;[316] more specifically, the hanging of six soldiers 'at the end of an house' in Kilkenny about Easter 1642.[317] Despite the best efforts of contemporary Catholic and Butlerite writers to deny these claims, it proved difficult to clear his name, and in Protestant literature of the eighteenth century he was still associated with the memory of massacre.[318] It is possible to trace the main source of this negative view of the viscount. As one of his posthumous defenders acknowledged in 1662, one text more than any other had besmirched Mountgarret, the anonymously authored *An abstract of some few of those barbarous cruel masacres and murthers of the Protestants and the English in some parts of Ireland, committed since the 23 of October 1641*, a pamphlet which first appeared in 1652 and was re-published in 1660.[319] This was especially influential because, following the Protestant victory in the wars of the 1640s, it drew attention to the sort of horror stories that the Catholics wished most to suppress after their defeat. Accordingly, instead of acknowledging the relative bloodlessness of Mountgarret's Kilkenny uprising in 1641, *An abstract* and subsequent Protestant histories looked to discredit the viscount and all his officers by drawing attention to the evidence of certain murders and other outrages that took place in the county.

There is not much doubt that Mountgarret was unfairly maligned. Examining the evidence it appears that none of the outrages that were later attributed to him were actually his responsibility, neither the general massacre across the south, reports of which were hugely exaggerated, nor the hanging of the six soldiers in Kilkenny, which an English Protestant eye-witness said was done by Captain Thomas Butler of Tubbrid, not by the viscount.[320] It seems, then, that the later seventeenth-century tradition of Mountgarret as a Papist tyrant was nothing more than a posthumous invention – one, moreover, that was completely out of step with earlier Protestant views of his role. Prior to his death many Irish Protestants had seen him rather as a moderate who preferred a negotiated settlement of Catholic grievances to an all-out religious war. Depositions made in 1642–4 and 1651–2 by survivors of the rebellion in Kilkenny referred repeatedly to his coming to the aid of various 'distressed Protestants' of the county. Even Mountgarret's most ardent critic, the Church of Ireland vicar of Kilmocahill, the Revd John Moore, had to admit that he owed his life to Viscount Richard for having given him a safe conduct out of the shire.[321] As seen already, Mountgarret's reported response to the demand

315 Rushworth, *Historical collections IV*, 169.   **316** Cox, *Hibernia Anglicana*, 94–5.   **317** Borlase, *History*, 117.   **318** E.g., Ledwich, *Antiquities*, ii, 465.   **319** It was derived from Henry Jones' book, *A remonstrance of divers remarkable passages concerning the church and kingdome of Ireland* (London 1642); see T. Barnard, '1641: A bibliographical essay', in Mac Cuarta (ed.), *Ulster 1641*, 173–86.   **320** TCD, Ms 812, fol. 299.   **321** Ibid., ff 197r–199r.

for a massacre of Protestants in Kilkenny city, threatening to 'pistol him [that] made any such request', brought some comfort to Protestants confined in the city.[322] He was as good as his word. Probably his most famous action during the rebellion was his shooting dead of 'one Cantwell' (and wounding of others) for involvement in the murder of a Protestant woman in Kilkenny city in December 1641.[323] The shooting caused shock across the Butler territories, for his victim was no common soldier but, as other sources record, the gentleman Richard Cantwell, brother of John, the prior of Holy Cross Abbey in Tipperary, the latter someone who the viscount 'much respected'.[324] Cantwell was not the only over-zealous rebel that Mountgarret killed. According to an eye witness, Nicholas Plunkett, a Meath Catholic who arrived in Kilkenny in 1642, Viscount Richard 'with his own hands killed one of the Irish that attempted to plunder … the English' in the county that summer.[325] More usually, of course, his efforts to safeguard captive Protestant settlers did not require such severity. Either during or after the siege of Castlecomer he allowed Richard Butler to set at liberty 'divers English' prisoners in the north of the county, provided Butler entered into a bond to guarantee their future peaceful behaviour.[326] His attitude to Protestant captives was probably best articulated by his eldest son, Edmund of Baleen, while campaigning in Co. Limerick in March 1642, who stated that he and his father 'did infinitely abhor and interdict the killing [of] any English but such as did resist them'.[327]

Probably the surest proof that his later vilification was unjustified is provided by that most famous of anti-Catholic texts, Sir John Temple's *History of the general rebellion in Ireland*, which appeared in 1646. Throughout its blood-spattered pages Mountgarret and Co. Kilkenny are barely mentioned, and this though it would have greatly served Temple's purpose to denigrate both as much as possible, given the centrality of the Kilkenny Confederation in British as well as Irish affairs at the time of publication. Indeed Temple's only atrocity story to feature the viscount depicts him in a favourable light, telling of how two leading Catholic gentlemen from Co. Carlow repeatedly entreated him to authorise the 'death and torture' of Anne Butler nee Colclough, because she and her family were 'rank puritan Protestants', 'to which malicious provocation the said lord did not hearken'.[328]

Viscount Richard was an old man when he took charge of the local uprising. It had been forty years since he had last seen military action, when serving under his father, the second viscount, and his father-in-law, the earl of Tyrone, at the end of the Elizabethan wars.[329] With precious little experience of command (thanks largely to the post-1603 government policy of excluding Catholic

322 Ibid., fol. 221.   **323** R.S., *A collection*, 11.   **324** Hickson (ed.), *Ireland*, ii, 250–1; Carte, *Ormond*, ii, 154.   **325** J.T. Gilbert (ed.), 'Nicholas Plunkett's account of the war and rebellion in Ireland', HMC, *Second Report* (London 1874), 231.   **326** TCD, Ms 812, fol. 293.   **327** H.W. Gillman, 'The rise and progress in Munster of the Rebellion, 1642', *JCHAS*, 2nd series 1/12 (Dec. 1895), 15–16.   **328** Temple, *History*, 196–8. Anne was a daughter of Sir Thomas Colclough of Tintern Abbey, Co. Wexford.   **329** Chapter 4 above.

lords and gentry from army positions), he had great difficulty curbing the excesses of many of those who served under him. The fact that he was forced to kill at least two of his underlings in 1641–2 betrays the fragility of his authority as much as it reveals his good intentions towards Protestant captives. Some of the worst excesses of the Catholic rebels in Munster occurred because his claims to over-all leadership were rejected by the lords of the province, and indiscipline ran riot in the ensuing vacuum. Even in Co. Kilkenny the old viscount was not always able to impose his will, such was the extent of sectarian disorder. Despite his instructions that all peaceable Protestant settlers be left unmolested, many of the gentry were quick to commit acts of plunder. As John Comerford of Ballyburr led his followers to believe, the object of the uprising was 'to banish the English [Protestants] and seize upon their goods'.[330] In the north of the shire, at Bawnmore in Galmoy barony, the Catholic landlord John Bryan allegedly plundered and drove away his most prosperous Protestant tenants; in the south, at Ballyreddy in Iverk and Ballybrazil in Ida, Robert Freney and Richard Strange did much the same; while in neighbouring counties, where the number of Protestants to be plundered was greater, Kilkenny gentry such as Robert Gall and Jasper Grant were to the fore in attacks.[331] The best recorded example of local looting concerns Richard Butler of Castlecomer, a great supporter of Mountgarret, who had the goods of various Protestant settlers brought to his little castle at Cownefeely, and there stored inside the bawn wall, entirely for his own benefit, and this despite being aware of the viscount's strong disap-proval of plunder.[332] At least Butler avoided the use of violence (one survivor later recalled that many Idough Protestants owed their lives to his mercy).[333] The same could not be said of three minor gentlemen living in 'Purcell's coun-try', Pierce Den and William and Edmund Archdekin, who at Muccully com-mitted 'cruelty' as well as 'robbery' on their English Protestant neighbours.[334]

The limit of Mountgarret's influence was especially evident when he was absent from the shire. Prisoners from Queen's County who had been seized and brought to the 'dark dungeon' of Kilkenny jail just before Christmas 1641 were subsequently dragged out and hanged 'without resistance of any' early in January 1642, at the behest of Colonel Florence Fitzpatrick, the chief rebel in Upper Ossory, who authorised this as soon as Mountgarret had gone into Munster.[335] Small wonder the countess of Ormond fled from Kilkenny Castle at precisely this time, with Fitzpatrick and his ilk beginning to 'murmur' at 'the favours showed by the said lady unto the English'.[336]

Mountgarret's ability to restrain his followers was greatly reduced in spring 1642, when conflict intensified across southern Ireland, and for the space of a

---

330 TCD, Ms 812, fol. 289.   **331** Ibid., Ms 812, ff 209–10; ibid., Ms 820, ff 10, 12, 316–7; Fitzpatrick, *Waterford*, 21–2.   **332** TCD, Ms 812, fol. 298r. He and his family may likewise have received cattle belonging to Protestant settlers in Queen's County (ibid., Ms 815, fol. 60v).   **333** Ibid., Ms 812, fol. 293r.   **334** Ibid., ff 170r, 217r.   **335** TCD. Ms 812, fol. 202v. Fitzpatrick's exploits in Laois are detailed in ibid., Ms 815, ff 16v, 21r–22r, 23v–27r, 31r, 61v.   **336** HMC, *Ormonde MSS*, 2nd series, ii, 369.

few fateful weeks he seems to have lost all control of events in the Kilkenny area. Two separate episodes of massacre of local Protestant groups are recorded during the month of May, involving those settled about Graiguenamanagh (2–3 May) and Gowran (*c*.15–22 May).[337] The catalyst for these grim events was provided by developments to the north and east of the shire, where the Catholic interest had suffered a series of setbacks since the beginning of the year. Commencing in February government troops commanded by the earl of Ormond and Sir Charles Coote had pursued a brutal policy of scorched earth in parts of Cos. Kildare and Wicklow, killing hundreds of non-combatant Catholics in an attempt to create a secure Protestant zone around Dublin and the Pale. On 6 April a detachment of Ormond's army, led by Sir Patrick Wemyss, had penetrated deep into Co. Carlow, towards Cloghgrenan Castle and the borders with Kilkenny, killing as many as 50 natives, whether 'rebels' or not.[338] Encouraged by this show of strength, and possibly reinforced, the garrison at Ballinakill in Queen's County broke out and raided into Idough, where it was later claimed 'an old woman of ninety years old' was burned alive 'in her own house'.[339] Not to be outdone, the Catholic forces subsequently hanged several Protestants who were still living in the area as a reprisal, five at Ballyragget on the orders of Edward Butler of Urlingford, including 'an old man, an old woman and a boy', and six at Kilkenny, in this case all soldiers, former members of the Castlecomer garrison, who were taken to the city for execution by the aforementioned Captain Thomas Butler.[340] A declaration later made by one Protestant onlooker strongly suggests that these reprisal killings occurred without the consent of Mountgarret. The viscount, the account states, was furious over the deaths at Ballyragget, and railed at his son, Edward Butler, who subsequently dared not 'come into his father's sight for hanging the said five prisoners'.[341]

Mountgarret hoped to rebut the government's advance at source. Abandoning his plans to seize Duncannon,[342] he assembled 'all the strength he could muster' and marched out of Kilkenny towards Dublin, a precipitate decision, as 'a moiety', or half, of his army went almost totally unarmed. On 15 April he observed Ormond's force near Athy in Co. Kildare. Despite the advice of Hugh Mc Phelim O'Byrne to fall back, on account of the 'rawness' of the men and their shortage of weapons, Mountgarret and Lord Ikerrin 'were of a contrary sense'. In the ensuing battle, fought at Kilrush, the Catholic forces were routed, losing 600–700 killed.[343] Immediately Mountgarret forfeited all credibility as a military leader. Not only had he lost, and lost heavily, but as his scattered forces beat a hasty retreat it seemed as though they had left the ground free for Ormond and Coote to advance virtually unopposed. Had he but lis-

---

337 A third, the undated hanging by Provost Marshal Cantwell of seven Protestants arrested at Ballyburr, probably belongs to this period also (TCD, Ms 812, fol. 221r).   338 Cox, *Hibernia*, 105.   339 R.S., *A collection*, 16.   340 TCD, Ms 812, fol. 299.   341 Ibid., fol. 331r.   342 Lord Esmond had expected Mountgarret to attack Duncannon sometime after 1 April (Bod Lib, Carte Ms 3, fol. 28).   343 Gilbert (ed.), *Contemporary history*, i, pt. 1, 29–30; HMC, *Ormonde MSS*, ii, 6.

tened to his advisers (as Ormond, no soldier either, listened to his),[344] then the Catholic population of the south might not have felt so endangered and the subsequent severity meted out to Protestants in parts of Co. Kilkenny might have been avoided.

Groups of Protestants still living in rural areas of the shire were rounded up and imprisoned shortly after the return of Catholic troops from Kilrush. Thus, late in April 1642 Colonels Edmund Butler of Baleen and Walter Bagenal of Dunleckny sent out men 'to apprehend the English' in the vicinity of Graiguenamanagh and the Rower, while 'about the beginning of May' between 35 and 40 English Protestant settlers were taken on the orders of Sir Walter Butler of Paulstown and Pierce Butler of Barrowmount and jailed in Gowran.[345] The presence of so many senior military figures in the east of the county shows how the Catholic forces were being amassed thereabouts, presumably in antic-ipation of a government attack. In this heightened atmosphere the presence of clusters of English Protestants was a security concern, all the more so when it was realised that one of the most prominent of the settlers, William Stone of Graigue, was a servant of Sir Charles Coote. Stone had earlier been interviewed over drinks by Edmund Butler and Walter Bagenal and boasted openly that he would have his day on the rebels when rescue arrived. Subsequent observation sealed his fate, as he was discovered in communication with government forces down river at Duncannon. To Bagenal's mind, of all the local Protestants 'there was one (naming William Stone) that the whole country would be the worse for', should he remain alive. Accordingly on 2 May Bagenal issued a warrant for Stone's execution in which it was explicitly stated that Stone was 'a spy' who would act as 'a guide to the enemy' in the event of an attack.[346] Without further ado, Stone was seized in his boat in the River Barrow by Garret McCody,[347] taken to Tinnahinch and there hanged 'towards evening' by Gibbon and Garret Forstall, household servants of Mountgarret's brother, James Butler.[348] With that all killings should have ended. However, within hours many other Protestants were dead, the victims of a nighttime massacre carried out by local Catholic tenants.

An Irish witness, Sarah Bolger, a native of Graiguenamanagh, later recalled that sometime before nightfall on 2 May Colonel Edmund Butler and his uncle, James of Tinnahinch had left the area, stating that she had seen them riding away on horseback towards Kilkenny.[349] It is likely that Colonel Walter Bagenal also departed, probably in a different direction, as no survivor, Protestant or Catholic, mentioned seeing him during the ensuing events. With no senior military figure on the spot to restrain the passions of local tenants and servants, the Protestants were easy prey, and their neighbours fell upon them with astonishing speed. In

344 W. Kelly, 'John Barry: An Irish Catholic royalist in the 1640s', in Ó Siochrú (ed.), *Kingdoms in crisis*, 146–7.   **345** TCD, Ms 812, ff 133r, 287.   **346** Hickson, *Ireland*, ii, 58–9; TCD, Ms 812, fol. 251r.   **347** Ibid., fol. 133r.   **348** Ibid., ff. 255r, 265r.   **349** Ibid., ff 263–5. This provides the main source for the next two paragraphs, with additional details from ibid., ff 133r, 251r, 255r.

the words of Sarah Bolger 'that same night, about midnight, Dermot O'Dogheran and Knogher More, servants to James Butler [of Tinnahinch]' crossed the bridge to Graiguenamanagh, 'knocked at the door and took away her husband', the English carpenter and joiner, Walter Shirley. Within little more than an hour she saw him hanged from a tree on the Tinnahinch side of the Barrow. 'John, the servant of John Stone, was also hanged on the same tree', while 'a little way from thence' they hanged Joseph Valentine, Sarah's brother-in-law. 'All the rest of the English', about six in all, being gathered together in full view of these killings, were then led away towards New Ross. They never reached the town, but were murdered along the way by Garret Kavanagh, a Gaelic piper, and his gang, their bodies dumped in the river.

The Graiguenamanagh massacre appalled the military leadership in Kilkenny, not least because it represented a flagrant disregard of its authority by the 'lower orders'. One of those murdered, Sarah Bolger's husband Walter Shirley, had been on good terms with both Walter Bagenal and James Butler before his death, having made a gate for Tinnahinch Castle and 'some pistol and carbine stocks for Colonel Bagenal and others' of the Catholic officers. Bagenal had granted Shirley a protection, or pass, in return for these services, which document he signed and delivered to Shirley on 2 May, sometime before William Stone was hanged. Shirley's subsequent murder was an insult to Bagenal's postition, cast-ing doubt on his ability to safeguard persons under his care; as such, it besmirched his reputation and undermined his honour as a gentleman and man of his word. Immediately on hearing news of the murders the military leader-ship determined to punish those responsible. An investigation was conducted in which the piper Kavanagh was identified as the main culprit. As one of his more fortunate accomplices later testified, 'Edmund Butler, son to ye Lord Mountgarret, did after[wards] hang the said piper for that fact'. The rest, of course, managed to evade detection, but they evidently got the leadership's message, for they took no part in the next outrage to occur in the area, the slaughter of 35 Protestants from Gowran who passed through Graiguenamanagh sometime between 15 and 22 May.[350]

It is impossible to be certain precisely how or why this group of religious victims was killed. However, one fact seems clear: hoping to avoid a repetition of the events of 2–3 May, the military leadership in east Co. Kilkenny took pre-cautions to guarantee their safe passage out of the shire. Thus it was arranged that the party would be removed from Gowran jail and given an escort through Graiguenamanagh and across the Barrow towards New Ross by Morris Kelly, ensign to Pierce Butler of Barrowmount. 'Bound two and three together' they made it safely to 'within a musket shot of [New] Ross', where Kelly gave them over to the charge of James Duffe, the captain of a foot company in the town. At this point extant accounts of the massacre diverge significantly. Some Protestant survivors state that they were to be taken only as far as New Ross

---

350 Ibid., fol. 133r.

(presumably to await shipping and evacuation); others, however, remarked that Ensign Kelly's orders were to find and recruit someone to convey the group further down river, to Duncannon Fort. Of course, from a purely military perspective, it made a great deal of sense to deliver the prisoners to Duncannon, thereby saving food in Kilkenny while helping to diminish Lord Esmond's supplies in the beleaguered government garrison; nevertheless, whatever Kelly's orders, the prisoners got only a little further before being killed. Having at first refused to take charge of the party, Captain Duffe and seven or eight of his men, 'with swords and batts in their hands', drove their victims to a woodland about a mile below New Ross where, it was reported, they murdered everyone except a woman and her four children. Kelly subsequently claimed that, on returning to New Ross three days afterwards and learning of the killings, he resigned his commission in disgust 'and never bore arms after'. If he was telling the truth, few believed him. His animosity towards English Protestants was too well known. In November 1641, for example, he had boasted that 'within a month' no Protestant would be alive in Kilkenny. Thus, though not actually present at the killing of the Gowran Protestants in May 1642, ten years later he was tried and executed by the Cromwellian authorities for suspected complicity in planning the slaughter.[351]

The timing of these atrocities is striking, occurring either side of a national ecclesiastical congregation of the Catholic bishops that met in Kilkenny city on 10–13 May at the invitation of Bishop Rothe. Asserting that the war against the Dublin government was lawful, just and 'pious', because Dublin Castle had fallen into the hands of 'unlawful usurpers, oppressors, and enemies of Catholics' who undermined 'the prerogative and royal rights of our gracious king' and 'the liberties and rights of Ireland', the prelates nonetheless feared the growth of anarchy. The congregation accordingly gave lengthy consideration to the collapse of order and the high incidence of sectarian and agrarian violence around the country. Reports of the bloodshed at Graiguenamanagh must have given an added urgency to discussions, which culminated with the delegates reaffirming the decision of the earlier synod of Kells (22 March) to pass sentence of excommunication against those guilty of pillaging or murder.[352] The grim fate of the Gowran Protestants near New Ross, happening just days after the congregation broke up, emphasised the need for the clergy to commit themselves to political action and make reality of their fine words.

Mountgarret welcomed the bishops' intervention. Though he never admitted it, it was beyond his power to restore order unaided. Traditional noble lordship, as it had operated in Co. Kilkenny during his youth, was no longer sufficient to keep the actions of the gentry and peasantry in check. The only way to prevent the worst excesses of religious discord was through close cooperation with bishops and senior churchmen. They alone enjoyed the moral author-

---

351 Ibid., ff 287r, 319r, 321r, 323r.   352 BL, Stowe Ms 82, ff 271–4; Healy, *History*, 330–1; Forrestal, *Catholic synods*, 103–4.

ity to convince ordinary Catholic men and women of the error of terrorising defenceless Protestants and the executive power to silence the ravings of over-zealous priests prepared to incite violence in order to rid their parishes of 'the heretics'. Once the church hierarchy became involved, atrocities ceased.

The new political structures for Catholic Ireland that emerged from the May gathering gave formal expression to the enhanced role of the church in secular affairs.[353] Until such time as a national assembly could meet, it was proposed that a general, or supreme, council made up of clergy, nobility and commons should rule the country from Kilkenny. Additionally, an oath of association, administered by clergy, was to be imposed on the Catholic population to bind them to the council's orders.[354] At the bishops' request, early in June an assembly of the lords and gentry from three of the four provinces gathered at Kilkenny (no representatives came from Connaught) to ratify and legitimise the new arrangements, and a series of 'acts, orders and constitutions' were adopted to regularise and harmonise the Catholic war effort while safeguarding landlord interests across the island.[355] On 11 June the first supreme council of what was now called the 'Confederate Catholics' began its sittings for the governance of the country.[356]

As Micheál Ó Siochrú has argued,[357] although no list of its membership survives, the first supreme council of the Confederates almost certainly included Mountgarret in the role of elder statesman. His conspicuousness apart,[358] various circumstantial facts lend weight to the suspicion that he sat on the first council. Because of his disastrous showing at the battle of Kilrush, he was persuaded to relinquish senior military office. Pending the arrival from France of General Thomas Preston, the post of commander-in-chief of the new national army of 4,500 men was given to Colonel Hugh McPhelim O'Byrne – which meant, of course, that Mountgarret was free to concentrate on more overtly political duties. Furthermore, it was only on 23 July, ten days after the disbandment of the first supreme council, that Viscount Richard again intervened in the war, travelling to Wexford town from where he made an ill-considered attempt to prise Duncannon Fort away from government control.[359] His political importance to the Confederates was confirmed in October, when he was elected president of the supreme council, a position that made him effective head of state for the national Catholic government.

353 For what follows see esp. Ó Siochrú, *Confederate Ireland*, 40–4. **354** The supreme council probably altered this later to enable lay officials to perform the task; hence James Bryan became a commissioner for the oath in Co. Kilkenny 'sometime after 1642' (ibid., 48n). **355** PRO, SP 63/260/67, ff 234–53. **356** The use of the term 'confederate' was interesting, hearkening back to the early days of the insurrection in the south-east, when in January 1642 (to the best of my knowledge) it was first used by a military delegation from Cos. Kilkenny, Tipperary, and Wexford, headed by Edmund Butler of Baleen and Richard Butler of Kilcash, who required the mayor and aldermen of Waterford to support 'the holy war of the Confederate Catholiques' (TCD, Ms 820, ff 15–16). **357** Ó Siochrú, *Confederate Ireland*, 42n. **358** E.g., his signature heads the sederunt of an important letter sent by the Kilkenny Catholics to the earl of Clanricarde on 11 June: U. Bourke, *Clanricarde memoirs* (London 1757), 171–2. **359** Hogan (ed.), *Letters and papers*, 91.

At this juncture the lives of Mountgarret and the local population entered a dramatic new phase, as Kilkenny became for seven years the administrative centre of a Catholic Irish state, its destiny inseparable from that of the Confederation to which it played host. There is little to be gained by prolonging this present study beyond autumn 1642, which, in regard to the story here told, marks an obvious end-point. Kilkenny, since 1610 or thereabouts the spiritual capital of the Irish Catholicism (through the work of Bishop David Rothe), now acted as its secular capital also. For the local gentry, the continuous drip-drip-drip of disempowerment that had corroded their status for more than a generation was at last stopped, and they threw themselves into the task of making the Confederate government work. Thus, Viscount Mountgarret and the Co. Kilkenny gentry occupied many of the senior and middling positions in the Confederate administration: Mountgarret was president until 1646; Richard Shee was secretary; Mountgarret, George Cantwell and one C. Bryan were army commissioners; Charles Greene of Kilkenny, a local English Catholic, was master of stores; and Thomas Cantwell of Cantwell's Court, Peter Shortal of Kilbline, Peter Rothe fitz John of Kilkenny (the former MP), and George Greene were judges, or resident commissioners, of the Confederate courts of justice.[360] In addition they took up what was probably a disproportionate number of military positions in the Confederate Leinster army, with as many as ten companies, or troops, being commanded by Colonel Walter Butler, Major Pierce Butler, and Captains Grace, Forstall, Drilling, Butler, Comerford, Nash, and Purcell in 1646.[361]

Most of all, however, this study also ends in 1642 because the Catholic uprising and the formation of the Confederacy represented the end of Ormond power in the area. Mountgarret, not the earl, occupied Kilkenny Castle, the chief seat of the Butler family, and the profits of the Ormond estate were sequestered to finance the war against the earl's Protestant army in Dublin. Henceforth for several years the traditional overlord was unable to influence the local community in any way, and was forced, reluctantly, to admit his loss of position by negotiating with the viscount and other leaders of the local Catholic community, his former subjects and inferiors. It would be eighteen long years, until the Stewart Restoration of 1660, before the Ormond lordship would be reborn in the county.

CONCLUSION

It might seem mistaken to identify the founding of the Confederacy as signalling the end of Ormond rule in Co. Kilkenny. There is, after all, an established school of thought that attributes the ultimate failure of the Confederates to the residual influence in Kilkenny after 1641 of the twelfth earl (and later marquis)

---

360 *Eighteenth report of the deputy keeper of the public records in Ireland* (Dublin 1886), 18; *Twentieth report* (Dublin 1888) 26, 29. **361** *CSPI, 1633–47,* 537, 539, 573.

of Ormond. Originating with certain Catholic treatises that were written after the Confederate defeat,[362] and subsequently repeated in the work of some distinguished historians,[363] this tradition contends that many of the most important Confederate leaders, from the president, Mountgarret, down, were somehow in the earl's power. Dubbed 'Ormondists', Viscount Richard and his allies have been represented invariably as always eager to cut a deal with the great Protestant magnate, even if doing so meant neutering the military capability of the Confederacy and jeopardising its chances of extracting the maximum concessions for Catholicism from the crown, solely because Ormond found their demands unpalatable. The root cause of Ormond's influence, apparently, was the continuing attachment of many of the lords and gentry of the Kilkenny area to the earl as their customary overlord and master. Accordingly, the most recent exponent of this view asserts that 'although not entirely his creatures' significant elements of the Confederate leadership were nonetheless his 'clients', and were 'inevitably drawn to the earl ... by traditional loyalty'.[364]

It need hardly be said that historians should at all times endeavour to avoid telescoping events, whereby what happened later is allowed, illogically, to set the context for what had happened earlier. Yet this is precisely the trouble with the 'Ormondist' thesis. Because during 1643–6 Mountgarret and his allies became increasingly anxious to negotiate a peace settlement with Ormond as the king's chosen representative in Ireland, and because Ormond did exert intermittent pressure on the Confederacy from his Dublin base, the previously dire state of Ormond's relations with the viscount and the Kilkenny community, in 1641–2, has been totally ignored. Consequently, the reasons underpinning the strained nature of the 1643 truce and the subsequent negotiations have not been fully appreciated. The convoluted peace talks of 1643–6 took place despite the relationship that existed between Ormond and his Catholic kin, not because of it.

Mutual alienation and mistrust, not rapprochement, was the inevitable consequence of events in Co. Kilkenny during the 1641 uprising. As soon as the revolt began the insurgents had made the Ormond estate a chief target for attack. For the insurrection to succeed it had been necessary to secure the estate as quickly as possible, so that as early as 2 December 1641 it was known in Clonmel that 'all of my lord of Ormond's cattle' in Kilkenny had been seized and some of his lands occupied.[365] At Market Castle, Dunmore, and Kilderry skirmishes seem to have taken place with the supporters (or sub-tenants) of the earl's English

362 Two treatises are usually cited: *Aphorismicall discovery of treasonable faction*, written after 1652, and printed in Gilbert (ed.), *Contemporary history*, i, 39–40; and Bishop French's *The unkinde desertor of loyall men and true frinds*, first published at Louvain in 1676, and later reprinted in *The historical works of Nicholas French* (2 vols., Dublin 1846), ii, 154. **363** E.g., Kelly, '"Most illustrious cavalier" or "unkinde desertor"?', 20; 'An Irish catholic royalist', 149; J. Ohlmeyer, *Civil war and restoration in the three Stuart kingdoms: the career of Randal MacDonell, marquis of Antrim* (Cambridge 1993; Dublin 2001), 164–5; 'Ireland Independent: Confederate foreign policy and international relations during the mid-seventeenth century', in Ohlmeyer (ed.), *Ireland*, 102. See also T. Fitzpatrick, *The bloody bridge and other papers relating to the insurrection of 1641* (Dublin 1903), 276. **364** Kelly, 'An Irish catholic royalist', 149. **365** HMC, *Egmont MSS*, i, 153.

Protestant tenants-in-chief, William Alfrey, Oliver Wheeler and Sir John Temple respectively. In each case hostile occupants had been driven away, forced to seek refuge with the countess of Ormond at Kilkenny Castle, and the property was ransacked.[366] In contrast to earlier uprisings that had threatened his ancestors, none of Ormond's traditional gentry clients lifted a finger in defence of his land; quite the opposite, in fact. The rebellion had general gentry support. Several of those who had been gentlemen-tenants of Ormond land – persons such as Patrick Purcell (Earl James' tenant at Clashduff), Piers Shortal (tenant of Maddock's mill), Thomas Butler (Tubbrid), Theobald Butler (Coolaghmore), Gilbert Butler (Glenpipe), and John Bryan (hereditary tenant of Bawnmore) – became prominent Catholic rebels and helped to organise the Confederate seizure of the earl's estate.[367] As shown above, the traumatic flight of the countess of Ormond and her Protestant followers to Waterford in early 1642 was not helped, but impaired and aggravated, by a number of local gentlemen who were both kinsmen and former clients, that is, the very sort who would once have served the house of Ormond instinctively, without hesitation.

Earl James himself acknowledged that his authority had collapsed. In a letter to London written in late 1641 he stated that, 'I have in my power particular[ly] suffered much … they rob to the very gates of Kilkenny, where I have my principal dwelling'.[368] His rental for Easter 1642, a hitherto neglected source, demonstrates that only a handful of his tenants continued to recognise his rights as overlord by paying rent to his wife, the countess, at Kilkenny and later at Carrick, before she escaped to Dublin in March.[369] During these first few months of the war concern for the safety of his wife and children consumed the earl. In his earliest letter about the Kilkenny rising he expressed his concern at having left Countess Elizabeth and their offspring 'defenceless' behind him;[370] by February 1642, having not seen or heard from his family for three months, he was inclined to think the worst. Writing to Viscount Gormanston, a senior Catholic lord who he hoped might exercise a moderating influence over the Kilkenny rebels, he swore that 'if they [the countess and children] shall receive injury by men', he would have his revenge on men, not on women and children.[371] Gormanston's reply was hardly encouraging. Instead of promising to act as a protector, the Pale lord expressed his approval of the rebels' decision to hold Ormond's family as 'pledges' (hostages).[372] By the beginning of March Earl James was convinced he would never see his wife and children again, and his surviving correspondence expresses nothing but hatred for his former subjects

366 As the depositions of Thomas Rothe and William Rothe – tenants at Glashare and Inchakilly respectively – make plain, the rebels plundered Ormond's Irish as well as his English tenants (HMC, *Ormonde MSS*, 2nd series, ii, 369–70). For details of the attacks on the Temple and Wheeler leaseholds, see ibid., 367–8, 370; TCD Ms 812, ff 20–3, 202–8. See also NLI, Ms 2506, ff 185r–188r. 367 Ibid.; TCD Ms 812, ff 166, 168, 181, 183. 368 Carte, *Ormond*, v, 267. 369 The tenants who paid her rent before she sailed from Waterford were James Comerford, Richard Comerford, Joseph Wheeler (who paid in corn), Oliver Wheeler, Sir Edward Butler of Duiske, 'Mr St Leger', and Richard Tobin. Sir Richard Butler of Knocktopher paid her in Dublin at Easter (NLI, Ms 2506, ff 185r–188r). 370 Carte, *Ormond*, v, 267. 371 Ibid., 292. 372 Ibid., 293.

in Kilkenny. 'By the help of God', he said, he would prosecute the war against the insurgents 'constantly', 'neither sparing the rebel because he is my kinsman or was [once] my friend', and he denounced the 'papists' for having done nothing except commit acts of wholesale 'rapine, barbarism and murder'.[373] Usually historians when commenting on the savage campaign waged by government forces in Leinster in spring 1642 blame the slaughter on Ormond's second-in-command, the justifiably notorious Sir Charles Coote. Given the earl's state of mind at the time of the campaign, this should perhaps be reconsidered.

Further evidence of the total collapse of Ormond/Kilkenny relations was provided at the battle of Kilrush. The English under Ormond's command were astonished (and impressed) by the malevolence the earl bore towards Mountgarret and the rest of his relatives, and the king later praised his bloodlust as 'a great comfort' to the state and 'a terror to the rebels'.[374] Especially esteemed was Ormond's declared intention to kill his brother, Richard of Kilcash, who had dared to enter the battlefield against him: Ormond 'made diligent enquiry after him as after a traitor'.[375] Richard evaded his grasp, only for another senior Butler, the baron of Dunboyne's brother, to satisfy the earl's thirst for vengeance when his head was brought in by Ormond's troops after the battle.[376]

A high level of animosity between the earl and the Kilkenny Catholic leadership continued for months, even years, to come. On 15 November 1642 a local gentleman named John Purcell was arrested in the Pale. On examination he revealed the extent of ill feeling now separating the different strands of the Butler dynasty, stating that Mountgarret and the Catholics of the lineage 'do all extremely inveigh against … Ormond for separating himself from them.' So great was their hatred for Earl James that Purcell reckoned he would need a strong bodyguard for his protection when he ventured south, as 'many hundreds' of the rebels in Kilkenny had taken an oath to kill the earl the next time they encountered him in the field.[377] Ormond for his own part allowed personal spite to interfere with his conduct of the war. The following December a detachment of his army broke off from an attack on New Ross to lay waste to Mountgarret's estate in Co. Wexford; there seems to have been little strategic value to the raid, other than to strike a blow at the old viscount's wealth and standing.[378]

It was, therefore, against a backdrop of hatred and mistrust, *not* one of covert clientage that the Confederate leadership entered into discussions with Ormond in the course of 1643. The talks were instigated by Ormond, who in mid-May

---

373 HMC, *Egmont MSS*, i, 166.   **374** Carte, *Ormond*, v, 292–3, 308–9, 312–3.   **375** HMC, *Ormonde MSS*, ii (London 1899), 7.   **376** Ibid., p.6. Given this episode, it is hard to accept the suggestion of one historian that Lord Dunboyne would have been 'sympathetic' to Ormond in early 1643 (Ó Siochrú, *Confederate Ireland*, 65 n.42).   **377** HMC, *Ormonde MSS, 1543–1700*, 53.   **378** NA, Paulet (Fitzpatrick) Papers, M 3179. This should not be confused with Ormond's later assault on New Ross, on 18 March 1643, for which see C.P. Meehan, *The Confederation of Kilkenny* (revised edn., Dublin 1905), Appendix, 293–7, and A.C. Miller, 'The battle of Ross: a controversial military event', *Irish Sword* 10 (1971).

despatched the Catholic royalist John Barry to Kilkenny in order to investigate the potential for dialogue.[379] In theory, of course, it should not have taken long for the two sides to reach an agreement, for following the outbreak of the English Civil War in summer 1642 they both claimed to act on behalf of 'his sacred majesty' the king. In reality, however, exploratory talks dragged on for months, until eventually, on 15 September, a one-year ceasefire rather than a permanent peace was concluded. For the record, it was only after the signing of this truce that a few gentry identifiable as 'Ormondists' emerged from the shadows to work on their master's behalf in Kilkenny. They numbered no more than five persons out of a local gentry community of several hundred:[380] the two knights, and brothers, Sir Edward Butler of Duiske (future Viscount Galmoy) and Sir Richard Butler of Knocktopher; and three of the earl's erstwhile domestic servants, his physician Dr Gerald (or Garret) Fennell, his estate manager Edward Comerford, and his business agent Patrick Archer.

Contrary to historians' assumptions, prior to the signing of the ceasefire none of these enjoyed much influence in the Kilkenny area. Sir Richard Butler had rendered only the minimum amount of assistance to the countess of Ormond's Protestant evacuees in December 1641, for fear of retaliation, and had kept a low profile ever since. Sir Edward Butler had lived as a recluse from the very beginning of hostilities, as estranged from the Confederate leadership as he was from his two rebel sons. His vain attempt to prevent the Graiguenamanagh massacre in May 1642 might have been more effective had he enjoyed a better relationship with the Catholic insurgents. Edward Comerford was slow to respond to the various demands of the Confederate government, and was probably just a marginal figure in the county.[381] The only 'Ormondist' to enjoy a position of influence was Fennell, who was elected to a seat on the Confederate supreme council in October 1642. Yet even Fennell's capacity to serve Ormond was highly constrained. In March 1642 one of his letters to Ormond had been intercepted by Viscount Mountgarret, who suspected him of being a spy, after which his attempts to send messages to Dublin were necessarily limited, lest 'he may suffer by it'.[382] He remained under suspicion (and surveillance) for a long time to come. A letter written to him by Ormond on 30 September 1643 concedes that Fennell had managed to provide little or no intelligence to the marquis since Mountgarret's discovery of their correspondence. The message, a mere five sentences, provides a revealing insight into Ormond's real standing in his former territories. In the frankest of terms he explained his reasons for not having contacted Fennell sooner. It would have been dangerous, he said, to have written directly 'in this open way', without using a code; dangerous, that is, to Fennell, for the marquis fully realised that the Kilkenny and Tipperary population had turned against him, and were liable to harm those who continued to

---

379 Kelly, 'An Irish Catholic royalist', 148. **380** A sixth, the Franciscan, Peter Walsh, appeared in 1646: J. Brennan, 'Peter Walsh and the Confederation of Kilkenny', *OKR* 4/2 (1990), 760–6. **381** *Twentieth report of the deputy keeper*, 26. **382** Gilbert, *Contemporary history*, i, 40; HMC, *Egmont MSS*, i, 166–7.

be associated with him.[383] (Eventually, in 1646, his links to Ormond cost Fennell his place on the Confederate council.)

Ormond's brief little note to Fennell provides an appropriate end-point to this study. Instead of suggesting that the marquis exercised any influence in Kilkenny, it shows that the Ormond lordship, based on widespread feudal clientage and traditional bonds of affinity, was no longer effective. The prolonged peace talks that consumed so much of the next two-and-a-half years did not lead to any reassertion of Ormond's right to rule in his ancestral territories; indeed, the subject was diplomatically ignored in the various negotiations. The marquis had even to forego his entitlement to rent from the Ormond estate. His lands remained fenced off from him, firmly under Confederate control. As a result, chronically short of cash in Dublin, he was forced to turn every which way for monetary support. Eventually, as new research has shown, he accepted assistance from members of the Protestant party in Ireland who were sympathetic to the English parliamentarians, and he did this even as he negotiated with the Confederates on behalf of the king.[384] Indeed, his leanings towards some of the hated 'Puritans' seriously compromised the royalist cause, only increasing Catholic suspicion of him in Kilkenny at a time when King Charles needed him to win the Confederates' trust and secure the intervention of an Irish Catholic army in the second civil war in England.[385]

Of course, the frustration of the talks had far-reaching consequences. Agreement was reached too late (March 1646) to prevent the king's defeat at Naseby at the hands of Oliver Cromwell and the New Model Army (June 1645); too late also to prevent the subsequent parliamentary seizure of the strategically vital ports of Bristol (September 1645) and Chester (February 1646). By the time Ormond and the Confederates finally agreed peace terms the game was already up for all concerned. Within a few months of the peace in Ireland, Rinuccini, the papal nuncio, who hoped to lead the Kilkenny Confederation into a holy war against Protestant heresy, overthrew Mountgarret and the 'peace party'. Within a few years the Stewart monarchy was swept away, and Britain and Ireland stood on the brink of a republican dictatorship that would be controlled by the forces of Protestant fundamentalism.

Perhaps if the king had chosen someone other than Ormond to be his chief negotiator in Ireland, events might have turned out differently. Then again, if Ormond had behaved as his ancestors had done, and sought to retain the loyalty of his traditional followers in Co. Kilkenny and the mid-south, peace talks would not have been necessary and loyalist elements among the southern Irish Catholics might have succeeded in their desire to save the house of Stewart and so break free of their marginalized position in the Three Kingdoms.

---

383 B.M. Mansfield, 'The marquis of Ormonde to Dr Fennell', *Butler Soc. Jn.* 2/4 (1985), 391. 384 Little, 'The marquess of Ormond', 83–99.   385 Ó Siochrú, *Confederate Ireland*, ch. 2–3; R. Armstrong, 'Ormond, the Confederate peace talks and Protestant royalism', in Ó Siochrú (ed.), *Kingdoms in crisis*, 122–40.

Conclusion

It is important to place the fall of the Ormond lordship after 1614 in its proper perspective. When in 1631 Walter, eleventh earl of Ormond, made his most famous remark, objecting to the government's plans to proceed with the confiscation and plantation of part of his inheritance in north Tipperary, on the grounds that he was the first of the Anglo-Irish, or 'Old English', to be treated as if he were 'mere Irish',[1] he was being deliberately disingenuous. Nearly seventy years previously, during the 1560s (while Walter was a child), his fellow Anglo-Irish the Cheevers of Maston had been confronted by the threat of state-sanctioned confiscation of their land on the grounds that they lacked proper English legal title to it. So too had Walter's uncle, Sir Edmund Butler of Cloghgrenan, who as seen in Chapter 3, had gone out into revolt in 1569 rather than lose part of Idrone, Co. Carlow, to an opportunistic, and highly arbitrary, government forfeiture.[2] Since then several other prominent Anglo-Irish families had had lands confiscated by the state: for instance, following the accession of James I in 1603 the Nugents of Delvin had lost possession of land in Co. Longford, and an official attempt had also been made to dispossess the Fitzgeralds of the Decies of their estate in Co. Waterford.[3] Earl Walter, then, was most definitely *not* the first 'Old English' lord to be confronted by a New English central administration determined to deprive him of land as if he were 'mere Irish', denying him title to it at English law.

Yet there was something in his aspersion all the same: finally, after a hundred years of crown support in which the earldom of Ormond had gone from strength to strength, it had been suddenly reduced to the level of any other Irish lordship. Its special status as an Anglo-Irish satellite of the English crown had ended, and its palatine liberty in Tipperary, the last secular liberty in Ireland, had gone, abol-

---

1 Bod. Lib., Carte Ms 30, fol. 259. His comments have become a common feature of various academic studies of the early seventeenth century, e.g. A. Clarke, 'Selling royal favours, 1624–32', *NHI* iii, 242; C. Russell, *The causes of the English civil war* (Oxford 1990), 55; Kelly, 'Ormond and Strafford', 90. 2 Canny, *Elizabethan conquest*, ch. 4. 3 R. Gillespie, 'A question of survival: the O'Farrells and Longford in the seventeenth century', in R. Gillespie & G. Moran (ed.), *Longford: essays in county history* (Dublin 1991), 15–16; Lambeth Palace Library, Ms 610, ff 87r–88v. In Co. Cork between *c.*1590 and 1618 the Barrys Oge of Rincorran struggled to secure their title to their shrivelling estate against the intrusive activities of local English administrators: K. Nicholls, 'The development of lordship in County Cork, 1300–1600', in P. O'Flanagan & C. G. Buttimer (ed.), *Cork: history & society* (Dublin 1993), 184–5.

ished in 1621. Once very wealthy, the earldom had fallen massively into debt due
to crown interference in its affairs. The fact that part of its territory was sched-
uled for plantation set the seal on its demotion into the ranks of the 'mere Irishry'.
Like many lordships before it, and in spite of its long record of loyalty to the
crown, the earldom of Ormond had been humbled by the English reconquest of
Ireland. The apparent improvement of the political status of the earldom after
Walter's death was only a mirage. Debts continued to pile up. Part of the price
required by the state of Walter's grandson and successor, Earl James, for renewing its support to him was his full cooperation in the north Tipperary plantation
scheme.[4] That James eventually acquiesced in the government's demands[5] amply
testified to the fact that the era of Ormond autonomy in Kilkenny and Tipperary
was finished. Following the initial government assult on the earldom in 1614 it
had become increasingly important that the earls avoid further a confrontation
with the state. The Ormond lordship had been subjugated.

It is truly remarkable that the lordship had avoided capitulation and retained
its independence for as long as it did. At times in the hundred-year period following the establishment of a new line of earls by Piers Ruadh Butler in 1515
the Ormond country around Kilkenny had enjoyed a charmed existence. The
earls' political abilities, and their close ties to the monarchy, had enabled them
to protect their territory from a multitude of dangers. Under the boy-king
Edward VI the plans of the Irish administration to profit from the wardship of
'Black' Thomas, the tenth earl, hoping to seize Kilkenny Castle as a vicregeal
residence and establish royal garrisons in the Butlers' outlying fortresses, had
been diverted fairly easily in London, where the family had influence. In the
reign of Elizabeth I Kilkenny had not experienced the full horrors of martial
law (and its attendant government execution squads) until 1582–3, something
that had set it apart from its nearest neighbours in the south, as thousands of
people were summarily put to death across Wexford, Wicklow, Carlow, Kildare,
Queen's County, King's County, Limerick and Cork during the 1550s, '60s
and '70s.[6] During the Nine Years War Kilkenny and east Tipperary had seemed
like a haven of peace and plenty in a land ravaged by war and famine. The local
population may even have increased, as refugees from other less well defended
regions poured in seeking sanctuary.

Across the country the power and prestige of the earls had grown accordingly, reaching its peak under Thomas, the tenth earl, who had dominated affairs
in Elizabethan Ireland at a time when many other Irish lords were weakened
by the strain of government expansion and some had collapsed. In stark contrast to developments within other Irish lordships, it had not been until the
beginning of the seventeenth century that the earls of Ormond had lost con-

---

4 Bod. Lib., Carte Ms 30, fol. 266.   **5** While still Viscount Thurles, James had supported Earl
Walter's objections to the plantation scheme (J.P. Prendergast, 'The projected plantation of Ormond
by King Charles I', *JKHAS* i (1849–51), 401), and as Kelly has shown, James did not finally consent to it until 1637 (Kelly, 'Ormond and Strafford', 94–5).   **6** Edwards, 'Beyond reform', 15–21;
'Ideology and experience'.

trol of local government personnel in Kilkenny, finally seeing their gentry clients displaced by outsiders imposed by Dublin. Thus, in a period of enormous political and social dislocation, the Ormond lordship had for a long time been characterised by continuity and stability, especially in its heartland, in the Nore river valley and the midland basin of Co. Kilkenny. But the disruption, when it came, came swiftly.

The dramatic decline of the earldom after 1614, and especially its collapse after 1633, points up one of the great under-explored themes of early seventeenth century Irish history – the continuing vitality of feudalism. Far from being some crumbling anachronism inherited from the Middle Ages, the principles of feudalism were deeply embedded in the Kilkenny community. Successive earls of Ormond had placed great store by the network of feudal relations that tied most sections of society to their leadership, and once the twelfth earl, James Butler, rejected the system in his search for immediate financial gain, he was himself rejected by local society. His reliance on the central power of the government left him more like Achilles than Apollo, unsteady on his feet as he turned away from the traditional responsibilities of lordship. Feudalism had more to do with social bonding and patterns of conduct than simple economics. Discontent with the new earl produced a refashioning of the Butler lordship after 1633, with the local community transferring its allegiance to Earl James's grand-uncle, Richard, Viscount Mountgarret, who, despite his difficulties with the Protestant colonial government in Dublin, was well connected in England, and was more willing than James to seek redress of local grievances – by outright opposition to the executive, if necessary.

And so it was that Ormond rule in Kilkenny and east Tipperary collapsed under what some historians have depicted as a pragmatic modernising earl – James Butler, twelfth earl of Ormond, who, on succeeding to the title, is considered to have recognised the new circumstances of post-conquest Ireland and renegotiated the political place of his earldom in the country with the new chief governor, his ally Sir Thomas Wentworth. It is interesting that in cultivating his relationship with Wentworth, for a time Ormond displayed what one scholar has dubbed an almost feudal sense of obligation towards his friend and patron.[7] If only he had been as mindful of his own obligations at home in Kilkenny he could have served his own interests more effectively. Had he shown a little less enthusiasm for Wentworth's pursuit of 'thorough' state power, he might have helped to avert the crisis that erupted in 1641 by keeping Kilkenny and east Tipperary neutral and under his control. The Ormond lordship had always enjoyed a strategic significance in Irish politics; invariably, whoever governed Kilkenny had national influence. By modernising as he did, throwing his territories open to the divisive policies of the central government, Ormond's pragmatism was shortsighted. In the longer term it cost him dearly. Whatever his financial gains during the 1630s, he entered the 1640s still enormously in debt, and following the out-

---

7 Kelly, 'Ormond and Strafford', 96.

break of full-scale civil war his finances were more precarious than ever before, as his rental income shrivelled up and his lands were seized by Mountgarret's Confederate Catholics.[8] His ability to extricate himself (and the monarchy he represented) from the political maze of 1640s Ireland was severely hampered by the memory of his behaviour under Wentworth. Having supported the governor's double-cross of the Catholic MPs in the 1634 parliament, and gone on to profit from the dispossession of Mountgarret, the O'Brennans and many others in Idough in 1635–6, he inevitably presented himself to his Catholic neighbours and kindred as an unprincipled turncoat. His subsequent use of coercion in Kilkenny, his eviction of tenants, and his cooperation with the north Tipperary plantation scheme increased the opprobrium directed against him, so much so that his capacity to serve the crown was severely limited. To paraphrase John Lowe, at a time of monumental mistrust between Irish Catholics and the Stewart regime, Ormond was a singularly unsuitable agent of the king.[9] His reputation as the 'Unkinde Desertor' of the Catholic Anglo-Irish had already been born, and he found it impossible to shake off.[10] Had the Cromwellian Republic that replaced Charles I not collapsed in the late 1650s Ormond would never have attained greatness. That he did so eventually was due more to accident than design.

The twelfth earl's loss of authority in Co. Kilkenny before 1642 points up one of the most important aspects of political life in Tudor and early Stewart Ireland – outside the walls of Dublin Castle, in the provinces, power was aristocratic, and as such it was personal. The personality of lords was crucial to the success or failure of lordship. For more than a century after 1515 successive earls of Ormond had attempted to impress their authority upon the local gentry on a one-to-one basis, like little monarchs holding court at the castles of Kilkenny and Carrick, where allies and supporters were honoured and erring members of the local elite privately censured.

The eighth earl, Piers Ruadh, a traditional gaelicised warlord, had sought to impress local landowners and merchants with his military prowess, suggesting he alone should have their support, as only he could guarantee them protection. Like other warlords, he was prepared to use intimidation to secure compliance, but even so he was careful not to push the Kilkenny gentry too hard. Among other things he made the inhabitants of neighbouring Wexford take the strain of maintaining his troops rather than risk alienating the Kilkenny elite with excessive military taxes. Lordship was about giving as well as taking, and the more a lord was able to give, the greater his power and influence. Piers offered the gentry the chance to profit through military expansion.

His son and grandson respectively, the ninth and tenth earls, built extensively on the foundations he bequeathed them, allowing the local elite to par-

8 R. Gillespie, 'The Irish economy at war, 1641–52', in Ohlmeyer (ed.), *Ireland*, 178–9; Little, 'The marquess'.   9 J. Lowe, 'Charles I and the confederation of Kilkenny', *IHS*, 14/53 (March 1964), 10.   10 French, *The unkinde desertor,* passim; T. Barnard, 'Irish images of Cromwell', in R.C. Richardson (ed.), *Images of Oliver Cromwell* (Manchester 1990), 183; Ó Ciardha, '"The unkinde deserter" and "The Bright Duke"', 177–93.

ticipate in their affairs and share in their prosperity. It was entirely in the earls'
own interests to honour the principles of good lordship. By retaining the loyalty of Kilkenny and the mid-south they were able to secure the favour of successive Tudor monarchs, who recognised that a strong Ormond lordship might
help reduce English security costs in Ireland – in turn the ninth and tenth earls
saw to it that their leading servants in Kilkenny and Tipperary had access to the
monarchy in London.

Lineage mattered enormously, but successful lordship demanded other qual-
ities – certainly, to rule Kilkenny and east Tipperary effectively it was not
enough to be head of the Butlers. As some senior Butlers discovered for themselves during the later sixteenth century, obedience was not automatic. The
local gentry and merchants stayed loyal to the tenth earl, 'Black' Thomas,
because he responded to the popular demand for protection – protection from
the excesses committed by his own brethren and some of the soldiers in the
Butler army, and protection from the officers of the state who, from the 1560s
onwards, showed an increasing disinclination to tolerate local autonomy. At
times Earl Thomas's defence of local interests was risky, especially when it meant
trying to block royal policy-makers in Dublin, but because of his high standing with Elizabeth I he was usually sure of his ability to prevail against even the
most senior government officials. His efforts on behalf of the Kilkenny gentry
proved worthwhile. As a rule, the county elite were willing to forgive his occasional aberrations, and they gave him steadfast support against the Butler rebels
of 1569 and 1596–7. In 1600 they raised a large ransom to buy his freedom from
captivity, and twelve of the local gentry gave themselves up as hostages to his
captors as a guarantee that the money would be collected, surely one of the
most remarkable episodes in the history of Elizabethan Ireland. After his death
aged 83 in 1614, Earl Thomas passed into popular memory as a great lord who
had also been a good lord. As one writer remembered him many years later,
the tenth earl, 'by name Black Thomas', had been 'a happy and a glorious earl,
hospiciously noble, and had many depending on his bounty and good nature'.
As well as being 'highly esteemed by Queen Elizabeth, King James and the
councils of England and Ireland', the earl had earned the regard of 'the people
of both kingdoms', having 'succoured the distressed' and provided 'a prop to
such as could not stand by themselves'. Though highly idealised and verging
on hagiography, the text in which this recollection of the earl appears (written
in 1676) is a powerful testament to the potential of feudal lordship for popularity, a fact often forgotten by historians.[11]

The tenth earl's successor, Earl Walter, was also highly regarded in the
county, as following the establishment of the Stewart monarchy under James
I, he too tried to defend the old order against government aggression. As far
as we can tell, his zeal in the Catholic cause did not alarm the local community of Kilkenny, who remembered him after his death as 'good, godly and

11 French, *The unkinde desertor*, 193–4.

virtuous'.[12] It did, of course, alarm the state authorities. Yet his subsequent problems with the crown, his disinheritance, imprisonment and impoverishment, did not destroy his capacity for leadership. When he returned to Kilkenny in 1628 he was enthusiastically accepted as overlord by the local inhabitants. Mounting debts and poverty did not prevent him exercising authority, and when he held discussions with government officials in the final years of his life he argued his case from a position of strength, not weakness – hence his defiance of the north Tipperary plantation project. The Ormond lordship, for all its financial difficulties, was still operative, because the incumbent earl continued to enjoy local support.

Ultimately, the failure of Walter's grandson, Earl James, to exercise personal influence as overlord exposes the unworkability of his supposedly pragmatic alliance with Lord Deputy Wentworth and his support for Wentworth's pursuit of 'thorough' state power. In early seventeenth-century Ireland more government did not mean better government, for state policies followed a strong sectarian colonialist direction. The Catholic Anglo-Irish community to which Earl James belonged by birth had been increasingly excluded from central and local government since the early 1600s; Wentworth's alliance with him did not reverse the trend towards the protestantisation and anglicisation of power, for the young earl was a Protestant, and following his compact with Wentworth, Kilkenny's Catholics remained cut off from Dublin and London, their hopes for a restoration of their former privileges undone. And yet their participation was necessary for the successful expansion of state control, if only because the crown lacked suitable English Protestants to represent it in local government in the mid-south. The men who dominated the county administration in Kilkenny in the 1620s and '30s – Patrick Wemyss, Henry Staines, Oliver Wheeler, Sir Cyprian Horsfall – were all newcomers to the area, colonial adventurers with few connections in county society. Confined to their hands, the enforcement of government seemed intrusive, an imposition by outsiders, whereas in the past its impact had been moderated and acclimatised through traditional gentry involvement.

'Thorough' government along the lines envisaged by Wentworth, brooking no devolution and riding roughshod over established regional interests, was only possible so long as Wentworth held the reins of power. Had Wentworth not been expendable, perhaps James Butler, twelfth earl of Ormond, would have continued to prosper in spite of his mounting disrepute inside his ancestral territories. But like so many chief governors before him, Wentworth was expendable. His sudden fall in 1640–1 laid bare the rashness of Earl James' cooperation with policies designed to replace regional power with undiluted central power. The Catholics of Kilkenny, a region of the country ostensibly under his sway, rose in revolt against him and the policies he embodied, perceiving him as a treacherous freebooter who had 'made the noble house of Ormond an infamous den of rapine'.[13] In doing so, the local Catholic community brought the Ormond lordship to a sudden and violent end.

12 Ibid., 26. 13 Ibid., 193.

Lands, squires and gentry

The principal landowners in County Kilkenny in 1640

(Total acreage of the county: 263,000 acres. All acreages according to 1654
Plantation measure)

Magnates	Acres	Manors	Castles
The earl and countess of Ormond[1]	66,760	15	25
Lesser lords			
Christopher Wandesford of Castlecomer[2]	21,620	1	1
Richard Butler, 3rd Viscount Mountgarret	17,440	6	3
Robert Walsh of Castlehowell	11,020	5	4
John Grace of Courtstown	9,840	1	3
Sir Edward Butler of Duiske	9,310	1	2
Squires			
The bishop of Ossory	5,700	7	4
Thomas Shortal of Ballylorcaine	5,380	3	3
Henry Archer of Muccully	5,250	2	3
Robert Rothe of Tullaghmaine	4,620	2	4
Robert Shee of Upper Court	4,300	1	5
John Cantwell of Cantwell's Court	3,590	5	3
Oliver Wheeler of Kilkeasy	3,480	1	2

1 According to the Cromwellian Book of Survey and Distribution (NLI, Ms 975) the earl and countess held only 59,420 acres in the county in 1641. This figure cannot be accepted. The Ormond lands in the barony of Kells, amounting to approximately 3,140 acres (1641 measure) were almost entirely omitted by the Cromwellian surveyors. Moreover, an account made c.1667 for the duke of Ormond by Thomas Elliott, the deputy-surveyor of Ireland (NLI, Ms 2560), draws attention to a further 1,930 acres overlooked in the Survey Book of Distribution. It is interesting to note that these lands werte included in the Civil Survey, the original of which was available to Elliott, and their subsequent omission from the Book of Distribution is an indication of the shoddy quality of the transcriptions made by the Book's compilers. Furthermore, there is reason to believe that an additional 1,780 acres or so (situated respectively at Rathlogan, Rosbercon, Ballytarsney, Doornane, Polroane, Kells, Cottrellsgrove and Cloghasty) were likewise in Ormond hands in 1641; not only do some of them appear in the Ormond rental for 1642 (NLI, Ms 2506, fol. 187v), but the others were part of the estate in 1618 (CPRIJI, 455–9), and thereafter there is no record of their transfer out of the dynasty's hands. Finally, the estate of 490 acres at Kilderry apportioned to Sir John Temple in the Book of Survey and Distribution was in fact held by Sir John on lease from the earl (NLI, Ms 2506, fol. 187v). 2 The Book of Survey and Distribution is hopelessly inaccurate about the Wandesford estate, omitting most of the townlands and half of the acreage confirmed to Christopher Wandesford by royal grant in 1639. For the full listing see McCall, *Family of Wandesford*, Appendix.

Sir Walter Butler of Paulstown	3,240	1	2
Thomas Den of Grenan	3,210	2	2
Peter Strange of Dunkitt	3,140	1	2
Philip Purcell of Ballyfoyle	3,040	2	3
Sir Edmund Blanchville of Blanchvillestown[3]	2,950	1	2
Richard Strange of Drumdowney	2,930	1	2
John Bryan of Bawnmore	2,840	2	2
The O'Ryans of Farren O'Ryan	2,800	0	5

Gentry

Thomas Walsh of Listerlin	2,390	1	2
David Butler of Kirrehill	2,320	1	1
Edmund Daton of Kilmodally	2,260	1	1
Thomas Freney of Ballyready	2,080	1	1
Peter Shortal of Kilbleine	1,920	1	3
John O'Dea-Fitzgerald of Gurteens	1,870	1	2
Edmund Fitzgerald of Brownesford	1,770	1	2
Oliver Shortal of Upper Clara	1,690	3	3
William Gall of Gallskill	1,670	1	2
Sir Cyprian Horsfall of Inishnag	1,620	1	2
Pierce Butler of Callan	1,610	1	2
John Comerford of Ballybur	1,550	1	2
Redmund Archdekin of Cloghlea	1,540	1	1
Robert Forstall of Kilferagh	1,530	1	1
Michael Cowley of Radestown	1,460	1	2
George St Leger of Tullaghanbroge	1,400	1	1
David Rothe of Kilkenny	1,340	(unclear)	
William Comerford of Inchyhologhan	1,300	1	2
James Kelly of Gowran	1,300	0	2
Pierce Butler of Barrowmount	1,210	1	1
William Sweetman of Castle Eve	1,210	1	3
Richard Barron Fitzgerald of Burnchurch	1,200	1	2
David Grant of Corluddy	1,150	1	2
Gerald Grace of Legan & Ballylinch	1,140	1	2
John Leonard of Flemingstown	1,130	(unclear)	
John Archdekin of Rahinrothe	1,110	2	2
Pierce Walsh of Grangeowney	1,100	1	1
Edmund Howling of Dirrenahinch	1,070	1	2
David Tobyn of Cahirlesky	1,070	1	1
Foulk Den of Fiddown	1,050	1	2
William Walton of Walton's Grove	1,050	1	1
Col. Richard Butler of Butlerswood	1,040	1	1
Pierce Archdekin of Kilmurry	1,030	1	1
Richard Butler of Castlecomer	1,030	1	1
Philip Walsh of Knockmugline	1,000	(unclear)	

---

3 Because Sir Edmund was declared a 'lunatic' by the authorities, the estate was effectively controlled for many years before his death by his eldest son and heir, Gerald Blanchville (Carrigan, *Ossory*, iii, 415).

John Grace of Garryhiggin	980	I	I
Pierce Butler of Annagh	930	I	I
William Drilling of Kilberegan	900	I	I
Nicholas Aylward of Aylwardstown	870	0	I
Richard Butler of Kilcash, Co. Tipperary	850	(unclear)	
Sir Nicholas White of Leixlip, Co. Kildare	850	I	2
Robert Shortal of Tubbrid	810	I	I
Nicholas Purcell of Ballsallagh	760	0	I
John Walsh of Ballyconnaght	750	(unclear)	
Edmund Grant of Poleraine	720	0	I
James Tobyn of Killaghy, Co. Tipperary	720	0	I
James Sweetman of Hodsgrove	700	0	3
Garret Blanchville of Kilmidimoge	640	I	I
Walter Archer of Corbettstown	630	I	I
James Butler of Danginspiddoge	630	I	I
Richard Grant of Rathkieran	620	0	I
Marcus Knaresborough of Kilkenny	620	0	I
James Forstall of Forstallstown	590	0	I
Peter Forstall of Kilmacnogue	590	0	I
John Rochford of Killary	590	I	I
John Aylward of Kilculiheen	580	(unclear)	
Sir Richard Butler of Knocktopher	580	I	3
James Comerford of Ballymack	580	I	2
Edmund Grace of Kilrindowney	570	I	I
Richard Lawless of Talbot's Inch	570	I	I
Peter Shee of Kilkenny	570	0	I
Philip Purcell of Foulkesrath	550	0	I
William Walsh of Ballinrea	550	0	I
James Walsh of Corbehy	540	0	I
Thomas Grant of Ballinabooley	510	0	I
Edmund Purcell of Esker	500	0	I

The demography of the Kilkenny elite

A sample taken of the generation of landlords and merchants who died before 1640

Extracted from extant Funeral Entries and Inquisitions Post Mortem

Father's date of death	Deceased father's name	CHILDREN				Age of heir/ heiress (if known)
		Total	Male	Female	Non-survivors	
1594	G. Blanchville	9	6	3	4	9
1602	2nd Viscount Mountgarret	16	8	8	2	Over 21
1616	J. Rochford	13	7	6	–	14
1621	D. Fitzgerald	8	5	3	–	30
1622	L. Shee	8	2	6	–	Over 21
1626	W. Archer	6	5	1	–	Over 21
1627	W. Lawless	5	3	2	–	Over 21
1628	J. Bryan	9	5	4	–	Over 21
1629	E. Daton	10	6	4	–	c.30
1630	P. Butler	6	4	2	1	Minor
1632	N. Langton	11	8	3	1	43
1632	Idem (2nd marriage)	14	4	10	5	26
1632	W. Purcell	8	3	5	–	21
1633	J. Shee	3	1	2	–	Over 21
1634	P. Den	16	12	4	–	Over 21
1635	R. Cowley	6	5	1	–	Over 21
1635	V. Knatchbull ★	4	3	1	–	–
1635	J. Shortal	7	5	2	–	28
1635	J. Walsh	0	0	0	–	–
1635	Idem (2nd marriage)	5	3	2	1	28
1636	E. Butler	13	5	8	–	20
1636	R. Purcell	10	5	5	–	40
1636	J. Walsh	8	5	3	–	–
1637	R. Comerford	14	3	11	6	c.47
1637	O. Grace	6	4	2	–	Minor
1637	P. Walsh	7	4	3	3	Minor
1638	F. Crispe ★	7	1	6	–	–
1638	T. Merry	2	1	1	–	Minor
1638	H. Shee	4	2	2	–	9
1639	R. Pembroke	4	1	3	2	Over 21
1639	H. Staines ★	1	0	1	–	Over 21
1640	W. Best ★	0	0	0	–	–

Note: those marked ★ = New English

Results

2. Average number of children (a) per marriage (all cases) 7.4
           (b) per Anglo-Irish marriage: 8.0
           (c) per New English marriage: 3.0
2. *Infertility* percentage of barren marriages: 6%
3. Infant *mortality* children pre-deceasing their fathers – (a) minimum (whole sample):10% (b) maximum (omitting unknowns): 29%
4. *Sex ratio* percentage of male children born: 53%; percentage of female children born: 47%
5. *Successional problems* Succession by a minor: (a) minimum (entire sample): 25%; b) maximum (excluding unknown cases): 30%

Sheriffs of County Kilkenny, 1515–1642[1]

1514–15	Sir Piers Butler of Pottlerath[2]	1542	Roland Fitzgerald of Burnchurch[12]
1515	Sir John Grace of Courtstown[3]		
1516	Sir Piers Butler of Pottlerath, nominal earl of Ormond[4]	1543	James Sweetman of Castle Eve[13]
		1544	Patrick Purcell of Ballyfoyle[14]
1518	Roland Fitzgerald of Burnchurch[5]	1549	James Comerford of Ballymack[15]
1523	Roland Fitzgerald of Burnchurch[6]	1551–2	John Fitzgerald of Burnchurch, killed in office[16]
1524	Roland Fitzgerald of Burnchurch[7]	1555	James Comerford of Ballymack[17]
1525	Fulk Den of Grenan[8]	1558	James Comerford of Ballymack[18]
1526	Fulk Den of Grenan		
1527	Fulk Den of Grenan	1559	James Comerford of Ballymack, killed in office[19]
1528	Fulk Den of Grenan		
1531	Fulk Den of Grenan[9]	1560	Lewis Bryan of Bawnmore[20]
1532	Oliver Grace of Courtstown[10]	1562	Patrick Sherlock of Burnchurch[21]
1535	Roland Fitzgerald of Burnchurch[11]	1564	William Sweetman of Castle Eve[22]

1 In the following list of sheriffs I have attempted to corroborate, extend and (where necessary) revise the work of the antiquarian and genealogist, G.D. Burtchaell who, in his book *Members of parliament for the county and city of Kilkenny* (Dublin 1888), gave an extensive but sometimes inaccurate shrieval register (ibid., Appendix vii, 249–50). Although he made use of some of the official archives that were subsequently lost in the 1922 fire at the Dublin PRO, Burtchaell did not always read the material carefully. It is fortunate that transcripts by other scholars have survived to facilitate a proper check of his findings. 2 Burtchaell, *Members*, 249. 3 Grace, *Memorials*, i, unpaginated pedigree. 4 NA, Ferguson MSS, Exchequer Memoranda Rolls, Henry VIII, 38. 5 Ibid., 53. 6 Ibid., 67. 7 Ibid. 8 Ibid., 113. Although Burtchaell claims that Den was sheriff for the entire period 1526–32 (Burtchaell, *Members*, 249), it is likely that he speculated for the period 1529–30. No shrieval list survives among the exchequer proffers for those years. All that can safely be said is that the 1530 incumbent was the same as that for 1529; sadly, his name is not recorded (NA, Ferguson MSS, Exchequer Memoranda Rolls, Henry VIII, 136). 9 Ibid., 152. 10 Burtchaell, *Members*, 249. 11 *CPRI, Henry VIII–Eliz. I*, 15. Burtchaell names him as sheriff in 1536, but this may only refer to the end of the 1535–6 shrieval year. 12 *COD*, iv, no. 281. 13 Ibid., no. 307; NA, Ferguson MSS, Exchequer Memoranda Rolls, Henry VIII, 222. 14 Ibid., 284. 15 *Ir. Fiants*, Edward VI, nos. 248, 504; *CPRI, Henry VIII–Eliz. I*, 206; *COD*, v, no. 14 (1) 16 *Ir. Fiants*, Philip & Mary, no. 162; PRO, SP 61/4/72. 17 *COD*, v, no. 54. 18 Burtchaell, *Members*, 249–50. 19 Comerford was appointed on 24 January (*CPRI, Henry VIII–Eliz. I*, 416), and was named on subsequent commissions of martial law and muster and array during March, April and May (NA, Lodge MSS, Articles, etc., 94). He was still serving on 17 August (*Ir. Fiants, Eliz. I*, no. 128). 20 NA, Ferguson MSS, Exchequer Memoranda Rolls, Eliz. I, 85. Burtchaell dated his office to 1561, but the reference in Ferguson clearly refers to 1560–1. 21 Sherlock was appointed on 27 January anno 3 Eliz. I, i.e. 1562 (ibid.), and was pardoned with some of his posse, including 'the captain of the sheriff's kerne', Gerald Archdekin of Bawnballymore (alias Bawnballinlogh), on 25 February following

1565	Gerald Blanchville of Blanchvillestown[23]	1584	Francis Lovell of Lismacteige[39]
1566	James Butler, baron of Dunboyne[24]	1585	Thomas Cantwell of Cantwell's Court[40]
1567	Thomas Masterson of Kilkenny[25]	1586	Walter Walsh of Castlehowell[41]
1568	Patrick Sherlock[26]	1587	Francis Lovell of Lismacteige[42]
1569	John Cantwell of Cantwell's Court, killed in office[27]	1588	Richard Shee of Kilkenny[43]
1570	Oliver Grace of Ballylinch[28]	1589	Piers Butler of Duiske[44]
1571	Patrick Sherlock[29]	1590	John Grace of Grace's Court[45]
1572	Walter Gall of Gallstown[30]	1591	John Sweetman of Castle Eve[46]
1573	Walter Gall of Gallstown[31]	1592	Richard Fitzgerald of Burnchurch[47]
1574	Walter Butler of Paulstown[32]	1594	Thomas Cantwell of Cantwell's Court[48]
1575	Thomas Den of Grenan[33]	1595	Piers Butler of Duiske[49]
1576	Patrick Sherlock of St. Katherine's, Waterford[34]	1596	Richard Butler of Paulstown[50]
1577	Richard Fitzgerald of Burnchurch[35]	1602	Oliver Grace[51]
1578	Patrick Sherlock of St. Katherine's, Waterford[36]	1604	Richard Fitzgerald of Burnchurch[52]
1579	Walter Walsh of Castlehowell[37]	1605	Captain Denis Daly[53]
1582	Francis Lovell of Dublin[38]	1606	David Serment of Lismacteige
		1608	Lucas Shee of Upper Court[54]
		1609	Cyprian Horsfall of Kilkenny[55]

(*Ir. Fiants*, Eliz. I, no. 406). **22** Named as a martial law commissioner on 14 July (HMC, *Haliday MSS*, 138). **23** Carrigan, *Ossory*, iii, 414–15. **24** 'Sheriff for the time being', *c*.1566. Unfortunately the date on the fiant was damaged (*Ir. Fiants*, Eliz. I, no. 953). **25** Appointed sheriff after 7 Oct. 1567 and before 20 Oct., when he was granted a martial law commission (ibid., nos. 1185, 1196). **26** Burtchaell, *Members*, 249–50 **27** Sheriff Cantwell received a commission for martial law on 10 Feb. 1569 (*Ir. Fiants*, Eliz. I, no. 1261). He was still exercising his office on 3 Nov., but was killed by rebels shortly afterwards (Chapter 3 above, and *COD*, v, no. 157). Burtchaell named him as sheriff for 1568, but this probably refers to the old style year, beginning in March. **28** Burtchaell, *Members*, 249–50, where Grace is entered incorrectly for 1571. **29** *COD*, v, no. 185. **30** He had been appointed in October (PRO, SP 63/38/24, inclosure i). **31** He was still sheriff on 26 June 1574, but was replaced before 26 October. His sub-sheriff was Patrick St Leger of Kilkenny, a clerk (*Ir. Fiants*, Eliz. I, nos. 2417, 2486). **32** Ibid., no. 2700. **33** NA, Ferguson MSS, Repertory to Memoranda Rolls, Edward VI–Elizabeth I, 176. **34** He had a commission for martial law on 19 Nov. 1576 (*Ir. Fiants*, Eliz. I, no. 2937). **35** He is named as 'late sheriff' of the county in a document dated 9 Feb. 1580 (*Cal. Carew MSS*, 1575–88, no. 297), but it seems logical that he filled the office in 1577–8. **36** He was acting sheriff of Kilkenny on 10 Oct. 1578 (PRO, SP 63/63/7); *Cal. Carew MSS*, 1575–88, no. 109). Burtchaell names Richard Butler as sheriff, but I can find no evidence to corroborate this. **37** Walsh was picked by Lord Justice Pelham on 25 Nov. 1579 (ibid., no. 178). He was granted a commission of martial law on 1 May 1580 (*Ir. Fiants*, Eliz. I, no. 3636). **38** Lovell was sworn as sheriff on 1 Dec. 1582, and served until 30 Sept. 1583: PRO, SP 63/108/34. His sub-sheriff was Patrick Shortal of Ballyvonte (*Ir. Fiants*, Eliz. I, no. 3960). **39** PRO, SP 63/107/13. **40** Cantwell received a commission of martial law on 30 Jan. 1585 (*Ir. Fiants*, Eliz. I, no. 4601). **41** Ibid., no. 4993. **42** He received a commission for martial law on 14 Jan. (ibid., nos. 4955, 5060). **43** Shee became a martial law commissioner on 2 Feb. 1589 (ibid., no. 5292). **44** Burtchaell, *Members*, 249–50. **45** PRO, SP 63/161/39; ibid., SP 63/170/25. **46** Burtchaell, *Members*, 249–50, dates his office to 1592, but 1591–2 seems more plausible. **47** Bod. Lib., Ms Talbot b.10/38: according to this, a memorandum of exchequer proceedings in 1595, Fitzgerald filled the shrievalty on 1 April 1593. **48** Burtchaell, *Members*, 249–50. **49** *COD*, vi, no. 99 (2). **50** *Cal. Carew MSS*, 1589–1600, no. 260 (v). **51** Burtchaell, *Members*, 249–50. **52** NLI, Ms 4147. **53** NA, Ferguson MSS, Equity Exchequer Orders, 1604–18, 31. **54** Ibid., 190 and 197. **55** Recorded as the 'late sheriff' when he appeared in exchequer *c*.1611 (ibid., Ferguson MSS, Abstracts of Exchequer Orders, 1592–1657, 129). If Burtchaell is correct in giving Edmund Walsh as sheriff for 1610, then 1609–10 is the latest that Horsfall can have held the post.

1610	Edmund Walsh of Castlehowell[56]	1623	Thomas Shortal of
1613	John Butler fitz John of Callan[57]		Rathardmore[67]
1614	Thomas Daniel of Kilkenny[58]	1624	Oliver Shortal of Highrath[68]
1615	Sir Oliver Shortal of	1629	John Tobyn of Killaghy[69]
	Ballylorcaine[59]	1630	Walter Walsh fitz Robert of
1616	Clement Daniel of Kilkenny[60]		Castlehowell[70]
1617	Walter Gall of Gallstown[61]	1631	Sir Edward Butler of Duiske[71]
1618	Henry Staines of Dublin[62]	1632	Patrick Wemyss of Dunfert[72]
1619	John Butler fitz John of Callan[63]	1633	Joseph Wheeler of Stonecarthy[73]
1620	John Butler fitz John of Callan[64]	1634	Patrick Wemyss of Dunfert[74]
1621	John Butler fitz John of Callan[65]	1636	Patrick Wemyss of Dunfert[75]
1622	Sir Oliver Shortal of	1640	Sir Edward Butler of Duiske[76]
	Ballylorcaine[66]	1641	Sir Cyprian Horsfall of Inishnag[77]

56 Burtchaell, *Members*, 249–50. He was the second son of Walter Walsh, the former sheriff.   **57** NAI, Ferguson MSS, Abstracts of Exchequer Orders, 1592–1657, 152, 156, 160.   **58** Ibid., 194.   **59** Burtchaell, *Members*, 249–50, who dates his shrievalty to 1616 rather than 1615–16.   **60** Confusion abounds over his name. Although Burtchaell renders it as Baggott (Burtchaell, *Members*, p.250), there is reason to suspect that he meant Clement Ragget, who could not have been sheriff of the county as he was one of the five mayors of Kilkenny city in 1616 (NLI, Ms 2531, pp 100–1). Another source, a copy of an exchequer document lost in the 1922 fire, names the sheriff as 'Clement Dayell', which surely stands for Daniel (W. Carrigan, 'Walsh Mountain history', *JWSEIAS* 16 (1913), p.132). Perhaps crucially, the Daniels were a local Protestant family.   **61** Ibid.   **62** Ibid. See also NA, Ferguson MSS, Abstracts of Exchequer Orders, 1592–1657, 241.   **63** Ibid., 250 and 263; John Ryland's Library, Manchester, Ms 246, fol. 41r; and Cambridgeshire (Huntingdon) RO, Ms DDM 70/31, where it is recorded that Butler was still expected to present his shrieval accounts on 28 July 1622.   **64** Ibid.   **65** Ibid.   **66** NA, Ferguson MSS, Abstracts of Exchequer Orders, 1592–1657, 268. The sub-sheriff was Richard Pembroke of Kilkenny (ibid., 302), whom Burtchaell wrongly identified as sheriff. The bailiff of the shire while Sir Oliver held the shrievalty was Henry Edwards (St Peter's College, Wexford, Hore MSS: Exchequer Memoranda Rolls, 1614–66: 64). My thanks to Brian Donovan for this reference.   **67** NA, Ferguson MSS, Abstracts of Exchequer Orders, 1592–1657, 314.   **68** W. Carrigan, 'Walsh Mountain history', *JWSEIAS* 16 (1913), 132.   **69** NA, Ferguson MSS, Equity Exchequer Orders, 1618–38, 90. Ferguson later incorrectly refers to him as Edward Tobyn (ibid., 277).   **70** Ibid.   **71** He is described as 'late sheriff' in a document commencing 1 Sept. 1632 (NLI, D. 3928).   **72** Wemyss served as sheriff from 1 Sept. 1632 to 29 Sept. 1633 (NLI, D. 3687, 3928); see also KCA, Ms CR/F/1: Irishtown Corporation Book, 1538–1661, fol. 10r.   **73** Burtchaell, *Members*, 250, who names him as sheriff for 1634 rather than 1633–4.   **74** Wemyss was reappointed sheriff by royal commission on 7 July 1634 (NLI, D. 3941), and again on 23 Dec. 1634 (ibid., D. 3978).   **75** Although difficult to read, Wemyss appears to be named sheriff in the preamble to the sheriff's court roll for 19 April–4 July 1637 (ibid., D. 4052). The same source also records that Piers Grace and William McTeige were two of his bailiffs.   **76** Burtchaell, *Members*, 250.   **77** Ibid.

Bibliography

MANUSCRIPT SOURCES

Ireland

Birr Castle, County Offaly
Earl of Rosse MSS — Notes of 1616 castle chamber proceedings (NLI microfilm)

Clonalis House, County Roscommon
O'Conor Don Ms 6.4HN002 — Archdekin's annals of Kilkenny, 1568–83

Genealogical Office, Dublin
Ms 2 — Non-payment of fees for funeral certificates, 1633–4
Ms 45 — Clarencieux grant of arms to Richard Shee of Kilkenny, 1582
Ms 164 — Includes pedigree of the Tobyns and Shees
MSS 170–1 — Pedigree of the Mountgarret and Paulstown Butlers, etc.

Kilkenny Corporation Archives
CR/B — Corporation grants, 1406–1596
CR/C — Copies and translations of documents, 1223–1690
CR/F — Includes the Irishtown Corporation Book, 1538–1661
CR/I — Corporation leases, c.1500–1685
CR/J — Accounts, receipts & orders of payment, 1577–c.1685
CR/K — Letters and petitions, 1547–c.1649

National Archives of Ireland, Dublin
Chancery MSS — Catalogue of deeds in chancery, including a collection of deeds concerning the Dobbin, Walsh and White families in Inistioge and Thomastown, 1483–1608
C 415 — Pakenham-Walsh deposit, including pardon of alienation to Edward Waton of the Grove, 1629
Co. 1759 — View of frank pledge for Durrow manor, 1635
CP — Salved Chancery Pleadings
D 19,307 — Fitzpatrick deed naming Richard Archdekin and others as feoffees, 1616
Ferguson MSS — Collection of abstracts taken from the records of the Irish court of exchequer, including the memoranda rolls, Henry VIII–Eliz. I (4 vols.); the revenue exchequer orders, 1592–1657 (1 vol.); and the equity exchequer orders, 1604–67 (3 vols)
Lodge MSS — Records of the rolls of the Irish chancery
M 481 — Ainsworth abstracts, containing chancery proceedings re Robert Butler, c.1505, and the earl of Ormond, 1618
M 530 (7) — Ainsworth abstract of a chancery case involving Nicholas White and John Aylward, 1567
M 594 — Money due from the earl of Ormond to the free school of the diocese of Ossory, early 17th century
M 2445 — Letter book of Lord Deputy Falkland, 1629–33

347

M 2448	Petitions to Lord Deputy Wentworth, 1638
M 2590	Sir Henry Farnham Burke's notes on the Ormond Butlers
M 2816	Copy of the cartulary of Sir Richard Shee
M 2835	Particulars of the estate of Piers Butler of Callan, 1662
M 3172–85	Paulet (Fitzpatrick) MSS, with material concerning Lord Mountgarret and the Butlers of Knocktopher, 1639–40
M. 3237	Copy of the Gowran charter, 1608
Prim MSS	Miscellaneous collection of antiquarian notes about Kilkenny city and county, including copies and abstracts of corporation leases (1537–1681) and genealogical information on local families.
RC 5/4–5	Transcripts of deeds & wills recited in chancery inquisitions, Co. Kilkenny (2 vols)
RC 6/1–2	Chancery Decrees, Ireland, Henry VIII–Charles II
RC 9/7	Reportories to exchequer inquisitions, Co. Kilkenny, Henry VIII–William III
RC 10/7	Transcripts of deeds & wills recited in exchequer inquisitions, Cos. Kildare & Kilkenny
RC 12/1	Reportory to exchequer decrees, 1609–67
RC 17/4	Index to the Irish Fiants of James I
RE 209	Copy of the Irish accounts of the earl of Essex, 1574
T 2621	Three acquittances for procurations due to the bishop of Ossory out of St John's Abbey, Kilkenny, 1602–8
T 7427	Abstracts of administrations granted to intestates (A–C) in the prerogative court, 1595–1802
Thrift Abstracts	Abstracts of chancery bills and pleadings
999/447	Copies of Waterford wills by Julian Walton

National Library of Ireland

D 2000–4200	Ormond Deeds
D 27542	Copy of the Thomastown charter, 1553
Ms 975	Books of Survey & Distribution, Co Kilkenny
Ms 2145	Shee Papers (badly damaged)
Ms 2153	Gaelic genealogy of the Shees of Upper Court, 1617
Ms 2181	Graves Papers
Ms 2301–3	Ormond correspondence
MSS 2482–3	Miscellaneous Ormond letters, mainly undated
MSS 2485–6	More miscellaneous Ormond letters
MSS 2506–9	Ormond rentals and accounts
Ms 2531	Material for the history of Kilkenny city, compiled in the 18th century
MSS 2543–4	Ormond estate surveys
Ms 2549	Ormond household accounts, 1630–2
Ms 2551	Miscellaneous Ormond estate records
Ms 2556 (10)	Extract of the 1536/7 act of Irish parliament repealing a 1468 act in favour of Edmund and Theobald Butler
Ms 2560	Extracts from the 1654 Civil Survey concerning the Ormond estate
Ms 8013	Papers of Sir Nathaniel Rich, 1620–5
Ms 8099	Fitzpatrick (Castletown) papers
Ms 8315 (9)	Pedigree of the Graces of Courtstown
Ms 9011	Pedigree of the Shees of Kilkenny & Upper Court
Ms 11,044 (1)–(15)	Tipperary liberty records
Ms 11,045 (1)–(25)	Ormond prise wine papers
Ms 11,046 (1)–(59)	Papers concerning the Ormond/Preston dispute
Ms 11,048 (2) –(9)	Miscellaneous Ormond documents re Kilkenny city, 1595–1631
Ms 11,053 (9), (13)	Papers regarding the Ormond/Gowran dispute, 1608–11, and a 17th–century description of Inistioge
Ms 11,061	Ormond estate papers
Ms 11,063 (1)	Ormond rentals and accounts

Ms 11,064 (5)	Ormond tithes, 1625
Ms 13,236–7	Lismore papers
Ms 13,678	J.G. Prim's notes on the antiquities of Kilkenny
Ms 20,625	Fitzgerald papers, including a 1510 deed involving Edmund Butler of Clonmel
Ms 22,318	Letter to Lord Deputy Sidney, 1575
Prior-Wandesford MSS	Deeds and accounts re Castlecomer, *c.*1500–1653

Representative Church Body Library, Dublin

St Werburgh's Church Muniments	Includes Ormond indenture with Roger Nott of London, 1635

Royal Irish Academy, Dublin.

Ms D.5.3 (4)	Arbitration of Mountgarret/Fitzpatrick dispute, 1559

St Kieran's College, Kilkenny

Carrigan MSS	Genealogical notes of Co Kilkenny families (NLI microfilm)

St Peter's College, Wexford

Hore MSS	Transcripts of exchequer memoranda rolls (NLI microfilm)

Trinity College, Dublin

Ms 660	Account of Lord Deputy Sidney's southern campaign, 1569
Ms 672	Commissioners of the peace, Co Kilkenny, *c.*1621
Ms 812	1641 Depositions for Cos Carlow & Kilkenny
Ms 842	Robert Rothe's Register, or Pedigree, of the house of Ormond, 1616
Ms 2512	Common Pleas entry book (fines), 1603–24
Ms 10,724	Ormond papers: copies of royal letters, 1573–1702
Ms 10,726 (1)–(2)	Correspondence re Ormond/Middlesex relations, 1637

Northern Ireland

Public Record Office of Northern Ireland, Belfast

D 3078	Duke of Leinster papers, with pre-1534 Co Kilkenny deeds

England

Alnwick Castle, Northumberland

Ms 476 GC 26	*c.*1587 treatise of Ireland (NLI microfilm)

Bodleian Library, Oxford University

Bankes Papers	Miscellaneous Irish items
Carte MSS	Ormond, Fitzwilliam & Wandesford correspondence
Rawlinson MSS	Various Irish documents
Talbot (Malahide) MSS	Miscellaneous 16th-century deeds and transcripts
Ms Add. C. 286	Wandesford/Radcliffe correspondence, 1636–40
Ms Eng. Hist. c. 304	Register of Wentworth warrants, 1633–5

British Library, London

Add Ms 4756	Entry Book of the 1622 Commission for Ireland
Add Ms 5754	Irish messenger's book, 1588
Add Ms 7042	Henry VII's charter for Kilkenny market, 1509
Add Ms 15,914	Ormond letter, 1576
Add Ms 19,843	Register of Kilkenny statutes staple, 1639–41
Add Ms 37,53	Government of Ireland papers, 1582–1608
Add Ms 47,172	Court of castle chamber entry book
Cotton MSS Titus B XII–XIII	Irish political correspondence, temp. Elizabeth I
Cotton Ms Vesp F XII	Includes undated Ormond correspondence

Egerton Ms 80   Includes copy of *c*.1641 Arundel case re Idough
Egerton Ms 2618   Ormond's letter to Philip IV of Spain, 1623
Egerton Ms 3048   English privy council minute book, 1573–86
Harleian Ms 430   Wentworth petition book, 1637/8
Sloane Ms 3827   Mountgarret letter, 1613, & Gernon's discourse, 1620
Stowe Ms 755   Letter by Lady Mountgarret, 1613

Cambridge University Library
Ms Dd. III. 84 (1)   Sir Edward Waterhouse's account of Ireland
Ms Mm. I. 32   Diary of John Hooker, 1568–9
Ms Kk. I. 15   Irish rebellion papers, 1590s, with Ormond letters

Cambridgeshire County Record Office, Cambridge
Ms R 52/15/1   Computus Roll for Ormond manors in England, 1506/7

Cambridgeshire County Record Office, Huntingdon
Manchester MSS   Irish government papers, 1614–24

Cheshire County Record Office, Chester
Ms DCC 14   Cowper (Crewe) MSS, with orders re Col. John Butler, 1642

Chester City Record Office
Ms ML/6   17th-century Mayor's letter book (various references)
Ms SB/10   Chester Sheriff's book, with customs entries, 1550s

Essex County Record Office, Chelmsford
Ms D/DL Z9   Loftus commonplace book, early 17th century

Gloucestershire County Record Office, Gloucester
Berkeley Muniments   Four deeds involving the Ormond Butlers, 1517–69

Gonville & Caius College Library, Cambridge
Ms 525/697   Pedigree of the Butlers of Ormond

Guildhall Library, London
Ms 9051/5   London archdeaconry court, register of wills, 1594–1604

Hampshire County Record Office, Winchester
Herriard MSS   Billeting arrangements for Capt. John Butler, 1628

Humberside County Record Office, Beverley
Ms DDCC 132/15   Ormond recognizance, 1631

Kent Archives Office, Maidstone
Sackville MSS   Irish papers of Lionel Cranfield, earl of Middlesex, 1608–40
De L'Isle & Dudley MSS   Irish papers of Sir Henry Sidney, 1556–78

Lambeth Palace Library, London
Ms 250   Lambeth MSS, with a journal of the Ile de Rhe expedition, 1627
Ms 611   Carew MSS, with *c*.1560 valuation of Co. Kilkenny lands
MSS 626 & 635   Sir George Carew's Irish genealogies (UCC microfilm)
Ms 3361   Household book of the earl of Middlesex, 1621–2

National Maritime Museum, Greenwich
Ms And. 44   Ship's journal of the *Fellowship* of Bristol, 1642

Northamptonshire County Record Office, Northampton
Ms FH 127   Finch-Hatton MSS: Account of the state of Ireland, 1599
Ormond (Kilkenny) MSS   English papers of the Ormond Butlers, with stray Irish deeds

Nottingham University Library
Clifton MSS   Includes Wandesford letters, 1630s
Middleton MSS   Estate papers of the Ridgeways, earls of Londonderry

Oxfordshire Archives Office, Oxford
Valentia MSS   Includes Ormond/Annesley bond, 1638

Public Record Office, London
C 66   Chancery Patent Rolls
E 122   Customs Accounts
E 163/15/12   Allowances for stores, 1597
E 190   Port Books
HCA   High Court of Admiralty papers
SP 60–63   Irish State Papers, Henry VIII–Charles I

John Ryland's Library, Manchester
Ms 246   Clerk of the Pells records for Leinster, 1622
Ms 887   Earl of Cork's will, mentioning Bennettsbridge, 1642.

Sheffield City Library
Wentworth Woodhouse Muniments,   Strafford MSS: Lord Deputy Wentworth's papers, 1632–41
  (WWM, Str. P.)
WWM Add.   Wentworth Irish deeds

Surrey County Record Office, Guildford
Ms LM 1330/73   Details of Kilkenny troops billeted at Guildford, 1628

East Sussex County Record Office, Lewes
Ms SAU 1321   1637 case of a Sussex recusant who died in Co Kilkenny

Yorkshire Archaeological Society, Leeds
Ms DD5/38/2   Duke of Leeds MSS, with Wandesford letters, 1640–53
Ms 514/S   Transcripts of documents about Sir Cyprian Horsfall

Scotland

Glasgow University Library
Ms Hunter 3   Royal warrant for the attainder of Thomas Comerford, 1570

PRINTED PRIMARY SOURCES

Acts of the privy council of England, 1542–1631, ed. J.R. Dasent et al. (32 vols, London 1890–1907).
John Ainsworth & Edward MacLysaght (ed.), 'The Power-O'Shee papers', *Anal. Hib.*, 20 (1959).
John Ainsworth (ed.), 'Abstracts of 17th century Irish wills in the Prerogative Court of Canterbury', *JRSAI*, 78 (1948).
— (ed.), 'The Power papers', *Anal. Hib.*, 25 (1967).
— (ed.), 'The Corporation Book of the Irishtown of Kilkenny, 1537–1628', *Anal. Hib.*, 28 (1978).
Ancient Irish histories: the works of Spenser, Campion, Hanmer and Marleburrough (2 vols, Dublin 1809).
Annals of Loch Cé: a chronicle of Irish affairs, 1014–1590, ed. William Hennessy (2 vols, London 1871).
Annals of the kingdom of Ireland by the Four Masters, ed. John O'Donovan (7 vols, Dublin 1851).
Anon., *Leycester's Commonwealth* (1641 edn.).
Anon. 'The complaints of Shane O'Neill', *Ulster Journal of Archaeology*, 2 (1854).
Anon. (ed.), 'Note of particulars extracted from the Kilkenny Corporation records relating to the Miracle Plays, 1580 to 1639', *RHAAI Jn.*, 4th series, 6/2 (1884).
John C. Appleby (ed.), *Calendar of material relating to Ireland in the High Court of Admiralty Examinations, 1536–1641* (IMC, Dublin 1992).
Daniel Beaufort, *Memoir of a map of Ireland* (Dublin 1792).
William Brereton, *Travels in Holland & the United Provinces, England, Scotland & Ireland*, ed. E. Hawkins (Chetham Soc., Manchester 1844).

Eric St John Brooks (ed.), *Knights' fees in Cos. Wexford, Carlow & Kilkenny* (IMC, Dublin 1950).
James Buckley (ed.), 'A vice-regal progress through the South and West of Ireland, 1567', *WSEIAS* 12 (1909).
—— (ed.), 'Monumenta Sepulchra', *WSEIAS* 16 (1913).
Hubert Butler (ed.), 'Occupants of Ormond houses in Kilkenny, 1641–61', *Butler Soc. Jn.*, 7 (1977).
Richard Butler (ed.), *The annals of Thady Dowling* (Irish Archaeological Soc., 1849).
Calendar of Border papers, 1560–1603, ed. J. Bain (2 vols, Edinburgh 1894–6).
Calendar of Carew MSS preserved at Lambeth Palace Library, 1515–1624, ed. J.S. Brewer et al. (6 vols, London 1867–73).
Calendar of the Irish patent rolls of James I (facsimile edn., IMC, Dublin 1966).
Calendar of patent and close rolls of Chancery in Ireland, Henry VIII–Eliz. I, Eliz. I, and Charles I, ed. James Morrin (3 vols, Dublin 1861–3).
Calendar of patent rolls, Eliz. I, 1558–80 (8 vols, London 1939–86).
Calendar of state papers, domestic, 1547–1695, ed. R. Lemon & M.A.E. Green et al. (82 vols, London 1856–1992).
Calendar of state papers, foreign, 1547–89 (23 vols, London 1861–1950).
Calendar of state papers, Ireland, 1509–1670, ed. H.C. Hamilton et al. (24 vols., London 1860–1912).
Calendar of state papers, Rome, 1558–78, ed. J.M. Rigg (2 vols, London 1917–26).
Calendar of state papers, Spanish, 1550–1603, ed. R. Tyler & M.A.S. Hume (8 vols, London 1892–9).
Calendar of state papers, Venetian, 1509–1619 (15 vols, London 1867–1909).
William Camden, *History of the most renowned and victorious princess Elizabeth, late queen of England*, ed. Wallace T. MacCaffrey (London 1970).
James Carney (ed.), *Poems on the Butlers* (Dublin 1945).
William Carrigan (ed.), 'Scraps of Walsh Mountain history', published in six parts in *WSEIAS* 9–10, 12, 14 and 16 (1909–13).
Richard Caulfield (ed.), *The Council Book of the Corporation of Youghal* (Guildford 1878).
J.P. Collier (ed.), *The Egerton papers* (Camden Soc., London 1840).
Arthur Collins (ed.), *Letters & memorials of state* (2 vols, London 1746).
Thomas Comber, *The life of Christopher Wandesford* (London 1778).
Patrick J. Corish (ed.), 'Two reports on the Catholic church in Ireland in the early 17th century', *Archivium Hibernicum*, xxii (1959).
Bernadette Cunningham (ed.), 'Clanricard letters', *Galway Arch. & Hist. Soc. Jn.*, 48 (1996).
Edmund Curtis (ed.), *Calendar of Ormond deeds, 1172–1603* (6 vols., IMC, Dublin 1932–43).
John Davies, *A Discovery of the true causes why Ireland was never entirely subdued, 1612* (facsimile edn., Shannon 1969).
'Deeds deposited by Edward J. French', *43rd report of the deputy keeper of the public records of Ireland* (Dublin 1912).
John Dymock 'A treatise of Ireland', ed. Richard Butler, *Tracts relating to Ireland*, ii (Dublin 1843).
R. Dudley Edwards (ed.), 'The Chichester Letter Book, 1612–14', *Anal. Hib.*, 8 (1938).
'Extracts from the Cartulary of Sir Richard Shee', *57th report of the deputy keeper of the public records in Ireland* (Dublin 1927).
C.L. Falkiner (ed.), 'The Parliament of Ireland under the Tudor sovereigns: supplementary paper', *PRIA* 25 C (1904/5).
—— (ed.), 'Barnaby Rich's Remembrances of the State of Ireland, 1612', *PRIA* 26 C (1906).
—— (ed.), 'William Farmer's Chronicles of Ireland, 1594–1613', *EHR* 22 (1907).
Hugh Fenning (ed.), 'Irishmen ordained at Lisbon, 1587–1625 and 1641–60', *Collectanea Hibernica*, 31–32 (1989–90).
Thomas G. Fewer & K.W. Nicholls (ed.), 'The will of Robert Forstall of Kilferagh, 1645', *Decies* 48 (1993).
J.F.M. Ffrench (ed.), 'Southern forts in 1624', *WSEIAS* 5 (1899).
C.H. Firth (ed.), 'Letters of William Wandesford to Sir Rowland Wandesford', *EHR* 9 (1894).
Cathaldus Giblin (ed.), 'Catalogue of Irish material in the Nunziatura di Fiadra', *Collectanea Hibernica*, i (1958).
John T. Gilbert (ed.), 'Nicholas Plunkett's account of the war and rebellion in Ireland since the year 1641', HMC, *Second Report* (London 1874).
—— (ed.), *A contemporary history of affairs in Ireland, 1641–52* (3 vols, Dublin 1879).
—— (ed.), *The history of the Irish Confederation and the war in Ireland, 1641–9* (7 vols, Dublin 1882–91).
H.W. Gillman (ed.), 'The rise and progress in Munster of the rebellion, 1642', *JCHAS*, 2nd series, i (1895).

James Graves (ed.), 'Report of a commission established to ascertain the damage mutually inflicted in the feud between the earls of Ormond and Desmond', *KSEIAS*, 1st series, i, Pt. 2 (1850).

— (ed.), 'Letter from the earl of Ormond to the lord lieutenant of Ireland, circa 1567', *KSEIAS*, 2nd series, i, Pt. 1 (1856).

— (ed.), 'Letter from General Preston to the marquis of Ormond, 1643', *KSEIAS*, 2nd series, i, Pt. 1 (1856).

— (ed.), 'Anonymous account of the early life and marriage of James, 1st duke of Ormonde', *RHAAI Jn.*, 2nd series, iv, Pt. 2 (1863).

— (ed.),'Unpublished Geraldine documents, pt. 2: the earls of Desmond', *RHAAI Jn.*, 3rd series, i (1869).

— (ed.), 'Grant to the Cistercian Abbey of the Vale of the Blessed Saviour by Donal Reagh Kavanagh, and a treaty of friendship between the MacMurroughs and the earls of Ormond, 1525', *RHAAI Jn.*, 4th series, vi, Pt. 1 (1883).

Margaret C. Griffith (ed.), *Calendar of inquisitions formerly in the office of the Chief Remembrancer of the Exchequer* (IMC, Dublin 1991).

A.B. Grosart (ed.), *The Lismore papers* (10 vols, London 1886–8).

J. Hagen (ed.), 'Miscellanea Vaticano-Hibernica', *Archivium Hibernicum*, v (1916).

Mary Hickson, *Selections from old Kerry records* (1st series, London 1872).

Historical Manuscripts Commission publications

  Bath MSS (5 vols, London 1904–80).

  De L'Isle & Dudley MSS (6 vols, London 1925–66).

  Downshire MSS (4 vols, London 1924–42).

  Egmont MSS (2 vols, London 1905–9).

  Haliday MSS: The Irish Privy Council Book, 1556–71 (London 1897).

  Hastings MSS (4 vols, London 1928–47).

  Irish Franciscan MSS (London 1906).

  Ormonde MSS (11 vols, London 1895–1920)

  Pepys MSS (London 1911)

  Rutland MSS (4 vols, London 1888–1905).

  Sackville (Cranfield) MSS (2 vols, London 1940–66).

  Salisbury MSS (23 vols, London 1888–1973).

  Shrewsbury & Talbot MSS (2 vols, London 1966–71).

James Hogan & N. McNeill O'Farrell (ed.), *The Walsingham Letter Book, May 1578–Dec. 1579* (IMC, Dublin 1959).

James Hogan (ed.), *Letters & papers relating to the Irish rebellion, 1642–46* (IMC, Dublin 1936).

Edmund Hogan (ed.), *The description of Ireland, anno 1598* (Dublin 1878).

Denzil Hollis (ed.), *Calendar of the Bristol Apprentice Book, pt. 1, 1532–42* (Bristol Record Soc., 1949).

H.F. Hore & James Graves (ed.), *The social state of south-east Ireland in the 16th century* (Special Annuary of the RHAAI, Dublin 1870)

H.F. Hore (ed.), 'Sir Henry Sidney's Memoir of his government of Ireland', *Ulster Journal of Archaeology*, 3, 5 and 8 (1855, 1857 and 1860).

—, 'The hosting against the northern Irish in 1566', *Ulster Journal of Archaeology*, 1 (1853).

Inquisitionum in Officio Rotulorum Cancellariae Hiberniae asservatum reportorium: Lagenia (Dublin 1826).

Brian Jackson (ed.), 'A document on the parliament of 1613 from St Isidore's College, Rome', *Anal. Hib.*, 33 (1986).

Charles Jackson (ed.), *The autobiography of Mrs Alice Thornton of East Newton, Yorkshire* (Surtees Soc., 62 (1875)).

Brendan Jennings (ed.), *Wadding papers, 1614–38* (IMC, Dublin 1953).

Journals of the Irish house of commons, 1613–66 (Dublin 1796).

Journals of the Irish house of lords, 1634–98 (Dublin 1779).

William Knowler (ed.), *The earl of Strafford's letters & dispatches* (2 vols, London 1739).

C.T. Lamacraft (ed.), *Irish funeral entries* (special volume of *Irish Memorials of the Dead*, vii 1907–9)

H.J. Lawlor (ed.), 'Calendar of the *Liber Ruber* of the diocese of Ossory', *PRIA* 27 C (1908).

John Lodge (ed.), *Desiderata curiosa hibernica* (2 vols, Dublin 1772).

A.K. Longfield (ed.), *Fitzwilliam accounts, 1560–65* (IMC, Dublin 1960).

John Lowe (ed.), *The letter book of the earl of Clanricarde, 1643–7* (IMC, Dublin 1983).

Charles MacNeill (ed.), *Liber Primus Kilkenniensis* (IMC, Dublin 1931).

— (ed.), 'Lord Chancellor Gerrard's notes of his Report of Ireland', *Anal. Hib.*, 2 (1931).

— (ed.), *The Tanner letters* (IMC, Dublin 1943).

— (ed.), 'The Perrot papers: the letter book of Lord Deputy Sir John Perrot, 9 July 1584–26 May 1586', *Anal. Hib.*, 12 (1943).

W.D. Macray (ed.), 'Transcripts from Rawlinson Ms C 98', *KSEIAS Jn.*, 2nd series, 1 (1856–7).
N.E. McClure (ed.), *The letters of John Chamberlain* (2 vols, Philadelphia, 1939).
P.F. Moran (ed.), *Spiciligium Ossoriense* (3 vols., 1874–84).
— (ed.), *The Analecta of David Rothe, bishop of Ossory* (Dublin 1884).
Fynes Moryson, *An itinerary containing his ten years travels* (4 vols, Glasgow 1907–8).
Kenneth W. Nicholls (ed.), 'Late medieval Irish annals: Two Fragments', *Peritia*, 2 (1983).
John O'Donovan (ed.), 'The Irish correspondence of James Fitzmaurice of Desmond', *KSEIAS Jn.*, 2nd series, 2 (1858–9).
Mary O'Dowd (ed.), 'Irish concealed lands papers', *Anal. Hib.*, 31 (1984).
Richard O'Farrell & Robert O'Connell, *Commentarius Rinuccinianus, de sedis apostolicae legatione ad foederatos Hiberniae Catholicos, 1645–9*, ed. Stanislaus Kavanagh (6 vols, IMC, Dublin 1932–49).
Tomas O'Laidhin (ed.), *Sidney state papers, 1565–70* (IMC, Dublin 1962).
'Old Waterford wills, No. 8: William Dobbin, 1663', *WSEIAS Jn.*, 11 (1908)
Anne O'Sullivan & Padraig O'Riain (ed.), *Poems on marcher lords from a 16th century Tipperary manuscript* (Irish Texts Soc., Dublin 1987).
William O'Sullivan (ed.), 'Correspondence of David Rothe and James Ussher, 1619–23', *Collectanea Hibernica*, xxxvi–xxxvii (1994/5).
Jocelyn Otway-Ruthven, 'Liber Primus Kilkenniensis: Corrigenda', *Anal. Hib.*, 26 (1970).
Liam Price (ed.), 'Armed forces of the Irish chiefs in the early 16th century', *JRSAI* 62 (1932).
D.B. Quinn (ed.), 'Ormond papers 1480–1535 in the Public Record Office, London, and the British Museum', appendix to *COD*, iv (Dublin 1937).
— (ed.), 'Calendar of the Irish Council Book, 1581–6', *Anal. Hib.*, 24 (1967).
— (ed.), 'Additional Sidney state papers, 1566–70', *Anal. Hib.*, 26 (1970).
E. Ralph & N.M. Hardwick (ed.), *Calendar of the Bristol Apprentice Book, pt. 2, 1542–52* (Bristol 1980).
F.J. Routledge (ed.), 'Journal of the Irish house of lords in Sir John Perrot's parliament', *EHR*, 29 (1914).
John Rushworth, *Historical collections IV, April 164–Dec. 1642* (London 1708 edn.).
W.H. Rylands (ed.), *The visitation of Buckinghamshire, 1634* (Harleian Soc., 1909).
W.A. Sargeant (ed.), 'Old records of the Corporation of Waterford', *WSEIAS Jn.*, 1–2 (1894–6).
R.C. Simington (ed.), *Civil survey for County Waterford, Muskerry & Kilkenny City* (IMC, Dublin 1942).
John Smyth, *The lives of the Berkeleys, 1066–1618*, ed. Sir John MacLean (2 vols, Gloucester 1883).
W.J. Smyth (ed.), *Herbert correspondence* (IMC, Dublin 1963).
W.L. Spiers (ed.), 'The note book and account book of Nicholas Stone', *Walpole Soc. Jn.*, 7 (1919).
R.R. Steele (ed.), *Tudor & Stuart royal proclamations* (2 vols, Oxford 1910).
Thomas Stafford, *Pacata Hibernica* [London 1633], ed. Standish O'Grady (2 vols, London 1896).
P.D. Vigors (ed.), 'Rebellion 1641–2 described in a letter of Rev. Urban Vigors to Rev. Henry Jones', *JCHAS*, 2nd series, 2 (1896).
Patrick Watters (ed.), 'Entries in the Kilkenny Corporation records regarding Lord Wentworth's visit in 1637', *JRSAI*, 4th series, 6/2 (1884).
R.B. Wernham (ed.), *List & analysis of state papers, foreign, 1589–June 1593* (6 vols., London 1964–84).
T.D. Whitaker (ed.), *The life & original correspondence of Sir George Radcliffe* (London 1810).
Newport B. White (ed.), *Irish monastic & episcopal deeds, 1200–1600* (IMC, Dublin 1936).
— (ed.), *Extents of Irish monastic possessions, 1540–1* (IMC, Dublin 1943).
Herbert Wood (ed.), *The chronicle of Ireland (1584–1608) by Sir James Perrot* (IMC, Dublin 1933).

SELECT SECONDARY SOURCES

G.P.V. Akrigg, *Jacobean pageant: the court of King James I* (London 1962)
Richard Bagwell, *Ireland under the Tudors* (3 vols., London 1885–90)
Idem, *Ireland under the Stuarts* (3 vols., London 1909–16)
T.B. Barry, E. Culleton & C.A. Empey, 'Kells Motte, County Kilkenny', *PRIA* 84 C (1984).
J.C. Beckett, 'The Confederation of Kilkenny reviewed', in J.C. Beckett, *Confrontations: studies in Irish history* (Belfast 1972).
—, *The cavalier duke: a life of James Butler, 1st duke of Ormond* (Belfast 1990).
Matthew Boland, 'The decline of the O'Kennedys of Ormond', *Tipperary Historical Jnl.* (1994).
John Bossy, 'The Counter-Reformation and the people of Catholic Ireland, 1596–1641', *Historical Studies VIII* (Dublin 1971)
Karl Bottigheimer, 'Why the Reformation failed in Ireland: *une question bien posée*', *Jn. of Ecclesiastical History*, 36 (1985).

John Bradley & Con Manning, 'Excavations at Duiske Abbey, Graiguenamanagh, County Kilkenny', *PRIA* 81 C (1981).

Brendan Bradshaw, *The dissolution of the religious orders in Ireland under Henry VIII* (Cambridge 1974)

—, 'Cromwellian Reform and the Origins of the Kildare Rebellion, 1533–4', *Transactions of the Royal Historical Soc.*, 5th series, 27 (1977).

—, 'Sword, word and strategy in the Reformation in Ireland', *Historical Jn.*, 21 (1978).

—, *The Irish constitutional revolution of the 16th century* (Cambridge 1979).

Ciaran Brady & Raymond Gillespie (ed.), *Natives & newcomers: the making of Irish colonial society, 1534–1641* (Dublin 1986).

Ciaran Brady, 'Faction and the origins of the Desmond rebellion of 1579', *IHS*, 22/88 (Sept. 1981).

Idem, 'Conservative subversives: the community of the Pale and the Dublin administration, 1581–6', in P.J. Corish (ed.), *Historical Studies XV: Radicals, rebels & establishments*, (Belfast 1985)

—, 'Court, Castle & Country: the framework of government in Tudor Ireland', in Brady & Gillespie (ed.), *Natives & newcomers* (Dublin 1986).

—, 'Thomas Butler, earl of Ormond (1531–1614) and Reform in Tudor Ireland', in C. Brady (ed.), *Worsted in the game: losers in Irish history* (Dublin 1989).

—, *The chief governors: the rise and fall of reform government in Tudor Ireland, 1536–88* (Cambridge 1994).

—, 'England's defence and Ireland's reform: the dilemma of the Irish viceroys, 1541–1641', in Brendan Bradshaw & John Morrill (ed.), *The British problem, c.1534–1707: state formation in the Atlantic archipelago* (London 1996).

James Brennan, 'Peter Walsh and the Confederation of Kilkenny', *Old Kilkenny Review*, 4/2 (1990).

Lady Burghclere [Winifred Gardner], *The life of James, 1st duke of Ormonde* (2 vols, London 1912).

George D. Burtchaell, 'The family of Rothe of Kilkenny', *RHAAI Jn.*, 4th series, 7 (1886).

—, 'The Geraldines of County Kilkenny, Pt. 1: the Barons of Burnchurch', *JRSAI* 22 (1892).

George Butler, 'The battle of Affane', *Irish Sword* 8 (1967/8).

Harriet J. Butler & Harold Edgeworth Butler, *The Black Book of Edgeworthstown* (Dublin 1929).

Hubert Butler, 'An Anti-English Butler', *Butler Soc. Jn.*, 1 (1968).

—, 'Colonel Walter Butler', *Butler Soc. Jn.*, 7 (1977).

W.F.T. Butler, 'The descendants of James, 9th earl of Ormond', *JRSAI* 59 (1929)

Conrad Cairns, 'Guns and castles in Tipperary', *Irish Sword* 16 (1985).

—, *Irish tower houses: a County Tipperary case study* (Athlone 1987).

Nicholas Canny, 'The treaty of Mellifont and the reorganisation of Ulster, 1603', *Irish Sword* 9 (1969).

—, 'The flight of the earls, 1607', *IHS*, 17 (1971).

—, *The Elizabethan conquest of Ireland: a pattern established, 1565–76* (Hassocks 1976).

—, 'Why the Reformation failed in Ireland: *une question mal posée*', *Jnl. of Ecclesiastical History*, 30 (1979).

—, 'Protestants, planters and apartheid in early modern Ireland', *IHS*, 25/98 (Nov. 1986).

—, *From Reformation to Restoration: Ireland, 1534–1660* (Dublin 1987).

—, 'Irish, Scottish and Welsh responses to centralisation, *c.*1530–1640: a comparative perspective', in Alexander Grant & Keith J. Stringer (ed.), *Uniting the kingdom: the making of British history* (London 1995).

Vincent Carey, 'The end of the Gaelic political order: the O'More lordship of Laois, 1536–1603', in Padraig Lane & William Nolan (ed.), *Laois: history & society* (Dublin 1998).

—, *Surviving the Tudors: the 'Wizard' earl of Kildare and English rule in Ireland* (Dublin 2002)

Charles Carlton, *Charles I: The personal monarch* (paperback edn., London 1984).

William Carrigan, *The history & antiquities of the diocese of Ossory* (4 vols, Dublin 1905).

Thomas Carte, *The life of James, 1st duke of Ormonde* (3 vols., London 1735–6; 6 vols., Oxford 1851).

Aidan Clarke, 'The army and politics in Ireland, 1625–30', *Studia Hibernica* 4 (1964).

—, *The Old English in Ireland, 1625–42* (London 1966).

—, *The Graces* (Dublin 1968).

—, 'The Irish economy, 1600–60', *NHI*, iii (1976).

—, 'Pacification, plantation and the Catholic question, 1603–23', *NHI*, iii (1976).

—, 'Selling royal favours, 1624–32', *NHI*, iii (1976).

—, 'The government of Wentworth, 1632–40', *NHI*, iii (1976).

—, 'The genesis of the Ulster rising of 1641', in Peter Roebuck (ed.), *Plantation to partition: essays in Ulster history* (Belfast 1981).

—, 'The 1641 depositions', in Peter Fox (ed.), *Treasures of the Library: Trinity College, Dublin* (Dublin 1986).

—, 'Sir Piers Crosby, 1590–1646: Wentworth's "tawney ribbon"', *IHS*, 26/102 (Nov. 1988)

—, 'The 1641 rebellion and anti-popery in Ireland', in B. MacCuarta (ed.), *Ulster 1641: aspects of the rising*

(Belfast 1993).

J.T. Cliffe, *The Yorkshire gentry from the Reformation to the Civil War* (London 1969)

P.J.M. Comerford, 'The Comerford family: how origins became confused', *Old Kilkenny Review*, 24 (1972).

Patrick J. Corish, 'The rising of 1641 and the Catholic Confederacy, 1641–5', *NHI*, iii (Oxford 1976).

—, 'Ormond, Rinuccini and the Confederates, 1645–9', *NHI*, iii (Oxford 1976).

—, *The Catholic community in the 17th and 18th centuries* (Dublin 1981).

—, 'David Rothe, bishop of Ossory, 1618–50', *Butler Soc. Jn.*, 2/3 (1984).

John G. Crawford, *Anglicising the government of Ireland: the Irish privy council and the expansion of Tudor rule, 1556–78* (Dublin 1994).

Donal F. Cregan, 'Irish Catholic admissions to the English inns of court, 1558–1625', *Irish Jurist*, v (1970).

—, 'The Confederation of Kilkenny', in Brian Farrell (ed.), *The Irish parliamentary tradition* (Dublin 1973).

—, 'The Confederate Catholics of Ireland: the personnel of the Confederation, 1642–9', *IHS*, 29/116 (Nov. 1995).

Gerard Crotty, 'Seals of the house of Ormond', *Old Kilkenny Review*, 3/2 (1985).

Neil Cuddy, 'The revival of the entourage: the bedchamber of James I, 1603–25', in D. Starkey et al., *The English court* (London 1987)

L.M. Cullen, 'The social and economic evolution of south Kilkenny in the 17th and 18th centuries', *Decies*, 13 (Jan. 1980).

Bernadette Cunningham, 'Native culture and political change in Ireland, 1580–1640', in Brady & Gillespie (ed.), *Natives & newcomers*.

Edmund Curtis, 'Some medieval seals out of the Ormond archives', *JRSAI* 66 (1936).

John J. Curtis, 'The Butler revolt of 1569', unpublished M.A. thesis, St Patrick's College, Maynooth, 1983.

Richard Cust & Ann Hughes (ed.), *Conflict in early Stuart England: studies in religion and politics, 1603–42* (London 1989).

Barbara Donagan, 'A courtier's progress: greed and consistency in the life of the earl of Holland', *Historical Jn.*, 19/2 (1976).

John Doyle, 'The water mills of Kilkenny', *Old Kilkenny Review*, 3/2 (1985).

Patrick Duffy, David Edwards & Elizabeth FitzPatrick (ed.), *Gaelic Ireland: land, lordship and settlement, c.1250–c.1650* (Dublin 2001).

Lord Dunboyne, 'Carve's Butler families of 1641', *Butler Soc. Jn.*, 6 (1975/6)

R. Dunlop, 'The plantation of Munster, 1584–9', *EHR*, 3 (1888)

—, 'The plantation of Leix and Offaly', *EHR*, 6 (1891)

David Edwards, 'Malice aforethought? The death of the 9th earl of Ormond, 1546', *Butler Soc. Jn.*, 3/1 (1987).

—, 'The Butler revolt of 1569', *IHS*, 28/111 (May 1993).

—, 'Beyond reform: martial law and the Tudor reconquest of Ireland', *History Ireland*, 5/2 (Summer 1997).

—, 'Further comments on the strange death of the 9th earl of Ormond', *Butler Soc. Jn.*, 4/1 (1997).

—, 'In Tyrone's shadow: Feagh MacHugh O'Byrne, forgotten leader of the Nine Years War', in Conor O'Brien (ed.), *Feagh McHugh O'Byrne: The Wicklow Firebrand* (Rathdrum 1998).

—, 'The MacGiollapadraigs (Fitzpatricks) of Upper Ossory, 1532–1641', in Lane & Nolan (ed.), *Laois.*

—, 'Ideology and experience: Spenser's *View* and martial law in Ireland', in Hiram Morgan (ed.), *Political ideology in Ireland, 1541–1641* (Dublin 1999).

—, 'The poisoned chalice: the Ormond inheritance, sectarian division and the rise of James Butler, 1614–1642', in Barnard & Fenlon (ed.), *The Dukes.*

—, 'Collaboration without Anglicisation: the MacGiollapadraig lordship and Tudor reform', in Duffy, Edwards & FitzPatrick (ed.), *Gaelic Ireland.*

Steven G. Ellis, 'The Kildare rebellion and the early Henrician Reformation', *Historical Jn.*, 19 (1976).

—, 'Tudor policy and the Kildare ascendancy in the lordship of Ireland, 1496–1534', *IHS*, 20 (1976/7).

—, 'Thomas Cromwell and Ireland, 1532–40', *Historical Jn.*, 23 (1980).

—, 'Henry VIII, rebellion and the rule of law', *Historical Jn.*, xxiv (1981).

—, *Reform and revival: English government in Ireland, 1470–1534* (London 1984).

—, 'John Bale, Bishop of Ossory, 1552–3', *Butler Soc. Jn.*, 2/3 (1984).

—, *Tudor Ireland: crown, community and the conflict of cultures, 1470–1603* (London 1985).

—, *Ireland in the age of the Tudors* (London 1998)

C.A. Empey & Katherine Simms, 'The ordinances of the White Earl and the problem of coign in the middle ages', *PRIA* 75 C (1975).

C.A. Empey, 'The Butler lordship', *Butler Soc. Jn.*, 1 (1970/1).

—, 'Ormond deeds in the National Library of Ireland', *Butler Soc. Jn.*, 7 (1977).

—, 'Medieval Knocktopher: a study in manorial settlement, Pt. 2', *Old Kilkenny Review*, ii (1983).

—, 'From rags to riches: Piers Butler, 8th earl of Ormond, 1515–39', *Butler Soc. Jn.*, 2/3 (1984)

— (ed.), *A worthy foundation: St Canice's cathedral, Kilkenny* (Dublin 1985)

—, 'Medieval Thurles: origin and development', in William Corbett & William Nolan (ed.), *Thurles: the cathedral town* (Dublin 1989)

Richard H.A.J. Everard, 'The family of Everard', *Irish Genealogist*, 7 (1988).

Cyril Falls, *Elizabeth's Irish wars* (London 1950)

—, 'Black Tom of Ormonde', *Irish Sword*, 5 (1961/2)

Lord Walter Fitzgerald, 'The O'Mores and their territory of Laois', *Kildare Archaeological Soc. Jn.*, 6 (1909–11).

S.A. FitzMaurice, 'Cloghgrenan and the Butlers', *Old Kilkenny Review*, 18 (1966).

Alan Ford, *The Protestant Reformation in Ireland, 1590–1641* (Frankfurt 1985).

—, 'The Protestant Reformation in Ireland', in Brady & Gillespie (ed.), *Natives & newcomers.*

—, 'James Ussher and the Godly Prince in early seventeenth-century Ireland', in Morgan (ed.), *Political ideology.*

Raymond Gillespie, 'Harvest crises in early 17th century Ireland', *IESH*, 11 (1984).

—, 'The origins and development of an Ulster urban network, 1600–41', *IHS*, 21/93 (May 1984).

—, 'The end of an era: Ulster and the outbreak of the 1641 rising', in Brady & Gillespie (ed.), *Natives & newcomers.*

—, 'Meal and money: the harvest crisis of 1621–4 and the Irish economy', in E.M. Crawford (ed.), *Famine: the Irish experience, 900–1900* (Edinburgh 1989).

—, 'The religion of the first duke of Ormonde', in Barnard & Fenlon (ed.), *The Dukes.*

—, *The transformation of the Irish economy, 1500–1700* (Dublin 1991).

Sheffield Grace, *Memorials of the family of Grace* (2 vols., privately printed, London 1823).

James Graves, 'The ancient tribes and territories of Ossory', *KSEIAS Jn.*, 1st series, 1/2, (1850).

—, 'The records of the ancient borough towns of County Kilkenny', *KSEIAS Jn.*, 2nd series, 1/1 (1856).

—, 'The Shee Alms House, Kilkenny', *KSEIAS Jn.*, 2nd series, 3/2 (1861).

—, 'The taking of the earl of Ormond, 1600', *KSEIAS Jn.*, 2nd series, 3–5 (1861–2, 1865).

—, 'A 16th century standing cup presented by Elizabeth I to Bishop Jonas Wheeler', *RHAAI Jn.*, 4th series, 3/2 (1875).

Christopher Haigh (ed.), *The reign of Elizabeth I* (London 1984).

Helga Robinson Hammerstein, 'Aspects of the Continental education of Irish students in the reign of Elizabeth I', *Historical Studies VIII* (Dublin 1971).

William Hayes, 'Dermot O'Hurley's last visit to Tipperary', *Tipperary Historical Jn.* (1992).

L.W. Henry, 'The earl of Essex and Ireland, 1599', *BIHR*, 32/85 (May 1959).

James Hughes, 'Sir Edmund Butler of the Dullough', *RHAAI Jn.*, 4th series, 1 (1870).

J.J. Hughes, 'Inistioge', *Old Kilkenny Review*, 2 (1949).

E.W. Ives, *Faction in Tudor England* (Historical Association, London 1979).

—, *Anne Boleyn* (Oxford 1986).

Donald Jackson, 'The taking of the earl of Ormonde, 1600', *Butler Soc. Jn.*, 1/6 (1975–6).

H.A. Jefferies, 'The Irish parliament of 1560: the Anglican reforms authorised', *IHS*, 26/102 (Nov. 1988).

W.J. Jones, 'The crown and the courts in England, 1603–25', in A.G.R. Smith (ed.), *The reign of James VI and I* (London 1973).

H.F. Kearney, 'The court of wards and liveries in Ireland, 1622–41', *PRIA* 57 C (1954–6).

—, *Strafford in Ireland, 1633–41* (Manchester 1959).

William J. Kelly, '"Most illustrious cavalier" or "Unkinde deserter"?: James Butler, 1st duke of Ormonde, 1610–88', *History Ireland* 1/2 (Summer 1993).

—, 'James Butler, 12th earl of Ormond, the Irish government and the Bishops' Wars, 1638–40', in John R. Young (ed.), *Celtic dimensions of the British Civil Wars* (Edinburgh 1997).

—, 'Ormond and Strafford, pupil and mentor?', *Butler Soc. Jn.*, 4/1 (1997)

Joe Kennedy, 'Cromwell in Callan', *Old Kilkenny Review*, new series, 3 (1984)

Colm Kenny, 'The exclusion of Catholics from the legal profession in Ireland, 1537–1829', *IHS*, 25/100 (1987).

John Kirwan, 'Thomas Butler, 10th earl of Ormond: his early career and rise to prominence, Pt. 1', *Butler Soc. Jn.*, 3/4 (1994).

—, 'Thomas Butler, etc., Pt. 2', *Butler Soc. Jn*, 4/1 (1997)

Peter Lake, 'Anti-popery: the structure of a prejudice', in R. Cust & A. Hughes (ed.), *Conflict in early Stuart England* (London 1989)

Colm Lennon, *Richard Stanihurst, the Dubliner, 1547–1618* (Dublin 1981)

—, 'The Counter-Reformation in Ireland, 1542–1641', in Brady & Gillespie (ed.), *Natives & newcomers*.

—, *The lords of Dublin in the age of Reformation* (Dublin 1989).

—, 'Political thought of Irish Counter-Reformation churchmen: the testimony of the *Analecta* of Bishop David Rothe', in Morgan (ed.), *Political thought*.

D.M. Loades, *The Tudor court* (London 1986).

Roger Lockyer, *Buckingham: the life and political career of George Villiers, 1st duke of Buckingham, 1592–1628* (London 1981).

—, *The early Stuarts: a political history of England, 1603–42* (London 1989).

A.K. Longfield, *Anglo-Irish trade in the 16th century* (London 1929).

John Lowe, 'Charles I and the Confederation of Kilkenny', *I.H.S.*, xiv, No. 53 (March 1954).

James F. Lydon, 'The middle nation', in J. Lydon (ed.), *The English in medieval Ireland* (Dublin 1982)

Michael MacCarthy-Murrough, *The Munster plantation: English migration to southern Ireland, 1583–1641* (Oxford 1986).

John McCavitt, *Sir Arthur Chichester, lord deputy of Ireland, 1605–16*, (Belfast 1998).

Idem, "Good planets in their several spheares': the establishment of the assize circuit in early 17th century Ireland', *Irish Jurist*, 24 (1989).

Idem, 'Lord Deputy Chichester and the 'Mandates' policy in Ireland, 1605–7', *Recusant History*, 20/3 (1991)

Brid McGrath, 'The membership of the Irish house of commons, 1613–15', unpublished M.Littt. thesis, Trinity College, Dublin (1986).

Gearoid Mac Niocaill, *Irish population before Petty: problems and possibilities* (Dublin 1981).

—, 'Socio-Economic problems of the late medieval Irish town', in D. Harkness & M. O'Dowd (ed.), *Historical Studies XIII* (Belfast 1981).

Conleth Manning, 'The Inistioge Priory cloister arcade', *Old Kilkenny Review*, new series, 1/3 (1976).

Brocard M. Mansfield, 'Elizabeth, Lady Thurles (1588–1673)', *Butler Soc. Jn.*, 3/1 (1986/7).

C.R. Mayes, 'The early Stuarts and the Irish peerage', *EHR*, 73 (1958).

H.B. McCall, *The family of Wandesford of Kirklington & Castlecomer* (London 1904).

Aileen McClintock, 'The earls of Ormond and Tipperary's role in the governing of Ireland, 1603–41', *Tipperary Historical Jn.*, 1 (1988).

Lawrence McCorristine, *The revolt of Silken Thomas: a challenge to Henry VIII* (Dublin 1987).

C.P. Meehan, *The Confederation of Kilkenny* (revised ed., Dublin 1905).

Helen Miller, *Henry VIII and the English nobility* (Oxford 1986).

T.W. Moody, 'The Irish parliament under Elizabeth I and James I', *PRIA*, 45 C (1939).

Donal Moore, 'English action, Irish reaction: the MacMurrough Kavanaghs, 1530–1630', unpublished M.A. thesis, St Patrick's College, Maynooth, 1985.

P.F. Moran, 'The bishops of Ossory', *Ossory Arch. Soc. Jn.*, 3 (1883).

Hiram Morgan, *Tyrone's rebellion: the outbreak of the Nine Years War in Tudor Ireland* (Dublin 1993).

—, 'Faith and fatherland in sixteenth century Ireland', *History Ireland*, 3/2 (Summer 1995).

—, 'British policies before the British state', in Bradshaw & Morril (ed.), *The British problem, c.1534–1707: state formation in the Atlantic archipelago* (London 1996).

— (ed.), *Political ideology in Ireland, 1541–1641* (Dublin 1999).

Thomas Morrissey, *James Archer of Kilkenny: an Elizabethan Jesuit* (Dublin 1979).

John Mulholland, 'The trial of Alice Butler, abbess of Kilculiheen, 1532', *Decies* 25 (1984).

J.C.J. Murphy, 'The ten civic families of Kilkenny', *Old Kilkenny Review*, vii (1954).

N. Murphy, 'The O'Brennans and the ancient territory of Hy-Duach', *Ossory Archaeological Soc. Jn.*, 1 (1874–9).

W.G. Neely, 'A social and economic history of Kilkenny City, 1391–1843', unpublished Ph.D. thesis, Queen's University, Belfast (1987).

Kenneth W. Nicholls, *Gaelic and gaelicised Ireland in the Middle Ages* (Dublin 1972).

—, 'The Kavanaghs, 1400–1700', *Irish Genealogist*, 5 (1974–9), 6 (1980–3).

—, *Land, law and society in 16th century Ireland* (Dublin 1976).

—, 'Further notes on Ormond material in the National Library', *Butler Soc. Jn.*, 7 (1977).

—, 'Anglo-French Ireland and after', *Peritia*, 1 (1982).

—, 'Gaelic landowners in Tipperary in the light of the surviving Irish deeds', in W. Nolan & T.G. McGrath (ed.), *Tipperary: history & society* (Dublin 1985).

—, 'Gaelic society and economy in the high middle ages', *NHI*, ii (Oxford 1987).
—, 'The development of lordship in County Cork, 1300–1600', in P. O'Flanagan & C.G. Buttimer (ed.), *Cork: history & society* (Dublin 1992).
William Nolan, *Fassadinin: land, settlement and society in south-east Ireland, 1600–1850* (Dublin 1979).
William Nolan & Kevin Whelan (ed.), *Kilkenny: history & society* (Dublin 1991).
Eamonn O'Ciardha, '"The Unkinde Desertor" and the "Bright Duke": contrasting views of the dukes of Ormonde in the Irish royalist tradition', in Barnard & Fenlon (ed.), *The Dukes*.
Mary O'Dowd, 'Land inheritance in early modern Sligo', *IESH*, 10 (1983).
—, 'Gaelic economy and society', in Brady & Gillespie (ed.), *Natives & newcomers* (Dublin 1986).
—, 'Land and lordship in 16th and early 17th century Ireland', in P. Roebuck & R. Mitchison (ed.), *Economy & society in Scotland and Ireland, 1500–1939* (Edinburgh 1988).
Fearghus O'Fearghaill, 'The Catholic Church in County Kilkenny, 1600–1800', in Nolan & Whelan (ed.), *Kilkenny*.
Owen O'Kelly, *The place-names of County Kilkenny* (Kilkenny Arch. Soc., 1985 edn.).
J. Canon O'Leary & E. O'Leary, *A history of the Queen's County* (2 vols., Dublin 1907).
Micheál O'Siochru, *Confederate Ireland: a political and constitutional analysis* (Dublin 1999).
Hans Pawlisch, *Sir John Davies and the conquest of Ireland: a study in legal imperialism* (Cambridge 1985).
Linda Levy Peck (ed.), *The mental world of the Jacobean court* (Cambridge 1991).
Michael Perceval-Maxwell, 'Protestant faction, the impeachment of Strafford, and origins of the Irish civil war', *Canadian Journal of History*, 17 (1982).
—, 'Ulster 1641 in the context of political developments in the three kingdoms', in Brian MacCuarta (ed.), *Ulster 1641: aspects of the rising* (Belfast 1993).
Margaret Phelan, 'Sir Thomas Wentworth's visit to Kilkenny, August 1637', *Butler Soc. Jn.*, 2/2 (1982).
Menna Prestwich, *Cranfield: politics and profits under the early Stuarts* (Oxford 1966).
J.G.A. Prim, 'The family of Cowley of Kilkenny', *KSEIAS*, 2nd series, 4 (1861).
—, 'Kilkenny inns and taverns', *Old Kilkenny Review*, 3 (1950)
Liam Price, 'The Byrnes' Country in the 16th century', *JRSAI*, 66 (1936)
Coslett Quinn, 'Nicholas Walsh and his friends: a forgotten chapter in the Irish reformation', *Butler Soc. Jn.*, 2/3 (1984)
D.B. Quinn & K.W. Nicholls, 'Ireland in 1534', *NHI*, iii (Oxford 1976).
D.B. Quinn, 'The Irish parliamentary subsidy in the 15th and 16th centuries', *PRIA* 42 C (1934/5).
—, 'Anglo-Irish local government, 1485–1534', *IHS*, 1 (1939)
—, 'The early interpretation of Poynings' Law, 1496–1534', *IHS*, 2 (1941).
—, 'Agenda for Irish history: Ireland from 1461 to 1603', *IHS*, 4 (1945).
—, 'Henry VIII and Ireland, 1509–34', *IHS*, 12 (1961).
—, *The Elizabethans and the Irish* (Ithaca 1966).
—, 'Aristocratic autonomy, 1460–94', *NHI*, ii (Oxford 1987).
—, 'The hegemony of the earls of Kildare, 1494–1520', *NHI*, ii (Oxford 1987).
—, '"Irish" Ireland and "English" Ireland', *NHI*, ii (Oxford 1987).
—, 'The re-emergence of English policy as a major factor in Irish affairs, 1520–34', *NHI*, ii (Oxford 1987).
Terence Ranger, 'Richard Boyle and the making of an Irish fortune, 1588–1614', *IHS*, 10/39 (March 1957).
Conrad Russell, 'The British problem and the English civil war', *History*, 72 (1987).
—, 'The British background to the Irish rebellion of 1641', *Historical Research* 61 (1988).
—, *The fall of the British monarchies, 1637–42* (Oxford 1991).
Vera M. Rutledge, 'Court-Castle faction and the Irish viceroyalty: the appointment of Oliver St John as lord deputy of Ireland in 1616', *IHS*, 26/103 (1989).
C.R. Sasso, 'The Desmond rebellions, 1569–73 and 1579–83', Ph.D. thesis, Loyola University of Chicago, 1980.
Kevin Sharpe, 'The earl of Arundel, his circle and the opposition to the duke of Buckingham, 1618–28', in K. Sharpe (ed.), *Faction & parliament* (London 1978).
—, 'The image of virtue: the court and household of Charles I, 1625–42', in D. Starkey et al., *The English court* (London 1987).
Anthony J. Sheehan, 'The overthrow of the plantation of Munster, October 1598', *Irish Sword*, 15 (1982).
—, 'The killing of the earl of Desmond, November 1583', *JCHAS* 88 (1983).
—, 'The recusancy revolt of 1603: a reinterpretation', *Archivium Hibernicum*, 38 (1983).
—, 'Official reaction to the native land claims in the plantation of Munster', *IHS* 23/92 (Nov. 1983).
—, 'Irish towns in a period of change, 1558–1625', in Brady & Gillespie (ed.), *Natives & newcomers*.

W.J. Smyth, 'Territorial, social and settlement hierarchies in 17th century Kilkenny', in Nolan & Whelan (ed.), *Kilkenny*.

Johann P. Sommerville, 'Ideology, property and the Constitution', in R. Cust & A. Hughes (ed.), *Conflict in early Stuart England* (London 1989).

—, 'James I and the divine right of kings: English politics and continental theory', in Levy Peck (ed.), *The mental world*.

David Starkey et al., *The English court from the Wars of the Roses to the Civil War* (London 1987).

David Starkey, *The reign of Henry VIII: personalities and politics* (London 1985).

—, 'Which age of reform?', in C. Coleman & D. Starkey (ed.), *Revolution reassessed* (Oxford 1986).

—, 'Court and government', in Coleman & Starkey (ed.), *Revolution reassessed* (Oxford 1986).

—, 'Intimacy and innovation: the rise of the Privy Chamber, 1485–1547', In D. Starkey et al., *The English court* (London 1987)

Lawrence Stone, *The crisis of the aristocracy* (Oxford 1965).

—, *An open elite? England 1540–1880* (abridged edn., Oxford 1986)

Victor Treadwell, 'The Irish parliament of 1569–71', *PRIA*, 66 C (1966/7).

—, 'Sir John Perrot and the Irish parliament of 1585–6', *PRIA*, 85 C (1985).

Julian C. Walton, 'The merchant communities of Waterford in the 16th and 17th centuries', in Paul Butel & L.M. Cullen (ed.), *Cities & merchants* (Dublin 1986).

A.E.J. Went, 'A short history of the fisheries of the River Nore', *RSAI Jnl.*, lxxxv (1955).

Dean Gunther White, 'Henry VIII's Irish kerne in France and Scotland, 1544–5', *Irish Sword*, iii (1957/8).

—, 'The reign of Edward VI in Ireland: some political, social and economic aspects', *IHS*, xiv (1964/5).

Glanmor Williams, *Renewal and Reformation: Wales, c.1415–1642* (Oxford 1993).

Penry Williams, *The Tudor regime* (Oxford 1979).

Philip Wilson, *The beginnings of modern Ireland* (Dublin 1914).

Pam Wright, 'A change in direction: the ramifications of a female household, 1558–1603', in D. Starkey et al., *The English court* (London 1987).

Index